P9-EDF-328

MANAGEMENT OF INFORMATION SECURITY

Dr. Michael E. Whitman, CISSP
Herbert J. Mattord, CISSP
Kennesaw State University

THOMSON
COURSE TECHNOLOGY

Australia • Canada • Mexico • Singapore • Spain • United Kingdom • United States

THOMSON
™
COURSE TECHNOLOGY

Management of Information Security

by Michael E. Whitman, Ph.D., CISSP and Herbert J. Mattord, M.B.A., CISSP

Senior Vice President, Publisher:
Kristen Duerr

Executive Editor:
Jennifer Locke

Product Manager:
Alyssa Pratt

Developmental Editor:
Lynne Raughley

Production Editor:
Brooke Brooth, Trillium Project Management

Associate Product Manager:
Mirella Misiaszek

Editorial Assistant:
Amanda Piantedosi

Marketing Manager:
Jason Sakos

Text Designer:
Books By Design

Cover Designer:
Nancy Goulet

Senior Manufacturing Coordinator:
Laura Burns

Compositor:
GEX Publishing Services

To Rhonda, Rachel, and Alex, thank you for your loving support. To Meghan, welcome to our family.

—MEW

For my family.

—HJM

Table of Contents

Chapter 3
Planning for Contingencies 63

Section III–Policy and Programs
Chapter 4
Information Security Policy. 105

Appendix A
Appendix: NIST SP 800-26, Security Self-Assessment Guide for Information Technology Systems, and the Human Firewall Council's Security Management Index Survey 249

Section IV–Protection
Chapter 7
Risk Management: Identifying and Assessing Risk 285

Section V–People and Projects
Chapter 10
Personnel and Security. 413

Chapter 11

Chapter 12

Preface

AS GLOBAL NETWORKS CONTINUE TO EXPAND, the interconnections between them become ever more vital to the smooth operation of communication and computing systems. However, escalating incidences of virus and worm attacks and the success of criminal attackers illustrate the weaknesses in current information technologies and the need for heightened system security.

In attempting to secure current systems and networks, organizations must draw on the pool of current information security practitioners. These same organizations will count on the next generation of professionals to have the correct mix of skills and experiences to develop more secure computing environments in the future. Students of technology must learn to recognize the threats and vulnerabilities present in existing systems. They must also learn how to design and develop the secure systems that will address these threats in the future.

The purpose of this textbook is to fill the increasing need for a quality academic textbook in the discipline of Information Security. While there are dozens of quality publications on information security and assurance for the practitioner, there are fewer textbooks that provide the student with a focus on information security management. By creating a book specifically oriented toward students of information systems management, we hope to close this gap. Specifically, there is a clear need for disciplines such as Information Systems, Criminal Justice, Political Science, and Accounting Information Systems to understand the foundations of management of information security and the development of managerial strategy for information security. The fundamental tenet of this textbook is that information security in the modern organization is a management problem, and not one that technology alone can answer; it is a problem that has important economic consequences and for which management is accountable.

Approach

The book provides a management overview of information security and a thorough treatment of the administration of information security. It can be used to support course delivery for information security driven programs targeted at Information Technology students as well as IT management and technology management curricula aimed at business or technical management students.

Certified Information Systems Security Professionals Common Body of Knowledge — Because the authors are Certified Information Systems Security Professionals (CISSP), the CISSP knowledge domains have had an influence in the design of the text. Although care was taken to avoid producing another CISSP study guide, the authors' backgrounds have resulted in a treatment that ensures that much of the CISSP Common Body of Knowledge (CBK), especially in the area of management of information security, has been integrated into the text to some degree.

Chapter Scenarios — Each chapter opens with a short story that follows the same fictional company as it encounters various information security issues. The final part of each chapter is a conclusion to the scenario and offers a few discussion questions to round out each scenario. These questions give the student and the instructor an opportunity to discuss the issues that underlay the content.

Viewpoints — An essay from an information security practitioner or academic is included in each chapter. These sections provide a range of commentary that illustrate interesting topics or share personal opinions, giving the student a wider view on the topics in the text.

Offline and Threat Management Boxes — These sections highlight interesting topics and detailed technical issues, allowing the student to delve more deeply into certain topics. Each chapter includes one Threat Management feature, and Offline boxes are included as needed.

Hands-On Learning — At the end of each chapter, students will find a Chapter Summary and Review Questions, as well as Exercises and Case Exercises which give them the opportunity to examine the information security arena outside the classroom. Using the Exercises, the student can research, analyze, and write to reinforce learning objectives and deepen their understanding of the text. With the Case Exercises, students use professional judgment, powers of observation, and elementary research to create solutions for simple information security scenarios.

Author Team

Michael Whitman and Herbert Mattord have jointly developed this text to merge knowledge from the world of academic study with practical experience from the business world.

Michael Whitman, Ph.D., CISSP is an Associate Professor of Information Systems in the Computer Science and Information Systems Department at Kennesaw State University, Kennesaw, Georgia, where he is also the Director of the Master of Science in Information Systems and the Director of the KSU Center for Information Security Education and Awareness (*infosec.kennesaw.edu*). He and Herbert Mattord are the authors of *Principles of Information Security* from Course Technology. Dr. Whitman is an active researcher in Information Security, Fair and Responsible Use Policies, Ethical Computing, and Information Systems Research Methods. He currently teaches graduate and undergraduate courses in Information Security, Local Area Networking, and Data Communications. He has published articles in the top journals in his field, including *Information Systems Research*, the *Communications of the ACM*, *Information and Management*, the *Journal of International Business Studies*, and the *Journal of Computer Information Systems*. He is an active member of the Information Systems Security Association, the Computer Security Institute, the Association for Computing Machinery, and the Association for Information Systems. Dr. Whitman has also co-authored a Lab Manual, "The Hands-On Information Security Lab Manual," from Thomson Learning Custom Publishing. He and Professor Mattord are also frequent presenters at Course University seminars.

Herbert Mattord, M.B.A. CISSP recently completed 24 years of IT industry experience as an application developer, database administrator, project manager, and information security practitioner to join the faculty at Kennesaw State University. He and Michael Whitman are the authors of *Principles of Information Security* from Course Technology. During his career as an IT practitioner, he has been an adjunct professor at Kennesaw State University; Southern Polytechnic State University in Marietta, Georgia; Austin Community College in Austin, Texas; and Texas State University: San Marcos. He currently teaches undergraduate courses in Information Security, Data Communications, Local Area Networks, Database Technology, Project Management, and Systems Analysis & Design. He is the coordinator for the department's Certificate in Information Security and Assurance, and is also an active member of the Information Systems Security Association and the Association for Computing Machinery. He was formerly the Manager of Corporate Information Technology Security at Georgia-Pacific Corporation, where much of the practical knowledge found in this and his earlier textbook was acquired.

Structure

The textbook is organized into sections based on the management functions of Planning, Policy, People, Projects, and Protection, and consists of twelve chapters and an Appendix.

Unit I—INTRODUCTION

Chapter 1—Introduction to Management of Information Security
The opening chapter establishes the foundation for understanding the field of information security by explaining the importance of information technology and identifying who is responsible for protecting an organization's information assets. Students learn the definition and key characteristics of information security, as well as the differences between information security management and general management.

UNIT II—PLANNING

Chapter 2—Planning for Security
This chapter explains the importance of planning and describes the principal components of organizational planning and information security system implementation planning.

Chapter 3—Planning for Contingencies
This chapter describes the need for contingency planning and explores the major components. It illustrates how to create a simple set of contingency plans using business impact analysis, and how to prepare and execute a test of those plans.

UNIT III—POLICY AND PROGRAMS

Chapter 4—Security Policy
This chapter defines information security policy and describes its central role in a successful information security program. Research has shown that there are three major types of information security policy; the chapter explains what goes into each type, and demonstrates how to develop, implement, and maintain various types of information security policies.

Chapter 5—Developing Security Programs

Chapter 5 explores the various organizational approaches to information security and provides an explanation of the functional components of the information security program. Students learn how to plan and staff an organization's information security department based on the size of the organization and other factors, as well as how to evaluate the internal and external factors that influence the activities and organization of an information security program. The chapter also identifies and describes the typical job titles and functions performed in the information security program, and concludes with an exploration of the creation and management of a security education, training, and awareness program.

Chapter 6—Security Management Models and Practices

This chapter describes the components of the dominant information security management models, including U.S. government-sanctioned models, and discusses how to customize them for a specific organization's needs. Students learn how to implement the fundamental elements of key information security management practices and gain an understanding of emerging trends in the certification and accreditation of U.S. federal IT systems.

Appendix—NIST SP 800-26, Security Self-Assessment Guide for Information Technology Systems and the Human Firewall Council's Security Management Index Survey

The appendix reproduces an essential security management model from the NIST library and the Human Firewall Council Security Management Index.

UNIT IV—PROTECTION

Chapter 7—Risk Assessment

Chapter 7 defines risk management and its role in the organization, and demonstrates how to use risk management techniques to identify and prioritize risk factors for information assets. The risk management model presented here assesses risk based on the likelihood of adverse events and the effects on information assets when events occur. The chapter concludes with a brief discussion on how to document the results of the risk identification process.

Chapter 8—Risk Management and Control

This chapter presents essential risk mitigation strategy options and opens the discussion on controlling risk. This includes identifying risk control classification categories, using existing conceptual frameworks to evaluate risk controls, and formulating a cost benefit analysis. Students learn how to maintain and perpetuate risk controls. As an alternative to the approach presented in the early parts of the chapter, the OCTAVE method of managing risk is discussed.

Chapter 9—Protection Mechanisms

Chapter 9 introduces students to the world of technical risk controls by exploring access control approaches, including authentication, authorization, and biometric access controls as well as firewalls and the common approaches to firewall implementation. The technical control approaches for dial-up access, intrusion detection systems, and cryptography are also covered.

UNIT V—PEOPLE AND PROJECTS

Chapter 10—Personnel and Security

This chapter expands upon the discussion of the skills and requirements for information security positions introduced in Chapter 5. It explores the various information security professional certifications, and identifies which skills are encompassed by each. The second half of the chapter explores the implementation of information security constraints—used to control employee behavior and prevent misuse of information—on an organization's human resources processes.

Chapter 11—Law and Ethics

In this chapter, students learn about the legal environment and its relationship to information security. The chapter describes the major national and international laws that affect the practice of information security, as well as the role of culture in ethics as it applies to information security.

Chapter 12—Security Project Management

The final chapter covers project management within the discipline of information security. It provides basic project management techniques as well as guidance on applying project management principles to an information security program.

Instructor Resources

A variety of teaching tools have been prepared to support this textbook and offer many options to enhance the classroom learning experience:

Electronic Instructor's Manual — The Instructor's Manual includes suggestions and strategies for using this text, such as advice for lecture topics. The Instructors Manual also includes answers to the review questions and suggested solutions to the exercises at the end of each chapter.

Figure Files — Figure files allow instructors to create their own presentations using figures taken from the text.

PowerPoint Presentations — This book comes with Microsoft PowerPoint slides for each chapter. These are included as a teaching aid for classroom presentation, to make available to students on the network for chapter review, or to be printed for classroom distribution. Instructors can add their own slides for additional topics they introduce to the class.

Lab Manual — Thompson Learning Custom Publishing is producing a lab manual to accompany this book, which is written by one of the authors. Contact your Course Technology sales representative for more information.

Curriculum Model for Programs of Study in Information Security and Assurance — In addition to the texts authored by this team, a curriculum model for programs of study in Information Security and Assurance is available from the Kennesaw State University Center for Information Security Education and Awareness (http://infosec.kennesaw.edu). This document provides details on designing and implementing security coursework and curricula in academic institutions, as well as guidance and lessons learned from the authors' perspective.

ExamView — ExamView®, the ultimate tool for objective-based testing needs, is a powerful objective-based test generator that enables instructors to create paper, LAN or Web-based tests from testbanks designed specifically for their Course Technology text. Instructors can utilize the ultra-efficient QuickTest Wizard to create tests in less than five minutes by taking advantage of Course Technology's question banks, or customize their own exams from scratch.

Acknowledgments

The authors would like to thank their families for their support and understanding for the many hours dedicated to this project, hours taken in many cases from family activities. Special thanks to Carola Mattord, doctoral student of English at Georgia State University. Her reviews of early drafts and suggestions for keeping the writing focused on the students resulted in a more readable manuscript.

Contributors

Several Kennesaw State University students also assisted in the preparation of the textbook, and we thank them for their contributions. They are listed in each Threat Management feature where they made their contributions.

Reviewers

We are indebted to the following individuals for their respective contributions of perceptive feedback on the initial proposal, the project outline, and the chapter-by-chapter reviews of the text:

- Denise Padavano, Peirce College
- George Proeller, Colorado Technical University
- Bill Schiano, Bentley College
- Bill Uminowicz, DeVry University

Special Thanks

The authors wish to thank the Editorial and Production teams at Course Technology. Their diligent and professional efforts greatly enhanced the final product:

- Alyssa Pratt, Product Manager
- Lynne Raughley, Developmental Editor
- Jennifer Locke, Executive Editor
- Brooke Booth, Production Editor
- Mirella Misiazcek, Associate Product Manager

In addition, several professional and commercial organizations and individuals have aided the development of the textbook by providing information and inspiration, and the authors wish to acknowledge their contribution:

- The Human Firewall Council
- NetIQ Corporation.
- The viewpoint authors:
  - Morgan Alexander-LeStat
  - Henry Bonin
  - George Hulme
  - Lee Imrey
  - Steve Kahan
  - Eng-Kiat Koh
  - Chris Pick
  - Bruce Schneier
  - Krizi Trivisani
  - Todd Tucker
- The many students who contributed to the Threat Management essays
- Steven Kahan, Executive Vice President of Marketing, NetIQ Corporation
- Charles Cresson Wood
- Our colleagues in the Department of Computer Science and Information Systems, Kennesaw State University
- Professor Merle King, Chair of the Department of Computer Science and Information Systems, Kennesaw State University

Our Commitment

The authors are committed to serving the needs of the adopters and readers. We would be pleased and honored to receive feedback on the textbook and its supporting materials. You can contact us through Course Technology at mis@course.com.

Foreword
By Charles Cresson Wood

Over the last 23 years that I've worked in the information security field, I've had an opportunity to perform risk assessments for over 125 different organizations around the world. No matter how large the organization, no matter how well-respected the organization, and no matter how high-tech the public's view of the organization, in all cases I find that management doesn't take information security seriously enough. In part this is because information security is still a relatively new field, and we don't yet understand many things about it. In part this is because top management often doesn't know much, and doesn't care to know much, about information systems technology, and in part this is because top management has been making traditional tradeoff decisions, where security loses when up against other objectives such as low cost, increased speed, user-friendliness, time to market with a new product, etc.

Times have changed dramatically, except top management, in most cases, hasn't yet appreciated how different things are. For example, consider the case of Arthur Andersen, once one of the largest and most highly-regarded public accounting firms in the world. Andersen did some auditing and consulting work for Enron, now a discredited and largely defunct energy trading concern. A US government Securities & Exchange Commission investigation into Enron's accounting practices caused certain Andersen employees to destroy documents which might have been relevant to the investigation. Aside from the fact that Andersen staff may have been involved in "cooking the books" along with Enron accounting staff, there was a major misunderstanding about the document destruction policy at Andersen. Certain staff believed they were doing the right thing when they destroyed thousands of pounds of Enron documents. Of course, document destruction is an important part of the information security field. If these staff members had received much better training about this document destruction policy, Andersen might still be in existence today. So here we have a misunderstanding about, and a lack of adequate training in, information security leading to the downfall of one the world's finest accounting firms. And still top management erroneously believes that information security is a relatively unimportant issue not worthy of considerable attention.

Additionally, please consider a recent poll conducted by Harris Interactive which indicated that fully 79% of the American public believes that their personal information will be shared with other organizations without their permission. Apparently Americans don't believe businesses and government agencies when they publish privacy policies. Americans think these policies are just "window dressing," or something to please the auditors and regulators. What we have here is a major trust problem, where customers don't believe what businesses and government agencies say about the handling of private data. This is indicative of a serious failure on the part of these organizations; they have failed to convince customers that they will dutifully respect privacy rights. At the same time, an earlier study performed by the same organization (then called Louis Harris Associates) indicated that the take-up or adoption rate for new electronic services such as Internet business would double when adequate privacy safeguards were added. In other words, customers will be twice as likely to place an order online if they feel comfortable that their personal information will be adequately protected. Yet top management often doesn't allocate sufficient resources to information security, for instance by establishing a Chief Privacy Officer, and the net result is that sales suffer. Top management so often doesn't appreciate how doing a good job in the information security realm will lead to a variety of tangible business benefits like competitive advantage. If being able to double the level of sales isn't important to top management, what is?

Information security now needs to be recognized as a regular part of every modern organization. People need to have information security in their job descriptions, departments need to have information security in their mission statements, and outsourcing firms need to have information security in their contracts. Every personal computer needs to be outfitted with a virus detection software package, a personal firewall, and related software. End users need to be trained about information security, for instance, told what to do when their machine is infected with a computer virus. End users are now on the front line of the information security war. And a war it is, because new, more complex, and more aggressive ways to compromise information systems security are being developed every day.

Information security cannot be something that is left to the technologists within the Information Technology department. End users, for example, must deal with telephone callers who are seeking to get information through what is called social engineering. Also known as masquerading or spoofing, this technique involves leading users to believe that the caller is somebody other than who they really are. A caller could say they were from the IT department, that they need to have the user's user-ID and fixed password in order to correct a problem with the network. While it may sound unbelievable, unless they are told not to divulge such information, studies have shown that a large percentage of the user population will simply reveal their user-ID and password.

Everybody who comes into contact with sensitive, valuable, or critical information needs to know about information security. This means that the janitor needs to know how to dispose of confidential documents that may have been thrown away in the trash. This means that the temporary staff person who is answering the telephone at the front desk needs to know what information he or she can divulge to outsiders. This means that outsourcing firms must know how to respond to a hacker break-in so that losses are minimized, so that the subscribing organization's good reputation is maintained, and so that the subscribing firm's business activity can proceed without undue interruption. In other words, information security must be approached with a team of individuals, all consistently using the same approaches to security, each with their own special part to play.

In this context, I welcome this new textbook to train our future leaders. Every person working in modern businesses or government agencies will need to know some practical information about information security. If they cover information security at all, too many of the current college classes get bogged-down in the technology. While the technology is interesting, it is an overview, a holistic perspective, that is needed so that future leaders can understand the importance of and the ways to use information security. Information security is multi-disciplinary, multi-departmental, and increasingly multi-organizational in its scope. Future business leaders must appreciate how information security fits in with the other activities performed by the organizations where they will work.

The need for this information security knowledge gets more pressing every year. The US Federal Bureau of Investigation teams up with the Computer Security Institute every year to do a survey about computer crime. The most recent survey indicated that quantified losses due to computer crime were up 42% over the year before (apparently this still isn't serious enough to get many top managers to pay attention). Yet still 50% of the respondents to this survey don't have something as simple as a policy informing them where they should report violations and incidents. If workers at an organization don't even know to whom and when they should report a violation or an incident, then there is no chance that management will know what is really happening when it comes to information security. If management doesn't know what's happening, then there will be no hope that they will be able to adequately manage the problem. In the interests of adequately managing this problem, this book helps by talking about best practices that can help management figure out what's happening, and from there, determine the best way to address the problems.

Charles Cresson Wood, CISA, CISSP
Independent Information Security Consultant
Sausalito, California

Introduction to the Management of Information Security

1

If this is the information superhighway, it's going through a lot of bad, bad neighborhoods.

DORIAN BERGER, 1997[1]

ONE MONTH INTO HER NEW JOB at Random Widget Works, Inc. (RWW), Iris Majwabu left her office early one afternoon to attend a meeting of the Information Systems Security Association (ISSA). The new job was a promotion from her previous position as an information security risk manager.

Although she had paid her dues to the organization last year, this occasion marked Iris's first ISSA meeting. With a mountain of pressing matters on her cluttered desk, Iris didn't know why she was making this meeting a priority. She sighed. As the first Chief Information Security Officer (CISO) of RWW, she already spent many hours in business meetings, followed by long hours at her desk as she pressed on in defining her new position at the firm.

In the ISSA meeting room she saw Charley Moody, her supervisor at her previous job at Sequential Label and Supply. Charley had been promoted to CIO almost a year ago.

"Hi, Charley," she said.

"Hello, Iris." They shook hands warmly. "How are things at the new office?"

"So far," she replied, "things are going well—I think."

Charlie noticed her hesitancy. "You think?" he said. "Okay, tell me what's really going on."

Iris explained. "I am struggling to get a consensus from the management team about the problems that we have. I'm told that information security is a priority, but everything is in disarray. Any ideas that are brought up, especially my ideas, are chopped to bits before they're even formally proposed. There's no established policy covering our information security needs, and it seems that we have little hope of getting one approved. The information security budget covers my salary plus funding for one technician in the network department. The IT managers act like I'm a waste of their budget, and they do not seem to take security issues as seriously as I do. It's like trying to drive a herd of cats!"

"It sounds like we need to talk," Charley said. "But not now; the meeting is about to start. Here's my card—call me tomorrow and we'll arrange to get together for coffee."

LEARNING OBJECTIVES

Upon completion of this material, you should be able to:

- Recognize the importance of information technology and understand who is responsible for protecting an organization's information assets
- Know and understand the definition and key characteristics of information security
- Know and understand the definition and key characteristics of leadership and management
- Recognize the characteristics that differentiate information security management from general management

Introduction

In today's global markets, business operations are enabled by technology. From boardroom to mailroom, businesses make deals, ship goods, track client accounts, and inventory company assets, all by means of information technology (IT). Information technology is the vehicle that stores and transports information—a company's most valuable resource—from one business unit to another. But what happens if the vehicle breaks down, even for a little while? Business deals fall through, shipments are lost, and company assets become even more vulnerable to threats from both inside and outside.

In the past, the business manager's response to this possibility was to proclaim, "We have technology people to handle technology problems." Such a response was valid when technology was confined to the climate-controlled rooms of the data center and information processing was centralized. In the last 20 years, however, technology has permeated every facet of the business environment. Businesses now move when employees move, from office to office or from city to city. Since businesses have become more fluid, the concept of *computer security* has been replaced by the concept of *information security*. Because this new concept covers a broader range of issues, from the protection of data to the protection of human resources, information security is no longer the sole responsibility of a small, dedicated group of people in the company; rather, it is the responsibility of every employee, and especially managers.

Astute business managers increasingly recognize the critical nature of information security. In response to this growing awareness, businesses are creating new positions to solve the newly perceived problems. The emergence of technical managers, like Iris in the opening scenario of this chapter, allows for the creation of professionally managed information security teams whose main objective is the protection of information assets.

Organizations must realize that information security funding and planning decisions involve more than just technical managers, such as information security managers or members of the information security team. Rather, the process should involve three distinct groups of decision makers, or **communities of interest**:

- Information security managers and professionals
- Information technology managers and professionals
- Nontechnical business managers and professionals

Through a process of constructive debate, these three groups work to find consensus on an overall plan to protect the organization's information assets.

The communities of interest fulfill the following roles:

- The **information security community** protects the organization's information assets from the many threats they face.
- The **information technology community** supports the business objectives of the organization by supplying and supporting information technology appropriate to the business' needs.
- The nontechnical **general business community** articulates and communicates organizational policy and objectives and allocates resources to the other groups.

Working together, these communities make collective decisions about how to most effectively secure the organization.

As the discussion between Iris and Charley illustrates, managing a successful information security program takes time, resources, and a lot of effort. All three communities within the organization must understand that information security is about risk: identifying, measuring, and mitigating—or, at a minimum, documenting—the risk of operating information assets.

What Is Security?

Understanding the technical aspects of information security requires that you know the definitions of certain information technology terms and concepts. This knowledge enables you to more effectively communicate with the IT and information security communities.

In general, **security** is defined as "the quality or state of being secure—to be free from danger."[2] To be secure is to be protected from adversaries or other hazards. National security, for example, is a system of multilayered processes that protects the sovereignty of a state, its assets, resources, and people. Achieving an appropriate level of security for an organization also depends on a multilayered system.

Security is often achieved by means of several strategies usually undertaken simultaneously or used in combination with one another. While each strategy has its own focus and builds on its own specializations, the various strategies share many common elements. From a management perspective, each must be properly planned, organized, staffed, directed, and controlled. Examples of the specialized areas of security include the following:

- **Physical security**, which encompasses strategies to protect people, physical assets, and the workplace from various threats including fire, unauthorized access, or natural disasters

- **Personal security,** which overlaps with physical security in the protection of the people within the organization
- **Operations security,** which focuses on securing the organization's ability to carry out its operational activities without interruption or compromise
- **Communications security,** which encompasses the protection of an organization's communications media, technology, and content, and its ability to use these tools to achieve the organization's objectives
- **Network security,** which addresses the protection of an organization's data networking devices, connections, and contents, and the ability to use that network to accomplish the organization's data communication functions

Each of these areas contributes to the information security program as a whole.

This textbook bases its definition of information security on the standards published by the Committee on National Security Systems (CNSS), formerly known as the National Security Telecommunications and Information Systems Security Committee (NSTISSC).[3] **Information security** (InfoSec) is the protection of information and its critical elements, including the systems and hardware that use, store, and transmit that information. Figure 1-1 shows that information security includes the broad areas of information security management (the topic of this book), computer and data security, and network security. At the heart of the study of information security is the concept of policy (discussed in detail in Chapter 4). Policy, awareness, training, education, and technology are vital concepts for the protection of information and for keeping information systems from danger. The **C.I.A. triangle,** which is the basis of the CNSS model of information security, has been the industry standard for computer security since the development of the mainframe.

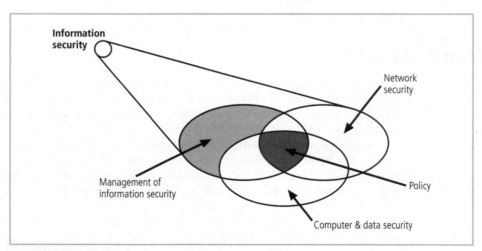

FIGURE 1-1   Components of Information Security

The C.I.A. triangle is founded on three desirable characteristics of information—confidentiality, integrity, and availability—that are as important today as they were when first put forth. However, present-day needs have made these three concepts alone inadequate, because they are limited in scope and cannot encompass the constantly changing environment of the IT industry. The threats to these three characteristics of information have evolved into a vast collection of potential dangers, including accidental or intentional damage, destruction, theft, unintended or unauthorized modification, or other misuses from human or other threats. This new environment of constantly evolving threats has necessitated the development of a more robust model of the characteristics of information. The updated model addresses the complexities of the current information security environment and the rapidly changing modern information technology industry. The C.I.A. triangle, therefore, has expanded into a more comprehensive list of critical characteristics of information, covered later in this chapter.

NSTISSC Security Model

The CNSS document called *National Training Standard for Information Security Professionals,* identified as NSTISSI No. 4011 (see *http://www.nstissc.gov/html/library.html*), presents a comprehensive model of information security. It is rapidly becoming the standard for many aspects of the security of information systems.

The NSTISSC security model, as shown in Figure 1-2, illustrates three dimensions central to the discussion of information security. If we extend the relationship among the three dimensions represented by the axes, we end up with a $3 \times 3 \times 3$ cube with 27 cells. Each of these cells represents an area of intersection among these three dimensions that must be addressed to secure information systems. When using this model to design or review any information security program, you must make sure that each of the 27 cells is properly addressed by each of the three communities of interest. For example, the cell representing the intersection between the technology, integrity, and storage areas is expected to include controls or safeguards addressing the use of *technology* to protect the *integrity* of information while in *storage*. Such a control might consist of a host intrusion detection system (HIDS), which alerts the security administrators when a critical file is modified.

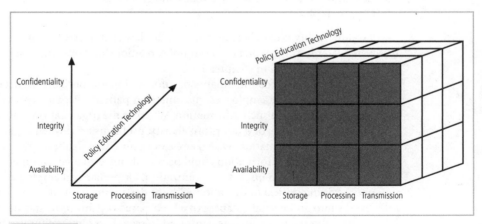

FIGURE 1-2 NSTISSC Security Model

While the NSTISSC model covers the three dimensions of information security, it omits discussion of detailed guidelines and policies that direct the implementation of controls. And in fact, merely having technical controls, policies, or education programs in place is inadequate. The main purpose of this model is to identify gaps in the coverage of an information security program.

Another weakness of using this model is to view it from a single perspective. The HIDS control in the preceding example addresses only the needs and concerns of the information security community, leaving out the needs and concerns of the broader IT and general business communities. In practice, thorough risk reduction requires that controls of all three types (policy, education, and technical) be created and communicated among all three communities. These controls can come about only through a process that includes consensus building and constructive conflict to reflect the balancing act that each organization faces as it designs and executes an information security program. Later chapters of this book will elaborate on these issues.

Key Concepts of Information Security

To better understand the management of information security, you must become familiar with the key characteristics of information that make it valuable to an organization. The C.I.A. triangle model mentioned earlier provides the first three of these characteristics (confidentiality, integrity, and availability).

Confidentiality

Confidentiality of information ensures that only those with sufficient privileges and a demonstrated need may access certain information. When unauthorized individuals or systems can access information, confidentiality is breached. To protect the confidentiality of information, a number of measures are used, including:

- Information classification
- Secure document storage
- Application of general security policies
- Education of information custodians and end users
- Cryptography

Confidentiality is closely related to another key characteristic of information, privacy (discussed later in this chapter). The complex relationship between these two characteristics is discussed in detail in Chapter 11.

In an organization, confidentiality of information is especially important for personal information about employees, customers, or patients. People expect that an organization will closely guard such information. Whether the organization is a federal agency, a commercial enterprise, or a nonprofit charity, problems arise when organizations disclose confidential information. Disclosure can occur either deliberately or by mistake. For example, confidential information could be mistakenly e-mailed to someone *outside* the organization rather than *inside* the organization. Or perhaps an employee discards a document containing critical information without destroying it. Or maybe a hacker successfully breaks into an internal database of a Web-based organization and steals sensitive information about clients, such as names, addresses, or credit card information.

Integrity

Integrity is the quality or state of being whole, complete, and uncorrupted. The integrity of information is threatened when it is exposed to corruption, damage, destruction, or other disruption of its authentic state. Corruption can occur while information is being entered, stored, or transmitted.

Many computer viruses and worms, for example, are designed to corrupt data. For this reason, the key method for detecting an integrity failure of a file system from an attack by a virus or worm is to look for changes in one file's state as indicated by the file's size, or in a more advanced operating system, the file's hash value (file hashing is discussed later in this section) or checksum.

The corruption of a file, however, does not always result from deliberate attacks. Faulty programming or even noise in the transmission channel or media can cause data to lose its integrity. For example, a low voltage state in a signal carrying a digital bit (a one or zero) can cause the receiving system to record the data incorrectly.

To compensate for internal and external threats to the integrity of information, systems employ a variety of error control techniques, including redundancy bits and check bits. During each transmission, algorithms, hash values, and the error-correcting codes ensure the integrity of the information. Data that has not been verified in this manner is retransmitted or otherwise recovered.

As noted earlier, one way to ensure information integrity is by means of **file hashing**. File hashing uses a special algorithm that evaluates the bits in a file and then computes a single representative number called a hash value. The **hash value** is different for each combination of bits. If the computer system performs the same hashing algorithm on the file and arrives at a different number than the file's recorded hash value, then it knows that the file has been compromised. Because information is of little or no value or use if its integrity cannot be verified, information integrity is a cornerstone of information security.

Availability

Availability is the characteristic of information that enables user access to information without interference or obstruction and in a useable format. A *user* in this definition may be either a person or another computer system. Availability does not imply that the information is accessible to *any* user; rather, it means availability to *authorized* users.

To understand this concept more fully, consider the contents of a library—in particular, research libraries that require identification for access to the library as a whole or to certain collections. Library patrons must present the required identification before accessing the collection. Once patrons are granted access, they expect to be able to locate and access resources in the appropriate languages and formats.

Privacy

The information that is collected, used, and stored by an organization is to be used only for the purposes stated to the data owner at the time it was collected. This definition of **privacy** does not focus on freedom from observation (the meaning usually associated with the word), but rather means that information will be used only in ways known to the person providing it. Many organizations collect, swap, and sell personal information as a commodity. It is now possible to collect and combine information on individuals from separate sources, which has yielded detailed databases whose data might be used in ways not agreed to, or even communicated to, the original data owner. Many people have become aware of these practices and are looking to governments for protection of their privacy.

Identification

An information system possesses the characteristic of **identification** when it is able to recognize individual users. Identification is the first step in gaining access to secured material, and it serves as the foundation for subsequent authentication and authorization. Identification and authentication are essential to establishing the level of access or authorization that an individual is granted. Identification is typically performed by means of a user name or other ID.

Authentication

Authentication occurs when a control provides proof that a user possesses the identity that he or she claims. Examples include the use of cryptographic certificates to establish Secure Sockets Layer (SSL) connections, or the use of cryptographic hardware tokens like SecurID cards to confirm a user's identity.

Authorization

After the identity of a user is authenticated, a process called **authorization** provides assurance that the user (whether a person or a computer) has been specifically and explicitly authorized by the proper authority to access, update, or delete the contents of an information asset. An example of this control is the activation and use of access control lists and authorization groups in a networking environment. Another example is a database authorization scheme to verify that the user of an application is authorized for specific functions such as read, write, create, and delete.

Accountability

The characteristic of **accountability** exists when a control provides assurance that every activity undertaken can be attributed to a named person or automated process. For example, audit logs that track user activity on an information system provide accountability.

THREAT MANAGEMENT

Ping of Death

Definition

The Ping of Death is a denial-of-service (DoS) attack that was once widely seen. While it is now rarely encountered because network product vendors have engineered the vulnerability out of currently used products, it can serve as an example of how vulnerabilities can be exploited and become attacks. This DoS attack is essentially an operating system vulnerability that takes advantage of the Internet Protocol's need to fragment large packets. Internet Protocol (IP) packets, as defined by the standard for TCP/IP in RFC-791, can be up to 65,535 ($2^{16} - 1$) octets long, which includes the header length (typically 20 octets if no IP options are specified). Most current network products do not allow packets that large, and are thus immune to the Ping of Death. Packets too big to be handled by the underlying layer—that is, packets that exceed a device's maximum transmission unit (MTU)—are fragmented into smaller packets, which are then reassembled by the

(continued)

receiver. For example, in most Ethernet routers and switches, the MTU is 1500 bytes. Each of these packet fragments contains an offset value that indicates where it belongs within the larger packet.

Therein lies the vulnerability. It is possible to combine a valid offset value with a valid fragment size so that the total size is greater than 65,535, the maximum packet size. Machines don't process a packet until they have all fragments and have tried to reassemble them into the original packet, so an oversized packet can cause an overflow of 16-bit internal variables, which can lead to system crashes, reboots, kernel dumps, and other problems. This kind of attack is commonly associated with the network diagnostic protocol, the Internet Control Message Protocol (ICMP). In common usage, many people call the use of ICMP pinging by association with the operating system command used to generate an ICMP message, ping. Pinging, however, is not the only means of generating an oversized packet.

Ping of Death attacks were once common because most platforms were susceptible to them, the identity of the sender could be easily spoofed (impersonated), and they required no more knowledge than the target system's IP address. Today most networking devices and operating systems have been effectively patched, rendering this exploit less popular than it once was.

Detection/Testing for Vulnerability

This type of attack uses a weakness in your system, rather than planting an executable or launching an obvious attack. There is no way to "detect" a Ping of Death attack in progress, but you can test to see if your system is vulnerable. On a system running Windows 95 or NT, run the following command:

```
ping -l 65510 your.host.ip.address
```

The message on the Windows 95 system will be "Request Timed Out." This means that the ping wasn't answered, either because the machine is ignoring you or because it's dead. Follow up with another ping without specifying a packet size:

```
ping your.host.ip.address
```

If the host responds to this second ping, it is immune to the Ping of Death. If the device is running and has ICMP enabled and it does not respond, it has been taken out of service by the attack.

Protection

Since bringing down a network or firewall can be part of a larger, multilevel attack, you should take this exploit seriously, even with so few network devices in service that are vulnerable. The best way to protect your system and network from Ping of Death attacks is to install updated patches for all network devices, based on each device's operating system. If no patch is available for your system, you should block all ICMP traffic using other network defenses, such as firewalls. A firewall does not detect any Ping of Death attacks, however, and although a properly kept log should show any attempts to ping your systems, it is merely a temporary solution. Attackers can still send invalid packets to a Web server or FTP service.

(continued)

Another potential solution is to block only fragmented pings. This strategy would allow 64-byte pings through on almost all systems, while blocking any larger ones.

The best solution is to patch your operating system and test it often for all known vulnerabilities. In this regard, the Ping of Death is illustrative of attacks in general; most attacks exploit system vulnerabilities that can be easily corrected but are often ignored until an attack forces system owners to close the loophole by updating their systems.

For more information, see the Ping of Death information page at *http://www.insecure.org/sploits/ping-o-death.html* or the CERT Advisory at *http://www.cert.org/advisories/CA-1996-26.html*.

Contributed by Art McLellelan, David Kabzinki, Eric Friebolin, Ginny Hudson, and Steve Lieb.

A successful information security program combines the conceptual elements described above to reduce risk to its information assets. The art of accomplishing meaningful reductions in risk requires communication and cooperation among all three communities of interest. In other words, securing information technology can be achieved only through careful management and dynamic leadership.

What is Management?

To make the information security process more effective, it is important to understand certain core principles of management. In its simplest form, **management** is the process of achieving objectives using a given set of resources. A **manager** is "someone who works with and through other people by coordinating their work activities in order to accomplish organizational goals."[4] A manager's job is to marshal and administer resources, coordinate the completion of tasks, and handle the many roles necessary to complete the desired objectives. A manager has many roles to play within organizations, including the following:

- Informational role: Collecting, processing, and using information that can affect the completion of the objective
- Interpersonal role: Interacting with superiors, subordinates, outside stakeholders, and other parties that influence or are influenced by the completion of the task
- Decisional role: Selecting from among alternative approaches, and resolving conflicts, dilemmas, or challenges.

The Difference Between Leadership and Management

The distinction between a leader and a manager arises in the execution of organizational tasks.

The leader influences employees so that they are willing to accomplish objectives. He or she is expected to *lead by example* and demonstrate personal traits that instill a desire in others to follow. In other words, leadership provides purpose, direction, and motivation to those that follow.

By comparison, a manager administers the resources of the organization. He or she creates budgets, authorizes expenditures, and hires employees. This distinction between a leader and a manager is important because leadership may not always be a function of a manager, and nonmanagers are often assigned to leadership roles. Many times, however, managers fulfill both the role of management and leadership.

Characteristics of a Leader

What makes a good leader? The U.S. military uses the following list of 14 leadership traits as a teaching tool for its officer corps to identify potential leaders:

1. Bearing – maintaining professional carriage and appearance
2. Courage – proceeding in the face of adversity
3. Decisiveness – making and expressing decisions in a clear and authoritative manner
4. Dependability – performing and completing tasks in a reliable and predictable manner
5. Endurance – withstanding mental, physical, and emotional hardship
6. Enthusiasm – displaying sincere interest in and exuberance for the accomplishment of tasks
7. Initiative – identifying and accomplishing tasks in the absence of specific guidance
8. Integrity – being of sound moral fiber, and good ethical worth
9. Judgment – using sound personal decision making to determine effective and appropriate solutions
10. Justice – being impartial and fair in exercising authority
11. Knowledge – possessing a base of information gained through experience or education
12. Loyalty – expressing open support and faithfulness to one's organization and fellow employees
13. Tact – dealing with a situation without undue personal bias or creating offense
14. Unselfishness – performing duties by placing the welfare of others and the accomplishment of the mission first

The private sector typically uses a shorter list of such traits, such as drive, desire to lead, honesty and integrity, self-confidence, cognitive ability, and knowledge of the business.[5]

The U.S. military also provides an action plan for the improvement of an individual's leadership abilities:

1. Know yourself and seek self-improvement.
2. Be technically and tactically proficient.
3. Seek responsibility and take responsibility for your actions.
4. Make sound and timely decisions.
5. Set the example.
6. Know your [subordinates] and look out for their well-being.
7. Keep your subordinates informed.
8. Develop a sense of responsibility in your subordinates.
9. Ensure the task is understood, supervised, and accomplished.
10. Build the team.
11. Employ your [team] in accordance with its capabilities."[6]

A key characteristic of a leader is concern for subordinates as well as strong motivation for accomplishing organizational objectives. A characteristic of leadership is the exhibition of the principles of *be…know…and do…*.

As a leader you must *BE* a person of strong and honorable character; committed to professional ethics; an example of individual values; and able to resolve complex ethical dilemmas. You must *KNOW* the details of your situation, the standards to which you work, yourself, human nature, and your team. You must *DO* by providing purpose, direction, and motivation to your teams."[7]

Behavioral Types of Leaders

There are three basic behavioral types of leaders: the *autocratic*, the *democratic*, and the *laissez-faire*.

Autocratic leaders reserve all decision-making responsibility for themselves, and are more *"do as I say"* types of managers. Such a leader typically issues an order to accomplish a task, and does not usually seek or accept alternative viewpoints. The democratic leader works in the opposite way, typically seeking input from all interested parties, requesting ideas and suggestions, and then formulating a position that can be supported by a majority. Each of these two diametrically opposed positions has both strengths and weaknesses. The autocratic leader can be more efficient in that he or she is not constrained by the necessity to accomodate alternative supporting viewpoints. The democratic leader can be the less efficient, because valuable time can be spent in discussion and debate when planning for the task. By contrast, the autocratic leader can also be the less effective if the knowledge possessed by the leader is less than sufficient for the task. The democratic leader can be more effective when dealing with very complex topics and those in which subordinates have strongly held opinions.

The laissez-faire leader is also known as the *"laid-back"* leader. While both autocratic and democratic leaders tend to be action-oriented, the laissez-faire leader tends to sit back and allow the process to develop as it goes, only making minimal decisions to avoid bringing the process to a complete halt.

Effective leaders function with a combination of these styles, shifting approaches as situations warrant. For example, depending on the circumstances, a leader will solicit input when the situation permits, make autocratic decisions when immediate action is required, or allow the operation to proceed if it is progressing in an efficient and effective manner.

Characteristics of Management

The management of tasks leading to the accomplishment of any objective requires certain basic skills. These skills are referred to as management characteristics, functions, principles, or responsibilities. Two basic approaches to management exist:

- Traditional management theory uses the core principles of planning, organizing, staffing, directing, and controlling (POSDC).
- Popular management theory categorizes the principles of management into planning, organizing, leading, and controlling (POLC).

The following discussion uses POLC to examine the skills that managers must employ when dealing with tasks. Figure 1-3 shows an overview of these elements and illustrates how the elements are conceptually related.

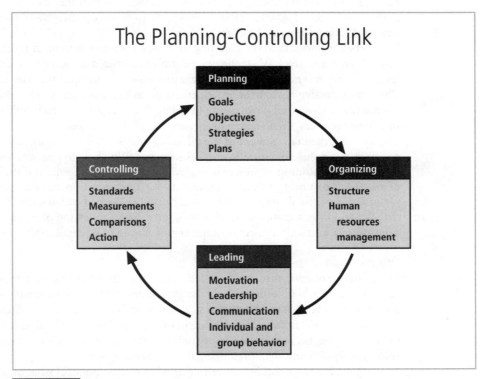

FIGURE 1-3 The Planning-Controlling Link[8]

Planning

The process that develops, creates, and implements strategies for the accomplishment of objectives is called **planning**. Several different approaches to planning are examined more thoroughly in later chapters and throughout this book. There are three levels of planning:

- *Strategic planning* occurs at the highest levels of the organization and for a longer period of time, usually five or more years.
- *Tactical planning* focuses on production planning and integrates organizational resources at a level below the entire enterprise and for an intermediate duration (such as one to five years).
- *Operational planning* focuses on the day-to-day operation of local resources, and occurs in the short or immediate term.

As Iris experiences in the opening story, lack of planning causes confusion and frustration among managers and staff.

The general approach to planning begins with the creation of strategic plans for the entire organization. The resulting plan is then divided up into planning elements appropriate for each major business unit of the organization. These business units in turn create business plans that meet the requirements of the overall organizational strategy, and these plans are communicated to mid-level managers so that they can create tactical plans at their levels. Supervisors use the tactical plans to create operational plans that guide the day-to-day operations of the organization.

To better understand the planning process, an organization must thoroughly define its goals and objectives. While the exact definition varies depending on context, the term **goal** refers to the end result of a planning process—for example, the goal line in football. The term **objective** refers to an intermediate point that allows us to measure progress toward the goal—a first down, using the football analogy. If you accomplish all objectives in a timely manner, then you are likely to accomplish your goal.

By itself, the management of the planning function within an organization encompasses an entire field of study. It involves understanding how to plan and relies on an integral understanding of project management. Project management is the management of all aspects of a project from inception, through organization and start-up, task completion, and eventual wrap-up. It involves the entire suite of activities necessary to ensure that the project is accomplished with the appropriate application of resources, including time, money, and staff. Project management is discussed in detail in Chapter 12.

Organization

The principle of management dedicated to the structuring of resources to support the accomplishment of objectives is called **organization**. It includes organizing departments and their associated staff, the storage of raw materials to facilitate manufacturing, and the information to aid in the accomplishment of the task. Recent definitions of organization include staffing, because organizing people so as to maximize their productivity is not substantially different than organizing time, money, or equipment.

Organizing tasks requires determining what is to be done, in what order, by whom, by which methods, and according to what timeline. These activities are typically considered a part of project management, and are discussed in later chapters of this book. Defining organizational units and establishing departmental responsibilities and reporting relationships among staff may be outside the authority of any individual manager. What may be within a manager's domain are the creation of project teams and internal departments, and the assignment of specific staff to specific positions. The selection and retention of security personnel, and the role of the information security department in the selection and retention of other personnel, is covered in Chapters 5 and 10.

Leadership

As noted earlier, **leadership** encourages the implementation of the planning and organizing functions. It includes supervising employee behavior, performance, attendance, and attitude. Leadership generally addresses the direction and motivation of the human resource.

Control

Monitoring progress toward completion, and making necessary adjustments to achieve the desired objectives, requires the exercise of **control**. In general, the control function serves to assure the organization of the validity of the plan. The manager ensures that sufficient progress is made, that impediments to the completion of the task are resolved, and that no additional resources are required. Should the plan be found invalid in light of the operational reality of the organization, the manager takes corrective action. The controlling function also determines what must be monitored as well as applies specific **control tools** to gather and evaluate information.

Four categories of control tools exist:

- *Information control tools* affect organizational communications, which is the flow of information throughout the entire organization, whether manual or automated.

- *Financial control tools* guide the expenditure of monetary resources, including total cost of ownership (TCO), return on investment (ROI), and cost-benefit analysis (CBA), along with the ordinary and expected budget process. The use of budgets as financial controls, as developed in planning, directly affects all operational functions. Project management brings a specific focus to certain financial controls that measure progress and performance. Being *on time* and *under budget* are two important controls used to regulate the progress of a project.

- *Operational control tools* evaluate the efficiency and effectiveness of business processes. The use of graphical control tools such as PERT, Gantt charts, and process flow, along with others discussed in Chapter 12, regulate the function of projects and operations.

- *Behavioral control tools* regulate the efficiency and effectiveness of human resources; they include supervision, performance evaluations, and discipline. Supervision refers to the immediate oversight, guidance, and instruction of employees. Performance evaluations are the periodic assessment of general job performance. Discipline is the method by which the manager deals with unapproved behavior.

Each of these tool categories relies on the use of cybernetic control loops, often called negative feedback. They all use performance measurements, comparison, and corrective action, an approach that is illustrated in Figure 1-4. In this figure, the cybernetic control process begins with a measurement of actual performance, which is then compared to the expected standard of performance as determined by the planning process. If the standard is being met, the process is allowed to continue toward completion. If an acceptable level of performance is not being met, either the process is corrected to achieve satisfactory results, or the expected level of planned performance is redefined.

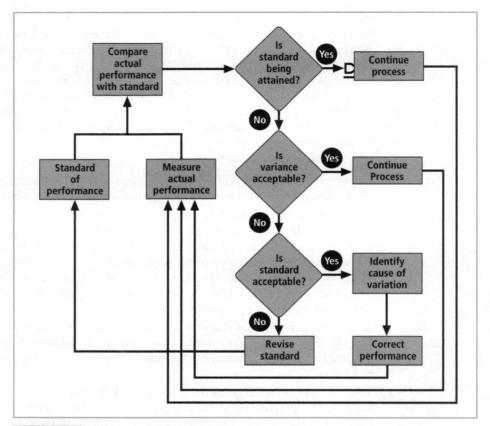

FIGURE 1-4 The Control Process

Understanding the four core principles discussed above enables managers to focus their energies and efforts in the right direction, using tried and true management methods. Ultimately, management success is measured by how a manager solves problems.

Solving Problems

All managers face problems in the course of the organization's day-to-day operation. Whether a problem is low or high profile, the same basic process can be used to solve it. Time pressures often constrain decision making when problems arise, however. The process of gathering and evaluating the necessary facts may be beyond available capabilities. Nevertheless, the methodology described in the following steps can be used as a basic blueprint for resolving many operational problems.

Step 1: Recognize and Define the Problem

The most frequent flaw in problem solving is failing to completely define the problem. Begin by clearly defining exactly which problem needs to be solved. For example, if Iris receives complaints at RWW about the receipt of a large number of unsolicited commercial e-mails (also known as spam), she must first determine whether the complaints are valid. Are employees receiving unsolicited spam, or have they signed up for notifications and mailing lists?

Step 2: Gather Facts and Make Assumptions

To understand the background and events that shape the problem, a manager can gather facts about the organizational, cultural, technological, and behavioral factors that are at the root of the problem. He or she can then make assumptions about the methods that are available to solve the problem. For example, by interviewing several employees, Iris might determine that several employees are receiving a large quantity of unsolicited e-mail. She might also determine that each of these employees has accessed approved vendor support sites, which require an e-mail sign-in process. In such a case, Iris would suspect that the problem of excessive e-mail is, in fact, the result of employees providing their company e-mail addresses, which are being improperly used by the site owners.

Step 3: Develop Possible Solutions

The next step is to begin formulating possible solutions. Managers can use several methods to generate ideas. One of these is brainstorming, a process where a number of individuals air as many ideas as possible in a short time, without regard for their practicality. The group then reviews and filters the ideas to identify any feasible options. Problem solvers can also interview experts, or perform research into solutions using the Web, magazines, journals, or books. In any case, the goal is to develop as many solutions as possible. In the preceding example, once Iris locates the source of the spam e-mails, she can speak with the e-mail server and firewall administrators, and then turn to her CISSP reading list. She might contact several of her friends from the local ISSA chapter, as well as spend time surfing security-related Web sites. After a few hours, Iris could have dozens of pages of information that might be useful in solving this problem.

Step 4: Analyze and Compare the Possible Solutions

Each proposed solution must be examined and ranked as to its likely success in solving the problem. This analysis may include reviewing economic, technological, behavioral, and operational feasibilities:

- To review economic feasibility, you compare the costs and benefits of possible solutions.
- To review technological feasibility, you address the organization's ability to acquire the technology needed to implement a candidate solution.
- To review behavioral feasibility, you assess a candidate solution according to the likelihood that subordinates will adopt and support a solution, rather than resisting it.
- To review operational feasibility, you assess the organization's ability to integrate a candidate solution into its current business processes.

Using these methods, you can compare and contrast various proposals. In the spam example, Iris might immediately eliminate any overly expensive solutions, throw out some technical solutions incompatible with RWW's systems, and narrow the field to three alternatives: (1) do nothing, and accept the spam as a cost of doing business; (2) have the e-mail administrator change the users' accounts; or (3) have the firewall administrator filter access to and traffic from the spam sites. Iris could then discuss these alternatives with all administrators involved. Each of the remaining three solutions is feasible, is inexpensive, and does not negatively affect RWW's overall operations.

Step 5: Select, Implement, and Evaluate a Solution

Once a solution is chosen and implemented, you must evaluate it to determine its effectiveness in solving the problem. It is important to monitor the chosen solution carefully so that if it proves ineffective, it can be cancelled or altered quickly. In Iris's case, she might decide to implement the firewall filters to reduce the spam, as most of it comes from a few common sources. She might also decide to require the affected employees to attend an e-mail security policy training program, where they can be reminded of the importance of controlling when and where they release company e-mail addresses. In addition, these employees might be required to submit periodic reports regarding the status of the e-mail problem.

VIEWPOINT

Information Security: On the Cusp of a Management Evolution

By Steve Kahan

The field of information security is today in the midst of a transformation. Until recently, the industry has been dominated by technical experts responding to technical issues as they provide information services, and confined to areas of computer and network operations. It is now evolving quickly into a management discipline that gets boardroom attention—one that involves managing people and processes, as well as technology. This evolution is the result of several major changes in our global, Internet-connected environment.

Information security breaches and the damage they cause have risen dramatically in the past few years. Computer security vulnerabilities and reported attacks more than doubled from 2001 to 2002. It has been estimated that the worldwide financial impact of such activities reached $13.2 billion in 2001 alone.

We are also seeing a surge of new government regulations covering all kinds of industries and aimed at setting standards for cyber security and privacy. The increase in security breaches, along with these new regulations, have spurred an increase in internal audits among private and public organizations worldwide seeking to comply with regulatory requirements and leading practices.

Security professionals are recognizing that technology alone cannot solve the problem of securing our nation's vital information assets. An increasing number of academic programs are focusing on information security, and books such as this one are beginning to articulate and codify the discipline of information security management.

(continued)

Outside of the academic world, efforts by organizations such as the Human Firewall Council, of which I am president, have helped raise the awareness and visibility of security management issues. The term "human firewall" refers to the idea that the people within an organization, if made aware and properly educated, will support information security efforts and form a layer of protection (much like a firewall) to prevent and deter threats to a company's critical information assets. Through the Human Firewall's Security Management Index and Security Awareness Index surveys and reports, we have begun to provide the measurements necessary to feed the growth of information security as a management discipline.

This is an exciting time to be involved in the study and practice of information security management. As a reader and a participant in the evolution of information security, you are among the pioneers setting the standards that will guide security professionals in the years to come.

Steve Kahan

President, Human Firewall Council

More information on the Human Firewall Project, including the Human Firewall Manifesto, can be found at http://www.humanfirewall.org.

Principles of Information Security Management

As noted earlier, information security management is one of the three communities of interest functioning in most organizations. As part of the management team, it operates like all other management units by using the common characteristics of leadership and management discussed earlier in this chapter. However, the goals and objectives of the information security management team differ from those of the IT and general management communities in that they are focused on the secure operation of the organization.

Because information security management is charged with taking responsibility for a specialized program, certain characteristics of its management are unique to this community of interest. These unique features extend the basic characteristics of general leadership and management and, as such, form the basis for the balance of this book.

The extended characteristics of information security are known as the six *P*s. Each is defined and examined briefly here.

Planning

Planning in InfoSec management is an extension of the basic planning model discussed earlier in this chapter. Included in the InfoSec planning model are activities necessary to support the design, creation, and implementation of information security strategies, as they exist within the IT planning environment

The business strategy is translated into the IT strategy, which is in turn converted into the InfoSec strategy. For example, the CIO uses the IT objectives gleaned from the business unit plans to create the organization's IT strategy. The IT strategy then informs the planning efforts for each IT functional area. Depending on the location of the InfoSec function in the organization, the IT strategy may be used for information security planning.

The CISO works with the appropriate security managers to develop operational security plans. These security managers consult with security technicians to develop tactical security plans. Each of these plans is usually coordinated across the IT functions of the enterprise and placed into a master schedule for implementation. The overall goal is to create plans that support long-term achievement of the overall organizational strategy. If all goes as planned, the entire collection of tactical plans results in accomplishment of operational goals, and the entire collection of operational goals results in accomplishment of subordinate strategic goals; this helps to meet the strategic goals and objectives of the organization as a whole.

Several types of InfoSec plans exist, including incident response planning, business continuity planning, disaster recovery planning, policy planning, personnel planning, technology rollout planning, risk management planning, and security program planning including education, training and awareness. Each of these plans has unique goals and objectives, and each benefits from the same organized methodical approach. Each of these planning areas is discussed in detail in later chapters of this book.

Another basic planning consideration unique to InfoSec is locating the InfoSec department within the organization structure. This topic is discussed in Chapter 5.

Policy

The set of organizational guidelines that dictates certain behavior within the organization is called **policy**. In InfoSec, there are three general categories of policy:

- *Enterprise information security policy* (EISP) sets the tone for the InfoSec department and the InfoSec climate across the organization. This policy is developed within the context of the strategic IT plan. The CISO typically drafts the program policy, which is usually supported and signed by the CIO or the CEO.

- An *issue-specific security policy* (ISSP) is a set of rules that defines acceptable behavior within a specific technology, such as e-mail or Internet usage.

- *System-specific policies* (SSSPs) are technical and/or managerial in nature and control the configuration and/or use of a piece of equipment or technology. For example, an access control list (ACL) is an SSSP that defines the accesses permitted for the specified device.

Programs

Programs are the operations conducted within InfoSec, which are specifically managed as separate entities. A security education training and awareness (SETA) program is one such entity. SETA programs are managed to provide critical information to employees to either improve their current level of security knowledge or maintain it. Other programs that may emerge include a physical security program, complete with fire, physical access, gates, guards, and so on. Each organization may have one or more security programs that must be managed.

Protection

The protection function is executed via a set of risk management activities, including risk assessment and control, as well as protection mechanisms, technologies, and tools. Each of these mechanisms represents some aspect of the management of specific controls in the overall information security plan.

People

People are the most critical link in the information security program. As discussed in the Viewpoint section, it is imperative that managers continuously recognize the crucial role that people play in the information security program. This aspect of InfoSec includes security personnel and the security of personnel, as well as aspects of the SETA program mentioned earlier.

Project Management

The final component is the application of thorough project management discipline to all elements of the information security program. Whether is the task is to roll out a new security training program or to select and implement a new firewall, it is important that the process be managed as a project. This effort involves identifying and controlling the resources applied to the project, as well as measuring progress and adjusting the process as progress is made toward the goal.

Chapter Summary

- In today's global markets, business operations are enabled by technology.
- Since businesses and technology have become more fluid, the concept of computer security has been replaced by the concept of information security.
- From an information security perspective, organizations often contain three communities of interest: information security managers and professionals, information technology managers and professionals, and nontechnical managers and professionals.
- Security is achieved via many routes, with several approaches usually undertaken singly or used in combination with one another.
- Specialized areas of security include the following:
  - Physical security
  - Personal security
  - Operations security
  - Communications security
  - Network security
- The C.I.A. triangle is based on three desirable characteristics of information: confidentiality, integrity, and availability.
- The CNSS (formerly the NSTISSC) presents a comprehensive model of information security that is rapidly becoming the evaluation standard for many aspects of the security of information systems.
- In its simplest form, management is the process of achieving objectives by using resources.
- The important distinction between a leader and a manager is that a leader influences employees so that they are willing to accomplish objectives, whereas a manager creates budgets, authorizes expenditures, and hires employees.

- The U.S. military uses a list of 14 leadership traits as a teaching tool for its officer corps, while the private sector typically uses a shorter list of such traits.
- Key characteristics of a leader are concern for employees as well as strong motivations for accomplishing organizational objectives.
- There are three basic behavioral types of leaders: the autocratic, the democratic, and the laissez-faire.
- Basic management skills are sometimes referred to as management characteristics, functions, principles, or responsibilities.
- The traditional approach to management theory uses the core principles of planning, organizing, staffing, directing, and controlling (POSDC).
- One approach to management theory categorizes the principles of management into planning, organizing, leading, and controlling (POLC).
- The process that develops, creates, and implements strategies for the accomplishment of objectives is called planning. There are three levels of planning: strategic, tactical and operational.
- The principle of management dedicated to the structuring of resources to support the accomplishment of objectives is called organization.
- Leadership includes supervising employee behavior, performance, attendance, and attitude.
- Exercising control involves monitoring progress toward completion and making necessary adjustments to achieve the desired objectives.
- Problem solving is a multistep process that involves defining the problem, developing and analyzing possible solutions, and then selecting, implementing, and evaluating the best solution.
- Information security management operates like all other management units, but the goals and objectives of the InfoSec management team are different in that they focus on the secure operation of the organization.

Review Questions

1. A globally interconnected commercial world has emerged from the technical advances that created the Internet. Has its creation increased or decreased the need for organizations to maintain secure operation of their systems? Why?
2. Which trend in IT has eliminated the "we have technology people to handle technology problems" approach as method for securing systems?
3. List and describe an organization's three communities of interest that engage in efforts to solve InfoSec problems. Give two or three examples of who might be in each community.
4. What is the definition of security? How is a secure state usually achieved?
5. List and describe the specialized areas of security.
6. What is the definition of information security? What essential protections must be in place to protect information systems from danger?
7. What is the C.I.A. triangle? Define each of its component parts.
8. Why is the C.I.A. triangle significant? Is it widely referenced?
9. Describe the CNSS security model. What are its three dimensions?

10. What is the definition of privacy as it relates to information security? How is this definition of privacy different from the everyday definition? Why is this difference significant?

11. Define the InfoSec processes of identification, authentication, authorization, and accountability.

12. What is management and what is a manager? What roles do managers play as they execute their responsibilities?

13. Are leadership and management similar? How are they different?

14. List and describe the behavioral types of leadership. Are they usually found in their pure form?

15. What are the characteristics of management based on the popular approach to management? Define each characteristic.

16. What are the three types of general planning? Define each.

17. List and describe the four categories of control tools.

18. List and describe the five steps of the general problem-solving process.

19. List and describe the extended characteristics of information security management.

20. Define project management. Why is project management of particular interest in the field of information security?

Exercises

1. Using a Web browser and search engine, find the Web site of the Committee on National Security Systems (CNSS), formerly the National Security Telecommunications and Information Systems Security Committee (NSTISSC). Locate the documentation library and browse the index. When was the site last updated? Which one or two documents would be of most interest to you now?

2. Think of an organization that uses information technology, but would not need to provide for information security on those systems. Describe that environment and explain why information security is not a factor for that organization.

3. Assume that a security model is needed for the protection of information in your class. Using the CNSS model, examine each of the cells and write a brief statement on how you would address the components represented in that cell.

4. Consider the information stored on your personal computer. Do you, at this moment, have information stored in your computer that is critical to your personal life? If that information became compromised or lost, what effect would it have on you?

5. Using the Web, identify the senior executive officer, the chief information officer, and the chief information security officer for your school or your current employer. Note that some organizations may use different titles for these personnel, so look for the closest approximate that can be found.

Case Exercises

Charley and Iris made an appointment to meet for a working lunch the next week. Charley sat down the day before the meeting to jot down his thoughts about good advice for Iris.

1. Based on your reading of the chapter and what you now know about the issues, list at least three things Iris could do.

2. Among the things listed in your advice to Iris, which one thing is the most important? Why?

Endnotes

1. Henry Ehrlich. *The Wiley Book of Business Quotations.* New York: John Wiley and Sons, 1998.
2. Merriam-Webster. "security." Merriam-Webster Online. [Cited 1 February 2002]. Available from the World Wide Web at http://www.m-w.com/cgi-bin/dictionary.
3. National Security Telecommunications and Information Systems Security. *National Training Standard for Information Systems Security (InfoSec) Professionals.* June 20, 1994, file 4011, [Cited February 1, 2002]. Available from the World Wide Web at http://www.nstissc.gov/Assets/pdf/4011.pdf.
4. Coulter Robbins. *Management 7th ed.* Upper Saddle River, NJ: Prentice Hall, 2002.
5. Coulter Robbins. *Management 7th ed.* Upper Saddle River, NJ: Prentice Hall, 2002: Chapter 16.
6. *Military Leadership.* FM 22-100. July 1990: p. 5.
7. *Military Leadership*, FM 22-100, July 1990: p. 53.
8. From the lecture notes of Dr. Louis Jourdan, Clayton College and State University. [Cited April 15, 2003]. Available from the World Wide Web at http://business.clayton.edu/ljourdan/mgmt3101ic/

Planning for Security

2

IRIS WAS A LITTLE UNEASY. WHILE THIS WASN'T HER first meeting with Mike Edwards, the Chief Information Officer, it was her first planning meeting. Around the table, the other IT department heads were casually chatting, drinking their coffee. Iris stared at her notepad, where she had carefully written "Strategic Planning Meeting" and nothing else.

Mike entered the room followed by his assistants. Stan, his lead executive assistant, was loaded down with stacks of copied documents, which he and the other assistants began handing out around the table. Iris took her copy and scanned the title: Random Widget Works, Inc., Strategic Planning Document, Information Technology Division, FY 2004–2008.

Mike began, "As you know, it's annual planning time again. You just got your copies of the multiyear IT strategic plan. Last month you each received your numbered copy of the company strategic plan." Iris remembered the half-inch-thick document she had carefully read and then locked in her filing cabinet.

Mike continued, "I'm going to go through the IT vision and mission statements, and then review the details of how the IT plan will allow us to meet the objectives articulated in the strategic plan. In 30 days you'll submit your draft plans back to me for review. Don't hesitate to come by to discuss any issues or questions."

Later that day, Iris dropped by Mike's office to discuss her planning responsibilities. This duty was not something he had briefed her about yet. Mike apologized, "I'm sorry, Iris. I meant to spend some time outlining your role as security manager. I'm afraid I can't do it this week; maybe we can start next week, by reviewing some key points I want you to make sure are in your plan."

The next day Iris and Charley Moody had planned lunch.

After they ordered, Iris said, "We just started on our strategic planning project and I'm developing a security strategic plan. You know, I've never worked up one of these from scratch before. Got any good advice on what to look for?"

Charley responded, "Sure. Coincidentally, when we're finished eating, I have something for you in my car that might help."

After they finished lunch, the pair went out to the parking lot. Inside Charley's trunk were two cardboard boxes, marked "BOOKS." He opened one and rummaged around for a few seconds. "Here," he said, handing her a textbook.

Iris read the title out loud. "*Strategic Planning.*"

"This one is from a planning seminar I did a while back. I have a later edition, but there really isn't much difference between the two. I was cleaning out some of my redundant books. I was going to donate these to the library book sale. It's yours if you want it. It might help out with your planning project."

Charley slammed the trunk shut and then said, "Read over the first few chapters—that'll give you the basics. Then sit down with your planning documents from corporate management and from IT. For each goal of the CEO and CIO you can identify, think about what your department needs to do to meet it. Then write up how you think the company as whole and your team in particular could satisfy that objective. Once you've listed the objectives and a way to meet them, you can go back and describe the resources you'll need to make it happen."

Iris said, "That's it?"

Charley shook his head. "There's more to it than that, but this exercise will get you started. Once you reach that point, I can share some of what I know about how to frame your plans and format them for use in the planning process."

LEARNING OBJECTIVES

Upon completion of this material, you should be able to:

- Recognize the importance of planning and describe the principal components of organizational planning
- Know and understand the principal components of information security system implementation planning as it functions within the organizational planning scheme

Introduction

Chapter 1, the only chapter in Unit I, discussed information security management within the context of general management, covering many of the elements of management as they apply to information security. Unit II, *Planning*, delves more deeply into organizational planning and the process of planning for information security. Unit II is divided into two chapters (see Figure 2-1): Chapter 2 addresses the topics of organizational planning and planning for information security systems, and Chapter 3 covers the concept of contingency planning.

FIGURE 2-1 Information Security Planning

In general, the success of an organization depends on proper organizational planning. In fact, it's difficult to overstate the essential nature of planning in business and organizational management. In a setting where there are continual constraints on resources, both human and financial, good planning enables an organization to make the most out of the resources at hand. While some planning is always viewed as essential, some organizations spend too much time, money, and human effort on planning with too little return to justify their investment. Each organization must balance the benefits of the chosen degree of planning effort against the costs of the effort.

Planning usually involves many interrelated groups and organizational processes. They may be internal or external to the organization, and can include employees, management, stockholders, other outside stakeholders, the physical environment, the political and legal environment, the competitive environment, and the technological environment, among other things. Each of these factors will likely affect the manner in which planning is conducted and implemented. The major components of a strategic plan—the vision statement, mission statement, strategy, and hierarchical and departmental plans—are discussed in this chapter in further detail.

Developing the organizational plan for information security depends on the same planning process. Because the information security community of interest seeks to influence the broader community in which it operates, to be effective the information security planner should know how the organizational planning process works so that participation in this process can yield meaningful results. While CISOs and information security managers can usually generate an urgent response to a current threat, they would be well advised to ensure the long-term viability of the information security program by utilizing a portion of the resources allocated via routine planning. Before we can explore the positioning of information security within an organization's planning processes, however, we must first define the concept of organizational planning.

The dominant means of managing resources in modern organizations, planning entails the enumeration of a sequence of actions intended to achieve specific goals, and then controlling the implementation of these steps. Planning provides direction for the organization's future. Without specific and detailed planning, organizational units would attempt to meet objectives independently, with each unit being guided by its own initiatives and ideas. Such an uncoordinated effort will not only fail to meet objectives, but also result in an inefficient use of resources. Planning, when conducted by the various segments of the organization, provides a uniform script that increases efficiency and reduces waste and duplication of effort.

Organizational planning should be undertaken using a top-down process in which the organization's leaders choose the direction and initiatives that the entire organization should pursue. Initially, the organizational plan contains few specific detailed objectives; instead, it outlines general objectives.

The primary goal of the organizational planning process is the creation of detailed plans—that is, systematic directions on how to meet the organization's objectives. This task is accomplished with a process that begins with the general and ends with the specific.

Components of Organizational Planning

To implement effective planning, an organization's leaders must first develop documents that explicitly state the organization's ethical, entrepreneurial, and philosophical perspectives. In recent years, the critical nature of the first of these perspectives—the ethical perspective—has come sharply into focus. Recent events, such as the widely publicized problems at companies such as Enron and WorldCom, illustrate the importance of an organization having solid and well-articulated ethical underpinnings. While ethical failures of this magnitude are, one hopes, not universal, many organizations have begun to critically review the documents that establish their ethical foundations.

When an organization's foundational documents do not match the demonstrated ethical, entrepreneurial, and philosophical approaches of its management teams, the developmental plan, which is guided by its mission statement, vision, values, and strategy, becomes unmanageable.

Mission

The **mission statement** explicitly declares the business of the organization and its intended areas of operations. It is, in a sense, the organization's identity card. For example:

> Random Widget Works Inc. designs and manufactures quality widgets and associated equipment and supplies for use in modern business environments.

Not the 12-page sleeping pill you expected? A mission statement should be concise, should reflect both internal and external operations, and should be robust enough to remain valid for a period of four to six years. Simply put, the mission statement must explain *what* the organization does and for *whom.*

Many organizations encourage or require each division or major department—including the information security department—to generate its own mission statement. These mission statements can be as concise as the one above, and express a general commitment to the importance of the confidentiality, integrity, and availability of information, or they can provide a more detailed description of the function of the information security department, as shown in the following example. This mission statement appears in *Information Security Roles and Responsibilities Made Easy.*

"The Information Security Department is charged with identifying, assessing, and appropriately managing risks to Company X's information and information systems. It evaluates the options for dealing with these risks, and works with departments throughout Company X to decide upon and then implement controls that appropriately and proactively respond to these same risks. The Department is also responsible for developing requirements that apply to the entire organization as well as external information systems in which Company X participates (for example, extranets) [these requirements include policies, standards, and procedures]. The focal point for all matters related to information security, this Department is ultimately responsible for all endeavors within Company X that seek to avoid, prevent, detect, correct, or recover from threats to information or information systems.

These threats include, but are not limited to:
- Unauthorized access to information
- Unauthorized use of information
- Unauthorized disclosure of information
- Unauthorized diversion of information
- Unauthorized modification of information
- Unauthorized destruction of information
- Unauthorized duplication of information
- Unavailability of information"[1]

Vision

The second component of the planning landscape is the **vision statement**. In contrast to the mission statement, which expresses what the organization is, the vision statement expresses what the organization wants to become. Vision statements should therefore be ambitious; after all, they are meant to express the aspirations of the organization and to serve as a means for visualizing its future. In other words, the vision statement is the best-case scenario for the organization's future. Many organizations mix or combine the vision statement and the mission statement. RWW's vision statement might be:

Random Widget Works will be the preferred manufacturer of choice for every business's widget equipment needs, with an RWW widget in every machine they use.

This is a very bold, ambitious vision statement. Even though it may not seem very realistic, vision statements aren't meant to be probable, only possible.

Values

The third component is the **values statement**. The trust and confidence of stakeholders and the public are important factors for any organization. By establishing a formal set of organizational principles, standards, and qualities in a values statement, as well as benchmarks for measuring behavior against these published values, an organization makes its conduct and performance standards clear to its employees and the public. The quality management movement of the 1980s and 1990s amply illustrated that organizations with strong values can earn greater loyalty from customers and employees.

Microsoft has a formal employee mission and values statement published on its Web site, as shown in Figure 2-2.

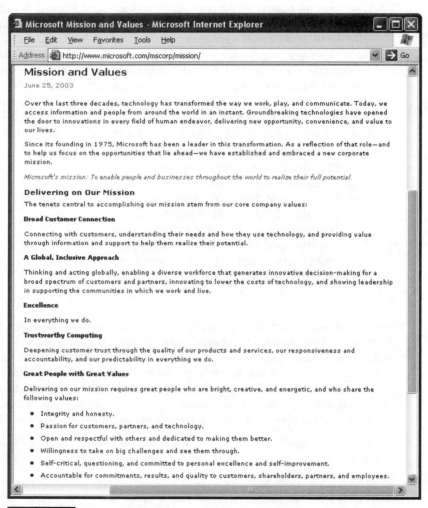

FIGURE 2-2 Microsoft's Mission and Values

Integrity, honesty, passion, and respectfulness are significant parts of Microsoft's corporate philosophy. A values statement for RWW might take the following form:

"RWW values commitment, honesty, integrity, and social responsibility among its employees, and is committed to providing its services in harmony with its corporate, social, legal, and natural environments."

Taken together, the mission, vision, and values statements provide the philosophical foundation for planning and guide the creation of the strategic plan.

Strategy

Strategy, or **strategic planning**, is the basis for the long-term direction taken by the organization. Strategic planning in general guides organizational efforts, and focuses resources toward specific, clearly defined goals, in the midst of an ever-changing environment.

In short, strategic planning is a disciplined effort to produce fundamental decisions and actions that shape and guide what an organization is, what it does, and why it does it, with a focus on the future.[2]

As you learned in Chapter 1, a clearly directed strategy flows from top to bottom, and a systematic approach is required to translate it into a program that can inform and lead all members of the organization, down to the lowest-ranked employee. As shown in Figure 2-3, strategic plans formed at the highest levels of the organization are translated into more specific strategic plans for intermediate layers of management. These plans are then converted into tactical planning for supervisory managers and eventually provide direction for the operational plans undertaken by the nonmanagement members of the organization. This multilayered approach encompasses two key objectives: general strategy and overall strategic planning. First, general strategy is translated into specific strategy; second, overall strategic planning is translated into lower-level tactical and operational planning. Each of these steps is discussed below.

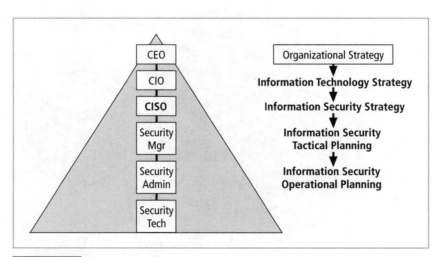

FIGURE 2-3   Top-Down Strategic Planning for Information Security

Planning for the Organization

After an organization develops a general strategy, it must create an overall strategic plan by extrapolating that general strategy into specific strategic plans for major divisions. Each level of each division translates those objectives into more specific objectives for the level below. For example, a CEO might develop the following general statement of strategy:

Providing the highest-quality health care service in the industry.

To execute this broad strategy and turn the general statement into action, the executive team (sometimes called the C-level of the organization, as in CEO, CFO, CIO, and so on) must first define individual responsibilities. The allocation of these responsibilities should maintain the integrity of the overall strategic plan. For example, the Chief Information Officer (CIO) might translate the previous general statement into this more specific statement:

Providing high-level health care information service in support of the highest-quality health care service in the industry.

The Chief Operations Officer (COO) might derive a different strategic goal, which focuses more on his or her specific responsibilities:

Providing the highest-quality medical services.

For the Chief Information Security Officer (CISO), the CIO's goal might be translated as follows:

Ensuring that health care information services are provided securely and in conformance with all state and federal information processing, information security, and privacy statutes, specifically including HIPPA compliance.

Figure 2-4 provides a visual representation of this example.

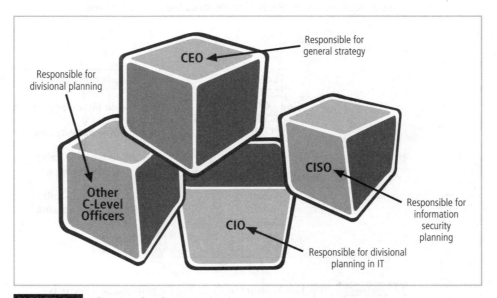

FIGURE 2-4   Planning for the Organization

The translation of goals from the strategic level to the next lower level is perhaps more art than science. It relies on the executive's ability to know and understand the strategic goals of the entire organization, to know and appreciate the strategic and tactical abilities of each unit within the organization, and to negotiate with peers, superiors, and subordinates. This mix of skills helps to achieve the proper balance in articulating goals that fall within performance capabilities.

Planning Levels

Once the organization's overall strategic plan is translated into strategic goals for each major division or operation, such as the Information Security group, the next step is to translate these strategies into tasks with specific, measurable, achievable, and time-bound objectives. Strategic planning then begins a transformation from general, sweeping statements toward more specific and applied objectives. Strategic plans are used to create tactical plans, which are in turn used to develop operational plans. Figure 2-5 illustrates the various planning levels discussed in this section.

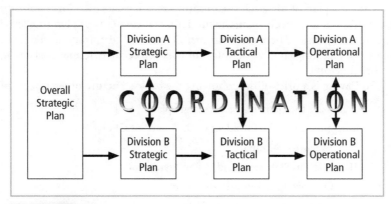

FIGURE 2-5   Planning Levels

Tactical planning has a more short-term focus than strategic planning, usually one to three years. It breaks down each applicable strategic goal into a series of incremental objectives. Each objective should be specific and ideally will have a delivery date within a year. Budgeting, resource allocation, and manpower are critical components of the tactical plan. Although these components may be discussed in general terms at the strategic planning level, they are crucial at the tactical level because they must be in place before the tactical plan can be translated into the operational plan. Tactical plans often include project plans and resource acquisition planning documents (such as product specifications), project budgets, project reviews, and monthly and annual reports.[3]

Because tactical plans are often oriented around projects, some organizations no longer call this process tactical planning; instead, they refer to it as project planning or intermediate planning. The CISO and the security managers use the tactical plan to organize, prioritize, and acquire resources necessary for the major projects and to provide support for the overall strategic plan.

Managers and employees use operational plans, which are derived from the tactical plans, to organize the ongoing, day-to-day performance of tasks. An operational plan includes clearly identified coordination activities that span department boundaries, communications requirements, weekly meetings, summaries, progress reports, and associated tasks. These plans are carefully designed to reflect the organizational structure, with each subunit, department, or project team conducting its own operational planning and reporting components. Frequent communication and feedback from the teams to the project managers and/or team leaders and then up the various management levels will make the planning process as a whole more manageable and successful.

For example, operational planning within information security may encompass such objectives as the selection, configuration, and deployment of a firewall, or the design and implementation of a security education, training, and awareness (SETA) program. Each of these tasks needs effective tactical planning that covers its entire development life cycle.

Planning and the CISO

The first priority of the CISO and information security manager should be the structure of a strategic plan. While each organization may have its own format for the design and distribution of a strategic plan, the fundamental elements of planning are the same for all types of enterprises. There are a number of excellent text, trade, and reference books on enterprise planning, and the serious information security manager is encouraged to explore this topic.

Following is a brief outline showing the basic structure of a strategic plan.

"What are the elements of a strategic plan?

Introduction by the President of the Board or CEO

I.   Executive Summary

II.   Mission Statement and Vision Statement

III.   Organizational Profile and History

IV.   Strategic Issues and Core Values

V.   Program Goals and Objectives

VI.   Management/Operations Goals and Objectives

VII.   Appendices (optional) [strengths, weaknesses, opportunities, and threats (SWOT) analyses, surveys, budgets, etc.]"[4]

You have already learned about some of the components in this outline. Those areas not previously discussed are very straightforward, such as the organizational profile, history, and appendices; they originate in studies conducted by the organization or highlight information about the environment in which the organization operates. These supplements may help the organization to identify new directions or eliminate directions that are less profitable than originally anticipated. Information security planners can consult studies such as the CSI/FBI survey, the Threats to Information Security study (described in detail later in this chapter), the Human Firewall Council's Security Management and Security Awareness Indices, and internal risk assessments to help identify trends of interest or relevance to the organization. These documents are key resources that can identify areas of concern that should be addressed by the information security strategic plan.

Some additional tips for planning follow:

"1. Create a compelling vision statement that frames the evolving plan, and acts as a magnet for people who want to make a difference.
2. Embrace the use of a balanced scorecard approach, which demands the use of a balanced set of measures and cause-and-effect thinking.
3. Deploy a draft high-level plan early, and ask for input from stakeholders in the organization.
4. Make the evolving plan visible.
5. Make the process invigorating for everyone.
6. Be persistent.
7. Make the process continuous.
8. Provide meaning.
9. Be yourself.
10. Lighten up and have some fun." [5]

VIEWPOINT

Planning for Security

By Eng-Kiat Koh, Encentuate, Inc.

With an increasing number of applications in the enterprise and more access modes available, organizations now face the opposing challenges of providing convenient access while tightening security, creating a huge dichotomy for their IT departments. A survey of 500 U.S. companies by the Computer Security Institute revealed that 80% of them had been attacked, with combined reported losses of $455 million.[6] Financial fraud and theft of proprietary information accounted for more than $250 million of the losses. The number of reported computer breaches increased a thousand times from 1999 to 2002.[7] Clearly, this issue is a growing problem that shows no sign of abating.

Good security requires a comprehensive defense, encompassing infrastructure, process, and people. Many organizations focus only on infrastructure defense—but that leaves the other avenues wide open for attack. It is important that you address all aspects of total defense; if you don't, your vulnerabilities will be exploited.

Infrastructure security requires that enterprises protect all infrastructure layers, not just the perimeter. Many enterprises focus on perimeter defense, but this approach assumes that the biggest threat comes from the outside, which is inaccurate: The 2002 CSI/FBI survey indicates that an average external attack causes $57,000 in damage, while an insider attack costs on average $2.7 million! In addition, the best firewalls and perimeter defense cannot stop what appears to be a legitimate user from gaining access. To counter these threats, enterprises need to strengthen security at all infrastructure layers, particularly at the application layers where the value at risk is the highest. For this reason, strong identity management is now considered central to good infrastructure security. Figure 2-6 depicts the various layers that require protection.

(continued)

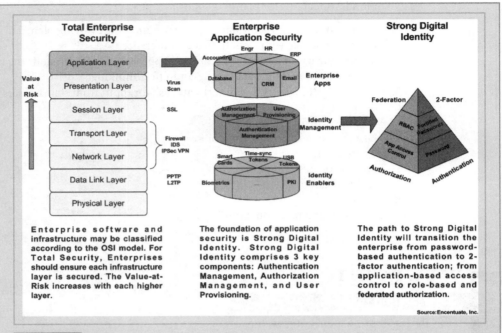

FIGURE 2-6 Enterprise Security Layers

Good infrastructure security needs to be augmented with good security processes and policies. For starters, enterprises should have well-established and well-communicated policies. A good policy should have the following characteristics:

- It should clearly identify the assets to be protected.
- It should clearly identify the required security measures and the responsibilities of each user group.
- It should clearly identify who is responsible for implementing, monitoring, and funding the security initiatives.
- It should include a training policy for employee awareness.

Finally, enterprises should recognize that the weakest link in the security chain is probably their own employees. A common form of attack comes via social engineering. In a recent Computer Technology Industry Association survey, more than 63% of computer breaches could be traced to human errors.[8] It is therefore important not only to raise awareness of security policies, but also to ensure that employees—especially those charged with implementing security initiatives—are well trained.

Ultimately, security is only as good as the weakest link. When planning for security, enterprises have to adopt total defense, or risk being attacked. Eighty percent protection is just not good enough.

Eng-Kiat Koh is a Principal Consultant with Encentuate, Inc., which provides enterprise identity management solutions.

Planning for Information Security Implementation

The CIO and CISO play important roles in translating overall strategic planning into tactical and operational information security plans. Depending on the information security function's placement within the organizational chart (discussed in detail in Chapter 5), the roles of the CIO and the CISO may differ. Most commonly, the CISO directly reports to the CIO.[9] In that case, the CIO charges the CISO and other IT department heads with creating and adopting plans that are consistent and supportive of the entire organizational strategy. The CIO must also ensure that the various IT functional areas in the organization provide broad support for the plan, and that no areas are omitted or ignored.

The CISO (often called the Information Security Department Manager) plays a more active role in the development of the planning details than does the CIO. Consider the job description for the Information Security Department Manager from *Information Security Roles and Responsibilities Made Easy:*

" ▪ Creates a strategic information security plan with a vision for the future of information security at Company X (utilizing evolving information security technology, this vision meets a variety of objectives such as management's fiduciary and legal responsibilities, customer expectations for secure modern business practices, and the competitive requirements of the marketplace)

▪ Understands the fundamental business activities performed by Company X and, based on this understanding, suggests appropriate information security solutions that uniquely protect these activities

▪ Develops action plans, schedules, budgets, status reports, and other top management communications intended to improve the status of information security at Company X"[10]

Once the organization's overall strategic plan has been translated into IT and information security departmental objectives by the CIO, and then further translated into tactical and operational plans by the CISO, the implementation of information security can begin.

Implementation of information security can be accomplished in two ways: bottom-up or top-down. These two basic approaches are illustrated in Figure 2-7.

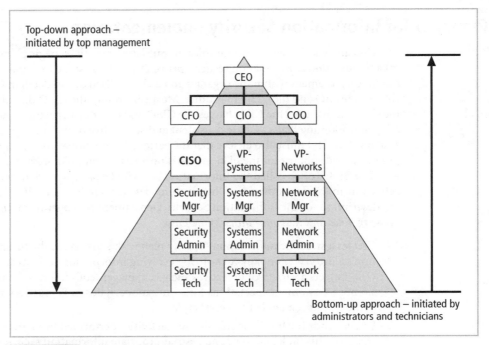

Top-down approach –
initiated by top management

Bottom-up approach – initiated by
administrators and technicians

FIGURE 2-7   Approaches to Security Implementation

The **bottom-up approach** might begin as a grass-roots effort in which systems administrators attempt to improve the security of their systems. The key advantage of this approach is that it utilizes the technical expertise of the individual administrators, who work with the information systems on a daily basis. System and network administrators possess in-depth knowledge that can greatly enhance the state of information security in the organization. These professionals know and understand many of the threats to their systems and the mechanisms needed to successfully protect them. Unfortunately, this approach seldom works, as it lacks a number of critical features, such as coordinated planning from upper management, coordination between departments, and the provision of sufficient resources.

The **top-down approach**, in contrast, features strong upper management support, a dedicated champion, usually assured funding, a clear planning and implementation process, and the ability to influence organizational culture. High-level managers provide resources; give direction; issue policies, procedures, and processes; dictate the goals and expected outcomes of the project; and determine who is accountable for each of the required actions. The most successful top-down approach also incorporates a formal development strategy referred to as the systems development life cycle.

For any top-down approach to succeed, high-level management must buy into the effort and provide all departments with their full support. Such an initiative must have a **champion**—ideally, an executive with sufficient influence to move the project forward, ensure that it is properly managed, and push for its acceptance throughout the organization. Typically, the champion of a far-reaching information security program is the Chief Information Officer or another senior executive such as the Vice President of Information Technology (VP-IT).

Without this high-level support, many mid-level administrators fail to dedicate enough resources to the project or dismiss it as a low priority.

Involvement and support of the end users is also critical to the success of this type of effort. Because the process and outcome of the initiative most directly affect these individuals, they must be included in the information security planning process. Key end users should be assigned to developmental teams, known as **joint application development** teams (JAD). A successful JAD must be able to survive employee turnover; that is, it should not be vulnerable to changes in personnel. For this reason, the processes and procedures must be documented and integrated into organizational culture. They must be adopted *and promoted* by the organization's management. These attributes are seldom found in projects that begin as bottom-up initiatives.

The success of information security plans can be enhanced by using the processes of system analysis and design, a discipline that is an integral part of most academic curricula in the information technology field. The following sections provide a brief treatment of this topic, but are not designed to replace a more thorough study of the discipline.

Introduction to the Systems Development Life Cycle

The general **systems development life cycle (SDLC)** is a popular methodology for the design and implementation of an information system in an organization. A **methodology** is a formal approach to solving a problem based on a structured sequence of procedures. Using a methodology ensures a rigorous process and increases the likelihood of achieving the desired final objective. Sometimes the SDLC is used to develop custom applications or to manage the integration or deployment process of a purchased package solution. A variation of this methodology, used to create a comprehensive security posture, is called the SecSDLC; you will learn more about this technique later in this chapter.

Using a methodology increases the probability of success, and organizations often repeatedly reuse a successful methodology. This tried-and-true approach is combined with sound project management practices to develop key milestones, allocate resources, select personnel, and perform the tasks needed to accomplish the project final objective.

Before you learn about the particulars of a formal SDLC, you should understand the basics of the general SDLC on which it relies. This traditional SDLC is widely recognized as consisting of six phases. If you have taken a systems analysis and design course, you may have been exposed to a model consisting of fewer or greater number of phases. In fact, different versions of the SDLC range from three to twelve stages, all of which can be mapped into the six phases presented here. The precise number of phases is not as significant as the repeatable nature of the process that the SDLC inculcates in the project team. It's worth restating that having a guide in the form of a well-designed SDLC makes the process more repeatable and more likely to succeed.

System projects may be initiated in response to specific conditions or combinations of conditions. The impetus to begin a SDLC-based project may be **event-driven**—that is, started in response to some event in the business community, inside the organization, or within the ranks of employees, customers, or other stakeholders. Alternatively, it could be **plan-driven**—that is, the result of a carefully developed planning strategy. Either way, once an organization recognizes the need for a project, the use of a methodology can ensure that development proceeds in an orderly, comprehensive fashion. At the end of each phase, a **structured review** or *reality check* takes place, during which the team and its management-level reviewers decide whether the project should be continued, discontinued, outsourced, or postponed until additional expertise or organizational knowledge is acquired.

The six phases of the traditional waterfall model SDLC are discussed in the sections that follow. The term *waterfall model* indicates that the work products of each phase fall into the next phase to serve as its starting point.

Investigation

The first phase, the **investigation phase**, is the most important. It identifies the problem that the system being developed will solve. The investigation phase begins with an examination of the event or plan that initiated the process. During this phase, the objectives, constraints, and scope of the project are specified. A preliminary cost-benefit analysis is developed to evaluate the perceived benefits and the appropriate costs for those benefits.

At the conclusion of this stage, and at the end of every subsequent phase, a **feasibility analysis** is performed. This analysis assesses one or more of the various approaches to understand the economic, technical, and behavioral feasibility of the process to be performed, and ensures that its implementation is worth the organization's time and effort. Figure 2-8 visualizes the end result of a feasibility analysis process.

FIGURE 2-8   Feasibility Analysis

Analysis

The **analysis phase** begins with the information learned during the investigation phase. It assesses the organization's readiness, its current systems status, and its capability to implement and then support the proposed systems. Analysts determine what the new system is expected to do and how it will interact with existing systems. This phase ends with the documentation of the findings and a feasibility analysis update.

Logical Design

In the **logical design phase**, the information obtained during the analysis phase is used to develop a proposed system-based solution for the business problem. In any such solution, it is imperative that the first and driving factor be the business need. Then, based on the business need, the team can select systems and applications capable of providing the needed services. Finally, based on all of the previous factors, the team can select specific types of technical controls that might prove useful when implemented as a physical solution. The logical design, therefore, serves as the blueprint for the desired solution. It is implementation independent, meaning that it contains no references to specific devices, vendors, or products. Instead, it addresses how the proposed system will solve the problem at hand. In this stage, analysts generate a number of alternative solutions, each with corresponding strengths and weaknesses, and estimates of costs and forecasts of benefits, which allows for a general comparison of available options. In the end, a feasibility analysis is performed for each remaining viable candidate system solution.

Physical Design

During the **physical design phase**, the team selects specific technologies that support the alternatives identified and evaluated in the logical design. The selected components are evaluated further as a make-or-buy decision (develop in-house or purchase from a vendor). When all possibilities have been thoroughly considered, a final design is chosen. This design must integrate the various required components and technologies. After another feasibility analysis, the entire solution is presented to the management reviewers and end-user representatives for approval.

Implementation

In the **implementation phase**, the organization's software engineers develop any software that is not to be purchased and take steps to create integration modules. The customized elements are tested and documented, and the purchased components are ordered, received, and tested. Once integrated, the system elements undergo further testing. As functional systems components are developed, users are trained and supporting documentation is created. When all components have been tested individually, they are installed and tested as a system. A feasibility analysis is conducted again, and the users are then presented with the system for a performance and acceptance testing.

Maintenance

The **maintenance phase** is the longest and most expensive phase of the process. It consists of the tasks necessary to support and modify the system for the remainder of its useful life cycle. Even though formal development may conclude during this phase, the life cycle of the project continues until the process begins again with a new version of the investigation phase. Periodically, the system is tested for compliance, and the feasibility of continuance versus discontinuance is evaluated. Upgrades, updates, and patches are managed. As the needs of the organization change, the systems that support the organization must also adapt to the new environment. It is important that both those who manage systems and those who support them continually monitor the effectiveness of the systems in relation to the organization's circumstances. When the current system can no longer support the changed mission of the organization, it is replaced after a new systems development project is completed.

The Security Systems Development Life Cycle (SecSDLC)

The traditional SDLC described in the previous section has been adapted to support the specialized implementation of a security project, in a variation called the **security systems development life cycle (SecSDLC)**. While this process may differ in several specific activities, the overall methodology is the same. The SecSDLC process involves the identification of specific threats and the risks that they represent, and the subsequent design and implementation of specific controls to counter those threats and assist in the management of the risk. It turns information security into a coherent program rather than a series of responses to individual threats and attacks. Figure 2-9 shows the phases in the SecSDLC.

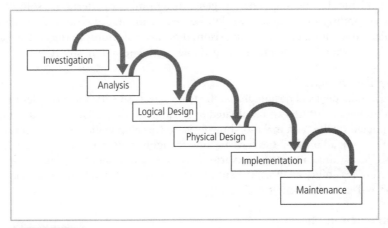

FIGURE 2-9 Phases of the SecSDLC

Investigation in the SecSDLC

The investigation phase of the SecSDLC begins with a directive from upper management specifying the process, outcomes, and goals of the project, as well as its budget and other constraints. Frequently, this phase begins with the affirmation or creation of security policies on which the security program of the organization is or will be founded. Teams of managers, employees, and consultants are assembled to analyze problems, define their scope, specify goals and objectives, and identify any additional constraints not covered in the enterprise security policy. (A more complete treatment of information security policy is presented in Chapter 4.) Finally, an organizational feasibility analysis determines whether the organization has the resources and commitment to conduct a successful security analysis and design.

It is unfortunate, but many information security projects are initiated in response to a significant negative event within an organization. While these circumstances may not be the ideal conditions under which to begin work on an organization's information security posture, the SecSDLC team should emphasize that improvement is now under way.

Analysis in the SecSDLC

In the analysis phase, the documents from the investigation phase are studied. The development team created during the investigation phase conducts a preliminary analysis of existing security policies or programs, along with documented current threats and associated controls. This phase also includes an analysis of relevant legal issues that could affect the design of the security solution. Increasingly, privacy laws are a major consideration when making decisions about information systems that manage personal information. Recently, many state legislatures have made illegal certain computer-related activities that were once unregulated, so a detailed understanding of these issues is vital.

The risk management task also begins in this stage. Risk management is the process of identifying, assessing, and evaluating the levels of risk facing the organization—specifically, the threats to the organization's security and to the information stored and processed by the organization. Ponder the words of the famous Chinese General Sun Tzu:

> "If you know the enemy and know yourself, you need not fear the result of a hundred battles. If you know yourself but not the enemy, for every victory gained you will also suffer a defeat. If you know neither the enemy nor yourself, you will succumb in every battle."[11]

You begin the analysis process by getting to know your enemy. In information security, the enemy is the threats and attacks that your systems face as they provide services to your organization and its customers.

To better understand the analysis phase of the SecSDLC, you should know something about the kinds of threats facing organizations in the modern, connected world of information technology. In this context, a **threat** is an object, person, or other entity that represents a constant danger to an asset. While each enterprise's categorization of threats will almost certainly vary, threats are relatively well researched and consequently fairly well understood. To better understand the numerous threats facing an organization, a scheme has been developed to group threats by their respective activities. This model consists of 12 general categories that represent real and present dangers to an organization's information and systems. The following sections, and Table 2-1, identify and describe each of these 12 categories of risk.

Acts of Human Error or Failure. This category includes acts performed without intent or without malicious purpose. When people use information systems, sometimes mistakes happen. Inexperience, improper training, the making of incorrect assumptions, and other circumstances can cause these problems.

Compromises to Intellectual Property. The owner of intellectual property has the right to control proprietary ideas, as well as their tangible or virtual representation. Information about an organization's intellectual property can be of great interest to its competitors and can be accidentally or deliberately disseminated to those outside the organization.

Deliberate Acts of Espionage or Trespass. This threat covers a well-known and broad category of electronic and human activities that can breach the confidentiality of information. When an unauthorized individual gains access to information that an organization is trying to protect, the act is categorized as a deliberate act of espionage or trespass.

Deliberate Acts of Information Extortion. Information extortion occurs when an attacker or formerly trusted insider steals information from a computer system and then demands compensation for its return or for an agreement to not disclose the information. This practice is common in credit card number theft.

Deliberate Acts of Sabotage or Vandalism. This threat originates with an individual or group of individuals who intend to deliberately sabotage the operations of a computer system or business, or who perform acts of vandalism to either destroy an asset or damage the image of the organization. These threats can range from petty vandalism by employees to Web page defacement by outside persons or groups.

Deliberate Acts of Theft. Theft is the illegal taking of another's property, whether physical, electronic, or intellectual.

Deliberate Software Attacks. Deliberate software attacks occur when an individual or group designs software—often called malicious code or software, or malware—to attack a vulnerable system. Some of the more common types of malicious code are viruses, worms, Trojan horses, logic bombs, and back doors.

Deviations in Quality of Service by Service Providers. This category includes situations in which a product or service is not delivered as expected. The organization's information system depends on the successful operation of many interdependent support systems, including power grids, telecommunications networks, parts suppliers, service vendors, and even the janitorial staff and garbage haulers.

The threat of irregularities from power utilities is common. When they occur they can lead to several types of power fluctuations:

- A voltage levels spike (a momentary increase)
- A surge (a prolonged increase)
- A momentary low voltage or sag
- A more prolonged drop in voltage, called a brownout
- A complete loss of power for a moment, called a fault
- A more lengthy loss, known as a blackout

Forces of Nature. Forces of nature (known as *force majeure*) or acts of God pose some of the most dangerous threats imaginable, because they can occur with very little warning. They include fire, flood, earthquake, and lightning, as well as volcanic eruption and insect infestation.

Technical Hardware Failures or Errors. Technical hardware failures or errors occur when a manufacturer distributes equipment containing a known or unknown flaw. These defects can cause the system to perform outside of expected parameters, resulting in unreliable service or lack of availability.

Technical Software Failures or Errors. This category of threats comes from software with known or unknown, hidden faults. These faults may range from bugs to untested failure conditions.

Technological Obsolescence. When the infrastructure becomes antiquated or outdated, it leads to unreliable and untrustworthy systems that may be difficult to maintain without extensive investment of resources.

TABLE 2-1 Threats to Information Security[12]

Categories of threat	Examples
1. Acts of human error or failure	Accidents, employee mistakes
2. Compromises to intellectual property	Piracy, copyright infringement
3. Deliberate acts of espionage or trespass	Unauthorized access and/or data collection
4. Deliberate acts of information extortion	Blackmail of information disclosure
5. Deliberate acts of sabotage or vandalism	Destruction of systems or information
6. Deliberate acts of theft	Illegal confiscation of equipment or information

TABLE 2-1 Threats to Information Security[12] (continued)

Categories of threat	Examples
7. Deliberate software attacks	Viruses, worms, macros, denial-of-service
8. Deviations in quality of service from service providers	Power and WAN service issues
9. Forces of nature	Fire, flood, earthquake, lightning
10. Technical hardware failures or errors	Equipment failure
11. Technical software failures or errors	Bugs, code problems, unknown loopholes
12. Technological obsolescence	Antiquated or outdated technologies

The preceding list of threats may be manifested as attacks against the assets of the organization. An **attack** is an act or event that exploits a vulnerability. It is accomplished by a **threat agent** that damages or steals an organization's information or physical asset. An **exploit** is a technique or mechanism used to compromise a system. A **vulnerability** is an identified weakness of a controlled system in which necessary controls are not present or are no longer effective. A technical attack may involve the use of an exploit to achieve the compromise of a controlled system, whereas a non-technical attack may involve natural events or less sophisticated approaches. The following list outlines some types of technical attacks:

- Malicious code: The execution of viruses, worms, Trojan horses, and active Web scripts with the intent to destroy or steal information.

- Hoaxes: A waste of time and resources, or an attack masked in a seemingly legitimate message.

- Back doors: A feature left behind by system designers or maintenance staff or installed by malicious code.

- Password crack: Attempting to reverse-calculate or guess a password. Password attacks include dictionary attacks, brute force attacks, and man-in-the-middle attacks (see below).

- Brute force: The application of computing and network resources to try every possible combination of characters to crack a password.

- Dictionary: An attack that narrows the field of possible password values by selecting specific accounts as targets using a list of commonly used passwords (the dictionary) with which to guess, instead of random combinations.

- Denial-of-service (DoS) and distributed denial-of-service (DDoS): Sending a large number of connection or information requests to a target, thereby blocking other, legitimate traffic. When multiple systems are organized into a simultaneous attack, it is categorized as a DDoS.

- Spoofing: A technique used to gain unauthorized access to computers, whereby the intruder sends network-level messages to a computer with an IP address indicating that the message is coming from a trusted host.

- Man-in-the-middle: Also known as a TCP hijacking attack. An attacker commandeers a network connection session, and then can read and perhaps modify the data transferred in that connection.

- Spam: Unsolicited commercial e-mail, the electronic equivalent of junk mail.
- Mail bombing: The routing of large quantities of e-mail to the target.
- Sniffer: A program or device that can monitor data traveling over a network.
- Social engineering: The use of social skills to convince people to reveal access credentials or other valuable information.
- Buffer overflow: An application error that occurs when more data is sent to a buffer than it can handle.
- Timing: An attack that enables an attacker to extract secrets maintained in a security system by observing the time it takes the system to respond to various queries.[13]

The last step in knowing the enemy is to find some method of prioritizing the risk posed by each category of threat and its related methods of attack. This can be done by adopting threat levels from an existing study of threats or by creating your own categorization of threats for your environment based on scenario analyses.

To manage risk, you must identify and assess the value of your information assets. This iterative process must include a classification and categorization of all elements of an organization's systems: people, procedures, data and information, software, hardware, and networking elements. As you assign each organizational asset to a category, you can pose certain questions to help develop the weighting criteria for an information asset valuation or impact evaluation:

- Which information asset is the most critical to the success of the organization?
- Which information asset generates the most revenue?
- Which information asset has the highest profitability?
- Which information asset would be the most expensive to replace?
- Which information asset would be the most expensive to protect?
- Which information asset would be the most embarrassing or cause the greatest liability if revealed?

It is important that the list include enough categories to allow for various priority levels, because the next step is to rank the components based on criteria driven by the categorization. It is also important that the categories be comprehensive (i.e. all information assets must fit somewhere) and mutually exclusive (i.e. each asset must fall into only one category). For example, if an organization has a public key infrastructure certificate authority (a software application that provides cryptographic key management services), it could be placed in the asset list as "Software, Application" or "Software, Security" using purely technical standards. In this case, it should be placed as "Software, Security" because this kind of software, which is part of the security infrastructure, must be carefully protected. Ultimately, it is more important to have a comprehensive set of categories than a mutually exclusive set, as it may be difficult to entirely avoid overlapping categories.

The next challenge in the analysis phase is to review each information asset for each threat it faces and create a list of vulnerabilities. As indicated earlier, vulnerabilities are specific avenues that threat agents can exploit. They represent the "chinks in the armor" of the information asset—a flaw or weakness in an information asset, a security procedure, or a control that could be exploited either accidentally or on purpose to breach security.

As the analysis phase continues, the next task is to assess the relative risk for each of the information assets via a process called **risk assessment** or **risk analysis**. Risk assessment assigns a comparative risk rating or score to each specific information asset. While this number does not mean anything in absolute terms, it is useful in gauging the relative risk introduced by each vulnerable information asset and allows us to make comparative ratings later in the risk control process. Risk assessment is covered in detail in Chapter 7.

Risk management is the part of the analysis phase that identifies vulnerabilities in an organization's information systems and takes carefully reasoned steps to assure the confidentiality, integrity, and availability of all components in the organization's information system. Risk management is covered in detail in Chapter 8.

Design in the SecSDLC

The SecSDLC design phase actually consists of two distinct phases: the logical design and the physical design.

In the logical design phase, team members create and develop the blueprint for security, and they examine and implement key policies that influence later decisions. At this stage, critical contingency plans for incident response are developed. Next, a feasibility analysis determines whether the project should continue in-house or should be outsourced.

In the physical design phase, team members evaluate the technology needed to support the security blueprint, generate alternative solutions, and agree on a final design. The security blueprint may be revisited to keep it synchronized with the changes needed when the physical design is completed. Criteria for determining the definition of successful solutions are also prepared during this phase, as are designs for physically securing the technological solutions. At the end of this phase, a feasibility study should determine the readiness of the organization for the proposed project, and then the champion and users should be presented with the design. At that point, the interested parties have a chance to approve (or not approve) the project before implementation begins.

During the logical and physical design phases, a security manager may seek to use established security models to guide the design process. Security models provide frameworks for ensuring that all areas of security are addressed; organizations can adapt or adopt a framework to meet their own information security needs. A number of information security frameworks have been published. One good source of framework documents is the Computer Security Resource Center of the National Institute for Standards and Technology (NIST; csrc.nist.gov). These documents, which are publicly available at no charge, have withstood the test of time and have been broadly reviewed by government and industry professionals. Other references include *Information Technology—Code of Practice for Information Security Management,* which was originally published as the British Standard BS 7799 and can be purchased at www.bsi-global.com/Corporate/17799.xalter. This code of practice was adopted as an international standard by the International Organization for Standardization (ISO) and the International Electrotechnical Commission (IEC) as ISO/IEC 17799 in 2000 as a framework for information security. A revised version of the British Standard, identified as BS7799-2:2002, has been released to bring it into compliance with the international revisions included in the ISO/IEC 17799 standard. A good place to start collecting information about this standard is at the NIST FAQ page found at http://csrc.nist.gov/publications/secpubs/otherpubs/reviso-faq.pdf.

One of the design elements (or redesign elements, in the case of some projects) of the information security program is the organization's information security policy. The meaning of the term "security policy" differs depending on the context in which it is used. Governmental agencies, for example, discuss security policy in terms of national security and interaction with foreign states. In another context, a security policy can be part of a credit card agency's method of processing credit card numbers. In general, a security policy consists of a set of rules that protects an organization's assets. An **information security policy** provides rules for the protection of the information assets of an organization. As stated in Chapter 1, the task of the information security program is to protect the *confidentiality, integrity, and availability* of information and information systems, whether in transit, storage, or processing. This task is accomplished by applying policy, education and training programs, and technology. Management must define three types of security policies, based on National Institute of Standards and Technology Special Publication 800-14: general or enterprise information security policy, issue-specific security policies, and systems-specific security policies. Each of these is covered in additional detail in Chapter 4.

Another integral part of the information security program to be designed is the **security education, training, and awareness (SETA)** program. The responsibility of the CISO, the SETA program is a control measure designed to reduce accidental security breaches by employees. As mentioned earlier, employee errors represent one of the top threats to information assets; for this reason, it is well worth expending resources to develop programs to combat this problem. SETA programs are designed to supplement the general information security education and training programs that are already in place. Good practice dictates that the systems development life cycle include user training during the implementation phase. Employee training should be managed so as to ensure that all employees are trained properly.

The SETA program consists of three elements: security education, security training, and security awareness. An organization may not be capable of or willing to undertake all three of these elements, so it may outsource them to local educational institutions. The purpose of SETA is to enhance security by the following means:

> "1) Improving awareness of the need to protect system resources; 2) developing skills and knowledge so computer users can perform their jobs more securely; and 3) building in-depth knowledge, as needed, to design, implement, or operate security programs for organizations and systems."[14]

As the design phase continues, attention turns to the design of the controls and safeguards used to protect information from attacks by threats. The terms **control** and **safeguard** are often used interchangeably. There are three categories of controls: managerial controls, operational controls, and technical controls.

Managerial controls cover security processes that are designed by the strategic planners and performed by security administration of the organization. They set the direction and scope of the security process and provide detailed instructions for its conduct. Management controls address the design and implementation of the security planning process and security program management. These controls also address risk management and security controls reviews (discussed in detail in Chapters 7 and 8). Management controls further describe the necessity and scope of legal compliance and the maintenance of the entire security life cycle.

Operational controls deal with the operational functionality of security in the organization. They cover management functions and lower-level planning, such as disaster recovery and incident response planning. In addition, these controls address personnel security, physical security, and the protection of production inputs and outputs. Operational controls also provide structure to the development of education, training, and awareness programs for users, administrators, and management. Finally, they address hardware and software systems maintenance and the integrity of data.

Technical controls address those tactical and technical issues related to designing and implementing security in the organization. Here the technologies necessary to protect information are examined and selected. Whereas operational controls address specific operational issues, such as developing controls and integrating them into the business functions, technical controls address the specifics of technology selection and the acquisition (make or buy) of certain technical components, including logical access controls, such as those related to identification, authentication, authorization, and accountability. Technical controls also address the development and implementation of audit trails for accountability and cryptography to protect information in storage and transit. Finally, they cover the classification of assets and users, so as to facilitate the authorization levels needed.

To the expanded categories used to classify the SecSDLC system components, we add another dimension to represent the sensitivity and security priority of the data and the devices that store, transmit, and process the data. Examples of such data classifications include confidential data, internal data, and public data. The opposite of the data classification scheme is the personnel security clearance structure, which identifies the level of information individuals are authorized to view based on their "need to know."

Another element of the design phase is the creation of essential preparedness documents. Managers in the IT and information security communities are usually called on to provide strategic planning to assure the organization of continuous information systems availability.[15] In addition, the managers of the organization must be ready to act when an attack occurs. Plans for handling attacks, disasters, or other types of incidents go by various names: business continuity plans, disaster recovery plans, incident response plans, or just contingency plans. In large, complex organizations, each of these named plans may represent separate but related planning functions, differing in scope, applicability, and design. In a small organization, the security administrator (or systems administrator) may have one simple plan, which consists of a straightforward set of media backup and recovery strategies, and a few service agreements from the company's service providers. The sad reality is that many organizations have a level of planning that is woefully deficient.

Incident response, disaster recovery, and business continuity planning are all components of contingency planning. **Contingency planning (CP)** is the entire planning conducted by the organization to prepare for, react to, and recover from events that threaten the security of information assets in the organization and to provide for the subsequent restoration to normal business operations. Organizations need to develop disaster recovery plans, incident response plans, and business continuity plans as subsets of the overall CP. **Incident response planning (IRP)** is the planning process associated with the identification, classification, response, and recovery from an incident. **Disaster recovery planning (DRP)** is the planning process associated with the preparation for and recovery from a disaster, whether natural or human-made. **Business continuity planning (BCP)** is the planning process associated with ensuring that critical business functions continue if a catastrophic incident or disaster occurs. These critical building blocks of response planning are presented in Chapter 3.

As the design phase progresses, attention turns to **physical security**, which addresses the design, implementation, and maintenance of countermeasures intended to protect the physical resources of an organization. Physical resources include people, hardware, and the supporting system elements and resources associated with the management of information in all its states—transmission, storage, and processing. Many technology-based controls can be circumvented if an attacker gains physical access to the devices being controlled. For example, when employees fail to secure a server console, the operating system running on that computer becomes vulnerable to attack. Some computer systems are constructed in such a way that it is easy to steal the hard drive and the information it contains. As a result, physical security should receive as much attention as logical security in the security development life cycle. For further discussions of the dimension of physical security, consult one of the many fine text, trade, or reference books on the subject.

Implementation in the SecSDLC

The SecSDLC implementation phase is similar to the corresponding phase of the traditional SDLC. The security solutions are acquired (made or bought), tested, implemented, and retested. Personnel issues are evaluated, and specific training and education programs are conducted. Finally, the entire tested package is presented to upper management for final approval.

The information security systems software or application systems selection process is not appreciably different from that for general IT needs. Vendors should be provided with detailed specifications, and they should in turn provide detailed information about products and costs. As in IT system implementation, it is essential to establish clear specifications and rigorous test plans to assure a high-quality implementation.

Perhaps the most important element of the implementation phase is the management of the project plan. While it has not been mentioned until this point, project management is a process that underlies all phases of the SecSDLC. The execution of the project plan proceeds in three steps:

1. Planning the project
2. Supervising the tasks and action steps within the project plan
3. Wrapping up the project plan

The project plan can be developed in any number of ways. Each organization must determine its own project management methodology for IT and information security projects. Whenever possible, information security projects should follow the organizational practices of project management. If your organization has not established clearly defined project management practices, the following pages supply general guidelines on recommended practices. Project management and its relationship to information security are described in detail in Chapter 12.

Information security is a field with a vast array of technical and nontechnical requirements. For this reason, the project team should include individuals who are experienced in one or multiple requirements of both the technical and nontechnical areas. Many of the same skills needed to manage and implement security are needed to design it. Members of the development team fill the following roles:

- The champion: A senior executive who promotes the project and ensures its support, both financially and administratively, at the highest levels of the organization.
- The team leader: A project manager—perhaps a departmental line manager or staff unit manager—who understands project management, personnel management, and information security technical requirements.
- Security policy developers: Individuals who understand the organizational culture, existing policies, and requirements for developing and implementing successful policies.
- Risk assessment specialists: Individuals who understand financial risk assessment techniques, the value of organizational assets, and the security methods to be used.

- Security professionals: Dedicated, trained, and well-educated specialists in all aspects of information security from both technical and nontechnical standpoints.

- Systems administrators: Individuals with the primary responsibility for administering the systems that house the information used by the organization.

- End users: The individuals whom the new system will most directly affect. Ideally, a disparate group of users from various departments and levels, and with varying degrees of technical knowledge, will assist the team in applying realistic controls in ways that do not disrupt the essential business activities they seek to safeguard.

Just as each potential employee and each potential employer look for the best fit during the hiring process, so each organization should thoroughly examine its options when staffing the information security function. When implementing information security in an organization, many human resource issues must be addressed. First, the entire organization must decide how to position and name the security function within the organization. Second, the information security community of interest must plan for the proper staffing (or adjustments to the staffing plan) for the information security function. Third, the IT community of interest must understand how information security affects every role in the IT function and adjust job descriptions and documented practices accordingly. Finally, the general management community of interest must work with the information security professionals to integrate solid information security concepts into the personnel management practices of the organization as a whole.

It takes a wide range of professionals to support a diverse information security program. Because a good security plan is initiated from the top down, senior management is the key component and vital force driving the successful implementation of an information security program. To develop and execute specific security policies and procedures, additional administrative support is required. Finally, technical expertise is necessary to implement the details of the security operation.

The various roles and the titles used to easily refer to them have already been used in this textbook. Until now, an approximate definition for these roles has been adequate. At this point, however, more precise descriptions of the professionals involved in information security are warranted.

- **The Chief Information Officer (CIO)** is the senior technology officer responsible for aligning the strategic efforts of the organization into action plans for the information systems or data processing division of the organization.

- **The Chief Information Security Officer (CISO)**, sometimes called the Manager for Security, the Security Director, or a similar title, is responsible for the assessment, management, and implementation of securing the information in the organization.

- **Security Managers** are accountable for ensuring the day-to-day operation of the information security program, accomplishing the objectives identified by the CISO, and resolving issues identified by technicians.

- **Security Technicians** are technically qualified individuals tasked to configure firewalls and intrusion detection systems (commonly referred to as IDSs), implement security software, diagnose and troubleshoot problems, and coordinate with systems and network administrators to ensure that security technology is properly implemented.

- **Data Owners** are responsible for the security and use of a particular set of information.

- **Data Custodians** work directly with data owners and are responsible for the storage, maintenance, and protection of the information.

- **Data Users** are systems users who work with the information to perform their daily jobs supporting the mission of the organization. Everyone in the organization is responsible for the security of data, so data users are included here as individuals with an information security role.

The various roles and players in information security implementation across the organization are presented in depth in Chapter 10.

Many organizations look for job applicants who have professional certifications so that they can more easily identify these individuals' proficiency. Unfortunately, most existing certifications are relatively new and not fully understood by hiring organizations. The certifying bodies continue to work diligently to educate the general public on the value and qualifications of their certificate recipients. Employers are trying to understand the match between certifications and the position requirements, and the candidates are trying to gain meaningful employment based on their newly received certifications.

Considered the most prestigious certification for security managers and CISOs, the Certified Information Systems Security Professional (CISSP) is one of two certifications offered by the International Information Systems Security Certification Consortium (ISC)²; see http://www.isc2.org. The Systems Security Certified Practitioner (SSCP) is the other.

The System Administration, Networking and Security Organization, better known as SANS (www.sans.org), developed a series of technical security certifications in 1999, known as the GIAC (www.giac.org). At that time, no technical certifications existed. Anyone who wished to work in the technical security field could obtain only networking or computing certifications, such as the Microsoft Certified Systems Engineer (MCSE) or Certified Novell Engineer (CNE) certification. Today, the GIAC family of certifications can be pursued independently or combined to earn the comprehensive certification, GIAC Security Engineer (GSE). Like the SSCP, the GIAC Information Security Officer (GISO) is an overview certification that combines basic technical knowledge with understanding of threats, risks, and best practices.

One of the newest certifications in the information security discipline is the Security Certified Professional (SCP) certification (www.securitycertified.net/). It provides two tracks: Security Certified Network Professional (SCNP) and Security Certified Network Architect (SCNA). Both are designed for the security technician and have dominant technical components; the latter certification also emphasizes authentication principles.

The ICSA certifications were among the first vendor-sponsored certifications. TruSecure Corporation, a well-known security organization, is promoting the ICSA security practitioner tracks. This vendor-neutral approach focuses on providing "certifications that are skills- and knowledge-based, technology specific, and pragmatic."[16]

CompTIA (www.comptia.com), the company that established the first vendor-neutral professional IT certifications, the A+ series, has recently defined the body of knowledge required for its next certification. The Security + certification is similar to the Network + certification and to many others in its focus on key skills necessary to perform security, without being tied to a particular software or hardware vendor package.

The Certified Information Systems Auditor (CISA) certification, while not specifically a security certification, contains many information security components. The Information Systems Audit and Control Association and Foundation promotes this certification for auditing, networking, and security professionals. It has recently created a new certification, the Certified Information Security Manager (CISM), which was still being defined as this book was being written.

A thorough discussion of information security industry certification approaches and programs appears in Chapter 10.

Maintenance and Change in the SecSDLC

The maintenance and change phase, though last, is perhaps most important, given the flexibility and persistence of many of the threats facing the modern organization. Today's information security systems need constant monitoring, testing, modifying, updating, and repairing. Traditional applications systems that are developed within the framework of the SDLC are not designed to anticipate a vicious attack that requires some degree of application reconstruction as a normal course of operation. In security, the battle for stable, reliable systems is a defensive one. As new threats emerge and old threats evolve, the information security profile of an organization requires constant adaptation to prevent threats from successfully penetrating sensitive data.

Once the information security program is implemented, it must be operated, properly managed, and kept up-to-date by means of established procedures. If the program is not adjusting adequately to the changes in the internal or external environment, it may be necessary to begin the cycle again. The CISO determines whether the information security group can adapt adequately and maintain the information security profile of the organization, or whether the macroscopic process of the SecSDLC must start anew to redevelop a fundamentally different information security profile. It is less expensive and more effective when an information security program is able to deal with change. Note that, even when an information security program is adapting and growing, those processes of maintenance and change mirror the overall process of the SecSDLC, differing only in scope. As deficiencies are found and vulnerabilities pinpointed, projects to maintain, extend, or enhance the program follow the SecSDLC steps. Therefore, for maintenance, the steps include investigation, analysis, design, and implementation.

While a systems management model is designed to manage and operate systems, a maintenance model is intended to complement a systems management model and focus organizational effort on system maintenance. Figure 2-10 presents one recommended approach for dealing with information security maintenance. This figure gives a framework for the discussion of maintenance that follows. The recommended maintenance model consists of five subject areas or domains:

External Monitoring. The objective of external monitoring within the maintenance model shown in Figure 2-10 is to provide early awareness of new and emerging threats, threat agents, vulnerabilities, and attacks, thereby enabling the creation of an effective and timely defense.

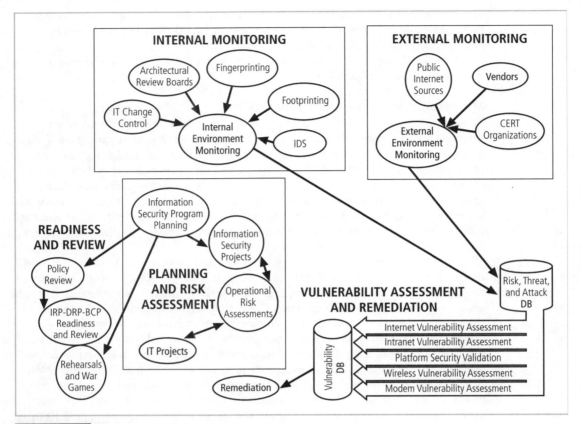

FIGURE 2-10   Maintenance Model

Internal Monitoring. The primary goals of internal monitoring are to maintain an informed awareness of the state of all of the organization's networks, information systems, and information security defenses. This status must be communicated and documented, especially the status of the parts of information systems that are connected to the external network.

Planning and Risk Assessment. The primary objective of planning and risk assessment is to keep a wary eye on the entire information security program. It is achieved in part by identifying and planning ongoing information security activities that further reduce risk. Also, the risk assessment group identifies and documents risks introduced by both IT projects and information security projects. Furthermore, it identifies and documents risks that may be latent in the present environment.

Vulnerability Assessment and Remediation. The primary goal of vulnerability assessment and remediation is the identification of specific, documented vulnerabilities and their timely remediation. It is accomplished by:

- Using documented vulnerability assessment procedures to safely collect intelligence about networks (internal and public-facing), platforms (servers, desktops, and process control), dial-in modems, and wireless network systems;

- Documenting background information and providing tested remediation procedures for the reported vulnerabilities; and

- Tracking, communicating, and reporting to management the itemized facts about the discovered vulnerabilities and the success or failure of the organization to remediate them.

Readiness and Review. The primary objectives of readiness and review are to keep the information security program functioning as designed and, it is hoped, continuously improve it over time.

Vulnerability assessment involves the physical and logical assessment of the vulnerabilities present in both information security and related nonsecurity systems. This analysis is most often accomplished with penetration testing. In **penetration testing**, security personnel simulate or perform specific and controlled attacks to compromise or disrupt their own systems by exploiting documented vulnerabilities. This kind of testing is commonly performed on network connections from outside the organization, as security personnel attempt to exploit vulnerabilities in the organization's system from the attacker's standpoint. Penetration testing is often conducted by consultants or outsourced contractors, who are commonly referred to as **white-hat hackers**, **ethical hackers**, **tiger teams**, or **red teams**. What they are called is less important than what they do, which is critical. Information security administrators who have not looked at their systems through the eyes of an attacker are failing to maintain readiness. The best procedures and tools to use in penetration testing and other vulnerability assessments are the procedures and tools of the hacker community. Fortunately, many intrusion detection systems detect the signatures of these tools and can alert information security management to their use.

One maintenance issue that must be settled in the SecSDLC is the selection of a systems management model. To assist the information security community in managing and operating the ongoing security program, a systems management model must be adopted. In general, systems management models are frameworks that structure the tasks of managing a particular set of activities or business functions. The framework discussed below is a modification of the ISO network management model.

The ISO network management model provides structure to the administration and management of networks and systems by covering five areas:

- Fault management
- Configuration and change management
- Accounting and auditing management
- Performance management
- Security program management

In its original form, the ISO model is not directly applicable to the management of an information security program, but it can be modified to reflect the various administrative tasks in most information security programs. The five areas of the ISO model in a security management are discussed in the following sections.

Fault Management. In the ISO model, fault management involves identifying, tracking, diagnosing, and resolving faults in the system. Information security fault management involves identifying faults in the applied information security profile and then addressing them. Another aspect of fault management is the monitoring and resolution of user complaints.

Configuration and Change Management. Configuration management is the administration of various components involved in the security program. Change management is the administration of changes in the strategy, operation, or components of the information security program. Both configuration and change management administration focus on making technical as well as nontechnical changes. Technical changes affect the technology implemented to support security in the hardware, software, and data components; nontechnical changes affect procedures and people.

Accounting and Auditing Management. The next category in the ISO security management model involves chargeback accounting and systems monitoring. Chargeback accounting happens when organizations internally charge their departments for system use. While chargebacks are seldom used today, certain kinds of resource usage are commonly tracked—such as those on a computing system (such as a server or a desktop computer) or human effort-hours—to recover IT costs from non-IT units of the organization. Accounting management involves monitoring the use of a particular component of a system. In networking, this monitoring may simply determine which users are using which resources. However, in security, it may be easy to track which resources are being used but difficult to determine who is using them. At that point, accounting management begins to overlap with performance management (discussed below). With accounting management you begin to determine optimal points of systems use as indicators for upgrade and improvement.

Auditing is the process of reviewing the use of a system not to determine its performance, but rather to determine whether misuse or malfeasance has occurred.

Performance Management. Because many information security technical controls are implemented on common IT processors, they are affected by the same factors as most computer-based technologies. It is therefore important to monitor the performance of security systems and their underlying IT infrastructure to determine whether they are effectively and efficiently doing the job they were intended to do. Some information security control systems, such as Internet usage monitors that look for inappropriate utilization of Internet resources, operate as pass-by devices.

Security Program Management. Once an information security program is functional, it must be operated and managed. The ISO five-area framework provides some structure for a management model, but it focuses on ensuring that various areas are addressed, rather than guiding the actual conduct of management. To assist in the actual management of information security programs, a formal management standard can provide some insight into the processes and procedures needed. It could be based on the BS7799/ISO17799 model or the NIST models described earlier in this chapter.

Comparing the SDLC and the SecSDLC

Table 2-2 summarizes the steps performed in both the SDLC and the SecSDLC. Since SecSDLC is based on the SDLC, the steps in the cycles are similar, and those common to both cycles are identified in the second column. The third column shows the security issues unique to the SecSDLC.

TABLE 2-2 SDLC and SecSDLC Phase Summary

	Steps common to the SDLC and the SecSDLC	Steps unique to the SecSDLC
Phase 1: Investigation	<ul><li>Outline project scope/goals</li><li>Estimate costs</li><li>Evaluate existing resources</li><li>Analyze feasibility</li></ul>	<ul><li>Define project process and goals and document them in the program security policy</li></ul>
Phase 2: Analysis	<ul><li>Assess current system against plan developed in Phase 1</li><li>Develop preliminary system requirements</li><li>Study integration of new system with existing system</li><li>Document findings and update feasibility analysis</li></ul>	<ul><li>Analyze existing security policies and programs</li><li>Analyze current threats and controls</li><li>Examine legal issues</li><li>Perform risk analysis</li></ul>
Phase 3: Logical Design	<ul><li>Assess current business needs against plan developed in Phase 2</li><li>Select applications, data support, and structures</li><li>Generate multiple solutions for selection of best</li><li>Document findings and update feasibility analysis</li></ul>	<ul><li>Develop security blueprint</li><li>Plan incident response actions</li><li>Plan business response to disaster</li><li>Determine feasibility of continuing and/or outsourcing the project</li></ul>
Phase 4: Physical Design	<ul><li>Select technologies to support solutions developed in Phase 3</li><li>Select the best solution</li><li>Decide whether to make or buy components</li><li>Document findings and update feasibility analysis</li></ul>	<ul><li>Select technologies needed to support security blueprint</li><li>Develop definition of successful solution</li><li>Design physical security measures to support technological solutions</li><li>Review and approve project</li></ul>
Phase 5: Implementation	<ul><li>Develop or buy software</li><li>Order components</li><li>Document system</li><li>Train users</li><li>Update feasibility analysis</li><li>Present system to users</li><li>Test system and review performance</li></ul>	<ul><li>Buy or develop security solutions</li><li>At end of phase, present tested package to management for approval</li></ul>
Phase 6: Maintenance	<ul><li>Support and modify system for its useful life</li><li>Test periodically for compliance with business needs</li><li>Upgrade and patch as necessary</li></ul>	<ul><li>Constantly monitor, test, modify, update, and repair to respond to changing threats</li></ul>

THREAT MANAGEMENT

The SYN Flood

Definition

In 1996, the IT world became aware of a new style of denial-of-service (DoS) attacks on Internet sites. DoS attacks prevent people from using systems or networks, often by overwhelming the systems with seemingly harmless activities. One type of DoS attack is the Transmission Control Protocol (TCP) SYN flood, which sends TCP connection requests faster than the server can process them, thereby overloading the targeted server. The resulting "flood" causes the server to quit responding to legitimate requests to open new connections with valid clients. The "SYN" in "SYN flood" stands for the synchronization flag found in TCP headers.

How the SYN Flood Works

A TCP SYN flood attack takes advantage of the way in which the TCP protocol establishes a new connection. Using port scanning software, the attacker determines which ports have servers listening, and then chooses a source address to impersonate. An attack tool employs a raw socket to create phony TCP and IP headers and form an impersonated client source address. This address is paramount to the SYN flood's success; with it, the attacker can deluge the server with what appear to be valid new connections. These spoofed or impersonated packets enter the server's queue, but the connection is never completed—leaving these new connections in the queue until the request for connection expires, which is determined by the server's configuration settings. Because the source address does not exist or cannot respond, the server will never receive an acknowledgment (ACK message) from the client. Thus, without the client's acknowledgment, the request for connection will remain in the server's connection queue until it times out.

In a SYN flood, the location of the attacking system is obscured because the source addresses in the SYN packets are often impersonated. When the packet arrives at the target server system, there is no way to determine its true source. Another damaging aspect of this kind of attack is that only a few of these packets ever need to be sent to the server, making a SYN flood easy to carry out even using a slow dial-up (e.g. PPP or SLIP) connection. Additionally, the Linux-based attack tool permits the attacker to choose which system to target, how many packets to send, which ports to attack, how often to send packets, and how long to continue the attack.

Detection

A specific TCP SYN flood will most likely be detected by client systems attempting to access one of the services on the victim system. To verify that such an attack is occurring, a server administrator should check the state of the server system's network traffic. Too many connections in the state "SYN_RECEIVED" could indicate that the system is under attack. Automated intrusion detection tools can also detect a SYN flood.

Response

In most cases, the victim of a SYN flood attack will experience difficulty in accepting any new incoming network connections. In these situations, the attack does not affect either existing incoming connections or the ability to originate outgoing network connections.

(continued)

In some worst-case scenarios, however, the system may exhaust memory, crash, or be rendered otherwise inoperative. To stop a detected attack, the server's administrator must close all of the open connections to the server.

Protection/Prevention

A generally accepted solution to guarding against a SYN flood attack using the current IP technology does not yet exist. Nevertheless, proper router configuration to disallow outgoing spoofing or impersonation activities can make your site a good neighbor to others by assuring that all outbound network traffic carries only the authentic IP addresses of the sending router and can reduce the likelihood that a site will be the source of one of these attacks. Also, the implementation of specialized techniques such as micro blocks, SYN cookies, RST cookies, and stack tweaking can aid in the prevention of the SYN flood attack.

The timeout value controls how long a request waits in the connection queue until an acknowledgment is received. Shortening this interval can help when used with longer queue lengths because the spoofed packets are quickly removed from the queue. This solution affects new outgoing connections, however, so remote users with slow links to the server might never get connected.

The best solution may be to modify the TCP implementation so as to reduce the amount of information stored for each in-progress connection, and to check the return route of any new connection. If the return route differs from that of the received packets (which is normal during this attack), the connection should be dropped.

For more information, refer to the Cert Advisory on TCP SYN Flooding and IP Spoofing Attacks at www.cert.org/advisories/CA-1996-21.html.

Contributed by Daniel Baer, Joe Dawson, Gary Greenewalt, and Brian Schultheiss.

Chapter Summary

- Planning is central to the management of any organization.
- Planning is based on the preparation, application, and control of a sequence of action steps to achieve specific goals.
- To develop and implement effective planning, a number of documents representing the philosophical, ethical, and entrepreneurial perspectives of the company are first created—namely, the mission statement, the vision statement, the values statement, and strategy.
- Security can begin either as a grass-roots effort (a bottom-up approach) or with plans formulated by senior management (a top-down approach).
- The systems development life cycle (SDLC) is a methodology for the design and implementation of an information system in an organization. A methodology is a formal approach to solving a problem based on a structured sequence of procedures.
- Using a methodology ensures a rigorous process, and increases the likelihood of achieving the desired final objective.

- The process of phased system development described by the traditional SDLC can be adapted to support the specialized implementation of a security project by using the security systems development life cycle (SecSDLC). The fundamental process is the identification of specific threats and the risks that they represent to the organization, followed by the design and implementation of specific controls to counter those threats and assist in the management of the risks.

- The investigation phase of the SecSDLC begins with a directive from upper management, dictating the process, outcomes, and goals of the project, as well as its budget and other constraints.

- In the analysis phase, the team examines existing security policies or programs, along with documented current threats and associated controls. This phase also includes an analysis of relevant legal issues that could affect the design of the security solution. Risk management begins in this stage as well. Risk management is the process of identifying, assessing, and evaluating the levels of risk facing the organization—specifically, threats to the organization's security and to the information stored and processed by the organization.

- Analysis begins with knowing your enemy. In information security, the enemy consists of the threats and attacks that your systems face.

- The design phase includes two distinct phases: the logical design and the physical design. In the logical design phase, blueprints for security are created, and key policies that influence later decisions are examined and implemented. In the physical design phase, the security technology needed to support this blueprint is evaluated, alternative solutions are generated, and a final design is determined.

- The maintenance and change phase, though last, is perhaps most important, given the flexibility and persistence of many of the threats facing the modern organization. Once the information security program is implemented, it must be operated and properly managed through the establishment of procedures. Additional procedures are needed to keep the organization safe as change occurs.

Review Questions

1. Describe the essential parts of planning. How does the existence of resource constraints affect the need for planning?
2. What are the three common layers of planning? How do they differ?
3. Who are the stakeholders? Why is it important to consider their views when planning?
4. What is a mission statement? Why is it important? What does it contain?
5. What is a vision statement? Why is it important? What does it contain?
6. What is a values statement? Why is it important? What does it contain?
7. What is strategy?
8. Describe top-down strategic planning. How does it differ from bottom-up strategic planning? Which is usually more effective in implementing security in a large, diverse organization?
9. Describe the planning role of the CISO. How does that role differ from the planning role of the CIO?
10. How does the SecSDLC differ from the more general SDLC?
11. What is the primary objective of the SecSDLC? What are its major steps, and what are the major objectives of each step?
12. What is a threat in the context of information security? How many categories of threats exist as presented in this chapter?
13. What is the difference between a threat and an attack?

14. How can a vulnerability be converted into an attack? What label would we give to the entity that performs this transformation?

15. What name is given to an attack that makes use of viruses and worms? What name is given to an attack that does not actually cause damage other than wasted time and resources?

16. What questions might be asked to help identify and classify information assets? Which is the most useful question in the list?

17. What name is given to the process of assigning a comparative risk rating to each specific information asset? What are the uses of such a rating?

18. What term is used to describe the provision of rules intended to protect the information assets of an organization?

19. What term is used to describe the control measure that reduces security incidents among members of the organization by familiarizing them with relevant policies and practices in an ongoing manner?

20. What are the three categories of information security controls? How is each used to reduce risk for the organization?

Exercises

1. Using a Web search engine, find an article from a reputable source published within the past six months that reports on the relative risk that comes from inside the organization as opposed to risk that comes from external sources. If the article notes that this relative risk is changing, how is it changing and to what does the article attribute the change?

2. Using a Web search engine, find five examples of corporate vision statements, corporate mission statements, and corporate goals. Do these examples express concern for the security of corporate information?

3. Search your institution's published documents, including its Web pages. Locate its mission statement, vision statement, and strategic goals. Identify any references to information security. Also look for any planning documents related to information security.

4. Using a Web browser, go to http://gocsi.com. Search for the link offering a free copy of the latest CSI/FBI study. Summarize the key points and bring your summary to class to discuss with your fellow students.

5. Go to the library and search through recent newspaper articles about your area. How many examples of threats to information security can you find in the last week?

Case Exercises

During the Random Widget's CIO strategic planning meeting…

CIO Mike Edwards discussed and expanded upon the details of how the information technology division would enable RWW to achieve each of its strategic goals. As he was finishing his review of the document, Mike made a crucial point: "Make sure you don't let this planning document get out. These documents are not to leave the building."

Iris asked, "Shouldn't they be labeled 'Confidential' then?"

"What do you mean, Iris?" Mike asked.

Iris replied, "I've been working on a data classification scheme for RWW along with the systems administrators. We have a draft that uses three data classification levels for the company. Every piece of information in the company is categorized as 'Confidential,' 'Sensitive,' or 'Public.'"

This document should be clearly labeled 'Confidential' to prevent it from being released by mistake."

After a moment's thought Mike exclaimed, "Excellent! Please send copies of the draft data classification scheme to all department heads immediately." He turned to Stan, his assistant, and said, "Please have new covers that label this plan as 'Confidential' prepared by noon today, and have one of your people replace each cover with the revised, properly marked cover before the end of business today."

1. Create definitions of "Confidential," "Sensitive," and "Public" for RWW. Create a list of examples of documents that should be labeled with each classification.

2. Design a labeling scheme (cover sheet, stamp, or other scheme) to associate with this classification system.

Endnotes

1. Charles Cresson Wood. *Information Security Roles and Responsibilities Made Easy.* Houston, TX: PentaSafe, 2002:46.
2. What is strategic planning? *The Alliance FAQs.* http://www.allianceonline.org/faqs.html. Accessed 02/21/03.
3. David Molta. *Planning Network Services.* http://web.syr.edu/~djmolta/ist753/planning.htm.
4. Michael Allison and Jude Kaye. *Strategic Planning for Nonprofit Organizations.* http://www.nonprofitgeorgia.org/faq-planning.html.
5. Brian Ward. *Planning as Doing.* http://www.refresher.com/!bwplanning.html.
6. 2002 CSI/FBI Computer Crime and Security Survey.
7. CERT. In: A survey of digital security. *The Economist,* Oct. 26–Nov. 1, 2002.
8. John Leyden. *The Register.* www.theregister.co.uk/content/55/29827.htm. March 19, 2003.
9. Charles Cresson Wood. *Information Security Roles and Responsibilities Made Easy.* Houston, TX: PentaSafe, 2002:96.
10. Charles Cresson Wood. *Information Security Roles and Responsibilities Made Easy.* Houston, TX: PentaSafe, 2002:58.
11. Sun Tzu. . *The Art of War.* Trans. by Samuel B. Griffith. Oxford, UK: Oxford University Press, 1988.
12. Michael Whitman. Enemy at the gates: threats to information security. *Communications of the ACM,* accepted March 26, 2002; in press.
13. David Brumley and Dan Boneh. *Remote Timing Attacks are Practical.* http://crypto.stanford.edu/~dabo/papers/ssl-timing.pdf. July 31, 2003.
14. National Institute of Standards and Technology. *An Introduction to Computer Security: The NIST Handbook.* SP 800-12.
15. William R. King and Paul Gray. *The Management of Information Systems.* Chicago: Dryden Press, 1989:359.
16. Trusecure. TICSA certification. *Trusecure Online.* http://www.truesecure.com/solutions/certifications/ticsa/. July 22, 2002.

Planning for Contingencies

3

A WEEK AFTER THE STRATEGIC PLANNING meeting, Iris was just finishing a draft of the information security strategic plan. Satisfied with her progress thus far, she activated the calendar on her desktop computer and began reviewing her schedule, hoping to find a good day and time to meet with Mike about contingency planning. During their last luncheon, her friend Charley had warned her not to let too much time pass before addressing the issue again. She knew he was right. It simply wasn't a good idea to put off discussing such an important project until the end of the month, as Mike had suggested during last week's strategic planning meeting. Having a plan in place in case of an emergency just made good business sense, even if planning for the unexpected was not perceived as a high priority by many of her management peers.

Suddenly, the building's fire alarm went off. Heart pumping, Iris left her office. With or without a contingency plan, it was her responsibility to assess this situation as quickly and as safely as possible. Was there an incident? A disaster? Or was it simply a false alarm? As she quickly moved down the line of cubicles, Iris called for everyone who had not yet left the floor to leave by way of the nearest exit. Then she rushed to the floor's fire control panel, which was located in the elevator lobby. A blinking light showed that one heat-sensitive sprinkler head had been activated. Iris waited a moment to see whether any other blinking lights came on. None did, but the existing light stayed on. It seemed that she was dealing with an incident, and not a disaster.

She headed down the hall to the place shown on the fire panel where the sprinkler had been triggered. Hearing voices coming from the break station, Iris turned the corner, and saw Harry and Joel from the accounting department. Their offices were located right next to the break station. Harry was inspecting what had once been the coffee pot, while Joel held a fire extinguisher. Both were wet and irritated. The room smelled of scorched coffee and was filled with smoke. To her relief, there was no more fire.

"Is everyone all right?" she asked.

"Yeah," Harry replied, "but our offices are a mess. There's water everywhere."

Joel shook his head in disgust. "What a time for this to happen. We were just getting ready to finish the quarterly reports, too."

"Never mind that. As long as you're both okay. You guys need to make a trip home so you can get changed . . ."

Iris was interrupted by Mike Edwards, who had just joined them. "What happened?" he asked.

Iris shrugged. "It's a minor incident, Mike, everything's under control. The fire department will be here any minute . . ."

"Incident? Incident?" Joel said in dismay as he pointed at his desk, where steam rose from his soaked CPU, and a pile of drenched reports littered the floor. "This isn't an incident. *This* is a disaster!"

LEARNING OBJECTIVES

Upon completion of this material, you should be able to:

- Understand the need for contingency planning
- Know the major components of contingency planning
- Create a simple set of contingency plans, using business impact analysis
- Prepare and execute a test of contingency plans
- Understand the unified contingency plan approach

Introduction

Chapter 2 introduced the topic of planning and provided some specifics about planning for the organization in general and for planning the information security program in particular. This chapter focuses on planning for the unexpected event, when the use of technology is disrupted and business operations come close to a standstill. Because technology drives business, planning for an unexpected event is usually undertaken by managers from both the information technology and information security communities of interest, who analyze the entire technological infrastructure of the organization. For a plan to gain the support of all members of the organization, it must also be sanctioned and actively supported by the general business community of interest.

The need to have a plan in place that systematically addresses how to identify, contain, and resolve an unexpected event was identified in the earliest days of information technology. As noted in NIST Special Publication 800-18, *Guide for Developing Security Plans for Information Technology Systems,* when an unexpected event occurs, "Procedures are required that will permit the organization to continue essential functions if information technology support is interrupted."[1] Some organizations—particularly, for national security reasons, federal agencies—are charged by law or other mandate to have such procedures in place at all times.

Business organizations of various sizes should also prepare for the unexpected. In general, a business organization's ability to weather losses caused by an unexpected event depends on proper planning and execution of such a plan; without a workable plan, an unexpected event can cause severe damage to an organization's information resources and assets from which it may never recover. As noted by The Hartford insurance company: "On average, over 40% of businesses that don't have a disaster plan go out of business after a major loss like a fire, a break-in, or a storm."[2] Therefore, the development of a plan for handling unexpected events should be a high priority for all managers.

What Is Contingency Planning?

The overall process of preparing for unexpected events is called **contingency planning (CP)**. CP is the process by which the information technology and information security communities of interest position their organizations to prepare for, detect, react to, and recover from events that threaten the security of information resources and assets, both human and natural. The main goal of CP is the restoration to normal modes of operation with minimal cost and disruption to normal business activities after an unexpected event—in other words, to make sure things get back to the way they were. Ideally, CP should ensure continuous information systems availability to the organization even in the face of the unexpected.[3]

CP consists of three major components, each of which is discussed in detail in the next section of this chapter:

- Incident response plan (IRP)
- Disaster recovery plan (DRP)
- Business continuity plan (BCP)

The IRP focuses on the immediate response to an incident. Any unexpected event is treated as an incident, unless and until a response team deems it to be a disaster. Then the DRP, which focuses on restoring operations at the primary site, is invoked. If operations at the primary site cannot be quickly restored—for example, when the damage is major or will affect the organization's functioning over the long term—the BCP occurs concurrently with the DRP, enabling the business to continue at an alternate site, until the organization is able to resume operations at its primary site or select a new primary location.

Depending on the size and business philosophy of an organization, information technology and information security managers can either (1) create and develop these three CP components as one unified plan or (2) create the three separately in conjunction with a set of interlocking procedures that enable continuity. Typically, larger, more complex organizations create and develop the CP components separately, as the functions of each component differ in scope, applicability, and design. Smaller organizations tend to adopt a one-plan method, consisting of a straightforward set of recovery strategies.

Ideally, the CIO, systems administrators, CISO, and key IT and business managers should be actively involved during the creation and development of all three CP components, as well as during the distribution of responsibilities among the three communities of interest. To ensure continuity across all of the CP processes, contingency planners should follow this six-step process when creating each of the three CP components:[4]

1. Identify the mission- or business-critical functions. Each organization must identify those areas of operation that must continue to allow for the ongoing operation of the organization. These areas must be prioritized from most critical to least critical to permit optimal allocation of resources (time, money, personnel, and so on) in the event of a disaster.
2. Identify the resources that support the critical functions. For each function, the organization must identify which resources that function depends upon. These resources could include people, computing capability, applications, data, services, physical infrastructure, and documentation (forms, reports, and so on).
3. Anticipate potential contingencies or disasters. Organizations hypothesize about potential disasters and determine which functions they would affect.
4. Select contingency planning strategies. This step involves identifying methods of dealing with each potential disaster scenario and outlining a plan to prepare for and react to that disaster.
5. Implement the selected strategy. Once contingency planning strategies have been selected, the organization must make the appropriate preparations, draft the strategies, and train employees. Many of these tasks continue even after the plans are developed and put into place.
6. Test and revise contingency plans. All CP components, including the IRP, should be tested periodically because flaws will likely crop up in the plan and in its implementation.

Four teams of individuals are involved in contingency planning and contingency operations:

- The *CP team* collects information about information systems and the threats they face, and creates the contingency plans for incident response, disaster recovery, and business continuity. The CP team often consists of a coordinating manager and representatives from each of the other three teams.
- The *incident response team* manages and executes the incident response plan by detecting, evaluating, and responding to incidents.
- The *disaster recovery team* manages and executes the disaster recovery plan by detecting, evaluating, and responding to disasters, and by reestablishing operations at the primary business site.
- The *business continuity team* manages and executes the business continuity plan by setting up and starting off-site operations in the event of an incident or disaster.

As indicated earlier, in larger organizations these teams are distinct entities, with non-overlapping membership, although the latter three teams have representatives on the CP team. In smaller organizations, the four teams may include overlapping groups of people.

As illustrated in the opening scenario of this chapter, many organizations' contingency plans are woefully inadequate. CP often fails to receive the high priority necessary for the efficient and timely recovery of business operations during and after an unexpected event. The fact that many organizations do not place an adequate premium on CP does not mean that it is unimportant, however. The Computer Security Resource Center (CSRC) at the National Institute for Standards and Technology (NIST) describes the need for this type of planning as follows:

> These procedures (contingency plans, business interruption plans, and continuity of operations plans) should be coordinated with the backup, contingency, and recovery plans of any general support systems, including networks used by the application. The contingency plans should ensure that interfacing systems are identified and contingency/disaster planning coordinated.[5]

As you learn more about CP, you may notice that it shares certain characteristics with risk management and the SecSDLC methodology. Many information technology and information security managers are already familiar with these processes; they can readily adapt their existing knowledge to the CP process.

Components of Contingency Planning

As noted earlier, CP includes three major components: incident response, disaster recovery, and business continuity plans (see Figure 3-1). Whether an organization adopts the one-plan method or the multiple-plan method with interlocking procedures, each of these CP components must be addressed and developed in its entirety. The following sections describe each component in detail, and discuss when and how each should be used. They also consider how to determine which plan is best suited for the identification, containment, and resolution of any given unexpected event.

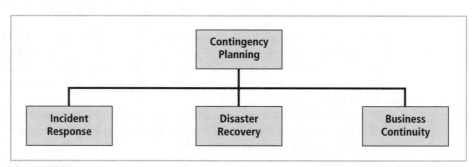

FIGURE 3-1   Contingency Planning Hierarchies

Incident Response Plan

The **incident response plan (IRP)** comprises a detailed set of processes and procedures that anticipate, detect, and mitigate the effects of an unexpected event that might compromise information resources and assets. In CP, an unexpected event is called an **incident**. An incident occurs when an attack (natural or human-made) affects information resources and/or assets, causing actual damage or other disruptions. **Incident response (IR)**, then, is a set of procedures that commence when an incident is detected. IR must be carefully planned and coordinated, because organizations heavily depend on the quick and efficient containment and resolution of incidents. The IRP is usually activated when an incident causes minimal damage—according to criteria set in advance by the organization—with little or no disruption to business operations.

The scenario at the beginning of this chapter depicts an incident and not a disaster, despite Joel's declaration otherwise. By now, it should be clear why a technology manager, like Iris, must become involved in assessing the damage to two drenched accounting offices and the break room. Because the incident at RWW was determined by Iris to have caused minimal damage, a corresponding IR would have been activated, if RWW had a properly developed IRP. If the fire had spread beyond the break room, triggered the sprinkler systems throughout the building, and caused employee injuries, then an IRP (even if RWW had one) would not have been adequate to deal with the situation. Instead, it would be necessary to initiate the disaster recovery plan and the business continuity plan, both of which are discussed later in this chapter.

When one of the threats identified in Chapter 2 turns into a valid attack, it is classified as an information security incident, but only if it has all of the following characteristics:

- It is directed against information assets.
- It has a realistic chance of success.
- It threatens the confidentiality, integrity, or availability of information resources and assets.

The prevention of threats and attacks has been intentionally omitted from this discussion because guarding against such possibilities is entirely the responsibility of the information security department. It is important to understand that *IR is a reactive measure, not a preventive one.*

The responsibility for creating an organization's IRP usually falls to the CISO. With the aid of other managers and systems administrators on the CP team, the CISO should select members from each community of interest to form an independent IR team, which executes the IRP. The roles and responsibilities of the members of the IR team should be clearly documented and communicated throughout the organization. The IRP also includes an alert roster, which lists certain critical agencies to be contacted during the course of an incident.

Using the six-step CP process, discussed in the previous section, the CP team creates the IRP, and the IR procedures take shape. For every incident scenario, the CP team creates three sets of incident-handling procedures:

1. During the incident: The planners develop and document the procedures that must be performed during the incident. These procedures are grouped and assigned to individuals. Systems administrators' tasks differ from managerial tasks, so members of the planning committee must draft a set of function-specific procedures.
2. After the incident: Once the procedures for handling an incident are drafted, the planners develop and document the procedures that must be performed immediately after the incident has ceased. Again, separate functional areas may develop different procedures.

3. Before the incident: The planners draft a third set of procedures, those tasks that must be performed to prepare for the incident. These procedures include the details of the data backup schedules, disaster recovery preparation, training schedules, testing plans, copies of service agreements, and business continuity plans, if any. At this level, the business continuity plan could consist of just additional material on a service bureau that stores data off-site via electronic vaulting, with an agreement to provide office space and lease equipment as needed.

Figure 3-2 presents an example of pages from the IR plan that support each of these phases. Once these sets of procedures are clearly documented, the IR portion of the IRP is assembled and the critical information as outlined in these planning sections is recorded.

Before an Attack
Users
1. Don't put suspicious diskettes in your system. Check your system before booti...
2. Don't download free games or u... system without authorization fr... Services department.
3. Don't open attachments in unso... Make sure all attachments are fr... party by confirming the origin i...
4. Don't forward messages that as... warn others of a virus or threat.

Technology Services
1. Ensure virus protection software... properly configured, and update...
2. Automate whenever possible. Provide awareness and training... users on proper use of the e-ma... antivirus software.

After an Attack
Users
1. Scan your computer thoroughly for any additional viruses.
2. Review e-mail (TITLES ONLY, D... REOPEN attachments) for sus...
3. Write down everything you we... before you detected the virus.
4. Verify that your antivirus softw... definitions are up-to-date.

Technology Services
1. Conduct an incident recovery i...
2. Interview all users detecting th...
3. Verify that all systems antiviru... definitions are up-to-date.
4. Reconnect quarantined users t...
5. Brief all infected users on prop... procedures.
6. File the incident recovery inves... Notify all users that this partic... of virus has been detected, an... antivirus software and definiti...

During an Attack
Users
1. If your antivirus software detects an attack, it will delete the virus or quarantine the file that carries it. Record any messages that your antivirus software displays and notify Technology Services immediately.
2. If your computer begins behaving unusually or you determine that you have contracted a virus through other means, turn your computer off immediately, by pulling the plug. Notify Technology Services immediately.

Technology Services
1. If users begin reporting virus attacks, record the information provided by the users.
2. Temporarily disconnect those users from the network at the switch.
3. Begin scanning all active systems for that strain of virus.
4. Deploy a response team to inspect the users' system.

FIGURE 3-2 Incident Response Planning

Preparing to Plan

Planning for an incident and the responses to it require a detailed understanding of the information systems and the threats they face. Later in this chapter, you will learn about a process called business impact analysis (BIA), which provides the data used to develop the IRP. The IR planning team seeks to develop a series of predefined responses that will guide the team and information security staff through the incident response steps. Predefining incident responses enables the organization to react to a detected incident quickly and effectively, without confusion or wasted time and effort.

The IR team consists of professionals who are capable of handling the information systems and functional areas affected by an incident. For example, imagine a firefighting team responding to an emergency call. Rather than responding to the fire as individuals, each member of the team has a specific role to perform, so that the team acts as a unified body that assesses the situation, determines the appropriate response, and coordinates the response. Similarly, each member of the IR team must know his or her specific role, work in concert with other team members, and execute the objectives of the IRP.

Incident Detection

The challenge for every IR team is determining whether an event is the product of routine systems use or an actual incident. **Incident classification** is the process of examining a possible incident, or **incident candidate**, and determining whether it constitutes an actual incident. Classifying an incident is the responsibility of the IR team. Initial reports from end users, intrusion detection systems, host- and network-based virus detection software, and systems administrators are all ways to track and detect incident candidates. Careful training in the reporting of an incident candidate allows end users, the help desk staff, and all security personnel to relay vital information to the IR team. Once an actual incident is properly identified, the members of the IR team can effectively execute the corresponding procedures from the IRP.

A number of occurrences signal the presence of an incident candidate. Unfortunately, these same events can result from an overloaded network, computer, or server, and some are similar to the normal operation of these information assets. Other incident candidates mimic the actions of a misbehaving computing system, software package, or other less serious threat. To help make the detection of actual incidents more reliable, D. L. Pipkin has identified three categories of incident indicators: possible, probable, and definite.[6]

Possible Indicators.   The following four types of incident candidates are considered *possible* actual incidents:

1. Presence of unfamiliar files: For example, users might discover unfamiliar files in their home directories or on their office computers. Administrators might also find unexplained files that do not seem to be in a logical location or owned by an authorized user.
2. Presence or execution of unknown programs or processes: For example, users or administrators might detect unfamiliar programs running, or processes executing, on office machines or network servers.
3. Unusual consumption of computing resources: For example, consumption of memory or hard disk space might suddenly spike or fall. Many computer operating systems, including Windows 2000, Windows XP, and many UNIX variants, allow users and administrators to monitor CPU and memory consumption. Most computers also have the ability to monitor hard drive space. In addition, servers maintain logs of file creation and storage.
4. Unusual system crashes: Computer systems can crash. Older operating systems running newer programs are notorious for locking up or spontaneously rebooting whenever the operating system is unable to execute a requested process or service. You are probably familiar with systems error messages such as "Unrecoverable Application Error," "General Protection Fault," and the infamous Windows NT "Blue

Screen of Death." However, if a computer system seems to be crashing, hanging, rebooting, or freezing more frequently than usual, the cause could be an incident candidate.

Probable Indicators.   The four types of incident candidates described below are *probable* indicators of actual incidents:

1. Activities at unexpected times: If traffic levels on the organization's network exceed the measured baseline values, an incident candidate is probably present. If this activity surge occurs when few members of the organization are at work, this probability becomes much higher. Similarly, if systems are accessing drives, such as floppy and CD-ROM drives, when the end user is not using them, an incident may also be occurring.
2. Presence of new accounts: Periodic review of user accounts can reveal an account (or accounts) that the administrator does not remember creating or that are not logged in the administrator's journal. Even one unlogged new account is an incident candidate. An unlogged new account with root or other special privileges has an even higher probability of being an actual incident.
3. Reported attacks: If users of the system report a suspected attack, there is a high probability that an attack has occurred, which constitutes an incident. The technical sophistication of the person making the report should be considered.
4. Notification from IDS: If the organization has installed and correctly configured a host- or network-based intrusion detection system (IDS), then notification from the IDS indicates that an incident might be in progress. However, IDSs are seldom configured optimally and, even when they are, tend to issue many false positives or false alarms. The administrator must then determine whether the notification is real or is the result of a routine operation by a user or other administrator.

Definite Indicators.   The five types of incident candidates described below are *definite* indicators of an actual incident. That is, they clearly signal that an incident is in progress or has occurred. In these cases, the corresponding IR must be activated immediately.

1. Use of dormant accounts: Many network servers maintain default accounts, and there often exist accounts from former employees, employees on a leave of absence or sabbatical without remote access privileges, or dummy accounts set up to support system testing. If any of these accounts begins accessing system resources, querying servers, or engaging in other activities, an incident is almost certain to have occurred.
2. Changes to logs: The smart systems administrator backs up system logs as well as system data. As part of a routine incident scan, systems administrators can compare these logs to the online versions to determine whether they have been modified. If they have, and the systems administrator cannot determine explicitly that an authorized individual modified them, an incident has occurred.
3. Presence of hacker tools: Network administrators sometimes use system vulnerability and network evaluation tools to scan internal computers and networks to determine what a hacker can see. These tools are also used to support research into attack profiles. All too often, however, they are used by employees, contractors, or outsiders with local network access to hack into systems. To combat this problem, many organizations explicitly prohibit the use of these tools without written permission from the CISO, making any unauthorized installation a policy violation. Most organizations that engage in penetration-testing operations require that all tools in this category be confined to specific systems, and that they not be used on the general network unless active penetration testing is under way.

4. Notifications by partner or peer: If a business partner or another connected organization reports an attack from your computing systems, then an incident has occurred.
5. Notification by hacker: Some hackers enjoy taunting their victims. If an organization's Web pages are defaced, it's an incident. If an organization receives an extortion request for money in exchange for its customers' credit card files, an incident is in progress.

Occurrences of Actual Incidents.   When the following actual incidents are confirmed, the corresponding IR must be immediately activated:

1. Loss of availability: Information or information systems become unavailable.
2. Loss of integrity: Users report corrupt data files, garbage where data should be, or data that just looks wrong.
3. Loss of confidentiality: You are notified of sensitive information leaks, or information you thought was protected has been disclosed.
4. Violation of policy: If organizational policies addressing information or information security have been violated, an incident has occurred.
5. Violation of law: If the law has been broken and the organization's information assets are involved, an incident has occurred.

Incident Response

Once an actual incident has been confirmed and properly classified, the IR team moves from the detection phase to the reaction phase. The steps in the IR are designed to stop the incident, mitigate its effects, and provide information for the recovery from the incident. In the incident response phase, a number of action steps taken by the IR team and others must occur quickly and may take place concurrently. An effective IRP prioritizes and documents these steps to allow for efficient reference in the midst of an incident. These steps include notification of key personnel, the assignment of tasks, and documentation of the incident.

Notification of Key Personnel.   As soon as the IR team determines that an incident is in progress, the right people must be immediately notified in the right order. Most response organizations, such as firefighters or the military, maintain an alert roster for all emergencies. An **alert roster** is a document containing contact information on the individuals to be notified in the event of an actual incident.

There are two ways to activate an alert roster: sequentially and hierarchically. A **sequential roster** requires that a contact person call each and every person on the roster. A **hierarchical roster** requires that the first person call designated other people on the roster, who in turn call designated other people, and so on. Each approach has both advantages and disadvantages. The hierarchical system is quicker, because more people are calling at the same time, but the message can become distorted as it is passed from person to person. The sequential system is more accurate, but slower because a single contact person provides each responder with the message.

The **alert message** is a scripted description of the incident and consists of just enough information so that each responder knows what portion of the IRP to implement without impeding the notification process. It is important to recognize that not everyone is on the alert roster—only those individuals who must respond to a specific actual incident. As with any part of the IRP, the alert roster must be regularly maintained, tested, and rehearsed if it is to remain effective.

During this phase other key personnel not on the alert roster, such as general management, must be notified of the incident as well. This notification should occur only after the incident has been confirmed, but before media or other external sources learn of it. In addition, some incidents are disclosed to the employees in general, as a lesson in security, and some are not, as a measure of security. Furthermore, other organizations may need to be notified, if it is determined that the incident is not confined to internal information resources, or if the incident is part of a larger-scale assault. For example, during Mafiaboy's distributed denial-of-service attack on multiple high-visibility Web-based vendors in late 1999, many of the target organizations reached out for help. In general, the IR planners should determine in advance whom to notify and when, and should offer guidance about additional notification steps to take as needed.

Documenting an Incident.   As soon as an incident has been confirmed and the notification process is under way, the team should begin to document it. The documentation should record the *who, what, when, where, why,* and *how* of each action taken while the incident is occurring. This documentation serves as a case study after the fact to determine whether the right actions were taken and if they were effective. It also proves, should it become necessary, that the organization did everything possible to prevent the spread of the incident. Legally, the standards of due care will protect the organization, should an incident adversely affect individuals inside and outside the organization, or other organizations that use the target organization's systems. Incident documentation can also be used as a simulation in future training sessions on future versions of the IRP.

Incident Containment Strategies.   One of the most critical components of IR is stopping the incident or containing its scope or impact. Incident containment strategies vary depending on the incident, and on the amount of damage caused. Before an incident can be stopped or contained, however, the affected areas must be identified. Now is not the time to conduct a detailed analysis of the affected areas; those tasks are typically performed after the fact, in the forensics process. Instead, simple identification of what information and systems are involved determines the containment actions to be taken. Incident containment strategies focus on two tasks: stopping the incident and recovering control of the affected systems.

The IR team can stop the incident and attempt to recover control by means of several strategies. If the incident originates outside the organization, the simplest and most straightforward approach is to disconnect the affected communication circuits. Of course, if the organization's lifeblood runs through that circuit, this step may be too drastic; if the incident does not threaten critical functional areas, it may be more feasible to monitor the incident and contain it another way. One approach used by some organizations is to dynamically apply filtering rules to limit certain types of network access. For example, if a threat agent is attacking a network by exploiting a vulnerability in the Simple Network Management Protocol (SNMP), then applying a blocking filter for the commonly used IP ports for that vulnerability will stop the attack without compromising other services on the network. Depending on the nature of the attack and the organization's technical capabilities, ad hoc controls can sometimes gain valuable time to devise a more permanent control strategy. Other containment strategies include the following:

- Disabling compromised user accounts
- Reconfiguring a firewall to block the problem traffic
- Temporarily disabling the compromised process or service
- Taking down the conduit application or server—for example, the e-mail server
- Stopping all computers and network devices

Obviously, the final strategy is used only when all system control has been lost, and the only hope is to preserve the data stored on the computers so that operations can resume normally once the incident is resolved. The IR team, following the procedures outlined in the IRP, determines the length of the interruption.

Consider the chapter-opening scenario again. What if, instead of a fire, the event had been a virus attack? And what if the key incident response personnel had been home sick, on vacation, or otherwise not there? Think how many people in your class or office aren't there on a regular basis. Many businesses involve travel, with employees going off-site to meetings, seminars, training, vacations, or other diverse requirements. In considering these possibilities, the importance of preparedness becomes clear. Everyone should know how to handle an incident, not just the CISO and systems administrators.

Incident Escalation. An incident may increase in scope or severity to the point that the IRP cannot adequately handle it. As important as knowing how to handle an incident is knowing at what point to hit the panic button and escalate the incident to a disaster, or to transfer the incident to an outside authority such as law enforcement or another public response unit. Each organization will have to determine, during the business impact analysis, the point at which an incident is deemed a disaster. These criteria must be included in the incident response plan. The organization must also document when to involve outside responders, as discussed in other sections. Escalation is one of those things that once done cannot be undone, so it is important to know when and where it should be used.

Incident Recovery

Once the incident has been contained, and system control has been regained, incident recovery can begin. As in the incident response phase, the first task is to inform the appropriate human resources. Almost simultaneously, the IR team must assess the full extent of the damage so as to determine what must be done to restore the systems. Each individual involved should begin recovery operations based on the appropriate incident recovery section of the IRP.

The immediate determination of the scope of the breach of confidentiality, integrity, and availability of information and information assets is called **incident damage assessment**. Incident damage assessment can take days or weeks depending on the extent of the damage. The damage can range from minor (a curious hacker snooped around) to severe (the infection of hundreds of computer systems by a worm or virus). System logs, intrusion detection logs, configuration logs, and other documents, as well as the documentation from the incident response, provide information on the type, scope, and extent of damage. Using this information, the IR team assesses the current state of the information and systems, and compares it to a known state. Individuals who document the damage from actual incidents must be trained to collect and preserve evidence, in case the incident is part of a crime or results in a civil action.

Once the extent of the damage has been determined, the recovery process begins. This process involves the following steps:[7]

- Identify the vulnerabilities that allowed the incident to occur and spread. Resolve them.

- Address the safeguards that failed to stop or limit the incident, or were missing from the system in the first place. Install, replace, or upgrade them.

- Evaluate monitoring capabilities (if present). Improve detection and reporting methods, or install new monitoring capabilities.

■ Restore the data from backups. The IR team must understand the backup strategy used by the organization, restore the data contained in backups, and then use the appropriate recover processes from incremental backups or database journals to recreate any data that was created or modified since the last backup.

■ Restore the services and processes in use. Compromised services and processes must be examined, cleaned, and then restored. If services or processes were interrupted in the course of regaining control of the systems, they need to be brought back online.

■ Continuously monitor the system. If an incident happened once, it could easily happen again. Hackers frequently boast of their exploits in chat rooms and dare their peers to match their efforts. If word gets out, others may be tempted to try the same or different attacks on your systems. It is therefore important to maintain vigilance during the entire IR process.

■ Restore the confidence of the members of the organization's communities of interest. The IR may wish to issue a short memorandum outlining the incident, and assuring all that the incident was handled and the damage was controlled. If the incident was minor, say so. If the incident was major or severely damaged systems or data, reassure the users that they can expect operations to return to normal as soon as possible. The objective of this communication is to prevent panic or confusion from causing additional disruption to the operations of the organization.

Before returning to its routine duties, the IR team must conduct an **after-action review (AAR)**. The after-action review entails a detailed examination of the events that occurred from first detection to final recovery. All key players review their notes and verify that the IR documentation is accurate and precise. All team members review their actions during the incident and identify areas where the IR plan worked, didn't work, or should improve. This exercise allows the team to update the IRP. The AAR can serve as a training case for future staff. It also brings the IR team's actions to a close.

Law Enforcement Involvement

When an incident violates civil or criminal law, it is the organization's responsibility to notify the proper authorities. Selecting the appropriate law enforcement agency depends on the type of crime committed. The Federal Bureau of Investigation (FBI), for example, handles computer crimes that cross state lines. The U.S. Secret Service investigates crimes involving U.S. currency, counterfeiting, credit cards, and identity theft. The U.S. Treasury Department has a bank fraud investigation unit, and the Securities and Exchange Commission has investigation and fraud control units as well. However, the heavy case loads of these agencies means that they typically prioritize those incidents that affect the national critical infrastructure or that have significant economic impact. The FBI Web site, for example, states that the FBI Computer Intrusion Squad:

> … pursues the investigation of cyber-based attacks, primarily unauthorized access (intrusion) and denial-of-service, directed at the major components of this country's critical information, military, and economic infrastructures. Critical infrastructure includes the nation's power grids and power-supply systems, transportation control systems, money transfer and accounting systems, defense-related systems, and telecommunications networks. Additionally, the Squad investigates cyber attacks directed at private industry and public institutions that maintain information vital to national security and/or the economic success of the nation.[8]

In other words, if the crime isn't directed at or doesn't affect the national infrastructure, the FBI may not be able to assist the organization as effectively as state or local agencies can. However, in general, if a crime crosses state lines, it becomes a federal matter. The FBI may also become involved at the request of a state agency, if it has the resources to spare.

Each state, county, and city in the United States has its own law enforcement agencies. These agencies enforce all local and state laws and handle suspects and security crime scenes for state and federal cases. Local law enforcement agencies rarely have computer crimes task forces, but the investigative (detective) units are quite capable of processing crime scenes and handling most common criminal violations, such as physical theft or trespassing, damage to property, and the apprehension and processing of suspects in computer-related crimes.

Involving law enforcement agencies has both advantages and disadvantages. Such agencies are usually much better equipped at processing evidence than a business organization. Unless the security forces in the organization have been trained in processing evidence and computer forensics, they may do more harm than good when attempting to extract information that can lead to the legal conviction of a suspected criminal. Law enforcement agencies are also prepared to handle the warrants and subpoenas necessary when documenting a case. They are adept at obtaining statements from witnesses, affidavits, and other required documents. For all these reasons, law enforcement personnel can be a security administrator's greatest allies in prosecuting a computer crime. It is therefore important to become familiar with the appropriate local and state agencies, before you have to make a call announcing a suspected crime. Most state and federal agencies offer awareness programs, provide guest speakers at conferences, and offer programs such as the InfraGard program of the FBI's National Information Protection Center (www.infragard.net). These agents clearly understand the challenges facing security administrators.

The disadvantages of law enforcement involvement include possible loss of control of the chain of events following an incident, including the collection of information and evidence, and the prosecution of suspects. An organization that wishes to simply reprimand or dismiss an employee should not involve a law enforcement agency in the resolution of an incident. Additionally, the organization may not hear about the case for weeks or even months due to heavy caseloads or resource shortages. A very real issue for commercial organizations when involving law enforcement agencies is the taking of equipment vital to the organization's business as evidence. Assets can be removed, stored, and preserved to prepare the criminal case. Despite these difficulties, if the organization detects a criminal act, it has the legal obligation to notify the appropriate law enforcement officials. Failure to do so can subject the organization and its officers to prosecution as accessories to the crimes or for impeding the course of an investigation. It is up to the security administrator to ask questions of law enforcement agencies to determine when each agency wishes to be involved, and specifically which crimes will be addressed by each agency.

Disaster Recovery

The next vital part of CP is disaster recovery planning. The IT community of interest, under the leadership of the CIO, is often made responsible for disaster recovery planning, including aspects that are not necessarily technology-based.

Disaster recovery planning entails the preparation for and recovery from a disaster, whether natural or human-made. In some cases, actual incidents detected by the IR team may escalate to the level of disaster, and the IRP may no longer be able to handle the effective and efficient recovery from the loss. For example, if a malicious program evades containment actions and infects and disables many or most of an organization's systems and its ability to function, the DRP is activated. Sometimes events are by their nature immediately classified as disasters, such as an extensive fire, flood, damaging storm, or earthquake.

As you learned earlier in this chapter, the CP team creates the DRP. In general, an incident is categorized as a disaster when either of two criteria is met: (1) the organization is unable to contain or control the impact of an incident or (2) the level of damage or destruction from an incident is so severe that the organization cannot quickly recover from it. The distinction between an actual incident and an immediate disaster may be subtle. The CP team must document in the DRP whether an event is classified as an incident or a disaster. This determination is critical because it determines which plan is activated. The key role of a DRP is defining how to reestablish operations at the location where the organization is usually located.

Disaster Classifications

A DRP can classify disasters in a number of ways. The most common method is to separate natural disasters, such as those described in Table 3-1, from human-made disasters. *Acts of terrorism,* including cyber-terrorism or hactivism, *acts of war,* and those *acts of man* that may begin as incidents and escalate into disasters are all examples of human-made disasters.

Another way of classifying disasters is by speed of development. **Rapid-onset disasters** occur suddenly, with little warning, taking the lives of people and destroying the means of production. Rapid-onset disasters may be caused by earthquakes, floods, storm winds, tornadoes, or mud flows. **Slow-onset disasters** occur over time and slowly degrade the capacity of an organization to withstand their effects. Hazards causing these disaster conditions typically include droughts, famines, environmental degradation, desertification, deforestation, and pest infestation.[9]

Table 3-1   Acts of God and Their Effects on Information Systems

Fire	Damages the building housing the computing equipment that constitutes all or part of the information system. Also encompasses smoke damage from the fire and water damage from sprinkler systems or firefighters. Can usually be mitigated with fire casualty insurance or business interruption insurance.
Flood	Can cause direct damage to all or part of the information system or to the building that houses all or part of the information system. May also disrupt operations by interrupting access to the buildings that house all or part of the information system. Can sometimes be mitigated with flood insurance or business interruption insurance.
Earthquake	Can cause direct damage to all or part of the information system or, more often, to the building that houses them. May also disrupt operations by interrupting access to the buildings that house all or part of the information system. Can sometimes be mitigated with specific casualty insurance or business interruption insurance, but is usually a specific and separate policy.

Table 3-1	Acts of God and Their Effects on Information Systems (continued)
Lightning	Can directly damage all or part of the information system or its power distribution components. Can also cause fires or other damage to the building that houses all or part of the information system. May also disrupt operations by interrupting access to the buildings that house all or part of the information system as well as the routine delivery of electrical power. Can usually be mitigated with multipurpose casualty insurance or business interruption insurance.
Landslide or mudslide	Can damage all or part of the information system or, more likely, the building that houses them. May also disrupt operations by interrupting access to the buildings that house all or part of the information system as well as the routine delivery of electrical power. Can sometimes be mitigated with casualty insurance or business interruption insurance.
Tornado or severe windstorm	Can directly damage all or part of the information system or, more likely, the building that houses them. May also disrupt operations by interrupting access to the buildings that house all or part of the information system as well as the routine delivery of electrical power. Can sometimes be mitigated with casualty insurance or business interruption insurance.
Hurricane or typhoon	Can directly damage all or part of the information system or, more likely, the building that houses them. Organizations located in coastal or low-lying areas may experience flooding (see previous page). May also disrupt operations by interrupting access to the buildings that house all or part of the information system as well as the routine delivery of electrical power. Can sometimes be mitigated with casualty insurance or business interruption insurance.
Tsunami	Can directly damage all or part of the information system or, more likely, the building that houses them. Organizations located in coastal areas may experience tsunamis. May also cause disruption to operations by interrupting access or electrical power to the buildings that house all or part of the information system. Can sometimes be mitigated with casualty insurance or business interruption insurance.
Electrostatic discharge (ESD)	Can be costly or dangerous when it ignites flammable mixtures and damages costly electronic components. Static electricity can draw dust into clean-room environments or cause products to stick together. The cost of ESD-damaged electronic devices and interruptions to service can range from a few cents to millions of dollars for critical systems. Loss of production time in information processing due to the effects of ESD is significant. While not usually viewed as a threat, ESD can disrupt information systems and is not usually an insurable loss unless covered by business interruption insurance.
Dust contamination	Can shorten the life of information systems or cause unplanned downtime.

Planning for Disaster

To plan for disaster, the CP team engages in scenario development and impact analysis, along the way categorizing the level of threat that each potential disaster poses. When generating a disaster recovery scenario, start first with the most important asset—people. Do you have the human resources with the appropriate organizational knowledge to restore business operations? Organizations must cross-train their employees to ensure that operations and a sense of normalcy can be restored. In addition, the DRP must be tested regularly so that the DR team can lead the recovery effort quickly and efficiently. The key points that the CP team must build into the DRP include the following:

1. Clear delegation of roles and responsibilities: Everyone assigned to the DR team should be aware of his or her duties during a disaster. Some team members may be responsible for coordinating with local services, such as fire, police, and medical personnel. Some may be responsible for the evacuation of company personnel, if required. Others may be assigned to simply pack up and leave.

2. Execution of the alert roster and notification of key personnel: These notifications may extend outside the organization to include the fire, police, or medical services mentioned earlier, as well as insurance agencies, disaster teams such as those of the Red Cross, and management teams.

3. Clear establishment of priorities: During a disaster response, the first priority is always the preservation of human life. Data and systems protection is subordinate when the disaster threatens the lives, health, or welfare of the employees or members of the community. Only after all employees and neighbors have been safeguarded can the disaster recovery team attend to protection of other organizational assets.

4. Documentation of the disaster: Just as in an incident response, the disaster must be carefully recorded from the onset. This documentation is used later to determine how and why the disaster occurred.

5. Inclusion of action steps to mitigate the impact of the disaster on the operations of the organization: The DRP should specify the responsibilities of each DR team member, such as the evacuation of physical assets or making sure that all systems are securely shut down, to prevent further loss of data.

6. Inclusion of alternative implementations for the various systems components, should primary versions be unavailable: These components include stand-by equipment, either purchased, leased, or under contract with a disaster recovery service agency. Developing systems with excess capacity, fault tolerance, auto-recovery, and fail-safe features facilitates a quick recovery. Something as simple as using Dynamic Host Control Protocol (DHCP) to assign network addresses instead of using static addresses can allow systems to quickly and easily regain connectivity without technical support. Networks should support dynamic reconfiguration; restoration of network connectivity should be planned. Data recovery requires effective backup strategies as well as flexible hardware configurations. System management should be a top priority. All solutions should be tightly integrated and developed in a strategic plan to provide continuity. Piecemeal construction can result in a disaster after the disaster, as incompatible systems are unexpectedly thrust together.

As part of DRP readiness, each employee should have two types of emergency information cards in his or her possession at all times. The first lists personal emergency information—the person to notify in case of an emergency (next of kin), medical conditions, and a form of identification. The second comprises a set of instructions on what to do in the event of an emergency. This snapshot of the DRP should contain a contact number or hotline for calling the organization during an emergency, emergency services numbers (fire, police, medical), evacuation and assembly locations (storm shelters, for example), the name and number of the disaster recovery coordinator, and any other needed information.

Crisis Management

The DRP must also include reference to another process that many organizations plan for separately—**crisis management**, or the action steps taken during and after a disaster. Crisis management entails a set of focused steps that deal primarily with the people involved. The DR team works closely with the crisis management team to assure complete and timely communication during a disaster. According to Gartner Research, the crisis management team is responsible for managing the event from an enterprise perspective and covers the following major activities:

- Supporting personnel and their loved ones during the crisis
- Determining the event's impact on normal business operations and, if necessary, making a disaster declaration
- Keeping the public informed about the event and the actions being taken to ensure the recovery of personnel and the enterprise
- Communicating with major customers, suppliers, partners, regulatory agencies, industry organizations, the media, and other interested parties [10]

The crisis management team should establish a base of operations or command center near the site of the disaster as soon as possible. It should include individuals from all functional areas of the organization to facilitate communications and cooperation. The crisis management team is charged with two key tasks:

1. Verifying personnel status: Everyone must be accounted for, including individuals who are on vacations, leaves of absence, and business trips.
2. Activating the alert roster: Alert rosters and general personnel phone lists are used to notify individuals whose assistance may be needed, or to simply tell employees not to report to work, until the disaster is over.

The crisis management team should plan an approach for releasing information in the event of a disaster, and should perhaps even have boilerplate scripts prepared for press releases. Advice from Lanny Davis, former counselor to President Bill Clinton, is very clear. When beset by damaging events, tell the whole story as soon as possible directly to the affected audience. This can be summed up with the pithy statement, "Tell It Early, Tell It All, Tell It Yourself," which is the subtitle of an autobiographical book by Davis. [11]

Responding to the Disaster

When a disaster strikes and the DRP is activated, actual events can at times overwhelm even the best of plans. To be prepared, the CP team should incorporate a degree of flexibility into the DRP. If the physical facilities are intact, the DR team should begin the restoration of systems and data to work toward full operational capability. If the organization's facilities are destroyed, alternative actions must be taken until new facilities can be acquired. When a disaster threatens the viability of an organization at the primary site, the disaster recovery process becomes a business continuity process, which is described in detail later in this chapter.

VIEWPOINT

Counterattack

By Bruce Schneier

Counterattacks must be an idea whose time has come, because they are being talked about everywhere. The entertainment industry has floated a bill that would give it the ability to break into other people's computers if it suspects copyright violation. Several articles have been written about automated law enforcement, where both governments and private companies use computers to automatically find and target suspected criminals. And Tim Mullen and other security researchers are talking about "strike back," where the victim of a computer assault automatically attacks the perpetrator.

The common theme here is vigilantism: citizens and companies taking the law into their own hands and going after their assailants. Viscerally, it has a certain appeal. But it's a horrible idea, and one that society after society has eschewed.

Our society does not give us the right of revenge, and wouldn't work very well if it did. Our laws give us the right to justice, in either the criminal or civil context. Justice is all we can expect if we want to enjoy our constitutional freedoms, personal safety, and an orderly society.

Anyone accused of a crime deserves a fair trial. He deserves the right to defend himself, the right to face his accuser, the right to an attorney, and the right to be held innocent until proven guilty.

Vigilantism flies in the face of these rights. It punishes people before they have been found guilty. An angry mob lynching a suspected murderer is wrong, even if that person is actually guilty. The Motion Picture Association of America (MPAA) disabling a computer because its owner is suspected of copying a movie is wrong, even if the movie *was* copied. Revenge is a basic human desire, but revenge becomes justice only if carried out by the state.

And the state has more motivation to be fair. The Recording Industry Association of America (RIAA) sent a cease-and-desist letter to an Internet service provider (ISP) asking it to remove certain files that were the copyrighted works of George Harrison. The RIAA simply Googled for the string "harrison" and went after everyone who turned up. Vigilantism is wrong because the vigilante could be wrong. The goal of a state legal system is justice; the goal of the RIAA was expediency.

Strike-back systems are much the same. The idea is that if a computer is attacking yours—sending you viruses, acting as a DDoS zombie, and so on—you can forcibly shut that computer down or remotely install a patch. Such an action might be satisfying in many ways, but it's legally and morally wrong.

Imagine you're a homeowner, and your neighbor has some kind of device on the outside of his house that makes noise. A lot of noise. All day and all night. Enough noise that any reasonable person would claim it to be a public nuisance. Even so, it is not legal for you to take matters into your own hand and stop the noise.

Destroying property is not a recognized remedy for stopping a nuisance, even if it is causing you real harm. Your remedies are to (1) call the police and ask them to turn the noise off, break it, or insist that the neighbor turn it off or (2) sue the neighbor and ask the court to enjoin him from using that device (unless the noise problem can be fixed) and award you damages for your aggravation. Vigilante justice is simply not an option, no matter how right you believe your cause to be.

(continued)

This is law, not technology, so there are all sorts of shades of gray. Factors to consider when assessing the morality or legality of an action are the interests at stake in the original attack; the nature of the property, liberty, or personnel threatened by the counterattack; the risk of being wrong; and the availability and effectiveness of other measures. The RIAA bill is at one extreme because copyright is a limited property interest, and there is a great risk of wrongful deprivation of use of the computer, and of the user's privacy and security. A strike-back attack that disables a dangerous Internet worm is perhaps more justifiable. Clearly this is something that the courts will have to sort out.

In 1789, the Declaration of the Rights of Man and of the Citizen said that the following: "No person shall be accused, arrested, or imprisoned except in the cases and according to the forms prescribed by law. Anyone soliciting, transmitting, executing, or causing to be executed any arbitrary order shall be punished." And also: "As all persons are held innocent until they shall have been declared guilty, if arrest shall be deemed indispensable, all harshness not essential to the securing of the prisoner's person shall be severely repressed by law."

Neither the interests of systems administrators on the Internet nor the interests of companies like Disney should be allowed to trump these rights.

Security expert Bruce Schneier (schneier@counterpane.com) is the author of *Beyond Fear: Thinking Sensibly About Security in an Uncertain World*, Copernicus Books, 2003.

Business Continuity Planning

Business continuity planning ensures that critical business functions can continue if a disaster occurs. Unlike the DRP, which is usually managed by the IT community of interest, the business continuity plan (BCP) is most properly managed by the CEO of an organization. The BCP is activated and executed concurrently with the DRP when the disaster is major or long term and requires fuller and complex restoration of information and IT resources. If a disaster has rendered the current business location unusable, there must be a plan to allow the business to continue to function. While the BCP reestablishes critical business functions at an alternate site, the DRP team focuses on the reestablishment of the technical infrastructure and business operations at the primary site. Not every business needs such a plan, or such facilities. Some small companies or fiscally sound organizations may be able to simply cease operations until the primary facilities are restored. Manufacturing and retail organizations may not have this option, however, because they depend on continued operations for revenue. Thus these entities must have a BCP in place so as to quickly relocate operations with minimal loss of revenue.

The identification of critical business functions and the resources to support them is the cornerstone of BCP. When a disaster strikes, these functions are the first to be reestablished at the alternate site. The CP team needs to appoint a group of individuals to evaluate and compare the various alternatives and to recommend which strategy should be selected and implemented. The strategy selected usually involves some form of off-site facility, which should be inspected, configured, secured, and tested on a periodic basis. The selection should be reviewed periodically to determine whether a better alternative has emerged or whether the organization needs a different solution.

Continuity Strategies

A CP team can choose from several continuity strategies in its planning for business continuity. The determining factor is usually cost. In general, three exclusive-use options exist:

- Hot Sites: A **hot site** is a fully configured computer facility, with all services, communications links, and physical plant operations. It duplicates computing resources, peripherals, phone systems, applications, and workstations. Essentially, this duplicate facility needs only the latest data backups and the personnel to function. If the organization uses one of the data services listed in the following sections, a hot site can be fully functional within minutes. Not surprisingly, it is the most expensive alternative available. Other disadvantages include the need to provide maintenance for all the systems and equipment at the hot site, as well as physical and information security. However, if the organization requires a 24/7 capability for near real-time recovery, the hot site is the optimal strategy.

- Warm Sites: A **warm site** provides many of the same services and options as the hot site, but typically software applications either are not included or are not installed and configured. It frequently includes computing equipment and peripherals with servers but not client workstations. A warm site offers many of the advantages of a hot site, but at a lower cost. The disadvantage is that it requires several hours—perhaps days—to make a warm site fully functional.

- Cold Sites: A **cold site** provides only rudimentary services and facilities. No computer hardware or peripherals are provided. All communications services must be installed after the site is occupied. A cold site is an empty room with standard heating, air conditioning, and electrical service. Everything else is an added cost option. Despite these disadvantages, a cold site may better than nothing. Its primary advantage relates to cost. The most useful feature of this approach is to reduce contention for suitable floor space should a widespread disaster strike, but some organizations are prepared to struggle to lease new space rather than pay maintenance fees on a cold site.

There are also three shared-use contingency options:

- Timeshares: A **timeshare** operates like one of the three sites described above, but is leased in conjunction with a business partner or sister organization. It allows the organization to provide a disaster recovery/business continuity option, while reducing its overall costs. The primary disadvantage is the possibility that more than one timeshare participant might need the facility simultaneously. Other disadvantages include the need to stock the facility with the equipment and data from all organizations involved, the complexity of negotiating the timeshare with the sharing organizations, and the possibility that one or more parties might exit the agreement or sublease their options. Operating under a timeshare is much like agreeing to co-lease an apartment with a group of friends. One can only hope that the organizations remain on amicable terms, as they all could potentially gain physical access to each other's data.

- Service Bureaus: A **service bureau** is a service agency that provides a service for a fee. In the case of disaster recovery/continuity planning, this service is the provision of physical facilities in the event of a disaster. Such agencies also frequently provide off-site data storage for a fee. Contracts with service bureaus can specify exactly what the organization needs under what circumstances. A service agreement usually guarantees space when needed, even if the service bureau must acquire additional space in the event of a widespread disaster. In this sense, it resembles the rental car provision in a car insurance policy. The disadvantage is that service contracts must be renegotiated periodically and rates can change. This option can also be quite expensive.

- Mutual Agreements: A **mutual agreement** is a contract between two organizations in which each party agrees to assist the other in the event of a disaster. It stipulates that each organization is obligated to provide the necessary facilities, resources, and services until the receiving organization is able to recover from the disaster. This arrangement can be a lot like moving in with relatives or friends—and it doesn't take long for an organization to wear out its welcome. Many organizations balk at the idea of having to fund (even in the short term) duplicate services and resources. Still, mutual agreements between divisions of the same parent company, between subordinate and senior organizations, or between business partners may be a cost-effective solution when both parties to the agreement have a mutual interest in each other's continued operations and both have similar capabilities and capacities.

In addition to these six basic strategies, some specialized alternatives are available, such as a rolling mobile site configured in the payload area of a tractor/trailer or externally stored resources, such as a rental storage area containing duplicate or older equipment. These alternatives are similar to the Pre-positioning of Overseas Material Configured to Unit Sets (POM-CUS) sites of the Cold War era, in which caches of materials to be used in the event of an emergency or war were stored awaiting the need for them. An organization might arrange with a prefabricated building contractor for immediate, temporary facilities (mobile offices) on site in the event of a disaster.

Off-Site Disaster Data Storage.   To get any of these sites up and running quickly, the organization must be able to move data into the new site's systems. There are a number of options (in addition to traditional backup methods) for getting operations up and running quickly:

- Electronic vaulting: The bulk batch-transfer of data to an off-site facility. This transfer is usually conducted via leased lines or through data communications services that are provided for a fee. The receiving server archives the data as it is received. Some disaster recovery companies specialize in **electronic vaulting** services.

- Remote journaling: The transfer of live transactions to an off-site facility. It differs from electronic vaulting in two ways: (1) only transactions are transferred, not archived data, and (2) the transfer takes place online and in much closer to real time. While electronic vaulting is akin to a traditional backup, with a dump of data to the off-site storage, **remote journaling** involves online activities on a systems level, much like server fault tolerance, where data is written to two locations simultaneously.

- Database shadowing: The storage of duplicate online transaction data, along with the duplication of the databases at the remote site on a redundant server. **Database shadowing** combines electronic vaulting with remote journaling, by writing multiple copies of the database simultaneously in two separated locations.

Timing and Sequence of CP Elements

As indicated earlier, the IRP focuses on immediate response, but if the incident escalates into a disaster, the IRP may give way to the DRP and BCP, as illustrated in Figure 3-3. The DRP typically focuses on restoring systems after disasters occur, and as such is closely associated with the BCP. The BCP occurs concurrently with the DRP when the damage is major or long term, requiring more than simple restoration of information and information resources, as illustrated in Figure 3-4.

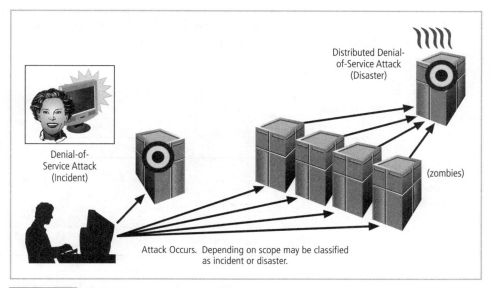

FIGURE 3-3 Incident Response and Disaster Recovery

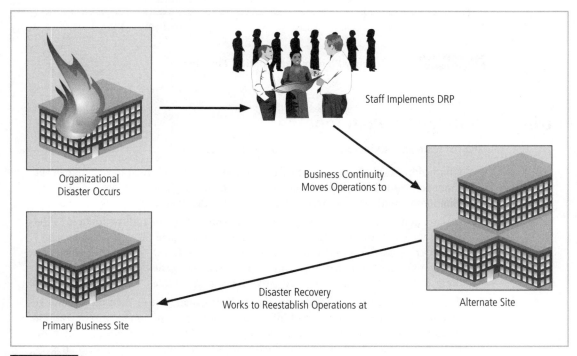

FIGURE 3-4 Disaster Recovery and Business Continuity Planning

Some experts may argue that the three elements of CP are so closely linked that they are indistinguishable. In fact, each has a distinct place, role, and planning requirement. Furthermore, each component (IRP, DRP, and BCP) comes into play at a specific time in the life of an incident. Figure 3-5 illustrates this sequence and shows the overlap that may occur. How the plans interact and the ways in which they are brought into action are discussed in the sections that follow.

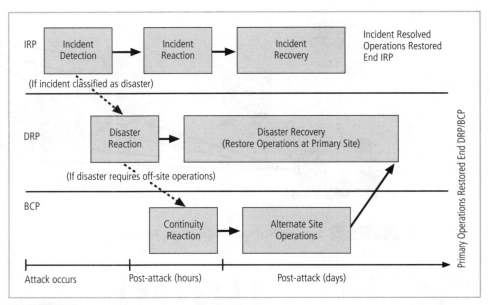

FIGURE 3-5 Contingency Plan Implementation Timeline

Putting a Contingency Plan Together

The CP team should include the following personnel:

- Champion: As with any strategic function, the CP project must have a high-level manager to support, promote, and endorse the findings of the project. This **champion** could be the CIO, or ideally the CEO/President.

- Project manager: A champion provides the strategic vision and the linkage to the power structure of the organization, but does not manage the project. A **project manager**—possibly a mid-level manager or even the CISO—leads the project, putting in place a sound project planning process, guiding the development of a complete and useful project, and prudently managing resources.

- Team members: The **team members** should be the managers or their representatives from the various communities of interest: business, information technology, and information security. Business managers supply details of their activities and insight into those functions critical to running the business. Information technology managers supply information about the at-risk systems and provide technical content for IRPs, DRPs, and BCPs. Information security managers oversee the security planning and provide information on threats, vulnerabilities, attacks, and recovery requirements.

Figure 3-6 depicts the major project modules performed by the contingency planning project team.

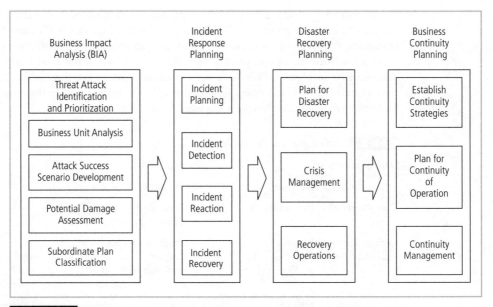

FIGURE 3-6   Major Tasks in Contingency Planning

Business Impact Analysis

The **business impact analysis (BIA)**, the first phase in the CP process, provides the CP team with information about systems and the threats they face. The BIA is a crucial component of the initial planning stages, as it provides detailed scenarios of the effects that each potential attack could have on the organization.

One of the fundamental differences between a BIA and the risk management processes discussed in Chapters 7 and 8 is that risk management focuses on identifying the threats, vulnerabilities, and attacks to determine which controls can protect the information. The BIA assumes that these controls have been bypassed, have failed, or have otherwise proved ineffective, and that the attack was successful.

The CP team conducts the BIA in the following stages, which are shown in Figure 3-6 and described in the sections that follow:

1. Threat attack identification and prioritization
2. Business unit analysis
3. Attack success scenario development
4. Potential damage assessment
5. Subordinate plan classification

Threat Attack Identification and Prioritization

An organization that has followed the SecSDLC outlined in Chapter 2, and the risk management process described in Chapters 7 and 8, will have already identified and prioritized threats facing it. To conduct the BIA, these organizations need simply update the threat list and add one piece of information, the attack profile.

An **attack profile** is a detailed description of the activities that occur during an attack. The example attack profile shown in Table 3-2 includes preliminary indications of the attack, as well as the actions taken and the outcome. Such a profile must be developed for every serious threat that the organization faces, whether natural or human-made, deliberate or accidental. This document is useful in later planning stages to provide indicators of attacks. It is used here to determine the extent of damage that could result to a business unit if the attack were successful.

Table 3-2   Example Attack Profile

Date of analysis:	*June 23, 2004*
Attack name/description:	*Malicious code via e-mail*
Threat/probable threat agents:	▪ *Vandalism/script kiddies* ▪ *Theft/experienced hacker*
Known or possible vulnerabilities:	▪ *Emergent weakness in e-mail clients* ▪ *Inappropriate actions by employees, contractors, and visitors using e-mail clients* ▪ *Emergent weakness in e-mail servers or gateways*
Likely precursor activities or indicators:	*Announcements from vendors and bulletins*
Likely attack activities or indicators of attack in progress:	▪ *E-mail volume measurements may show variances* ▪ *Unusual system failures among clients* ▪ *Unusual system failures among servers* ▪ *Notification from e-mail recipients who may be ahead of us in attack life cycle*
Information assets at risk from this attack:	*All connected systems due to blended attack model now prevalent*
Damage or loss to information assets likely from this attack:	▪ *Denial-of-service for some clients almost certain* ▪ *Denial-of-service for servers possible* ▪ *Possible losses of data depending on nature of attack*
Other assets at risk from this attack:	*None likely*
Damage or loss to other assets likely from this attack:	*None likely*
Immediate actions indicated when this attack is under way:	▪ *Disconnect e-mail gateway(s)* ▪ *Update e-mail gateway filtering patterns and apply* ▪ *Update and distribute client filtering patterns* ▪ *Isolate all infected servers* ▪ *Isolate all infected clients* ▪ *Begin server recovery actions for infected servers* ▪ *Begin client recovery actions for infected clients*
Follow-up actions after this attack was successfully executed against our systems:	*Review pattern update timing and procedure to assure adequacy*
Comments:	*None at this time*

Business Unit Analysis

The second major BIA task is the analysis and prioritization of business functions within the organization. Each business department, unit, or division must be independently evaluated to determine how important its functions are to the organization as a whole. For example, recovery operations would probably focus on the IT department and network operation before turning to the personnel department's hiring activities. Likewise, recovering a manufacturing company's assembly line is more urgent than recovering its maintenance tracking system. This is not to say that personnel functions and assembly line maintenance are not important to the business, but unless the organization's main revenue-producing operations can be restored quickly, other functions are irrelevant.

Attack Success Scenario Development

Once the threat attack profiles have been developed and the business functions prioritized, the BIA team must create a series of scenarios depicting the effects of an occurrence of each threat on each prioritized functional area. This step can be a long and detailed process; as such occurrences may have implications for many functions. Attack profiles should include scenarios depicting a typical attack, including its methodology, indicators of an attack, and broad consequences. Once the attack profiles are completed, the business function details can be integrated with the attack profiles. Then **attack success scenarios** with more detail are added to the attack profile, including alternative outcomes—best, worst, and most likely. This level of detail allows planners to address each possibility in turn.

Potential Damage Assessment

From these detailed scenarios, the BIA planning team must estimate the cost of the best, worst, and most likely outcomes by preparing an **attack scenario end case**. It will allow the organization to identify what must be done to recover from each possible case. At this time the team does not attempt to determine how much to spend on the protection of business units—this issue is analyzed during risk management. The costs determined at that time include the actions of the response team members (described in the following sections) as they act to quickly and effectively recover from any incident or disaster. These cost estimates can persuade management representatives throughout an organization of the importance of planning and recovery efforts.

Subordinate Plan Classification

Once the potential damage has been assessed, and each scenario and attack scenario end case has been evaluated, a subordinate plan must be developed or identified from among existing plans already in place. Some of these related plans may already be part of standard operating procedures, such as file recovery from backup. Other plans may be in place as part of existing DRP or BCP projects. Because most attacks are not disastrous and therefore fall into the category of incident response, the BIA team will likely develop a number of new subordinate plans that are meant to be exclusively used at the incident level. Those scenarios that do qualify as disastrous are likely addressed in the DRP or BCP.

Each attack scenario end case is categorized as disastrous or not. The difference between the two classifications reflects whether the organization is able to take effective action during the event to combat the attack's effects. Attack end cases that are disastrous find members of the organization waiting out the attack and planning to recover from it after the attack ends. In a typical disaster recovery operation, the lives and welfare of the employee are the highest priority, as most disasters involve fires, floods, hurricanes, tornadoes, and the like. Other disasters include the following events:

- Electrical blackouts affecting a city or region
- Attacks on service providers that result in a loss of communications to the organization (either telephone or Internet)
- Massive, malicious-code attacks that sweep through the organization before they can be contained

Combining the DRP and the BCP

Because the DRP and BCP are closely related, most organizations prepare the two at the same time, and may combine them into a single planning document. Such a comprehensive plan must be able to support the reestablishment of operations at two different locations—one immediately at an alternate site, and one eventually back at the primary site. Therefore, although a single planning team can develop the combined DRP/BRP, execution of the plan requires separate execution teams.

The planning process for the DRP/BCP should be tied to, but distinct from, the IRP. As noted earlier in the chapter, an incident may escalate into a disaster when it grows dramatically in scope and intensity. It is important that the three processes be so tightly integrated that the reaction teams can easily make the transition from incident response to disaster recovery and business continuity planning.

One useful resource is the Business Continuity Plan template provided by the Federal Agency Security Practices section of the CSRC at NIST (http://fasp.nist.gov/). Although it is labeled as a contingency plan, this Web page provides a template DRP/BCP, complete with instructions designed for Department of Justice (DOJ)–related agencies. The instructions specifically describe the approach taken for the template, allowing easy conversion to suit many public and private organizations. Table 3-3 provides the table of contents for this document.

Table 3-3   Contingency Plan Template

Contents

1.	Executive Summary
2.	Introduction
	2.1 Purpose
	2.2 Scope
	2.3 Plan Information
3.	Contingency Plan Overview
	3.1 Applicable Provisions and Directives
	3.2 Objectives
	3.3 Organization
	3.4 Contingency Phases
	3.4.1 Response Phase
	3.4.2 Resumption Phase
	3.4.3 Recovery Phase
	3.4.4 Restoration Phase
	3.5 Assumptions
	3.6 Critical Success Factors and Issues

Table 3-3 Contingency Plan Template (continued)

	3.7 Mission-Critical Systems/Applications/Services
	3.8 Threats
	3.8.1 Probable Threats
4.	System Description
	4.1 Physical Environment
	4.2 Technical Environment
5.	Plan
	5.1 Plan Management
	5.1.1 Contingency Planning Workgroups
	5.1.2 Contingency Plan Coordinator
	5.1.3 System Contingency Coordinators
	5.1.4 Incident Notification
	5.1.5 Internal Personnel Notification
	5.1.6 External Contact Notification
	5.1.7 Media Releases
	5.1.8 Alternate Site(s)
	5.2 Teams
	5.2.1 Damage Assessment Team
	5.2.2 Operations Team
	5.2.3 Communications Team
	5.2.4 Data Entry and Control Team
	5.2.5 Off-Site Storage Team
	5.2.6 Administrative Management Team
	5.2.7 Procurement Team
	5.2.8 Configuration Management Team
	5.2.9 Facilities Team
	5.2.10 System Software Team
	5.2.11 Internal Audit Team
	5.2.12 User Assistance Team
	5.3 Data Communications
	5.4 Backups
	5.4.1 Vital Records/Documentation
	5.5 Office Equipment, Furniture, and Supplies
	5.6 Recommended Testing Procedures
6.	Recommended Strategies
	6.1 Critical Issues
	6.1.1 Power
	6.1.2 Diversification of Connectivity
	6.1.3 Offsite Backup Storage
7.	Terms and Definitions
8.	Appendices
Appendix A	Contingency Plan Contact Information
Appendix B	Emergency Procedures
Appendix C	Team Staffing and Tasking
Appendix D	Alternate Site Procedures

Table 3-3 Contingency Plan Template (continued)

Appendix E	Documentation List
Appendix F	Software Inventory
Appendix G	Hardware Inventory
Appendix H	Communications Requirements
Appendix I	Vendor Contact Lists
Appendix J	External Support Agreements
Appendix K	Data Center/Computer Room Emergency Procedures and Requirements
Appendix L	Plan Maintenance Procedures
Appendix M	Contingency Log

Source: (http://csrc.nist.gov/fasp/FASPDocs/contingency-plan/contingencyplan-template.doc).

Sample Disaster Recovery Plan

Figure 3-7 shows another example of what may be found in a disaster recovery plan. This document provides a sample disaster recovery plan adapted from one provided by the Texas State Library and Archives State and Local Records Management Division.[12]

FIGURE 3-7 Sample Disaster Recovery Plan

5. Locations of in-house emergency equipment and supplies (attach map or floor plan with locations marked):

Batteries _____

Badges (employee identification) _____

Camera /Film _____

Cut-off Switches and Valves:

Electric _____

Gas _____

Water _____

Sprinkler System (if separate) _____

Extension Cords (heavy-duty) _____

Fire Extinguishers _____

Flashlights _____

Ladders _____

Mops/Sponges/Buckets/Brooms _____

Nylon Monofilament _____

Packing Tape/String/Sissors _____

Paper Towels (white) _____

Plastic Trash Bags _____

Rubber Gloves _____

Transistor Radio (battery powered) _____

3

6. Sources of off-site equipment and supplies (if maintained on-site, note location):

Item:	Contact/Company:	Number:

Cellular Phone _____

Dehumidifiers _____

Drying Space _____

Dust Masks _____

Fans _____

Fork Lift _____

Freezer/Wax Paper _____

Freezer Space/Refrigeration Truck _____

Fungicides _____

Generator (portable) _____

Hard Hats _____

Pallets _____

Plastic Milk Crates _____

Pumps (submersion) _____

Rubber Boots _____

Safety Glasses _____

Trash Can (all sizes) _____

Vacuum/Freeze Drying Facilities _____

Waterproof Clothing _____

Wet-Dry Vacuum _____

4

7. Salvage Priority List:

Attach a copy of the records retention schedule identifying all vital/essential records series. The location and record medium of the preservation duplicate for each vital records series should be noted.

It is also very helpful if other records series are reviewed to determine their priority for salvage should a disaster occur. The following questions can be helpful in determining priorities:

1. Can the records be replaced? At what cost?
2. Would the cost of replacement be less or more than restoration of the records?
3. How important are the records to the agency?
4. Are the records duplicated elsewhere?

To simplify this process, priorities may be assigned as follows:

1. Salvage at all costs.
    (example, records that are historically valuable or non-vital records that are important to agency operations and very difficult to recreate)

2. Salvage if time and resources permit.
    (example, records that are less important to the agency or somewhat easier to recreate)

3. Dispose of as part of general cleanup.
    (example, records that do not need to be salvaged because they are convenience copies and the record copy is at another location)

8. Agency Disaster Recovery Procedures:

Attach a list of specific procedures to be followed in the event of a disaster in you agency, including responsibilities of in-house recovery team members.

9. Follow-up Assessment:

A written report, including photographs, should be prepared after recovery and attached to a copy of the disaster plan. The report should note the effectiveness of the plan, and should include an evaluation of the sources of supplies and equipment, and of any off-site facilities used.

(Adapted from *Basic Guidelines for Disaster Planning in Oklahoma*)

5

FIGURE 3-7   Sample Disaster Recovery Plan (continued)

The plan has nine major sections, each of which is outlined below. Many organizations—particularly ones with multiple locations and hundreds of employees—would find this plan too simple. Nevertheless, the basic structure provides a solid starting point for any organization.

1. Name of agency: The first section identifies the department, division, or institution to which this particular plan applies. This identification is especially important in organizations that are large enough to require more than one plan.

2. Date of completion or update of the plan and test date: Self-explanatory.

3. Agency staff to be called in the event of a disaster: This roster should be kept current; it will not help the organization to have a list of employees who are no longer with the company. This section should also identify key support personnel such as building maintenance supervisors, physical security directors, legal council, and the starting points on the alert roster. A copy of the alert roster (also known as the telephone tree) should be attached.

4. Emergency services to be called (if needed) in event of a disaster: While dialing 911 will certainly bring police, fire, and ambulance services, the organization may have equally pressing needs for emergency teams from the gas, electric, and water companies. This section should also list electricians, plumbers, locksmiths, and software and hardware vendors.

5. Locations of in-house emergency equipment and supplies: This section should include maps and floor plans with directions to all critical in-house emergency materials, including shut-off switches and valves for gas, electric, and water. It should also provide directions to key supplies including first aid kits, fire extinguishers, flashlights, batteries, and a stash of office supplies. It is a good idea to place a disaster pack on every floor in an unlocked closet or readily accessible location. These items should be inventoried and updated as needed.

6. Sources of off-site equipment and supplies: These items include contact sources for mobile phones, dehumidifiers, industrial equipment such as forklifts and portable generators, and other safety and recovery components.

7. Salvage priority list: While the IT director may have just enough time to grab the last on-site backup before darting out the door in the event of a fire, most likely additional materials can be salvaged if recovery efforts permit. In this event, recovery teams should know what has priority. This list should specify whether to recover hard copies or if the effort should be directed toward saving equipment. Similarly, it specifies whether the organization should focus on archival records or recent documents. The plan should include the locations and priorities of all items of value to the organization. When determining priorities, ask questions such as the following: Are these records archived elsewhere (i.e., off-site), or is this the only copy? Can these records be reproduced if lost, and if so, at what cost? Is the cost of replacement more or less than the cost of the value of the materials? It may be useful to create a simple rating scheme for materials. Data classification labels can be adapted to include disaster recovery information. For example, some records may be labeled "Salvage at all costs," "Salvage if time and resources permit," or "Do not salvage."

8. Agency disaster recovery procedures: This very important section outlines the specific assignments given to key personnel, including the disaster recovery team, to be performed in the event of a disaster. If these duties differ by type of disaster, it may be useful to create multiple scenarios, each listing the duties and responsibilities of

the parties involved. It is equally important to make sure that all personnel identified in this section have a copy of the DRP stored where they can easily access it, and that they are familiar with their responsibilities.

9. Follow-up assessment: The final section details what is to be accomplished after disaster strikes—specifically, what documentation is required for recovery efforts, including mandatory insurance reports, required photographs, and the after-action review format.

Testing Contingency Plans

An untested plan is no plan at all. Very few plans are executable as initially written; instead, they must be tested to identify vulnerabilities, faults, and inefficient processes. Once problems are identified during the testing process, improvements can be made, and the resulting plan can be relied on in times of need. Five strategies[13] can be used to test contingency plans:

- Desk check
- Structured walk-through
- Simulation
- Parallel testing
- Full interruption

Desk Check

The simplest kind of validation involves distributing copies of the appropriate plans to all individuals who will be assigned roles during an actual incident. Each of these people performs a **desk check** by reviewing the plan and creating a list of correct and incorrect components. While not a true test, this strategy is a good way to review the perceived feasibility and effectiveness of the plan.

Structured Walk-Through

In a **structured walk-through**, all involved individuals walk through the steps they would take during an actual event. This exercise can consist of an on-site walk-through, in which everyone discusses their actions at each particular location and juncture, or it may be more of a "chalk talk," in which all involved individuals sit around a conference table and discuss in turn their responsibilities as the incident unfolds.

Simulation

In a **simulation**, each involved person works individually, rather than in a group setting, to simulate the performance of each task. The simulation stops short of performing the actual physical tasks required, such as installing the backup data or disconnecting a communications circuit. The major difference between a walk-through and a simulation is that individuals work on their own tasks and are responsible for identifying the faults in their own procedures.

Parallel Testing

In **parallel testing**, individuals act as if an actual incident occurred, and begin performing their required tasks and executing the necessary procedures, without interfering with the normal operations of the business. Great care must be taken to ensure that the procedures performed do not halt the operations of the business functions, thereby creating an actual incident.

Full Interruption

In **full-interruption** testing, the individuals follow each and every procedure, including the interruption of service, restoration of data from backups, and notification of appropriate individuals. This exercise is often performed after normal business hours in organizations that cannot afford to disrupt or simulate the disruption of business functions. Although full-interruption testing is the most rigorous testing strategy, it is unfortunately too risky for most businesses.

At a minimum, organizations should conduct periodic walk-throughs (or chalk talks) of each of the CP component plans. A failure to update these plans as the business and its information resources change can erode the team's ability to respond to an incident, or possibly cause greater damage than the incident itself. If this sounds like a major training effort, note that the author Richard Marcinko, a former Navy SEAL, provides a few relevant quotations to motivate teams:[14]

- The more you sweat in training, the less you bleed in combat.
- Training and preparation hurts.
- Lead from the front, not the rear.
- You don't have to like it; just do it.
- Keep it simple.
- Never assume.
- You are paid for your results, not your methods.

THREAT MANAGEMENT

IP Spoofing

IP spoofing is the crafting of abnormal packets with false Internet Protocol (IP) addresses in the source address field. An abnormal packet is one that violates IP packet standards as defined by the IETF in RFCs 791, 793, and 1918. Such a packet could result from a technical glitch, such as a malfunctioning router, or it could be purposefully created. Abnormal packets are sometimes created to bypass a firewall or intrusion detection system, or to crash systems.

Spoofing an IP address makes it difficult to track an attack to its source IP address. Attackers may use addresses from reserved IP number ranges or, more commonly, regular addresses that belong to someone else. Another type of IP spoofing attack, called a land attack, uses packets with the source and destination addresses set to the same value. Normal packets always have different source and destination addresses, so network devices should be configured to reject any packet where those values are the same as well as those showing a source from a reserved number range.

(continued)

IP Spoofing Detection

According to the CERT Advisory on IP Spoofing Attacks (www.cert.org/advisories/CA-1995-01.html), the presence of a packet on an external interface whose source and destination IP addresses both use an organization's local domain indicates that an attack is in progress. Another way to identify an IP spoofing attack is to check the process accounting logs of systems in the internal network. This review might uncover a log entry in the victim machine showing a remote access. The easiest way to detect an IP spoofing attack is to use tools—such as Argus, tcpdump, and arpwatch—that monitor the packets flowing through the network, checking their IP addresses.

Organizations can be good Internet neighbors and help prevent users on their networks from launching IP spoofing attacks by incorporating a few techniques identified by the SANS Institute (www.sans.org/dosstep/), such as implementing egress filtering to stop spoofed IP packets from leaving the network. This tactic can prevent the organization's network from being used as the source of spoofed communications. Ensure that routers and firewalls are configured to forward IP packets only if those packets are using the network's source IP address.

If you are not able to implement this technique because you are unsure which address space is in use at your site, then you should, at a minimum, deny private and reserved source IP addresses. Table 3-4 lists source addresses that should be filtered.

Table 3-4   Reserved IP Addresses

Private and Reserved Space Addresses with Subnet Mask	Reserved Use
0.0.0.0/8	Historical broadcast
10.0.0.0/8	RFC 1918 private network
127.0.0.0/8	Loopback
169.254.0.0/16	Link local networks
172.16.0.0/12	RFC 1918 private network
192.0.2.0/24	TEST-NET
192.168.0.0/16	RFC 1918 private network
224.0.0.0/4	Class D multicast
240.0.0.0/5	Class E reserved
248.0.0.0/5	Unallocated
255.255.255.255/32	Broadcast address

(continued)

IP Spoofing Protection

Packet filtering is a layer of defense used by network firewalls. It examines packets to ascertain their source IP addresses. If the IP source is on a list of approved origination IP addresses, then the firewall lets the packet through to the protected network. The packet's payload is not examined for malicious code, however, so a packet containing damaging code could slip through and be executed behind the firewall. Consequently, additional layers of network protection must be instituted to protect a network against IP spoofing:

- An application-level filter (also known as an assured pipeline, application gateway, or proxy server) examines the entire packet, including the data payload. It looks at the payload to determine the nature of its data request. If the data request is legitimate, the application-level filter allows the packet to pass through the firewall. If the data request is identified as hacker code, the packet is trapped and removed. Unfortunately, the high cost of a proxy server may be prohibitive.

- Enabling encryption avoids the need for IP address source authentication. Authenticated and authorized users will be connected and their packets will be protected in transit. You can enable encryption using virtual private networks (VPNs).

- Adjusting the settings of your network configuration adds a protective layer. You can configure your network firewall to reject packets from the outside that have an IP source address that is within your protected network.

- Shutting down all nonessential network connectivity offers additional protection. You can restrict or block unused or unwanted technologies that are vulnerable or insecure, such as Telnet, FTP, X Windows, and DNS zone transfers. The additional benefit here is that this option makes your network less complex and simpler to manage.

A Single Continuity Plan

As mentioned at the beginning of this chapter, it is not uncommon for small to medium-sized organizations to place all three CP component plans—IRP, DRP, and BCP—into one document. This approach supports concise planning and encourages smaller organizations to develop, test, and use IR/DR plans.

Figure 3-8 shows a sample unified contingency plan, based on analyses of the IRPs and DRPs of dozens of organizations.

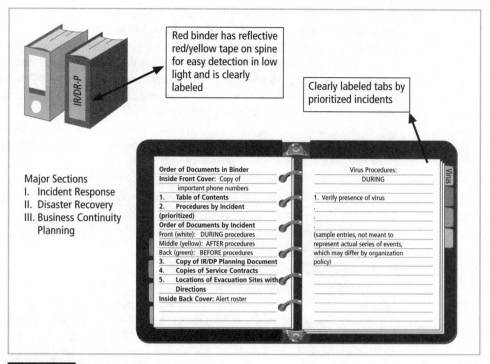

FIGURE 3-8 Contingency Plan Format

A closing thought: Just as in all organizational efforts, iteration results in improvement. A formal implementation of this methodology is continuous process improvement (CPI). Each time the organization rehearses its plans, it should learn from the process, improve the plans, and then rehearse again. Each time an incident or disaster occurs, the organization should review what went right and what went wrong. Through the ongoing evaluation and improvement, the organization continues to move forward, and continually improves upon the process, so that it can strive for an even better outcome.

Chapter Summary

- Planning for unexpected events is usually the responsibility of managers from both the information technology and information security communities of interest.
- For a plan to be seen as valid by all members of the organization, it must be sanctioned and actively supported by the general business community of interest.

- Some organizations are required by law or other mandate to have CP procedures in place at all times, but all business organizations should prepare for the unexpected.

- Contingency planning (CP) is the process by which the information technology and information security communities of interest position their organizations to prepare for, detect, react to, and recover from events that threaten the security of information resources and assets, both human and artificial.

- CP is made up of three major components: The incident response plan (IRP), the disaster recovery plan (DRP), and the business continuity plan (BCP).

- Organizations can either create and develop these three CP components as one unified plan, or they create the three elements separately in conjunction with a set of interlocking procedures that enable continuity.

- To ensure continuity during the creation of the CP components, a six-step CP process is used:
  1. Identify the mission- or business-critical functions.
  2. Identify the resources that support the critical functions.
  3. Anticipate potential contingencies or disasters.
  4. Select contingency planning strategies.
  5. Implement the selected strategy.
  6. Test and revise contingency plans.

- Three teams of individuals are involved in contingency planning and contingency operations: The contingency planning team, the incident response team, and the disaster recovery team.

- The incident response plan is a detailed set of processes and procedures that plan for, detect, and resolve the effects of an unexpected event on information resources and assets.

- For every scenario identified, the CP team creates three sets of procedures—for before, during, and after the incident—to detect, contain, and resolve the incident.

- Incident classification is the process by which the IR team examines an incident candidate and determines whether it constitutes an actual incident.

- Three categories of incident indicators are used: possible, probable, and definite. Possible indicators include the presence of unfamiliar files, the presence or execution of unknown programs or processes, the unusual consumption of computing resources, and unusual system crashes.

- Probable indicators include activities at unexpected times, the presence of new accounts, reported attacks, and notification from an IDS.

- Definite indicators include use of dormant accounts, changes to logs, the presence of hacker tools, notifications by partner or peer, and notification by hacker.

- When any one of the following happens, an actual incident is in progress: Loss of availability, loss of integrity, loss of confidentiality, violation of policy, or violation of law.

- When an actual incident violates civil or criminal law, the organization must notify the proper authorities for further action. Selecting the appropriate law enforcement agency depends on the type of crime committed.

- Disaster recovery planning encompasses preparation for handling and recovering from a disaster, whether natural or human-made.

- The DRP must include crisis management, the action steps taken during and after a disaster.

- Business continuity planning ensures that critical business functions continue if a catastrophic incident or disaster occurs. Business continuity plans can include provisions for hot sites, warm sites, cold sites, timeshares, service bureaus, and mutual agreements.

- The CP team should include a champion, a project manager, and team members.

- Business impact analysis (BIA) entails an investigation and assessment of the effects that various attacks can have on the organization.
- All plans must be tested to identify vulnerabilities, faults, and inefficient processes. Five testing strategies can be used to test contingency plans: Desk check, structured walk-through, simulation, parallel testing, and full interruption testing.

Review Questions

1. What is the name for the broad process of planning for the unexpected? What are its three primary components?
2. Which two communities of interest are usually associated with contingency planning? Which community must give authority to ensure broad support for the plans?
3. What percentage of businesses that do not have a disaster plan go out of business after a major loss, according to The Hartford Insurance Company?
4. List the six-step CP process as defined by the NIST. Why is it the recommended standard approach to the process?
5. List and describe the three teams that perform the planning and execution of the CP plans and processes. What is the primary role of each?
6. Define the term *incident* as used in the context of IRP. How is it related to the concept of incident response?
7. List and describe the three criteria used to determine whether an actual incident is occurring.
8. List and describe the three sets of procedures used to detect, contain, and resolve an incident.
9. List and describe the four IR planning steps.
10. List and describe the actions that should be taken during an incident response.
11. What is an alert roster? What is an alert message? Describe the two ways they can be used when activated.
12. List and describe several containment strategies given in the text. On which two tasks do they focus?
13. What is an incident damage assessment? What is it used for?
14. Should law enforcement agencies be involved in all incidents? In general, how is this decision made?
15. What is a disaster recovery plan, and why is it important to the organization?
16. List and describe two rapid-onset disasters. List and describe one slow-onset disaster. How would you respond differently to the two types of disasters?
17. What is a business continuity plan, and why is it important?
18. What is a business impact analysis and what is it used for?
19. Why should continuity plans be tested and rehearsed?
20. Which types of organizations might use a unified continuity plan? Which types of organizations might use the various contingency planning components as separate plans? Why?

Exercises

1. Using a Web search engine, search for the terms "disaster recovery" and "business continuity." How many responses do you get for each term? Note how many companies do not distinguish between the two.

2. Go to csrc.nist.gov. Under "Publications," search for Special Publication (SP) 800-34 Contingency Planning Guide for Information Technology Systems, June 2002. Download and review this document. Summarize the key points for an in-class discussion.

3. Using a Web search engine, visit one of the popular disaster recovery/business continuity sites such as www.disasterrecoveryworld.com/, www.drj.com/, www.drie.org/, www.drii.org/, or csrc.nist.gov. Search for the terms "hot site," "warm site," and "cold site." Do the descriptions provided match those of the text? Why or why not?

4. Using the format provided in the text, design an incident response plan for your home computer. Include actions to be taken if each of the following events occurs:
   - Virus attack
   - Power failure
   - Fire
   - Burst water pipe
   - ISP failure

   What other scenarios do you think are important to plan for?

5. Look for information on incident response on your institution's Web site. Does your institution have a published plan? Identify the areas in an academic institution's contingency planning that might differ from those of a "for-profit" institution.

Case Exercises

...Iris tried not to smile. She explained, "Of course, it isn't technically a disaster, but I understand what you mean. How much information is lost?"

Joel looked at her in dismay. "Lost? All of it! We had just saved the report and sent it to the department print server!"

Iris asked, "Where did you save it—to your local drive or to the department share?"

Joel tried to remember. "I think it was to the G: drive. Why?"

"Well, the G: drive is on a machine at the end of the hall, which doesn't have a water-based fire suppression system. It's probably fine. And if you did save it to your local drive, there's about an 80% chance we can get it anyway. I doubt the water damaged the hard drive itself." Iris continued, "We were lucky this time. If the fire had spread to the next room, the paper file storage could have been destroyed."

1. Extrapolate on the case. At what point could this incident have been declared a disaster? What would Iris have done differently if it had?

2. Identify the procedures that Joel could have taken to minimize the potential loss in this incident. What would he need to do different in the event of a disaster, if anything?

Endnotes

1. NIST. *Special Publication 800-18: Guide for Developing Security Plans for Information Technology Systems.* December 1998. Accessed May 13, 2003. http://csrc.nist.gov/publications/nistpubs/800-18/Planguide.doc, p. 31.

2. *Why You Need a Disaster Recovery Plan.* Accessed May 13, 2003. http://sb.thehartford.com/reduce_risk/disaster_recovery.asp.

3. William R. King and Paul Gray. *The Management of Information Systems.* Chicago: Dryden Press, 1989:359.

4. NIST. *Special Publication 800-12: An Introduction to Computer Security: The NIST Handbook.* October 1995. Accessed February 10, 2002. http://csrc.nist.gov/publications/nistpubs/800-12/.

5. NIST. *Special Publication 800-18: Guide for Developing Security Plans for Information Technology Systems.* December 1998. Accessed May 13, 2003. http://csrc.nist.gov/publications/nistpubs/800-18/Planguide.doc, p. 31.

6. Donald L. Pipkin. *Information Security: Protecting the Global Enterprise.* Upper Saddle River, NJ: Prentice Hall PTR, 2000:256.

7. Donald L. Pipkin. *Information Security: Protecting the Global Enterprise.* Upper Saddle River, NJ: Prentice Hall PTR, 2000:285.

8. Federal Bureau of Investigation. *Technology Crimes (San Francisco).* Available from the World Wide Web at http://www.fbi.gov/contact/fo/sanfran/sfcomputer.htm.

9. International Federation of Red Cross and Red Crescent Societies. *Disaster Preparedness Training Programme.* Accessed March 1, 2003. http://www.ifrc.org/what/dp/manual/introdp.pdf.

10. Roberta Witty. What is crisis management? *Gartner Online,* September 19, 2001. [Cited June 26, 2002]. Available from the World Wide Web at http://security1.gartner.com/story.php.id.152.jsp.

11. Lanny J. Davis. *Truth to Tell: Tell It Early, Tell It All, Tell It Yourself: Notes from My White House Education.* New York: Free Press, May 1999.

12. Texas State Library and Archives State and Local Records Management Division. *Example Disaster Recovery Plan.* Accessed May 21, 2003. http://www.tsl.state.tx.us/slrm/disaster/recovery_plan.pdf.

13. Ronald L. Krutz and Russell Dean Vines. *The CISSP Prep Guide: Mastering the Ten Domains of Computer Security.* New York: John Wiley and Sons, 2001:288.

14. Richard Marcinko and John Weisman. *Designation Gold.* New York: Pocket Books, 1998: preface.

Information Security Policy

4

> Each problem that I solved became a rule which served afterwards to solve other problems.
>
> **RENE DESCARTES (1596–1650), "DISCOURS DE LA METHODE"**

IRIS WAS RETURNING FROM LUNCH when she ran into Susan Weinstein, one of RWW's senior account executives, who was accompanied by a man whom Iris did not know. Susan introduced him as Bob Watson, a prospective client. As they were chatting, Iris noticed Bob's distracted demeanor and Susan's forced smile and unusually stiff manner.

We didn't get the account, Iris realized.

A few minutes later, she saw why the meeting between RWW's account executive and new client did not go well. In the cubicle across the hall from Susan's office, two programmers were having lunch. Tim had his feet propped up on the desk. In one hand was a half-eaten hamburger; in the other, he held several playing cards. John had made himself comfortable by taking off his shoes. Next to his elbow was an open container of coffee, which he had placed in the open tray of the PC's CD-ROM drive. On the desk between the two employees was a small pile of coins.

Iris went into her office and pulled the company's policy manual off the shelf. She had already become familiar with RWW's policies, but for the next steps she had in mind, she needed specifics. As she read the sections on workplace behavior, however, Iris found that the policy manual didn't seem to cover Tim's and John's behavior. She did not find policies about alerting employees to meetings with prospective clients, eating and drinking in the workplace, or specifics about practices that supported data protection and other information security necessities.

Before Iris left for home that evening, she typed up her notes and scheduled an early meeting for the morning with her boss, Mike Edwards. Iris had some concrete concerns about the behavior of the staff and the omissions from the policy manual. As she left for home, she thought, *I think seeing Tim and John playing cards and lunching in may have cost us a new account.* Her thoughts continued, "Our company is growing, and things are getting more complicated than they were just a few months ago. I'll suggest to Mike that it's time for us to set up a policy review committee."

LEARNING OBJECTIVES

Upon completion of this material, you should be able to:

- Define information security policy and understand its central role in a successful information security program
- Recognize the three major types of information security policy and know what goes into each type
- Develop, implement, and maintain various types of information security policies

Introduction

The previous chapters of this book explained the relevance and role of information security in the modern organization (Chapter 1) and described the various planning activities that can augment the effectiveness of information security programs (organizational planning in Chapter 2 and contingency planning in Chapter 3). This chapter focuses on information security policy: what it is, how to write it, how to implement it, and how to maintain it.

The success of any information security program lies in policy development. In 1989, the National Institute of Standards and Technology (NIST) addressed this point in Special Publication SP 500-169, *Executive Guide to the Protection of Information Resources:*

> The success of an information resources protection program depends on the policy generated, and on the attitude of management toward securing information on automated systems. You, the policy maker, set the tone and the emphasis on how important a role information security will have within your agency. Your primary responsibility is to set the information resource security policy for the organization with the objectives of reduced risk, compliance with laws and regulations and assurance of operational continuity, information integrity, and confidentiality.[1]

Policy is the essential foundation of an effective information security program. As stated by Charles Cresson Wood, in his widely referenced book *Information Security Policies Made Easy*,

> The centrality of information security policies to virtually everything that happens in the information security field is increasingly evident. For example, system administrators cannot securely install a firewall unless they have received a set of clear information security policies. These policies will stipulate the type of transmission services that

should be permitted, how to authenticate the identities of users, and how to log security-relevant events. An effective information security training and awareness effort cannot be initiated without writing information security policies because policies provide the essential content that can be utilized in training and awareness material.[2]

Why Policy?

A quality information security program begins and ends with policy.[3] Properly developed and implemented policies enable the information security program to function almost seamlessly within the workplace. Although information security policies are the least expensive means of control to execute, they are often the most difficult to implement. Policy controls cost only the time and effort that the management team spends to create, approve, and communicate them, and that employees spend integrating the policies into their daily activities. Even when the management team hires an outside consultant to assist in the development of policy, the costs are minimal compared to the other forms of control, especially technical controls.

Some basic rules must be followed when shaping a policy:

- Policy should never conflict with law.
- Policy must be able to stand up in court, if challenged.
- Policy must be properly supported and administered.

Recognizing that policy is often difficult to implement, Bergeron and Bérubé have proposed guidelines for the formulation of computer policy. The same guidelines are directly applicable to information security policy:

1. All policies must contribute to the success of the organization.
2. Management must ensure the adequate sharing of responsibility for proper use of information systems.
3. End users of information systems should be involved in the steps of policy formulation.[4]

Bergeron and Bérubé further note that policy must be tailored to the specific needs of the organization and, while it is an admirable goal for policies to be complete and comprehensive, the existence of too many policies or policies that are too complex can lower end-user satisfaction.[5]

One implementation model that emphasizes the role of policy in an information security program is the **bull's-eye model**. Because it provides a proven mechanism for prioritizing complex changes, the bull's-eye model has become widely accepted among information security professionals. In this model, issues are addressed by moving from the general to the specific, always starting with policy. That is, the focus is on systemic solutions instead of individual problems. Figure 4-1 illustrates the four layers of the bull's-eye model:

1. Policies—the outer layer in the bull's-eye diagram
2. Networks—the place where threats from public networks meet the organization's networking infrastructure; in the past, most information security efforts have focused on networks, and until recently information security was often thought to be synonymous with network security
3. Systems—computers used as servers, desktop computers, and systems used for process control and manufacturing systems

4. Applications—all applications systems, ranging from packaged applications, such as office automation and e-mail programs, to high-end enterprise resource planning (ERP) packages, to custom application software developed by the organization

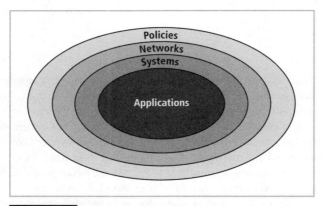

FIGURE 4-1 The Bull's-Eye Model

Whether via the use of the bull's-eye model or any other methodology, until sound and usable IT and information security policy is developed, communicated, and enforced, no additional resources should be spent on controls other than policy. Charles Cresson Wood summarizes the need for policy as follows:

... policies are important reference documents for internal audits and for the resolution of legal disputes about management's due diligence [and] policy documents can act as a clear statement of management's intent...[6]

Policy, Standards, and Practices

Policy is defined as "a plan or course of action, as of a government, political party, or business, intended to influence and determine decisions, actions, and other matters."[7] In other words, policies comprise a set of rules that dictates acceptable and unacceptable behavior within an organization. Policies must also specify the penalties for unacceptable behavior and define an appeal process. An example of a policy would be an organization's prohibiting the viewing of inappropriate Web sites at the workplace. To execute this policy, the organization must implement a set of standards that clarify and define exactly what is inappropriate in the workplace and to what degree the organization will act to stop the inappropriate use. A **standard** is a more detailed statement of what must be done to comply with policy. In the implementation of such an inappropriate-use policy, the organization might create a standard that all inappropriate content will be blocked and then list the material that is considered inappropriate. Later in the process, technical controls and their associated procedures might be established such that the network blocks access to pornographic Web sites. **Practices**, **procedures**, and **guidelines** explain how employees are to comply with policy. Figure 4-2 illustrates the relationship among policies, standards, and practices.

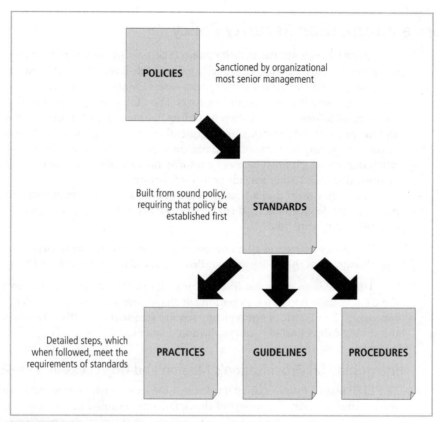

FIGURE 4-2 Policies, Standards, and Practices

For policies to be effective, they must be properly disseminated via printed per-sonnel manuals, organizational intranets, and periodic supplements. All members of the organization must read, understand, and agree to abide by the organization's poli-cies. In addition, policies require constant modification and maintenance. As the needs of the organization evolve, so must its policies.

To produce a complete information security policy, management must define three types of information security policies. These three types are based on NIST Special Publi-cation 800-14, which outlines the requirements of writing policy for senior managers. (This document, which is discussed in greater detail later in this chapter, is recommended for professionals involved in creating policy and can be found at http://csrc.nist.gov/pub-lications/nistpubs/800-14/800-14.pdf.) The three types of policy are as follows:

- Enterprise information security program policy
- Issue-specific security policies
- System-specific security policies

Each of these policy types is found in most organizations. The usual procedure is to create the highest level of policy first, the enterprise security policy. After that, general security policy needs are met by developing issue- and system-specific policies. The three types of policy are described in detail in the following sections.

Enterprise Information Security Policy

An **enterprise information security policy (EISP)**—also known as a security program policy, general security policy, IT security policy, high-level information security policy, or more simply, information security policy—sets the strategic direction, scope, and tone for all of an organization's security efforts. The EISP assigns responsibilities for the various areas of information security, including maintenance of information security policies and the practices and responsibilities of end users. In particular, the EISP guides the development, implementation, and management requirements of the information security program, which must be met by information security management, IT development, IT operations, and other specific security functions.

This policy must directly support the organization's vision and mission statements. It must also be defensible if legal challenges to it arise. Thus, the organization must ensure that two criteria are met:

- The policy exists and all members of the organization are informed of it.
- Violations of the policy are handled in a standard and consistent way.

The EISP is an executive-level document, drafted by the CISO in consultation with the CIO. Usually two to ten pages long, it shapes the security philosophy in the IT environment. The EISP does not typically require frequent or routine modification, unless the strategic direction of the organization changes.

Integrating an Organization's Mission and Objectives into the EISP

The EISP plays a number of vital roles, not the least of which is to state the importance of information security in support of the organization's mission and objectives. As demonstrated in the organizational and information security planning processes discussed in Chapter 2, information security strategic planning derives from the IT strategic policy, which is itself derived from the organization's strategic planning. Unless the EISP directly reflects this association, the policy will likely become confusing and counterproductive.

How can the EISP be crafted to reflect the organization's mission and objectives? Suppose that an academic institution's mission statement promotes academic freedom, independent research, and the relatively unrestricted pursuit of knowledge. This institution's EISP should reflect great tolerance for the use of organizational technology, a commitment to protecting the intellectual property of the faculty, and a degree of understanding for study delving into what could be called esoteric areas. The EISP should not contradict the organizational mission statement. For example, if the academic institution's mission statement supports the unrestricted pursuit of knowledge, then the EISP should not restrict access to pornographic Web sites or specify penalties for such access. Such a policy would directly contradict the academic institution's mission statement and, therefore, would be unenforceable.

EISP Elements

Although the specifics of EISPs vary from organization to organization, most EISP documents should include the following elements:

- An overview of the corporate philosophy on security

- Information on the structure of the information security organization and individuals who fulfill the information security role
- Fully articulated responsibilities for security that are *shared by all members* of the organization (employees, contractors, consultants, partners, and visitors)
- Fully articulated responsibilities for security that are *unique to each role* within the organization

The components of a good EISP are shown in Table 4-1.[8]

TABLE 4-1 Components of the EISP

Component	Description
Statement of Purpose	Answers the question, "What is this policy for?" Provides a framework that helps the reader to understand the intent of the document. Can include text such as the following: "This document will: - Identify the elements of a good security policy - Explain the need for information security - Specify the various categories of information security - Identify the information security responsibilities and roles - Identify appropriate levels of security through standards and guidelines This document establishes an overarching security policy and direction for our company. Individual departments are expected to establish standards, guidelines, and operating procedures that adhere to and reference this policy while addressing their specific and individual needs."[9]
Information Technology Security Elements	Defines information security. For example: "Protecting the confidentiality, integrity, and availability of information while in processing, transmission, and storage, through the use of policy, education and training, and technology…" This section can also lay out security definitions or philosophies to clarify the policy.
Need for Information Technology Security	Provides information on the importance of information security in the organization and the obligation (legal and ethical) to protect critical information whether regarding customers, employees, or markets.
Information Technology Security Responsibilities and Roles	Defines the organizational structure designed to support information security within the organization. Identifies categories of individuals with responsibility for information security (IT department, management, users) and their information security responsibilities, including maintenance of this document.
Reference to Other Information Technology Standards and Guidelines	Lists other standards that influence and are influenced by this policy document, perhaps including relevant laws (federal and state) and other policies.

Example EISP

Charles Cresson Wood, the author of *Information Security Policy Made Easy*, includes a sample information security policy (or EISP) in his book. Table 4-2 shows the specific components of this model EISP, which, when combined with the framework described in Table 4-1, provide detailed guidance for the creation of an organization-specific EISP. In his version, Wood also provides a justification for each policy statement and the target audience.

TABLE 4-2 Information Security Policy (EISP) Document Elements

1. Protection of Information

Policy:	Information must be protected in a manner commensurate with its sensitivity, value, and criticality.
Commentary:	This policy applies regardless of the media on which information is stored, the locations where the information is stored, the systems technology used to process the information, or the people who handle the information. This policy encourages examining the ways information flows through an organization. The policy also points to the scope of Information Security management's work throughout, and often even outside, an organization.
Audience:	Technical staff

2. Use of Information

Policy:	Company X information must be used only for the business purposes expressly authorized by management.
Commentary:	This policy states that all nonapproved uses of Company X information are prohibited.
Audience:	All

3. Information Handling, Access, and Usage

Policy:	Information is a vital asset and all accesses to, uses of, and processing of Company X information must be consistent with policies and standards.
Commentary:	This policy sets the context for a number of other information security policies. Such a statement is frequently incorporated into the first set of policies and summary material oriented toward users and members of the top management team. It is necessary for these people to appreciate how information has become a critical factor of production in business. This policy motivates the need for information security measures and to create a new understanding of the importance of information systems in organizations.
Audience:	All

TABLE 4-2 Information Security Policy (EISP) Document Elements (continued)

4. Data and Program Damage Disclaimers

Policy:	Company X disclaims any responsibility for loss or damage to data or software that results from its efforts to protect the confidentiality, integrity, and availability of the information handled by computers and communications systems.
Commentary:	This policy notifies users that they cannot hold Company X liable for damages associated with management's attempts to secure its system.
Audience:	End users

5. Legal Conflicts

Policy:	Company X information security policies were drafted to meet or exceed the protections found in existing laws and regulations, and any Company X information security policy believed to be in conflict with existing laws or regulations must be promptly reported to Information Security management.
Commentary:	This policy creates a context for the requirements specified in an information security policy document. Sound policies go beyond laws and regulations, or at least ensure that an organization will meet the requirements specified by laws and regulations. This policy acknowledges support for laws and regulations, and expresses an intention to stay in compliance with existing laws and regulations. The policy is suitable for both internal information security policies and those made available to the public.
Audience:	End users

6. Exceptions to Policies

Policy:	Exceptions to information security policies exist in rare instances where a risk assessment examining the implications of being out of compliance has been performed, where a standard risk acceptance form has been prepared by the data owner or management, and where this form has been approved by both Information Security management and Internal Audit management.
Commentary:	Management will be called upon to approve certain exceptions to policies. This policy clarifies that exceptions will be granted only after a risk acceptance form has been completed, signed, and approved. The form should include a statement where the data owner or management takes responsibility for any losses occurring from the out-of-compliance situation. The existence of such a form provides an escape value that can be used to address those situations where users insist on being out of compliance with policies. It is desirable to make all out-of-compliance situations both known and documented. This means that if there were to be a loss that occurred as a result of the situation, management could demonstrate to a judge or jury that it was aware of the situation, examined the risks, and decided to waive the relevant policy or standard.
Audience:	Management

TABLE 4-2 Information Security Policy (EISP) Document Elements (continued)

7. Policy Nonenforcement

Policy:	Management's nonenforcement of any policy requirement does not constitute its consent.
Commentary:	This policy notifies policy statement readers that they should not expect out-of-compliance conditions to be continued only because management has not yet enforced the policy. This policy eliminates any claim that local management may state that an out-of-compliance condition should remain as it is because the condition has been in existence for a considerable period of time.
Audience:	End users

8. Violation of Law

Policy:	Company X management must seriously consider prosecution for all known violations of the law.
Commentary:	This policy encourages the prosecution of abusive and criminal acts. While a decision to prosecute will be contingent on the specifics of the case, management should not dismiss prosecution without review. This policy may be important in terms of communicating to those would-be perpetrators of abusive or criminal acts. Many computer crimes are not prosecuted and perpetrators often know this, expecting victim organizations to terminate them and suppress the entire affair.
Audience:	Management

9. Revocation of Access Privileges

Policy:	Company X reserves the right to revoke a user's information technology privileges at any time.
Commentary:	This policy notifies users that they jeopardize their status as authorized users if they engage in activities that interfere with the normal and proper operation of Company X information systems, that adversely affect the ability of others to use these information systems, or that are harmful or offensive to others. For example, crashing the system could be expected to be harmful to other users, and would subject the perpetrator to disciplinary action including privilege revocation. The policy attempts to broadly describe an ethic for computing. Rather than specifying all of the adverse things that people could do, such as crashing a system, this policy is discreet and at a high level. This policy may give management latitude when it comes to deciding about privilege revocation.
Audience:	End users

TABLE 4-2 Information Security Policy (EISP) Document Elements (continued)

10. Industry-Specific Information Security Standards

Policy:	Company X information systems must employ industry-specific information security standards.
Commentary:	This policy requires systems designers and other technical staff to employ industry-standard controls. For example, in banking, encryption systems should use industry-specific systems for key management. Other industry-specific controls are relevant to the medical services industry, the aerospace and defense community, and other industry groups.
Audience:	Technical staff

11. Use of Information Security Policies and Procedures

Policy:	All Company X information security documentation, including, but not limited to, policies, standards, and procedures, must be classified as "Internal Use Only," unless expressly created for external business processes or partners.
Commentary:	This policy prevents workers from disclosing to outsiders the specifics of how Company X secures its information and systems. These details may be used to compromise Company X information and systems.
Audience:	All

Review and Evaluation

1. Security Controls Enforceability

Policy:	All information systems security controls must be enforceable prior to being adopted as a part of standard operating procedure.
Commentary:	Controls that are not enforced have a tendency to become useless. For example, if management has a policy about clean desks by locking up all sensitive materials after work, and it is not enforced, then employees quickly learn to ignore the policy. This policy is intended to require management to review the enforcement of controls, an issue that may not occur before adopting a control. A definition of the word "enforceable" may be advisable in some instances. For a control to be enforceable, it must be possible for management to clearly determine whether staff is in compliance with the control, and whether the control is effectively doing its intended job. The policy is purposefully vague about what constitutes standard operating procedure. This permits the policy to apply to a wide variety of circumstances, regardless of whether the control is documented, specific to a certain department, or used in an experimental way. In some instances, this policy may require the control designers to add a monitoring mechanism that reports on the status of the control. For example, encryption boxes from some vendors have lights that indicate that they are working, as they should.
Audience:	Management and technical staff

Source: Charles Cresson Wood. *Information Security Policies Made Easy*, 9th ed. NetIQ Corporation, 2003: 31–34. Used with permission.

The formulation of program policy in the EISP establishes the overall information security environment. As noted earlier, any number of specific issues may require policy guidance beyond what can be offered in the EISP. The next level of policy document, the issue-specific policy, delivers this needed specificity.

Issue-Specific Security Policy

A sound **issue-specific security policy (ISSP)** provides detailed, targeted guidance to instruct all members of the organization in the use of technology-based systems. The ISSP should begin by introducing the organization's fundamental technological philosophy. It should assure the member of the organization that the purpose of the policy is not to establish a legal foundation for persecution or prosecution, but rather to provide a common understanding of the purposes for which an employee can and cannot use the technology. Once this understanding is established, employees are free to use the technology without seeking approval for each type of use. This type of policy serves to protect both the employee and the organization from inefficiency and ambiguity.

An effective ISSP accomplishes the following goals:

- It articulates the organization's expectations about how its technology-based system should be used.
- It documents how the technology-based system is controlled and identifies the processes and authorities that provide this control.
- It indemnifies the organization against liability for an employee's inappropriate or illegal use of the system.

An effective ISSP is a binding agreement between parties (the organization and its members) and shows that the organization has made a good-faith effort to ensure that its technology will not be used in an inappropriate manner. Every organization's ISSP has three characteristics:

- It addresses specific technology-based systems.
- It requires frequent updates.
- It contains an issue statement explaining the organization's position on a particular issue.[10]

An ISSP may be drafted to cover many topics, including these:

- Use of electronic mail
- Use of the Internet and the World Wide Web
- Specific minimum configurations of computers to defend against worms and viruses
- Prohibitions against hacking or testing organization security controls
- Home use of company-owned computer equipment
- Use of personal equipment on company networks
- Use of telecommunications technologies (fax, phone)
- Use of photocopying equipment

Components of the ISSP

Table 4-3 describes the typical ISSP components. Each of these components is, in turn, discussed on the pages that follow. The specific situation of the particular organization dictates the exact wording of the security procedures as well as issues not covered within these general guidelines.

TABLE 4-3 Framework for Issue-Specific Policies

1. Statement of Purpose
    a. Scope and Applicability
    b. Definition of Technology Addressed
    c. Responsibilities

2. Authorized Access and Usage of Equipment
    a. User Access
    b. Fair and Responsible Use
    c. Protection of Privacy

3. Prohibited Usage of Equipment
    a. Disruptive Use or Misuse
    b. Criminal Use
    c. Offensive or Harassing Materials
    d. Copyrighted, Licensed, or Other Intellectual Property
    e. Other Restrictions

4. Systems Management
    a. Management of Stored Materials
    b. Employer Monitoring
    c. Virus Protection
    d. Physical Security
    e. Encryption

5. Violations of Policy
    a. Procedures for Reporting Violations
    b. Penalties for Violations

6. Policy Review and Modification
    a. Scheduled Review of Policy
    b. Procedures for Modification

7. Limitations of Liability
    a. Statements of Liability
    b. Other Disclaimers

Source: Michael E. Whitman, Anthony M. Townsend, and Robert J. Alberts. Considerations for an effective telecommunications-use policy. *Communications of the ACM*, June 1999; 42(6):101–109.

Statement of Purpose

The ISSP should begin with a clear statement of purpose that outlines the scope and applicability of the policy. It should address the following questions: What purpose does this policy serve? Who is responsible and accountable for policy implementation? What technologies and issues does the policy document address?

Authorized Access and Usage of Equipment

This section of the policy statement explains who can use the technology governed by the policy and for what purposes. Recall that an organization's information systems are the exclusive property of the organization, and users have no particular rights of use. Each technology and process is provided for business operations. This section defines "fair and responsible use" of equipment and other organizational assets, and it addresses key legal issues, such as protection of personal information and privacy. As strictly interpreted, the policy makes any use for any purpose not explicitly identified a misuse of equipment. When it is management's intention to allow some, selective, extra-organizational uses, such as using company systems and networks for noncommercial personal e-mail, that use must be allowed for in the policy.

Prohibited Usage of Equipment

While the previous section specifies what the issue or technology *can* be used for, this section outlines what it *cannot* be used for. Unless a particular use is clearly prohibited, the organization cannot penalize employees for it. For example, the following actions might be prohibited: personal use, disruptive use or misuse, criminal use, offensive or harassing materials, and infringement of copyrighted, licensed, or other intellectual property. Note: The ISSP sections called Authorized Access and Usage of Equipment and Prohibited Usage of Equipment might be more efficiently combined into a section entitled Appropriate Use Policy.

Systems Management

This section of the ISSP focuses on the users' relationships to systems management. A company may wish to issue specific rules regarding the use of e-mail and electronic documents, and storage of those documents, as well as guidelines about authorized employer monitoring, and the physical and electronic security of e-mail and other electronic documents. The Systems Management section should specify users' and systems administrators' responsibilities, so that all parties know what they are accountable for.

Violations of Policy

This section specifies the penalties and repercussions of violating the usage and systems management policies. Penalties should be laid out for each type or category of violation. This section should also provide instructions on how to report observed or suspected violations, either openly or anonymously, because some employees may fear that powerful individuals in the organization could discriminate against, single out, or otherwise retaliate against someone who reports violations. Anonymous submissions are often the only way to convince individual users to report the unauthorized activities of other, more influential employees.

Policy Review and Modification

Every policy should contain procedures and a timetable for periodic review. This section should outline a specific methodology for the review and modification of the ISSP, so as to ensure that users always have guidelines that reflect the organization's current technologies and needs.

Limitations of Liability

The final section offers a general statement of liability or a set of disclaimers. If an individual employee is caught conducting illegal activities with organizational equipment or assets, management does not want the organization to be held liable for that situation. Therefore, if employees violate a company policy or any law using company technologies, the company will not protect them and is not liable for their actions, assuming that the violation is not known or sanctioned by management.

Implementing the ISSP

A number of approaches for creating and managing ISSPs are possible. Three of the most common are described here:

- Create a number of independent ISSP documents, each tailored to a specific issue.
- Create a single comprehensive ISSP document that aims to cover all issues.
- Create a modular ISSP document that unifies policy creation and administration, while maintaining each specific issue's requirements. This approach results in a modular document with a standard template for structure and appearance, in which certain aspects are standardized, while others—including much of the content—are customized for each issue. The end result is several independent ISSP documents, all derived from a common template and physically well managed and easy to use.

Table 4-4 describes the advantages and disadvantages of each approach.

TABLE 4-4 ISSP Approaches

Approach	Advantages	Disadvantages
Individual Policy	Clear assignment to a responsible department Written by those with superior subject matter expertise for technology-specific systems	Typically yields a scattershot result that fails to cover all of the necessary issues Can suffer from poor policy dissemination, enforcement, and review
Comprehensive Policy	Well controlled by centrally managed procedures assuring complete topic coverage Often provides better formal procedures than when policies are individually formulated Usually identifies processes for dissemination, enforcement, and review	May over-generalize the issues and skip over vulnerabilities May be written by those with less complete subject matter expertise

TABLE 4-4 ISSP Approaches (continued)

Approach	Advantages	Disadvantages
Modular Policy	Often considered an optimal balance between the individual ISSP and the comprehensive ISSP approaches Well controlled by centrally managed procedures, assuring complete topic coverage Clear assignment to a responsible department Written by those with superior subject matter expertise for technology-specific systems	May be more expensive than other alternatives Implementation can be difficult to manage

The recommended approach is the modular policy, which offers a balance between issue orientation and policy management. The policies created via this approach are individual modules, each created and updated by the individuals who are responsible for a specific issue. These individuals report to a central policy administration group that incorporates these specific issues into an overall policy.

VIEWPOINT

Information Security Policies: Turning People into the First Line of Defense

By Chris Pick

In my career as a security professional, I served as an information security consultant for Ernst and Young for many years and wrote hundreds of policies for organizations in almost every market around the world. Typically, these policies are collected as printed documents in a rather large, three-ring binder that sits imposingly on the shelf. And that's the problem with most security policies. Too many policies simply stay on the shelf gathering dust—never making an impact on what actually happens in the day-to-day operations of an organization.

I'm convinced that most organizations are sincere in their efforts to create policies based on legal requirements to document controls and to ensure a passing grade for regulatory audits. But in many cases these policies simply were created to put a check in the box. They have never been "operationalized"—that is, translated into technical configurations—nor have they been communicated in a way that people understand what they should be doing as part of their job each day. Thus, a lot of effort is spent developing and publishing policies that few employees ever actually read, let alone act upon.

This situation of "policy impotence" is, however, changing in today's more security-sensitive environment. Since the tragedy on September 11, 2001, and the advent of costly computer viruses, our world is rapidly becoming more regulated, with new laws specifying how information must be handled and safeguarded. As a consequence, making security policy "operational" is no longer a nice-to-have, but a must-do for any private and public organization today.

(continued)

Recognizing these challenges, three years ago some industry colleagues and I began a national awareness campaign called the Human Firewall initiative. The name was chosen to acknowledge the fact that information security critically depends on people to be effective. The Human Firewall campaign recognizes that the support of each and every worker who comes in contact with sensitive, valuable, or critical information is essential for effective information security.

A primary principle of the Human Firewall is the acceptance of responsibility—both individual and collective—for helping to ensure that safe policies and procedures are followed and become second nature among people handling sensitive or critical information. It recognizes that one of our major goals must be to change the attitudes and behavior of people involved in information security according to those specific guidelines and policies that best fit their organizations.

Through the Human Firewall's Web site at www.humanfirewall.org, more than 4000 organizations have been able to benchmark their security awareness and policy management capabilities and get recommended guidelines on how to change people from a liability into their first line of defense.

Chris Pick is the Vice President of Strategic Marketing at NetIQ Corporation.

System-Specific Policy

While issue-specific policies are formalized as written documents readily identifiable as policy, system-specific policies (SysSPs) sometimes have a different look. SysSPs often function as standards or procedures to be used when configuring or maintaining systems. For example, such a document might describe the configuration and operation of a network firewall. This document could include a statement of managerial intent; guidance to network engineers on selecting, configuring, and operating firewalls; and an access control list that defines levels of access for each authorized user. SysSPs can be separated into two general groups, management guidance and technical specifications, or they may combine these two types of SysSP content into a single policy document, as in the preceding example.

Management Guidance SysSPs

A management guidance SysSP document is created by management to guide the implementation and configuration of technology as well as to address the behavior of people in the organization in ways that support the security of information. For example, while the specific configuration of a firewall belongs in the technical specifications SysSP, the process of constructing and implementing the firewall must follow guidelines established by management. An organization might not want its employees to have access to the Internet via the organization's network, for instance; in that case, the firewall would have to be implemented according to this rule.

Firewalls are not the only area that may require system-specific policies. Any technology that affects the confidentiality, integrity, or availability of information must be assessed to evaluate the trade-off between improved security and restrictions.

System-specific policies can be developed at the same time as ISSPs, or they can be prepared in advance of their related ISSPs. Before management can craft a policy informing users what they can do with the technology and how they may do it, it might be necessary for system administrators to configure and operate the system. Some organizations may prefer to develop ISSPs and SysSPs in tandem, so that operational procedures and user guidelines are created simultaneously.

Technical Specifications SysSPs

While a manager may work with a systems administrator to create managerial policy as described in the preceding section, the system administrator may in turn need to create a different type of policy to implement the managerial policy. Each type of equipment requires its own set of policies, which are used to translate the management intent for the technical control into an enforceable technical approach. For example, an ISSP may require that user passwords be changed quarterly; a systems administrator can implement a technical control within a specific application to enforce this policy. The screen shots in Figure 4-3 illustrate network operating systems configured to implement a password change requirement.

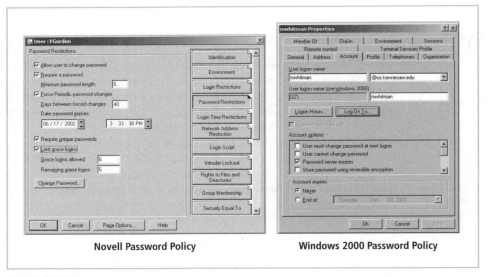

Novell Password Policy   Windows 2000 Password Policy

FIGURE 4-3 Password SysSP

There are two general methods of implementing such technical controls: access control lists and configuration rules.

Access Control Lists

Access control lists (ACLs) include the user access lists, matrices, and capability tables that govern the rights and privileges of users. ACLs can control access to file storage systems, object brokers, or other network communications devices. A capability table specifies which subjects and objects that users or groups can access; in some systems, capability tables are called user profiles or user policies. These specifications frequently take the form of complex matrices, rather than simple lists or tables.

The Microsoft Windows NT/2000 and Novell Netware families of systems translate ACLs into configuration sets that administrators can use to control access to their systems. The level of detail and specificity (often called granularity) may vary from system to system, but in general ACLs enable administrations to restrict access according to user, computer, time, duration, or even a particular file. This range gives a great deal of control to the administrator. In general, ACLs regulate the following aspects of access:

- *Who* can use the system
- *What* authorized users can access
- *When* authorized users can access the system
- *Where* authorized users can access the system from
- *How* authorized users can access the system

Restricting who can use the system requires no explanation. To restrict what users can access—for example, which printers, files, communications, and applications—administrators assign user privileges, such as the following:

- Read
- Write
- Create
- Modify
- Delete
- Compare
- Copy

This list is not exhaustive, but represents the key ACL privilege types. Figures 4-4 and 4-5 show how the ACL security model has been implemented by Novell and Microsoft operating systems, respectively.

The Directory "Mongo" provides information via this ACL about who can access the directory and what rights these users have within the directory.

FIGURE 4-4 Novell Netware ACL

The list of "built-in" groups specifies which rights individual users have to and within a particular system.

FIGURE 4-5 Windows 2000 ACLs

Configuration Rules

Configuration rules are the specific configuration codes entered into security systems to guide the execution of the system when information is passing through it. Rule-based policies are more specific to the operation of a system than ACLs are, and they may or may not deal with users directly. Many security systems require specific configuration scripts telling the systems which actions to perform on each set of information they process. Examples include firewalls, intrusion detection systems (IDSs), and proxy servers. Figures 4-6 and 4-7 show how this security model has been implemented by Checkpoint in a firewall rule set and by TripWire in an IDS rule set, respectively.

Action specifies whether the packet from Source: is accepted (allowed through) or dropped.

Track specifies whether the processing of the specified packet is written to the system logs.

Rule 7 states that any traffic coming in on a specified link (Comm_with_ Contractor) requesting a Telnet session will be accepted, but logged. This rule also implies that non-Telnet traffic will be denied.

FIGURE 4-6 Firewall Configuration Rules

This section defines which security levels are to be used and who is to be notified if that level file is modified.

```
################################################################### #
# This Policy was created by the Tripwire Policy Resource Center  # #
# Created on: Mon Mar 25 21:54:27 GMT 2002                        # #
#        Copyright (C) 2001, Tripwire Inc. Reprinted with permission  #
################################################################### #
@@section global
SYSTEMDRIVE="C:" ;
BOOTDRIVE="C:" ;
SYSTEMROOT="C:\\Winnt" ;
PROGRAMFILES="C:\\Program Files" ;
IE5="C:\\Program Files\\Plus!\\Microsoft Internet" ;
# Email Recipients # #
SIG_HIGHEST_MAILRECIPIENTS  = "Administrator" ;
SIG_HIGH_MAILRECIPIENTS     = "Administrator" ;
SIG_MED_MAILRECIPIENTS      = "Administrator" ;
SIG_LOW_MAILRECIPIENTS      = "Administrator" ;
# Security Levels # #
SIG_LOW      = 33 ;     # Non-critical files that are of minimal security impact
SIG_MED      = 66 ;     # Non-critical files that are of significant security impact
SIG_HIGH     = 100 ;    # Critical files that are significant points of vulnerability
SIG_HIGHEST  = 1000 ;   # Super-critical files.  Mostly used for the TCB section.
@@section NTFS
{
```

FIGURE 4-7 IDS Configuration Rules

<table>
<tr><td>

This section looks for unauthorized modifications to Internet Explorer Registry edits, most likely due to virus or hacker efforts.

</td><td>

```
rulename = "IE 5.01 Registry keys",
  severity = $ (SIG_HIGHEST),
  emailto  = $ (SIG_HIGHEST_MAILRECIPIENTS),
  recurse  = true
}
{
  $ (HKLM_CCS_SM_CBadApps)                           -> $ (REG_SEC_HIGHEST) ;
  $ (HKLM_CRYPT)                                     -> $ (REG_SEC_HIGHEST) ;
  $ (HKLM_CRYPTINIT)                                 -> $ (REG_SEC_HIGHEST) ;
  $ (HKLM_CRYPTMSG)                                  -> $ (REG_SEC_HIGHEST) ;
  $ (HKLM_CRYPTSIGN)                                 -> $ (REG_SEC_HIGHEST) ;
  $ (HKLM_EventSystem)                               -> $ (REG_SEC_HIGHEST) ;
  $ (HKLM_SW_IE_Setup)                               -> $ (REG_SEC_HIGHEST) ;
  $ (HKLM_WHM)                                       -> $ (REG_SEC_HIGHEST) ;
  $ (HKLM_WIE)                                       -> $ (REG_SEC_HIGHEST) ;
  $ (HKLM_WIE_INF_Setup)                             -> $ (REG_SEC_HIGHEST) ;
  $ (HKLM_WMM)                                       -> $ (REG_SEC_HIGHEST) ;
}
#         Snippet Name: A Nimda Virus Rule                            # #
#        Snippet Author: support@tripwire.com                        # #
#       Snippet Version: 1.0.0                                       # #
#                   Nimda#                                           # #
@@section NTFS
{
```

</td></tr>
<tr><td>

This section defines the rules necessary to detect and react to the Nimda virus.

</td><td>

```
rulename = "Nimda File Scan",
Severity = 100
}
{
$ (SYSTEMROOT)\ZaCker.vbs -> $ (IgnoreNone);
$ (SYSTEMROOT)\MixDaLaL.vbs -> $ (IgnoreNone);
$ (SYSTEMDIR)\ZaCker.vbs -> $ (IgnoreNone);
$ (SYSTEMDIR)\MixDaLaL.vbs -> $ (IgnoreNone);
}
```

</td></tr>
</table>

FIGURE 4-7   IDS Configuration Rules (continued)

Combination SysSPs

Many organizations choose to create a single document that combines elements of both the management guidance SysSP and the technical specifications SysSP. While this document can be somewhat confusing to the users of the policies, it is very practical to have the guidance from both perspectives in a single place. If this approach is employed, care should be taken to articulate the required actions carefully as the procedures are presented.

Guidelines for Policy Development

It is often useful to view policy development as a two-part project. The first part of the project designs and develops the policy (or redesigns and rewrites an outdated policy), and the second part establishes management processes to perpetuate the policy within the organization. The former is an exercise in project management, whereas the latter requires adherence to good business practices.

The Policy Project

Like any IT project, a policy development or redevelopment project should be well planned, properly funded, and aggressively managed to ensure that it is completed on time and within budget. One way to accomplish this goal is to use a systems development life cycle (SDLC). You are already familiar with a variant of the SDLC, the SecSDLC, from Chapter 2. The following discussion expands the SecSDLC model to encompass projects in policy development. You will learn more about project management in the realm of information security in Chapter 12.

When a policy development project is undertaken, the project can be guided by the SecSDLC process. The following sections describe the tasks that could be included in each phase of the SecSDLC.

Investigation Phase

During the investigation phase the policy development team should obtain the following elements:

- Support from senior management, because any project without it has a reduced chance of success. Only with the support of top management will a specific policy receive the attention it deserves from the intermediate-level managers who must implement it, and from the users who must comply with it.
- Support and active involvement of IT management, specifically the CIO. Only with the CIO's active support will technology area managers be motivated to participate in policy development and support the implementation efforts to deploy it once created.
- The clear articulation of goals.
- The participation of the correct individuals from the communities of interest affected by the recommended policies. Assembling the right team, by ensuring the participation of the proper representatives from the groups that will be affected by the new policies, is very important. The team must include representatives from the legal department, the human resources department, and end users of the various IT systems covered by the policies, as well as a *project champion* with sufficient stature and prestige to accomplish the goals of the project, and a capable project manager to see the project through to completion.
- A detailed outline of the scope of the policy development project, and sound estimates for the cost and scheduling of the project.

Analysis Phase

The analysis phase should include the following activities:

- A new or recent risk assessment or IT audit documenting the current information security needs of the organization. This risk assessment should include any loss history, as well as past lawsuits, grievances, or other records of negative outcomes from information security areas.
- The gathering of key reference materials—including any existing policies—in addition to the items noted above. Sometimes policy documents that affect information security will be housed in the Human Resources department as well as the accounting, finance, legal, or corporate security department.

According to Charles Cresson Wood:

> Some who are facing significant time or resource constraints will be tempted to skip the above-mentioned data gathering processes. Whenever data gathering is significantly abbreviated, the likelihood that management will reject the resulting document increases. It is through this data gathering process that management's view of information security can be identified, the policies that already exist, the policies that need to be added or changed, how management enforces policies, the unique vulnerabilities that the organization faces, and other essential background information. If serious consideration has not been given to this background information, it is unlikely that a newly written information security policy will be responsive to the true needs of the organization.[11]

Design Phase

During the design phase, the team must create a plan to distribute, and verify the distribution of, the policies. The members of the organization must explicitly acknowledge that they have received and read the policy. Otherwise, an employee can claim never to have seen a policy. In that case, unless the manager can produce strong evidence to the contrary, any enforcement action, such as dismissal for inappropriate use of the Web, can be overturned and punitive damages might be awarded to the former employee. The simplest way to document acknowledgment of a written policy is to attach a cover sheet that states "I have received, read, understood, and agreed to this policy." The employee's signature and date provides a paper trail of his or her receipt of the policy.

Some situations preclude a formal documentation process. Take, for instance, student use of campus computer labs. Most universities have stringent policies on what students can and cannot do in a computer lab. These policies are usually posted on the Web, in the student handbook, in course catalogs, and in a number of other locations, including bulletin boards in the labs. For the policies to be enforceable, however, some mechanism must be established that captures the student's acknowledgment of the policy. This is frequently accomplished with a banner screen that displays a brief statement warning the user that the policy is in place, and that use of the system constitutes acceptance of the policy. The user must then click an OK button or press a key to get past the screen. This method can be ineffective if the acknowledgment screen does not require any unusual action to move past it, however; this kind of acknowledgment screen is often called a *blow-by screen*.

In the past, companies used banners or pop-up windows to display *end-user license agreements (EULAs)*. A EULA, which is usually presented on a screen to the user during software installation, spells out fair and responsible use of the software being installed. At one time, EULAs were typically presented on blow-by screens, with an instruction like "Hit any key to agree," so that users could install the software without explicitly agreeing to the restrictions on software use, thus negating the software company's legal claim. Today, most EULA screens require that the user click a button, press a function key, or type words to agree to the terms of the EULA. Similar methods are used on network and computer logins to reinforce acknowledgement of the system use policy. Figure 4-8 provides an example of a EULA screen that requires specific user input.

FIGURE 4-8   End-User License Agreement for Microsoft Office XP

Specifications for any automated tool used for the creation and management of policy documents will also be included in the design as will revisions to feasibility analysis reports based on improved costs and benefits as the design is clarified.

Implementation Phase

In the implementation phase, the policy development team actually writes the policies. This can be a challenging process, but you don't have to come up with a good policy document from scratch. There are a number of resources at your disposal, including these:

- The Web, where you can search for other, similar policies. The point here is not to advocate wholesale copying of these policies, but rather to encourage you to look for ideas on what should be contained in your policy. For example, dozens of policies available on the Web describe fair and responsible use of various technologies. What you may not find, however, are policies that relate to sensitive internal documents or processes.
- Government sites such as http://csrc.nist.gov, and http://fasp.nist.gov/fasp/, which contain a number of sample policies and policy support documents, including SP 800-12, *An Introduction to Computer Security: The NIST Handbook.* While these policies are typically directed toward or applicable to federal government Web sites, you may be able to adapt some sections to meet your organization's needs.
- Professional literature. Several authors—most notably, Charles Cresson Wood—have published books on the subject. Of particular note is Wood's *Information Security Policies Made Easy,*[12] which not only provides more than 1000 pages of policies, but also makes those policies available in electronic format, complete with permission to use them in internal documents. Exercise caution when using such resources, however; it is extremely easy to take large sections of policy and end up with a massive document that is neither publishable nor enforceable.

- Peer networks. Other information security professionals have to write similar policies and implement similar plans. Attend meetings like those offered by the Information Systems Security Association (www.issa.org), and ask your peers (as Iris in the chapter-opening vignette did).
- Professional consultants. Policy is one area of information security that can certainly be developed in-house, but if you simply cannot find the time to develop your own policy, then hiring outside consultants may be your last option. Keep in mind that no consultant can know your organization as thoroughly as you do, and the consultant may simply design generic policies that you can then adapt to your specific situation.

During the implementation phase, the policy development team must also ensure that certain criteria are met:

- Make certain that policies are enforceable. An unenforceable policy—such as employees being prohibited from discussing personal matters with coworkers—is an ineffective policy.
- Provide for policy distribution. This effort is not always as straightforward as you might think. Posting a policy on a bulletin board is insufficient, unless another policy requires the employees to read the bulletin board on a specified schedule (daily, weekly, and so forth). Unless the policy actually reaches the end users, it cannot be enforced. Unlike in civil or criminal law, ignorance of policy, where policy is inadequately distributed, is considered an acceptable excuse. In some cases, policies must be read aloud and/or provided in other languages or formats.
- Make certain that policy is written at a reasonable reading level, with minimal technical jargon and management terminology. A useful tool in determining this reading level is the readability statistics offered in most productivity suite applications like Microsoft Word. Figure 4-9 presents the readability statistics for this section.

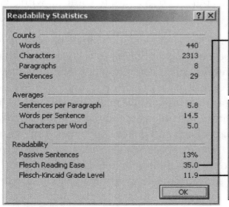

FIGURE 4-9 Readability Statistics for Policy

Maintenance Phase

During the maintenance phase, the policy development team monitors, maintains, and modifies the policy as needed to ensure that it remains effective as a tool to meet changing threats. The policy should have a built-in mechanism through which users can report problems with the policy, preferably anonymously.

Automated Tools

The need for effective policy management has led to the emergence of a class of software tools that support policy development, implementation, and maintenance. At the forefront of these tools is the VigilEnt Policy Center (VPC), a centralized policy approval and implementation system. VPC allows policy developers to create policy, manage the approval process with multiple individuals or groups, and distribute approved policy throughout their organizations. VPC assesses readers' understanding of the policy and electronically records reader acknowledgments. In this way, it reduces or eliminates the need to distribute hard copies of documents that might go unread, and to manage multiple policy receipt acknowledgment forms. Tools like VPC keep policies confidential, behind password-protected intranets, and generate periodic reports indicating which employees have and have not read and acknowledged the policies. Figure 4-10 illustrates the VigilEnt Policy Center methodology.

FIGURE 4-10 The VigilEnt Policy Center

This description of VPC is taken from NetIQ product literature:

NetIQ's VigilEnt Policy Center allows you to manage and implement all of your policies enterprise-wide through an automated Web-based solution. You can keep policies up-to-date, easily changing and distributing them automatically via a Web browser. Moreover, VigilEnt Policy Center provides you with the tools necessary to track user compliance statements and measure understanding and awareness of your entire workforce.

When policies are created and distributed without software automation tools, it is often not clear where a policy has originated, and which manager approved it. However, with tools such as VPC, the primary manager responsible for the policy has his or her name prominently displayed on the policy, along with the date of approval. This identification can make managers reluctant to implement policies using automated software tools, because it can associate a particular manager with new restrictions or rules. This hesitancy is a difficult hurdle to overcome but can be addressed by evaluating managerial job performance on achieved objectives—in this case, an effective policy process—rather than on the basis that an unobserved failure is a success.

The *Information Securities Policy Made Easy* Approach

The following sections, used with permission of the author and publisher of *Information Security Policies Made Easy (ISPME)* referenced earlier,[13] discusses another approach to policy development.

Gathering Key Reference Materials

Information security policies should be largely driven by the nature of the information handled by the organization. One should acquaint him- or herself with the nature of the information handled by the organization. A good source for this information, also known as metadata, is a data dictionary. Overviews of internal information systems prepared for top executives, board members, merger and acquisition candidates, and strategic partners also may be useful background to the policy writing effort. Because information systems change so rapidly, available documentation is likely to be outdated. Knowledgeable workers should be interviewed to accurately identify the nature of the information currently being handled by the organization, including what information is sensitive, what information is valuable, and what information is critical.

When developing a set of information security policies, a recent risk assessment or an information technology audit should be referenced that clearly indicates the organization's current information security needs. A loss history documenting the specifics of recent incidents may be helpful in terms of identifying areas in need of further attention. Lawsuits, formal written grievances, and other disputes may identify areas that should be addressed in a policy document. To identify further problem areas, meetings with interested parties such as the in-house legal counsel, the director of Physical Security, the chief information officer, the Internal Audit director, and the director of Human Resources are advised.

To identify the policy areas needing further attention, copies of all other relevant and current organizational policy documents should be collected. Relevant policies include application systems development policies, computer operations policies, computer equipment acquisition policies, human resources policies, information system quality control policies, and physical security policies. If obtainable, policies from other organizations in the same industry can provide useful background information. If the organization is a subsidiary or affiliate of another organization, then the parent organization's policies should be obtained and used as reference material. If the organization is a participant in an electronic data interchange, value-added network, a multi-organizational Internet commerce arrangement, or any other multi-organizational networks, the policies of these networks should be obtained and reviewed.

Some who are facing significant time or resource constraints will be tempted to skip the above-mentioned data gathering processes. Whenever data gathering is significantly abbreviated, the likelihood that management will reject the resulting document increases. It is through this data gathering process that management's view of information security can be identified, the policies that already exist, the policies that need to be added or changed, how management enforces policies, the unique vulnerabilities that the organization faces, and other essential background information. If serious consideration has not been given to this background information, it is unlikely that a newly written information security policy will be responsive to the true needs of the organization.

Another major reason to do a good deal of background research in preparation for policy writing is to ensure that the requirements defined in the policy document are consistent with management's intentions. One of the fastest ways to lose credibility for an information security policy writing effort is to propose a policy that is clearly inconsistent with existing organizational norms. For example, employees at a high-tech company routinely downloaded games from the Internet and played these games on their powerful workstations during breaks and after-hours. Top management knew of and tacitly approved of these activities. At the same time, a published policy indicated that no personal use of the corporation's information systems would be tolerated. This glaring inconsistency caused a large majority of the workers at this company to dismiss the policy document as irrelevant.

Another important reason to spend considerable time on background research is to identify and define the organization's business-related strategic directions. A new or revised policy document needs to be consistent with these strategic directions if top management is going to approve and support the policy. For example, suppose an organization decides it wants to once again centralize its currently decentralized information systems activities. A policy document that stresses many activities to be performed by a group of decentralized information security coordinators would then be inconsistent with management's intentions, and consequently would be unlikely to be approved.

Yet another reason to thoroughly research the current situation before beginning the policy writing process is to identify the internal information systems architecture. An information security policy document should be consistent with and fully support an existing information systems architecture. This is not addressing information security architecture, but an information systems architecture. An information security policy document is typically developed after an information systems architecture is already in place. The development of an information security policy document will permit an information security architecture to be developed. For example, a policy about permissible access through an Internet firewall will enable a security architecture to be specified. It will also enable an appropriate firewall product to be chosen and implemented.[14]

Defining a Framework for Policies

After the above-mentioned reference materials have been collected, a list should be compiled that contains topics to be covered in a new or more comprehensive information security policy document. The first draft of the list should include policies that are intended for immediate adoption and those that are intended for adoption in the future. In most cases, the level of detail in this list will be inconsistent, and at this stage in the process, this should not be cause for concern. For example, the list might include telecommuting and password construction with a minimum of 10 characters. When a high-level outline is prepared, the level of detail should be standardized. For more information, see "Preparing a Coverage Matrix" [next section].

Next, an attempt should be made to define the ways in which the organization intends to express information security policies. For example, policies may be placed in a standard operating procedures manual. Alternatively, the director of the Information Security department may periodically issue electronic mail memos summarizing policies. It is common for privacy policies to be posted on the Internet. Because workers are bombarded by communications from many people through many different communication channels, it is essential that information security policies be repeatedly sent through multiple communication channels. [...] The channels used to express a policy will determine how the policy should be written. For example, if videotape will be used, then an abbreviated colloquial style should be employed. If a policy document will reside on an intranet Web server, then a more graphic and hypertext-linked style is appropriate.

The ways that the organization currently uses or intends to use information security policies should be examined. Policies may be used to guide information system acquisition efforts, drive information technology audit plans, and assist users in securely operating their desktop computers. [...] Defining the uses of policies will identify the audiences to whom policies will be addressed. For more information about identifying audiences, see "Preparing a Coverage Matrix" [next section].

Determining the uses for policies will also focus attention on those areas that most need to be addressed. Other uses soon will be apparent after the policy document has been distributed. This should not be considered poor planning, but should be considered a successful initiative that has unforeseen contributions to the organization. In some instances, the uses of a policy document will be initially unknown, but these uses can be quickly identified through a series of meetings with interested parties.

Study of the style in which existing policies are written, the use of certain words, the conventional format for documenting policies, the system for numbering and naming policies, and the linkages between policies and other management directives like procedures and standards should be completed. For example, existing policies may use the word "must" consistently. To maintain consistency, the information security policies also should use the word "must." Likewise, the existing policies may have a military-style numbering system or something entirely different. The issuance of an information security policy document will be controversial by nature. Do not give critics additional ammunition by failing to be consistent with internal policy style guidelines, whether these guidelines are written or unwritten.

Part of the study of the existing policies and how they are used should entail a review of the level of detail appropriate for the organization's policy statements. The organization may have defined existing policies in very specific terms, in which case many detailed information security policies may be appropriate. Alternatively, the organization may have defined policies in very high-level terms, in which case only a brief overall information security statement may be appropriate. Both of these alternatives may simultaneously exist in that separate policies are provided to different audiences. The level of detail is in part driven by the extent to which management trusts workers to use their judgment, the extent to which specific documentation requirements are being observed, and the extent to which the topics being addressed are new to the involved audiences.

Information about the expression, use, style, and level of detail found in internal policies is rarely documented, but it can be obtained by examining existing policy statements. In very large organizations there may even be a document that provides directions on the policy writing process. In some large organizations, in-house staff in a Policy and Planning group can help with the policy writing effort. Whether explicit written guidance or in-house consulting assistance is available, to ensure their prompt adoption, new and revised information security policies should be written in a manner that resembles and is at least in a form indistinguishable from existing policies.[15]

Preparing a Coverage Matrix

After preparing a rough list of the areas needing attention, and after becoming acquainted with the ways in which the organization expresses and uses policies, the policies found in this guide now can be used. At this point the additional topics to be covered should be evaluated. Review the policy titles or the policies themselves, but skip the accompanying commentaries. This task is generally done most rapidly with the hardcopy guide and a marker such as a yellow highlighter.

[…] categories should be developed that uniquely respond to the organization's needs. Alternatively, categories reflecting the areas to be addressed may be patterned after an internal audit report or an information security guide that management values. Another way to segment the controls would be broad control objectives such as "avoid," "prevent," "deter," "detect," "mitigate," "recover," and "correct."

At this point, a draft high-level outline reflecting the topics to be addressed should be developed. This outline is best if accompanied by a brief explanation with examples of topics to be covered in each section. The explanation can be only a sentence or two and just enough to provide a preview of the topics included. At this point, distribution of the high-level outline to interested parties is recommended, and the constructive feedback received should then be integrated with the high-level outline.

At this point, a determination must be made of the proper audiences to which these messages are to be addressed. Often policies will be directed at several significantly different audiences because each audience has distinctly different needs. For example, end users might receive a small booklet containing the most important information security policies that they need to keep in mind. The focus could be on desktop computer information security issues. At the same time, systems developers and other technical staff might receive a considerably longer document that provides much more detail, perhaps focusing on security as part of a standard systems development methodology. Management may get yet another document that deals primarily with the tasks of information owners.

While separate documents for separate audiences may sound like too much effort, the additional work is not great if a list of the essential messages to be communicated has been made. This list now can be split by audience, and it is this splitting process that is discussed in the next few paragraphs. The development and maintenance of separate documents for separate audiences is much easier if all of these documents are placed on an intranet. Using browser links, those who read the policy can be quickly provided with only the information that is relevant to them. For example, at a large bank, an intranet is used to segment the information security policies by job title. People need to read only those policies that directly apply to their own job. This intranet implementation also provides a key word search mechanism and an index, both of which help readers quickly find policies relevant to their current circumstances. Intranets can also now be used to administer quizzes to ensure that policies were understood.

When more than two audiences will be addressed by separate policy documents, it is recommended that a "coverage matrix" be prepared before actually writing the first draft policy documents. This can be achieved by preparing a separate detailed outline for each of the identified audiences. A coverage matrix is simply an organizational tool to ensure that all the appropriate information security policy messages are presented to all the appropriate audiences. It is a way of looking at the work to be done and can bring order to what otherwise may be a complicated policy writing effort. Once the topics to be communicated have been identified, and organized in a coverage matrix, the preparation of policy documents will be relatively easy and straightforward.

A coverage matrix in its simplest form is a two-dimensional table. It can, for instance, use the primary audiences to which the policies are directed as row identifiers, and policy categories as column headings. These policy categories are the major sections appearing in the above-mentioned high-level outline. The cells in the center of the matrix should be filled with reference numbers, each referring to a policy found in this guide and perhaps elsewhere.

Because there will probably be many columns but only a few rows, a standard coverage matrix with the row headings filled in for audiences, with blank column headings for policy categories, and with blank cells in the middle for specific policies, is recommended. Such a template coverage matrix then can be photocopied many times to save considerable time creating coverage matrices. If seeing only one portion of the coverage matrix at any one moment is acceptable, it is often more time-efficient if a spreadsheet program is used to construct and manipulate a coverage matrix. Use of a spreadsheet program also makes the generation of professional-looking hardcopy easier, just as it makes updates more straightforward.

Often only two or three audiences will be needed. Two possible audiences could be end users and computer-literate technical staff. Using another approach, three possible audiences could be end users, management, and computer support. In almost every instance, there will be a significant amount of overlap in the messages directed to each of these audiences. Make every attempt to minimize the number of audiences while at the same time recognizing the needs of different groups to receive different information.

[Figure 4-11] provides an example of a matrix that can be developed. The policy numbers appearing in this matrix are placeholders and are deliberately not the result of an analysis. Each organization will need to prepare its own coverage matrix, inserting policy numbers in the relevant cells to reflect its own unique business and information systems environment.

If the development of this type of a coverage matrix seems too time-consuming, a similar table using broad categories such as those found in the table of contents to this guide can be prepared.

An alternative approach provides what could be considered a middle ground between a single policy and separate policies for different audiences. In this case, a broad umbrella policy document can apply to all staff, while separate specialized policy documents can be used to address audiences such as information owners, systems developers, telecommuters, and other target audiences. With this approach there is a basic set of rules that applies to everyone, but then there are also special policies that apply only to selected audiences. At larger organizations with intranets, this approach is increasingly common.

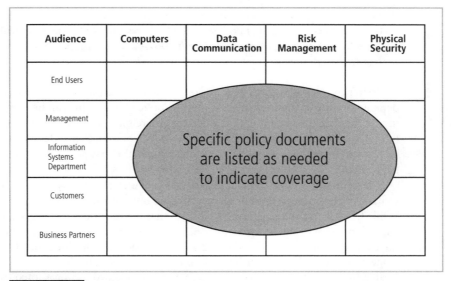

Audience	Computers	Data Communication	Risk Management	Physical Security
End Users				
Management				
Information Systems Department				
Customers				
Business Partners				

Specific policy documents are listed as needed to indicate coverage

FIGURE 4-11 A Sample Coverage Matrix

Source: Charles Cresson Wood. *Information Security Policies Made Easy.* NetIQ Corporation, 2003. http://www.netiq.com/products/pub/ispme.asp.

In an effort to save time, some people often anticipate there will be only one audience. This one-size-fits-all approach may work for the first few policy statements that an organization issues, but the more sophisticated the information security effort, the less applicable this approach will become. It will often save a significant amount of time if the different audiences are targeted from the beginning of a policy writing effort, rather than having to keep modifying a one-size-fits-all policy that was originally intended to meet the needs of multiple audiences. The various audiences will also appreciate the use of separate documents. If separate documents are employed, they will not need to be repeatedly notified about changes that in many cases will not apply to them. The use of separate documents will permit differential treatment without confusion. For example, the rules for third-party access to an organization's information systems can be quite different from the rules for permanent employee access.

Just because there are different audiences for policies does not necessarily imply that there should be different documents. It is possible to have different chapters or sections in an information security manual devoted to different audiences. This approach is attractive because all the policies are then found in one document rather than several. Having all information security policies in a single manual facilitates maintenance and revisions. It is also attractive because individuals often find themselves falling into two or more of the audiences. For example, an individual may be both a general user and a systems developer.

Now the policy numbers should be written directly into the body of the coverage matrix. The process of filling in the body of the coverage matrix often highlights the fact that certain audiences are not being adequately addressed, just as it often indicates that certain areas need additional policies to be truly responsive to the organization's needs. If outlines for policy documents to different audiences were prepared, but no coverage matrix was used, these discrepancies may not have been revealed.

[…]

After the overall topics to be covered have been clarified through a coverage matrix, a detailed outline of the soon-to-be-prepared policy documents can be compiled. Depending on the management at the organization, there may be a need to get interested parties to review a detailed outline. If no such review is required, then a detailed outline may not be needed. In this case, using the coverage matrix, the first policy documents can begin to be drafted.

Anyone who noticed a great deal of political uncertainty associated with the policy writing process may wish to prepare a detailed outline and subject it to a review process. While this may delay the process, it ensures that the resulting document is on target and truly responsive to the organization's needs. Where only one audience is being addressed, the coverage matrix can be dispensed with, but a detailed outline is needed. Either a coverage matrix or a detailed outline is important. Without one or the other, weeks of wasted time writing policies on topics that are not needed or not wanted by management are at risk.

At this point, a decision on the categories to be employed in the policy document must be made. The categories in the coverage matrix or the detailed outline will do, although they will often be modified during the subsequent review process. The use of a large number of subtitles is recommended. This will assist readers in their efforts to quickly locate topics of interest. This will permit readers to skip sections that do not pertain to them.

In those cases where a very large policy document is being developed, or if a significant amount of complexity must be addressed in the policy document, a mind map can be used. Mind maps are graphical representations of the relationships between ideas. They generally use circles to represent ideas and arrows to represent the relationship between ideas. A mind map can be readily converted into a complex outline that can be used to develop a draft policy document. Various guides and software programs are available to assist with the drawing and revision of mind maps.

After the policy writing process is complete, the coverage matrix, outlines, and related working papers should be saved. In a year or two a revised policy document will probably be needed. It will save a lot of time if the person writing revised policies can consult the original working papers. The coverage matrix and related working papers may also serve as important information in a court case, should there ever be any allegations that management did not seriously think about the risks and the policy messages that needed to be communicated.

Similarly, the working papers should be retained for a year or two because internal and external auditors may wish to review them. Having the working papers in an accessible storage location can also be important if a member of the management team claims that his or her comments were not integrated into the final draft policy document.[16]

Making Critical Systems Design Decisions

Before a final version of a policy document can be published, management often needs to make a number of security-related systems design decisions. Examples of these decisions include the:

- Groups of users [who] will be given Internet access.
- Frequency that they will need access, whether continuous, regular, or occasional.
- Type of access they will need, whether electronic mail, Web surfing, file transfer, remote logon, or chat rooms.
- Type of access control, whether dynamic passwords, fixed passwords, or smart cards.
- Types of user activity that will be monitored, whether files transferred, Web sites visited, or hours per day of usage.

Identification of these and other systems design decisions is ordinarily indirect. Typically a draft policy document that incorporates a number of suggested options will be prepared. Unfortunately, in an effort to expedite the policy writing process, alternative solutions are not highlighted. As a result, management may approve of a policy document incorporating decisions with far-reaching implications, many of which were unappreciated at the time of the approval. This may lead to excessive costs for information security as the initial approaches described in the policy document soon need to be replaced or revised. It may also mean that the policy document needs to be changed much sooner than it otherwise would be.

If the project schedule and resources permit, the fundamental systems design decisions should be highlighted. If a paper draft of the policy is going to be circulated for comment, this could be accomplished by using footnotes or endnotes that describe the options and the pros and cons of each. Wording reflecting the different design decisions can be incorporated into the body of the draft document. Seeing the options in context will often help management make these decisions. If the draft policy is going to be placed on an intranet server with restricted access to selected interested parties, certain words can be highlighted and links can be used to illuminate options and supporting justifications.

In organizations that have been attending to information security for some time, management will have already seriously considered all the necessary fundamental systems design options. In these cases, a policy writing effort will simply involve documenting the decisions already made, and choosing appropriate ways to express these decisions in the form of policies. In these cases, there will be no need for a separate review of the critical systems design issues as discussed above. Instead, the focus can be on the extension of these existing design decisions to new information systems such as extranets, and to new technologies such as new programming languages.[17]

Structuring Review, Approval, and Enforcement Processes

Once the first draft of the information security policy document has been written, a few colleagues should review [it]. After the changes are made in response to feedback from these colleagues, the policy document should be sent to interested internal parties such as Internal Audit management and the Intellectual Property attorney. After a few critical allies have made changes, it is ready for review by the Information Security management committee. The next release of the draft can involve distribution to a much larger body of interested parties—for example, all information owners and all people employed in

Information Systems. This review process is advisable because it builds on support from critical players, pre-selling the document to these critical players, and building support from these same critical players.

Many review cycles, each with more changes to the policy document, are often necessary. This should be viewed as standard procedure, and should in no way be taken as a personal insult. Multiple reviews are in part a reflection of the fact that the information security policy development process is highly political, emotionally charged, and highly unstructured. Input should be welcomed with an appreciation that this iterative review process makes the policies more clear, concise, and responsive to prevailing conditions. Two appendices to this guide provide additional information on this process. For more information, see "Checklist of Steps in the Policy Development Process" [below].

The final step in the review process is the signature of the general manager, president, chief executive officer, or chairman of the board. A brief message indicating that compliance is expected as a condition of continued employment should be found on the first page of a policy document, or the opening Web page if the policy is posted on an intranet server. This message should be signed by the top executive in a readily visible place so that the reader can have no doubt that the policy document is strongly supported by top management. If there is no realistic chance of getting the chief executive involved, the signature of the chief information officer may suffice. Settling for the approval of a middle-level manager is not recommended. The signature of Information Security management is generally insufficient to show top management adoption and support. While obtaining top management approval may sound like unnecessary marketing, experience has shown that a top management signature and accompanying message about expected compliance is critical to widespread adoption. Before management approves a policy document, it should already have been reviewed and edited several times by various parties within the organization. Perhaps the most desirable review body is an information security management committee.

An information security management committee is generally composed of representatives from departments within the organization who are interested in information security. Participants include members from the Information Security, Internal Audit, Risk Management, Physical Security, Information Systems, Human Resources, Legal, Finance, and Accounting departments, and various user departments. Such a committee typically oversees the work of the Information Security department. This management committee is used to filter and refine proposed policies, procedures, organizational structures, and other information security initiatives so that they will be readily adopted and implemented throughout the organization. In most cases, Information Security management will write a draft version of an information security policy, then submit it to the management committee for review and approval. If the organization does not yet have a management committee, development of an information security policy is an excellent time to propose the formation of such a committee. The committee is generally made up of five to eight individuals who have relevant expertise, who view themselves as influential in the information security area, and who can represent their own department or area of expertise. For more information about such a committee, see *Information Security Roles and Responsibilities Made Easy.* [...]

In some cases, a separate information security policy development committee is formed. Such a committee could be formed regardless of the existence of an information security management committee. This development committee may be a subcommittee of the management committee. If a development committee is created, it should not actually write the policy. Policies written by committees are often a combination of inconsistent ideas and poorly organized thoughts that never seem to coherently come together into an integrated and understandable document. Instead, the first draft policy should be written by a single technically competent individual who has good writing skills and is familiar with the organization's business activities. If a single individual, who may be on the development committee, will be responsible for writing the first draft policy, a development committee can be most useful. In this case, the development committee can be used for such things as identifying the topics needing to be addressed, preparing a high-level outline, identifying the ways that the policy will be communicated, and [providing] editing suggestions.

In the absence of either of the two committees mentioned immediately above, special early review cycles with Internal Audit, Human Resources, and Legal management are highly recommended. These departments are important allies of Information Security and will be called upon to enforce an information security policy. If a draft policy does not have the blessings of these departments, it is unlikely to be taken seriously after it is issued. For this reason, some will meet with senior members of these departments prior to writing a first draft policy, just to ensure that everybody is in agreement about what should go into a policy document. Such meetings can take place even though representatives of these departments are found on one or both of the two committees previously mentioned.

While preparing new information security policies, an adequate enforcement process must exist or soon will exist. If policies cannot be enforced they will, in all probability, not be effective. To have policies that are not enforced may be worse than not having policies at all. This is because the policies may teach workers hypocrisy and tolerance for inappropriate behaviors. Having policies that are not enforced may also lull management into thinking that information security problems have been addressed when the reality is something else.

Management often believes that workers will naturally behave in a manner that is in the best interests of the organization. This is a dangerous and ill-advised assumption. Although policies are unlikely to affect the personal values of workers, management uses policies to give workers the opportunity to conduct themselves in a manner consistent with organizational values. Policies tell workers what is expected of them—that is, if they want to continue their employment. Assuming there will always be a variance between personal values and organizational values, policies will be taken seriously only if effective compliance mechanisms are in place.

In advance of the issuance of new policies, ways to achieve compliance should be discussed with the Internal Audit or Information Technology Audit department. These might include compliance-checking tools such as software license management systems. Also consider the difficulty and advisability of conducting periodic manual compliance check efforts. The manner and means for the accomplishment of these compliance checks also should be envisioned in advance. Human Resources policies, such as a disciplinary process and an employee performance evaluation process, will need to be discussed in advance of writing policies.

Compliance in many instances can be assisted when computerized tools are used to 141sure agreements (NDAs) can be found on an intranet server accessible to all employees. Whenever an NDA is needed, a user can simply print the relevant form found on this server. The ready availability of tools such as this will help users translate information security policies into action.

Policy enforcement need not be painful. Consider using special procedures to make a point. For example, if confidential information is left on top of a desk, the information can be taken and a receipt provided indicating how the worker can retrieve it. The second time confidential material is left out, the worker and the worker's manager both must retrieve the information. The third time requires the worker, the worker's manager, and a vice president. A fourth time could be reason to discontinue the worker's employment.

Enforcement actions are often more effective if workers are aware of what activities would be information security policy violations, and exactly what penalties would be encountered if they were caught. Establishing clear expectations through an information security awareness program is a very important part of an effective and enforceable set of policies. Such awareness programs might, for example, clearly state that business information is the property of Company X, and that it must not to be copied, modified, deleted, or used for unintended purposes without management approval.

[…] It should not be the intent to catch people and discipline the offending worker. While punishment should be used for offenders as necessary, it is not the intent of enforcement mechanisms to generate large numbers of out-of-compliance notices. If a large number of people are out of compliance, this is an indication that the policies and related awareness programs have been ineffective. In these situations, the intention behind the policies may need to be communicated more effectively, or the policies may need to be modified to better reflect the organizational culture or prevailing operating circumstances.[18]

Checklist of Steps in the Policy Development Process

This checklist is intended to provide a quick overview of the major steps associated with the development, refinement, and approval of an internal information security policy document. For a list of steps to complete after a policy document has been produced, see "Next Steps" [next section]. Many of the following steps can be pursued simultaneously or in an order different than the following:

1. Perform a risk assessment or information technology audit to determine your organization's unique information security needs. These needs must be addressed in a policy document.
2. Clarify what the word "policy" means within your organization so that you are not preparing a "standard," "procedure," or some other related material.
3. Ensure that roles and responsibilities related to information security are clarified, including responsibility for issuing and maintaining policies.
4. Convince management that it is advisable to have documented information security policies.
5. Identify the top management staff who will be approving the final information security document and all influential reviewers.
6. Collect and read all existing internal information security awareness material and make a list of the included bottom-line messages.
7. Conduct a brief internal survey to gather ideas that stakeholders believe should be included in a new or updated information security policy.
8. Examine other policies issued by your organization, such as those from Human Resources management, to identify prevailing format, style, tone, length, and cross-references. The goal is to produce information that conforms with previous efforts.
9. Identify the audience to receive information security policy materials and determine whether [each person will] get a separate document or a separate page on an intranet site.

10. Determine the extent to which the audience is literate, computer knowledgeable, and receptive to security messages. This includes understanding the corporate culture surrounding information security.

11. Decide whether some other awareness efforts must take place before information security policies are issued. For example, one effort might show that information itself has become a critical factor of production.

12. Using ideas from the risk assessment, prepare a list of absolutely essential policy messages that must be communicated. Consult the policy statements as well as the sample policies found in this book.

13. If there is more than one audience, match the audiences with the bottom-line messages to be communicated through a coverage matrix. [...]

14. Determine how the policy material will be disseminated, noting the constraints and implications of each medium of communication. An intranet site is recommended. [...]

15. Review the compliance checking process, disciplinary process, and enforcement process to ensure that they all can work smoothly with the new policy document.

16. Determine whether the number of messages is too large to be handled all at one time, and if so, identify different categories of material that will be issued at different times.

17. Have an outline of topics to be included in the first document reviewed by several stakeholders. An information security management committee is the ideal review board.

18. Based on comments from the stakeholders, revise the initial outline and prepare a first draft. [...]

19. Have the first draft document reviewed by the stakeholders for initial reactions, presentation suggestions, and implementation ideas.

20. Revise the draft in response to comments from stakeholders. Expect this step to [be repeated] several times.

21. Request top management approval on the policy. Changes may be necessary, in which case this step may [be repeated] several times.

22. Prepare extracts of the policy document for selected purposes—for example, for a form signed by users receiving new or renewed user IDs and passwords.

23. Develop an awareness plan that uses the policy document as a source of ideas and requirements.

24. Create a working papers memo indicating the disposition of all comments received from reviewers, even if no changes were made.

25. Write a memo about the project, what you learned, and what needs to be fixed so that the next version of the policy document can be prepared more efficiently, better received by the readers, and more responsive to the unique circumstances facing your organization.

26. Prepare a list of next steps that will be required to implement the requirements specified in the policy document. [These steps] can include the development of an information security architecture, manual procedures documents, and technical information security standards, and acquisition of new products, hiring new technical staff, and other matters.[19]

Next Steps

There are many paths available after an information security policy has been approved. The following list of suggested next steps provides some answers, but it is not intended to provide a comprehensive list of all possible next steps. Each of these suggested next steps are commonly encountered, although not all the items will apply to all organizations. These suggestions should be used as a starting point when creating an information security policy implementation project plan. The suggestions are organized in a rough chronological order, and may be addressed individually. A better alternative would be to pursue several of these steps at the same time in order to make significant progress.

There will typically be many other projects that are initiated as a result of preparing an information security policy document. For example, a policy preparation effort may have illuminated the fact that an existing information security requirement is obsolete. A specific example might involve callback technology for dial-in access to an organization's networks. If this requirement is widely subscribed to within the organization, an effort to adopt a more current alternative may be yet another project to add to a project plan. Continuing with this specific example, dynamic password tokens could be used instead of callback systems.

Post Policies to Intranet or Equivalent—The new document should be placed on the Company X intranet, and links to related documents should be added. Multiple indexes should be prepared so that users can quickly locate material of interest. A key word search facility should be added. Other electronic bulletin board equivalents, such as a Human Resources kiosk, could include the document. [...]

Develop a Self-Assessment Questionnaire—The essential requirements found in the new information security policy document should be extracted and reformatted in the form of a questionnaire. Internal Audit then should issue the questionnaire to department managers. Responses to the questionnaire will highlight those areas where departments are out of compliance and where additional control enhancements are needed. Based on the results of the survey, remedial projects can be proposed. The questionnaire can be used as part of a regular compliance-checking internal audit process. [...]

Develop Revised User ID Issuance Form—A form is used at many organizations as a way to document management approval prior to the issuance of a user ID. [...] A summary of the critical ideas in the new information security policy document should be included as part of this form along with words such as "the user mentioned below has read and agrees to abide by Company X information security policies as a condition of [his or her] continued use of Company X information systems." All new or reissued user IDs should then be enabled only after the form is signed.

Develop Agreement to Comply with Information Security Policies Form—A legal document reflecting an agreement by employees to comply with information security policies should be drafted, edited, and later approved by management. This form should be signed by all workers, or at the very least by all newly hired or retained workers. An awareness program should be initiated to publicize the existence of the new policy document and to get signed forms. [...]

Develop Tests to Determine if Workers Understand Policies—A set of tests or quizzes can be developed to determine if workers understand the essential points covered in an information security policy document. These tests and quizzes can be used to determine what additional training and awareness material needs to be developed and delivered.

The tests and quizzes also can be used as gateways to certain privileges. For example, only after a worker passes a test or a quiz will telecommuting privileges be enabled. [...]

Assign Information Security Coordinators—Many centralized Information Security departments are understaffed and cannot handle all the information security jobs that need to be done. To assist in the implementation of the controls described in the new policy document, decentralized information security coordinators should be assigned. System administrators, systems managers, network managers, and other technical staff often serve in this part-time capacity. Coordinators serve as a local liaison with the central information security group, interpreting policies for a department or division. [...]

Train Information Security Coordinators—Before the information security coordinators can be expected to do substantive work, they should receive a training course. A half-day course should be developed to acquaint them with the requirements defined in the new information security policy document, existing organizational resources, and the best ways to deal with a variety of problems such as power failures, hacker intrusions, and computer virus infections. A handbook for local information security coordinators is also recommended. [...]

Prepare and Deliver a Basic Information Security Training Course—A brief training course should be prepared and presented to all employees at Company X. The policy document can be the primary source of ideas for a training and awareness course. A variety of other material, such as the corporate code of conduct, should also be drawn upon when preparing this course. After this course has been presented several times, it can be revamped, then recorded by videotape or computer-based training software. In some instances, separate audiences may need different training courses. Possible audiences include new hires going through orientation, current employees in need of additional training, system administrators, network administrators, and others likely to be designated as information security coordinators, and systems analysts, application programmers, systems-related project managers, systems quality assurance staff, and other technical staff who will not be serving in an information security coordinator capacity. [...]

Develop Application-Specific Information Security Policies—Certain highly sensitive applications will need additional application-specific policies and procedures. Now that the new information security policy document has been prepared, more detailed policies and related requirements for high-risk application systems should be developed. Certain computing environments, not just applications, such as Internet electronic commerce, may warrant more detailed policies and procedures. The conceptual hierarchy described below can be used to describe the linkage between these application-specific documents and the new information security policy. [...]

Develop a Conceptual Hierarchy of Information Security Requirements—The information security area is complex, and this complexity shows up in various documents that define information security requirements. In many organizations, these include standards, guidelines, policies, procedures, and architectures. A general information security policy document should be at the top of a conceptual hierarchy, with application-related information security policy documents falling underneath. Standards, guidelines, procedures, and other documents should be controlled by the general organization-wide information security policy statement. A conceptual hierarchy should indicate when certain documents apply, which documents take precedence when a conflict exists, and which documents are current or outdated. This conceptual hierarchy will be useful for training and awareness purposes, and can be posted to the Company X information security intranet page. [...]

Assign Information Ownership and Custodianship—Management ownership of specific types of information should be assigned according to the requirements defined in the new information security document. After ownership roles have been assigned, custodianship roles should come next. In many instances, these efforts will be a natural transition to the compilation of a corporate data dictionary, an electronic document management system, or a similar project. [...]

Establish an Information Security Management Committee—To supervise the various information security initiatives now under way, a committee should be formed with middle-level managers from each of the major divisions at Company X. This committee will ensure that current and proposed information security activities are consistent with business objectives. The committee will serve as a sounding board for proposals, prior to presenting these same proposals to top management. The committee ordinarily would meet once a quarter, and would not provide any technical assistance to the Information Security department. [...] A mission statement and related details about such a committee can also be found in the book *Information Security Roles and Responsibilities Made Easy*.

Develop an Information Security Architecture Document—Even though the basic rules for information security are specified in a policy document, in most cases there is a need to put together a grand vision for designing secure systems. The larger an organization, the more the need for a document such as this. Complexity is much more of a problem in these organizations. An architecture should specify the controls that will be used now and in the near future, and provide a plan for the migration to controls to be adopted in the near future. Some organizations also use an architecture document as a place to specify certain approved information security products and vendors. An architecture deals with system interfaces, technical standards, and other more technical considerations than a policy document. [...][20]

Automating Policy Enforcement Through Policy Servers

At many organizations, the complexity of information systems is overwhelming the ability of staff to manage these systems. To deal with this complexity, new expert systems tools are being introduced. For example, some firewalls include an expert system that will tell the person doing the installation whether a configuration inadvertently has created a serious security vulnerability. To deal with this increased complexity, organizations will need to have more centralized network management systems that play an increasing array of information security roles. For example, network management systems can, and in some organizations do, act as a conduit for the relay of intrusion detection information to a network operator on duty.

An interesting new development along these lines is called a policy server. Policy servers take organization-specific policies and code them in a special machine-readable language that then can be accessed by a wide variety of operating systems, access control packages, and network management systems. Examples of these policies or rules include the minimum number of characters in a password, the maximum number of logon attempts before a connection will be severed, and whether attachments to electronic mail files will be passed through firewalls. In many ways a policy server is expected to be like an active data dictionary because it will be called upon to provide definitive instructions from a centralized point. In the near future, suites of products from a single vendor, and suites from a combination of vendors, will start to perform some of the rationalizing and centralizing tasks of a policy server.

To prepare their organizations for these upcoming developments, consideration should be given to how the policies they develop today will be put into the computer models of tomorrow. Attempts should be made to be as logical and straightforward as possible. Not only will this help the readers understand how to behave when it comes to information security, but it will also help tomorrow's programmers in their efforts to create computer-enforced rules. Attempts also should be made to achieve the most cross-organization, cross-network, cross-system, and cross-platform coordination of information security policies. This will also reduce complexity and permit the organization to more readily adopt new policy enforcement tools.[21]

SP 800-18: *Guide for Developing Security Plans for Information Technology Systems Policy Management*

NIST's Special Publication 800-18 reinforces this approach to policy management. Because policies are living documents that constantly change and grow, organizations cannot simply create such an important set of documents and then shelve them. Instead, these documents must be properly disseminated (distributed, read, understood, and agreed to) and managed. Good management practices for policy development and maintenance make for a more resilient organization. For example, all policies, including security policies, undergo tremendous stress when corporate mergers and divestitures occur. In these situations changes happen quickly, and employees suffer uncertainty and are faced with many distractions; these stresses can reveal weaknesses in management of security policies. When two companies come together as one, but still have separate policies, it can be very difficult to implement security controls. Likewise, when one company with unified policies splits into two, the policy needs of both spin-offs change and must be accommodated.

To policies current and viable, there must be an individual responsible for scheduling reviews, defining review practices and procedures, and ensuring that policy and revision dates are present.

Responsible Individual

Just as information systems and information security projects must have a champion and manager, so must policies. The policy champion and manager is called the policy administrator. Typically this person is a mid-level staff member who is responsible for the creation, revision, distribution, and storage of the policy. Note that the policy administrator does not necessarily have to be technically oriented. While practicing information security professionals require extensive technical knowledge, policy management and policy administration require only a moderate technical background. The policy administrator solicits input both from the technically adept information security experts and from the business-focused managers in each community of interest. In turn, he or she notifies all affected members of the organization when the policy is modified.

It is rather disheartening when a policy that requires hundreds of staff-hours of development time is inserted into a three-ring binder and then placed on a manager's bookcase to gather dust. A good policy administrator can prevent this fate by making sure that the policy document and all subsequent revisions to it are appropriately distributed. The policy administrator must be clearly identified on the policy document as the primary contact for providing additional information or suggesting revisions to the policy.

Review Schedule

In a changing environment, policies can retain their effectiveness only if they are periodically reviewed for currency and accuracy, and modified to keep them current. As stated in Chapter 3, to ensure **due diligence**, an organization must demonstrate that it is continually attempting to meet the requirements of the market in which it operates. This applies to both public (government, academic, and nonprofit) and private (commercial and for-profit) organizations. For this reason, any policy document should contain a properly organized schedule of reviews. Typically a policy should be reviewed at least annually. The policy administrator should solicit input from representatives of all affected parties, management and staff, and then use this input to modify the document accordingly.

Review Procedures and Practices

To facilitate policy reviews, the policy administrator should implement a mechanism by which individuals can easily make recommendations for revisions to the policies and other related documentation. Recommendation methods could include e-mail, office mail, or an anonymous drop box. If the policy is controversial, the policy administrator may feel that anonymous submission of information is the best way to determine the suitability of the policy as perceived by employees. Many employees feel intimidated by management and will hesitate to voice honest opinions about a policy in a more open forum.

Once the policy has come up for review, all comments should be examined and management-approved changes should be implemented. Additional review methods could involve including representative users in the revision process and allowing for direct comment on the revision of the policy. In reality, most policies are drafted by a single responsible individual and are then reviewed, or "signed into law," by a higher-level manager. This method should not preclude the collection and review of employee input, however.

Policy and Revision Date

In some organizations, policies are drafted and published without a date, leaving users of the policy unaware of its age or status. This practice can create problems, including legal ones, if employees are "complying" with an out-of-date policy. Such problems are particularly common in a environment that is characterized by high turnover. Ideally, the policy document should include its date of origin, along with the dates, if any, of revisions. Some policies may need a "sunset clause," particularly if they govern information use for a short-term association with second-party businesses or agencies. The inclusion of such an expiration date prevents a temporary policy from becoming a permanent mistake.

A Final Note on Policy

Lest the reader believe that the only reason to have policies is to avoid litigation, it is important to emphasize their preventive nature. Policies exist first and foremost to inform employees of what is and is not acceptable behavior in the organization. Their development is meant to improve employee productivity and to prevent potentially embarrassing situations. In a worst-case scenario, an employee could be fired for failure to comply with a policy. If the organization cannot verify that the employee was in fact properly educated on the policy, as described earlier in the chapter, the employee could sue the organization for wrongful termination. Lawsuits cost money, and the organization could be so financially devastated that it has to go out of business. Other employees will then lose their livelihoods, and no one wins.

In reality, most employees inherently want to do what is right. If properly educated on what is acceptable and what is not, they will choose to follow the rules for acceptable behavior. Most people prefer systems that provide fair treatment. If they know the penalties for failure to comply, no outrage will arise when someone is caught misbehaving and the penalties are applied. Knowing what is prohibited, what the penalties are, and how penalties will be enforced is a preventive measure that should free employees to focus on the business at hand.

Policy represents law applied within the business, with the exception of the legal defense that "what is not prohibited is permitted." While the reverse is true in law, policy must be clear; there is no default of "what is not permitted is prohibited."

THREAT MANAGEMENT

Teardrop Attack

Teardrop is a program that launches a denial-of-service attack on the target system. This hacker tool, which is quite easy for script kiddies (novices with few real computer skills who use scripts written by expert hackers) to use, can be downloaded at any hacker Web site. It works by sending improper IP fragments with improper headers to targeted Windows 95, 98, and NT systems, or Linux boxes.

How a Teardrop Attack Works

Teardrop sends IP packets that have irregular byte numbers, taking advantage of a bug in Windows whereby the system will overlap the improper IP fragments during reassembly. The IP layer in such systems checks for packets that are too long, but not for those that are too short or that are misaligned. A typical IP packet contains a specific number of bytes. These bytes are broken into even parts, so when the IP fragments come in they are typically labeled as bytes 0 to 1023, bytes 1024 to 2047, and bytes 2048 to 3071. The Teardrop program sends bytes with overlapping positions—for example, 0 to 1200, 800 to 2200, and 1900 to 3071. The overlapping packets cause problems in the memory stack: When the stack gets such a fragment, it allocates memory for the fragment and inserts an end pointer for the stack. The IP layer then allocates memory for the next fragment, which is supposed to be the same size as the first fragment. The IP layer expects the second fragment to start at the end pointer. In a proper IP reassembly operation, the needed memory is equal to the end address of the packet thus far, minus the offset for the new fragment; the result should be larger than zero. The problem occurs when the second fragment is assembled; the fragment that is overlapped makes a stack that points inside the first stack. The memory pointers adjust to start at the beginning of the second stack, but now the IP address has a memory pointer inside a stack. As a result, the memory calculation is negative. When the system tries to allocate more memory for the next packet, it creates another negative memory calculation, which may crash the system. As more and more overlapping IP packets come into the system, they generate

(continued)

correspondingly more negative memory variables, which causes the system to slow down greatly or crash because of a lack of memory.

Detecting a Teardrop Attack

Finding the sources of forged IP datagrams in a large, high-speed network is difficult due to the design of the IP protocol and the lack of sufficient processing capability in most high-speed, high-capacity router implementations. Hackers can implement Teardrop attacks against large sophisticated sites using resources as limited as a dial-up modem. Detecting such attacks is often a matter of identifying their effects—frequent crashes, or restarts, with no other apparent cause.

Monitoring

Because Teardrop attacks are executed remotely via a connection that utilizes the TCP/IP protocol suite, monitoring the status of the network and server is one of the best ways to detect such attacks. When an attack is in progress, it usually generates a higher than normal volume of traffic on the network. Therefore, one way of monitoring for teardrop attacks is to continuously watch the level of traffic across key segments of the network and compare the observed traffic levels to a baseline.

Responding to a Teardrop Attack

When faced with a Teardrop attack, there is usually little that you can do. Many times the users targeted by such an attack do not recognize what is happening until it is too late. The first indication that something has gone wrong is the appearance of the "blue screen of death"—and the only way to respond to this outcome is to reboot.

Protecting Against Teardrop Attack

There are numerous ways to minimize the likelihood that a Teardrop attack will cripple your network. The first and most important step you can take is to apply any available patches and updates to your servers and applications; then configure your server so that it's secure, and install protective devices such as a firewall. To stay up-to-date about ways to fight attacks, you can join relevant mailing lists, search information from organizations such as CERT, purchase commercial software from companies such as ISS, read magazines, and discuss with other administrators how they protect their systems from various types of attacks.

References:

ftp://ftp.microsoft.com/bussys/winnt/kb/Q154/1/74.TXT
http://advanced.comms.agilent.com/routertester/member/journal/3teardrop.htm
http://www.sans.org/y2k/DdoS.html

Contributed by Lee Burnette, Cecilia Fly, Irfan Ali, and Masato Yoshino.

Chapter Summary

- A quality information security program begins and ends with policy.
- Policy drives the performance of personnel in ways that enhance the information security of an organization's information assets.
- Developing proper guidelines for an information security program is a management problem, not a technical one. The technical aspect of an information security program is merely one part of the entire program and should be dealt with only after management has created relevant policies.
- Although information security policies are the least expensive means of control to execute, they are often the most difficult to implement. Policy controls cost only the time and effort that the management team spends to create, approve, and communicate them, and that employees spend to integrate the policies into their daily activities.
- The information security policy must satisfy several criteria:
- Policy should never conflict with law.
- Policy must stand up in court, when it is challenged.
- Policy must be properly supported and administered.
- Guidelines for the formulation of information security policy are as follows:
- Recognize that all policies must contribute to the success of the organization.
- Management must ensure the adequate sharing of responsibility.
- End users of information systems should be involved in the policy development process.
- A policy is a statement of the organization's position that is intended to influence and determine decisions and actions and that is used to control the actions of people and the development of procedures.
- A policy may be viewed as a set of rules that dictates acceptable and unacceptable behavior within an organization.
- Policies must contain information on what is required and what is prohibited; on the penalties for violating policy; and on the appeal process.
- For a policy to be effective, it must be properly disseminated to those responsible for implementing it.
- Management must define three types of information security policies:
- Enterprise information security program policy, which sets the strategic direction, scope, and tone for all security efforts. The EISP must be based on and must support the organization's vision and mission statement.
- Issue-specific information security policies, which provide guidance to all members of an organization regarding the use of information technology.
- System-specific information security policies, which guide the management and technical specifications of particular technologies and systems.

Review Questions

1. What is information security policy? Why it is critical to the success of the information security program?
2. Of the controls or countermeasures used to control information security risk, which is viewed as the least expensive? What are the primary costs of this type of control?
3. List and describe the three challenges in shaping policy.
4. List and describe the three guidelines for sound policy, as stated by Bergeron and Bérubé.
5. Describe the bull's-eye model. What does it say about policy in the information security program?
6. Are policies different from standards? In what way?
7. Are policies different from procedures? In what way?
8. For a policy to have any effect, what must happen after it is approved by management? What are some ways to accomplish this?
9. Is policy considered static or dynamic? Which factors might determine this status?
10. List and describe the three types of information security policy as described by NIST SP 800-14.
11. For what purpose is an enterprise information security program policy (EISP) designed?
12. For what purpose is an issue-specific security policy (ISSP) designed?
13. For what purpose is a system-specific security program policy (SysSP) designed?
14. To what degree should the organization's values, mission, and objectives be integrated into the policy documents?
15. List and describe four elements that should be present in the EISP.
16. List and describe three purposes that the ISSP serves in the organization.
17. What should be the first component of an ISSP when it is presented? Why? What should be the second major heading, in your opinion? Why?
18. List and describe three common ways in which ISSP documents are created and/or managed.
19. List and describe the two general groups of material included in most SysSP documents.
20. List and describe the three approaches to policy development presented in the text. In your opinion, which is better suited for use by a smaller organization, and why? If the target organization were very much larger, which approach would be superior and why?

Exercises

1. Using the Internet and a browser, go to the International Information Systems Security Certifications Consortium Web site (www.isc2.org) and look for the information security common body of knowledge (CBK). When you review the list of 10 areas in the CBK, is policy listed? Why do you think this is so?
2. Search your institution's intranet or Web sites for its security policies. Do you find an enterprise security policy? What issue-specific security policies can you locate? Are all of these policies issued or coordinated by the same individual or office, or are they scattered throughout the institution?

3. Using the policies you located in Exercise 2, use the framework presented in this chapter and evaluate the comprehensiveness of each policy. Which areas are missing?

4. Using the framework presented in this chapter, draft a sample issue-specific security policy for an organization. At the beginning of your document, describe the organization for which you are creating the policy, and then complete the policy using the framework.

5. Using a Web browser, search for sample security policies. Identify five EISP and five ISSP sample policies, and bring them to class. Compare these with the framework presented in this chapter, and comment on the policies' comprehensiveness.

Case Exercises

Prior to the first meeting of the RWW Enterprise Policy Review Committee, Mike and Iris met in Mike's office to formulate a common IT and Information Security approach to the coming policy review cycle. Here is part of that conversation:

Mike motioned for Iris to sit down, and then said, "You've convinced me that IT and InfoSec policy are tightly integrated, and that InfoSec policy is critical to the enterprise. I would like you to join me as a member of the Enterprise Policy Review Committee. Okay?"

Iris, who knew how important policy was to her program's success, replied, "Sure. No problem."

Mike continued. "Good. We'll work together to make sure the EISP you've drafted gets equal status with the other top-level enterprise policies and that the second-tier issue and third-tier system policies are also referenced in all other top-level policies, especially those of the HR department."

Iris nodded. Mike went on, "I want you to take the current HR policy document binder and make a wish list of changes you need to be sure we get the right references in place. Let me see your HR policy change plan by the end of the week."

1. If the enterprise policy committee is not open to the approach that Mike and Iris want to use for structuring information security policies into three tiers, how should they proceed?

2. Should the CISO (Iris) be assessing HR policies? Why or why not?

Endnotes

1. http://csrc.nist.gov/publications/nistpubs/500-169/sp500-169.txt.
2. Charles Cresson Wood. *Information Security Policies Made Easy,* 9th ed. NetIQ Corporation, 2003: 1.
3. Charles Cresson Wood. Integrated approach includes information security. *Security,* February 2000; 37(2):43–44.
4. F. Bergeron and C. Bérubé. End users talk computer policy. *Journal of Systems Management,* December 1990; 41(12):14–17.
5. Ibid.
6. Charles Cresson Wood. *Information Security Policies Made Easy,* 9th ed. NetIQ Corporation, 2003: 1.
7. Merriam-Webster. Policy. *Merriam-Webster Online.* [Cited 24 June 2002]. Available from the World Wide Web at http://www.m-w.com/cgi-bin/dictionary.
8. Derived from a number of sources, the most notable of which is http://www.wustl.edu/policies/infosecurity.html.
9. Washington State University. *Information Security Policy.* Accessed 4/12/03. http://www.wustl.edu/policies/infosecurity.html.
10. Ibid.
11. Charles Cresson Wood. *Information Security Policies Made Easy,* 9th ed. NetIQ Corporation, 2003: 9.
12. Charles Cresson Wood. *Information Security Policies Made Easy.* NetIQ Corporation, 2003: 1. http://www.netiq.com/products/pub/ispme.asp.
13. Ibid.
14. Ibid.
15. Ibid.
16. Ibid.
17. Ibid.
18. Ibid.
19. Ibid.
20. Ibid.
21. Ibid.

Developing the Security Program

5

IRIS WAS LOOKING OVER THE freshly printed first issue of RWW's information security newsletter when Mike Edwards walked into her office.

"What's new, Iris?" he asked.

"See for yourself!" she replied with a grin, as she handed him her latest completed project.

"Very nice," he commented. "How close are you to publication?"

"We've just put it on the intranet, and we're going to run off a few dozen hard copies for our office. That's your copy."

"Thanks!" he said while he scanned the cover article. "What is this privacy situation all about?"

Mike was referring to the recent state law that mandated very specific definitions and penalties for computer-related crimes such as computer trespassing and theft of computer information. What had caught his attention was the clause providing penalties for the disclosure of some types of personal data such as Social Security numbers and account passwords. The penalties ranged from $500 to $5000 per incident, and even up to a year in jail.

Mike whistled and said, "We need to talk about this issue at the senior staff meeting. We should get the other departments involved to make sure we don't have any problems in complying with this law."

Iris nodded and said, "Maybe someone from corporate legal should be there, too."

"Good idea."

Then Mike asked about the newsletter's listing of information security training sessions. "Where did you get the training staff?" he asked.

"I've been meaning to talk to you about that," Iris said. "I'll teach the classes until my security manager, Tom, can take over. But we should ask the corporate training office about getting some of their staff up to speed on our topics."

"Sounds good. I'll get with Jerry tomorrow after the staff meeting," Mike replied.

LEARNING OBJECTIVES
Upon completion of this material you should be able to:

- Recognize and understand the organizational approaches to information security
- List and describe the functional components of the information security program
- Determine how to plan and staff an organization's information security program based on its size
- Evaluate the internal and external factors that influence the activities and organization of an information security program
- List and describe the typical job titles and functions performed in the information security program
- Describe the components of a security education, training, and awareness program and understand how organizations create and manage these programs

Introduction

Some organizations use the term "security program" to describe the entire set of personnel, plans, policies, and initiatives related to information security. Others may apply the term "information security" to the broader context of corporate or physical security. The term **information security program** is used in this book to describe the structure and organization of the effort that strives to contain the risks to the information assets of the organization.

Organizing for Security

Among the variables that determine how to structure an information security program are organizational culture, size, security personnel budget, and security capital budget. The first and most influential of these variables is the organizational culture. If upper management and staff perceive information security as being a waste of time and resources, the information security program will remain small and poorly supported. Efforts made by the information security staff will be viewed as contrary to the mission of the organization and detrimental to the organization's productivity. Conversely, where there is a strong, positive perception of information security, the information security program is likely to be larger and well supported, both financially and otherwise.

The organization's size and available resources also directly affect the size and structure of the information security program. Organizations with complex IT infrastructures and sophisticated system users are likely to require more information security support. Large, complex organizations may have entire divisions dedicated to information security, including a CISO, multiple security managers, multiple administrators, and many technicians. Such divisions might have specialized staff focusing on specific issues—for example, policy, planning, firewalls, and intrusion detection systems (IDSs). In general, the larger the organization, the larger the information security program. Smaller organizations, by contrast, may have a single security administrator, or they may assign the information security responsibilities to a systems or network administrator.

Another variable is the personnel budget for the information security program. The size of the information security budget typically corresponds to the size of the organization. Although no standard exists for the size of the information security budget and/or the number of security personnel in any given organization, measured industry averages are available. Industry averages vary widely and may be expressed in terms of information security budget per unit of revenue, in terms of information security staff per number of total employees in the organization, or as information security budget per unit of IT budget. Determining the industry average in any given case may be a challenge, but the reality is that regardless of the industry average, it is the management of the particular organization that has the most influence over this variable, for better or worse. In general, security programs are understaffed for the tasks they have been assigned. Top security managers must constantly struggle to create policy and policy plans, manage personnel issues, plan training, and keep the administrative and support staff focused on their assigned responsibilities and tasks. According to the article referenced in the following Offline, "Does Size Matter?,"

> as organizations get larger in size, their security departments are not keeping up with the demands of increasingly complex organizational infrastructures. Security spending per user and per machine declines exponentially as organizations grow, leaving most handcuffed when it comes to implementing effective security procedures.[1]

Office politics, the economy, and budget forecasts are just some of the factors that cause upper management to perform juggling acts with staffing levels. In today's environment, the information security programs in most organizations do not yet receive the support they need to function properly. That situation may change, however, because the current political climate and the many reported events regarding information security breaches are rapidly forcing organizational cultures to view information security as another critical function.

Another important variable is the capital and expense budget for physical resources dedicated to information security. This budget includes allocation of offices, computer labs, and testing facilities, as well as the general information security expense budget. Because the information security staff handle confidential information regarding security plans, policies, structures, designs, and a host of other items, it is prudent to provide this group with its own secured physical resources, including office space.

OFFLINE

Does Size Matter?

While many IT professionals may think they would be better off in the big IT departments of nationally renowned organizations, the fact is they may be better off at a smaller organization. Big organizations have large staffs, full-time and part-time security professionals, and more problems than the typical smaller organization. This section defines small, medium, large and very large organizations, and describes the problems inherent in each and how they are staffed to deal with them.

- The small organization has 10-100 computers. Most small organizations have a simple, centralized IT organizational model, and spend disproportionately more on security, averaging almost 20 percent of the total IT budget. The typical security staff in this organization is usually only one person (the lone ranger!), if in fact there is a full-time security professional. Much more frequently, information security is an additional duty of one of the IT staffers. However, financially the small organizations, including ones with the smallest budgets, spend more per user than medium- and large-sized organizations. "More than two-thirds say all or most of their security decisions are guided by management-approved policies, and 57 percent say that all or most of their responses to incidents were guided by a predefined IR plan."[2]

- The medium-sized organization has 100-1,000 computers, and has a smaller budget (averaging about 11 percent of the total IT budget), about the same security staff, and a larger need than the small organization. The medium-sized organization's security people must rely on help from IT staff to carry out security plans and practices. "Their ability to set policy, handle incidents in a regular manner and effectively allocate resources are, overall, worse than any other group. Considering their size, the number of incidents they recognize is skyrocketing. Some 70 percent of them had damages from security breaches, a 48 percent increase over small organizations."[3]

- The large organization has 1,000 to 10,000 computers. Organizations of this size have generally integrated planning and policy into the organizational culture; "eight in 10 organizations say at least some of their security decisions are guided by them."[4] Unfortunately, the large organization tends to spend substantially less on security (only about 5 percent of the total IT budget on average) creating issues across the organization, especially in the "people" areas.

- The very large organization has more than 10,000 computers, and large information security budgets, which grow faster than IT budgets. However, in these multimillion-dollar security budgets, the average amount per user is still less than in any other type of organization. "Where small organizations spend more than $5,000 per user on security, very large organizations spend about one-eighteenth of that, roughly $300 per user"; or approximately 6 percent of the total IT budget. The very large organization does a better job in the policy and resource management areas, although "only about a third of organizations in this demographic handled incidents according to an IR plan."[5]

Source: Andrew Briney and Frank Prince. Does size matter? *Information Security,* September 2002, 36–54.

Organizing an information security program poses several managerial challenges. Although the size of an organization influences the organization of its information security program, certain basic functions should occur in every organization, and thus these functions should be included in any budget allocation. Table 5-1 outlines the suggested functions for a successful information security program. These functions are not necessarily performed within the information security department, but they must be performed somewhere within the organization.

TABLE 5-1 Functions Needed to Implement the Information Security Program

Function	Description	Comments
Risk Assessment	Evaluates risk present in IT initiatives and/or systems	Identifies the sources of risk and may offer advice on controls that can reduce risk
Risk Management	Implements or oversees use of controls to reduce risk	Often paired with risk assessment
Systems Testing	Evaluates patches used to close software vulnerabilities and acceptance testing of new systems to assure compliance with policy and effectiveness	Usually part of the incident response and/or risk management functions
Policy	Maintains and promotes information security policy across the organization	Must be coordinated with organization-wide policy processes
Legal Assessment	Maintains awareness of planned and actual laws and their impact, and coordinates with outside legal counsel and law enforcement agencies	Almost always external to the information security and IT departments
Incident Response	Handles the initial response to potential incidents, manages escalation of actual incidents, and coordinates the earliest responses to incidents and disasters	Often cross-functional and drawn from multiple departments; should include middle management to manage escalation processes
Planning	Researches, creates, maintains, and promotes information security plans; often takes a project management approach to planning as contrasted with strategic planning for the whole organization	Must coordinate with organization-wide policy processes
Measurement	Uses existing control systems (and perhaps specialized data collection systems) to measure all aspects of the information security environment	Management relies on timely and accurate statistics to make informed decisions

TABLE 5-1 Functions Needed to Implement the Information Security Program (continued)

Function	Description	Comments
Compliance	Verifies that system and network administrators repair identified vulnerabilities promptly and correctly	Poses problems for good customer service because it is difficult to be customer-focused and to enforce compliance at the same time
Centralized Authentication	Manages the granting and revocation of network and system credentials for all members of the organization	Often delegated to the help desk or staffed in conjunction and co-located with the help desk function
Systems Security Administration	Administers the configuration of computer systems, which are often organized into groups by the operating system they run	Many organizations may have originally assigned all security functions to these groups outside of the information security function; this can be a source of conflict when organizations update their information security program
Training	Trains general staff in information security topics, IT staff in specialized technical controls, and internal information security staff in specialized areas of information security, including both technical and managerial topics	Some or all of this function may be carried out in conjunction with the corporate training department
Network Security Administration	Administers configuration of computer networks, often organized into groups by logical network area (i.e., WAN, LAN, DMZ) or geographic location	Many organizations may have originally assigned some security functions to these groups outside of the information security function, which may require close coordination or reassignment
Vulnerability Assessment	Locates exposure within information assets so these vulnerabilities can be repaired before weaknesses are exploited	Sometimes called the penetration testing team or the ethical hacking unit; often outsourced to consultant "tiger teams"

Security in Large Organizations

As observed in the Offline feature, the largest organizations have more than 1000 devices requiring security management.[6] Organizations of this size are likely to be staffed and funded at a level that enables them to accomplish most of the functions identified in Table 5-1. They will often create an internal organization to deal with the specific information security challenges they face. Not surprisingly, the security functions and organizational approaches implemented by larger organizations are as diverse as the organizations themselves. Information security departments in such organizations tend to form and re-form internal groups to meet long-term challenges even as they handle day-to-day security operations. Thus functions are likely to be split into groups in larger organizations; in contrast, smaller organizations typically create fewer groups, perhaps only having one general group representing the whole department.

One recommended approach is to separate the functions into four areas:

1. Functions performed by nontechnology business units outside of the information technology area of management control, such as
   - Legal
   - Training
2. Functions performed by IT groups outside of the information security area of management control, such as
   - Systems security administration
   - Network security administration
   - Centralized authentication
3. Functions performed within the information security department as a customer service to the organization and its external partners, such as
   - Risk assessment
   - Systems testing
   - Incident response
   - Planning
   - Measurement
   - Vulnerability assessment
4. Functions performed within the information security department as a compliance enforcement obligation, such as
   - Policy
   - Compliance
   - Risk management

It remains the CISO's responsibility to see that information security functions are adequately performed somewhere within the organization. As indicated in Figures 5-1 and 5-2, respectively, large and very large organizations typically have dedicated staffs—sometimes large ones—to support the security program. The deployment of full-time security personnel depends on a number of factors, including sensitivity of the information to be protected, industry regulations (as in the financial and health care industries), and general profitability. The more resources the company can dedicate to its personnel budget, the more likely it is to maintain a large information security staff. As shown in Figure 5-1, a typical large organization has on average 1 full-time administrator, 4 full-time administrators/technicians, and as many as 15 part-time staff members, who have information security duties in addition to their duties in other areas.[7] For example, a systems administrator of a Windows 2000 server may be responsible for maintaining both the server and the security applications running on it. The very large organization, as illustrated in Figure 5-2, may have more than 20 full-time security personnel, and 40 or more individuals with part-time responsibilities.[8]

FIGURE 5-1 Information Security Staffing in a Large Organization

FIGURE 5-2 Information Security Staffing in a Very Large Organization

Security in Medium-Sized Organizations

Medium-sized organizations have between 100 and 1000 machines requiring security management.[9] These organizations may still be large enough to implement the multi-tiered approach to security described previously for large organizations, though perhaps with fewer dedicated groups and more functions assigned to each group. In a medium-sized organization, more of the functional areas from Table 5-1 are assigned to other departments within IT, but outside of the information security department. Also, the central authentication function often gets handed off to systems administration personnel within the IT department.

Medium-sized organizations tend to ignore some of the functions from Table 5-1—in particular, when the information security department cannot staff a certain function and the IT or other department is not encouraged or required to perform that function in its stead. In these cases, the CISO must improve the collaboration among these groups, and must provide leadership in advocating decisions that stretch the capabilities of the organization.

As illustrated in Figure 5-3, the full- and part-time staff of the medium-sized organization is dramatically smaller than that of its larger counterparts. This organization may only have one full-time security person, with perhaps three individuals with part-time information security responsibilities.[10]

Security Manager

Security Administrator

Security Technician

1 full-time manager and partial support staff members

FIGURE 5-3   Information Security Staffing in a Medium-Sized Organization

Security in Small Organizations

Smaller organizations—those with fewer than 100 systems to supervise—face particular challenges.[11] Information security in the small organization often becomes the responsibility of a *jack-of-all-trades,* a single security administrator with perhaps with one or two assistants for managing the technical components. It is not uncommon in smaller organizations to have the systems or network administrators play these many roles. Such organizations frequently have little in the way of formal policy, planning, or security measures, and they commonly outsource their Web presence or electronic commerce operations. As a result, the security administrator most often deals with desktop management, virus protection, and local area network security issues.

Because resources in smaller organizations are often limited, the security administrator frequently turns to freeware or *hackerware* to lower the costs of assessing and implementing security. As noted in Chapter 9, these tools can be quite effective in both providing access to otherwise unavailable utilities and lowering the total cost of security.

In small organizations, security training and awareness is most commonly conducted on a one-on-one basis, with the security administrator providing advice to users as needed. Any published policies are likely to be issue-specific policies—for example, on Web and Internet use, and fair-and-responsible use of office equipment. Formal planning, when it happens, is usually part of the IT planning conducted by the Director of Information Systems or CIO.

To their advantage, small organizations avoid some threats precisely because of their size. Hacktivists, hackers, and other threat agents are less likely to go after smaller companies, opting instead to attack larger and more prestigious targets. Of course, it is not wise to gamble the future of the organization on its staying unnoticed. So, to use an old saying "There is no security in obscurity."

Threats from insiders are also less likely in an environment where every employee knows every other employee. In general, the less anonymity an employee has, the less likely he or she feels able to get away with mischief, abuse, or misuse of company assets.

The lack of resources available to the smaller organization's security administrators is somewhat offset by the lower risk of becoming a target. Figure 5-4 shows the challenges faced in smaller organizations, which typically have either one individual who has full-time duties in information security or, more likely, one individual who manages or conducts information security duties in addition to those of other functional areas, most likely IT. This individual may have partial supervision of one or two assistants.[12]

FIGURE 5-4   Information Security Staffing in a Smaller Organization

VIEWPOINT

Developing a Security Program

By Krizi Trivisani, CISSP

Getting started can be the hardest part of any journey—especially if you do not have a clear understanding of where to begin or where are you going. Developing an information

(continued)

security program can be an enormous task, and, as with a journey, it helps to have a map of the territory before you start. But it is important to remember that maps can—and do—change over time; thus your program must have a certain amount of flexibility built in. I like to think of my security architecture as living and breathing, able to adapt and change as threats evolve.

When developing a security program for an organization, it is essential to understand your environment, as it will be the biggest influence on how your program will work. The first question to ask is, "What are you trying to protect?" Identifying the data critical to your company's success—customer, financial, student, medical, and so on—will help you establish the "crown jewels" upon which you will focus your protective efforts.

Keep your organization's mission in mind and develop your security program to support it. For example, a bank may restrict access on a "need to know" basis, whereas a university may encourage full access and sharing across its network, save for a protective layer around the central systems required to manage the university itself. Select a security philosophy that works best at combating the challenges your organization faces.

Don't forget about legislation—the things you are required to do must be included in your plan. An alphabet soup of requirements—HIPAA, FERPA, GLB—is alive and well in security compliance. Make sure you know which ones affect you and take appropriate measures. The excuse "I didn't know we were covered" won't help you in court. Adhering to appropriate industry guidelines will also help you measure and track your program's progress and avoid pitfalls later.

Some organizations still spend more on coffee than they do on security. Completing a risk assessment with a cost-benefit analysis will help you determine where to best apply your scarce resources. The odds are good that you will not have enough money to create one security group that will be responsible for everything. Instead, find out who is doing security-related tasks in the organization and create relationships with them. Often they will be your best advocates, and having representatives from multiple departments will help create widespread security ownership.

Speaking of ownership, who are your stakeholders? Support from upper-level management is crucial to your program's success. The security office must have the proper level of authority and autonomy to protect the crown jewels from threats originating both inside and outside of the organization. Know who the decision makers are, and keep them informed on a regular basis.

Starting a security program also requires a change in culture. Most people resist change, so awareness and involvement should be integral elements in your program. Understand your organization's culture and tailor your efforts appropriately. In addition, look for resources outside of your organization. Some of your best allies may be other people in similar situations. Find other security professionals who are willing to share ideas. Join local chapters and national organizations to network, continue your professional development, and stay abreast of the latest trends.

Sir Winston Churchill once said, "Every day you may make progress. Every step may be fruitful. Yet there will stretch out before you an ever-lengthening, ever-ascending, ever-improving path. You know you will never get to the end of the journey. But this, so far from discouraging, only adds to the joy and glory of the climb."

Krizi Trivisani is the Director of Systems Security Operations and the Chief Security Officer at The George Washington University in Washington, D.C.

Placing Information Security Within An Organization

Although there are other valid models for placing the information security department within an organization, in large organizations this department is often located within the information technology department, headed by the CISO who reports directly to the top computing executive, or CIO. Such a structure implies that the goals and objectives of the CISO and CIO are closely aligned. In reality, this is not always the case. By its very nature, an information security program is sometimes at odds with the goals and objectives of the information technology department as a whole. On the one hand, the CIO, as the executive in charge of the organization's technology, manages the efficiency in the processing and accessing of the organization's information. Anything that limits access or slows information processing directly contradicts the CIO's mission. On the other hand, the CISO functions more like an internal auditor, with the information security department examining existing systems to discover information security faults and flaws in technology, software, and employees' activities and processes. At times, these activities may disrupt the processing and accessing of the organization's information. Because the goals and objectives of the CIO and the CISO may come in conflict, it is not difficult to understand the current movement to separate information security from the IT division.

The vision of separate IT and information security functions is shared by many executives. A 2002 survey conducted by Meta Group found that while only 3% of the consulting firm's clients positioned the information security department outside IT, the clients viewed this positioning as what a forward-thinking organization should do. The article "Where the Chief Security Officer Belongs" perhaps states this point more succinctly: "The people who do and the people who watch shouldn't report to a common manager."[13]

The challenge is to design a reporting structure for the information security program that balances the competing needs of each of the communities of interest. In many cases, the unit that executes the information security program is shoehorned into the organizational chart in a way that reflects its marginal status, and it may be shuffled from place to place within the organization with little attention being paid to how such organizational moves hinder its effectiveness. Organizations searching for a rational compromise will attempt to find a place for the information security program that allows it to balance policy enforcement with education, training, awareness, and customer service needs. This approach can help make information security part of the organizational culture.

There are many ways to position the information security program within an organization. In his book *Information Security Roles and Responsibilities Made Easy,* Charles Cresson Wood has compiled many of the best practices on information security program positioning from many industry groups. His chapter covering this topic, "Reporting Relationships," has been condensed here with his permission.

This [area] covers the generally accepted and frequently encountered reporting relationships for an Information Security Department. The pros and cons of twelve options are explored and six reporting relationships are recommended. Because there are many places in the organizational hierarchy where an Information Security Department could be situated, you should review the list of pros and cons for each option, thinking about what is most important in your organization. [...] You should then summarize these considerations in a memo, and after this memo is prepared, you will most likely be leaning in the direction of one of these reporting relationships. At that point in time, a clear and well-justified proposal for an Information Security Department reporting relationship can be formulated.

[…] In successful organizational structures, the Department reports high up in the management hierarchy. Reporting directly to top management is advisable for the Information Security Department Manager [or CISO] because it fosters objectivity and the ability to perceive what's truly in the best interest of the organization as a whole, rather than what's in the best interest of a particular department (such as the Information Technology Department). A highly placed executive in charge of information security will also be more readily able to gain management's attention, and this in turn will increase the likelihood that the Information Security Department will obtain the necessary budget and staffing resources. An Information Security Department that reports high up on the management ladder will also be more readily able to force compliance with certain requirements, such as a standard specifying consistent implementation of certain encryption technology.

In a few progressive organizations, being located high on the management ladder means that the Information Security Department Manager is a Senior Vice President who reports directly to the Chief Executive Officer (CEO). This is, for example, the organizational structure now found at a well-known credit card company. Having an Information Security Manager who reports directly to the CEO may also be appropriate for a short while until major improvements in the information security area have been made. This temporary reporting structure clearly communicates that information security is important and worthy of top management's attention.

Nonetheless, for a medium- to large-scale organization, the most common reporting structure involves one or two levels of management between the Information Security Department Manager and the CEO. In general, the smaller the number of intermediate levels of management, the greater the strategic importance of the information security function. It is important that the distance between the CEO and the Information Security Manager be minimized. […]

[…] If you are establishing an information security function for the first time, or if a major reorganization is under way, you should seriously think about which middle managers would best serve as the conduit for messages sent to the CEO. Other desirable attributes are:

- Openness to new ideas
- Clout with top management
- Respect in the eyes of a wide variety of employees
- Comfort and familiarity with basic information systems concepts
- Willingness to take a stand for those things that are genuinely in the long-term best interest of the organization

The ideal middle-level manager should report directly to the CEO, or as high up on the organizational hierarchy as possible. The manager's organizational unit will also need a credible day-to-day relationship with, or a strategic tie-in with, the information security function. For example, a Risk and Insurance Management Department would have such a tie-in, but an Assembly Line Operations Department most often would not. The candidates are many, but some common choices are the Executive Vice President Administrative Services, the Legal Department Manager (Chief Legal Officer), and the Chief Information Officer (CIO).

This [section] makes reference to six [figures that illustrate] Options 1 through 6. These six reporting relationships are explored in that sequence. After that, six other options, which are not as frequently encountered, are discussed. The six [figures] are illustrative of real-world organizations and are not in any way meant to be hypothetical or normative. Throughout [...] I have attempted to be descriptive rather than to propose a new paradigm, and in that respect, because these options are based on real-world experience, you can be assured that any one of these six initial options could be effective within your organization. The [figures] are also meant to convey an indication of good practice on which you can rely.

Option 1: Information Technology

In [Figure 5-5], you will note that in this organizational structure the Information Security Department reports to the Information Technology Department. [...] Here the Information Security Department Manager reports directly to the Chief Information Officer (CIO), or the Vice President of Information Systems. In this option, you will find the most common organizational structure. Various statistical studies show that over 50% of organizations use this reporting relationship. This option is desirable because the manager to whom the Information Security Department Manager reports generally has clout with top management, and understands (in broad and general terms) the information systems technological issues. This option is also advantageous because it involves only one manager between the Information Security Department Manager and the Chief Executive Officer (CEO). The option is additionally advisable because the Information Security Department staff, on a day-to-day basis, must spend a good deal of time with the Information Technology Department staff. In that respect, this option is convenient. Nonetheless, this option is flawed because it includes an inherent conflict of interest. When confronted with resource allocation issues, or when required to strike a trade-off, the CIO is likely to discriminate against the information security function. Other objectives such as cost minimization, user friendliness, or time-to-market with a new product or service will likely take precedence over information security. Another drawback of this option involves the implied conclusion that information security is strictly a technological issue, which clearly it is not. Although common, this organizational structure is not as desirable as several of the other options, and for that reason is not particularly recommended.

Note that [Figure 5-5] does not have information security reporting to a Computer Operations Manager, the Management Information Systems Manager, the Information Resources Manager, or some other manager who in turn reports to the CIO or the Vice President of Information Systems. This one additional level of middle management can make a world of difference for the Information Security Department. The CIO is dealing with the business uses of information systems—for example, using these systems to achieve strategic advantage. At the same time, the Computer Operations Manager is dealing with the bits and bytes of everyday computer operations and related technical matters. The CIO is more removed from the technology and is therefore better able to make appropriate trade-offs between security and competing objectives like response time. But, because that's what he or she knows and is measured by, the Computer Operations Manager in many cases will favor response time, ease of use, and other technical objectives rather than information security. Having an additional level of management also increases the likelihood that messages sent from the Information Security Department to the CEO will be corrupted in transit (the "whisper down the lane" problem). Other reasons not to pursue this organizational structure are covered below in "Option 8: Help Desk."

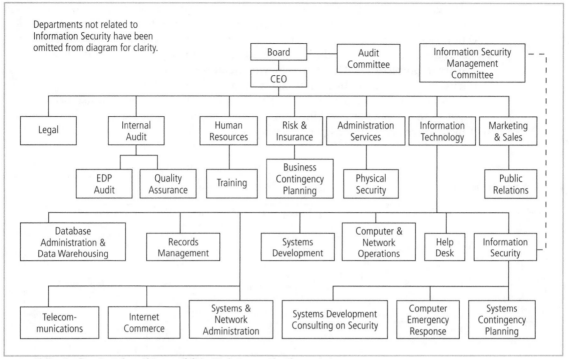

Departments not related to Information Security have been omitted from diagram for clarity.

From *Information Security Roles and Responsibilities Made Easy*, used with permission.

FIGURE 5-5 Wood's Option 1: Information Security Reports to Information Technology Department

In [Figure 5-5], you should note that the Information Security Department Manager also has a dotted-line reporting relationship with the Information Security Management Committee. Although they are highly recommended, both this dotted-line relationship and the Committee can be omitted for smaller organizations. A Committee of this nature is a good idea because it provides a sounding board, a management direction-setting body, and a communication path with the rest of the organization. A mission statement for this Committee can be found [in the book *Information Security Roles and Responsibilities Made Easy*]. Because this Committee is relevant no matter where the Information Security Department reports, it has been shown on all six [figures]. In fact, this Committee is relevant to every one of the options described in this chapter. A drawback of using a committee like this is that it may take longer to get management approval for certain initiatives, but the approval that is obtained is likely to be more lasting and more widely distributed throughout the organization.

Option 2: Security

Another popular option, which again is not necessarily recommended, involves the Information Security Department reporting to the Security Department. In this case, the information security function is perceived to be primarily protective in nature, and therefore comparable to the Physical Security Department as well as the Personnel Security and Safety Department. Where this organizational design prevails, you may occasionally find the Information Security Department is instead referred to as the Information Protection Department. Shown in [Figure 5-6], this approach is desirable because it facilitates communication with others who have both a security perspective and related security responsibilities. This may help with incident investigations as well as reaching practical solutions to problems like laptop computer theft (which involves a combination of physical and information security). This option is also desirable because it brings a longer-term preventive viewpoint to information security activities, which in turn is likely to lower overall information security costs.

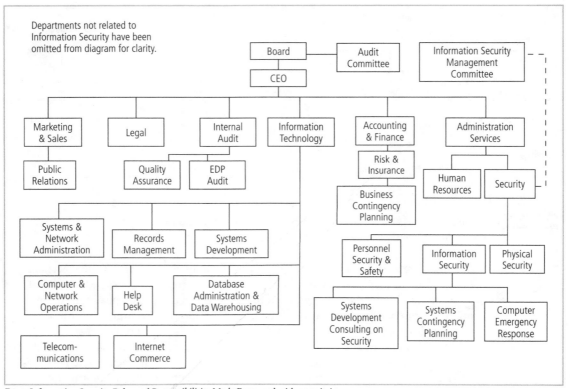

From *Information Security Roles and Responsibilities Made Easy,* used with permission.

FIGURE 5-6 Wood's Option 2: Information Security Reports to Broadly Defined Security Department

Nonetheless, there are some problems with this structure. Although the information security and physical security functions may at first seem to be philosophically aligned, there is a significant cultural difference between the two. For example, information security staff see themselves as high-tech workers, while physical security staff see themselves as participants in the criminal justice system. These cultural differences may cause some information security specialists to feel that it's not appropriate to be managed by a specialist in physical security, which will most often be the background of the Security Department Manager. This option is moreover undesirable because, at most firms, the budget for physical security has not increased much over the last few years, but the budget for information security has rapidly escalated; by combining these two departments under the Security Department umbrella, top management may underestimate the resources that the information security function will need. Option 2 is furthermore undesirable because the Security Department Manager will often lack an appreciation of information systems technology, and so may be a poor communicator with top management. This option is furthermore ill advised because it involves two middle managers in the communication path between the Information Security Department Manager and the CEO. To make it still less appealing, this option is likely to indirectly communicate that the Information Security Department is a new type of police; this perspective will make it more difficult for the Information Security Department to establish consultative relationships with other departments. On balance, this organizational structure is acceptable, but not as desirable as some of the other diagrams described.

Option 3: Administrative Services

Another way to do things, which is a significant improvement over both Option 1 and 2, is shown in [Figure 5-7]. Here the Information Security Department reports to the Administrative Services Department (which may also be called Administrative Support). In this case, the Information Security Department Manager reports to the Administrative Services Department Manager or the Vice President of Administration. This approach assumes that the Information Security Department is advisory in nature (also called a *staff function*), and performs services for workers throughout the organization, much like the Human Resources Department. This option is desirable because there is only one middle manager between the Information Security Department Manager and the CEO. The approach is also advisable because it acknowledges that information and information systems are found everywhere throughout the organization, and that workers throughout the organization are expected to work with the Information Security Department. This option is also attractive because it supports efforts to secure information no matter what form it takes (on paper, verbal, etc.), rather than viewing the information security function as strictly a computer- and network-oriented activity.

In many cases, depending on who fills the Administrative Services Vice President position, this option suffers because the Vice President doesn't know much about information systems technology, and this in turn may hamper his or her efforts to communicate with the CEO about information security. This option may also be ill advised for those organizations that could severely suffer, or even go out of business, if major information security problems were encountered. An Internet merchant (a "dot-com" firm) fits this billing. For these firms, this option doesn't give information security the prominence it deserves, nor does it give it the strategic and long-term focus that information security requires. Thus, with this option, the Information Security Department may be subject to more cost-cutting pressure from top management than it would with Option 4 or 5. On balance, though, for organizations that are not highly information intensive, such as a chain of restaurants, this is a desirable and recommended option.

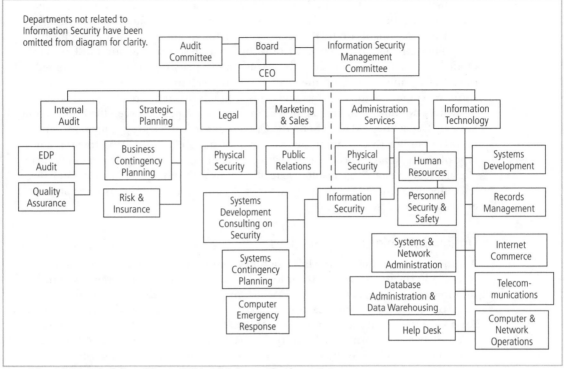

Departments not related to Information Security have been omitted from diagram for clarity.

From *Information Security Roles and Responsibilities Made Easy*, used with permission.

FIGURE 5-7   Wood's Option 3: Information Security Reports to Administrative Services Department

Option 4: Insurance and Risk Management

[Figure 5-8] shows how the Information Security Department can report to the Insurance and Risk Management Department. With this approach, the Information Security Department Manager would typically report to the Chief Risk Manager (CRM) or the Vice President of Risk and Insurance Management. This option is desirable because it fosters what is often called an integrated risk management perspective. With this viewpoint, a centralized perspective prioritizes and compares all risks across the organization. The application of this idea typically involves assessing the extent of potential losses and the likelihood of losses across all functional departments, including Information Security, Physical Security, Legal, Internal Audit, Customer Relations, Accounting and Finance, etc. The intention is to see the big picture and be able to allocate resources to those departments and risk management efforts that most need these resources. You are strongly urged to foster the integrated risk management viewpoint, even if the current or proposed organizational structure doesn't reflect it, because information security will often be shown to be a serious and largely unaddressed problem area deserving greater organizational resources and greater management attention. Beyond integrated risk management, this option is desirable because it involves only one middle manager between the Information Security Department Manager and the CEO.

The CRM is also likely to be prevention oriented, adopt a longer-term viewpoint, and is able to engage the CEO in intelligent discussions about *risk acceptance* (doing nothing), *risk mitigation* (adding controls), and *risk transfer* (buying insurance). A CRM is also likely to be comfortable thinking about the future and generating scenarios reflecting a number of different possibilities, including information security scenarios such as a denial-of-service (DoS) attack. The CRM, however, is often not familiar with information systems technology, and so may need some special coaching or extra background research from the Information Security Department Manager to make important points with the CEO. Another problem with this approach is that its focus is strategic, and the operational and administrative aspects of information security (such as changing privileges when people change jobs) may not get the attention that they deserve from the CRM. Nonetheless, on balance this is a desirable option and is recommended for organizations that are information intensive, such as banks, stock brokerages, telephone companies, and research institutes.

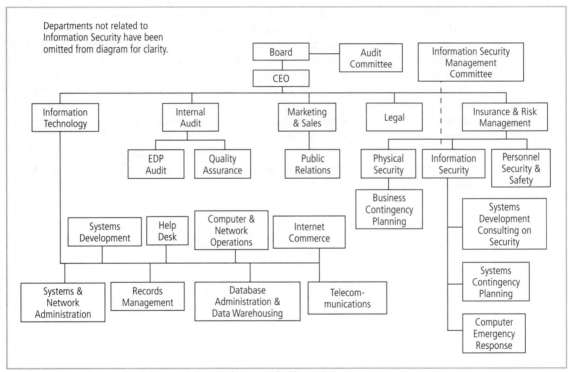

From *Information Security Roles and Responsibilities Made Easy*, used with permission.

FIGURE 5-8   Wood's Option 4: Information Security Reports to Insurance and Risk Management Department

Option 5: Strategy and Planning

In [Figure 5-9], you will find still another possible organizational structure found in the real world. Here the Information Security Department reports to the Strategy and Planning

Department. In this case, the Information Security Department Manager reports directly to the Vice President of Strategy and Planning. This option views the information security function as critical to the success of the organization. This option would be appropriate for an Internet merchant (a "dot-com" enterprise) or a credit card company, both of which are critically dependent on the success of the information security function. This option is desirable because it involves only one middle manager between the Information Security Department Manager and the CEO. It is thus just one step down from the option mentioned at the beginning of this chapter, where the Senior Vice President of Information Security reports directly to the CEO.

Option 5 is desirable because it underscores the need for documented information security requirements (policies, standards, procedures, etc.) that apply to the entire organization. Like Options 3 and 4, this reporting structure also acknowledges the multi-departmental and multidisciplinary nature of information security tasks such as risk analysis and incident investigations. This option is also advisable because the Information Security Department works with others that share a scenario-oriented view of the world (they often ask "what if..." questions). Another desirable aspect of this approach is that it implicitly communicates that information security is very importantly a management and people issue, not just a technological issue.

This same advantage can be a disadvantage if workers in the Information Technology Department consider the staff in the Information Security Department to be management oriented, and out of touch when it comes to the technology (of course, the work of the Information Security Department can clearly communicate that this is a misperception). One problem with this approach is that the focus is strategic, and the operational and administrative aspects of information security (such as changing privileges when people change jobs) may not get the attention that they deserve from the Vice President of Strategy and Planning. On balance, though, this is an advisable reporting relationship for the information security function, and should be something that the Information Department Manager is considering for the long run even if he or she is not proposing it today.

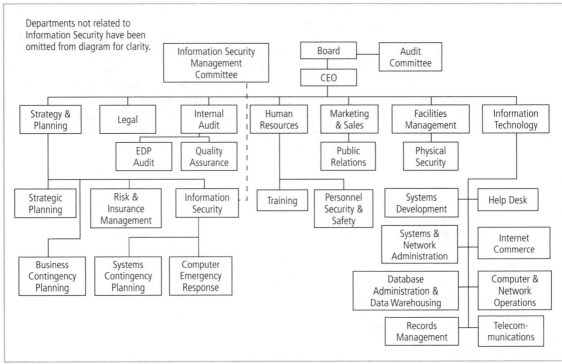

Departments not related to Information Security have been omitted from diagram for clarity.

From *Information Security Roles and Responsibilities Made Easy*, used with permission.

FIGURE 5-9   Wood's Option 5: Information Security Reports to Strategy and Planning Department

Option 6: Legal

[Figure 5-10] shows an unusual but nonetheless viable and recommended organizational structure. In this case the Information Security Department reports to the Legal Department. This option correctly emphasizes that information is the asset of primary concern, not information systems. This option thus places great emphasis on copyrights, patents, trademarks, and related intellectual property protection mechanisms. As they should, contracts—such as nondisclosure agreements (NDAs) and outsourcing agreements—will also get great attention with this organizational structure. With this option there is also great emphasis on compliance with laws, regulations, and ethical standards (like privacy). Information security is increasingly mandated by law, regulated, and affected by ethical standards, so Option 6 is really an organizational structure for the future. If your organization happens to be in a highly regulated industry, such as credit bureaus or defense contractors, then this organizational structure could be appropriate today. This option is desirable because access to top management is provided through only one middle manager—the Legal Department Manager, sometimes called the Chief Legal Officer (CLO). This manager is often quite articulate and credible and often a desirable carrier of Information Security Department messages to the CEO. This reporting structure is also advisable because the members of the Legal Department are comfortable with, and spend a lot of time developing, documentation such as policies and procedures; and documentation showing that the organization is in compliance with the information security standard of due care is increasingly important.

On the downside of Option 6 is the potential overemphasis on compliance, with the potential consequential underemphasis on other aspects of information security, such as access control administration. This organizational structure might also inadvertently lead to the Information Security Department doing compliance checking work, which presents a clear conflict of interest (as explained in "Option 7: Internal Audit"). Compliance checking should be performed by an Internal Auditing Department, not the Information Security Department. On balance, though, this organizational structure has much to recommend it, and will probably be encountered in an increasing number of organizations in the years ahead.

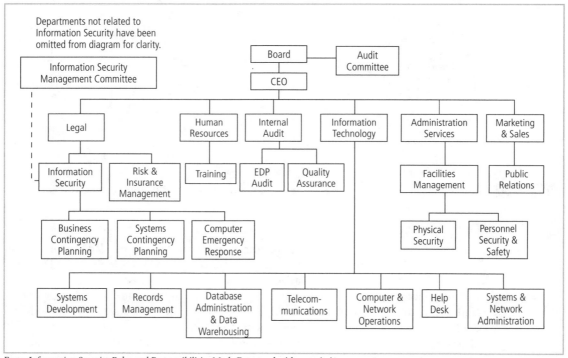

From *Information Security Roles and Responsibilities Made Easy*, used with permission.

FIGURE 5-10 Wood's Option 6: Information Security Reports to Legal Department

Option 7: Internal Audit

Although I have seen it in the real world, the Information Security Department should definitely not report to the Internal Audit Department. This is why you will not find a diagram for this option. In this case, the Information Security Department Manager reports to the Internal Auditing Department Manager. An examination of the mission statement for the Internal Audit Department [...] reveals that Internal Audit is charged with reviewing the work done by other units, including the Information Security Department. If the Information Security Department were to report to the Internal Audit Department, a conflict of interest would exist. Internal Audit would be tempted to exaggerate the good work of the Information Security Department so that the Internal Audit Department as a whole would look good. A controls-oriented Chief Internal Auditor may also be tempted to allocate more resources to an Information Security Department than are realistically warranted, and this in turn could create an undue security burden for the rest of the organization as well as a backlash that could take years to overcome. Reporting to the Internal Audit Department may also be contraindicated because Internal Audit often has adversarial relationships with other departments, and the perspectives that go along with those relationships could be unwittingly transferred to relationships between the Information Security Department and other departments. To foster smooth working relationships, an Information Security Department should instead be considered advisory in nature, and not a new type of auditor. The Internal Audit Department Manager may also lack sufficient technical expertise to understand what the Information Security Department is doing, and this may make it hard to convey messages from the Information Security Department Manager to the CEO. On the other hand, one advantage of reporting to the Internal Audit Department is that the Internal Audit Department Manager has a controls perspective and will at least in theory support what an Information Security Department is trying to do. Another reason in favor of reporting to Internal Audit is the tremendous clout that this group has with top management and the Board of Directors. Nothing in this paragraph is meant to discourage the Information Security Department from establishing a close and mutually beneficial working relationship with an Internal Audit Department, and such a good working relationship is characteristic of firms with successful information security efforts.

Just because there is no direct reporting relationship to EDP Audit (or Internal Audit for that matter) doesn't mean it isn't a good idea to have a dotted-line reporting relationship to the Audit Committee on the Board of Directors. This dotted-line relationship is intended to be a periodic reporting relationship as well as a safety valve. Information Security can provide quarterly reports about the status of information security to the Audit Committee. If the Committee doesn't like what they are hearing, they can then redirect the efforts of top managers. Likewise, if top management is relatively unreceptive to the Information Security Department's point of view, Information Security can take its concerns to the Audit Committee. This dotted-line reporting relationship doesn't currently exist in many organizations, but there are many efforts now under way to establish this type of relationship. Because it's unusual, this dotted-line relationship has been deliberately omitted from the six diagrams that go along with this chapter.

Option 8: Help Desk

Another option involves having the Information Security Department report to the Help Desk Department. In this case, the Information Security Department Manager reports to the Help Desk Department Manager. As is the case with reporting into the Internal Audit Department, this option was not presented in a diagram because it is not advised. A Help Desk Department is a lower-level technical group that does not get much top management attention or respect. Likewise, the Help Desk Department generally does not command many resources, and this scarcity of resources may be carried over into the Information Security Department. If the Information Security Department reported to the Help Desk Department, there would be at least two levels of middle management between the Information Security Department Manager and the CEO, and this could further hinder the acquisition of adequate resources. Another reason not to establish an organizational structure like this involves the Help Desk Department's customer focus and service orientation. While this may at first be perceived to be a desirable characteristic, it may also force the Information Security Department to opt for quick response, ease of use, and other objectives besides a high level of security. It could, nonetheless, be advantageous to report to the Help Desk Department in terms of mobilization after a break-in, for example, when it comes time to get a computer emergency response team (CERT) into action. This is because a Help Desk Department is on the front lines, and is often first to hear about a problem. This reporting structure could also be beneficial because the Help Desk Department's trouble ticket system could be directly tied into logs of information security problems. Analysis of these logs could provide the Information Security Department with important insight into problems as they are occurring. On balance, though, this reporting relationship, like reporting relationships to other lower-level departments, is strongly discouraged. Similar remarks could be offered for organizational designs involving the reporting of an Information Security Department into other subgroups within the Information Technology Department. Examples include the Computer Operations Department, the Systems Development Department, and the Records Management Department.

Option 9: Accounting and Finance Through IT

Another option involves the Information Security Department reporting to the Accounting and Finance Department through the Information Technology Department. This option is not recommended and is therefore not shown in a diagram. This very traditional organizational structure is a reflection of the early days of information systems where, at least in the commercial world, the computer was applied largely to accounting and finance tasks. The uses of computers and networks have expanded dramatically over the last few decades, and so the Information Technology Department should report higher in the organizational ladder, not through the Accounting and Finance Department. This option is undesirable for the reasons mentioned under "Option 1: Information Technology" (notably trade-offs with competing objectives). This option is furthermore undesirable because the Information Security Department would be buried deep in the organizational hierarchy, and would be therefore unlikely to get the resources and top management attention that it needs. While the Information Security Department is a staff (advisory service) department like the Accounting & Finance Department, it is growing much more rapidly than the Accounting and Finance Department. Integration with the Accounting and Finance Department may thus conceal this rapid growth rate from top management, which in turn could lead to underfunded information security efforts. Reporting to the Accounting and Finance Department may also cause the needs of the Information Security Department to be lost within, and overshadowed by, the needs of the Accounting and Finance Department. If the Information Security Department is combined with other activities in the Accounting and Finance Department, top management is likely to see the information security function as a back-office operation, and not a strategic issue worthy of top management attention. Reporting through the Accounting and Finance Department appears to some people to be advisable because the Accounting and Finance Department Manager is controls-oriented, but this in many cases does not compensate for the other deficiencies. In fact, reporting to the Accounting and Finance Department may put additional pressure on an Information Security Department to cut costs, a move that would pay off in the short run but that could spell serious problems in the long run.

Option 10: Human Resources

Still another possibility for the Information Security Department is reporting to the Human Resources Department. [...] There is a certain synergy that could be achieved when the Information Security Department is part of the Human Resources Department; this comes from both groups developing policies that must be followed by workers throughout the organization. For example, the Human Resources disciplinary process is used to deal with those who are not in compliance with information security policies. If the Human Resources Department also handles the staff training function, this synergy can be magnified. Nonetheless, this is generally considered an ill-advised organizational position for the Information Security Department because the Human Resources Department Manager often knows very little about information systems, and is therefore most often not a credible conduit for communications to top management. [...]

Option 11: Facilities Management

Yet another option for the Information Security Department involves reporting to the Facilities Management Department (sometimes called Buildings and Grounds). Since this option is not recommended, no diagram has been provided. This is a rare but occasion-ally encountered organizational structure that views the information security function as something similar to the building guards who help prevent burglary. With this organiza-tional structure, the Information Security Department is seen by top management as an asset protection function much like the Physical Security Department. [...]

Option 12: Operations

Under this approach, the Information Security Department Manager reports to the Chief Operating Officer (COO). This approach assumes that information security is a line management responsibility, and a topic that all department managers must consider in their day-to-day activities. While it is desirable to emphasize management's responsibili-ties, it is also true that information security is a staff function, a function that provides advice and guidance to other departments. [...]

Summary of Reporting Relationships

The Information Security Department at many organizations has been an unwelcome stepchild, handed back and forth between various groups, none of which felt as though they were its proper home. [...]

Smaller organizations will want to have a part-time Information Security Coordina-tor or Information Security Manager. [...] Small to medium-sized organizations will often require at least one full-time person, and medium-sized to large organizations will often require several full-time information security staff. [...] Since so few people are involved, in smaller organizations, the formal designation of a separate department will be considered to be unwarranted. But for all other organizations, no matter where the information security function happens to report, it is desirable to designate a separate department that has been formally recognized by top management. [...][14]

Components of the Security Program

The information security needs of any organization are unique to the culture, size, and budget of that organization. Determining what level the information security program operates on depends on the organization's strategic plan, and in particular on the plan's vision and mission statements. The CIO and CISO should use these two documents to formulate the mission statement for the information security program. Some guidance concerning the formulation of mission statements is provided by Charles Cresson Wood:

> A mission statement is a brief statement of objectives that describes what top management expects from the involved organizational unit. Although a broad-brush overview of activities is often helpful in a mission statement, specifics about these activities should instead appear in [associated] job description[s]. A mission statement should deal with a whole department or similar multi-person organizational unit, and should not talk about the objectives for a specific job title. [...] Likewise, a mission statement should not use any technical language, acronyms, or other jargon that will not be immediately understood by non-technical workers or top management.[15]

Two documents from the National Institute of Standards and Technology (NIST) also provide guidance for developing an information security program. The first is SP 800-14, *Generally Accepted Principles and Practices for Securing Information Technology Systems.* This document

> ...gives a foundation that organizations can reference when conducting multi-organizational business as well as internal business. Management, internal auditors, users, system developers, and security practitioners [sic] can use the guideline to gain an understanding of the basic security requirements most IT systems should contain. The foundation begins with generally accepted system security principles and continues with common practices that are used in securing IT systems.[16]

The second, and perhaps more important, NIST publication is SP 800-12, *An Introduction to Computer Security: The NIST Handbook.* This manual "provides a broad overview of many of the core topics included in computer [and information] security to help readers understand their computer security needs and develop a sound approach to the selection of appropriate security controls."[17] This handbook includes sections covering many topics, including the following:

- The elements of computer security
- Roles and responsibilities
- Common threats
- Common information security controls
- Risk management
- Security program management
- Contingency planning

Table 5-2 summarizes the essential program elements presented in these two NIST documents.

TABLE 5-2 Elements of a Security Program

Primary Element	Components
Policy	Program Policy, Issue-Specific Policy, System-Specific Policy
Program Management	Central Security Program, System-Level Program
Risk Management	Risk Assessment, Risk Mitigation, Uncertainty Analysis
Life-Cycle Planning	Security Plan, Initiation Phase, Development/Acquisition Phase, Implementation Phase, Operation/Maintenance Phase
Personnel/User Issues	Staffing, User Administration
Preparing for Contingencies and Disasters	Business Plan, Identify Resources, Develop Scenarios, Develop Strategies, Test and Revise Plan
Computer Security Incident Handling	Incident Detection, Reaction, Recovery, and Followup
Awareness and Training	SETA plans, Awareness Projects, and Policy and Procedure Training
Security Considerations in Computer Support and Operations	Help Desk Integration, Defending Against Social Engineering, and Improving System Administration
Physical and Environmental Security	Guards, Gates, Locks and Keys, and Alarms
Identification and Authentication	Identification, Authentication, Passwords, Advanced Authentication
Logical Access Control	Access Criteria, Access Control Mechanisms
Audit Trails	System Logs, Log Review Processes, and Log Consolidation and Management
Cryptography	TKI, VPN, Key Management, and Key Recovery

Source: National Institute of Standards and Technology. *Generally Accepted Principles and Practices for Securing Information Technology Systems.* NIST Publication 800-14. http://csrc.nist.gov/publications/nistpubs/800-14/800-14.pdf.

There is much overlap between the elements of Table 5-2 and the earlier list of functions of an information security program given in Table 5-1. Both resources should be used when reviewing the components of any specific information security program.

Information Security Roles and Titles

A study of information security positions by Schwartz, Erwin, Weafer, and Briney found that positions can be classified into one of three types: those that *define,* those that *build,* and those that *administer.*

Definers provide the policies, guidelines, and standards. [...] They're the people who do the consulting and the risk assessment, who develop the product and technical architectures. These are senior people with a lot of broad knowledge, but often not a lot of depth. Then you have the builders. They're the real techies, who create and install security solutions. [...] Finally, you have the people who operate and administrate the security tools, the security monitoring function, and the people who continuously improve the processes. [...] What I find is we often try to use the same people for all of these roles. We use builders all the time [...] If you break your InfoSec professionals into these three groups, you can recruit them more efficiently, with the policy people being the more senior people, the builders being more technical, and the operating people being those you can train to do a specific task.[18]

A typical organization has a number of individuals with information security responsibilities. While the titles used within any specific organization may be different from one organization to the next, most of the job functions fit into one of the following categories:

- Chief Information Security Officer (CISO)
- Security managers
- Security administrators and analysts
- Security technicians
- Security staffers
- Security consultants
- Security officers and investigators
- Help desk personnel

Each of these positions is discussed briefly here and more fully in Chapter 10.

Chief Information Security Officer

The CISO is primarily responsible for the assessment, management, and implementation of the program that secures the organization's information. This position may also be called the Manager for Security, the Security Administrator, or a similar title. The CISO usually reports directly to the CIO, although in larger organizations one or more layers of management may separate the two officers. Figure 5-11 shows that the CISO is the senior-most information security role.

Security Managers

Security managers are accountable for the day-to-day operation of the information security program. They accomplish objectives identified by the CISO, to whom they report as shown in Figure 5-11, and resolve issues identified by technicians, administrators, analysts, or staffers whom they supervise. Managing technology requires an understanding of it, but not necessarily a technical mastery in its configuration, operation, and fault resolution. Within the information security community, some team leaders or project managers may be responsible for management-like functions, such as scheduling, setting priorities, or administering any number of procedural tasks, but are not necessarily held accountable for making a particular technology function. The accountability for the actions of others is the hallmark of a true manager. The accountability found in true management roles can be used to differentiate between actual managers and other roles that may include the word "manager" in their job titles but, in fact, do not have such accountability.

FIGURE 5-11   Information Security Roles

Security Administrators and Analysts

The security administrator is a hybrid of a security technician (see the following section) and a security manager (described in the previous section). Such individuals have both technical knowledge and managerial skill. They are frequently called upon to manage the day-to-day operations of security technology, as well as to assist in the development and conduct of training programs, policy, and the like.

The security analyst is a specialized security administrator. In traditional IT, the security administrator corresponds to a systems administrator or database administrator, and the security analyst to a systems analyst. The systems analyst, in addition to performing his or her security administration duties, must analyze and design security solutions within a specific domain (firewall, IDS, antivirus program). Systems analysts must be able to identify users' needs and to understand the technological complexities and capabilities of the security systems they design.

Security Technicians

Security technicians are the technically qualified individuals who configure firewalls and IDSs, implement security software, diagnose and troubleshoot problems, and coordinate with systems and network administrators to ensure that security technology is properly implemented. A security technician is usually an entry-level position; some technical skills are required, however, which can make it difficult for those new to the field. It is difficult to get a job without experience, and experience comes with a job.

Just as in networking, security technicians tend to be specialized, focusing on one major security technology group (firewalls, IDSs, servers, routers, or software), and further specializing in one particular software or hardware package within that group, such as Checkpoint firewalls, Nokia firewalls, or Tripwire IDS. These technologies are sufficiently complex to warrant a high level of specialization. Security technicians who want to move up in the corporate hierarchy must expand their technical knowledge horizontally, gaining an understanding of the general, organizational issues of information security as well as all technical areas.

Security Staffers

"Security staffer" is a catchall title that applies to the individuals who perform routine watch-standing activities. It encompasses the people who watch intrusion consoles, monitor e-mail accounts, and perform other routine, yet critical roles that support the mission of the information security department.

Security Consultants

The information security consultant is typically an expert in some aspect of information security (disaster recovery, business continuity planning, security architecture, policy development, or strategic planning). He or she is usually brought in when the organization makes the decision to outsource one or more aspects of its security program. While it is usually preferable to involve a formal security services company, qualified individual consultants are available for hire.

Security Officers and Investigators

Occasionally, the physical security and information security programs are blended into a single organization. When that occurs, a series of roles are added to the combined program, including the roles of security officers and investigators. These roles are associated with what is known as the guards, gates, and guns (GGG) type of security.

Help Desk Personnel

An important part of the information security team is the help desk, which enhances the security team's ability to identify potential problems. When a user calls the help desk with a complaint about his or her computer, the network, or an Internet connection, the user's problem may turn out to be related to a bigger problem, such as a hacker, denial-of-service attack, or a virus.

Because help desk technicians perform a specialized role in information security, they have a need for specialized training. These staff members must be prepared to identify and diagnose both traditional technical problems and threats to information security. Being able to do so may cut precious hours off of an incident response.

Implementing Security Education, Training, and Awareness Programs

Once the information security program's place in the organization is established, planning for **security education, training, and awareness (SETA)** programs begins. The SETA program is the responsibility of the CISO and is designed to reduce the incidence of accidental security breaches by members of the organization, including employees, contractors, consultants, vendors, and business partners who come into contact with its information assets. As mentioned in Chapter 2, *acts of human error or failure* (known generally as *errors*) are among the top threats to information assets.

Awareness, training, and education programs offer two major benefits:

- They can improve employee behavior.
- They enable the organization to hold employees accountable for their actions.

Employee accountability is necessary to ensure that the acts of an individual do not threaten the long-term viability of the entire company. When employees recognize that the organization protects itself by enforcing accountability, they will be less likely to view these programs as punitive. In fact, when an organization does not enforce accountability, it increases the risk of incurring a substantial loss that might cause it to go out of business, putting the entire workforce out of jobs.

SETA programs enhance general education and training programs, by focusing on information security. For example, if an organization finds that many employees are using e-mail attachments in an unsafe manner, then those e-mail users must be trained or retrained. As a matter of good practice, all systems development life cycles include user training during both their implementation and their maintenance phases. Information security projects are no different; they require initial training programs as systems are deployed and occasional retraining as needs arise.

A SETA program consists of three elements: security education, security training, and security awareness. An organization may not be able or willing to undertake all of these components in-house and instead may outsource them to local educational institutions. The purpose of SETA is to enhance security in three ways:

- By building in-depth knowledge, as needed, to design, implement, or operate security programs for organizations and systems
- By developing skills and knowledge so that computer users can perform their jobs while using IT systems more securely
- By improving awareness of the need to protect system resources[19]

Table 5-3 shows the features of security education, training, and awareness within the organization.

TABLE 5-3 Framework of Security Education Training and Awareness

	Awareness	Training	Education
Attribute	"What"	"How"	"Why"
Level	Information	Knowledge	Insight
Objective	Recognition	Skill	Understanding
Teaching Method	Media • Videos • Newsletters • Posters, Inc.	Practical Instruction • Lecture • Case study workshop • Hands-on practice	Theoretical Instruction • Discussion seminar • Background reading
Test Measure	True/False Multiple Choice (identify learning)	Problem Solving (apply learning)	Eassay (interpret learning)
Inpact Timeframe	Short-term	Intermediate	Long-term

Source: National Institute of Standards and Technology. *An Introduction to Computer Security: The NIST Handbook.* SP 800-12. http://csrc.nist.gov/publications/nistpubs/800-12/.

Security Education

Some organizations may have employees within the information security department who are not prepared by their background or experience for the information security roles they are intended to play. When tactical circumstances allow and/or strategic imperatives dictate, these employees may be encouraged to use a formal education method. Resources that describe information security training programs include the NIST training and education site at http://csrc.nist.gov/ATE/training_&_education.html, the Virginia Alliance for Security Computing and Networking (VA SCAN) at http://www.vascan.org/training.html, and the National Security Agency (NSA)–identified Centers of Academic Excellence in Information Assurance Education (CAEIAE) at http://www.nsa.gov/isso/programs/nietp/newspg1.htm. Local resources might also provide information—for example, Kennesaw State's Center for Information Security Education and Awareness (http://infosec.kennesaw.edu).

Information security training programs must address the following issues:

- The information security educational components required of all *information security* professionals
- The general educational requirements that all *information technology* professionals must have

A number of institutions of higher learning, including colleges and universities, provide formal coursework in information security. Unfortunately, a recent review of such institutions offering formal programs in information security or computer security found that the majority of those granting degrees (bachelor's or master's) were, in reality, providing computer science or information systems degrees that included a few courses in information security. While some programs do offer depth and breadth in information security education, prospective students must carefully examine the curriculum before enrolling. Those planning for careers in information security should carefully review the number of courses offered, as well as the content of those courses.

The general IT educational curriculum needs to prepare students to work in an environment that values a secure and ethical computing environment. As noted by Irvin, Chin, and Frinke in the article "Integrating Security into the Curriculum,"

> An educational system that cultivates an appropriate knowledge of computer security will increase the likelihood that the next generation of IT workers will have the background needed to design and develop systems that are engineered to be reliable and secure.[20]

The need for improved information security education is so great that President Clinton issued Presidential Decision Directive 63, the Policy on Critical Infrastructure Protection, in May 1998. Among other things, it required the NSA to establish outreach programs like the CAEIAE. The CAEIAE program goal is "to reduce vulnerabilities in our National Information Infrastructure by promoting higher education in information assurance, and producing a growing number of professionals with IA expertise."[21] These initiatives are intended to increase not only the number of information security professionals, but also the information security awareness and educational knowledge of all technologists.

Developing Information Security Curricula

One reason that hybrid information technology/security programs have emerged is to fill the gap created by the lack of formal guidance from established curricula bodies. Established organizations that have developed and promoted standardized curricula, such as the Association of Computing Machinery (ACM), the Institute of Electrical and Electronics Engineers (IEEE), and the Accreditation Board for Engineering and Technology (ABET), do not have formal information security curricula models. For two-year institutions, however, the National Science Foundation (NSF) and the American Association of Community Colleges sponsored a workshop in 2002 that drafted recommendations for a report entitled *The Role of Community Colleges in Cybersecurity Education.* This report serves as a starting point for community colleges developing curricula in the field. A similar effort is currently under way for four-year institutions, but remains in its infancy.

Any institution designing a formal curriculum in information security must carefully map the expected learning outcomes of the planned curriculum to course learning objectives to establish the body of knowledge to be taught. This knowledge map, which can help potential students assess information security programs, identifies the skills and knowledge clusters obtained by the program's graduates. Graduate-level programs are more complex, and possibly more managerial in nature, depending on the program. For the undergraduate level, program planners examine the areas that graduates are expected to work in, and then define the required skills and knowledge.

Creating a knowledge map can be difficult because many academics are unaware of the numerous subdisciplines within the field of information security, each of which may have different knowledge requirements. For example, a student wanting a more managerial focus needs to be educated in policy, planning, personnel administration, and other relevant topics, and thus would want to take courses like the ones for which this textbook is written. In contrast, a student whose interests are more technical would want courses in specific hardware areas such as Windows Network Security, firewalls and IDSs, or remote access and authentication.

Because many institutions have no frame of reference for which skills and knowledge are required for a particular job area, frequently they refer to the certifications offered in that field (certification is discussed in Chapter 10). A more managerial program would examine certifications like the CISSP, CISM, or GISO; a more technical program would examine the specific GIAC or Security+ certifications. A balanced program takes the best of both programs and then maps the knowledge areas from each specialty area backward to specific courses.

Figure 5-12 shows the complex process of mapping information security positions to the roles that an individual performs and the corresponding core knowledge requirements of those roles. These roles (defined earlier) must then be carefully mapped to the role's required knowledge domains. For example, a CISO may need to have a working understanding of all knowledge areas, while a firewall administrator may need true expertise in only one or two areas. The depth of knowledge is indicated by a level of mastery using an established taxonomy of learning objectives or a simple scale such as "understanding → accomplishment → proficiency → mastery."

FIGURE 5-12 Information Security Knowledge Map

Once the knowledge areas are identified, common knowledge areas are aggregated into teaching domains, from which individual courses can be created. Courses should be designed so that the student can obtain the required knowledge and skills upon completion of the program. For example, in a program for firewall administrators, an introductory class (to supply understanding) might be followed by a technical security class (to supply accomplishment), which might be followed by a firewall administration class (to supply proficiency and mastery).

The final step is to identify the prerequisite knowledge for each class. Figure 5-13 provides examples of increasingly more technical classes with their knowledge areas and prerequisite requirements.

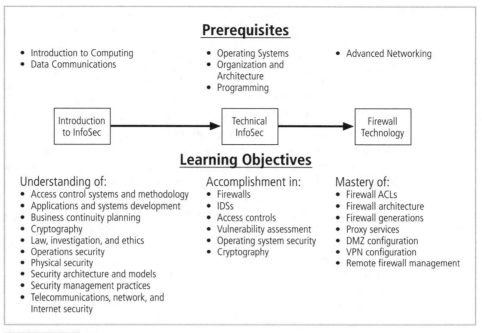

FIGURE 5-13   Technical Course Progression

Security Training

Security training involves providing members of the organization with detailed information and hands-on instruction to enable them to perform their duties securely. Management of information security can wither develop customized in-house training or outsource all or part of the training program.

As an alternative to in-house or outsourced formal training programs, organizations can subsidize or underwrite industry training conferences and programs offered through professional agencies such as SANS (www.sans.org), ISC² (www.isc2.org), ISSA (www.issa.org), and CSI (www.gocsi.org). Many of these programs are too technical for the average employee, but they may be ideal for the continuing education requirements of information security professionals.

A number of resources can help organizations put together SETA programs. The Computer Security Resource Center at NIST, for example, provides several very useful documents free of charge in its special publications area (http://csrc.nist.gov).

Among the most useful of these documents for information security practitioners and those developing training programs is NIST SP 800-16. This 188-page manual with extensive appendices describes training with an emphasis

> on training criteria or standards, rather than on specific curricula or content. The training criteria are established according to trainees' role(s) within their organizations, and are measured by their on-the-job performance. This emphasis on roles and results, rather than on fixed content, gives the Training Requirements flexibility, adaptability, and longevity…[22]

This approach makes the document a durable and useful guide. Although it is directed toward federal agencies and organizations, its overall approach applies to all kinds of organizations:

> Federal agencies and organizations cannot protect the integrity, confidentiality, and availability of information in today's highly networked systems environment without ensuring that each person involved understands their roles and responsibilities and is adequately trained to perform them.[23]

The Computer Security Act of 1987 requires federal agencies to provide mandatory periodic training in computer security awareness and accepted computer practices to all employees involved with the management, use, or operation of their computer systems. Other federal requirements for computer security training are contained in OMB Circular A-130, Appendix III, and OPM regulations.

Training is most effective when it is designed for a specific category of users. The more closely the training is designed to match the specific needs of the users, the more effective it is. Training includes teaching users not only what they should or should not do, but also how they should do it.

There are two methods for customizing training for users. The first is by functional background: general user, managerial user, and technical user. The second is by skill level: novice, intermediate, and advanced. Because traditional training models are accustomed to using skill level as course customization criteria, the more detailed discussion that follows focuses on the development of training by functional area.

Training for General Users

One method of ensuring that policies are read and understood by general users is to provide training on those policies. This strategy allows users to ask questions and receive specific guidance, and it allows the organization to collect the required letters of compliance. These general users also require training on the technical details of how to do their jobs securely, including good security practices, password management, specialized access controls, and violation reporting.

A convenient time to conduct this type of training is during employee orientation. During this critical time, employees are educated on a wide variety of organizational policies and on the expectations that the organization has for its employees. Because employees should have no preconceived notions or established methods of behavior at that point, they are more likely to be receptive to this instruction. This openness is balanced against their lack of familiarity with the systems or their jobs, so any particular issues that they might have questions about will not have arisen yet.

Training for Managerial Users

Management may have the same training requirements as the general user, but managers typically expect a more personal form of training, characterized by smaller groups and more interaction and discussion. In fact, managers often resist organized training of any kind. This is another area in which a champion can exert influence. Support at the executive level can convince managers to attend training events, which in turn reinforces the entire training program.

Training for Technical Users

Technical training for IT staff, security staff, and technically competent general users is more detailed than general user or managerial training, and may therefore require the use consultants or outside training organizations. There are three methods for selecting or developing advanced technical training:

- By job category—for example, technical users versus managers
- By job function—for example, accounting versus marketing versus operations functional areas
- By technology product—for example, e-mail client, database

Training Techniques

Good training techniques are as essential to successful training as thorough knowledge of the subject area. As explained by Charles Trepper in his article "Training Developers More Efficiently,"

> Using the wrong method can actually hinder the transfer of knowledge and lead to unnecessary expense and frustrated, poorly trained employees. Good training programs, regardless of delivery method, take advantage of the latest learning technologies and best practices. Recent developments include less use of centralized public courses and more on-site training. Training is often needed for one or a few individuals, not necessarily for a large group. Waiting until there is a large-enough group for a class can cost companies lost productivity. Other best practices include the increased use of short, task-oriented modules and training sessions, available during the normal work week, that are immediate and consistent. Newer concepts in training also provide students with the training they need when they need it—a practice often called just-in-time training.[24]

Delivery Methods

Selection of the training delivery method is not always based on the best outcome for the trainee. Often other factors—most usually budget, scheduling, and needs of the organization—come first. Table 5-4 lists the most common delivery methods.

TABLE 5-4 Training Delivery Methods

Method	Advantages	Disadvantages
One-on-One: A dedicated trainer works with each trainee on the areas specified.	<ul><li>Informal</li><li>Personal</li><li>Customized to the needs of the trainee</li><li>Can be scheduled to fit the needs of the trainee</li></ul>	Resource intensive, to the point of being inefficient
Formal Class: A single trainer works with multiple trainees in a formal setting.	<ul><li>Formal training plan, efficient</li><li>Trainees can learn from each other</li><li>Interaction with trainer is possible</li><li>Usually considered cost-effective</li></ul>	<ul><li>Relatively inflexible</li><li>May not be sufficiently responsive to the needs of all trainees</li><li>Difficult to schedule, especially if more than one session is needed</li></ul>

TABLE 5-4 Training Delivery Methods (continued)

Method	Advantages	Disadvantages
Computer-Based Training (CBT): Prepackaged software that provides training at the trainees workstation.	■ Flexible, no special scheduling requirements ■ Self-paced, can go as fast or as slow as the trainee needs ■ Can be very cost-effective	■ Software can be very expensive ■ Content may not be customized to the needs of the organization
Distance Learning/Web Seminars: Trainees receive a seminar presentation at their computers. Some models allow teleconferencing for voice feedback; others have text questions and feedback.	■ Can be live, or can be archived and viewed at the trainee's convenience ■ Can be low- or no-cost	■ If archived, can be very inflexible, with no mechanism for trainee feedback ■ If live, can be difficult to schedule
User Support Group: Support from a community of users is commonly facilitated by a particular vendor as a mechanism to augment the support for products or software.	■ Allows users to learn from each other ■ Usually conducted in an informal social setting	■ Does not use a formal training model ■ Centered on a specific topic or product
On-the-Job Training: Trainees learn the specifics of their jobs while working, using the software, hardware, and procedures they will continue to use.	■ Very applied to the task at hand. ■ Inexpensive	■ A sink-or-swim approach ■ Can result in substandard work performance until trainee gets up to speed
Self-Study (Noncomputerized): Trainees study materials on their own, usually when not actively performing their jobs.	■ Lowest cost to the organization ■ Places materials in the hands of the trainee ■ Trainees can select the material they need to focus on the most ■ Self-paced	■ Shifts responsibility for training onto the trainee, with little formal support

Selecting the Training Staff

To provide employee training, an organization can use a local training program, a continuing education department, or another external training agency. Alternatively, it can hire a professional trainer, a consultant, or someone from an accredited institution to conduct on-site training. It can also organize and conduct training in-house using its own employees. This last option should not be undertaken without careful consideration. A special set of skills and abilities are required to conduct effective training. Teaching a class of five or more peers (or subordinates) is very different than offering friendly advice to coworkers. The former effort may require the hiring of individuals with training experience.

Implementing Training

While each organization develops its own strategy based on the techniques discussed above, the following seven-step methodology generally applies:

Step 1: Identify program scope, goals, and objectives.
Step 2: Identify training staff.

Step 3: Identify target audiences.

Step 4: Motivate management and employees.

Step 5: Administer the program.

Step 6: Maintain the program.

Step 7: Evaluate the program.

This methodology, and the material that follows, is drawn from the previously referenced NIST document, *SP 800-12 An Introduction to Computer Security: The NIST Handbook.*

Identify Program Scope, Goals, and Objectives The scope of the security training program should encompass all personnel who interact with computer systems. Because users need training that relates directly to their use of particular systems, an organization-wide training program may need to be supplemented by more specific programs targeted at specific groups. Generally, the goal of a security training program is to sustain an appropriate level of protection for computer resources by increasing employee awareness of, and ability to fulfill, computer security responsibilities. More specific goals may need to be established as well. Objectives should be defined to meet the organization's specific goals.

Identify Training Staff Whether the trainer is an in-house expert or a hired professional, the organization should carefully match the capabilities of the training to the needs of the class. It is also vital that the trainer knows how to effectively communicate information and ideas.

Identify Target Audiences A security training program that distinguishes between groups of people, presents only the information needed by the particular audience, and omits irrelevant information yields the best results. In larger organizations, some individuals will fit into more than one group. In smaller organizations, it may not be necessary to draw distinctions between groups.

You can divide employees into groups for training by the following methods:

- Segment according to level of awareness. Separating individuals into groups according to level of awareness may require research to determine how well employees follow computer security procedures or understand how computer security fits into their jobs.
- Segment according to general job task or function. Individuals may be grouped as data providers, data processors, or data users.
- Segment according to specific job category. Many organizations assign individuals to job categories. As each job category generally has different job responsibilities, training for each will necessarily be different. Examples of job categories include general management, technology management, applications development, and security.
- Segment according to level of computer knowledge. Computer experts may find a program containing highly technical information more valuable than one covering management issues in computer security. Conversely, a computer novice would benefit more from a training program that presents fundamentals.
- Segment according to types of technology or systems used. Security techniques used for each off-the-shelf product or application system usually vary. The users of major applications normally require training specific to that application.

Motivate Management and Employees To successfully implement an awareness and training program, it is important to gain the *support* of both management and employees. For this reason, consideration should be given to using motivational techniques as part of the SETA program. Motivational techniques should demonstrate to management and employees how participation in the security training program benefits the organization. To motivate managers, for example, make them aware of the potential for losses and the role of training in computer security. Employees must understand how computer security benefits them and the organization and how it relates to their jobs.

Administer the Program Several important considerations apply when administering the security training program:

- Visibility. The visibility of a security training program plays a key role in its success. Efforts to achieve a highly prominent place in the organization should begin during the early stages of security training program development.

- Training methods. The methods used in the security training program should be consistent with the material presented and should be tailored to the specific audience's needs. Some training and awareness methods and techniques were listed earlier in the "Training Techniques" section.

- Training topics. Topics should be selected based on the audience's requirements.

- Training materials. In general, higher-quality training materials are more favorably received, but are more expensive. To reduce costs, you can obtain training materials from other organizations. Modifying existing materials is usually cheaper than developing them from scratch.

- Training presentation. Presentation issues to consider include the frequency of training (for example, annually or as needed), the length of presentations (for example, 20 minutes for general presentations, one hour for updates, or one week for an off-site class), and the style of presentation (for example, formal presentation, informal discussion, computer-based training, humorous).

Maintain the Program Efforts should be made to keep abreast of changes in computer technology and security requirements. A training program that meets an organization's needs today may become ineffective if the organization begins using a new application or changes its environment, such as by connecting to the Internet. Likewise, an awareness program can become obsolete if laws, organizational policies, or common usage practices change. For example, if an awareness program is training employees about a new policy for e-mail usage and uses examples from Eudora (a popular e-mail client program), it may be less effective if the organization switches to Outlook (another e-mail client program) in the meantime. Employees may discount the security training program, and by association the importance of computer security, if the program does not provide current information.

Evaluate the Program Organizations can evaluate their training programs by ascertaining how much information is retained, to what extent computer security procedures are being followed, and what are the attitudes toward computer security. The results of such an evaluation should help identify and correct problems. Some popular evaluation methods (which can be used in conjunction with one another) are described here:

- Using student evaluations to collect feedback from the trainees
- Observing how well employees follow recommended security procedures after being trained
- Testing employees on material after it has been covered in training
- Monitoring the number and kind of computer security incidents reported before and after the training program is implemented

Security Awareness

One of the least frequently implemented, but most effective security methods is the security awareness program. As noted in the NIST document SP 800-12,

> Security awareness programs: (1) set the stage for training by changing organizational attitudes to realize the importance of security and the adverse consequences of its failure; and (2) remind users of the procedures to be followed.[25]

A security awareness program keeps information security at the forefront of users' minds on a daily basis. Awareness serves to instill a sense of responsibility and purpose in employees who handle and manage information, and it leads employees to care more about their work environment. When developing an awareness program, there are certain important ideas to keep in mind:

- Focus on people both as part of the problem and as part of the solution.
- Refrain from using technical jargon; speak the language the users understand.
- Use every available venue to access all users.
- Define at least one key learning objective, state it clearly, and provide sufficient detail and coverage to reinforce the learning of it.
- Keep things light; refrain from "preaching" to users.
- Don't overload the users with too much detail or too great a volume of information.
- Help users understand their roles in information security and how a breach in that security can affect their jobs.
- Take advantage of in-house communications media to deliver messages.
- Make the awareness program formal; plan and document all actions.
- Provide good information early, rather than perfect information late.

OFFLINE

The Ten Commandments of Information Security Awareness Training

I. Information security is a people, rather than a technical, issue.
II. If you want them to understand, speak their language.
III. If they cannot see it, they will not learn it.
IV. Make your point so that you can identify it and so can they.
V. Never lose your sense of humor.
VI. Make your point, support it, and conclude it.
VII. Always let the recipients know how the behavior that you request will affect them.
VIII. Ride the tame horses.
IX. Formalize your training methodology.
X. Always be timely, even if it means slipping schedules to include urgent information.

Source: Mark B. Desman. The ten commandments of information security awareness training. *Information Systems Security*, January/February 2003, 11(6), 39–45.

As Susan Hansche indicates in her article "Designing a Security Awareness Program," good security awareness programs should be

...supported and led by example from management, simple and straightforward, a continuous effort. They should repeat important messages to ensure they get delivered. They should be entertaining, holding the users' interest and humorous where appropriate in order to make slogans easy to remember. They should tell employees what the dangers are (threats) and how they can help protect the information vital to their jobs.[26]

Hansche continues by noting that awareness programs should focus on topics that the employees can relate to, including

...threats to physical assets and stored information, threats to open network environments, [and] federal and state laws they are required to follow, including copyright violations or privacy act information. It can also include specific organization or department policies and information on how to identify and protect sensitive or classified information, as well as how to store, label, and transport information. This awareness information should also address who they should report security incidents to, whether real or suspect.[27]

Employee Behavior and Awareness

Security awareness and security training are designed to modify any employee behavior that endangers the security of the organization's information. By teaching employees how to properly handle information, use applications, and operate within the organization, you minimize the risk of accidental compromise, damage, or destruction of information. By making employees aware of threats to information security, the potential damage that can result from these threats, and ways that these threats can occur, you reduce the chance that they will not take such threats seriously. By making employees aware of policy, the penalties for failure to comply with policy, and the mechanism by which policy violations are discovered, you reduce the probability that an employee will try to get away with intentional misuse and abuse of information. As noted in Chapter 2, penalties for policy violations are effective only when (1) employees fear the penalty, (2) employees believe they may be caught, and (3) employees believe that, if caught, they will be penalized.

Security training and awareness activities can be undermined, however, if management does not set a good example. Failure of management—and especially upper management—to follow organizational policy will be quickly mirrored by the actions and activities of all employees. As an example, suppose Random Widget Works has a policy that all employees must wear identification badges in a visible location at all times. If, over time, employees observe that senior executives do not wear badges, then soon no one will wear a badge, and attempts to penalize employees for this failure will be compromised. Policy breaches by upper management are always perceived as a lack of support for the policy. For that reason, management must always lead by example, in whatever policies they expect the entire organization to comply with.

Employee Accountability

Effective training and awareness programs make employees accountable for their actions. The legal defense *ignorantia legis neminem excusat* (ignorance of the law excuses no one)

may not be valid in a criminal courtroom, but it does protect employees who are fighting policy violation penalties in labor disputes, administrative law hearings, or civil court cases. As described in Chapter 4, comprehensive and properly disseminated policies enable organizations to require employee compliance. Dissemination and enforcement of policy become easier when training and awareness programs are in place.

Demonstrating **due care** and **due diligence**—warning employees that misconduct, abuse, and misuse of information resources will not be tolerated and that the organization will not defend employees who engage in this behavior—can help indemnify the institution against lawsuits. Lawyers tend to seek compensation from employers, which have more assets than employees, and thus attempt to prove that the alleged conduct was not clearly prohibited by organizational policy, thereby making the organization liable for it.

Awareness Techniques

The NIST document SP 800-12, *An Introduction to Computer Security: The NIST Handbook,* describes the essentials of developing effective awareness techniques:

> Awareness can take on different forms for particular audiences. Appropriate awareness for management officials might stress management's pivotal role in establishing organizational attitudes toward security. Appropriate awareness for other groups, such as system programmers or information analysts, should address the need for security as it relates to their job. In today's systems environment, almost everyone in an organization may have access to system resources and therefore may have the potential to cause harm.
>
> A security awareness program can use many methods to deliver its message, including video tapes, newsletters, posters, bulletin boards, flyers, demonstrations, briefings, short reminder notices at log-on, talks, or lectures. Awareness is often incorporated into basic security training and can use any method that can change employees' attitudes. Effective security awareness programs need to be designed with the recognition that people tend to practice a *tuning out* process (also known as *acclimation*). For example, after a while, a security poster, no matter how well designed, will be ignored; it will, in effect, simply blend into the environment. For this reason, awareness techniques should be creative and frequently changed.[28]

Developing Security Awareness Components

Many security awareness components are available at low cost, or virtually no cost, except for the time and energy of the developer. Others can be very expensive if purchased externally. Security awareness components include the following items:

- Videos
- Posters and banners
- Lectures and conferences
- Computer-based training
- Newsletters
- Brochures and flyers
- Trinkets (coffee cups, pens, pencils, T-shirts)
- Bulletin boards

Several of these options are discussed in detail in the following sections.

The Security Newsletter A security newsletter is the most cost-effective method of disseminating security information and news to employees. Newsletters can be in the form of hard copy, e-mail, or intranet-based. Their topics can include new threats to the organization's information assets, the schedule for upcoming security classes, and the addition of new security personnel. The goal is to keep the idea of information security uppermost in users' minds and to stimulate them to care about security.

Consider the newsletter model illustrated in Figure 5-14. The following sections describe the components of this sample newsletter.

FIGURE 5-14   SETA Awareness Components: Newsletters

Cover page: The cover page should contain a title that evokes an image of security, such as *The Guardian*, *The Sentinel*, *The Protector*, or *A Higher Plane*. Graphics should be included, but sparingly. Clipart works well, as do company logos or designs. The cover should also contain standard literary denotations such as volume, issue, date, and so on, to allow for archiving, which provides proof of due care and due diligence in the event the process is audited. In addition, a simple index or table of contents should appear on the cover. While each issue's content will be distinct, in most cases the layout is standardized. Developing a template containing just the frame, page numbers, and a common back cover simplifies the creation of newsletters.

Back cover: The back cover is most often used to provide contact information for information security personnel, the help desk, physical security (law enforcement), and other quick reference items. It might also include editorial and author information.

Interior: The newsletter should contain articles of interest, gleaned from information security publications, along with local publications, summaries of policies, security-related activities, and the like. It might also include these items:

- Summaries of key policies (one per issue, to avoid overloading the reader)
- Summaries of key news articles (one or two each at the national, state, and local levels)
- A calendar of security events, including training sessions, presentations, and other activities
- Announcements relevant to information security, such as planned installations, upgrades, or deployment of new technologies or policies
- How-to's, such as
    - How to make sure virus definitions are up-to-date
    - How to report an incident
    - How to properly classify, label, and store information
    - How to determine whether e-mail is dangerous
    - How to secure the office before leaving (clean desk policies)
    - How to avoid tailgaters

The decision about how to publish the newsletter will vary according to organizational needs. Hard copies, especially in color, may be inordinately expensive, even if the institution owns its own reproduction equipment. Larger organizations may prefer to distribute color Portable Document Format (PDF) copies, or even HTML documents via e-mail or intranet. Some companies may choose to create an HTML Web site and e-mail links to users, rather than distributing hard copy or sending attachments.

The Security Poster A security poster series—which can be displayed in common areas, especially where technology is used—is a simple and inexpensive way to keep security on people's minds. The examples shown in Figure 5-15, along with eight others, were developed in one long afternoon, with the bulk of the time being spent looking for just the right clipart. Professionally developed graphic posters can be quite expensive, so in-house development may be the best solution (but don't simply copy someone else's work), especially if the organization has the ability to print on poster-sized paper. If not, most copy shops can enlarge letter-sized copies to poster size.

FIGURE 5-15 SETA Awareness Components: Posters

There are several keys to a good poster series:

- Varying the content and keeping posters updated
- Keeping them simple, but visually interesting
- Making the message clear
- Providing information on reporting violations

A variation on the poster series is the screen saver slideshow. Many modern operating systems allow you to create a rotating slideshow, which you can configure as a screen saver.

The Trinket Program This option is one of the most expensive security awareness programs. Trinkets may not cost much on a per-unit basis, but they can be expensive to distribute throughout an organization. Trinkets are everyday items with specialized security messages printed on them, as shown in Figure 5-16.

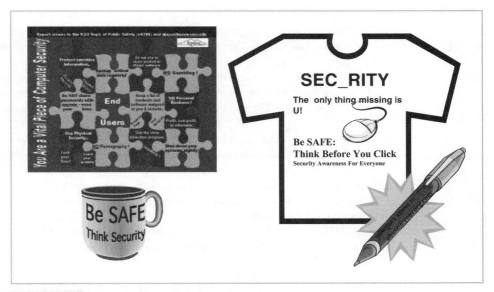

FIGURE 5-16   SETA Awareness Components: Trinkets

Several types of trinkets are commonly used:

- Pens and pencils
- Mouse pads
- Coffee mugs
- Plastic cups
- Hats
- T-shirts

Trinket programs can get people's attention at first, but the messages they impart will eventually be lost unless reinforced by other means.

Information Security Awareness Web Site   Organizations can establish Web pages or sites dedicated to promoting information security awareness, like Kennesaw State University's Web site at infosec.kennesaw.edu. As with other SETA awareness methods, the challenge lies in updating the messages frequently enough to keep them fresh. When new information is posted, employees can be informed via e-mail. The latest and archived newsletters can reside on the Web site, along with press releases, awards, and recognitions.

Some tips on creating and maintaining an educational Web site[29] are provided here:

1. See what's already out there. You don't have to reinvent the wheel. Look at what other organizations have done with their InfoSec awareness Web sites. Determine ownership, as you don't want to infringe on another organization's intellectual property. It's one thing to adopt a good idea; it's another thing to present it as your own. Where necessary, give credit where credit is due. A good rule of thumb is to look at a large number of sites, then design your site from memory using the best things you have seen.

2. Plan ahead. Design the Web site on paper before designing it on the computer. Standardize file naming conventions, file and image locations, and other development components, so that you don't have to recode links or pages because you changed your convention halfway through.

3. Keep page loading time to a minimum. Avoid large images and complex/long pages. Design for the lowest common denominator, typically a 640 × 480 display screen with VGA graphics. Use .jpg graphics wherever possible, as opposed to larger file formats.

4. Appearance matters. Create a themed "look and feel" for the pages, using templates and visually attractive formats. Keep quick links on the side, on the bottom, or in floating palettes.

5. Seek feedback. Ask others to review your work, and accept the best suggestions for improvement. Use statistical measurements to determine which parts of the Web site are used most frequently.

6. Assume nothing and check everything. Verify your standards by using other computers to view the documents. Try out the Web site with multiple browsers, platforms, and systems. Each may claim to use a standardized interpreter, but their idiosyncrasies may yield unexpected results.

7. Spend time promoting your site. Let everyone at the company know it's there. Send notifications when new content is posted. Posting information on a Web site can reduce e-mail traffic.

One final recommendation (not found in the aforementioned article) is to place your Web site on the intranet. You can then include phone numbers and information not generally released to the public, such as notices of breaches and violations, and company policies and procedures for handling problems.

Security Awareness Conference/Presentations Another means of renewing the information security message is to have a guest speaker or even a mini-conference dedicated to the topic—perhaps in association with Computer Security Day! Never heard of it? That's not surprising. Even through it's been around since 1988, Computer Security Day (November 30) is an underpromoted event, much like information security itself. (For more information see the Association for Computer Security Day at www.geocities.com/a4csd/index.html.) The guest speaker or speakers could discuss vital industry-specific information security issues. The drawbacks: Speakers seldom speak for free, and few organizations are willing to suspend work for such an event, even a half-day conference.

THREAT MANAGEMENT

Threat Management: Smurf Attack

Definition

A Smurf attack is a specific type of denial-of-service (DoS) attack that typically targets Internet Relay Chat (IRC) servers, but that can be directed toward any networking resource. Its name derives from the software that propagates the attack. Smurf attacks, like most DoS attacks, occur quickly with little warning and are almost impossible to

(continued)

trace. One of the most visible attacks targeted the Yahoo! Web site in February 2000, resulting in a loss of business for almost three hours. The hacker Mafiaboy was notorious for conducting DoS attacks against public sites, until his apprehension later in the year.

A Smurf attack is instigated via the creation of an ICMP packet, usually an echo or a Ping request packet that contains the victim's address in the return field. A massive barrage of these packets are sent to various "accomplices" on the network, each of which responds to the spoofed address, thereby creating an unmanageable level of traffic for the unsuspecting victim. The "accomplices" are typically unaware that they are contributing to this attack; they are usually high-load Internet servers belonging to other organizations.

Detection

To understand how to detect a Smurf attack or its identifying features, you must be familiar with attack signatures. An attack signature is a display of specific patterns that may indicate malicious intent. In a well-secured network, a network-based IDS monitors and analyzes all network traffic for attack signatures in real time using raw network packets as the data source. If a possible attack is identified, the IDS will send a notification to an administrator. It may also collect evidence or record the session for later forensic analysis, or terminate the connection.

To identify a Smurf attack, an IDS should recognize two possible attack signatures correlating to the two potential victims. The first victim's resources are exploited when response requests are sent to each network node. A network-based IDS should recognize the brief spike in traffic when all responses are returned to an identical address. The second victim is the target of the DoS attack. An IDS for the target victim should recognize a large number of responses, from a number of similar addresses, for which no request was sent (unilateral network traffic).

Response

An organization that has been hit with a Smurf attack has limited options for handling it. McAfee recommends taking the following steps:

- To stop new infections by scripts, batch executables, macro viruses, and worms, make sure your virus scanner is updated with a current pattern file and perform a systems scan to remove and/or quarantine the infectious elements.
- To control infected systems that are executing hostile programs, boot the systems to MS-DOS mode or use a boot diskette and a reputable command line scanner such as:

```
SCANPM/ADL/CLEAN/ALL
```

In addition, McAfee recommends that systems using Windows ME and XP disable the system restoration feature to remove this attack (www.mcafeeb2b.com/naicommon/download/dats/find.asp). Symantec also offers information on its site about Smurf attacks and remedies (www.symantec.com/avcenter/venc/data/pf/smurf.dos.attack.html).

According to the CERT advisory on Smurf attacks (www.cert.org/advisories/CA-1998-01.html), there is no easy solution for victims. Blocking traffic at the router may not prevent congestion between the victim's router and its Internet service provider (ISP). Instead, the victim may find it necessary to request that its ISP temporarily block this type of traffic. The CERT advisory also provides an appendix containing a list of

(continued)

vendors (e.g., Cisco, Data General, DEC, IBM, and Sun Microsystems) with specific recommendations for dealing with Smurf attacks on their products.

Protection and Prevention

Because of the nature of Smurf attacks, you must both protect against being used as an intermediary *in* a Smurf attack and prevent becoming the target *of* a Smurf attack.

One way to prevent your organization's use as an intermediary is to disable IP-directed broadcasts at your router, thereby denying IP broadcast traffic from other networks. IP-directed broadcast functionality is rarely necessary. In addition, you should disable IP-directed broadcasts on all of your routers, not just the ones used for your external network connectivity. For example, if you have four routers connecting eight LANs at your site, you should turn off IP-directed broadcasts on all four routers.

Another protective measure is to configure your operating system so as to prevent your machines from responding to ICMP packets sent to IP broadcast addresses. An intruder trying to launch a Smurf attack by high jacking your network as an intermediary could use your machines to send the ICMP echo request packet to the IP broadcast address of the local network. Because this traffic does not travel through a router to reach other machines on the local network, disabling IP-directed broadcasts on your routers will not stop it. Some operating systems can be configured to prevent a machine from responding to ICMP packets sent to IP broadcast addresses. Configuring machines so that they do not respond to these packets can prevent your machines from being exploited as intermediaries.

Unfortunately, there is no easy solution for anyone receiving the potentially large number of ICMP echo reply packets that constitutes a Smurf attack. The traffic from the intermediary could be blocked at the victim's router, but that will not necessarily prevent the congestion that occurs between the victim's router and its ISP. Victims receiving this traffic may need to request that their ISP temporarily block this type of traffic. In addition, some companies have developed devices that monitor ICMP traffic. When these devices detect numbers of ICMP packets above a certain threshold, the malicious packets are dropped, thereby blocking the attack.

Victims of Smurf attacks should contact any and all intermediaries and inform them of the attack and of the steps that should be taken to prevent future occurrences.

Contributed by Chad Austin, Bonnie May, Debbie McFarland, Randy Pafford, and Lynn Silvers.

Chapter Summary

- The term "information security program" is used to describe the structure and organization of the effort that contains risks to the information assets of the organization.

- In the largest organizations, specific InfoSec functions are likely to be performed by specialized groups of staff members; in smaller organizations, these functions may be carried out by all members of the department.

- Information security functions should be separated into four areas:
    - Functions performed by nontechnical areas of the organization outside of the information technology area of management control
    - Functions performed by IT groups outside of the information security area of management control
    - Functions performed within the information security department as a customer service to the organization and its external partners
    - Functions performed within the information security department as a compliance enforcement obligation
- Implementation of full-time security personnel will vary depending on a number of industry factors:
    - A typical large organization will have on average 1 full-time manager, 4 full-time technicians/administrators, and as many as 15 part-time staff members.
    - A very large organization may have more than 20 full-time security personnel and 40 or more individuals with part-time responsibilities.
    - A medium-sized organization may have only one full-time security person and as many as three individuals with part-time responsibilities.
    - Smaller organizations may have either one individual with full-time duties in information security or one individual who is a part-time manager.
- Information security positions can be classified into one of three areas: those that *define,* those that *build,* and those that *administer.*
- The SETA program is the responsibility of the CISO and is designed to reduce the incidence of accidental security breaches.
- SETA programs improve employee behavior and enable the organization to hold employees accountable for their actions.
- Training is most effective when it is designed for a specific category of users. Training includes teaching users not only what they should or should not do, but also how they should do it.
- There are two methods for customizing training for users: by functional background and by level of skill. Training delivery methods include one-on-one, formal classes, computer-based training, distance learning/Web seminars, user support groups, on-the-job training, and self-study (noncomputerized).
- A security awareness program can deliver its message via video tapes, newsletters, posters, bulletin boards, flyers, demonstrations, briefings, short reminder notices at logon, talks, or lectures.

Review Questions

1. What is an information security program?
2. What functions constitute a complete information security program?
3. What organizational variables can influence the size and composition of an information security program's staff?
4. What is the typical size of the security staff in a small organization? A medium-sized organization? A large organization? A very large organization?
5. Where can an organization place the information security unit? Where should (and shouldn't) it be placed?
6. Into what four areas should the information security functions be divided?

7. What are the five roles that an information security professional can assume?

8. What are the three areas of the SETA program?

9. What can influence the effectiveness of a training program?

10. What are some of the various ways to implement an awareness program?

11. Which two documents largely determine the shape of the information security program? Which other documents can assist in this effort?

12. What are the elements of a security program, according to NIST SP 800-14?

13. Information security positions can be classified into what three areas? What are the differences among them?

14. Describe the two overriding benefits of awareness, training, and education.

15. What is the purpose of a SETA program?

16. Which of the SETA program's three elements is the organization best prepared to offer? Which should it consider outsourcing?

17. How does training differ from education? Which is provided to the broader audience with regard to information security?

18. What are the various training program delivery methods?

19. Describe a sample seven-step methodology for implementing training.

20. When developing an awareness program, what priorities should you keep in mind?

Exercises

1. Using a Web browser, search for the term "security awareness." Describe the available materials and services.

2. Using a Web browser, go to http://csrc.nist.gov. Look for the link on the left side of the Web page called Security Awareness. Review SETA program resources. Describe the various materials that an organization could use in its programs.

3. Get the latest copy of your local Sunday paper. Look through the paper and circulars for advertisements for training and education in security- and technology-related areas. What are the costs of the advertised security specific training? Network certification? General computer training?

4. Design five security posters on various aspects of information security, using a graphics presentation program and clip art. Bring the posters to class and discuss the methods you used to develop your materials.

5. Examine your institution's Web site and identify full- and part-time information security jobs. Create an organizational chart showing the reporting structures for these individuals.

Case Exercises

Mike Edwards thanked the attorney from the corporate legal office for his presentation on the newly enacted state computer crime and privacy law, and then asked, "How should we comply and when does it take effect?" The attorney gave a full analysis of RWW's responsibilities.

Mike turned to his staff of department managers and said, "It's important that we comply with the new law. First, however, we need to determine how much it will cost us to comply with the password privacy area. I need from each of you a budget impact analysis that encompasses the effort needed to meet this new requirement."

1. What elements will each department manager have to consider to complete Mike's assignment?

2. How will a privacy law affect an organization like RWW? What other laws also affect privacy in the workplace?

Endnotes

1. Andrew Briney and Frank Prince. Does size matter? *Information Security,* September 2002, 36–54.

2. Ibid.

3. Ibid.

4. Ibid.

5. Ibid.

6. Ibid.

7. Ibid.

8. Ibid.

9. Ibid.

10. Ibid.

11. Ibid.

12. Ibid.

13. M. Hayes. Where the Chief Security Officer belongs. *InformationWeek,* February 25, 2002. Accessed May 4, 2003. http://www.informationweek.com/story/showArticle.jhtml?articleID=6500913.

14. Charles Cresson Wood. *Information Security Roles and Responsibilities Made Easy.* Houston: PentaSafe, 2002: 95–105. Used with permission.

15. Charles Cresson Wood. *Information Security Roles and Responsibilities Made Easy.* Houston: PentaSafe, 2002: 45. Used with permission.

16. National Institute of Standards and Technology. *Generally Accepted Principles and Practices for Securing Information Technology Systems.* NIST Publication 800-14. http://csrc.nist.gov/publications/nistpubs/800-14/800-14.pdf.

17. National Institute of Standards and Technology. *An Introduction to Computer Security: The NIST Handbook.* NIST Publication 800-12, 15. http://csrc.nist.gov/publications/nistpubs/800-12/handbook.pdf.

18. Eddie Schwartz, Dan Erwin, Vincent Weafer, and Andy Briney. Roundtable: InfoSec staffing help wanted! *Information Security Magazine Online,* April 2001. [Cited 22 July 2002]. http://www.infosecuritymag.com/articles/april01/features_roundtable.shtml.

19. National Institute of Standards and Technology. *An Introduction to Computer Security: The NIST Handbook.* SP 800-12. http://csrc.nist.gov/publications/nistpubs/800-12/.

20. C. Irvine, S-K. Chin, and D. Frincke. Integrating security into the curriculum. *Computer,* December 1998, 31(12), 25–30.

21. National InfoSec Education and Training Program (NIETP). Centers of Academic Excellence in Information Assurance Education. Accessed February 6, 2001. http://www.nsa.gov/isso/programs/coeiae/index.htm.

22. National Institute of Standards and Technology. *Information Technology Security Training Requirements: A Role- and Performance-Based Model.* http://csrc.nist.gov/publications/ nistpubs/800-16/800-16.pdf.

23. National Institute of Standards and Technology. *Information Technology Security Training Requirements: A Role- and Performance-Based Model.* http://csrc.nist.gov/publications/nistpubs/800-16/800-16.pdf.

24. Charles Trepper. Training developers more efficiently. *InformationWeekOnline.* http://www.informationweek.com/738/38addev.htm.

25. National Institute of Standards and Technology. *An Introduction to Computer Security: The NIST Handbook.* SP 800-12. http://csrc.nist.gov/publications/nistpubs/800-12/.

26. Susan Hansche. Designing a security awareness program: Part I. *Information Systems Security,* January/February 2001, 9(6), 14–23.

27. Ibid.

28. National Institute of Standards and Technology. *An Introduction to Computer Security: The NIST Handbook.* SP 800-12. http://csrc.nist.gov/publications/nistpubs/800-12/.

29. S. Plous. Tips on creating and maintaining an educational Web site. *Teaching of Psychology,* 2000, 27, 63–70.

Security Management Models and Practices

6

> Security can only be achieved through constant change, through discarding old ideas that have outlived their usefulness and adapting others to current facts.
>
> **WILLIAM O. DOUGLAS, U.S. SUPREME COURT JUSTICE (1898–1980)**

IRIS LOOKED AT THE MOUND OF documents on her desk. Each one was neatly labeled with its own acronym and number: NIST, ISO, Special Publication, and RFC. Her head was beginning to swim. She had not imagined that it would be quite so difficult to choose a security management model for her review of RWW's ongoing security program. She wanted an independent framework that would allow her to perform a thorough analysis of RWW's program.

Iris was almost finished skimming the stack when she found what she was looking for: a document that contained a self-assessment checklist with page after page of specific items important in the management of information security. She perused the list carefully. Using her Internet connection, Iris downloaded the full document, inserted a few minor changes, made copies for the managers who worked for her, and then scheduled a meeting.

At the meeting, Tom, the Manager of Risk Assessment and Policy, commented, "Gee, Iris, when did you have time to design this checklist?" Iris replied, "I didn't. I was lucky enough to find the perfect one for us. I changed just a few things to make it specific enough for our needs." She quickly outlined her plan. Using the checklist, each manager would indicate the progress that RWW had made in that area—specifically, whether policy had been created and, if so, whether it had been integrated into the company culture. Iris explained how to use the forms and noted when she expected the assessment to be complete.

"What happens once we're done?" one manager asked.

"That's when the real work begins," Iris said. "We'll establish priorities for improving the areas that need improvement, and sustaining the areas that are satisfactory. Then we'll determine whether we have the resources needed to accomplish that work; if not, I'll go to the CIO and request more resources."

LEARNING OBJECTIVES

Upon completion of this material, you should be able to:

- Select from the dominant information security management models, including U.S. government-sanctioned models, and customize them for a specific organization's needs
- Implement the fundamental elements of key information security management practices
- Follow emerging trends in the certification and accreditation of U.S. federal IT systems

Introduction

To create or maintain a secure environment, you must design a working security plan and then implement a management model to execute and maintain that plan. This effort may begin with the creation or validation of a security framework, followed by the development of an information security blueprint that describes existing controls and identifies other necessary security controls. The terms *blueprint* and *framework* are closely related: A **framework** is the outline of the more thorough **blueprint**, which serves as the basis for the design, selection, and implementation of all subsequent security controls, including information security policies, security education and training programs, and technological controls.

To design a security blueprint, most organizations draw upon established security models and practices. A **security model** is a generic blueprint offered by a service organization. Some of these models are proprietary, and are only available for high fees; others are relatively inexpensive, such as ISO standards; and some are free. Free models are available from the National Institute of Standards and Technology (NIST) and a variety of other sources. The model you choose must be flexible, scalable, robust, and sufficiently detailed.

Another way to create the blueprint is to look at the paths taken by other organizations. In this kind of *benchmarking,* you follow the best practices or industry standards. Benchmarking can provide details on *which* controls should be considered, but it does not provide implementation details that explain *how* controls should be put into action.

One way to select a methodology is to adapt or adopt an existing security management model or set of practices. A number of published information security models and frameworks exist, such as those from government organizations presented later in this chapter. Because each information security environment is unique, you may need to modify or adapt portions of several frameworks, because what works well for one organization may not precisely fit another.

Security Management Models

There are as many security management models and practices available as there are consultants who offer them. Among the most accessible places in which to find a quality security management model are U.S. federal agencies and international organizations. In fact, one of the most popular security management models has been ratified into an international standard. British Standard 7799 provides two components, each addressing a different area of security management practice:

- BS 7799:1, now known as ISO/IEC 17799, called *Information Technology—Code of Practice for Information Security Management.*
- BS 7799:2 called *Information Security Management: Specification with Guidance for Use.*

These documents are discussed in detail in the following sections. They are proprietary, and organizations wishing to adopt this model must purchase the rights to do so.

A number of alternative sources exist as well. The first and foremost of these are free documents provided by NIST's Computer Security Resource Center (http://csrc.nist.gov). This site houses many publications, including ones containing models and practices. You learned about some of these publications in earlier chapters of this book. Later in this chapter, you will learn more about the following NIST publications:

- NIST SP 800-12, *Computer Security Handbook*
- NIST SP 800-14, *Generally Accepted Security Principles and Practices*
- NIST SP 800-18, *Guide for Developing Security Plans*
- NIST SP 800-26, *Security Self-Assessment Guide for Information Technology Systems*
- NIST SP 800-30, *Risk Management for Information Technology Systems*
- Draft NIST SP 800-37, *Guidelines for the Security Certification and Accreditation of Federal Information Technology Systems*

Two supplemental resources are also discussed in this chapter:

- RFC 2196, *The Site Security Handbook*
- VISA, *U.S.A. Cardholder Information Security Program*

BS 7799 Part 1 (ISO 17799:2002 Standard): Code of Practice for Information Security Management

One of the most widely referenced and often discussed security models is *Information Technology—Code of Practice for Information Security Management,* which was originally published as **British Standard 7799.** In 2000, this code of practice was adopted as an international standard framework for information security by the International Organization for Standardization (ISO) and the International Electrotechnical Commission (IEC) as **ISO/IEC 17799.** While the details of ISO/IEC 17799 are available only to buyers of the standard, its structure and general organization are well known. For a summary description, see the section of this chapter entitled "The Ten Sections of ISO/IEC 17799."

The stated purpose of ISO/IEC 17799 is to "give recommendations for information security management for use by those who are responsible for initiating, implementing, or maintaining security in their organization. It is intended to provide a common basis for developing organizational security standards and effective security management practice and to provide confidence in inter-organizational dealings."[1] The international standards component is actually the first volume of the two-volume British Standard BS 7799. It offers an overview of the various areas of security and provides information on 127 controls over 10 broad areas. Volume 2 provides information on how to implement Volume 1 (17799) and how to set up an Information Security Management Structure (ISMS). Figure 6-1 overviews the entire certification process.

In the United Kingdom, these standards, when implemented correctly, are used to obtain the ISMS certification and accreditation, as determined by a BS 7799–certified evaluator. Many countries, including the United States, Germany, and Japan, have not formally adopted ISO/IEC 17799 as national policy, however. Groups within each of these countries claim that the methodology has some fundamental problems:

- The global information security community has not defined any justification for a code of practice as identified in the ISO/IEC 17799.
- ISO/IEC 17799 lacks "the necessary measurement precision of a technical standard."[2]
- There is no reason to believe that ISO/IEC 17799 is more useful than any other approach.
- ISO/IEC 17799 is not as complete as other frameworks.
- ISO/IEC 17799 is perceived as having been hurriedly prepared, given the tremendous impact that its adoption could have on industry information security controls.[3]

TECHNICAL DETAILS

The Ten Sections of ISO/IEC 17799

1. **Organizational Security Policy** is needed to provide management direction and support for information security.
2. **Organizational Security Infrastructure** objectives include:
   - Manage information security within the company
   - Maintain the security of organizational information processing facilities and information assets accessed by third parties
   - Maintain the security of information when the responsibility for information processing has been outsourced to another organization
3. **Asset Classification and Control** is needed to maintain appropriate protection of corporate assets and to ensure that information assets receive an appropriate level of protection.
4. **Personnel Security** objectives are:
   - Reduce risks of human error, theft, fraud or misuse of facilities
   - Ensure that users are aware of information security threats and concerns, and are equipped to support the corporate security policy in the course of their normal work
   - Minimize the damage from security incidents and malfunctions and learn from such incidents

5. **Physical and Environmental Security** objectives include:
   - Prevent unauthorized access, damage, and interference to business premises and information
   - Prevent loss, damage, or compromise of assets and interruption to business activities
   - Prevent compromise or theft of information and information processing facilities
6. **Communications and Operations Management** objectives are:
   - Ensure the correct and secure operation of information processing facilities
   - Minimize the risk of system failures
   - Protect the integrity of software and information
   - Maintain the integrity and availability of information processing and communication
   - Ensure the safeguarding of information in networks and the protection of the supporting infrastructure
   - Prevent damage to assets and interruptions to business activities
   - Prevent loss, modification, or misuse of information exchanged between organizations
7. **System Access Control** objectives in this area include:
   - Control access to information
   - Prevent unauthorized access to information systems
   - Ensure the protection of networked services
   - Prevent unauthorized computer access
   - Detect unauthorized activities
   - Ensure information security when using mobile computing and telecommunications networks
8. **System Development and Maintenance** objectives include:
   - Ensure security is built into operational systems
   - Prevent loss, modification, or misuse of user data in application systems
   - Protect the confidentiality, authenticity, and integrity of information
   - Ensure IT projects and support activities are conducted in a secure manner
   - Maintain the security of application system software and data
9. **Business Continuity Planning** counteracts interruptions to business activities and to critical business processes from the effects of major failures or disasters.
10. **Compliance** objectives include:
    - Avoid breaches of any criminal or civil law, statutory, regulatory, or contractual obligations and of any security requirements
    - Ensure compliance of systems with organizational security policies and standards
    - Maximize the effectiveness of and minimize interference to or from the system audit process

Source: Mark Merkow. Standardizing information systems security across the globe: a look at ISO17799. *Internet.com Online,* September 10, 2001. [Cited 24 June 2002]. Available from the World Wide Web at http://ecommerce.internet.com/news/insights/outlook/article/0,3371,10535_881531,00.html.

While ISO/IEC 17799 is certainly an interesting information security framework, at this time it is difficult to predict how it will affect small- and medium-sized U.S. organizations that do not operate in the European Union (EU). Perhaps only those organizations with an EU customer base will be required to adopt it; however, some indications suggest that this standard may have broader uses within other U.S. organizations.

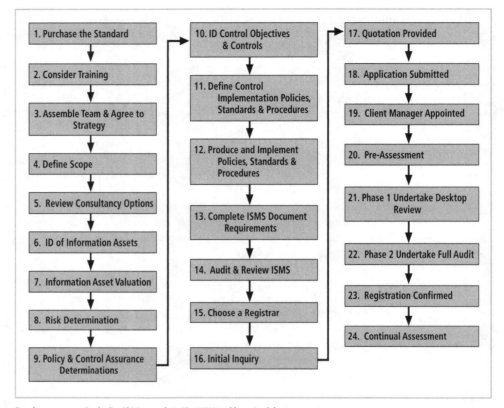

Based on a presentation by David Watson – http://iso17799world.com/auth.htm

FIGURE 6-1 Implementation of ISO 17799:2000

BS 7799 Part 2: The Information Security Management System

Part 2 of BS 7799 provides implementation details using a Plan-Do-Check-Act cycle, as described here and shown in Figure 6-2 in abbreviated form:

Plan:
1. Define the scope of the ISMS.
2. Define an ISMS policy.
3. Define the approach to risk assessment.
4. Identify the risks.
5. Assess the risks.
6. Identify and evaluate options for the treatment of risk.
7. Select control objectives and controls.
8. Prepare a Statement of Applicability (SOA).

Do:

9. Formulate a Risk Treatment Plan.
10. Implement the Risk Treatment Plan.
11. Implement controls.
12. Implement training and awareness programs.
13. Manage operations.
14. Manage resources.
15. Implement procedures to detect and respond to security incidents.

Check:

16. Execute monitoring procedures.
17. Undertake regular reviews of ISMS effectiveness.
18. Review the level of residual and acceptable risk.
19. Conduct internal ISMS audits.
20. Undertake regular management review of the ISMS.
21. Record actions and events that impact an ISMS.

Act:

22. Implement identified improvements.
23. Take corrective or preventive action.
24. Apply lessons learned.
25. Communicate results to interested parties.
26. Ensure improvements achieve objectives.[4]

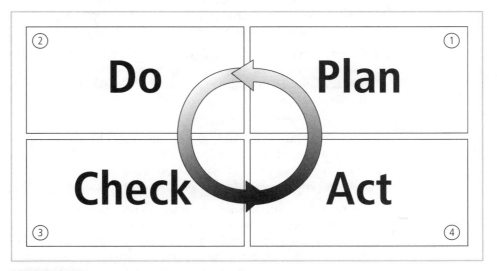

FIGURE 6-2   Plan – Do – Check – Act cycle of BS 7799:2

Although the newly revised Part 2 provides some implementation information, it simply specifies *what* must be done—not *how* to do it. As noted by Gamma Secure Systems, "The standard has an appendix that gives guidance on the use of the standard, in particular to expand on the Plan-Do-Check-Act concept. It is important to realize that there will be many Plan-Do-Check-Act cycles within a single ISMS all operating asynchronously at different speeds."[5]

The Security Management Index and ISO 17799

One way to determine how closely an organization is complying with ISO 17799 is to take the Human Firewall Council's survey, the **Security Management Index (SMI)**. The SMI (located at www.humanfirewall.org) asks 35 questions over the 10 domains of the ISO standard. According to the Web site, "This survey gathers metrics on how organizations manage security and enables information security officers to benchmark their practices against those of other organizations. The survey has been developed according to ISO 17799 international security standards to reflect best practices from a global perspective. The Security Management Index survey will help you measure your security management practices compared to other organizations in your industry and peer group."[6] The complete questionnaire is presented in the Appendix to Chapter 6.

To take advantage of the free metrics supplied in the Security Management Index, the Human Firewall Council recommends the following:

1. **Familiarize yourself with the 10 categories of security management.**
   These 10 categories correspond to leading practices as outlined by security industry analysts and security professional associations. Even if you are not familiar with ISO 17799, the 10 categories of security management in the survey represent a comprehensive way to organize and define the pertinent issues and challenges.

2. **Benchmark your organization's security management practices by taking the survey.**
   After completing the survey, you will receive your individual organization's score in a result screen that also shows how you compare your score to other organizations that have taken the survey. In Annex C of this report, you will find an example of how the results are displayed.

3. **Evaluate your results in each category to identify strengths and weaknesses.**
   Using these responses, you can readily see areas where your organization may be weaker or stronger compared to other organizations of your size, in your industry. Based on your scores you can then make a list of the areas that appear to need improvement and further attention.

4. **Examine the suggestions for improvement in each category in this report.**
   Along with descriptions of the aggregate results from the SMI survey to date, each of the category sections of this report contains suggested actions that would likely improve performance and scores for a particular area.

5. **Use your SMI results to gain support for improving security.**
   Security management and IT executives can use both their individual score and the survey's aggregate results to help persuade top management of the necessity for a more coherent, management-centric approach to security. It may help to make your case to executive management with a presentation and discussion of your scores from the Security Management Index in the context of your industry and peer group.[7]

RFC 2196 Site Security Handbook

While the Internet Engineering Task Force (IETF) promotes no particular architecture, the Security Area Working Group within the IETF has created RFC 2196, *Site Security Handbook.* (The Security Area Working Group acts as an advisory board for the protocols and areas developed and promoted through the Internet Society.) RFC 2196 provides a good functional discussion of important security issues and an overview of five basic areas of security, along with development and implementation details. It includes chapters on such critical topics as security policies, security technical architecture, security services, and security incident handling. For example, the architecture chapter begins by highlighting the importance of security policies, then expands into an examination of services, access controls, and other relevant areas. Table 6-1 gives the table of contents for RFC 2196.

TABLE 6-1   Table of Contents for RFC 2196, *Site Security Handbook*

1. Introduction

1.1 Purpose of This Work

1.2 Audience

1.3 Definitions

1.4 Related Work

1.5 Basic Approach

1.6 Risk Assessment

2. Security Policies

2.1 What Is a Security Policy and Why Have One?

2.2 What Makes a Good Security Policy?

2.3 Keeping the Policy Flexible

3. Architecture

3.1 Objectives

3.2 Network and Service Configuration

3.3 Firewalls

4. Security Services and Procedures

4.1 Authentication

4.2 Confidentiality

4.3 Integrity

4.4 Authorization

4.5 Access

4.6 Auditing

4.7 Securing Backups

TABLE 6-1   Table of Contents for RFC 2196, *Site Security Handbook* (continued)

5. Security Incident Handling

5.1 Preparing and Planning for Incident Handling

5.2 Notification and Points of Contact

5.3 Identifying an Incident

5.4 Handling an Incident

5.5 Aftermath of an Incident

5.6 Responsibilities

6. Ongoing Activities

7. Tools and Locations

8. Mailing Lists and Other Resources

9. References

NIST Security Models

Other approaches are described in the many documents available from NIST's Computer Security Resource Center (http://csrc.nist.gov). These documents are among the references cited by the U.S. government as reasons not to adopt ISO/IEC 17799 standards. They enjoy two notable advantages over many other sources of security information: (1) they are publicly available at no charge and (2) they have been available for some time and thus have been broadly reviewed by government and industry professionals. You can use the NIST SP documents listed earlier along with the comments provided below to help you design a custom security framework for your organization's information security program.

NIST Special Publication 800-12

SP 800-12, *The Computer Security Handbook,* is an excellent reference and guide for the routine management of information security. It provides little guidance, however, on the design and implementation of new security systems; use it as a supplement to gain a deeper understanding in the background and terminology of security. The following excerpt gives an idea of the kind of information found in SP 800-12:

> 800-12 draws upon the OECD's Guidelines for the Security of Information Systems, which was endorsed by the United States. It provides for:
>
> - Accountability—The responsibilities and accountability of owners, providers, and users of information systems and other parties [...] should be explicit.
>
> - Awareness—Owners, providers, users, and other parties should readily be able, consistent with maintaining security, to gain appropriate knowledge of and be informed about the existence and general extent of measures [...] for the security of information systems.
>
> - Ethics—The information systems and the security of information systems should be provided and used in such a manner that the rights and legitimate interest of others are respected.
>
> - Multidisciplinary—Measures, practices, and procedures for the security of information systems should take account of and address all relevant considerations and viewpoints. [...]

- Proportionality—Security levels, costs, measures, practices, and procedures should be appropriate and proportionate to the value of and degree of reliance on the information systems and to the severity, probability, and extent of potential harm. [...]
- Integration—Measures, practices, and procedures for the security of information systems should be coordinated and integrated with each other and other measures, practices, and procedures of the organization so as to create a coherent system of security.
- Timeliness—Public and private parties, at both national and international levels, should act in a timely coordinated manner to prevent and to respond to breaches of security of information systems.
- Reassessment—The security of information systems should be reassessed periodically, as information systems and the requirements for their security vary over time.
- Democracy—The security of information systems should be compatible with the legitimate use and flow of data and information in a democratic society.[8]

SP 800-12 also lays out NIST's philosophy on security management by identifying 17 controls organized into three categories. These three categories are described below:

The Management Controls section addresses security topics that can be characterized as managerial. They are techniques and concerns that are normally addressed by management in the organization's computer security program. In general, they focus on the management of the computer security program and the management of risk within the organization.

The Operational Controls section addresses security controls that focus on controls that are, broadly speaking, implemented and executed by people (as opposed to systems). These controls are put in place to improve the security of a particular system (or group of systems). They often require technical or specialized expertise and often rely upon management activities as well as technical controls.

The Technical Controls section focuses on security controls that the computer system executes. These controls are dependent upon the proper functioning of the system for their effectiveness. The implementation of technical controls, however, always requires significant operational considerations and should be consistent with the management of security within the organization.[9]

The 17 specific areas of control are discussed in more detail in the section on NIST SP 800-26 later in this chapter.

NIST Special Publication 800-14

NIST SP 800-14, *Generally Accepted Principles and Practices for Securing Information Technology Systems,* describes best practices and provides information on commonly accepted information security principles that can direct the security team in the development of a security blueprint. It also describes the philosophical principles that the security team should integrate into the entire information security process, expanding upon the components of SP 800-12. Table 6-2 shows the table of contents for NIST SP 800-14.

TABLE 6-2   Table of Contents for NIST SP 800-14, *Generally Accepted Principles and Practices for Securing Information Technology Systems*

1. Introduction

1.1 Principles

1.2 Practices

1.3 Relationship of Principles and Practices

1.4 Background

1.5 Audience

1.6 Structure of this Document

1.7 Terminology

2. Generally Accepted System Security Principles

2.1 Computer Security Supports the Mission of the Organization

2.2 Computer Security Is an Integral Element of Sound Management

2.3 Computer Security Should Be Cost-Effective

2.4 Systems Owners Have Security Responsibilities Outside Their Own Organizations

2.5 Computer Security Responsibilities and Accountability Should Be Made Explicit

2.6 Computer Security Requires a Comprehensive and Integrated Approach

2.7 Computer Security Should Be Periodically Reassessed

2.8 Computer Security Is Constrained by Societal Factors

3. Common IT Security Practices

3.1 Policy

    3.1.1 Program Policy

    3.1.2 Issue-Specific Policy

    3.1.3 System-Specific Policy

    3.1.4 All Policies

3.2 Program Management

    3.2.1 Central Security Program

    3.2.2 System-Level Program

3.3 Risk Management

    3.3.1 Risk Assessment

    3.3.2 Risk Mitigation

    3.3.3 Uncertainty Analysis

3.4 Life Cycle Planning

    3.4.1 Security Plan

    3.4.2 Initiation Phase

    3.4.3 Development/Acquisition Phase

    3.4.4 Implementation Phase

    3.4.5 Operation/Maintenance Phase

    3.4.6 Disposal Phase

TABLE 6-2 Table of Contents for NIST SP 800-14, *Generally Accepted Principles and Practices for Securing Information Technology Systems* (continued)

The more significant points made in NIST SP 800-14 are as follows:

1. **Security Supports the Mission of the Organization.** The implementation of information security is not independent of the organization's mission. On the contrary, *it is driven by it.* An information security system that is not grounded in the organization's mission, vision, and culture is guaranteed to fail. The information security program must support and further the organization's mission, which means that it must include elements of the mission in each of its policies, procedures, and training programs.

2. **Security Is an Integral Element of Sound Management.** Effective management includes planning, organizing, leading, and controlling activities. Security supports the planning function when information security policies provide input into the

organization initiatives, and it supports the controlling function when security controls enforce both managerial and security policies.

3. **Security Should Be Cost-Effective.** The costs of information security should be considered part of the cost of doing business, much like the cost of the computers, networks, and voice communications systems. None of these systems generates any profit, and they may not lead to competitive advantages. As discussed in Chapter 5, however, information security should justify its own costs. Security measures whose costs outweigh their benefits must be rationalized based on other business reasons (such as legal requirements).

4. **Systems Owners Have Security Responsibilities Outside Their Own Organizations.** Whenever systems store and use information from customers, patients, clients, partners, and others, the security of such data becomes a serious responsibility for the systems owners. Also, systems owners have the general duty to protect information assets on behalf of all stakeholders of the organization. These stakeholders may include shareholders in publicly held organizations, and the government and taxpayers in the case of public agencies and institutions.

5. **Security Responsibilities and Accountability Should Be Made Explicit.** Policy documents should clearly identify the security responsibilities of users, administrators, and managers. To be legally binding, such documents must be disseminated, read, understood, and agreed to. As described in Chapter 4, ignorance of the law is no excuse, but ignorance of policy can be. Any relevant legislation must also become part of the security program.

6. **Security Requires a Comprehensive and Integrated Approach.** As emphasized throughout this book, *security is everyone's responsibility.* Throughout each stage of the SecSDLC, the three communities of interest—information technology management and professionals, information security management and professionals, and the users, managers, administrators, and other stakeholders of the broader organization—should participate in all aspects of the information security program.

7. **Security Should Be Periodically Reassessed.** Information security that is implemented and then ignored lacks due diligence and is considered negligent. Security is an ongoing process. To remain effective in the face of a constantly shifting set of threats and a constantly changing user base, the security process must be periodically repeated. Continuous analyses of threats, assets, and controls must be conducted and new blueprints developed.

8. **Security Is Constrained by Societal Factors.** A number of factors influence the implementation and maintenance of security. Legal demands, shareholder requirements, and even business practices affect the implementation of security controls and safeguards, for example. While security professionals would prefer to isolate information assets from the Internet—the major source of threats to those assets— the business requirements of the organization may preclude this control measure.

Table 6-3 shows the principles for securing information technology systems from NIST SP 800-14. This table serves as a checklist for the blueprint process and provides a method to ensure that all key elements are present in the design of an information security program and that the planning efforts produce a blueprint for an effective security architecture.

TABLE 6-3   NIST SP 800-14, *Principles for Securing Information Technology Systems*

Principle 1.	Establish a sound security policy as the "foundation" for the design.
Principle 2.	Treat security as an integral part of the overall system design.
Principle 3.	Clearly delineate the physical and logical security boundaries governed by associated security policies.
Principle 4.	Reduce risk to an acceptable level.
Principle 5.	Assume that external systems are insecure.
Principle 6.	Identify potential trade-offs between reducing risk and increased costs and decreases in other aspects of operational effectiveness.
Principle 7.	Implement layered security (ensure no single point of vulnerability).
Principle 8.	Implement tailored system security measures to meet organizational security goals.
Principle 9.	Strive for simplicity.
Principle 10.	Design and operate an IT system to limit vulnerability and to be resilient in response.
Principle 11.	Minimize the system elements to be trusted.
Principle 12.	Implement security through a combination of measures distributed physically and logically.
Principle 13.	Provide assurance that the system is, and continues to be, resilient in the face of expected threats.
Principle 14.	Limit or contain vulnerabilities.
Principle 15.	Formulate security measures to address multiple overlapping information domains.
Principle 16.	Isolate public access systems from mission-critical resources (e.g., data, processes).
Principle 17.	Use boundary mechanisms to separate computing systems and network infrastructures.
Principle 18.	Where possible, base security on open standards for portability and interoperability.
Principle 19.	Use a common language in developing security requirements.
Principle 20.	Design and implement audit mechanisms to detect unauthorized use and to support incident investigations.
Principle 21.	Design security to allow for regular adoption of new technologies, including a secure and logical technology upgrade process.
Principle 22.	Authenticate users and processes to ensure appropriate access control decisions both within and across domains.
Principle 23.	Use unique identities to ensure accountability.

TABLE 6-3　NIST SP 800-14, *Principles for Securing Information Technology Systems* (continued)

Principle 24.	Implement least privilege. [process of granting the lowest level of access consistent with accomplishing the assigned role]
Principle 25.	Do not implement unnecessary security mechanisms.
Principle 26.	Protect information while being processed, in transit, and in storage.
Principle 27.	Strive for operational ease of use.
Principle 28.	Develop and exercise contingency or disaster recovery procedures to ensure appropriate availability.
Principle 29.	Consider custom products to achieve adequate security.
Principle 30.	Ensure proper security in the shutdown or disposal of a system.
Principle 31.	Protect against all likely classes of "attacks."
Principle 32.	Identify and prevent common errors and vulnerabilities.
Principle 33.	Ensure that developers are trained in how to develop secure software.

Source: National Institute of Standards and Technology. *Generally Accepted Principles and Practices for Securing Information Technology Systems.* SP 800-14. September 1996.

NIST Special Publication 800-18

NIST SP 800-18, *Guide for Developing Security Plans for Information Technology Systems,* provides detailed methods for assessing, designing, and implementing controls and plans for various-sized applications. It serves as a guide for the activities described in this chapter, and for the overall information security planning process. In addition, this document includes templates for major application security plans. As with any publication of this scope and magnitude, SP 800-18 must be customized to fit the particular needs of any organization. Table 6-4 shows the table of contents for SP 800-18.

TABLE 6-4　Table of Contents for NIST SP 800-18, *Guide for Developing Security Plans for Information Technology Systems*

1. Introduction

　　1.1 Background
　　1.2 Major Application or General Support System Plans
　　1.3 Relationship to Other NIST Security Documents
　　1.4 Purposes of Security Plans
　　1.5 Security Plan Responsibilities
　　1.6 Recommended Format
　　1.7 Advice and Comment on Plan
　　1.8 Audience
　　1.9 Organization of Document

2. System Analysis

　　2.1 System Boundaries
　　2.2 Multiple Similar Systems
　　2.3 System Category

TABLE 6-4 Table of Contents for NIST SP 800-18, *Guide for Developing Security Plans for Information Technology Systems* (**continued**)

TABLE 6-4 Table of Contents for NIST SP 800-18, *Guide for Developing Security Plans for Information Technology Systems* (continued)

6. MA Major Application—Technical Controls

6.MA.1 Identification and Authentication

    6.MA.1.1 Identification

    6.MA.1.2 Authentication

6.MA.2 Logical Access Controls (Authorization/Access Controls)

6.MA.3 Public Access Controls

6.MA.4 Audit Trails

7. GSS General Support System—Operational Controls

7.GSS.1 Personnel Controls

7.GSS.2 Physical and Environmental Protection

    7.GSS.2.1 Explanation of Physical and Environment Security

    7.GSS.2.2 Computer Room Example

7.GSS.3 Production, Input/Output Controls

7.GSS.4 Contingency Planning (Continuity of Support)

7.GSS.5 Hardware and System Software Maintenance Controls

7.GSS.6 Integrity Controls

7.GSS.7 Documentation

7.GSS.8 Security Awareness and Training

7.GSS.9 Incident Response Capability

8. GSS General Support System—Technical Controls

8.GSS.1 Identification and Authentication

    8.GSS.1.1 Identification

    8.GSS.1.2 Authentication

8.GSS.2 Logical Access Controls (Authorization/Access Controls)

8.GSS.3 Audit Trails

NIST Special Publication 800-26

NIST SP 800-26, *Security Self-Assessment Guide for Information Technology Systems,* describes 17 areas that span managerial, operational, and technical controls. These 17 areas, which are shown in Table 6-5, form the core of the NIST security management structure.

When working in these areas, be sure to consider the information processed by the system under review and evaluate the need for protective measures. Relate the information processed to each of the three basic information protection requirements (confidentiality, integrity, and availability). In addition, it is often helpful to categorize systems or groups of systems by sensitivity level. Three examples of such categories for sensitive unclassified information are described here:

- High: Extremely grave injury accrues to U.S. interests if the information is compromised; could cause loss of life, imprisonment, or major financial loss, or require legal action for correction
- Medium: Serious injury accrues to U.S. interests if the information is compromised; could cause significant financial loss or require legal action for correction
- Low: Injury accrues to U.S. interests if the information is compromised; would cause only minor financial loss or require only administrative action for correction

TABLE 6-5   Topic Areas Covered in NIST SP 800-26, *Security Self-Assessment Guide for Information Technology Systems*

Management Controls

1. Risk Management
2. Review of Security Controls
3. Life Cycle Maintenance
4. Authorization of Processing (Certification and Accreditation)
5. System Security Plan

Operational Controls

6. Personnel Security
7. Physical Security
8. Production, Input/Output Controls
9. Contingency Planning
10. Hardware and Systems Software
11. Data Integrity
12. Documentation
13. Security Awareness, Training, and Education
14. Incident Response Capability

Technical Controls

15. Identification and Authentication
16. Logical Access Controls
17. Audit Trails

Each of the topics shown in Table 6-5 emerged out of earlier documents and the knowledge and experience of information security professionals.

NIST Special Publication 800-30

NIST SP 800-30, *Risk Management Guide for Information Technology Systems,* provides a foundation for the development of an effective risk management program, containing both the definitions and the practical guidance necessary for assessing and mitigating risks identified within IT systems. The ultimate goal is to help organizations to better manage IT-related mission risks.[10]

This guide can help you develop or evaluate the risk management process. It is organized into five chapters, as shown in Table 6-6.

TABLE 6-6 Table of Contents for NIST SP 800-30, *Risk Management Guide for Information Technology Systems*

1. Introduction

2. Risk Management Overview

2.1	Importance of Risk Management
2.2	Integration of Risk Management into SDLC
2.3	Key Roles

3. Risk Assessment

3.1	Step 1: System Characterization
3.2	Step 2: Threat Identification
3.3	Step 3: Vulnerability Identification
3.4	Step 4: Control Analysis
3.5	Step 5: Likelihood Determination
3.6	Step 6: Impact Analysis
3.7	Step 7: Risk
3.8	Step 8: Control Recommendations
3.9	Step 9: Results Documentation

4. Risk Mitigation

4.1	Risk Mitigation
4.2	Risk Mitigation Strategy
4.3	Approach for Control Implementation
4.4	Control Categories
4.5	Cost-Benefit Analysis
4.6	Residual Risk

5. Evaluation and Assessment

| 5.1 | Good Security Practice |
| 5.2 | Keys For Success |

Appendix A	Sample Interview Questions
Appendix B	Sample Risk Assessment Report Outline
Appendix C	Sample Implementation Safeguard Plan Summary Table
Appendix D	Acronyms
Appendix E	Glossary
Appendix F	References

A Hybrid Security Management Model

As noted earlier in the discussion of the NIST Computer Security Handbook (SP 800-12), and enumerated in Table 6-5, there are three types of security controls:

- **Management controls** cover security processes that are designed by the strategic planners and executed by security administrators. Each of these topics is covered in greater detail in this textbook.
- **Operational controls** deal with the operational functionality of security in the organization.
- **Technical controls** address the tactical and technical issues of designing and implementing security in the organization.

Using these three sets of controls as a foundation, this book offers a synthesis of recommended practices, called the *Hybrid Information Security Framework*. Table 6-7 presents an overview of this approach.

TABLE 6-7   **A Hybrid Information Security Framework**

Management Controls

> Program Management
> System Security Plan
> Life Cycle Maintenance
> Risk Management
> Review of Security Controls
> Legal Compliance

Operational Controls

> Contingency Planning
> Security Education, Training, and Awareness
> Personnel Security
> Physical Security
> Production Inputs and Outputs
> Hardware and Software Systems Maintenance
> Data Integrity

Technical Controls

> Logical Access Controls
> Identification, Authentication, Authorization, and Accountability
> Audit Trails
> Asset Classification and Control
> Cryptography

Table 6-7 provides both a checklist and an outline for information security practitioners. When used as a checklist, it can, like NIST SP 800-26, help you ensure that your planning has included all areas requiring controls. When used as an outline, it provides a convenient way of categorizing project management plans within the overall information security blueprint.

VIEWPOINT

Information System Certification and Accreditation

By Morgan Lestat-Alexander

As a federal agency, the Centers for Disease Control and Prevention (CDC) is required by law to ensure that all of its information systems have been authorized to operate. This authorization is provided through a formal process known as certification and accreditation (C&A). C&A helps to ensure that agency management officials are aware of the risks inherent in the operation of a given system, approve of the current system security controls, and are willing to be held accountable for system breaches, exposure, or loss of service. Under the recently passed Federal Information Security Management Act (FISMA), C&A can also be used as part of the federal funding process; systems that are not accredited and that cannot demonstrate active security maintenance may lose funding and be subject to suspension or cancellation.

The C&A process for federal agencies is defined by NIST through the institute's special publications framework. The CDC has customized this framework into a life-cycle process specifically designed to support the agency's missions and goals. The result is a set of five major requirements that each system must satisfactorily complete before being authorized to operate:

- System characterization: A complete description of the system, its users, data, dependencies, architecture, components, and purpose
- System security plan: A definition of system security requirements and the controls currently deployed to meet those requirements
- Risk assessment: A formal analysis of the threats, vulnerabilities, and risks inherent in the operation of the system
- Security testing and evaluation: The verification of existing security controls and the technical evaluation of their effectiveness
- Plan of action and milestones: A mitigation plan that tracks identified system weaknesses, planned corrective measures, and progress against remediation goals

When a system achieves accreditation, it enters into a maintenance cycle of monitoring, support, and review. Over time, the needs of the agency and the system users will inevitably change. The underlying technologies that support the system may change, too. The C&A process manages all of these changes through regular periodic testing, change control management, system maintenance, and scheduled reaccreditation.

C&A processes, when used effectively, become living life-cycle management tools that ensure appropriate system security and provide a solid demonstration of an organization's commitment to due care and continued diligence.

Morgan Lestat-Alexander is a Senior Analyst with Northrop-Grumman Mission Systems providing contract support for the U.S. Centers for Disease Control and Prevention in Atlanta, Georgia.

Security Management Practices

In information security, two categories of benchmarks are used: standards of due care/due diligence and best practices. Best practices include a subcategory of practices—the so-called gold standard—that are generally regarded as "the best of the best."

Standards of Due Care/Due Diligence

For legal reasons, an organization may be forced to adopt a certain minimum level of security. When organizations adopt minimum levels of security in order to prepare for a future legal defense, they may need to show that they have done what any *prudent* organization would do in similar circumstances; this is known as a **standard of due care**. Implementing controls at this minimum standard, and maintaining them, demonstrates that an organization has performed **due diligence**. Due diligence requires that an organization ensure that the implemented standards continue to provide the required level of protection. Failure to support a standard of due care or due diligence can expose an organization to legal liability, provided it can be shown that the organization was negligent in its application or lack of application of information protection. This consideration is especially important when the organization maintains information about customers, including medical, legal, or other personal data.

The information security protection environment that an organization must maintain can be large and complex. It may, therefore, be impossible to implement best practices in all categories. Based on the budget assigned to the protection of information, it may also be financially impossible to provide security levels on par with those offered by organizations that can spend more money on information security. Information security practices are often viewed relatively; as noted by F. M. Avolio, "Good security now is better than perfect security never."[11] Some organizations might wish to implement the best, most technologically advanced controls available, but for financial or other reasons cannot do so. Ultimately, it is counterproductive to establish costly, state-of-the-art security in one area, only to leave other areas exposed. Instead, organizations must make sure that they have met a reasonable level of security in all areas, and that they have adequately protected all information assets, before improving individual areas to meet the highest standards.

Best Security Practices

Security efforts that seek to provide a superior level of performance in the protection of information are referred to as **best business practices** or simply *best practices*. Some organizations refer to them as **recommended practices**. Security efforts that are among the best in the industry are referred to as **best security practices (BSPs)**. These practices balance the need for information access with the need for adequate protection. They seek to provide as much security as possible for information and information systems while simultaneously demonstrating fiscal responsibility and ensuring ready information access. Of course, companies with best practices may not be the best in every area; they may have established an extremely high quality or successful security effort in only one area.

The federal government has established a Web site that provides government agencies with the opportunity to share their best security practices with other agencies (http://fasp.nist.gov). This project, known as the Federal Agency Security Project, was the result of the Federal Chief Information Officer Council's Federal Best Security Practices (BSP) pilot effort to identify, evaluate, and disseminate best practices for computer information protection and security. The FASP site contains agency policies, procedures, and practices; the CIO pilot BSPs; and, a Frequently Asked Questions (FAQ) section.[12]

While few commercial equivalents exist at this time, many of the BSPs discussed here are applicable to the area of information security in both the public and private sectors. BSPs are organized into the areas shown in Table 6-8, which describes each area and lists examples that can be found on the Web site.

TABLE 6-8   Federal Agency Best Security Practices

Area	Description	Examples
Audit Trail	A record of system activity by system or application processes and by user activity	■ Sample Generic Policy ■ High-Level Procedures for Audit Trails
Authorize Processing (C&A)	A method of assurance of the security of the system	■ Certification and Accreditation Documentation Performance Work Summary ■ Sample Generic Policy and High-Level Procedures for Certification/Accreditation ■ C&A of Core Financial System for USAID ■ How to Accredit Information Systems for Operation
Contingency Planning	Strategies for keeping an organization's critical functions operating in the event of disruptions, whether large or small	■ Contingency Planning Template ■ Contingency Planning Template Instructions ■ Sample Generic Policy and High-Level Procedures for Contingency Plans ■ Continuity of Operations from the U.S. Treasury
Data Integrity	Controls used to protect data from accidental or malicious alteration or destruction and to provide assurance to the user that the information meets expectations about its quality and integrity	■ How to Protect Against Viruses Using Attachment Blocking ■ Sample Generic Policy and High-Level Procedures for Data Integrity/Validation
Documentation	Descriptions of the hardware, software, policies, standards, procedures, and approvals related to the system document and formalized description of the system's security controls	■ Sample Generic Policy and High-Level Procedures for System Documentation

TABLE 6-8 Federal Agency Best Security Practices (continued)

Area	Description	Examples
Hardware and System Software Maintenance	Controls used to monitor the installation of, and updates to, hardware and software to ensure that the system functions as expected and that a historical record is maintained of changes	■ Configuration Management Plan ■ Interim Policy Document on Configuration Management ■ Sample Generic Policy and High-Level Procedures for Hardware and Application Software Security
Identification and Authentication	Technical measures that prevent unauthorized people (or unauthorized processes) from entering an IT system	■ Creating Strong Passwords ■ Password Cracking Information ■ Password Management Standard ■ Sample Generic Policy and High-Level Procedures for Passwords and Access Forms
Incident Response Capability	The capacity to provide help to users when a security incident occurs in a system	■ Computer Incident Response Team Desk Reference ■ Identification and Authentication on Agency Systems ■ Computer Virus Incident Report Form ■ Agency Computer Incident Response Guide ■ Sample Generic Policy and High-Level Procedures for Incident Response ■ Developing an Agency Incident Response Process
Life Cycle	IT system life cycles contain five basic phases: initiation, development and/or acquisition, implementation, operation, and disposal	■ Sample Generic Policy and High-Level Procedures for Life Cycle Security ■ Integrating Security into Systems Development Life Cycle
Logical Access Controls	System-based mechanisms used to designate who or what is to have access to a specific system resource and the type of transactions and functions that are permitted	■ Decision Paper on Use of Screen Warning Banner ■ Sample Warning Banner from the National Labor Relations Board
Network Security	Secure communication capability that allows one user or system to connect to another user or system	■ E-Mail Spam Policy ■ Network Perimeter Security Policy ■ Securing POP Mail on Windows Clients ■ How to Deploy Firewalls ■ Configuration of Technical Safeguards ■ Network Security Management Policy ■ How to Secure a Domain Name Server (DNS)

TABLE 6-8   Federal Agency Best Security Practices (continued)

Area	Description	Examples
Personnel Security	Human users, designers, implementers, and managers—how they interact with computers and the access and authorities they need to do their jobs	▪ Policy on Limited Personnel Use of Government Office Equipment ▪ Email Policy ▪ Internet Use Policy ▪ Limited Personnel Use of Government Equipment ▪ Nondisclosure Form ▪ Guidelines for Evaluating Information on Public Web Sites ▪ Receipt of Proprietary Information ▪ Sample Generic Policy and High-Level Procedures for Personnel Security ▪ Investigative Requirements for Contractor Employees
Physical and Environment Protection	Measures taken to protect systems, buildings, and related supporting infrastructures against threats associated with their physical environment	▪ Securing Portable Electronic Media Agency ▪ Sample Generic Policy and High-Level Procedures for Facility Protection
Production, Input/Output Controls	Covers topics ranging from user help desks to procedures for storing, handling, and destroying media	▪ Disk Sanitization Procedures ▪ Sample Generic Policy and High-Level Procedures for Marking, Handling, Processing, Storage, and Disposal of Data
Policy and Procedures	Formally documented security policies and procedures	▪ Internet Security Policy ▪ Telecommuting and Mobile Computer Security Policy ▪ Sample of Agency Large Service Application (LSA) Information Technology (IT) Security Program Policy ▪ Security Handbook and Standard Operating Procedures for the GSA
Program Management	Overall scope of the program (i.e., PDs, policies, and security program plans and guidance)	▪ IT Security Cost Estimation Guide from the Department of Education ▪ A Summary Guide: Public Law, Executive Orders, and Policy Documents ▪ Position Description for Computer System Security Officer

Source: http://fasp.nist.gov

VISA International Security Model

Another example of best practices is VISA International's Security Model. VISA International, the credit card processing vendor, promotes strong security measures among its business associates, and has established guidelines for the security of its information systems. VISA has developed two important documents that are designed to improve and regulate its information systems: *Security Assessment Process* and *Agreed Upon Procedures*. Both documents provide specific instructions on the use of the VISA Cardholder Information Security Program:[13]

- *Security Assessment Process* contains a series of recommendations for the detailed examination of an organization's systems with the eventual goal of integration into the VISA systems.
- *Agreed Upon Procedures* outlines the policies and technologies used to safeguard security systems that carry the sensitive cardholder information to and from VISA systems.

Using these documents, a security team can design a good security architecture. The downside to this approach is its very specific focus on systems that can or do integrate with VISA's systems, with the explicit purpose of transmitting cardholder-related information.

The Gold Standard

Best business practices are not sufficient for organizations that prefer to set the standard by implementing the most protective, most supportive, yet fiscally responsible standards they can. These organizations strive to achieve the gold standard. As noted earlier, the **gold standard** is a model level of performance that demonstrates industrial leadership, quality, and concern for the protection of information. The implementation of gold-standard security requires a great deal of support, in terms of both financial and personnel resources. While some public information on best practices is available, no published criteria for a gold standard exist. In reality, the gold standard is a level of security that is out of reach for most organizations. While many vendors claim to offer a gold standard in one product or service, such assertions are predominantly marketing hype.

Selecting Best Practices

Choosing which recommended practices to implement can pose a challenge for some organizations. In industries that are regulated by governmental agencies, government guidelines are often requirements that must be met. For other organizations, government guidelines merely serve as excellent sources of information about what steps other organizations are required to take to control information security risks, and can inform their selection of best practices.

When considering best practices for your organization, consider the following questions:

- Does your organization resemble the identified target organization of the best practice?
    - Are you in a similar industry as the target? A strategy that works well in manufacturing organizations might have little relevance to a nonprofit organization.
    - Do you face similar challenges as the target? If your organization lacks a functioning information security program, a best practice target that assumes such a program is in place has value.
    - Is your organizational structure similar to the target? A best practice proposed for a small office is not applicable to a multinational company.

- Are the resources you can expend similar to those required by the best practice? A best practice proposal that assumes unlimited funding has limited value if your program must deal with budget constraints.
- Are you in a similar threat environment as the one assumed by the best practice? Best practices that are months or even weeks old may not answer the current threat environment. To see how quickly obsolescence arises, merely consider the best practice for Internet connectivity required in the modern organization at the opening of the twenty-first century compared to best practices of five years ago.

Another source for best practices information is the Web site operated by the Computer Emergency Response Team (CERT) at Carnegie Mellon University (www.cert.org/security-improvement/), which presents a number of security improvement modules and practices in HTML and PDF formats. Similarly, Microsoft has published a set of best practices in security at its Web site (www.microsoft.com/privacy/safeinternet/security/best_practices/default.htm). Microsoft focuses on seven key tactics:

1. Use antivirus software.
2. Use strong passwords.
3. Verify your software security settings.
4. Update product security.
5. Build personal firewalls.
6. Back up early and often.
7. Protect against power surges and losses.

These resources are but a few of the many public and private organizations that promote solid best security practices. Investing a few hours in searching the Web will reveal dozens of other locations that offer additional information. In fact, finding information on security design is the easy part. Sorting through the collected mass of information, documents, and publications, however, can require a substantial investment in time and human resources. The goal is to obtain a clear methodology enabling the creation of a framework, which in turn leads to a blueprint for the development of a security system that provides specifics on the implementation of the necessary components in the areas of policy, education and training programs, and technology.

Benchmarking and Best Practices Limitations

The biggest problem with benchmarking in information security is that organizations don't talk to each other. That is, a successful attack is viewed as an organizational failure and is kept secret, insofar as possible. As a consequence, the entire industry suffers, because valuable lessons are not recorded, disseminated, and evaluated. Today, however, an increasing number of security administrators are joining professional associations and societies like the Information Systems Security Association (ISSA) and sharing their stories and lessons learned. An alternative to participating in this direct dialog is the publication of lessons learned. Individual security administrators are beginning to publish in security journals sanitized versions of the attacks on their organizations and information, in an effort to share what they have learned.

Another problem with benchmarking is that no two organizations are identical. Even if two organizations offer products or services in the same market, their size, composition, management philosophies, organizational culture, technological infrastructure, and budgets for security may differ dramatically. Even if they did exchange information, each might not be able to apply the strategies of the other. What organizations seek most are lessons that can help them strategically, rather than information about specific technologies they should adopt. Recall that security is a managerial problem, not a technical one. If it were a technical problem, then implementing the same technology would solve the problem regardless of industry or organizational composition. Because it is a managerial and people problem, however, the number and types of variables that affect the security of the organization will likely differ radically in any two organizations.

A third problem is that best practices are a moving target. What worked well two years ago may be completely worthless against today's threats. Security programs must continually keep abreast of new threats as well as methods, techniques, policies, guidelines, educational and training approaches, and, yes, technologies to combat them.

One final issue to consider is that knowing what was happening a few years ago, which is emphasized in benchmarking, doesn't necessarily tell you what to do next. While it's true that, in security, those who do not prepare for the attacks of the past will see them again, it's also true that preparing for past threats does not protect you against what lies ahead. It is important to be as prepared as possible to contain known threats, and then to focus efforts on monitoring the communications and new listings oriented toward systems and security administrators to determine what is coming and to learn how to prepare for it.

Baselining

Related to the concept of benchmarking is the process of baselining. A **baseline** is a "value or profile of a performance metric against which changes in the performance metric can be usefully compared."[14] An example is a baseline for the number of attacks per week that an organization experiences. In the future, this baseline can serve as a reference point to determine whether the average number of attacks is increasing or decreasing. *Baselining* is the process of measuring against established standards. In information security, it involves the comparison of security activities and events against the organization's future performance. Used in this way, baselining can provide the foundation for internal benchmarking. The information gathered for an organization's first risk assessment becomes the baseline for future comparisons.

When baselining it is useful to have a guide to the overall process. NIST offers two publications specifically written to support these activities:

- SP 800-27, *Engineering Principles for Information Technology Security (A Baseline for Achieving Security)*, June 2001
- SP 800-26, *Security Self-Assessment Guide for Information Technology Systems*, November 2001 (discussed elsewhere in this chapter)

Both of these documents are available at http://csrc.nist.gov/publications/nistpubs/index.html.

Baselining and researching best practices provide less detail for the design and implementation of a security program than does use of a complete methodology. Nevertheless, by baselining and using best practices, you can piece together the desired outcome of the security process, then work backward to achieve an effective design.

The Internet Security Task Force (www.ca.com/ISTF) also provides information on best practices. This task force is a collection of parties, both public and private, with a shared interest in the security of the Internet. It provides recommendations for security implementations. Another widely referenced source is CERT (www.cert.org). It promotes a series of security modules, and its Web site provides links to practices and implementation that make up a security methodology.

It may be worth your time and money to join professional societies that maintain information on best practices for their members. The Technology Manager's Forum (www.techforum.com) bestows annual best practice awards in a number of areas, including information security. The Information Security Forum (www.isfsecuritystandard.com) has a free publication titled *Standard of Good Practice* that outlines information security best practices.

Many organizations offer seminars and classes on best practices for implementing security. For example, the Information Systems Audit and Control Association (www.isaca.com) hosts such seminars on a regular basis. Similarly, the International Association of Professional Security Consultants (www.iapsc.org) has a listing of best practices, as does the Global Grid Forum (www.gridforum.org). You can also peruse Web portals for posted security best practices. Several free portals dedicated to security maintain collections of practices, such as SearchSecurity.com and NIST's Computer Resources Center.

The Gartner Group offers 12 questions as a self-assessment for best security practices. The questions are organized into three categories—people, processes, and technology— which loosely map to the managerial, operational, and technical areas of the NIST methodology. The 12 questions are given below:

People

1. Do you perform background checks on all employees with access to sensitive data, areas, or access points?

2. Would the average employee recognize a security issue?

3. Would they choose to report it?

4. Would they know how to report it to the right people?

Processes

5. Are enterprise security policies updated on at least an annual basis, employees educated on changes, and consistently enforced?

6. Does your enterprise follow a patch/update management and evaluation process to prioritize and mediate new security vulnerabilities?

7. Are the user accounts of former employees immediately removed on termination?

8. Are security group representatives involved in all stages of the project life cycle for new projects?

Technology

9. Is every possible route to the Internet protected by a properly configured firewall?

10. Is sensitive data on laptops and remote systems encrypted?

11. Do you regularly scan your systems and networks, using a vulnerability analysis tool, for security exposures?

12. Are malicious software scanning tools deployed on all workstations and servers?[15]

By completing this survey online (www.gartnerinfo.com/sec_diagnostic), an organization can compare its operations to those of other companies, providing a best practices comparison.

Emerging Trends in Certification and Accreditation

In security management, **accreditation** is the authorization of an IT system to process, store, or transmit information. It is issued by a management official and serves as a means of assuring that systems are of adequate quality. It also challenges managers and technical staff to find the best methods to assure security, given technical constraints, operational constraints, and mission requirements.[16] In the same vein, **certification** is defined as "the comprehensive evaluation of the technical and nontechnical security controls of an IT system to support the accreditation process that establishes the extent to which a particular design and implementation meets a set of specified security requirements." [17] Organizations pursue accreditation or certification to gain a competitive advantage, or to provide assurance or confidence to their customers. Federal systems require accreditation under OMB Circular A-130 and the Computer Security Act of 1987. Accreditation demonstrates that management has determined an acceptable risk level and provided resources to control unacceptable risk levels.

Accreditation and certification are not permanent. Just as standards of due diligence and due care require an ongoing maintenance effort, most accreditation and certification processes require reaccreditation or recertification every few years (typically every three to five years). For commentary on this topic, see the Viewpoint feature earlier in this chapter.

SP 800-37: Guidelines for the Security Certification and Accreditation of Federal IT Systems

NIST promotes a new System Certification and Accreditation Project designed to achieve three goals:

- Develop standard guidelines and procedures for certifying and accrediting federal IT systems, including the critical infrastructure of the United States
- Define essential minimum security controls for federal IT systems
- Promote the development of public- and private-sector assessment organizations and certification of individuals capable of providing cost-effective, high-quality security certifications based on standard guidelines and procedures

The security certification and accreditation (C&A) initiative offers several specific benefits:

- More consistent, comparable, and repeatable certifications of IT systems
- More complete, reliable information for authorizing officials—leading to better understanding of complex IT systems and their associated risks and vulnerabilities—and, therefore, to more-informed decisions by management officials
- Greater availability of competent security evaluation and assessment services
- More secure IT systems within the federal government [18]

Figure 6-3 shows the relationship between the primary publication SP 800-37 and other NIST publications.

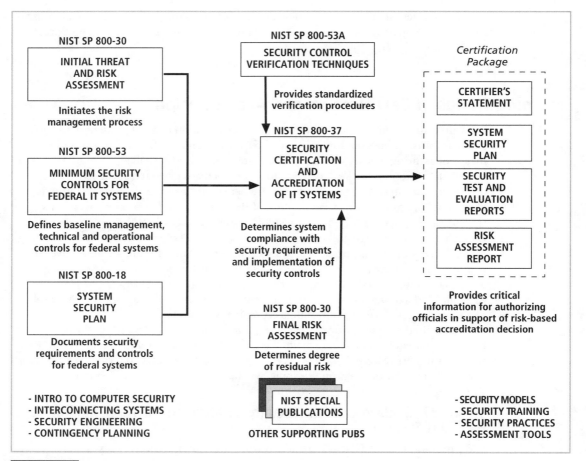

FIGURE 6-3   Special Publications Supporting SP 800-37

Source: R. Ross and M. Swanson. *Guidelines for the Security Certification and Accreditation of Federal Information Technology Systems. NIST SP 800-53.* October 2002.

800-37 focuses on a three-step security controls selection process:[19]

Step 1: Characterize the System
Obtain the following system-related information from the security plan:

- Accreditation boundary for the system and, if appropriate, the proposed decomposition of the system into subsystem components
- Criticality/sensitivity of the system (or subsystems, if appropriate) based on levels of concern for confidentiality, integrity, and availability
- External system exposure based on level of concern by system or by subsystem, if appropriate
- Internal system exposure based on level of concern by system or by subsystem, if appropriate

Step 2: Select the Appropriate Minimum Security Controls for the System
- Select minimum security controls from the standard package of basic controls
- Select additional minimum security controls (moderate/high levels), if appropriate, to create a supplemental package of controls based on increased levels of concern for confidentiality, integrity, and/or availability
- Create agency-specific or technology-driven security controls

Step 3: Adjust Security Controls Based on System Exposure and Risk Decisions
- Adjust the selected controls based on internal/external exposure and risk-based decisions; describe the controls in documented, allowable waivers

Systems are classified into one of three security certification levels:[20]

- Security Certification Level 1: The entry-level certification appropriate for low-priority (concern) systems. SCL-1 certifications typically employ agency-directed, independent assessments or basic security reviews of IT systems using questionnaires or specialized checklists, intended to demonstrate proper levels of implementation for these low levels of concern.
- Security Certification Level 2: The mid-level certification appropriate for moderate-priority (concern) systems. SCL-2 certifications call for independent assessments of IT systems building on the verification techniques and procedures from SCL-1 and adding more substantial techniques and procedures, as appropriate.
- Security Certification Level 3: The top-level certification appropriate for high-priority (concern) systems. SCL-3 certifications call for independent assessments of IT systems building on the verification techniques and procedures from SCL-1 and SCL-2 and employing the most rigorous verification techniques, as appropriate.

SP 800-53: Minimum Security Controls for Federal IT Systems

SP 800-53 is the second part of NIST's System Certification and Accreditation Project. Its purpose is to "establish a set of standardized, minimum security controls for IT systems addressing low, moderate, and high levels of concern for confidentiality, integrity, and availability."[21] It derives its information from a number of other federal documents, including NIST SP 800-26, Department of Defense (DoD) Policy 8500, Director of Central Intelligence Directive (DCID) 6-3, ISO/IEC Standard 17799, and General Accounting Office (GAO) Federal Information System Controls Audit Manual (FISCAM).

As in earlier NIST documents (especially SP 800-18), security controls in SP 800-53 are classified into the three familiar general categories of security controls: management, operational, and technical. Each of the three classes addresses various aspects of security topics, including "risk management, system development and acquisition, configuration management, system interconnection, personnel security, security awareness, education, and training, physical and environmental protection, media protection, contingency planning, hardware and system software maintenance, system and data integrity, documentation, incident response capability, identification and authentication, logical access, audit, and communications."[22] New to the C&A criteria is the concept of critical elements, which were initially defined in SP 800-26. Critical elements represent "important security-related focus areas for the system with each critical element addressed by one or more security controls."[23] As technology evolves, so will the set of security controls, requiring additional control mechanisms. Figure 6-4 describes the participants in the certification and accreditation process.

FIGURE 6-4 Participants in the Certification and Accreditation Process

NIST SP 800-53, *Minimum Security Controls for Federal Information Technology Systems*, and its companion publication, NIST SP 800-53A, *Techniques and Procedures for the Verification of Security Controls in Federal Information Technology Systems*, are expected to be published in late 2003 or early 2004.

THREAT MANAGEMENT

Man-in-the-Middle Attack

Introduction

Many types of attacks occur on public networks. One of the more damaging is the man-in-the-middle attack (MITM), also called TCP hijacking. The classic MITM attack works by convincing hosts that another computer on network, the so-called man-in-the-middle, is the host with which they wish to communicate.

Convincing the target hosts can be accomplished in two ways. One is a domain name spoof, used when the victim uses Domain Name Service (DNS) to perform address resolution (converting the name of a server to its numeric address) and the attacker can alter the DNS entries. This approach is sometimes called DNS poisoning. The other approach is performing a spoofing exploit with the address resolution protocol (ARP) that makes the victim think it knows the host address based on erroneous notifications from what seems to be the DNS. Both of these exploits target the establishment of the initial TCP session by the victim, who thinks they are connecting to a legitimate host; hence the name TCP hijacking.

(continued)

DNS Spoofing

There are two different ways to accomplish DNS spoofing. The first is to alter the DNS server itself. This redirects all traffic bound for a specific domain name to to any IP address the attacker desires. The second is to trick the victim by mimicking the DNS service when DNS resolution requests for a specific host are detected. The attacker's false reply, with a fake IP address for the requested host, arrives before the true reply from the legitimate DNS server, and the victim proceeds to connect to the spoofed host with the faked address.

ARP Spoofing

ARP spoofing involves constructing forged ARP request and reply packets. By sending forged ARP replies, a victim can be convinced to send packets destined for one host to a different host. When done properly, neither the victim nor the true host has any idea that this redirection took place. Once computers on a network have updated their ARP cache to send all packets destined for the true host to the attacker's host, all connection requests for the target host are routed to the attacker. The attacker can then either pretend to be the true host, or else act to establish a connection to the true host and monitor and record all of the traffic between the victim and the true host. This is all done in the background, without any computer on the LAN detecting what has happened. If the attacker monitors, records, and/or alters the traffic in the connection between the victim client and the victim host, it is an MITM attack.

Control Methods for Man-in-the-Middle-Attacks

The keys to controlling the MITM attacks are to establish a well-defined, policy-based network perimeter, keep all local network systems up-to-date with vendor patches, and secure the DNS infrastructure of the local network. Maintaining a solid program of network monitoring, network intrusion detection, and host intrusion detection can add additional protection. A properly configured firewall can prevent many spoofing exploits and can alert you to some warning signs of an attack, as well as provide forensic logging of network events in case an attack is successfully carried out. Establishing tight controls on how DNS systems are configured (especially the restriction of DNS Zone transfers) can restrict the ability of a network insider to carry out a MITM attack.

The use of cryptographic access control technologies greatly complicates the attacker's effort and raises the likelihood that the victim client can detect the deception. Cryptography in HTTPS and SSL is based on public key cryptography and thus HTTPS requires the trust of public key certificates. When a user of the victim client is prompted to respond to a dialog box indicating that the public key has changed or that there is a bad certificate or unknown certificate authority, the user may cancel the connection request or else raise an alarm. Therefore, system users should be made aware that these are warning signs of something gone wrong.

Response to Attack

- **Remain calm:** The intruder may have been in your computer for days or weeks, so another few hours will not make any difference. Calm and deliberate responses are required.
- **Take good notes:** You must take detailed, organized, and complete notes while handling the attack. The notes must contain answers to the questions Who, What, When, and Where.

(continued)

- **Notify the right people and get help:** Inform the right people about the incident and ask for further assistance. People with a need to know about the incidents must be notified. The well-meaning handler often becomes part of the incident itself. Make sure that this doesn't happen to you. Make sure of the facts before you pass them on.
- **Use out-of-band communications:** It is better to use telephone and faxes during the attack because the attacker might have full access, and might be able to read your e-mail. The attacker knows if you are using your computer; thus it is better not to use the computer.
- **Contain the problem:** In order to contain the problem and regain control, all communication between the compromised host and other hosts on the network must be stopped.
- **Make backups:** Make backups of the file system information. Make multiple full backups using at least two different methods.
- **Get rid of the problem:** First, you need to understand the cause of the incident. Which vulnerability did the intruder use to gain access? Once you find out the cause, you can reload a clean operating system and ensure the improvement of the system's defenses by installing the right software. You must harden the system by applying all of the latest patches, disabling any unnecessary services, and taking any other system-specific steps required. Once the system has been completely hardened, you can reconnect to the network. Follow up by performing a vulnerability analysis on all other systems in the local network, taking care to target similar systems to the victim host.
- **Get back in business:** Being attacked is a fairly normal occurrence and it can happen to anyone. Once the situation is under control, learn what lessons you can, and move on.

Contributed by Nicole Hart, Andrew Palmer, Josh Joiner, Fadi Meqbel

Chapter Summary

- A security model is a generic blueprint that has been offered by a service organization or institution for other organizations to follow.
- Among the most accessible places to find a quality security management model are U.S. federal agencies and international organizations.
- ISO/IEC 17799, *Information Technology—Code of Practice for Information Security Management,* was originally published as the British Standard BS 7799. It provides information security management recommendations to information security professionals.
- BS 7799:2 picks up where ISO/IEC 17799 leaves off. It provides information on how to implement Volume 1 (17799) and how to set up an Information Security Management Structure (ISMS).

- RFC 2196, *The Site Management Handbook,* provides an overview of five basic areas of security with detailed discussions on their development and implementation.
- The National Institute for Standards and Technology (NIST) provides several references that can assist in the design of a security framework:
  - SP 800-12, *Computer Security Handbook,* is an excellent reference and guide for the security manager or administrator in the routine management of information security.
  - SP 800-14, *Generally Accepted Security Principles and Practices,* provides recommended best practices and information on commonly accepted information security principles.
  - SP 800-18, *Guide for Developing Security Plans,* lays out the foundation for a comprehensive security blueprint and framework.
  - SP 800-26, *Security Self-Assessment Guide for Information Technology Systems,* includes assessment checklists organized into 17 areas that span managerial, operational, and technical controls.
  - SP 800-30, *Risk Management for Information Technology Systems,* lays out a foundation for the development of an effective risk management program.
- The Hybrid Information Security Framework is a synthesis of various reference sources.
- Due diligence entails the demonstration that the organization is ensuring that the implemented standards continue to provide the required level of protection.
- Security efforts that seek to provide a superior level of information protection are referred to as best business practices.
- When considering best practices for adoption in your organization, compare your organization to the example practice according to the following criteria: industry, organizational size, organizational structure, resources, and threat environment.
- A baseline is a value or profile of a performance metric against which changes in the performance metric can be usefully compared.
- Federal information systems are required to be accredited. NIST is promoting a new System Certification and Accreditation Project designed to develop standard guidelines. This consists of three steps:

  Step 1: Characterize the System

  Step 2: Select the Appropriate Minimum Security Controls for the System

  Step 3: Adjust Security Controls Based on System Exposure and Risk Decisions

  Systems are classified into one of three security certification levels.

Review Questions

1. What is an information security framework? How does it relate to the information security blueprint?
2. What is a security model? How might an information security professional use such a model?
3. Which information security model evolved from the BS 7799 model? What does it include?
4. What is an alternative model to the BS 7799 model (and its successor)? What does it include?
5. How many sections does the ISO/IEC 17799 include? What is the first of these sections?
6. What is the Security Management Index? Who is its sponsor? What does it accomplish?
7. Which organization sponsors RFC 2196? What does RFC 2196 provide?
8. What are the two primary advantages of NIST security models?

9. What is the name and purpose of NIST SP 800-12? What resources does it provide?

10. What is the name and purpose of NIST SP 800-14? What resources does it provide?

11. What is the name and purpose of NIST SP 800-18? What resources does it provide?

12. What is the name and purpose of NIST SP 800-26? What resources does it provide?

13. What is the name and purpose of NIST SP 800-30? What resources does it provide?

14. What is the Hybrid Security Model? What does it provide that is not in any single NIST, RFC, or ISO/IEC model?

15. What is the standard of due care? How does it relate to due diligence?

16. What is a best security practice? What is a good source for finding such best practices?

17. What is a gold standard in information security practices? Where can you find published criteria for it?

18. When selecting best practices, what criteria should you use?

19. What is benchmarking? What is baselining? How do they differ?

20. Which reference document describes the new initiative for certification and accreditation of federal IT systems?

Exercises

1. Visit the VISA Web site at www.usa.visa.com/business/merchants/cisp_index.html. Locate the document outlining the Cardholder Information Security Program. Compare this program to the NIST documents outlined in this chapter. Which areas are similar to those covered in the NIST documents, and which areas are different?

2. Compare the ISO 17799 outline with the NIST documents outlined in this chapter. Which areas, if any, are missing from the NIST documents? Identify the strengths and weaknesses of the NIST programs compared to the ISO standard.

3. Using a Web browser, search for the term "security best practices." Compare your findings to the best practices outlined in the NIST documents.

4. Using the list of Generally Accepted System Security Principles, look for examples within your institution that support (or do not support) each principle.

5. What other security models exist? Search the Web for "security models" and compare your findings to the models described in this chapter.

Case Exercises

Iris sighed as she completed her initial review of her staff's checklist results. She pulled out a notepad and began outlining the projects she foresaw, based on the shortcomings identified via the checklists. She was fortunate to have found a useful model for an information security review of her program.

1. Based on your understanding of the chapter, from which model did Iris draw her checklist?

2. Referring to the section in this chapter regarding best practices, what do you think Iris should do next?

Endnotes

1. National Institute of Standards and Technology. *Information Security Management, Code of Practice for Information Security Management.* ISO/IEC 17799. December 6, 2001.
2. Ibid.
3. Ibid.
4. T. Humphries. *The Newly Revised Part 2 of BS 7799.* Accessed May 27, 2003. http://www.gammassl.co.uk/bs7799/The%20Newly%20Revised%20Part%202%20of%20BS%207799ver3a.pdf.
5. *How 7799 Works.* Accessed May 27, 2003. http://www.gammassl.co.uk/bs7799/works.html.
6. Human Firewall Council. *Welcome to the Security Management Index.* Accessed May 1, 2003. http://www.humanfirewall.org/smi/.
7. Human Firewall Council. *The Alarming State of Security Management Practices Among Organizations Worldwide.* Accessed May 27, 2003. http://www.humanfirewall.org/SMIReport/SMIReport2003.pdf.
8. National Institute of Standards and Technology. *An Introduction to Computer Security: The NIST Handbook.* SP 800-12. October 1995.
9. Ibid.
10. National Institute of Standards and Technology. *Risk Management Guide for Information Technology Systems.* SP 800-30. January 2002.
11. F. M. Avolio. Best practices in network security. *Network Computing,* March 20, 2000.
12. *http://fasp.nist.gov.*
13. VISA. Cardholder Information Security Program. *Visa Online.* Cited June 24, 2002. Available from the World Wide Web at *http://www.usa.visa.com/business/merchants/cisp_index.html.*
14. *http://www.networkcomputing.com/netdesign/base2.html.*
15. Gartner Group. *Enterprise Security Diagnostic: Best Practices.* Accessed May 1, 2003. *https://www.garterinfo.com/sec_diagnostic/.*
16. National Institute of Standards and Technology. *Background.* Accessed May 27, 2003. http://csrc.nist.gov/sec-cert/ca-background.html.
17. Ibid.
18. Ibid.
19. R. Ross and M. Swanson. *Guidelines for the Security Certification and Accreditation of Federal Information Technology Systems.* NIST SP 800-53. October 2002.
20. Ibid.
21. National Institute of Standards and Technology. *Security Controls.* Accessed May 27, 2003. *http://csrc.nist.gov/sec-cert/ca-controls.html.*
22. Ibid.
23. Ibid.

Appendix: NIST SP 800-26, Security Self-Assessment Guide for Information Technology Systems, and the Human Firewall Council's Security Management Index Survey

A

NIST SP 800-26, Security Self-Assessment Guide for Information Technology Systems

The self-assessment questionnaire contains three sections: a cover sheet, questions, and notes. The cover sheet requires descriptive information about the major application, general support system, or group of interconnected systems being assessed.

The questions take a hierarchical approach to assessing a system by examining critical elements and subordinate questions. The critical element level is determined by the answers to the subordinate questions. The critical elements are derived primarily from OMB Circular A-130. The subordinate questions address the control objectives and techniques that can be implemented to satisfy the critical elements. Assessors will need to carefully review the levels of subordinate control objectives and techniques to determine which level has been reached for the related critical element. The control objectives were obtained from the list of source documents given in Appendix B. Note that there is some flexibility in implementing the control objectives and techniques. In some cases, not all control objectives and techniques may be needed to achieve the critical element.

The questionnaire section may be customized by the organization. An organization can add questions, require more descriptive information, and even pre-mark certain questions if applicable. For example, many agencies have personnel security procedures that apply to all systems within the agency. The level 1 and level 2 columns in the questionnaire can be pre-marked to reflect the standard personnel procedures in place. Additional columns may be added to reflect the status of the control (i.e., planned action date, not applicable, or location of documentation). The questionnaire should not have questions removed or questions modified to reduce the effectiveness of the control.

After each question, there appear a comment field and an initial field. The comment field can be used to note the reference to supporting documentation that is attached to the questionnaire or is obtainable for that question. The initial field can be used when a risk-based decision is made not to implement a control or if the control does not apply to the system.

At the end of each set of questions, there is also an area provided for notes. This area may be used to denote where in a system security plan specific sections should be modified. It can be used to document why a particular control objective is not being implemented fully or why it is overly rigorous. The notes section may be a good place to mark where follow-up work is needed or where additional testing (e.g., penetration testing or product evaluations) should be initiated. Additionally, the section may reference supporting documentation on how the control objectives and techniques were tested and a summary of findings.

Utilizing the Completed Questionnaire

The questionnaire can be used for two purposes. First, agency managers who know their agency's systems and security controls can use it to quickly gain a general understanding of where security for a system, group of systems, or the entire agency needs improvement. Second, the questionnaire can serve as a guide for thoroughly evaluating the status of security for a system. The results of such comprehensive reviews provide a much more reliable measure of security effectiveness and may be used to fulfill reporting requirements, prepare for audits, and identify resource needs.

Questionnaire Analysis

Because this questionnaire is a self-assessment, ideally the individuals who are assessing the system will be the owners of the system or will be responsible for operating or administering it. The same individuals who completed the assessment can conduct the analysis of the completed questionnaire. Alternatively, a centralized group, such as an agency's Information System Security Program Office, can conduct the analysis as long as the supporting documentation is sufficient. The results of the analysis should be placed in an action plan, and the system security plan should be created or updated to reflect each control objective and technique decision.

Action Plans

How the critical element will be implemented—that is, specific procedures, equipment installed and tested, and personnel trained—should be documented in an action plan. This action plan must contain projected dates, an allocation of resources, and follow-up reviews to ensure that remedial actions have been effective. Routine reports should be submitted to senior management on weaknesses identified, status of the action plans, and resources still needed.

Management, Operational, and Technical Controls

The results from the completed questionnaires' 17 control topic areas can be used to summarize an agency's implementation of management, operational, and technical controls. For the report to give an accurate picture, these results must be summarized by system type, rather than being compiled into an overall agency grade level. As an example, suppose ten systems were assessed using the questionnaire. Five of the ten systems assessed were major applications; the other five were general support systems. The summary should then separate the systems into general support systems and major applications.

By further separating the systems and control objectives into groups according to criticality, the report stresses which ones require more attention based on their sensitivity and criticality. Not all systems require the same level of protection, of course; the report should reflect that diversity. The use of percentages for describing compliance (i.e., 50% of the major applications and 25% of the general support systems that are deemed high in criticality have complete system security plans that were developed within the past three years) can be used as long as a distinct division is made between the types of systems being reported.

All, or a sampling of, the completed questionnaires can be analyzed to determine which controls, if implemented, would affect the most systems. For example, if viruses frequently plague systems, then a stricter firewall policy that prohibits attached files in e-mail may be a solution. Also, systemic problems should be culled out. If an agency sees an influx of poor password management controls in the questionnaire results, then possibly password checkers should be used, awareness material issued, and password-aging software installed.

The report should conclude with a summary of planned IT security initiatives. This summary should include goals, actions needed to meet those goals, projected resources, and anticipated dates of completion.

Questionnaire Cover Sheet

The cover sheet provides instruction on completing the questionnaire, standardizing how the completed evaluation should be marked, indicating how systems are named, and labeling the criticality of the system.

All completed questionnaires should be marked, handled, and controlled at the level of sensitivity determined by organizational policy. Note that the information contained in a completed questionnaire could easily identify where the system or group of systems is most vulnerable.

The cover sheet of the questionnaire begins with the name and title of the system to be evaluated. As explained in NIST SP 800-18, each major application or general support system should be assigned a unique name/identifier. The purpose and objectives of the assessment should be identified as well. The names, titles, and sponsoring organizations of the individuals who will perform the assessment should also be listed, and the organization should customize the cover page accordingly. Finally, the start and completion dates of the evaluation should appear on the cover sheet.

Criticality of Information

The level of sensitivity of information as determined by the program official or system owner should be documented using the table on the questionnaire cover sheet. The premise behind formulating the level of sensitivity is that systems supporting higher-risk operations would be expected to have more stringent controls than those supporting lower-risk operations.

The questions are separated into three major control areas: management controls, operational controls, and technical controls. The division of control areas in this manner complements three other NIST Special Publications: NIST SP 800-12, *An Introduction to Computer Security: The NIST Handbook* (Handbook); NIST SP 800-14, *Generally Accepted Principles and Practices for Securing Information Technology Systems* (Principles and Practices); and NIST SP 800-18, *Guide for Developing Security Plans for Information Technology Systems* (Planning Guide).

The method for answering the questions can be based primarily on an examination of relevant documentation and a rigorous examination and test of the controls. The five levels describing the state of the control objective provide a picture of each operational control; the determination of how well each one of these control objectives, however, is met is subjective. Criteria have been established for each of the five levels that should be applied when determining whether the control objective has fully reached one or more of these levels.

As stated previously, the critical elements are required to be implemented; the control objectives and techniques, however, tend to be more detailed and leave room for reasonable subjective decisions. If a particular control does not reasonably apply to the system, then "not applicable" or "NA" can be entered next to the question. Note that management controls focus on the management of the IT security system and the management of risk for a system; these techniques and concerns are normally addressed by management.

The Self-Assessment Guide Questions

To measure the progress of effectively implementing the needed security control, five levels of effectiveness are provided for each answer to the security control question:

- Level 1: control objective is documented in a security policy
- Level 2: security controls have been documented as procedures
- Level 3: procedures have been implemented
- Level 4: procedures and security controls are tested and reviewed
- Level 5: procedures and security controls are fully integrated into a comprehensive program

Each of the items shown in the following checklist is evaluated on this scale. Individuals using the guide will check the level that corresponds to their current readiness level.

Specific Control Objectives and Techniques	Level 1	Level 2	Level 3	Level 4	Level 5	Risk-Based Decision Made	Comments	Initials
Management Controls								
1. Risk Management								
1.1 Critical Element: **Is risk periodically assessed?**								
1.1.1 Is the current system configuration documented, including links to other systems?								
1.1.2 Are risk assessments performed and documented on a regular basis or whenever the system, facilities, or other conditions change?								
1.1.3 Has data sensitivity and integrity of the data been considered?								
1.1.4 Have threat sources, both natural and manmade, been identified?								
1.1.5 Has a list of known system vulnerabilities, system flaws, or weaknesses that could be exploited by the threat sources been developed and maintained current?								
1.1.6 Has an analysis been conducted that determines whether the security requirements in place adequately mitigate vulnerabilities?								
1.2 Critical Element: **Do program officials understand the risk to systems under their control and determine the acceptable level of risk?**								
1.2.1 Are final risk determinations and related management approvals documented and maintained on file?								

Specific Control Objectives and Techniques	Level 1	Level 2	Level 3	Level 4	Level 5	Risk-Based Decision Made	Comments	Initials
1.2.2 Has a mission/business impact analysis been conducted?								
1.2.3 Have additional controls been identified to sufficiently mitigate identified risks?								
2. Review of Security Controls								
2.1 Critical Element: **Have the security controls of the system and interconnected systems been reviewed?**								
2.1.1 Has the system and all network boundaries been subjected to periodic reviews?								
2.1.2 Has an independent review been performed when a significant change occurred?								
2.1.3 Are routine self-assessments conducted?								
2.1.4 Are tests and examinations of key controls routinely made i.e., network scans, analyses of router and switch settings, penetration testing?								
2.1.5 Are security alerts and security incidents analyzed and remedial actions taken?								
2.2 Critical Element: **Does management ensure that corrective actions are effectively implemented?**								
2.2.1 Is there an effective and timely process for reporting significant weaknesses and ensuring effective remedial actions?								

Specific Control Objectives and Techniques	Level 1	Level 2	Level 3	Level 4	Level 5	Risk-Based Decision Made	Comments	Initials
3. Life Cycle								
3.1 Critical Element: Has a system development life-cycle methodology been developed?								
Initiation Phase								
3.1.1 Is the sensitivity of the system determined?								
3.1.2 Does the business case document the resources required for adequately securing the system?								
3.1.3 Does the Investment Review Board ensure any investment request includes the security resources needed?								
3.1.4 Are authorizations for software modifications documented and maintained?								
3.1.5 Does the budget request include the security resources required for the system?								
Development/Acquisition Phase								
3.1.6 During the system design, are security requirements identified?								
3.1.7 Was an initial risk assessment performed to determine security requirements?								
3.1.8 Is there a written agreement with program officials on the security controls employed and residual risk?								

Specific Control Objectives and Techniques	Level 1	Level 2	Level 3	Level 4	Level 5	Risk-Based Decision Made	Comments	Initials
3.1.9 Are security controls consistent with and an integral part of the IT architecture of the agency?								
3.1.10 Are the appropriate security controls with associated evaluation and test procedures developed before the procurement action?								
3.1.11 Do the solicitation documents (e.g., request for proposals) include security requirements and evaluation/test procedures?								
3.1.12 Do the requirements in the solicitation documents permit updating security controls as new threats/vulnerabilities are identified and as new technologies are implemented?								
Implementation Phase								
3.2 Critical Element: **Are changes controlled as programs progress through testing to final approval?**								
3.2.1 Are design reviews and system tests run prior to placing the system in production?								
3.2.2 Are the test results documented?								
3.2.3 Is certification testing of security controls conducted and documented?								
3.2.4 If security controls were added since development, has the system documentation been modified to include them?								

Specific Control Objectives and Techniques	Level 1	Level 2	Level 3	Level 4	Level 5	Risk-Based Decision Made	Comments	Initials
3.2.5 If security controls were added since development, have the security controls been tested and the system recertified?								
3.2.6 Has the application undergone a technical evaluation to ensure that it meets applicable federal laws, regulations, policies, guidelines, and standards?								
3.2.7 Does the system have written authorization to operate either on an interim basis with planned corrective action or full authorization?								
Operation/Maintenance Phase								
3.2.8 Has a system security plan been developed and approved?								
3.2.9 If the system connects to other systems, have controls been established and disseminated to the owners of the interconnected systems?								
3.2.10 Is the system security plan kept current?								
Disposal Phase								
3.2.11 Are official electronic records properly disposed/archived?								
3.2.12 Is information or media purged, overwritten, degaussed, or destroyed when disposed or used elsewhere?								
3.2.13 Is a record kept of who implemented the disposal actions and verified that the information or media was sanitized?								

Specific Control Objectives and Techniques	Level 1	Level 2	Level 3	Level 4	Level 5	Risk-Based Decision Made	Comments	Initials
4. Authorize Processing (Certification and Accreditation)								
4.1 Critical Element: **Has the system been certified/recertified and authorized to process (accredited)?**								
4.1.1 Has a technical and/or security evaluation been completed or conducted when a significant change occurred?								
4.1.2 Has a risk assessment been conducted when a significant change occurred?								
4.1.3 Have rules of behavior been established and signed by users?								
4.1.4 Has a contingency plan been developed and tested?								
4.1.5 Has a system security plan been developed, updated, and reviewed?								
4.1.6 Are in-place controls operating as intended?								
4.1.7 Are the planned and in-place controls consistent with the identified risks and the system and data sensitivity?								
4.1.8 Has management authorized interconnections to all systems (including systems owned and operated by another program, agency, organization, or contractor)?								
4.2 Critical Element: **Is the system operating on an interim authority to process in accordance with specified agency procedures?**								

Specific Control Objectives and Techniques	Level 1	Level 2	Level 3	Level 4	Level 5	Risk-Based Decision Made	Comments	Initials
4.2.1 Has management initiated prompt action to correct deficiencies?								
5. System Security Plan								
5.1 Critical Element: **Is a system security plan documented for the system and all interconnected systems if the boundary controls are ineffective?**								
5.1.1 Is the system security plan approved by key affected parties and management?								
5.1.2 Does the plan contain the topics prescribed in NIST Special Publication 800-18?								
5.1.3 Is a summary of the plan incorporated into the strategic IRM plan?								
5.2 Critical Element: **Is the plan kept current?**								
5.2.1 Is the plan reviewed periodically and adjusted to reflect current conditions and risks?								
Operational Controls								
6. Personnel Security								
6.1 Critical Element: **Are duties separated to ensure least privilege and individual accountability?**								
6.1.1 Are all positions reviewed for sensitivity level?								
6.1.2 Are there documented job descriptions that accurately reflect assigned duties and responsibilities and that segregate duties?								

Specific Control Objectives and Techniques	Level 1	Level 2	Level 3	Level 4	Level 5	Risk-Based Decision Made	Comments	Initials
6.1.3 Are sensitive functions divided among different individuals?								
6.1.4 Are distinct systems support functions performed by different individuals?								
6.1.5 Are mechanisms in place for holding users responsible for their actions?								
6.1.6 Are regularly scheduled vacations and periodic job/shift rotations required?								
6.1.7 Are hiring, transfer, and termination procedures established?								
6.1.8 Is there a process for requesting, establishing, issuing, and closing user accounts?								
6.2 Critical Element: **Is appropriate background screening for assigned positions completed prior to granting access?**								
6.2.1 Are individuals who are authorized to bypass significant technical and operational controls screened prior to access and periodically thereafter?								
6.2.2 Are confidentiality or security agreements required for employees assigned to work with sensitive information?								
6.2.3 When controls cannot adequately protect the information, are individuals screened prior to access?								

Specific Control Objectives and Techniques	Level 1	Level 2	Level 3	Level 4	Level 5	Risk-Based Decision Made	Comments	Initials
6.2.4 Are there conditions for allowing system access prior to completion of screening?								
7. Physical and Environmental Protection								
7.1 Critical Element: Have adequate physical security controls been implemented that are commensurate with the risks of physical damage or access?								
7.1.1 Is access to facilities controlled through the use of guards, identification badges, or entry devices such as key cards or biometrics?								
7.1.2 Does management regularly review the list of persons with physical access to sensitive facilities?								
7.1.3 Are deposits and withdrawals of tapes and other storage media from the library authorized and logged?								
7.1.4 Are keys or other access devices needed to enter the computer room and tape/media library?								
7.1.5 Are unused keys or other entry devices secured?								
7.1.6 Do emergency exit and reentry procedures ensure that only authorized personnel are allowed to reenter after fire drills, etc?								
7.1.7 Are visitors to sensitive areas signed in and escorted?								
7.1.8 Are entry codes changed periodically?								

Specific Control Objectives and Techniques	Level 1	Level 2	Level 3	Level 4	Level 5	Risk-Based Decision Made	Comments	Initials
7.1.9 Are physical accesses monitored through audit trails and apparent security violations investigated and remedial action taken?								
7.1.10 Is suspicious access activity investigated and appropriate action taken?								
7.1.11 Are visitors, contractors, and maintenance personnel authenticated through the use of preplanned appointments and identification checks?								
Fire Safety Factors								
7.1.12 Are appropriate fire suppression and prevention devices installed and working?								
7.1.13 Are fire ignition sources, such as failures of electronic devices or wiring, improper storage materials, and the possibility of arson, reviewed periodically?								
Supporting Utilities								
7.1.14 Are heating and air-conditioning systems regularly maintained?								
7.1.15 Is there a redundant air-cooling system?								
7.1.16 Are electric power distribution, heating plants, water, sewage, and other utilities periodically reviewed for risk of failure?								
7.1.17 Are building plumbing lines known and do not endanger system?								
7.1.18 Has an uninterruptible power supply or backup generator been provided?								

Specific Control Objectives and Techniques	Level 1	Level 2	Level 3	Level 4	Level 5	Risk-Based Decision Made	Comments	Initials
7.1.19 Have controls been implemented to mitigate other disasters, such as floods, earthquakes, etc.?								
Interception of Data								
7.2 Critical Element: Is data protected from interception?								
7.2.1 Are computer monitors located to eliminate viewing by unauthorized persons?								
7.2.2 Is physical access to data transmission lines controlled?								
Mobile and Portable Systems								
7.3 Critical Element: Are mobile and portable systems protected?								
7.3.1 Are sensitive data files encrypted on all portable systems? (NIST SP 800-14)								
7.3.2 Are portable systems stored securely? (NIST SP 800-14)								
8. Production, Input/Output Controls								
8.1 Critical Element: Is there user support?								
8.1.1 Is there a help desk or group that offers advice?								
8.2 Critical Element: Are there media controls?								
8.2.1 Are there processes to ensure that unauthorized individuals cannot read, copy, alter, or steal printed or electronic information?								

Specific Control Objectives and Techniques	Level 1	Level 2	Level 3	Level 4	Level 5	Risk-Based Decision Made	Comments	Initials
8.2.2 Are there processes for ensuring that only authorized users pick up, receive, or deliver input and output information and media?								
8.2.3 Are audit trails used for receipt of sensitive inputs/outputs?								
8.2.4 Are controls in place for transporting or mailing media or printed output?								
8.2.5 Is there internal/external labeling for sensitivity?								
8.2.6 Is there external labeling with special handling instructions?								
8.2.7 Are audit trails kept for inventory management?								
8.2.8 Is media sanitized for reuse?								
8.2.9 Is damaged media stored and /or destroyed?								
8.2.10 Is hardcopy media shredded or destroyed when no longer needed?								
9. Contingency Planning								
9.1 Critical Element: Have the most critical and sensitive operations and their supporting computer resources been identified?								
9.1.1 Are critical data files and operations identified and the frequency of file backup documented?								
9.1.2 Are resources supporting critical operations identified?								

Specific Control Objectives and Techniques	Level 1	Level 2	Level 3	Level 4	Level 5	Risk-Based Decision Made	Comments	Initials
9.1.3 Have processing priorities been established and approved by management?								
9.2 Critical Element: **Has a comprehensive contingency plan been developed and documented?**								
9.2.1 Is the plan approved by key affected parties?								
9.2.2 Are responsibilities for recovery assigned?								
9.2.3 Are there detailed instructions for restoring operations?								
9.2.4 Is there an alternate processing site; if so, is there a contract or interagency agreement in place?								
9.2.5 Is the location of stored backups identified?								
9.2.6 Are backup files created on a prescribed basis and rotated off-site often enough to avoid disruption if current files are damaged?								
9.2.7 Is system and application documentation maintained at the off-site location?								
9.2.8 Are all system defaults reset after being restored from a backup?								
9.2.9 Are the backup storage site and alternate site geographically removed from the primary site and physically protected?								
9.2.10 Has the contingency plan been distributed to all appropriate personnel?								

Specific Control Objectives and Techniques	Level 1	Level 2	Level 3	Level 4	Level 5	Risk-Based Decision Made	Comments	Initials
9.3 Critical Element: **Are tested contingency/disaster recovery plans in place?**								
9.3.1 Is an up-to-date copy of the plan stored securely off-site?								
9.3.2 Are employees trained in their roles and responsibilities?								
9.3.3 Is the plan periodically tested and readjusted as appropriate?								
10. Hardware and System Software Maintenance								
10.1 Critical Element: **Is access limited to system software and hardware?**								
10.1.1 Are restrictions in place on who performs maintenance and repair activities?								
10.1.2 Is access to all program libraries restricted and controlled?								
10.1.3 Are there on-site and off-site maintenance procedures (e.g., escort of maintenance personnel, sanitization of devices removed from the site)?								
10.1.4 Is the operating system configured to prevent circumvention of the security software and application controls?								
10.1.5 Are up-to-date procedures in place for using and monitoring use of system utilities?								

Specific Control Objectives and Techniques	Level 1	Level 2	Level 3	Level 4	Level 5	Risk-Based Decision Made	Comments	Initials
10.2 Critical Element: **Are all new and revised hardware and software authorized, tested, and approved before implementation?**								
10.2.1 Is an impact analysis conducted to determine the effect of proposed changes on existing security controls, including the required training needed to implement the control?								
10.2.2 Are system components tested, documented, and approved (operating system, utility, applications) prior to promotion to production?								
10.2.3 Are software change request forms used to document requests and related approvals?								
10.2.4 Are there detailed system specifications prepared and reviewed by management?								
10.2.5 Is the type of test data to be used specified, i.e., live or made up?								
10.2.6 Are default settings of security features set to the most restrictive mode?								
10.2.7 Are there software distribution implementation orders including effective date provided to all locations?								
10.2.8 Is there version control?								
10.2.9 Are programs labeled and inventoried?								

Specific Control Objectives and Techniques	Level 1	Level 2	Level 3	Level 4	Level 5	Risk-Based Decision Made	Comments	Initials
10.2.10 Are the distribution and implementation of new or revised software documented and reviewed?								
10.2.11 Are emergency change procedures documented and approved by management, either prior to the change or after the fact?								
10.2.12 Are contingency plans and other associated documentation updated to reflect system changes?								
10.2.13 Is the use of copyrighted software or shareware and personally owned software/equipment documented?								
10.3 Critical Element: Are systems managed to reduce vulnerabilities?								
10.3.1 Are systems periodically reviewed to identify and, when possible, eliminate unnecessary services (e.g., FTP, HTTP, mainframe supervisor calls)?								
10.3.2 Are systems periodically reviewed for known vulnerabilities and software patches promptly installed?								
11. Data Integrity								
11.1 Critical Element: Is virus detection and elimination software installed and activated?								
11.1.1 Are virus signature files routinely updated?								
11.1.2 Are virus scans automatic?								

Specific Control Objectives and Techniques	Level 1	Level 2	Level 3	Level 4	Level 5	Risk-Based Decision Made	Comments	Initials
11.2 Critical Element: **Are data integrity and validation controls used to provide assurance that the information has not been altered and the system functions as intended?**								
11.2.1 Are reconciliation routines used by applications, i.e., checksums, hash totals, record counts?								
11.2.2 Is inappropriate or unusual activity reported, investigated, and appropriate actions taken?								
11.2.3 Are procedures in place to determine compliance with password policies?								
11.2.4 Are integrity verification programs used by applications to look for evidence of data tampering, errors, and omissions?								
11.2.5 Are intrusion detection tools installed on the system?								
11.2.6 Are the intrusion detection reports routinely reviewed and suspected incidents handled accordingly?								
11.2.7 Is system performance monitoring used to analyze system performance logs in real time to look for availability problems, including active attacks?								
11.2.8 Is penetration testing performed on the system?								
11.2.9 Is message authentication used?								

Specific Control Objectives and Techniques	Level 1	Level 2	Level 3	Level 4	Level 5	Risk-Based Decision Made	Comments	Initials
12. Documentation								
12.1 Critical Element: Is there sufficient documentation that explains how software/hardware is to be used?								
12.1.1 Is there vendor-supplied documentation of purchased software?								
12.1.2 Is there vendor-supplied documentation of purchased hardware?								
12.1.3 Is there application documentation for in-house applications?								
12.1.4 Are there network diagrams and documentation on setups of routers and switches?								
12.1.5 Are there software and hardware testing procedures and results?								
12.1.6 Are there standard operating procedures for all the topic areas covered in this document?								
12.1.7 Are there user manuals?								
12.1.8 Are there emergency procedures?								
12.1.9 Are there backup procedures?								
12.2 Critical Element: Are there formal security and operational procedures documented?								
12.2.1 Is there a system security plan? FISCAM SP-2.1								
12.2.2 Is there a contingency plan?								

Specific Control Objectives and Techniques	Level 1	Level 2	Level 3	Level 4	Level 5	Risk-Based Decision Made	Comments	Initials
12.2.3 Are there written agreements regarding how data is shared between interconnected systems?								
12.2.4 Are there risk assessment reports?								
12.2.5 Are there certification and accreditation documents and a statement authorizing the system to process?								
13. Security Awareness, Training, and Education								
13.1 Critical Element: Have employees received adequate training to fulfill their security responsibilities?								
13.1.1 Have employees received a copy of the rules of behavior?								
13.1.2 Are employee training and professional development documented and monitored? FISCAM SP-4.2								
13.1.3 Is there mandatory annual refresher training?								
13.1.4 Are methods employed to make employees aware of security, i.e., posters, booklets?								
13.1.5 Have employees received a copy of or have easy access to agency security procedures and policies?								
14. Incident Response Capability								
14.1 Critical Element: Is there a capability to provide help to users when a security incident occurs in the system?								

Specific Control Objectives and Techniques	Level 1	Level 2	Level 3	Level 4	Level 5	Risk-Based Decision Made	Comments	Initials
14.1.1 Is a formal incident response capability available?								
14.1.2 Is there a process for reporting incidents?								
14.1.3 Are incidents monitored and tracked until resolved?								
14.1.4 Are personnel trained to recognize and handle incidents?								
14.1.5 Are alerts/advisories received and responded to?								
14.1.6 Is there a process to modify incident handling procedures and control techniques after an incident occurs?								
14.2 Critical Element: Is incident related information shared with appropriate organizations?								
14.2.1 Is incident information and common vulnerabilities or threats shared with owners of interconnected systems?								
14.2.2 Is incident information shared with FedCIRC3 concerning incidents and common vulnerabilities and threats?								
14.2.3 Is incident information reported to FedCIRC, NIPC4, and local law enforcement when necessary?								
Technical Controls								
15. Identification and Authentication								
15.1 Critical Element: Are users individually authenticated via passwords, tokens, or other devices?								

Specific Control Objectives and Techniques	Level 1	Level 2	Level 3	Level 4	Level 5	Risk-Based Decision Made	Comments	Initials
15.1.1 Is a current list maintained and approved of authorized users and their access?								
15.1.2 Are digital signatures used and conform to FIPS 186-2?								
15.1.3 Are access scripts with embedded passwords prohibited?								
15.1.4 Is emergency and temporary access authorized?								
15.1.5 Are personnel files matched with user accounts to ensure that terminated or transferred individuals do not retain system access?								
15.1.6 Are passwords changed at least every ninety days or earlier if needed?								
15.1.7 Are passwords unique and difficult to guess (e.g., do passwords require alpha numeric, upper/lower case, and special characters)?								
15.1.8 Are inactive user identifications disabled after a specified period of time?								
15.1.9 Are passwords not displayed when entered?								
15.1.10 Are there procedures in place for handling lost and compromised passwords?								
15.1.11 Are passwords distributed securely and users informed not to reveal their passwords to anyone (social engineering)?								
15.1.12 Are passwords transmitted and stored using secure protocols/algorithms?								

Specific Control Objectives and Techniques	Level 1	Level 2	Level 3	Level 4	Level 5	Risk-Based Decision Made	Comments	Initials
15.1.13 Are vendor-supplied passwords replaced immediately?								
15.1.14 Is there a limit to the number of invalid access attempts that may occur for a given user?								
15.2 Critical Element: **Are access controls enforcing segregation of duties?**								
15.2.1 Does the system correlate actions to users?								
15.2.2 Do data owners periodically review access authorizations to determine whether they remain appropriate?								
16. Logical Access Controls								
16.1 Critical Element: **Do the logical access controls restrict users to authorized transactions and functions?**								
16.1.1 Can the security controls detect unauthorized access attempts?								
16.1.2 Is there access control software that prevents an individual from having all necessary authority or information access to allow fraudulent activity without collusion?								
16.1.3 Is access to security software restricted to security administrators?								
16.1.4 Do workstations disconnect or screen savers lock the system after a specific period of inactivity?								

Specific Control Objectives and Techniques	Level 1	Level 2	Level 3	Level 4	Level 5	Risk-Based Decision Made	Comments	Initials
16.1.5 Are inactive users' accounts monitored and removed when not needed?								
16.1.6 Are internal security labels (naming conventions) used to control access to specific information types or files?								
16.1.7 If encryption is used, does it meet federal standards?								
16.1.8 If encryption is used, are there procedures for key generation, distribution, storage, use, destruction, and archiving?								
16.1.9 Is access restricted to files at the logical view or field?								
16.1.10 Is access monitored to identify apparent security violations and are such events investigated?								
16.2 Critical Element: **Are there logical controls over network access?**								
16.2.1 Has communication software been implemented to restrict access through specific terminals?								
16.2.2 Are insecure protocols (e.g., UDP, FTP) disabled?								
16.2.3 Have all vendor-supplied default security parameters been reinitialized to more secure settings?								
16.2.4 Are there controls that restrict remote access to the system?								
16.2.5 Are network activity logs maintained and reviewed?								

Specific Control Objectives and Techniques	Level 1	Level 2	Level 3	Level 4	Level 5	Risk-Based Decision Made	Comments	Initials
16.2.6 Does the network connection automatically disconnect at the end of a session?								
16.2.7 Are trust relationships among hosts and external entities appropriately restricted?								
16.2.8 Is dial-in access monitored?								
16.2.9 Is access to telecommunications hardware or facilities restricted and monitored?								
16.2.10 Are firewalls or secure gateways installed?								
16.2.11 If firewalls are installed do they comply with firewall policy and rules?								
16.2.12 Are guest and anonymous accounts authorized and monitored?								
16.2.13 Is an approved standardized logon banner displayed on the system warning unauthorized users that they have accessed a U.S. Government system and can be punished?								
16.2.14 Are sensitive data transmissions encrypted?								
16.2.15 Is access to tables defining network options, resources, and operator profiles restricted?								
16.3 Critical Element: **If the public accesses the system, are there controls implemented to protect the integrity of the application and the confidence of the public?**								

Specific Control Objectives and Techniques	Level 1	Level 2	Level 3	Level 4	Level 5	Risk-Based Decision Made	Comments	Initials
16.3.1 Is a privacy policy posted on the Web site?								
17. Audit Trails								
17.1 Critical Element: **Is activity involving access to and modification of sensitive or critical files logged, monitored, and possible security violations investigated?**								
17.1.1 Does the audit trail provide a trace of user actions?								
17.1.2 Can the audit trail support after-the-fact investigations of how, when, and why normal operations ceased?								
17.1.3 Is access to online audit logs strictly controlled?								
17.1.4 Are off-line storage of audit logs retained for a period of time, and, if so, is access to audit logs strictly controlled?								
17.1.5 Is there separation of duties between security personnel who administer the access control function and those who administer the audit trail?								
17.1.6 Are audit trails reviewed frequently?								
17.1.7 Are automated tools used to review audit records in real time or near real time?								
17.1.8 Is suspicious activity investigated and appropriate action taken?								
17.1.9 Is keystroke monitoring used? If so, are users notified?								

Human Firewall Council's Security Management Index Survey

Security Management Index Scoring Methodology

The Security Management Index (SMI) is designed to assess an organization's management practices using a framework based on ISO 17799. The SMI respondent is asked to assess the organization's implementation of 99 security objectives for 33 security standards across the 10 domains of ISO 17799. For each objective, a respondent may choose one of the following degrees of compliance:

- Fully compliant: The standard objective has been fully implemented at the organization. Results in a score of 10 for the objective.
- Partially compliant: The standard objective has been partially implemented at the organization. Results in a score of 5 for the objective.
- Planned: The organization has made definite plans to implement the standard objective. Results in a score of 2 for the objective.
- Not compliant or planned: The standard objective has not been implemented (even partly) and there are no plans to implement it. Results in a score of 0 for the objective.
- Not applicable: The objective does not appear to apply to the organization. No score is given and the potential score of 10 is not incorporated in the calculation of the total score, as if the objective was not included in the index.

Each objective is also given a weight that is used to calculate the final index. The weights of high, medium and low are defined as follows:

- High: These objectives represent minimum standards to achieve for organizations at a low level of security maturity. These apply to all organizations, regardless of regulatory drivers or industry standards. Their relative weight is 3.
- Medium: These objectives represent basic standards to achieve for organizations at a moderate level of security maturity. These apply to all organizations, but may be driven by some regulations or industry standards. Their relative weight is 2.
- Low: These objectives represent advanced standards to achieve for organizations at a high level of security maturity. These are often driven by regulations or industry standards, but are highly recommended for all organizations and are part of ISO17799 among other generally accepted security practices. Their relative weight is 1.

These weights are then multiplied by each objective's score, the product of which is totaled to provide the index score for the organization.

The scoring methodology is designed to illustrate a great benefit from implementing minimum and basic security standards, although implementation of all standards are required for a score of 100%. As such, the following chart illustrates how an organization might progress in security management maturity by first implementing the minimum security standards (high weight objectives), then the basic standards (medium weight) and finally the advanced standards (low weight). The weights were designed explicitly to provide this type of maturity curve.

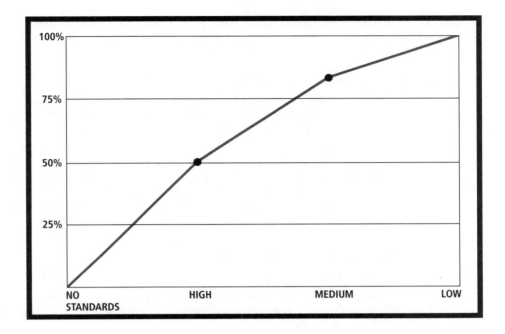

Questionnaire

I.   Security Policy

1. Information Security Policy
   The current information security policies within your organization:
   - ❏ Define information security objectives and illustrate the importance of security.
   - ❏ Provide a statement of management's intentions to support information security.
   - ❏ Define general responsibilities for employees.
   - ❏ Reference other corporate documents.
2. Information Security Policy
   When reviewing, evaluating, and distributing security policies, your organization:
   - ❏ Specifies a distinct information security owner who has the responsibility for update and maintenance of those policies.
   - ❏ Requires a review by business owners, legal and HR.

II.   Organizational Security

1. Information Security Infrastructure
   Your organization's information security infrastructure is supported by a(n):
   - ❏ Enterprise-wide security steering committee.
   - ❏ Information security representative from each business unit.
   - ❏ Allocation of information security responsibilities.
   - ❏ Information security advisor (for expert advice) or coordinator (to coordinate security knowledge sharing).
   - ❏ Documented points of contact with law enforcement, standards setting organizations, and service providers for both incident response support and security advice.

❑ Autonomous oversight of information security policy implementation.

❑ Performing risk assessments before granting access to external parties.

❑ Management review and approval for the development or implementation of any new information technologies.

2. Security of Third Party Access

   Third-party access is controlled in your organization by:

   ❑ Documenting the organization's security policy in the third-party contract.

   ❑ Educating third parties on the information classification program.

3. Outsourcing

   Outsourcing is controlled in your organization by:

   ❑ Communicating legal requirements for protecting your organization's information and information technologies and services.

   ❑ Educating outsourcers on their liabilities in regards to the security of your organization's information, technologies and services.

III. Asset Classification & Control

1. Accountability for Assets

   Your organization accounts for key information technology assets by:

   ❑ Recording the information and business ownership.

2. Information Classification

   Safeguarding information within your organization includes:

   ❑ A simple, effective guideline that indicates the degree of protection for each type of information asset.

   ❑ Handling and labeling procedures for physical media.

IV. Personnel Security

1. Security in Job Definition and Resourcing

   Your organization has policies and procedures in place that require:

   ❑ Information security roles and responsibilities included in all company job descriptions.

   ❑ All candidates for employment be adequately screened to ensure that their qualifications are accurate.

   ❑ All employees sign a confidentiality (non-disclosure) agreement to ensure that they understand their information handling responsibilities.

2. User Training

   An organizational-wide training program is in place for:

   ❑ Information security policy and procedure awareness and comprehension.

   ❑ Informing personnel of their legal responsibilities for security.

   ❑ Correct usage of information technologies including business applications.

3. Responding to Security Incidents and Malfunctions

   In response to a security incident or malfunction, a formal process exists in your organization that:

   ❑ Instructs employees on the correct method of handling security incidents.

   ❑ Instructs employees on the proper method for preserving the evidence necessary for forensic investigations.

   ❑ Disciplines employees who have violated security policies and procedures.

V. Physical and Environmental Security

1. Secure Areas
   Facilities are properly secured by:
   - ❑ Adequately establishing and monitoring a physical perimeter.
   - ❑ Logging and supervising physical entry by visitors.
   - ❑ Taking precautions (including proper layout and site selection) to secure against natural or man-made disasters.
   - ❑ Adequately controlling personnel or third parties working in secure areas.
   - ❑ Controlling delivery and loading areas and if possible, isolating them from information processing facilities.
   - ❑ Protecting equipment from power failures and other electrical anomalies.

2. Equipment Security
   Equipment is properly secured by:
   - ❑ Protecting power and telecommunications cabling from interception or damage.
   - ❑ Correctly maintaining equipment to ensure its continued availability and integrity.
   - ❑ Physically destroying storage devices containing sensitive information or securely overwriting sensitive data when disposing of those storage devices.

3. General Controls
   Your organization prevents the compromise or theft of information and information-processing facilities by requiring:
   - ❑ A clear desk policy for papers and removable storage media, and a clear screen policy for information processing facilities.
   - ❑ Equipment or information taken off site to be removed only with authorization, and proper logging is in place to control removal.

VI. Communications & Operations Management

1. Operational Procedures and Responsibilities
   Your organization ensures the correct and secure operation of information technologies by using:
   - ❑ Documented standard operating procedures including processing information, scheduling, error handling, support, and recovery.
   - ❑ A change management process.
   - ❑ An incident management process.
   - ❑ An enforceable segregation of duties policy.
   - ❑ A separation between the development and operational (production) facilities.

2. System Planning and Acceptance
   Your organization minimizes the risk that essential systems will fail by using acceptable:
   - ❑ Capacity planning.

3. Protection Against Malicious Software
   You organization protects the integrity and security of essential software and information by:
   - ❑ Using a policy requiring compliance with software licenses.
   - ❑ Using a policy for obtaining files and software from third parties.
   - ❑ Installing and regularly updating anti-virus detection and repair software.
   - ❑ Checking any files, electronic mail attachments, or downloads of uncertain origin for viruses before use.

4. Housekeeping

Your organization maintains the integrity and availability of essential information processing and communication services by:

- ❑ Implementing a backup and recovery process.
- ❑ Logging operator commands.
- ❑ Logging network and system faults.

5. Network Management

Your organization ensures the protection of networks and supporting infrastructure by:

- ❑ Establishing special controls to safeguard the confidentiality and integrity of data passing over public networks.
- ❑ Separating operational responsibility for the networks from the computer operations where possible.

6. Media Handling and Security

To prevent asset damage and business activity interruption, your organization's media should be controlled and physically protected by:

- ❑ Procedures for managing removable computer media such as CDs, disks, and printed reports.
- ❑ Securely storing system documentation.

7. Exchanges of Information and Software

Your organization prevents loss, modification, or misuse of information exchanges between organizations by utilizing the appropriate:

- ❑ Agreements between organizations for the exchange of information.
- ❑ Security precautions for electronic commerce.
- ❑ Security precautions for electronic mail.
- ❑ Security precautions for electronic office systems such as voice mail, mobile communications, video, and postal services.
- ❑ Security precautions for publicly available systems such as Web servers.

VII. Access Control

1. Business Requirement for Access Control

Your organization controls access to sensitive information by:

- ❑ Documenting policy and business requirements for controlling access to each business application.
- ❑ Establishing access control rules that grant permissions to each group of users.

2. User Access Management

Your organization prevents unauthorized access to information systems by:

- ❑ Using a formal user registration and de-registration procedure for granting access to all multi-user information systems.
- ❑ Controlling password allocation through a formal management process.

3. User Responsibilities

To prevent unauthorized user access, your organization requires users to:

- ❑ Follow good security practices in the selection and use of passwords.
- ❑ Ensure that unattended equipment automatically logs users out or securely locks the system from unauthorized use.

4. Network Access Control

The protection of networked services is enforced by:

❑ Authenticating all users from external connections.

❑ Requiring authentication for an automatic connection to a network, such as in trust relationships between computers.

5. Operating System Access Control

All access to computer resources is restricted by operating system controls that:

❑ Authenticate connections using terminal identification when it is important to ensure logins occur only from specific locations and/or computers or terminals.

❑ Require a unique, non-descript identifier for all authorized users.

❑ Employ effective password management systems that ensure quality passwords.

❑ Restrict and log all use of system utilities.

❑ Permit time-of-day connection limits to high-risk or sensitive applications.

6. Monitoring System Access and Use

All access and use of computer systems is monitored to detect unauthorized activities by:

❑ Recording all relevant security events in audit logs.

❑ Reviewing audit logs through an effective and routine process.

❑ Documenting and implementing procedures for monitoring the use of information technologies.

❑ Using a process to ensure that all system clocks are synchronized with an agreed standard.

7. Mobile Computing and Teleworking

Your organization has information security policies and procedures documented and implemented to control:

❑ The use of all mobile computing facilities including physical protection, access controls, cryptographic techniques, backups, and virus protection.

❑ All activities related to working remotely from a fixed site not located within your organization.

VIII. Systems Development and Maintenance

1. Security Requirements of Systems

Your organization specifies security requirements and specifications that:

❑ Reflect the business value of the information assets involved.

❑ Follow a risk assessment and risk management process to determine the acceptable controls.

2. Cryptographic Controls

Your organization uses cryptographic systems and techniques to protect the confidentiality, authenticity, or integrity of information by:

❑ Considering regulatory restrictions that may apply to the use of cryptographic algorithms in different parts of the world.

❑ Applying digital signatures to any form of legal or business document being processed electronically.

❑ Implementing a system for the management of cryptographic keys.

3. Security of System Files

System files are secured during IT projects and support activities by:

❑ Controlling program source libraries in the development process to restrict possible corruption or tampering.

4. Security in Development and Support Processes

In order to minimize the corruption of information systems, your organization controls the implementation of changes by:

❑ Using access controls to restrict the movement of programs and data from development into production.

❑ Testing the application system when a change in the operating system occurs to ensure that there is no adverse impact on operation or security.

❑ Conducting source code reviews to eliminate possible security vulnerabilities.

IX. Business Continuity Management

1. Aspects of Business Continuity Management

Your organization has a business continuity planning process in place that:

❑ Has produced a current, comprehensive, documented, and routinely-maintained business continuity plan for the entire organization.

❑ Requires the completion of a business impact analysis that identifies events and their associated risks.

❑ Requires a current prioritization of all business processes and supporting functions, including computer systems and applications.

❑ Ensures that the business continuity plan is routinely tested using effective techniques to assure that the plan is viable.

X. Compliance

1. Compliance with Legal Requirements

Your organization has implemented policies and procedures to ensure compliance with legal requirements that specifically address the:

❑ Data protection and privacy of personal information.

❑ Acceptable use of information technologies.

❑ International usage or transport of cryptographic controls.

2. Reviews of Security Compliance and Technical Compliance

Compliance procedures are in place that require the:

❑ Departmental managers to perform routine self-assessments to ensure that their areas comply with security policies and standards.

❑ Technical checking of information systems by independent experts for compliance with security standards and leading practices.

3. System Audit Considerations

Audit procedures are in place that require:

❑ Review of all operational systems to minimize the risk of business process disruptions.

❑ Restricted access to system audit tools to prevent misuse or compromise.

7

Risk Management: Identifying and Assessing Risk

IRIS MAJWABU AND MIKE EDWARDS SAT SIDE BY SIDE on the short flight to the nearby city where the RWW board of directors audit committee was meeting that afternoon. The two had been invited to present RWW's IT risk management program to the committee. The board's concerns stemmed from a recent briefing by the National Association of Corporate Directors, which focused on trends affecting the potential liability of board members in the area of information security in general and risk management in particular.

After the plane leveled off, Mike pulled out his copy of the presentation he planned to give that afternoon. He and Iris had been working on it for at least two weeks, and each knew the slides by heart. Iris was along to assist with the question-and-answer period that would follow Mike's presentation.

"They're not going to be happy campers when you're done," said Iris.

"Nope. They are likely to be a little unhappy. The CEO is worried about how they'll respond, and about what might come up at the full board meeting next month," Mike said. "I'm afraid the disconnection between IT and Internal Audit in this briefing may have some unexpected consequences."

Iris considered Mike's comment and what she knew about the weaknesses of the internal audit department's approach to the company's non-IT assets. Where Mike and Iris had built a sound, information-based approach to estimating and controlling IT risk, some of the other company divisions used less empirical methods.

"I think we should come out of this okay," Iris told Mike. "After all, the main concern of the Audit Committee members is the newfound perception of their liability for IT security and the effects it has on the issues of privacy. We have a solid risk management plan in place that's working well, in my opinion."

Mike looked up from his notes and said, "It's not us I'm worried about. I'm afraid we may create some discomfort and unwanted attention for our peers after the board sees the wide variety of risk management approaches used in other divisions."

LEARNING OBJECTIVES

Upon completion of this material, you should be able to:

- Define risk management and its role in the organization

- Begin using risk management techniques to identify and prioritize risk factors for information assets

- Assess risk based on the likelihood of adverse events and the effects on information assets when events occur

- Begin to document the results of risk identification

Introduction

Information security departments are created primarily to manage information technology (IT) risk. Managing risk is one of the key responsibilities of every manager within the organization. In any well-developed risk management program, two formal processes are at work:

- The first, risk identification and assessment, is discussed in this chapter.
- The second, risk control, is the subject of the next chapter.

Each manager in the organization, regardless of his or her affiliation with one of the three communities of interest, should focus on reducing risk as follows:

- General management must structure the IT and information security functions in ways that will result in the successful defense of the organization's information assets, including data, hardware, software, procedures, and people.
- IT management must serve the information technology needs of the broader organization and at the same time exploit the special skills and insights of the information security community.
- Information security management must lead the way with skill, professionalism, and flexibility as it works with the other communities of interest to balance the constant trade-offs between information system utility and security.

Risk Management

> If you know the enemy and know yourself, you need not fear the result of a hundred battles. If you know yourself but not the enemy, for every victory gained you will also suffer a defeat. If you know neither the enemy nor yourself, you will succumb in every battle.[1]

Chinese general Sun Tzu's observation, made more than 2400 years ago, continues to have direct relevance to the philosophy of information security today. Information security strategy and tactics are in many ways similar to those employed in conventional warfare. Information security managers and technicians are the defenders of information. A myriad of threats constantly attacks the organization's information assets. A layered defense is the foundation of any information security program. So, as Sun Tzu recommends, to reduce risk an organization must (1) know itself and (2) know its enemy. This means that managers from all three communities of interest must first understand where the weaknesses of their organization's operations lie; how the organization's information is processed, stored, and transmitted; and what resources are available. Only then can any strategic plan of defense be developed.

Knowing Ourselves

When operating any kind of organization, a certain amount of risk is always involved. Risk is inherent in hiring decisions, marketing products, and even in making decisions about where to place the building that houses the organization. Risk winds its way into the daily operations of every organization, and if it is not properly managed, it can cause operational failures that can lead to complete collapse.

For an organization to properly manage risk, managers should understand how information is processed, stored, and transmitted. Armed with this knowledge, they can then initiate an in-depth risk management program.

Note that the existence of a risk management program does not necessarily mean that assets are completely protected. Frequently, risk management mechanisms are implemented but are not subsequently maintained and kept current. Risk management is a process, which means the safeguards and controls that are devised and implemented, as described in Chapter 8, are not install-and-forget devices.

Knowing the Enemy

Once an organization becomes aware of its weaknesses, managers can then take up Sun Tzu's second dictum: Know the enemy. This means identifying, examining, and understanding the *threats* facing the organization's information assets. Managers must be prepared to fully identify those threats that pose risks to the organization and the security of its information assets. **Risk management** is the process of discovering and assessing the risks to an organization's operations and determining how those risks can be controlled or mitigated.

Accountability for Risk Management

All three communities of interest bear responsibility for the management of organization risks, and each has a particular strategic role to play.

- Information Security: Because the members of the information security community best understand the threats and attacks that introduce risk, they often take a leadership role in addressing risk.
- Information Technology: This group must help to build secure systems and ensure their safe operation. For example, IT operations create good backup methodologies to control the risk from hard drive failures.
- Management and Users: When properly trained and kept aware of the threats faced by the organization, this group plays a part in the early detection and response process. Members of this community also ensure that sufficient resources (money and personnel) are allocated to the information security and information technology groups to meet the security needs of the organization. For example, business managers must ensure that supporting records for orders remain intact in case of data entry error or transaction corruption. Users must be made aware of threats to data and systems, and educated on practices that minimize those threats.

All three communities of interest must work together to address every level of risk, ranging from full-scale disasters (whether natural or human-made) to the smallest mistake made by an employee. To do so, they must be actively involved in the following activities:

- Evaluating the risk controls
- Determining which control options are cost-effective
- Acquiring or installing the appropriate controls
- Overseeing processes to ensure that the controls remain effective
- Identifying risks, which includes:
  - Creating an inventory of information assets
  - Classifying and organizing those assets into meaningful groups
  - Assigning a value to each information asset
  - Identifying threats to the cataloged assets
  - Pinpointing vulnerable assets by tying specific threats to specific assets
- Assessing risks, which includes:
  - Determining the likelihood that vulnerable systems will be attacked by specific threats
  - Assessing the relative risk facing the organization's information assets, so that risk management and control activities can focus on assets that require the most urgent and immediate attention
  - Calculating the risks to which assets are exposed in their current setting
  - Looking in a general way at controls that might come into play for identified vulnerabilities and ways to control the risks that the assets face
  - Documenting the findings of risk identification and assessment
- Summarizing the findings, which involves stating the conclusions of the analysis stage of risk assessment in preparation for moving into the stage of controlling risk by exploring methods to mitigate risk

Figure 7-1 outlines the steps in the risk identification and assessment process.

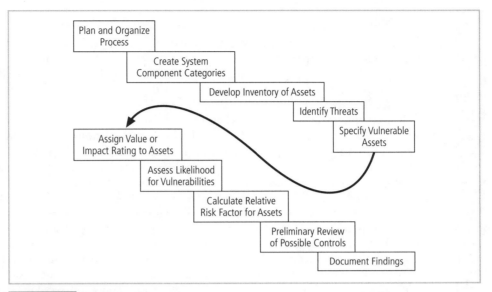

FIGURE 7-1 Risk Identification Process

THREAT MANAGEMENT

Tiny Fragment Attacks

Definition

The Tiny Fragment Attack occurs when an attacker misuses the fragmentation feature of the Internet Protocol to create very small fragments that can force elements of the TCP header into a separate packet. Some router or firewall controls examine only the first packet and allow the rest of the packets in the frame to follow without any further checking. Packets allowed past the control device without evaluation may be used in an exploit that can result in the loss of system control or loss of data integrity. Loss of system control may be further exploited via indirect attack against other information assets present on the local network.

Many Internet firewalls currently in use are simple routers that provide only packet filtering. This technique has little or no marginal cost and is also transparent to users and applications. Limiting its effectiveness is the fact that creating and maintaining packet-filtering rule sets is a complex undertaking. A complete packet-filtering rule set includes provisions for managing or restricting all needed Internet services, packet header formats, and specific values found in each field of a packet. The filtering rule set is usually long and complicated and is a challenge to manage and control. Once a rule set is defined and the network devices are configured, testing the configuration is another complex challenge. As the filtering rule grows in complexity and the original rules age and become dated, it becomes less effective and is therefore subject to attack.

(continued)

Remediation

Since the edge router is the most vulnerable device in most networks, it should be configured to perform packet reassembly before rule set evaluation. Additional controls such as firewalls and intrusion detection systems should be implemented behind the edge router within the screened subnet (if that is the deployed architecture of the network). Devices exposed to unfiltered outside traffic that do not perform packet reassembly usually pass potentially dangerous packets through.

In general, initially small packets are almost always malicious. It is prudent to enforce rules such that the first packet in any transmission is large enough to contain all of the header information. Any small packets should be located at the end of the transmission group. As a rule, all exposed networking devices must be kept up to date with the latest security patches and upgrades—this will help protect against emergent attacks.

Research into the tiny fragment attack has found that mitigation techniques take two general approaches. The first of these, known as the direct method, involves requiring the first fragment of any transmission series to be large enough to hold all the essential header information. The second, called the indirect method—considered much less effective—involves observing packets for fragmentation to force certain header fields out of the zero-offset fragment, with the intent of blocking later reassembly at the receiving host.

Contributed by Joe Leonardi, Kevin Sims, Andy Boldin, Tony Alexander, Anish Sikri

Risk Identification

Risk identification begins with the process of self-examination. At this stage, managers identify the organization's information assets, classify them into useful groups, and prioritize them by their overall importance. This can be a daunting task, but it must be done to identify weaknesses and the threats they present.

Creating an Inventory of Information Assets

The risk identification process begins with the identification of information assets, including people, procedures, data and information, software, hardware, and networking elements. This step should be done without pre-judging the value of each asset; values will be assigned later in the process. Table 7-1 is a model outline showing identified assets, which are subcategorized into risk management components.

TABLE 7-1 Organizational Assets Used in Systems

IT system components	Risk management components	
People	People inside an organization	Trusted employees Other staff
	People outside an organization	People at organizations we trust Strangers
Procedures	Procedures	IT and business standard procedures IT and business sensitive procedures
Data	Data/Information	Transmission Processing Storage
Software	Software	Applications Operating systems Security components
Hardware	Hardware	Systems and peripherals Security devices
Networking	Networking components	Intranet components Internet or Extranet components

Table 7-1 compares the standard IT system components (people, procedures, data and information, software, hardware, and networks) with an extended risk management breakdown of those components. The following list describes this breakdown more fully:

- *People* are divided into insiders (employees) and outsiders (non-employees). Insiders come in two categories: Either they hold trusted roles and have correspondingly greater authority and accountability, or they are regular staff without any special privileges. The group of outsiders consists of other users who have access to the organization's information assets.
- *Procedures* are split into two categories: IT and business standard procedures, and IT and business sensitive procedures. Sensitive procedures have the potential to enable an attack or to otherwise introduce risk to the organization. For example, the procedures used by a telecommunications company to activate new circuits pose special risks because they reveal aspects of the inner workings of a critical process that can be subverted by outsiders for the purpose of obtaining unbilled, illicit services.
- *Data* components account for information in all states: transmission, processing, and storage. These categories expand the conventional use of the term "data," which is usually associated with databases, not the full range of information used by modern organizations.
- *Software* elements can be inventoried in one of three categories: applications, operating systems, or security components. Software components that provide security controls may fall into the operating systems or applications category, but are differentiated by the fact that they are part of the information security control environment and must be protected more thoroughly than other systems components.

- *Hardware* is split into two categories: the usual systems devices and their peripherals, and the devices that are part of information security control systems. The latter must be protected more thoroughly than the former.
- *Networking* components are extracted from software and hardware because networking subsystems are often the focal point of attacks against a system. For this reason, they should be considered separately, rather than combined with general hardware and software components.

Identifying Hardware, Software, and Network Assets

Many organizations use purchased asset inventory systems to keep track of their hardware, network, and perhaps software components. Numerous packages are available in the market today, and it is up to the CISO or CIO to determine which package best serves the needs of the organization. Those organizations that do not use an automated inventory system must create an equivalent manual process.

Whether automated or manual, the inventory process requires a certain amount of planning. Most importantly, you must determine which attributes of each of these information assets should be tracked. That determination will depend on the needs of the organization and its risk management efforts, as well as the preferences and needs of the information security and information technology communities. When deciding which attributes to track for each information asset, consider the following list of potential attributes:

- Name: A list of all names commonly used for the device or program. Some organizations may have several names for the same product, and each of them should be cross-referenced in the inventory. This redundancy accommodates the usage across the organization and makes it accessible for everyone. No matter how many names you track or how you select a name, always provide a definition of the asset in question. It is wise to adopt naming standards that do not convey critical information to potential system attackers. For instance, a server named CASH1 or HQ_FINANCE may entice attackers to take a shortcut to those systems and go for the valuables first.
- IP address: An attribute that is useful for network devices and servers but rarely applies to software. You can, however, use a relational database and track software instances on specific servers or networking devices. Note that many larger organizations use the Dynamic Host Control Protocol (DHCP) within TCP/IP, which reassigns IP numbers to devices as needed, making the use of IP numbers as part of the asset identification process very difficult.
- MAC address: Also called an electronic serial number or hardware address. As per the TCP/IP standard, all network interface hardware devices have a unique number. The network operating system uses this number to identify specific network devices. The client's network software uses it to recognize traffic that it needs to process. In most settings MAC addresses can be a useful way to track connectivity, but they can be spoofed by some hardware/software combinations.
- Asset type: An attribute that describes the function of each asset. For hardware assets, develop a list of possible asset types that includes servers, desktops, networking devices, and test equipment. For software assets, develop a list that includes operating systems, custom applications by type (accounting, human resources, or payroll, to name a few), and packaged applications and/or specialty application (such as firewall programs). The degree of specificity is determined by the needs of the organization. Asset types can be recorded at two or more levels of specificity by first

recording one attribute that classifies the asset at a high level, and then adding attributes for more detail. For example, one server might be listed as follows:

DeviceClass = S (server)

DeviceOS = W2K (Windows 2000)

DeviceCapacity = AS (Advanced Server)

- Serial number: A number that uniquely identifies a specific device. Some software vendors also assign a software serial number to each instance of the program licensed by the organization.
- Manufacturer name: An attribute that can be useful for analyzing threat outbreaks when certain manufacturers announce specific vulnerabilities.
- Manufacturer's model or part number: A number that identifies exactly what the asset is. It can be very useful in later analysis of vulnerabilities, because some threats apply only to specific models of certain devices and/or software components.
  - Software version, update revision, or FCO number: Current information about software and firmware versions and, for hardware devices, the current **field change order** (FCO) number. A field change order occurs when a manufacturer performs an upgrade to a hardware component at the customer's premises. Tracking this information is particularly important when inventorying networking devices that function mainly through the software running on them. For example, firewall devices often have three versions: an operating system version, a software version, and a Basic Input/Output System (BIOS) firmware version. Depending on an organization's needs, the inventory may have to track each of those version values for each asset.
- Physical location: An attribute that does not apply to software elements. Nevertheless, some organizations may have license terms that indicate where software can be used.
- Logical location: An attribute that specifies where an asset can be found on the organization's network. The logical location is most applicable to networking devices and indicates the logical network segment (sometimes labeled a VLAN) that houses the device.
- Controlling entity: The organizational unit that controls the asset. A remote location's on-site staff may sometimes be placed in control of network devices; at other organizations, a central corporate group may control all network devices. The inventory should determine which group controls each specific asset, as the controlling group will want a voice in determining how much risk that device can tolerate and how much expense it can sustain to add controls.

Identifying People, Procedures, and Data Assets

Unlike hardware and software, human resources, documentation, and data information assets are not as readily identified and documented. Responsibility for identifying, describing, and evaluating these information assets should be assigned to managers who possess the necessary knowledge, experience, and judgment. As these assets are identified, they should be recorded via a reliable data-handling process like the one used for hardware and software.

The record keeping system should be flexible, allowing you to link assets to attributes based on the nature of the information asset being tracked. The following list describes some basic attributes for various classes of assets:

People

- Position name/number/ID: Avoid names; use position titles, roles, or functions
- Supervisor name/number/ID: Avoid names; use position titles, roles, or functions

- Security clearance level
- Special skills

Procedures

- Description
- Intended purpose
- Software/hardware/networking elements to which it is tied
- Location where it is stored for reference
- Location where it is stored for update purposes

Data

- Classification
- Owner/creator/manager
- Size of data structure
- Data structure used: For example, sequential or relational
- Online or offline
- Location
- Backup procedures

Consider carefully what should be tracked for specific assets. Often larger organizations find that that they can effectively track only a few valuable facts about the most critical information assets. For instance, a company may track only IP address, server name, and device type for its mission-critical servers. The organization might forgo additional attribute tracking on all devices, and completely omit the tracking of desktop or laptop systems.

Classifying and Categorizing Assets

Once the initial inventory is assembled, you must determine whether its asset categories are meaningful to the organization's risk management program. Such a review may cause managers to further subdivide the categories listed in Table 7-1 or to create new categories that more satisfactorily meet the needs of the risk management program. For example, if the category "Internet components" is deemed too general, it could be further divided into subcategories of servers, networking devices (routers, hubs, switches), protection devices (firewalls, proxies), and cabling.

The inventory should also reflect the sensitivity and security priority assigned to each information asset. A classification scheme should be developed (or reviewed, if already in place) that categorizes these information assets based on their sensitivity and security needs. Consider the following classification scheme for an information asset: *confidential, internal,* and *public.* Each of these classification categories designates the level of protection needed for a particular information asset. Some asset types, such as personnel, may require an alternative classification scheme that would identify the information security processes used by the asset type. For example, based on need-to-know and right-to-update, an employee might be given a certain level of security clearance, which identifies the level of information that individual is authorized to use. A more detailed discussion of classification schemes is provided later in this chapter in the section entitled "Data Classification Model."

Classification categories must be comprehensive and mutually exclusive. *Comprehensive* means that all inventoried assets fit into a category; *mutually exclusive* means that each asset is found in only one category. For example, an organization may have a public key infra-structure certificate authority, which is a software application that provides cryptographic key management services. Using a purely technical standard, a manager could categorize the application in the asset list of Table 7-1 as *software,* a general grouping with no special classification priority. Because the certificate authority must be carefully protected as part of the information security infrastructure, it should be categorized into a higher priority classification, such as *software/security component/cryptography,* and it should be verified that no overlapping category exists, such as *software/security component/PKI.*

Assessing Values for Information Assets

As each information asset is identified, categorized, and classified, a relative value must also be assigned to it. Relative values are comparative judgments made to ensure that the most valuable information assets are given the highest priority when managing risk. It may be impossible to know in advance—in absolute economic terms—what losses will be incurred if an asset is compromised; however, a relative assessment helps to ensure that the higher-value assets are protected first.

As each information asset is assigned to its proper category, posing the following basic questions can help you develop the weighting criteria to be used for information asset valuation or impact evaluation. You can use a worksheet, such as the one shown in Figure 7-2, to collect the answers for later analysis.

- **Which information asset is the most critical to the success of the organization?** When determining the relative importance of each information asset, refer to the organization's mission statement or statement of objectives. From this source, determine which assets are essential for meeting the organization's objectives, which assets support the objectives, and which are merely adjuncts. For example, a manufacturing company that makes aircraft engines may decide that the process control systems that control the machine tools on the assembly line are of the first order of importance. While shipping and receiving data entry consoles are important to those functions, they may be less critical if alternatives are available or can be easily arranged. Another example is an online organization such as Amazon.com. The Web servers that advertise the company's products and receive its orders 24 hours a day are essential, whereas the desktop systems used by the customer service department to answer customer e-mails are less critical.
- **Which information asset generates the most revenue?** The relative value of an information asset depends on how much revenue it generates—or, in the case of a nonprofit organization, how critical it is to service delivery. Some organizations have different systems in place for each line of business or service they offer. Which of these assets plays the biggest role in generating revenue or delivering services?
- **Which information asset generates the highest profitability?** Managers should evaluate how much profit depends on a particular asset. For instance, at Amazon.com, some servers support the book sales operations, others support the auction process, and still others support the customer book review database. Which of these servers contributes the most to the profitability of the business? Although important, the review database server does not directly generate profits. Note the distinction between revenues and profits: Some systems upon which revenues depend operate on thin or nonexistent margins and do not generate profits. In nonprofit organizations, you can determine what percentage of the agency's clientele receives services from the information asset being evaluated.

- **Which information asset is the most expensive to replace?** Sometimes an information asset acquires special value because it is unique. If an enterprise still uses a Model-129 keypunch machine to create special punch-card entries for a critical batch run, for example, that machine may be worth more than its cost, because spare parts or service providers may no longer be available. Another example is a specialty device with a long delivery time frame because of manufacturing or transportation requirements. Organizations must control the risk of loss or damage to such unique assets—for example, by buying and storing a backup device.
- **Which information asset is the most expensive to protect?** Some assets are by their nature difficult to protect, and formulating a complete answer to this question may not be possible until after the risk identification phase is complete, because the costs of controls cannot be computed until the controls are identified. However, you can still make a preliminary assessment of the relative difficulty of establishing controls for each asset.
- **Which information asset's loss or compromise would be the most embarrassing or cause the greatest liability?** Almost every organization is aware of its image in the local, national, and international spheres. The loss or exposure of some assets would prove especially embarrassing. Microsoft's image, for example, was tarnished when an employee's computer system became a victim of the QAZ Trojan horse capability, and the latest version of Microsoft Office was stolen.[2]

System Name: SLS E-Commerce		
Date Evaluated: February 2003		
Evaluated By: D. Jones		

Information assets	Data classification	Impact to profitability
Information Transmitted:		
EDI Document Set 1 — Logistics BOL to outsourcer (outbound)	Confidential	High
EDI Document Set 2 — Supplier orders (outbound)	Confidential	High
EDI Document Set 2 — Supplier fulfillment advice (inbound)	Confidential	Medium
Customer order via SSL (inbound)	Confidential	Critical
Customer service Request via e-maill (inbound)	Private	Medium
DMZ Assets:		
Edge Router	Public	Critical
Web server #1—home page and core site	Public	Critical
Web server #2—Application server	Private	Critical
Notes: BOL: Bill of Lading: DMZ: Demilitarized Zone EDI: Electronic Data Interchange SSL: Secure Sockets Layer		

FIGURE 7-2 Sample Asset Classification Worksheet

You may also need to identify and add other institution-specific questions to the evaluation process.

Listing Assets in Order of Importance

The final step in the risk identification process is to list the assets in order of importance. This goal can be achieved by using a weighted factor analysis worksheet similar to the one shown in Table 7-2. In this process, each information asset is assigned a score for each critical factor. Table 7-2 uses the NIST SP 800-30 recommended values of 0.1 to 1.0. (NIST SP 800-30, *Risk Management for Information Technology Systems,* is published by the National Institute of Standards and Technology and is covered in detail in Chapter 8. Your organization may choose to use another weighting system.) Each criterion has an assigned weight, showing its relative importance in the organization.

TABLE 7-2 Example Weighted Factor Analysis Worksheet

Information Asset	Criterion 1: Impact on Revenue	Criterion 2: Impact on Profitability	Criterion 3: Impact on Public Image	Weighted Score
Criterion weight (1–100); must total 100	30	40	30	
EDI Document Set 1—Logistics bill of lading to outsourcer (outbound)	0.8	0.9	0.5	75
EDI Document Set 2—Supplier orders (outbound)	0.8	0.9	0.6	78
EDI Document Set 2—Supplier fulfillment advice (inbound)	0.4	0.5	0.3	41
Customer order via SSL (inbound)	1.0	1.0	1.0	100
Customer service request via e-mail (inbound)	0.4	0.4	0.9	55

EDI: Electronic Data Interchange
SSL: Secure Sockets Layer

A quick review of Table 7-2 shows that the Customer order via SSL (inbound) data flow is the most important asset on this worksheet, and that the EDI Document Set 2—Supplier fulfillment advice (inbound) is the least critical asset.

Data Classification Model

Corporate and military organizations use a variety of classification schemes. Georgia-Pacific Corporation (G-P), for example, uses a corporate data classification scheme throughout the company that helps secure the confidentiality and integrity of its data. The G-P data classification scheme has three categories: confidential, internal, and external. Data owners must classify the information assets for which they are responsible. At least once a year, data owners must review these classifications to ensure that the data are still classified correctly and the appropriate access controls are in place.

In this company, information asset classifications are defined as follows:

- Confidential: The most sensitive G-P information assets that must be tightly controlled, even within the company. Access to information assets with this classification is strictly on a need-to-know basis or as required by the terms of a contract. Information assets with this classification may also be called "sensitive" or "proprietary."
- Internal: All internal information assets that do not meet the criteria for the confidential category. These assets can be viewed only by G-P employees, authorized contractors, and specific third parties.
- External: All information assets that have been approved by management for public release.[3]

As you might expect, the **U.S. military classification scheme** relies on a more complex categorization system than the schemes of most corporations. The military is perhaps the best-known user of data classification schemes. It has invested heavily in information security (InfoSec), operations security (OpSec), and communications security (ComSec). In fact, many developments in data communications and information security are the result of military-sponsored research and development.

For most information, the U.S. military uses a five-level classification scheme as defined in Executive Order 12958 and presented below:[4]

- Unclassified Data: Generally free for distribution to the public, and poses no threat to U.S. national interests.
- Sensitive But Unclassified (SBU) Data: "Any information of which the loss, misuse, or unauthorized access to, or modification of, might adversely affect U.S. national interests, the conduct of Department of Defense (DoD) programs, or the privacy of DoD personnel." Common designations include For Official Use Only, Not for Public Release, or For Internal Use Only.
- Confidential Data: "Any information or material the unauthorized disclosure of which reasonably could be expected to cause damage to the national security. Examples of damage include the compromise of information that indicates strength of ground, air, and naval forces in the United States and overseas areas; disclosure of technical information used for training, maintenance, and inspection of classified munitions of war; and revelation of performance characteristics, test data, design, and production data on munitions of war."
- Secret Data: "Any information or material the unauthorized disclosure of which reasonably could be expected to cause serious damage to the national security. Examples of serious damage include disruption of foreign relations significantly affecting the national security; significant impairment of a program or policy directly related to the national security; revelation of significant military plans or intelligence operations; compromise of significant military plans or intelligence operations; and compromise of significant scientific or technological developments relating to national security."
- Top Secret Data: "Any information or material the unauthorized disclosure of which reasonably could be expected to cause exceptionally grave damage to the national security. Examples of exceptionally grave damage include armed hostilities against the United States or its allies; disruption of foreign relations vitally affecting the national security; the compromise of vital national defense plans or complex cryptologic and communications intelligence systems; the revelation of sensitive intelligence operations; and the disclosure of scientific or technological developments vital to national

security." This classification comes with the general expectation of "crib to grave" protection, meaning that individuals entrusted with top secret information are expected to honor the classification of the information for life, even after they are no longer employed in the role that originally allowed them to access the information.

The military also has some specialty classification ratings, such as Personnel Information and Evaluation Reports, to protect related areas of information. Federal agencies such as the FBI and CIA also use specialty classification schemes, such as Need-to-Know and Named Projects. Obviously, Need-to-Know authorization allows access to information by individuals who need the information to perform their work. Named Projects are clearance levels based on a scheme similar to Need-to-Know. When an operation, project, or set of classified data is created, the project is assigned a code name. Next, a list of authorized individuals is created and assigned to either the Need-to-Know or the Named Projects category.

Most organizations do not need the detailed level of classification used by the military or federal agencies. Nevertheless, they may find it necessary to classify data to provide protection. A simple scheme can allow an organization to protect its sensitive information such as marketing or research data, personnel data, customer data, and general internal communications. A scheme such as the following could be adopted:

- Public: For general public dissemination, such as an advertisement or press release.
- For official use only: Not for public release but not particularly sensitive, such as internal communications.
- Sensitive: Important information that could embarrass the organization or cause loss of market share if compromised.
- Classified: Essential and confidential information, disclosure of which could severely damage the well-being of the organization.

Security Clearances

Another perspective on the data classification scheme is the personnel security clearance structure, in which each user of an information asset is assigned an authorization level that indicates the level of information classification he or she can access. This is usually accomplished by assigning each employee to a named role, such as data entry clerk, development programmer, information security analyst, or even CIO. Most organizations have developed a set of roles and corresponding security clearances, so that individuals are assigned authorization levels that correlate with the classifications of the information assets.

Beyond a simple reliance on the security clearance of the individual is the **need-to-know** principle. Regardless of one's security clearance, an individual is not allowed to view data simply because it falls within that individual's level of clearance. That is, after an individual is granted a security clearance but before he or she is allowed access to a specific set of data, that person must also meet the need-to-know requirement. This extra requirement ensures that the confidentiality of information is properly maintained.

Management of the Classified Information Asset

Managing an information asset includes considering the storage, distribution, portability, and destruction of that information asset. An information asset, such as a report, that has a classification designation other than unclassified or public must be clearly marked as such. The U.S. government, for example, uses color-coordinated cover sheets to protect classified information from the casual observer. As shown in Figure 7-3, every classified document should also contain the appropriate security designation at the top and bottom of each page. Classified documents must be available only to authorized individuals, which usually requires locking file cabinets, safes, or other such protective devices for hard copies and systems. When an individual carries a classified report, it should be inconspicuous and kept in a locked briefcase or portfolio, and in compliance with appropriate policies (for example, requirements for double-sealed envelopes, tamper-proof seals, etc.).

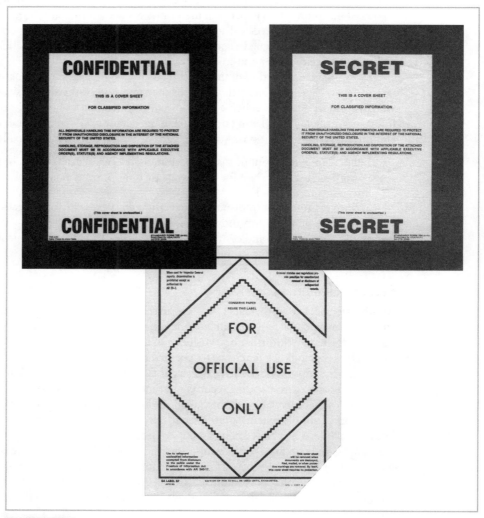

FIGURE 7-3 Military Data Classification Cover Sheets

To maintain the confidentiality of classified documents, managers can implement a risk management policy control known as the clean desk policy. This policy usually meets with resistance because it requires each employee to secure all information in its appropriate storage container at the end of every business day.

When copies of classified information are no longer valuable or too many copies exist, care should be taken to destroy them properly, usually after double signature verification. Documents should be destroyed by means of shredding, burning, or transfer to a service offering authorized document destruction. Policy should ensure that no classified information is inappropriately disposed of in trash or recycling areas. Otherwise, people who engage in **dumpster diving** may retrieve information and thereby compromise the security of the organization's information assets.

Threat Identification

As mentioned at the beginning of this chapter, the ultimate goal of risk identification is to assess the circumstances and setting of each information asset to reveal any vulnerabilities. Armed with a properly classified inventory, you can assess potential weaknesses in each information asset—a process known as **threat identification**.

Any organization typically faces a wide variety of threats. If you assume that every threat can and will attack every information asset, then the project scope becomes too complex. To make the process less unwieldy, each step in the threat identification and vulnerability identification processes is managed separately and then coordinated at the end. At every step the manager is called upon to exercise good judgment and draw on experience to make the process function smoothly.

Identify And Prioritize Threats and Threat Agents

Chapter 2 identified 12 categories of threats to information security, which are listed alphabetically in Table 7-3.

TABLE 7-3 Threats to Information Security

Threat	Example
Act of human error or failure	Accidents, employee mistakes
Compromises to intellectual property	Piracy, copyright infringement
Deliberate acts of espionage or trespass	Unauthorized access and/or data collection
Deliberate acts of information extortion	Blackmail for information disclosure
Deliberate acts of sabotage or vandalism	Destruction of systems or information
Deliberate acts of theft	Illegal confiscation of equipment or information
Deliberate software attacks	Viruses, worms, macros, denial-of-service
Forces of nature	Fire, flood, earthquake, lightning
Quality of service deviations from service providers	Power and WAN quality of service issues
Technical hardware failures or errors	Equipment failure
Technical software failures or errors	Bugs, code problems, unknown loopholes
Technological obsolescence	Antiquated or outdated technologies

Source: ©2003 ACM, Inc., Included here by permission.

Each of these threats presents a unique challenge to information security and must be handled with specific controls that directly address the particular threat and the threat agent's attack strategy. Before threats can be assessed in the risk identification process, however, each threat must be further examined to determine its potential to affect the targeted information asset. In general, this process is referred to as a threat assessment. Posing the following questions can help you understand the threat and its potential effects on an information asset:

- **Which threats present a danger to this organization's information assets in its current environment?** Not all threats endanger every organization, of course. You should examine each of the categories in Table 7-3, and eliminate any that don't apply to your organization. While it is unlikely that you can eliminate an entire category of threats, if you can, it speeds the threat assessment process. The Offline feature entitled "Threats to Information Security" describes the threats that some CIOs of major companies identified for their organizations. Although the Offline feature directly addresses only information security, note that a weighted ranking of threats should be compiled for any information asset that is at risk. Once you have determined which threats apply to your organization, you should identify particular examples of threats within each category, eliminating those that are not relevant. For example, a company with offices on the twelfth floor of a high-rise building in Denver, Colorado, might not be subject to flooding. Similarly, a firm with an office in Oklahoma City, Oklahoma, might not be concerned with landslides.
- **Which threats represent the gravest danger to the organization's information assets?** The amount of danger posed by a threat is sometimes difficult to assess. It may be simply the probability of a threat attacking the organization, or it may reflect the amount of damage that the threat could create or the frequency with which an attack can occur. During this preliminary assessment phase, the analysis is limited to examining the existing level of preparedness and improving the strategy of information security. The results give a quick overview of the components involved.

As you will discover in Chapter 8, you can use both quantitative and qualitative measures to rank values. Since information in this case is preliminary, the organization may wish to subjectively rank threats in order of danger. Alternatively, it may simply rate each of the threats on a scale of 1 to 5, with 1 designating insignificant threats and 5 designating highly significant threats.

OFFLINE

Threats to Information Security: Survey of Industry

What are the threats to information security according to top computing executives? A recent study by Whitman asked that very question. Based on the categories of threats presented earlier, more than 1000 top computing executives were asked to rate each threat category on a scale ranging from "not significant" to "very significant." The results were converted to a five-point scale, where 5 represented "very significant," and are shown under the heading "Mean" in the following table. Then the executives were also asked to identify the top five threats to their organization. Their responses were weighted, with five

(continued)

points assigned to a first-place vote and one point assigned to a fifth-place vote. The sum of weights is presented under the heading "Weight" in the table. The two ratings were then combined into a weighted rank.

Weighted Ranks of Threats to Information Security

	Threat	Mean	Standard Deviation	Weight	Weighted Rank
1.	Deliberate software attacks	3.99	1.03	546	**2178.3**
2.	Technical software failures or errors	3.16	1.13	358	**1129.9**
3.	Acts of human error or failure	3.15	1.11	350	**1101.0**
4.	Deliberate acts of espionage or trespass	3.22	1.37	324	**1043.6**
5.	Deliberate acts of sabotage or vandalism	3.15	1.37	306	**962.6**
6.	Technical hardware failures or errors	3.00	1.18	314	**942.0**
7.	Deliberate acts of theft	3.07	1.30	226	**694.5**
8.	Forces of nature	2.80	1.09	218	**610.9**
9.	Compromises to intellectual property	2.72	1.21	182	**494.8**
10.	Quality-of-service deviations from service providers	2.65	1.06	164	**433.9**
11.	Technological obsolescence	2.71	1.11	158	**427.9**
12.	Deliberate acts of information extortion	2.45	1.42	92	**225.2**

Another popular study also examines threats to information security. The Computer Security Institute, in cooperation with the Federal Bureau of Investigation (FBI), conducts an annual survey of computer crime. The following table shows its results from the last five years.

CSI/FBI Survey Results for Types of Attack or Misuse (1997–2003)

Type of Attack or Misuse		2003	2002	2001	2000	1999	1998	1997
1.	Virus	82%	85%	94%	85%	90%	83%	82%
2.	Insider abuse of Internet access	80%	78%	91%	79%	97%	77%	68%
3.	Laptop	59%	55%	64%	60%	69%	64%	58%
4.	Unauthorized access by insiders	45%	38%	49%	71%	55%	44%	40%
5.	Denial of service	42%	40%	36%	27%	31%	24%	–
6.	System penetration	36%	40%	40%	25%	30%	23%	20%
7.	Theft of proprietary information	21%	20%	26%	20%	25%	18%	20%
8.	Sabotage	21%	8%	18%	17%	13%	14%	14%

(continued)

CSI/FBI Survey Results for Types of Attack or Misuse (1997–2003)							
Type of Attack or Misuse	2003	2002	2001	2000	1999	1998	1997
9. Financial fraud	15%	12%	12%	11%	14%	14%	12%
10. Telecommunications fraud	10%	9%	10%	11%	17%	16%	27%
11. Telecommunications eavesdropping	6%	6%	10%	7%	14%	9%	11%
12. Active wiretap	1%	1%	2%	1%	2%	1%	3%

Source: R. Power. 2003 CSI/FBI Computer Crime and Security Survey. *Computer Security Issues & Trends,* 9(1), 2003, 1–20.

Frequency of Attacks

The number of attacks is also increasing. The average company reported between 10 and 15 attacks, up steadily every year from an average of 5 to 10 attacks in 1996. Unfortunately, the number of organizations reporting that they just don't know is also rising. The fact is, almost every company has experienced an attack. Whether that attack was successful depends on the company's security efforts; whether the perpetrators were caught or the organization was willing to report the attack is another matter entirely.

Source: Adapted from M. E. Whitman. Enemy at the gates: Threats to information security. *Communications of the ACM,* August 2003.

■ **How much would it cost to recover from a successful attack?** One of the calculations that guide corporate spending on controls is the cost of recovery operations if an attack occurs and is successful. At this preliminary phase, it is not necessary to conduct a detailed assessment of the costs associated with recovering from a particular attack. Instead, at this stage of threat identification, subjective ranking or listing of the threats based on the cost to recover is common. Alternatively, you could assign a rating for each threat on a scale of 1 to 5, with 1 representing "not expensive at all" and 5 representing "extremely expensive." If the information is available, a raw value (e.g., $5000, $10,000, or $2 million) can be assigned. In other words, the goal at this phase is to provide a rough assessment of the cost to recover operations should the attack interrupt normal business operations.

■ **Which threats would require the greatest expenditure to prevent?** Another factor that affects the danger posed by a particular threat is the amount it would cost to protect against that threat. Controlling for some threats has a nominal cost, as in protections from malicious code, while other protective strategies are very expensive, as in protections from forces of nature. Here again the manager ranks, rates, or attempts to quantify the level of danger associated with protecting against a particular threat, by using the same techniques outlined earlier for calculating recovery costs. Look at the Offline feature on expenditure for threats to see how some top executives recently handled this issue.

This list of questions may not cover everything that affects risk identification. An organization's specific guidelines or policies should influence the process and will inevitably require that some additional questions be answered.

OFFLINE

Expenditures for Threats to Information Security

The recent study by Whitman also asked computing executives to determine the priorities set in their organizations for expenditures geared toward threats to information security. Each executive responded by identifying his or her top five expenditures. These ratings were used to create a rank order of the expenses. The results are presented in the following table.

Weighted Ranking of Threat-Driven Expenditures

Top Threat-Driven Expenses	Rating
1. Deliberate software attacks	12.7
2. Acts of human error or failure	7.6
3. Technical software failures or errors	7.0
4. Technical hardware failures or errors	6.0
5. Quality-of-service deviations from service providers	4.9
6. Deliberate acts of espionage or trespass	4.7
7. Deliberate acts of theft	4.1
8. Deliberate acts of sabotage or vandalism	4.0
9. Technological obsolescence	3.3
10. Forces of nature	3.0
11. Compromises to intellectual property	2.2
12. Deliberate acts of information extortion	1.0

Source: Adapted from M. E. Whitman. Enemy at the gates: Threats to information security. *Communications of the ACM*, August 2003.

Vulnerability Assessment

Once you have identified the information assets of the organization and documented some threat assessment criteria, you can begin to review every information asset for each threat. This review leads to the creation of a list of vulnerabilities that remain potential risks to the organization. What are vulnerabilities? They are specific avenues that threat agents can exploit to attack an information asset. In other words, they are chinks in the asset's armor—a flaw or weakness in an information asset, security procedure, design, or control that can be exploited accidentally or on purpose to breach security. As an example, Table 7-4 analyzes the threats to and possible vulnerabilities of a DMZ router.

TABLE 7-4 Vulnerability Assessment of a DMZ Router

Threat	Possible Vulnerabilities
Deliberate software attacks	• Internet Protocol (IP) is vulnerable to denial-of-service attack • Outsider IP fingerprinting activities can reveal sensitive information unless suitable controls are implemented.
Acts of human error or failure	• Employees or contractors may cause an outage if configuration errors are made.
Technical software failures or errors	• Vendor-supplied routing software could fail and cause an outage.
Technical hardware failures or errors	• Hardware could fail and cause an outage • Power system failures are always possible
Quality-of-service deviations from service providers	• Unless suitable electrical power conditioning is provided, failure is probable over time
Deliberate acts of espionage or trespass	• Router has little intrinsic value, but other assets protected by this device could be attacked if it is compromised
Deliberate acts of theft	• Router has little intrinsic value, but other assets protected by this device could be attacked if it is compromised
Deliberate acts of sabotage or vandalism	• IP is vulnerable to denial-of-service attacks • Device may be subject to defacement or cache poisoning
Technological obsolescence	• If it is not reviewed and periodically updated, a device may fall too far behind its vendor support model to be kept in service
Forces of nature	• All information assets in the organization are subject to forces of nature unless suitable controls are provided
Compromises to intellectual property	• Router has little intrinsic value, but other assets protected by this device could be attacked if it is compromised
Deliberate acts of information extortion	• Router has little intrinsic value, but other assets protected by this device could be attacked if it is compromised

A list like the one in Table 7-4 must be created for each information asset to document how each possible or likely attack could be perpetrated against it. This list is usually long and shows all the vulnerabilities of the information asset. Some threats manifest themselves in multiple ways, yielding multiple vulnerabilities for that asset–threat pair. Of necessity, the process of listing vulnerabilities is somewhat subjective and is based on the experience and knowledge of the people who create the list. Therefore, the process works best when groups of people with diverse backgrounds work together in a series of brainstorming sessions. For instance, the team that reviews the vulnerabilities for networking equipment should include networking specialists, the systems management team that operates the network, information security risk specialists, and even technically proficient users of the system.

At the end of the risk identification process, a list of assets and their vulnerabilities has been developed. This list serves as the starting point (with its supporting documentation from the identification process) for the next step in the risk management process—risk assessment.

VIEWPOINT

Getting at Risk

By George V. Hulme

The risks that organizations face have never been higher. More systems are interconnected today than ever before, and there is only one constant to those systems: change. Aside from hackers, disgruntled employees, and corporate spies, a growing number of laws and regulations (such as Sarbanes-Oxley, Gramm-Leach-Bliley, and the Health Information Portability and Accountability Act) have forever changed the role of the information security professional as the gatekeeper of information and the manager of risk.

The role of the security professional is to help the organization manage risks poised against the confidentiality, integrity, and availability of its information assets. And the foundation of all information security programs begins and forever lives with the process of risk assessment. Risk isn't static. Rather, risk is fluid and evolves over time. A risk assessment conducted on the first day of the month can be quite different than the same assessment conducted several weeks later. The levels of risks for particular information systems can change as quickly as IT systems change. And geopolitical events such as war, economics, new employee hires, layoffs, and the steady introduction of new technologies all work to change the amount of risk faced by an organization.

The first task in risk assessment is to identify, assess, classify, and then decide on the value of digital assets and systems. Many believe that the most difficult aspect of risk assessment is uncovering the myriad system and configuration vulnerabilities that place systems at risk, but that's not so: An abundance of tools is available that can help automate that task. It's really deciding, organization-wide, the value of information and intellectual property that poses one of the most daunting challenges for the security professional. How much is the research and development data worth? How much will it cost the organization if it loses access to the accounting, or customer relationship management, systems for a day? Without knowing the value of information, and the systems that ensure its flow, it's impossible to make reasonable decisions about how much can reasonably be spent protecting that information. It makes little sense to spend $200,000 annually to protect information that wouldn't cost an organization more than $25,000 if exposed or lost. In a perfect world, with unlimited budgets and resources in hand, everything could be protected all of the time. But we don't live in a perfect world, and tough decisions need to be made. That means bringing together management, legal, human resources, physical security, and other groups in the organization. In assessing risk, you must decide what needs to be protected and how much that information is worth. Only then can reasonable decisions be made as to how to mitigate risk by implementing defensive measures and sound policy.

(continued)

During the risk assessment process, vulnerabilities to systems will inevitably be uncovered. The challenge here is to determine which ones pose the greatest threats to protected assets. It's a challenge that security professionals face every day. Does a low-risk vulnerability (something unlikely to be exploited) on a system holding highly valuable corporate information need to be remediated more quickly than a high-risk vulnerability (one that is easily, and likely to be, exploited) on a system holding information of little value? Maybe. It all depends. And each situation is different.

Risk can never be entirely eliminated; it can only be managed to levels that an organization can tolerate. The best way to keep risk low is to remain eternally vigilant by following a four-step process: (1) identify new assets, vulnerabilities, and threats; (2) assess and classify assets, vulnerabilities, and threats; (3) remediate and defend; and (4) return to Step 1.

George V. Hulme is the Senior Editor for Security at *InformationWeek* magazine.

Risk Assessment

Assessing the relative risk for each vulnerability is accomplished via a process called risk assessment. Risk assessment assigns a risk rating or score to each specific vulnerability. While this number does not mean anything in absolute terms, it enables you to gauge the relative risk associated with each vulnerable information asset, and it facilitates the creation of comparative ratings later in the risk control process.

Introduction to Risk Assessment

Figure 7-4 shows the factors that go into the risk-rating estimate for each of the vulnerabilities.

Risk is

The **likelihood** of the occurrence of a vulnerability

Multiplied by

The **value** of the information asset

Minus

The percentage of risk mitigated by **current controls**

Plus

The **uncertainty** of current knowledge of the vulnerability

---

FIGURE 7-4 Risk Identification Estimate Factors

The goal at this point is to create a method to evaluate the relative risk of each listed vulnerability. Chapter 8 describes how to determine more precise cost estimates for vulnerabilities as well as projected expenses for the controls that reduce the risks. For now, you can use the simpler risk model of Figure 7-4 to evaluate the risk for each information asset. The next section describes the factors used to calculate the relative risk for each vulnerability.

Likelihood

Likelihood is the overall rating—a numerical value on a defined scale—of the probability that a specific vulnerability will be exploited. NIST recommends in its Special Publication 800-30 that vulnerabilities be assigned a likelihood rating between 0.1 (low) and 1.0 (high). For example, the likelihood of an employee or system being struck by a meteorite while indoors would be rated 0.1, while the likelihood of receiving at least one e-mail containing a virus or worm in the next year would be rated 1.0. You could also choose to use a number between 1 and 100, but not zero, since vulnerabilities with a zero likelihood should have already been removed from the asset/vulnerability list. Whatever rating system you employ for assigning likelihood, use professionalism, experience, and judgment in determining the rating—and use it consistently. Whenever possible, use external references for likelihood values, after reviewing and adjusting them for your specific circumstances. For many asset/vulnerability combinations, existing sources have already determined their likelihood. For example,

- The likelihood of a fire has been estimated actuarially for each type of structure.
- The likelihood that any given e-mail will contain a virus or worm has been researched.
- The number of network attacks can be forecast depending on how many network addresses the organization has assigned.

Assessing Potential Loss

Using the information documented during the risk identification process, you can assign weighted scores based on the value of each information asset. The actual number used will vary according to the needs of the organization. Some groups use a scale of 1 to 100, with 100 being reserved for those information assets whose loss would stop company operations within a few minutes. Other recommended scales, including the one included in NIST SP 800-30, use assigned weights in broad categories, with all-important assets having a value of 100, low-criticality assets having a value of 1, and all other assets having a medium value of 50. Still other scales employ weights from 1 to 10, or assigned values of 1, 3, and 5 to represent low, medium, and high-valued assets, respectively. Alternatively, you can create unique weight values customized to your organization's specific needs.

To be effective, the values must be assigned by asking the questions listed earlier in the section entitled "Identify and Prioritize Threats and Threat Agents." These questions are restated here for easy reference:

- Which threats present a danger to this organization's assets in the given environment?
- Which threats represent the most danger to the organization's information?
- How much would it cost to recover from a successful attack?
- Which threats would require the greatest expenditure to prevent?

After reevaluating these questions, use the background information from the risk identification process and add to that information by posing yet another question:

- Which of the aforementioned questions is the most important to the protection of information from threats within this organization?

The answer to this question determines the priorities used in the assessment of vulnerabilities. Which is the most important to the organization—the cost to recover from a threat attack or the cost to protect against a threat attack? More generally, which of the threats has the highest probability of successful attack? Recall that the purpose of risk assessment is to look at the threats an organization faces in its current state. Once these questions are answered, move to the next step in the process: examining how current controls can reduce the risk faced by specific vulnerabilities.

Percentage of Risk Mitigated by Current Controls

If a vulnerability is fully managed by an existing control, it can be set aside. If it is partially controlled, estimate what percentage of the vulnerability has been controlled.

Uncertainty

It is not possible to know everything about every vulnerability, such as how likely an attack against an asset is to occur or how great an impact a successful attack would have. The degree to which a current control can reduce risk is also subject to estimation error. A factor that accounts for uncertainty must always be added to the equations; it consists of an estimate made by the manager using good judgment and experience.

Risk Determination

For the purpose of relative risk assessment, risk *equals* likelihood of vulnerability occurrence *times* value (or impact) *minus* percentage risk already controlled *plus* an element of uncertainty. As an example of how this equation works, consider the following scenario:

- Information asset A has a value score of 50 and has one vulnerability: Vulnerability 1 has a likelihood of 1.0 with no current controls. You estimate that assumptions and data are 90% accurate.
- Information asset B has a value score of 100 and has two vulnerabilities: Vulnerability 2 has a likelihood of 0.5 with a current control that addresses 50% of its risk; vulnerability 3 has a likelihood of 0.1 with no current controls. You estimate that assumptions and data are 80% accurate.

The resulting ranked list of risk ratings for the three vulnerabilities described above is as follows [(value times likelihood) minus risk mitigated plus uncertainty]:

- Asset A: Vulnerability 1 rated as $55 = (50 \times 1.0) - ((50 \times 1.0) \times .2) + ((50 \times 1.0) \times .1)$
- Asset B: Vulnerability 2 rated as $35 = (100 \times 0.5) - ((100 \times 0.5) \times .5) + ((100 \times 0.5) \times .2)$
- Asset B: Vulnerability 3 rated as $12 = (100 \times 0.1) - ((100 \times 0.5) \times .0) + ((100 \times 0.5) \times .2)$

Identify Possible Controls

For each threat and its associated vulnerabilities that have residual risk, create a preliminary list of control ideas. Residual risk is the risk that remains even after the existing control has been applied. *Controls, safeguards,* and *countermeasures* are all terms used to describe security mechanisms, policies, and procedures. These mechanisms, policies, and procedures counter attacks, reduce risk, resolve vulnerabilities, and otherwise improve the general state of security within an organization.

Three general categories of controls exist: policies, programs, and technical controls. You learned about policies in Chapter 4. **Programs** are activities performed within the organization to improve security; they include security education, training, and awareness programs. Technical controls—also known as security technologies—are the technical implementations of the policies defined by the organization.

Access Controls

Access controls specifically address admission of a user into a trusted area of the organization. These areas can include information systems, physically restricted areas such as computer rooms, and even the organization in its entirety. Access controls usually consist of a combination of policies, programs, and technologies.

Types of Access Controls

A number of approaches to, and categories of, access controls exist. They can be mandatory, no discretionary, or discretionary. Each category of controls regulates access to a particular type or collection of information, as explained below.

Mandatory Access Controls (MACs). MACs are required—obviously—and are structured and coordinated with a data classification scheme. When MACs are implemented, users and data owners have limited control over their access to information resources. MACs use a data classification scheme that rates each collection of information. Each user is also rated to specify the level of information that he or she may access. These ratings are often referred to as sensitivity levels.

In a variation of this form of access control called **lattice-based access control**, users are assigned a matrix of authorizations for particular areas of access. The level of authorization may vary depending on the classification authorizations that individuals possess for each group of information assets or resources. The lattice structure contains subjects and objects, and the boundaries associated with each subject/object pair are clearly demarcated. Lattice-based access control then specifies the level of access each subject has to each object, if any. With this type of control, the column of attributes associated with a particular object (such as a printer) is referred to as an **access control list (ACL)**. The row of attributes associated with a particular subject (such as a user) is referred to as a **capabilities table**.

Nondiscretionary Controls. Nondiscretionary controls are determined by a central authority in the organization and can be based on roles—called **role-based controls**—or on a specified set of tasks—called **task-based controls**. Task-based controls can, in turn, be based on lists maintained on subjects or objects. Role-based controls are tied to the role that a particular user performs in an organization, whereas task-based controls are tied to a particular assignment or responsibility.

The role- and task-based controls make it easier to maintain controls and restrictions, especially if the individual performing the role or task changes often. Instead of constantly assigning and revoking the privileges of individuals who come and go, the administrator simply assigns the associated access rights to the role or task. When individuals are subsequently assigned to that role or task, they automatically receive the corresponding access. The administrator can easily remove individuals' associations with roles and tasks, thereby revoking their access.

Discretionary Access Controls (DACs). DACs are implemented at the discretion or option of the data user. The ability to share resources in a peer-to-peer configuration allows users to control and possibly provide access to information or resources at their disposal. The users can allow general, unrestricted access, or they can allow specific individuals or sets of individuals to access these resources. As an example, suppose a user has a hard drive containing information to be shared with office coworkers. This user can elect to allow access to specific individuals by listing their names in the share control function.

Figure 7-5 shows an example of a DAC from a peer-to-peer network using Microsoft Windows.

FIGURE 7-5 Discretionary Access Control

Documenting the Results of Risk Assessment

The goal of the risk management process so far has been to identify information assets and their vulnerabilities and to rank them according to the need for protection. In preparing this list, a wealth of factual information about the assets and the threats they face is collected. Also, information about the controls that are already in place is collected. The final summarized document is the ranked vulnerability risk worksheet, as shown in Table 7-5. A review of this worksheet reveals similarities to the weighted factor analysis worksheet depicted in Table 7-2. The columns in the worksheet shown in Table 7-5 are used as follows:

- Asset: List each vulnerable asset.
- Asset Impact: Show the results for this asset from the weighted factor analysis worksheet. In our example, this value is a number from 1 to 100.
- Vulnerability: List each uncontrolled vulnerability.
- Vulnerability Likelihood: State the likelihood of the realization of the vulnerability by a threat-agent as indicated in the vulnerability analysis step. In our example, the potential values range from 0.1 to 1.0.
- Risk-Rating Factor: Enter the figure calculated by multiplying the asset impact and its likelihood. In our example, the calculation yields a number ranging from 0.1 to 100.

TABLE 7-5 Ranked Vulnerability Risk Worksheet

Asset	Asset Impact	Vulnerability	Vulnerability Likelihood	Risk-Rating Factor
Customer service request via e-mail (inbound)	55	E-mail disruption due to hardware failure	0.2	11
Customer service request via e-mail (inbound)	55	E-mail disruption due to software failure	0.2	11
Customer order via Secure Sockets Layer (SSL) (inbound)	100	Lost orders due to Web server hardware failure	0.1	10
Customer order via SSL (inbound)	100	Lost orders due to Web server ISP service failure	0.1	10
Customer service request via e-mail (inbound)	55	E-mail disruption due to SMTP mail relay attack	0.1	5.5
Customer service request via e-mail (inbound)	55	E-mail disruption due to ISP service failure	0.1	5.5
Customer service request via e-mail (inbound)	55	E-mail disruption due to power failure	0.1	5.5
Customer order via SSL (inbound)	100	Lost orders due to Web server denial-of-service attack	0.025	2.5
Customer order via SSL (inbound)	100	Lost orders due to Web server software failure	0.01	1
Customer order via SSL (inbound)	100	Lost orders due to Web server buffer overrun attack	0.01	1

Looking at Table 7-5, you may be surprised that the most pressing risk requires making the mail server or servers more robust. Even though the impact rating of the information asset represented by the customer service e-mail is only 55, the relatively high likelihood of a hardware failure makes it the most pressing problem.

Now that the risk identification process is complete, what should the documentation package look like? In other words, what are the deliverables from this stage of the risk management project? The risk identification process should designate what function the reports serve, who is responsible for preparing them, and who reviews them. The ranked vulnerability risk worksheet is the initial working document for the next step in the risk management process: assessing and controlling risk. Table 7-6 shows an example list of the worksheets that should have been prepared by an information asset risk management team to this point.

TABLE 7-6 Risk Identification and Assessment Deliverables

Deliverable	Purpose
Information asset classification worksheet	Assembles information about information assets and their impact on or value to the organization
Weighted criteria analysis worksheet	Assigns a ranked value or impact weight to each information asset
Ranked vulnerability risk worksheet	Assigns a risk-rating ranked value to each uncontrolled asset–vulnerability pair

Chapter Summary

- Risk management examines and documents an organization's information assets. Management is responsible for identifying and controlling the risks that an organization encounters. In the modern organization, the information security group often plays a leadership role in risk management.

- A key component of a risk management strategy is the identification, classification, and prioritization of the organization's information assets.

- Assessment is the identification of assets, including all of the elements of an organization's system: people, procedures, data and information, software, hardware, and networking elements.

- The human resources, documentation, and data information assets of an organization are not as easily identified and documented as tangible assets, such as hardware and software. These more elusive assets should be identified and described using knowledge, experience, and judgment.

- You can use the answers to the following questions to develop weighting criteria for information assets:
  - Which information asset is the most important to the success of the organization?
  - Which information asset generates the most revenue?
  - Which information asset generates the most profitability?
  - Which information asset would be the most expensive to replace?
  - Which information asset would be the most expensive to protect?
  - Which information asset would be the most embarrassing if compromised?
  - What questions should be added to cover the needs of the specific organization and its environment?

- After identifying and performing a preliminary classification of information assets, the threats facing an organization should be examined. There are 12 general categories of threats to information security.

- Each threat must be examined through a threat assessment process that addresses the following questions: Which of these threats exist in this organization's environment? Are most dangerous to the organization's information? Require the greatest expenditure for recovery? Require the greatest expenditure for protection?

- Each information asset is evaluated for each threat it faces; the resulting information is used to create a list of the vulnerabilities that pose risks to the organization. This process results in an information asset and vulnerability list, which serves as the starting point for risk assessment.

- The goal of risk assessment is the assignment of a risk rating or score that represents the relative risk for a specific vulnerability of a specific information asset.

- If any specific vulnerability is completely managed by an existing control, it no longer needs to be considered for additional controls.

- Controls, safeguards, and countermeasures should be identified for each threat and its associated vulnerabilities.

- In general, three categories of controls exist: policies, programs, and technologies.

- Access controls can be classified as mandatory, discretionary, or nondiscretionary.

- The risk identification process should designate what function the resulting reports serve, who is responsible for preparing them, and who reviews them. The ranked vulnerability risk worksheet is the initial working document for the next step in the risk management process: assessing and controlling risk.

Review Questions

1. What is risk management?
2. List and describe the key areas of concern for risk management.
3. Why is identification of risks, through a listing of assets and their vulnerabilities, so important to the risk management process?
4. According to Sun Tzu, what two things must be achieved to successfully secure information assets?
5. Who is responsible for risk management in an organization?
6. Which community of interest usually takes the lead in information asset risk management?
7. Which community of interest usually provides the resources used when undertaking information asset risk management?
8. In risk management strategies, why must periodic review be a part of the process?
9. Why do networking components need more examination from an information security perspective than from a systems development perspective?
10. What value would an automated asset inventory system have for the risk identification process?
11. Which information attributes are seldom or never applied to software elements?
12. Which information attribute is often of great value for networking equipment when DHCP is not used?
13. When you document procedures, why is it useful to know where the electronic versions are stored?
14. Which is more important to the information asset classification scheme, that it be comprehensive or that it be mutually exclusive?
15. What is the difference between an asset's ability to generate revenue and its ability to generate profit?
16. How many categories should a data classification scheme include? Why?
17. How many threat categories are listed in this chapter? Which do you think is the most common, and why?
18. What are vulnerabilities?
19. How do you identify vulnerabilities?
20. Examine the simplest risk formula and the risk formula presented in this chapter. Do other formulas exist and, if so, when are they used?

Exercises

1. If an organization has three information assets to evaluate for risk management purposes as shown in the accompanying data, which vulnerability should be evaluated for additional controls first? Which vulnerability should be evaluated last?

   Data for Exercise 1

   ▪ Switch L47 connects a network to the Internet. It has two vulnerabilities: (1) susceptibility to hardware failure, with a likelihood of 0.2, and (2) susceptibility to an SNMP buffer overflow attack, with a likelihood of 0.1. This switch has an impact rating of 90 and has no current controls in place. There is a 75% certainty of the assumptions and data.

   ▪ Server WebSrv6 hosts a company Web site and performs e-commerce transactions. It has Web server software that is vulnerable to attack via invalid Unicode values. The likelihood of such an attack is estimated at 0.1. The server has been assigned an impact value of 100, and a control has been implemented that reduces the impact of the vulnerability by 75%. There is an 80% certainty of the assumptions and data.

   ▪ Operators use the MGMT45 control console to monitor operations in the server room. It has no passwords and is susceptible to unlogged misuse by the operators. Estimates show the likelihood of misuse is 0.1. There are no controls in place on this asset, which has an impact rating of 5. There is a 90% certainty of the assumptions and data.

2. Using the Web, search for at least three tools to automate risk assessment. Collect information on automated risk assessment tools. What do they cost? What features do they provide? What are the advantages and disadvantages of each one?

3. Using the list of threats to information security presented in this chapter, identify and describe three instances of each threat not previously mentioned in the chapter.

4. Using the data classification scheme presented in this chapter, identify and classify the information contained in your personal computer or personal digital assistant. Based on the potential for misuse or embarrassment, what information is confidential, sensitive but unclassified, or suitable for public release?

5. Using the asset valuation method presented in this chapter, conduct a preliminary risk assessment on the information contained in your home. Answer each of the questions covered in the chapter. What would it cost if you lost all your data?

6. Using the Internet, locate the National Association of Corporate Directors' Web site. Describe its function and purpose. What does this association say about board member liability for information security issues?

Case Exercises

Mike and Iris were flying home from the meeting. The reaction of the Audit Committee members had not been as they had discussed on the way to the meeting.

"I'm glad they understood the situation," Mike said to Iris. "I'd like you to start revising our risk management documentation to make it a little more general. It sounds like the board will want to take our approach company-wide soon."

Iris nodded and pulled out her notepad to make herself a to-do-list.

1. What will Iris have on her to-do-list?

2. What resources can Iris call upon to assist her?

Endnotes

1. Sun Tzu. *The Art of War.* Translation by Samuel B. Griffith. Oxford, UK: Oxford University Press, 1988.
2. http://zdnet.com.com/2100-11-525083.html?legacy=zdnn.
3. Adapted from the *Georgia-Pacific Corporation Practices Guide.*
4. Executive Order 12958, *Classified National Security Information.* Accessed September 15, 2003. http://www.dss.mil/seclib/eo12958.htm.

Risk Management: Assessing and Controlling Risk

> Weakness is a better teacher than strength.
> Weakness must learn to understand the
> obstacles that strength brushes aside.
> **MASON COOLEY (1927–)**

IRIS OPENED THE DOOR TO THE manager's lounge and walked up to the counter to pick up a soda. Leaving the lounge, she saw Jane Harris—accounting supervisor of RWW—at a table, poring over a spreadsheet that Iris recognized.

"Hi, Jane," she said. "Can I join you?"

"Sure, Iris," she said. "Perhaps you can help me with this form Mike wants us to fill out."

Jane was working on the asset valuation worksheet that Iris had sent to all of the company managers. The worksheet contained a list of all of the information assets in Jane's department. Mike had asked each manager to provide four values for each item: its cost, its replacement value, its criticality to the company's mission, and a rank order, with the most important item being ranked number one. Mike hoped that Iris and the rest of the risk management team could use the data to build a consensus about the relative importance of various assets.

"What's the problem?" Iris asked.

"I understand these first two columns. But how am I supposed to decide what's the most important?"

"Well," Iris began, "with your accounting background, you could base your answers on some of the data you collect about each of these information assets. For this quarter, what's more important to senior management—revenue or profitability?"

"Profitability is almost always more important," Jane replied. "We have some systems that have lots of revenue, but operate at a loss."

"Well, there you go," Iris said. "Why not calculate the profitability margin for each listed item and use that to rate and rank them?"

"Oh, okay, Iris. Thanks for the idea." Jane started to make notes on her copy of the form.

LEARNING OBJECTIVES

Upon completion of this material, you should be able to:

- Understand and select from the risk mitigation strategy options to control risk
- Identify the risk control classification categories
- Use existing conceptual frameworks to evaluate risk controls, and formulate a cost-benefit analysis
- Maintain and perpetuate risk controls
- Understand the OCTAVE approach to managing risk, and locate more detailed information about it if and when necessary

Introduction

In the early days of information technology, corporations used IT systems mainly to gain advantages over their competition. Managers discovered that establishing a competitive business model, method, or technique allowed an organization to provide a product or service that was superior in some decisive way, thus creating a **competitive advantage**. But this is no longer true. The current IT industry has evolved from this earlier model to one in which almost all competitors operate at a similar level of automation. Because IT is now readily available to almost all organizations willing to make the investment, they can all react quickly to changes in the market. In today's highly competitive environment, managers now realize that investing in IT systems at a level that merely maintains the status quo is no longer sufficient to gain competitive advantage. In fact, even the implementation of new technologies will not necessarily enable an organization to maintain a competitive lead. Instead, the concept of **competitive disadvantage**—the state of falling behind the competition—has emerged as a critical factor. Effective IT-enabled organizations now quickly absorb emerging technologies, not to gain or maintain the traditional competitive advantage, but rather to avoid the possibility of losing market share when faltering systems make them unable to maintain the current standard of service.

To keep up with the competition, organizations must design and create a safe environment in which business processes and procedures can function effectively. This environment must maintain confidentiality and privacy and assure the integrity and availability of organizational data. These objectives are met via the application of the principles of risk management.

As discussed in Chapter 7, **risk management** is the process used by managers to identify vulnerabilities in an organization's information systems and to assure the confidentiality, integrity, and availability of all the components in the organization's information systems. When an organization depends on IT-based systems to remain viable, information security and the discipline of risk management move beyond theoretical discussions to become an integral part of the economic basis for making business decisions. These decisions are based on trade-offs between the costs of applying information systems controls and the benefits realized from the operation of secured, available systems.

The concepts in this chapter build on those developed in Chapter 7. Recall that Chapter 7 focused on the *identification* of risk and the assessment of its relative impact from all identified vulnerabilities. The primary result of that effort is a list of documented vulnerabilities, ranked by criticality of impact. In Chapter 8, working from that list, the goal is to *assess* options, estimate costs, weigh the relative merits of options, and gauge the benefits from various control approaches.

Controlling risk begins with a discussion of what risk mitigation strategies are and how to formulate them. The chosen strategy may include applying controls to some or all of the vulnerabilities from the ranked vulnerability worksheet prepared in Chapter 7. This chapter explores a variety of control approaches, and then discusses how such controls can be categorized. It also explains the critical concepts of cost-benefit analysis and residual risk, and describes control strategy assessment and maintenance.

Risk Control Strategies

When an organization's general management team determines that risks from information security threats are creating a competitive disadvantage, it empowers the information technology and information security communities of interest to control those risks. Once the project team for information security development has created the ranked vulnerability worksheet (see Chapter 7), the team must choose one of four basic strategies to control the risks that result from these vulnerabilities:

- Avoidance: Applying safeguards that eliminate or reduce the remaining uncontrolled risks for the vulnerability
- Transference: Shifting the risks to other areas or to outside entities
- Mitigation: Reducing the impact should an attacker successfully exploit the vulnerability
- Acceptance: Understanding the consequences and accepting the risk without any attempts at control or mitigation

Avoidance

Avoidance is the risk control strategy that attempts to prevent the exploitation of the vulnerability. It is the preferred approach, as it seeks to avoid risk rather than deal with it after it has been realized. Avoidance is accomplished through the following techniques:

- Application of policy
- Application of training and education
- Countering threats
- Implementation of technical security controls and safeguards

Application of Policy

As discussed in Chapter 4, the application of policy allows all levels of management to mandate that certain procedures always be followed. For example, if the organization needs to control password use more tightly, it can implement a policy requiring passwords on all IT systems. Note that policy alone may not be enough. Indeed, effective management always couples changes in policy with the training and education of employees, or an application of technology, or both.

Application of Training and Education

Communicating new or revised policy to employees may not be adequate to assure compliance. Awareness, training, and education are essential to creating a safer and more controlled organizational environment and to achieving the necessary changes in end-user behavior.

Countering Threats

Risks can be avoided by countering the threats facing an asset and by eliminating its exposure to threats. Eliminating a threat is difficult but possible. For example, when an organization becomes susceptible to **cyberactivism** or **hacktivism** (the use of computer-related technologies to advance a political agenda), it must take steps to avoid potential attacks. For example, McDonald's Corporation recently sought to reduce risks to its image by imposing stricter conditions on egg suppliers regarding the health and welfare of chickens.[1] This area had been a source of contention between animal rights activists and the corporation for many years. The new strategy, along with other changes made by McDonald's, has led to improved relationships with animal rights activists, which has reduced this company's exposure to the risk from cyberactivism.

Implementing Technical Controls and Safeguards

In the everyday world of information security, technical solutions are often required to effectively reduce risk. For example, systems administrators can configure systems to use passwords where policy requires them and where the administrators are both aware of the requirement and trained to implement it.

OFFLINE

The Human Firewall Project

By The Human Firewall Council

A consortium of security experts from government, private industry, associations and nonprofit organizations known as the Human Firewall Council is directing the Human Firewall campaign. The goal of the Council is to help educate people in organizations on how to better protect information assets from the perspective of changing human behavior: creating a "human firewall" as a complement to the usual technical firewalls and other network security devices and software designed to safeguard the enterprise.

(continued)

8 Essential Steps to Building a Human Firewall

1. Get top management buy-in and commitment. The Gartner Group has identified three major questions that executives and boards of directors need to answer when confronting information security issues:
   - Is our security policy enforced fairly, consistently, and legally across the organization?
   - Would our employees, contractors, and partners know if a security violation were being committed?
   - Would they know what to do about it if they did recognize a security violation?
2. Assign and clarify roles and responsibilities.
3. Create an action plan with a budget.
4. Develop and/or update information security policies.
5. Develop an organization-wide security awareness/education program.
6. Measure the progress of your security awareness/education efforts.
7. Adapt and improve your security awareness/education programs according to progress/feedback.
8. Develop an information security incident response team and plan.

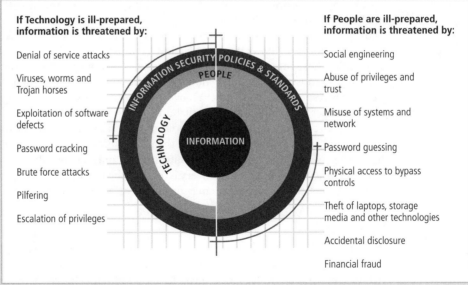

Source: www.humanfirewall.org.

FIGURE 8-1   Creating a Human Firewall

Source: HumanFirewall.org. Building a human firewall. *Human Firewall Online,* 2001 [Cited June 19, 2002]. Available from the World Wide Web at http://www.humanfirewall.org.

Transference

Transference is the control approach that attempts to shift the risk to other assets, other processes, or other organizations. This goal may be accomplished by rethinking how services are offered, revising deployment models, outsourcing to other organizations, purchasing insurance, or implementing service contracts with providers.

In the popular book *In Search of Excellence,* management consultants Tom Peters and Robert Waterman present a series of case studies of high-performing corporations. They assert that one of the eight characteristics of excellent organizations is that they "stick to their knitting. They stay reasonably close to the business they know."[2] What does this mean? It means that Kodak focuses on the manufacture of photographic equipment and chemicals, while General Motors focuses on the design and construction of cars and trucks. Neither company spends strategic energies on the technology for developing Web sites. They focus energy and resources on what they do best while relying on consultants or contractors for other types of expertise.

These lessons should be taken to heart whenever an organization begins to expand its operations, including information and systems management, and even information security. If an organization does not have adequate security management and administration experience, it should hire individuals or firms that provide such expertise. For example, many organizations want Web services, including Web presences, domain name registration, and domain and Web hosting. Rather than implementing their own servers, and hiring their own Webmasters, Web systems administrators, and even specialized security experts, however, savvy organizations hire an ISP or a Web consulting organization. This approach allows the organization to transfer the risk associated with the management of these complex systems to another organization that has more experience in dealing with those risks. A side benefit of specific contract arrangements is that the provider is responsible for disaster recovery and, through service-level agreements, for guaranteeing server and Web site availability.

Outsourcing, of course, is not without its own risks. It is up to the owner of the information asset, IT management, and the information security team to ensure that the disaster recovery requirements of the outsourcing contract are sufficient and have been met *before* they are needed for recovery efforts. If the outsourcer has failed to meet the contract terms, the consequences may be far worse than expected.

Mitigation

Mitigation is the control approach that attempts to reduce, by means of planning and preparation, the damage caused by the exploitation of vulnerability. This approach includes three types of plans, which you learned about in Chapter 3: the incident response plan (IRP), the disaster recovery plan (DRP), and the business continuity plan (BCP). Mitigation depends on the ability to detect and respond to an attack as quickly as possible.

Table 8-1 summarizes each of the three types of mitigation plans, including its characteristics and examples.

TABLE 8-1 Summaries of Mitigation Plans

Plan	Description	Example	When deployed	Timeframe
Incident Response Plan (IRP)	Actions an organization takes during incidents (attacks)	■ List of steps to be taken during disaster ■ Intelligence gathering ■ Information analysis	As incident or disaster unfolds	Immediate and real-time reaction
Disaster Recovery Plan (DRP)	■ Preparations for recovery should a disaster occur ■ Strategies to limit losses before and during disaster ■ Step-by-step instructions to regain normalcy	■ Procedures for the recovery of lost data ■ Procedures for the reestablishment of lost services ■ Shutdown procedures to protect systems and data	Immediately after the incident is labeled a disaster	Short-term recovery
Business Continuity Plan (BCP)	Steps to ensure continuation of the overall business when the scale of a disaster exceeds the DRP's ability to quickly restore operations	■ Preparation steps for activation of secondary data centers ■ Establishment of a hot site in a remote location	Immediately after the disaster is determined to affect the continued operations of the organization	Long-term operation

Acceptance

As described above, mitigation is a control approach that attempts to reduce the effects of an exploited vulnerability. In contrast, acceptance of risk is the choice to do nothing to protect an information asset and to accept the outcome from any resulting exploitation. It may or may not be a conscious business decision. The only use of the acceptance strategy that industry practices recognize as valid occurs when the organization has done the following:

■ Determined the level of risk posed to the information asset
■ Assessed the probability of attack and the likelihood of a successful exploitation of a vulnerability
■ Approximated the annual rate of occurrence of such an attack
■ Estimated the potential loss that could result from attacks
■ Performed a thorough cost-benefit analysis
■ Evaluated controls using each appropriate type of feasibility
■ Determined that the particular function, service, information, or asset did not justify the cost of protection

This control—or rather lack of control—assumes that it may be a prudent business decision to examine the alternatives and conclude that the cost of protecting an asset does not justify the security expenditure. Suppose it would cost an organization $100,000 per year to protect a server. The security assessment determined that for $10,000 it could replace the information contained in the server, replace the server itself, and cover associated recovery costs. Therefore, management may be satisfied with taking its chances and saving the money that would otherwise be spent on protecting this particular asset.

Note that if every risk of loss an organization identifies is handled through acceptance, it may reflect an inability to conduct proactive security activities and an apathetic approach to security in general. It is not acceptable for an organization to assume the policy that "ignorance is bliss" and hope to avoid litigation by pleading ignorance of the requirements of protecting employees' and customers' information. It is also unacceptable for management to hope that if they don't try to protect information, the opposition will imagine that little will be gained by an attack. The risks far outweigh the benefits of this approach, which usually ends in regret, as the exploitation of the vulnerabilities causes a seemingly unending series of information security lapses.

Now that you understand the four strategies that are used to control risk, you need to learn the next step in the risk management process: selection of the proper strategy to defend the specific vulnerability of a specific information asset.

Risk Control Strategy Selection

Risk control involves selecting one of the four risk control strategies for the vulnerabilities present within the organization. Figure 8-2 illustrates the process of deciding among the four strategies. As shown in this flowchart, after the information system is designed, you must ask whether the system has vulnerabilities that can be exploited. If the answer is yes, and a viable threat exists, examine what an attacker would gain from a successful attack. Then, estimate the expected loss the organization will incur if the vulnerability is successfully exploited. If this loss is within the range of losses the organization can absorb, or if the attacker's gain is less than the expected costs of the attack, the organization may choose to accept the risk. Otherwise, you must select one of the other control strategies.

For further guidance, some rules of thumb on strategy selection are presented below. When weighing the benefits of the various strategies, keep in mind that the level of threat and the value of the asset should play a major role in strategy selection.

- When a vulnerability (flaw or weakness) exists: Implement security controls to reduce the likelihood of a vulnerability being exercised.
- When a vulnerability can be exploited: Apply layered protections, architectural designs, and administrative controls to minimize the risk or prevent the occurrence of an attack.
- When the attacker's potential gain is greater than the costs of attack: Apply protections to increase the attacker's cost, or reduce the attacker's gain, by using technical or managerial controls.
- When the potential loss is substantial: Apply design principles, architectural designs, and technical and nontechnical protections to limit the extent of the attack, thereby reducing the potential for loss.[3]

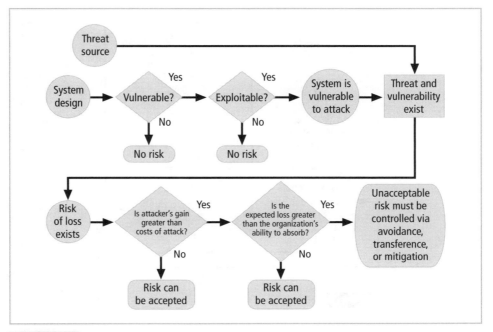

FIGURE 8-2 Risk-Handling Action Points

Evaluation, Assessment, and Maintenance of Risk Controls

Once a control strategy has been selected and implemented, the effectiveness of controls should be monitored and measured on an ongoing basis to determine their effectiveness and the accuracy of the estimated risk that will remain after all planned controls are in place. Figure 8-3 shows how this cyclical process is continuously used to ensure that risks are controlled.

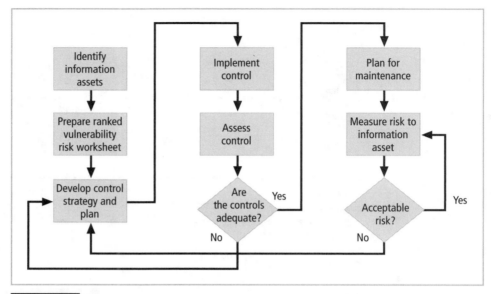

FIGURE 8-3   Risk Control Cycle

Categories of Controls

Controlling risk by means of avoidance, mitigation, or transference may be accomplished by implementing various types of controls or safeguards. Controls can be classified into one of four categories:

- Control function
- Architectural layer
- Strategy layer
- Information security principle

While other ways to categorize controls and safeguards certainly exist, the four categories given here illustrate the process that might be used and provide an opportunity to present information about the varieties of controls currently in use.

Control Function

Controls or safeguards designed to defend a vulnerable system are either preventive or detective. **Preventive controls** stop attempts to exploit a vulnerability by enforcing an organizational policy or a security principle, such as authentication or confidentiality. These controls use a technical procedure, such as encryption, or some combination of technical means and enforcement methods. **Detective controls** warn organizations of violations of security principles, organizational policies, or attempts to exploit vulnerabilities. These controls use techniques such as audit trails, intrusion detection, and configuration monitoring.

Architectural Layer

Some controls apply to one or more layers of an organization's technical architecture. Controls can be classified by the layer or layers in which they provide control. Some controls, such as firewalls, operate at the interface between architectural layers, such as between the external network and the extranet, or between the organization's wide area network (WAN) and a specific facility's local area network (LAN). Other controls, such as an organizational policy to always use nine or more characters for all passwords and SNMP shared-device passwords (or community strings), operate at all of the architectural layers simultaneously, from external networks to specific applications. Possible architectural layering models may include the following:

- Organizational policy
- External networks
- Extranets
- Demilitarized zones (DMZs)
- Intranets (WANs and LANs)
- Network devices that interact with network zones (switches, routers, firewalls, and hubs)
- Systems (computers for mainframe, server, and desktop use)
- Applications

Strategy Layer

Controls are sometimes classified by the risk control strategy they operate within: avoidance, mitigation, or transference. Note that the acceptance strategy is not an option because it involves the absence of controls.

Information Security Principle

Risk controls operate within one or more of the commonly accepted information security principles:

- Confidentiality: This principle is in use when the control provides assurance of the confidentiality of organizational data when it is stored, processed, or transmitted. An example is the use of Secure Sockets Layer (SSL) encryption technology to secure Web content as it moves from Web server to browser.
- Integrity: This principle is in use when the control provides assurance that the information asset properly, completely, and correctly receives, processes, stores, and retrieves data in a consistent and correct manner. One example is the use of parity or cyclical redundancy checks in data transmission protocols. A second example is the use of a product, such as Tripwire, that monitors the contents and structure of critical system files for unauthorized change.
- Availability: This principle is in use when the control provides assurance of ongoing access to critical information assets. An example of this kind of control is the deployment of a network operations center using a sophisticated network availability monitoring toolset, such as Tivoli, OpenView, or NetIQ, to guarantee optimum availability of network resources.

- Authentication: This principle is in use when the control provides assurance that users of information assets are, in fact, the entities (person or computer) they claim to be. Examples include the use of cryptographic certificates to establish SSL connections and the use of cryptographic hardware tokens such as SecurID cards as a second authentication of identity.
- Authorization: This principle is in use when the control provides assurance that a particular user (person or computer) has been specifically and explicitly authorized by the proper authority to access, update, or delete the contents of an information asset. One example of such a control is the activation and use of access control lists and authorization groups in the Windows networking environment. Another example is the use of a database authorization scheme to verify that users of an application are the designated users for each function.
- Accountability: This principle is in use when the control provides assurance that every activity undertaken can be attributed to a specific named person or automated process. An example of such a control is the use of audit logs to track when each user logged in and logged out of each computer.
- Privacy: This principle is in use when the control provides assurance that the procedures to access, update, or remove personally identifiable information comply with the applicable laws and policies for that kind of information.

THREAT MANAGEMENT

Buffer Overflow

Know what happens if a person tries to put ten gallons of water into a five-gallon container? The same thing that happens with a buffer overflow: Too much code is written to a memory buffer and the rest of the code "spills out," overwriting code in adjacent buffers. Buffer overflows have existed since the 1960s. The first major buffer overflow attack was the Morris worm, which took advantage of a service that gave information about users logged into a UNIX-based computer system. This worm shut down more than 6000 systems. Although good programming practice can usually eliminate the risk from buffer overflows, many software programs in use and being developed today continue to exhibit flaws related to this problem.

A buffer overflow is an application layer attack initiated by sending a string of code larger than the buffer on the target computer can handle. This string of code has a command attached to the end that can be treated as instructions that the program will carry out. If the intruder writing the buffer overflow code is highly skilled or uses the right tool, he or she can gain control of the target computer and force it to take any action, including sending private information such as password files, financial information, or anything else via e-mail. Buffer overflows are commonly used to place back doors onto the targeted systems.

Detecting a buffer overflow attack on a system is best done by an intrusion detection system. It is also possible to detect buffer overflow vulnerabilities with a vulnerability scanner. Intrusion detection systems detect buffer overflows in two ways: by using a protocol signature and by using a payload signature. A protocol signature is a technique that

(continued)

detects a buffer overflow by looking for anomalous traffic, such as remote traffic, targeted at services that should not be accessible to a remote user. Payload signatures detect buffer overflows by looking at the signatures of the actual exploitative code contained within the payload of the attack. Signatures detected in this way include the use of "no operation" instructions to pad the exploitative code, script signatures, and abnormal user data and responses.

When the intrusion detection system identifies a potential buffer overflow attack, there are two ways to respond: the administrator can wait until the intruder leaves or simply disconnect the intruder. The choice of how to respond depends on what the attacker is doing. If the intruder is lurking in an area that is not critical or sensitive or is merely scouting the system, waiting until the intruder leaves may be the best response. Once the attacker leaves, the administrator can simply remove the files the intruder has placed on the system and then patch the vulnerability that allowed the intrusion. When the intruder returns to activate the back door and finds that it is not working, preferably he or she will chalk it up to bad luck and move on. In contrast, pulling the plug and disabling the attack may alert the intruder, who may view it as a challenge. This tactic may be necessary, however, if the intruder is accessing critical systems or is otherwise likely to cause damage.

Intrusion detection systems must be regularly upgraded and patched. As stated earlier, many common programs are prone to buffer overflows, but all have patches available to repair this vulnerability. Even without an intrusion detection system, regularly checking for patches is the best way to protect a system from buffer overflows. A large list of known vulnerabilities can be found at http://online.securityfocus.com/archive/1.

Due to poor programming practices, buffer overflows continue to pose a serious threat to any computer attached to the Internet. Although intrusion detection systems offer some protection by finding the intruder before any damage is done, they are not infallible. Ultimately, the best protection from buffer overflows is prevention. With a little effort, systems can be easily safeguarded against most buffer overflows.

Contributed by Doan Thompson, Rob Mainella, Thuyen Nguyen, and Sutham Cheurprakobkit.

Feasibility Studies and Cost-Benefit Analysis

Before deciding on the strategy (avoidance, transference, mitigation, or acceptance) for a specific vulnerability, all readily accessible information about the economic and noneconomic consequences of the vulnerability must be explored. This exploration attempts to answer the question, "What are the actual and perceived advantages of implementing a control as opposed to the actual and perceived disadvantages of implementing the control?"

There are a number of ways to determine the advantages of a specific control, though the primary means is to determine the value of the information assets that it is designed to protect. There are also many ways to determine the disadvantages associated with specific risk controls. The following sections discuss some of the more commonly used techniques for making these choices. Note that some of these discussions involve dollar-denominated expenses and savings implied from economic cost avoidance, whereas other discussions deal with noneconomic feasibility criteria. **Cost avoidance** is the money saved by avoiding, via the implementation of a control, the financial ramifications of an incident.

Cost-Benefit Analysis

The criterion most commonly used when evaluating a project that implements information security controls and safeguards is economic feasibility. While any number of alternatives may solve a particular problem, not all of them will necessarily have the same economic feasibility. Most organizations can spend only a reasonable amount of time and money on information security, where the definition of reasonable differs from organization to organization, and even from manager to manager. Organizations are urged to begin this type of economic feasibility analysis by evaluating the worth of the information assets to be protected and the loss in value if those information assets became compromised by the exploitation of a specific vulnerability. Common sense dictates that an organization should not spend more to protect an asset than it is worth. This decision-making process is called a **cost-benefit analysis (CBA)** or an **economic feasibility study**.

Cost

Just as it is difficult to determine the value of information, so it is difficult to determine the cost of safeguarding it. Among the items that affect the cost of a control or safeguard are the following:

- Cost of development or acquisition of hardware, software, and services
- Training fees (cost to train personnel)
- Cost of implementation (installing, configuring, and testing hardware, software, and services)
- Service costs (vendor fees for maintenance and upgrades)
- Cost of maintenance (labor expense to verify and continually test, maintain, train, and update)

Benefit

The **benefit** is the value to the organization of using controls to prevent losses associated with a specific vulnerability. It is usually determined by valuing the information asset or assets exposed by the vulnerability and then determining how much of that value is at risk and how much risk exists for the asset. This result is expressed as the annualized loss expectancy, which is defined later in this chapter.

Asset Valuation

It is often necessary to assess the value of an information asset to determine how much benefit can be achieved by implementing a control. **Asset valuation** is the process of assigning financial value or worth to each information asset. Some argue that it is virtually impossible to accurately determine the true value of information and information-bearing assets. Perhaps this is one reason why insurance underwriters currently have no definitive valuation tables for assigning worth to information assets. As discussed in Chapter 7, the value of information differs within organizations and between organizations, based on the characteristics of information and the perceived value of that information. Much of the work of assigning value can draw on the preparations made in assessing the information assets, as done in the risk identification process completed in Chapter 7.

Assessing the value of information assets is among the most challenging activities in the information security program. Asset valuation involves estimation of real and perceived costs associated with the design, development, installation, maintenance, protection, recovery, and defense against loss and litigation. These estimates are calculated for every set of information-bearing systems or information assets. Some component costs are simple to determine, such as the cost to replace a network switch or the hardware needed for a specific class of server. Other costs are almost impossible to determine accurately, such as the dollar value of the loss in market share if information on a firm's new product offerings were released prematurely and the company lost its competitive edge. A further complication is the value that some information assets acquire over time that is beyond the **intrinsic value**—the essential worth—of the asset under consideration. This higher **acquired value** is the more appropriate value in most cases.

Asset valuation includes the following components:

- Value retained from the cost of creating the information asset: Information is created or acquired at some cost to the organization. This cost can then be calculated or estimated. One potential category of costs involved in creating an asset is software development; another category is data collection and processing. Many organizations have developed extensive cost-accounting practices to capture the costs associated with the collection and processing of data, as well as the costs of the software development and maintenance activities. For software development, this value includes the cost of the efforts of the many people involved in designing, testing, and resolving problems in the systems development life cycle for each application and system. Although this effort draws mainly on IT personnel, it also includes the user and general management community and sometimes the information security staff. In today's marketplace, with high programmer salaries and even higher contractor expenses, the average cost to complete even a moderately sized application can quickly escalate. For example, multimedia-based training averaging 350 hours of development for each hour of content will require total expenditures of as much as $10,000 per hour for multimedia-based training software.
- Value retained from past maintenance of the information asset: It is estimated that for every dollar spent to develop an application or to acquire and process data stored by the organization, many more dollars are spent on maintenance over the useful life of the data or software. If actual costs have not been recorded, the cost can be estimated in terms of the amount and level of the human resources required to continually update, support, modify, and service the applications and systems associated with a particular set of information.
- Value implied by the cost of replacing the information: Another important cost associated with the loss or damage to information is that associated with replacing or restoring the information. It includes the human resources time needed to reconstruct, restore, or regenerate the information from backups, independent transactions logs, or even hard copies of data sources. Most organizations rely on routine media backups to protect their information. If you find yourself estimating recovery costs, keep in mind that employees are occupied with routine work, and you may have to hire contractors to carry out this effort. Also, loss of real-time information may not be recoverable from a previous tape backup, unless the system process includes built-in journaling capabilities. To replace information in the system, the various sources of the information may have to be reconstructed, and the data reentered into the system and validated for accuracy. This restoration can take longer than it took to create the data initially, not to mention the need for simultaneous entry of new data.

- Value from providing the information: Separate from the cost of developing or maintaining the information is the cost of providing the information to those users who need it. Such costs include the values associated with the delivery of the information through databases, networks, and hardware and software systems. They also include the cost of the infrastructure necessary to provide access to and control of the information.

- Value acquired from the cost of protecting the information: Here a recursive dilemma arises. That is, the value of an asset is based in part on the cost of protecting it; the amount of money spent to protect an asset is based in part on the value of the asset. While this is a seemingly unending circle, it is possible to estimate the value of the protection for an information asset so as to better understand the value associated with its potential loss. The values listed above are easy to calculate with some precision. This value and those that follow are likely to be estimates of cost.

- Value to owners: How much is your Social Security number worth to you? Or your telephone number? Placing a value on information can be quite a daunting task. What value does the information have, beyond its costs? A market researcher collects data from a company's sales figures and determines that a new product offering has a strong potential market appeal to members of a certain age group. While the cost associated with the creation of this new information may be small, how much is the new information actually worth? It could be worth millions if it successfully captures new market share. Although the value of information to an organization, or how much of the organization's bottom line is directly attributable to that information, may be impossible to estimate, it is vital to understand the overall cost of protecting this information so as to better understand its value. Here again, estimating value may be the only method possible.

- Value of intellectual property: Related to the value of information is the specific consideration of the value of intellectual property. The value of a new product or service to a customer may ultimately be unknowable. How much would a cancer patient pay for a cure? How much would a shopper pay for a new flavor of cheese? What is the value of a poem? All of these examples could represent the intellectual property of an organization, yet their valuation is complex. A related but separate consideration is intellectual properties known as trade secrets. These intellectual information assets are so valuable that they are literally the primary assets of some organizations.

- Value to adversaries: How much would it be worth to an organization to know what the competition is doing? Many organizations now have established departments that deal in competitive intelligence, tasked with the assessment and estimation of the activities of the organization's competition. Even organizations in traditionally nonprofit industries can benefit from understanding what is going on in political, business, and competitive organizations. Stories of industrial espionage abound, including the urban legend of Company A encouraging its employees to hire on as janitors at Company B. As custodial workers, the employees could snoop through open terminals, photograph and photocopy unsecured documents, and rifle through internal trash and recycling bins. Such legends support a widely accepted concept: that information can have extraordinary value to the right individuals. Similarly, stories are circulated of how disgruntled employees, soon to be terminated, might steal information and present it to competitive organizations to curry favor and land new employment. Those who hire such applicants in an effort to gain from their larceny should consider whether benefiting from such a tactic is wise. After all, such thieves could presumably repeat their activities when they become disgruntled with their newest employers.

- Loss of productivity while the information assets are unavailable: For example, when a power failure occurs, effective use of UPS equipment can prevent data loss, but system users cannot create additional information. Instead, workers must resort to other activities until power is restored. Although this example does not entail an attack that damages information, it is an instance in which a threat (deviations in quality of service from service providers) affects an organization's productivity. The hours of wasted employee time, the cost of using alternatives, and the general lack of productivity can severely set back a critical operation or process.

- Loss of revenue while information assets are unavailable: Have you ever been in a retail store when your credit card wouldn't scan? How many times did the salesperson rescan the card before resorting to manually entering the numbers? How long did it take to enter the numbers manually in contrast to the quick swipe? What if the credit card verification process was off-line? Did the organization have a manual process to validate or process credit card payment in the absence of the familiar approval system? Many organizations have all but abandoned manual backups for automated processes. In some situations, businesses may even have to turn away customers because their automated payments systems are inoperative. While this scenario typically arises because of a failure of management to prepare (disaster recovery planning), it clearly illustrates the potential loss of revenue when information and information systems are unavailable. Most grocery stores no longer label each item with the price, because the UPC scanners and the related databases calculate the costs and inventory levels dynamically. Without these systems, could your grocery store sell goods? How much would the store lose if it could not? It has been estimated that "43 percent of all businesses that close their doors due to a disaster or crisis, even for one day, never reopen them again. An additional 28 percent fail during the next three to five years."[4] Imagine, instead of a grocery store, an online book retailer such as Amazon.com suffering a power outage. The entire operation is instantly closed. Even if Amazon's offering system were operational, what if the payment systems were off-line? Customers could make selections, but could not check out to complete their purchases. While dotcom businesses may be more susceptible to suffering a loss of revenue as a result of a loss of information, most organizations would be unable to conduct business if certain pieces of information were unavailable.

An organization must be able to place a dollar value on each collection of information and the information assets it owns. This value is based on the answers to these questions:

- How much did it cost to create or acquire the information?
- How much would it cost to recreate or recover the information?
- How much does it cost to maintain the information?
- How much is the information worth to the organization?
- How much is the information worth to the competition?

Once an organization has estimated the worth of various assets, it can begin to examine the potential loss that could occur from the exploitation of vulnerability or a threat occurrence. This process yields the estimate of potential loss per risk. The questions that must be asked at this stage include the following:

- What damage could occur, and what financial impact would it have?
- What would it cost to recover from the attack, in addition to the financial impact of damage?
- What is the single loss expectancy for each risk?

A **single loss expectancy (SLE)** is the calculation of the value associated with the most likely loss from an attack. This calculation takes into account both the value of the asset and the expected percentage of loss that would occur from a particular attack:

SLE = asset value (AV) $\times$ exposure factor (EF)

where EF is the percentage loss that would occur from a given vulnerability being exploited.

For example, if a Web site has an estimated value of $1,000,000 (as determined by asset valuation), and a sabotage or vandalism (hacker defacement) scenario indicates that 10% of the Web site would be damaged or destroyed in such an attack (the exposure factor), then the SLE for this Web site would be $1,000,000 $\times$ 0.10 = $100,000. This estimate is then used to calculate another value, annual loss expectancy, as discussed below.

As difficult as it is to estimate the value of information, the estimation of the probability of a threat occurrence or attack is even more difficult. There are not always tables, books, or records that indicate the frequency or probability of any given attack, though some sources are available for certain asset–threat pairs. For instance, the likelihood of a tornado or thunderstorm destroying a building of a specific type of construction within a specified region of the country is available to insurance underwriters. In most cases, however, an organization can rely only on its internal information to calculate the security of its information assets. Even if the network, systems, and security administrators have been actively and accurately tracking these threat occurrences, the organization's information will be sketchy at best. As a result, this information is usually estimated.

In most cases, the probability of a threat occurring is depicted in the form of a loosely derived table indicating the probability of an attack from each threat type within a given time frame (for example, once every ten years). This value is commonly referred to as the **annualized rate of occurrence (ARO)**. ARO is simply how often you expect a specific type of attack to occur. As you learned in Chapter 7, many types of attacks occur much more frequently than every year or two. For example, if a successful act of sabotage or vandalism occurs about once every two years, then the ARO would be 50% (0.5). In contrast, some kinds of network attacks can occur multiple times per second. To standardize calculations, you convert the rate to a yearly (annualized) value, which is expressed as the probability of a threat occurrence.

Once each asset's worth is known, the next step is to ascertain how much loss is expected from a single attack and how often such attacks might occur. Once those values are determined, you can calculate the overall loss potential per risk expressed as an **annualized loss expectancy (ALE)** using the values for the ARO and SLE from the previous sections.

ALE = SLE $\times$ ARO

To use our previous example, if SLE = $100,000 and ARO = 0.5, then

ALE = $100,000 $\times$ 0.5
ALE = $50,000

Thus, unless you increase the level of security on your Web site, the organization can expect to lose $50,000 per year, every year. Now, armed with a figure to justify its expenditures for controls and safeguards, the information security design team can deliver a budgeted value for planning purposes. Note that sometimes noneconomic factors are considered in this process, so that in some cases even when ALE amounts are not huge, control budgets can be justified.

The Cost-Benefit Analysis Formula

CBA (or economic feasibility) determines whether a control alternative is worth its associated cost. Such analyses may be performed before a control or safeguard is implemented, to determine whether the control is worth implementing, or after controls have been implemented and have been functioning for a time. Observation over time adds precision to the evaluation of the benefits of the safeguard and the determination of whether the safeguard is functioning as intended. While many CBA techniques exist, the CBA is most easily calculated using the ALE from earlier assessments.

CBA = ALE(pre-control) − ALE(post-control) − ACS

where

ALE(pre-control) = ALE of the risk before the implementation of the control
ALE(post-control) = ALE examined after the control has been in place for a period of time
ACS = annual cost of the safeguard

Once the controls are implemented, it is crucial to continue to examine their benefits, thereby determining when the controls must be upgraded, supplemented, or replaced. As Frederick Avolio states in his article "Best Practices in Network Security":

> Security is an investment, not an expense. Investing in computer and network security measures that meet changing business requirements and risks makes it possible to satisfy changing business requirements without hurting the business's viability.[5]

Other Feasibility Studies

Earlier in this chapter, the concept of economic feasibility was employed to justify proposals for information security controls. The next step in measuring how ready an organization is for the introduction of these controls is to determine the proposal's organizational, operational, technical, and political feasibility.

Organizational Feasibility

Organizational feasibility analysis examines how well the proposed information security alternatives will contribute to the efficiency, effectiveness, and overall operation of an organization. In other words, the proposed control approach for the vulnerability must contribute to the organization's strategic objectives. Above and beyond the impact on the bottom line, the organization must determine how the proposed alternatives will contribute to its business objectives. Does the implementation align well with the strategic planning for the information systems? Or does it require deviation from the planned expansion and management of the current systems? The organization should not invest in technology that changes its fundamental ability to explore certain avenues and opportunities. Suppose that, without considering the control's organizational feasibility, a university decides to implement a new firewall. It takes a few months for the technology group to learn enough about the firewall to completely configure it. A few months after the implementation begins, it is discovered that the firewall as configured does not permit outgoing Web-streamed media. If one of the business goals of the university is the pursuit of distance-learning opportunities, and the firewall prevents that type of communication, it has failed the organizational feasibility measure and should be modified or replaced.

Operational Feasibility

Operational feasibility addresses several key areas not covered in the other feasibility measures—namely, user acceptance and support, management acceptance and support, and the overall requirements of the organization's stakeholders. Operational feasibility is also known as **behavioral feasibility**, because it assesses the behavior of users. One of the fundamental principles of systems development is obtaining user buy-in on projects. If the users do not accept a new technology, policy, or program, it will inevitably fail. Users may not openly oppose a change, but if they do not support a control, they will find ways of disabling or otherwise circumventing it, creating yet another vulnerability. One of the most common methods of obtaining user acceptance and support is via **user involvement**. User involvement can be attained through three simple steps: communicate, educate, and involve.

Organizations should *communicate* with system users throughout information security improvement projects. The data shared in this fashion should include the timetables and implementation schedules, plus the dates, times, and locations of upcoming briefings and training. Those making the changes should let the affected parties know what the purpose of the proposed changes is and how they will enable everyone to work more securely.

In addition, users should be *educated* and trained on how to work under the new constraints while avoiding any negative performance consequences. One of the most frustrating things from the users' perspective is the implementation of a new program that prevents them from accomplishing their duties, with only a promise of eventual training.

Finally, those making changes should *involve* users by asking them what they want from the new systems and what they will tolerate from the new systems. One way to do so is to include selected representatives from the various constituencies in the development process.

Adherence to these three simple steps of communication, education, and involvement can reduce *resistance* to change and build *resilience* for change—that ethereal quality that allows workers to not only tolerate constant change but also accept it as a necessary part of the job.

Technical Feasibility

In addition to the straightforward cost and benefit feasibilities, the project team must consider the **technical feasibilities** associated with the design, implementation, and management of controls. Some safeguards, especially technology-based controls, are extremely complex to implement, configure, and manage. Technical feasibility examines whether the organization has or can acquire the technology necessary to implement and support the control alternatives. Does the organization have the hardware and software necessary to support a new firewall system? If not, can it be obtained?

Technical feasibility also examines whether the organization has the technological expertise needed to manage the new technology. Does the staff include individuals who are qualified (and possibly certified) to install and manage a new firewall system? If not, can staff be spared from their current obligations to attend formal training and education programs to prepare them to administer the new systems? Or must personnel be hired? In the current job environment, how difficult is it to find qualified personnel?

These issues must be examined in detail before acquiring a new set of controls. Unfortunately, many organizations rush into the acquisition of new safeguards, without completely examining the requirements involved in implementing and using these complex controls effectively.

Political Feasibility

Politics has been defined as "the art of the possible."[6] Within organizations, **political feasibility** defines what can and cannot occur based on the consensus and relationships among the communities of interest. The limits placed on an organization's actions or behaviors by the information security controls must fit within the realm of the possible before they can be effectively implemented, and that realm includes the availability of staff resources.

In some cases, resources are provided to the information security community directly under a budget apportionment model. The management and professionals involved in information security then allocate the resources to activities and projects using processes of their own design.

In other organizations, resources are first allocated to the IT community of interest. The information security team then must compete for resources in that context. Sometimes, the cost-benefit analysis and other forms of justification discussed in this chapter are used in a resource allocation process to make rational decisions about the relative merits of proposed activities and projects. Unfortunately, in other settings, these decisions are politically charged and do not focus on the pursuit of the greater organizational goals.

Another methodology for budget allocation requires the information security team to propose and justify use of the resources for activities and projects in the context of the entire organization. This approach requires that arguments for information security spending articulate the benefit of the expense for the whole organization, so that members of the organizational communities of interest can understand and perceive their value.

Alternatives to Feasability

Rather than using cost-benefit analysis or some other feasibility reckoning to justify an approach to control risk, you can approach risk management from a different angle. An organization might look to alternative justifications. Many of these have been described in earlier chapters (especially in Chapter 6). A short list of alternatives is provided here to jog your memory:

- Benchmarking is the process of seeking out and studying the practices used in other organizations that produce the results you desire in your organization. When benchmarking, an organization typically uses either metrics-based measures or process-based measures.
- Due care and due diligence occur when an organization adopts a certain minimum level of security as what any *prudent* organization would do in similar circumstances.

- Best business practices are a superior level of performance in the protection of information and are considered those that are among the best in the industry, balancing the need to access information with adequate protection.
- The gold standard is for those ambitious organizations in which the best business practices are not sufficient. They aspire to set the standard for their industry, and are thus said to be in pursuit of the gold standard.
- Government recommendations and best practices are useful for organizations that operate in industries that are regulated by governmental agencies, government recommendations are, in effect, requirements. For other organizations, government regulations serve as excellent sources for information about what other organizations may be doing, or are required to do, to control information security risks.
- A baseline is derived by comparing measured actual performance against established standards for the measured category.

Risk Management Discussion Points

Not every organization has the collective will or budget to manage each vulnerability through the application of controls. As a consequence, each organization must define the level of risk it is willing to live with.

Risk Appetite

Risk appetite defines the quantity and nature of risk that organizations are willing to accept, as they evaluate the trade-offs between perfect security and unlimited accessibility. For instance, a financial services company, regulated by government and conservative by nature, seeks to apply every reasonable control and even some invasive controls to protect its information assets. Other, less closely regulated organizations may also be conservative by nature, and seek to avoid the negative publicity and perceived loss of integrity caused by the exploitation of a vulnerability. A firewall vendor might install a set of firewall rules that are far more onerous than necessary, simply because being hacked would jeopardize its market. Other organizations may take on dangerous risks because of ignorance. The reasoned approach to risk is one that balances the expense (in terms of finance and the usability of information assets) against the possible losses if exploited.

James Anderson, vice president of information security at Inovant, the world's largest commercial processor of financial payment transactions, believes that information security in today's enterprise is a "well-informed sense of assurance that the information risks and controls are in balance." As this statement shows, the key for the organization is to find the balance in its decision-making processes and in its feasibility analyses, thereby assuring that its risk appetite is based on experience and facts, and not on ignorance or wishful thinking.

Residual Risk

When vulnerabilities have been controlled as much as possible, there is often remaining risk that has not been completely removed, shifted, or planned for, known as residual risk. To express it another way, "**Residual risk** is a combined function of (1) a threat less the effect of threat-reducing safeguards; (2) a vulnerability less the effect of vulnerability-reducing safeguards; and (3) an asset less the effect of asset value-reducing safeguards."[7] Figure 8-4 illustrates how residual risk persists even after safeguards are implemented.

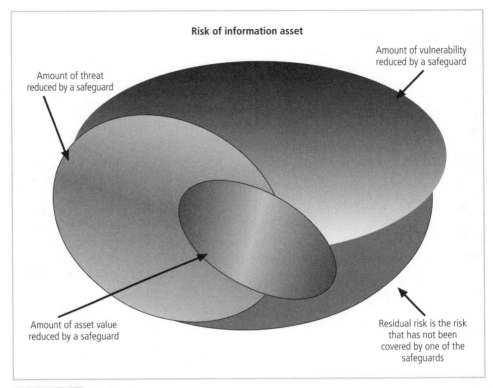

Risk of information asset

Amount of vulnerability reduced by a safeguard

Amount of threat reduced by a safeguard

Amount of asset value reduced by a safeguard

Residual risk is the risk that has not been covered by one of the safeguards

FIGURE 8-4   Residual Risk

The significance of residual risk must be judged within the context of an organization. Although it might seem counterintuitive, the goal of information security is not to bring residual risk to zero; rather, it is to bring residual risk into line with an organization's risk appetite. If decision makers have been informed of uncontrolled risks and the proper authority groups within the communities of interest decide to leave residual risk in place, then the information security program has accomplished its primary goal.

Documenting Results

When the risk management program of an organization has been completed, the result is that a series of proposed controls are prepared, each of which is justified by one or more feasibility or rationalization approaches. At a minimum, each information asset–threat pair should have a documented control strategy that clearly identifies any residual risk remaining after the proposed strategy has been executed. This control strategy articulates which of the four fundamental risk-reducing approaches will be used, how the various approaches might be combined, and justifies the findings by referencing the feasibility studies.

Some organizations document the outcome of the control strategy for each information asset–threat pair in an action plan. This action plan includes concrete tasks, with accountability for each task being assigned to an organizational unit or to an individual. It may include hardware and software requirements, budget estimates, and detailed timelines.

VIEWPOINT

Risk Management

By Dr. Michael E. Whitman, CISSP

According to an IT saying, there are 10 types of people in the world: those who understand binary and those who don't. In the world of information security, there are three types of people: those who understand the importance of information security, those who don't, and those who think they do but really don't. The third group represents the highest risk to the security of information.

The first group, one hopes, is us—the protectors of the information, the defenders of the realm, and the keepers of the gates. Those who get it know that information security is not really about technology, it's about people. More than 3000 years ago China defended itself from the nomadic barbarians to the north by building a massive wall. Legend has it that in the first 500 years of the wall's existence it was breached three times. Did these failures occur because the wall was not long enough, tall enough, or strong enough? No. In each instance, the invaders breached the Great Wall of China by bribing the gatekeeper.

As we see, security has always been a people problem. In fact, the top five threats to information security are all people problems:

1. Deliberate software attacks, such as viruses, worms, and denial-of-service attacks. All of these attacks are instigated and propagated by people. Hackers write viruses, and, in almost all cases, the viruses are spread by individuals who open attachments, fail to scan diskettes for viruses, or commit some other breach of security common sense.

2. Technical software failures or errors. Most technical software failures or errors are the fault of software developers. The rush to market software has resulted in inadequate or incomplete controls. Most college programming classes teach fundamental security and emphasize thorough testing. You test lines of code, then modules of code, then entire applications, and finally interactions of applications. Today's companies tend to create three levels of testers: (1) alpha testers are programmers who examine the software in-house; (2) beta testers are outsiders who either are brought in for testing or receive the software to evaluate; and (3) gamma testers are unofficial software testers—users who buy the software and then contact tech support when something goes wrong. In the case of the gamma testers, tech support logs the problems and then programmers resolve them with patches and upgrades.

3. Acts of human error or failure. This threat is self-explanatory. Humans may fail to follow established policy or procedures, or make mistakes because other humans didn't provide them with appropriate training, or make a mistake just because they are, after all, human.

4. Deliberate acts of espionage or trespass. It's hard enough to scratch out a meager profit, as many small to medium-sized companies do, without hackers trying to crash your e-business server, mangle your intranet servers, or worse.

5. Deliberate acts of sabotage or vandalism. Same as above.

The second group, those who don't understand the importance of information security, make up the bulk of the population in the InfoSec world. Security education, training, and awareness (SETA) programs are designed to help educate and inform people in this group. We struggle to inform, communicate, and involve them in information security, but they are many and we are few. Nonetheless, a noble battle ensues.

(continued)

The third group, those who think they know what's going on in information security but actually are sadly misinformed or misguided, represent the biggest threat. Some members of this group claim that security is a technology problem, which can be solved by attending technical conferences. Others claim that the problem is overstated and that the threat isn't that real; they are wrong. A manager at a major managed security services company recently told my class, "We tell our customers that an exposed server usually won't be on the Internet for more than 24 hours before it's scanned, hacked, infected, and/or crashed. In reality, it's about 4 hours!" And it's true; we recently ran a group of unprotected servers as a test, and all of them were infected with the Slammer worm before the day was over.

The people in the third group are the toughest to educate. They must be reeducated to dispel the bad information they currently hold on to. Until this reeducation happens, they pose the biggest threat to information security.

Here are a few words of wisdom:

Albert Einstein:

"Only two things are infinite, the universe and human stupidity, and I'm not sure about the former."

"Problems cannot be solved at the same level of awareness that created them."

Helen Keller:

"Science may have found a cure for most evils; but it has found no remedy for the worst of them all—the apathy of human beings."

"I am only one; but still I am one. I cannot do everything, but still I can do something; I will not refuse to do the something I can do."

Recommended Risk Control Practices

Assume that a risk assessment has determined that it is necessary to protect a particular asset from a particular threat, at a cost up to $50,000. Unfortunately most budget authorities focus on the *up to,* and then try to cut a percentage of the total figure to save the organization money. This tendency underlines the importance of developing strong justifications for specific action plans and providing concrete estimates in those plans.

Consider also that each control or safeguard affects more than one asset–threat pair. If a new $50,000 firewall is installed to protect the Internet connection infrastructure from the threat posed by hackers launching port-scanning attacks, the same firewall may also protect this Internet connection infrastructure, as well as other information assets, from other threats and attacks. The final choice may call for a balanced mixture of controls that provides the greatest value for as many asset–threat pairs as possible. This example reveals another facet of the problem: Information security professionals manage a dynamic matrix covering a broad range of threats, information assets, controls, and identified vulnerabilities. Each time a control is added to the matrix, it undoubtedly changes the ALE for the information asset vulnerability for which it has been designed, and it also may alter the ALE for other information asset vulnerabilities. To put it more simply, if you put in one safeguard, you decrease the risk associated with all subsequent control evaluations. To make matters worse, the action of implementing a control may change the values assigned or calculated in a prior estimate.

Between the impossible task associated with the valuation of information assets and the dynamic nature of the ALE calculations, it's no wonder that organizations typically look for a more straightforward method of implementing controls that doesn't involve such complex, inexact, and dynamic calculations. This preference has prompted an ongoing search for ways to design security architectures that go beyond the direct application of specific controls, where which each control is justified specifically for information asset vulnerability. Some of the alternatives that have been and continue to be developed are discussed below.

Qualitative Measures

The set of steps described previously used actual values or estimates to create a **quantitative assessment**. In some cases, an organization might determine that it cannot put specific numbers on these values. Fortunately, it is possible to repeat the risk assessment steps using estimates based on a **qualitative assessment**. For example, instead of placing a value of once every 10 years for the ARO, the organization might list all possible attacks on a particular set of information and rate each in terms of its probability of occurrence. This could be accomplished using scales, rather than specific estimates. For example, a scale might range from 0, representing no chance of occurrence, to 10, representing almost certain occurrence. Organizations may, of course, prefer other scales: 0–10, 1–5, 0–20. Using scales also relieves the organization of the burden of trying to determine exact values. These same scales can be used in any situation requiring a value, even in asset valuation. For example, instead of estimating that a particular piece of information is worth $1,000,000, you might value information on a scale of 1–20, where 1 indicates relatively worthless information and 20 indicates extremely critical information, such as a certain soda manufacturer's secret recipe or those 11 herbs and spices of a popular chicken vendor.

Delphi Technique

How do you calculate the values and scales used in either qualitative or quantitative assessment? An individual can pull the information together based on personal experience, but, as the saying goes, "two heads are better than one"—and a team of heads is better than two. One technique for accurately estimating scales and values is the Delphi technique. The **Delphi technique**, named for the oracle at Delphi, is a process whereby a group rates or ranks a set of information. The individual responses are compiled and then returned to the group for another iteration. This process continues until the entire group is satisfied with the result. This technique can be applied to the development of scales, asset valuation, asset or threat ranking, or any decision that can benefit from the input of more than one decision maker.

A Single-Source Approach to Risk Management

Until now, this book has presented a general treatment of risk management, synthesizing information and methods from many sources to provide a well-rounded treatment of the customary or usual approaches found as organizations manage risk. As an alternative, the next section of the text presents a comprehensive approach to risk management provided from a single source. The Operationally Critical Threat, Asset, and Vulnerability Evaluation (OCTAVE) Method is an InfoSec risk evaluation methodology that allows organizations to balance the protection of critical information assets against the costs of providing protective and detective controls. It can assist the organization by enabling an organization to measure itself against known or accepted good security practices, and then to establish an organization-wide protection strategy and information security risk mitigation plan. If, after reading the following section, you want more information, you can download the OCTAVE Method implementation guide from www.cert.org/octave/omig.html.

The OCTAVE Method*

From Appendix D of OCTAVE Method Implementation Guide Version 2.0 by C. Alberts and A. Dorofee, June 2001. Reprinted here with permission.

The Operationally Critical Threat, Asset, and Vulnerability Evaluation (OCTAVE) Method defines the essential components of a comprehensive, systematic, context-driven, self-directed information security risk evaluation.[8] By following the OCTAVE Method, an organization can make information-protection decisions based on risks to the confidentiality, integrity, and availability of critical information technology assets. The operational or business units and the IT department work together to address the information security needs of the organization.

Using a three-phase approach, the OCTAVE Method examines organizational and technology issues to assemble a comprehensive picture of the information security needs of an organization. The phases are described below:

- Phase 1: Build Asset-Based Threat Profiles. This is an organizational evaluation. Key areas of expertise within the organization are examined to elicit important knowledge about information assets, the threats to those assets, the security requirements of the assets, what the organization is currently doing to protect its information assets (current protection strategy practices), and weaknesses in organizational policies and practice (organizational vulnerabilities).
- Phase 2: Identify Infrastructure Vulnerabilities. This is an evaluation of the information infrastructure. The key operational components of the information technology infrastructure are examined for weaknesses (technology vulnerabilities) that can lead to unauthorized action.
- Phase 3: Develop Security Strategy and Plans. Risks are analyzed in this phase. The information generated by the organizational and information infrastructure evaluations (Phases 1 and 2) is analyzed to identify risks to the organization and to evaluate the risks based on their impact to the organization's mission. In addition, an organization protection strategy and risk mitigation plans for the highest priority risks are developed.

Important Aspects of the OCTAVE Method

In this section, some of the key aspects of the OCTAVE Method are highlighted.

Self-Direction

The OCTAVE Method is self-directed. A small, interdisciplinary team of the organization's personnel (called the analysis team) manages the process and analyzes all information. Thus, the organization's personnel are actively involved in the decision-making process. When organizations outsource risk assessments, they often detach from making decisions. They rely solely on the judgment of external experts. The organization's staff does not

---

* Special permission to reproduce "OCTAVE™ Method Implementation Guide: Appendix D," (c) 2001 by Carnagie Mellon University, is granted by the Software Engineering Institute.

know the underlying thinking process used by the experts. If the decisions recommended by the external experts are adopted without evaluation, the organization's staff will not understand the underlying risk assumptions or the different possibilities that might unfold. The responsibility has been shifted to the expert, who is not accountable. As a result, improvements are not institutionalized in the organization.

Analysis Team

The OCTAVE Method requires an analysis team to conduct the evaluation and to analyze the information. The analysis team is an interdisciplinary team comprising representatives from both the mission-related and information technology areas of the organization. Typically, the analysis team will contain a core membership of about three to five people, depending on the size of the overall organization and the scope of the evaluation. The basic tasks of the analysis team are:

- To facilitate the knowledge elicitation workshops of Phase 1
- To gather any supporting data that are necessary
- To analyze threat and risk information
- To develop a protection strategy for the organization
- To develop mitigation plans to address the risks to the organization's critical assets

Thus, the analysis team must have knowledge of the organization and its business processes (including mission-related processes and information technology processes), facilitation skills, and good communications skills. It is also important to note that the analysis team is responsible for analyzing information and for making decisions. The core members of the analysis team may not have all of the knowledge and skills needed during the evaluation. At each point in the process, the analysis team members must decide if they need to augment their knowledge and skills for a specific task. They can do so by including others in the organization or by using external experts. For example, when they are analyzing data from a vulnerability tool, the analysis team members might want to include a member of the organization who has significant information technology knowledge. Likewise, when the team is creating a protection strategy to address strategic security issues in the organization, they might want to include a manager who has knowledge of the organization and good planning skills.

Workshop-Based Approach

The OCTAVE Method uses a workshop-based approach for gathering information and making decisions. In Phase 1, key areas of expertise within the organization are examined in facilitated workshops (also called knowledge elicitation workshops). The analysis team facilitates these workshops. Participants in the workshops are from multiple organizational levels. The result is the identification of important information assets, the threats to those assets, the security requirements of the assets, what the organization is currently doing to protect its information assets (current protection strategy), and weaknesses in organizational policies and practice (organizational vulnerabilities).

The remainder of Phase 1, as well as Phases 2 and 3, include consolidation and analysis workshops to consolidate and analyze the information gathered during the Phase 1 knowledge elicitation workshops. The analysis team members participate in these workshops. The consolidation and analysis workshops yield information such as the key operational components of the information infrastructure, the risks to the organization, the protection strategy for the organization, and mitigation plans for addressing the risks to the critical assets.

Catalogs of Information
The OCTAVE Method relies upon the following major catalogs of information:

- Catalog of practices: A collection of good strategic and operational security practices
- Threat profile: The range of major sources of threats that an organization needs to consider
- Catalog of vulnerabilities: A collection of vulnerabilities based on platform and application

An organization that is conducting the OCTAVE Method evaluates itself against the above catalogs of information. During Phase 1, the organization uses the catalog of practices as a measure of what it is currently doing well with respect to security (its current protection strategy practices) as well as what it is not doing well (its organizational vulnerabilities). The analysis team also uses the catalog of practices when it creates the protection strategy for the organization during Phase 3. After the analysis team selects the critical assets for the organization, they use the threat profile to create the range of threat scenarios that affect each critical asset. This occurs at the end of Phase 1. The analysis team uses software tools to examine their information technology infrastructure for weaknesses (technology vulnerabilities) in Phase 2. The software tools incorporate a catalog of vulnerabilities to check the organization's systems, components, and devices for technology-based weaknesses. The tools used during Phase 2 of the evaluation are commercial tools or freeware tools. The OCTAVE Method does not require specialized software tools for the technology vulnerability evaluation.

Phases, Processes, and Activities
Each phase of the OCTAVE Method contains two or more processes. Each process is made of activities. The following list highlights the phases and processes of OCTAVE:

- Preparing for the OCTAVE Method
- Phase 1: Build Asset-Based Threat Profiles
    - Process 1: Identify Senior Management Knowledge
    - Process 2: Identify Operational Area Management Knowledge
    - Process 3: Identify Staff Knowledge
    - Process 4: Create Threat Profiles
- Phase 2: Identify Infrastructure Vulnerabilities
    - Process 5: Identify Key Components
    - Process 6: Evaluate Selected Components
- Phase 3: Develop Security Strategy and Plans
    - Process 7: Conduct Risk Analysis
    - Process 8: Develop Protection Strategy

Each of these is described in more detail in the following sections.

Preparing for the OCTAVE Method
Preparing for the OCTAVE Method creates the foundation for a successful or unsuccessful evaluation. The following are some keys to a successful evaluation:

- Getting senior management sponsorship: This is the most critical success factor for information security risk evaluations. Any successful evaluation will require the time of people in the organization. The OCTAVE Method is a workshop-based approach that requires staff members from key operational areas. Even senior managers need to participate in the evaluation. If senior managers support the process, people in the organization tend to participate actively. If senior managers do not support the process, then staff support for the evaluation will dissipate quickly. People will miss workshops, and the analysis team will not have the ability to convince people to attend. If people know that senior management is very interested in the results of the evaluation, then the analysis team will have the authority and backing to convince people to attend the workshops.

- Selecting the analysis team: The analysis team is responsible for managing the process and analyzing information. The members of the team need to have sufficient skills to lead the evaluation. They also need to know when and where to go outside the team to augment their knowledge and skills.
- Scoping the OCTAVE Method: The evaluation should include important operational areas, but the scope cannot get too big. If the scope is too broad, it will be difficult for the analysis team to analyze all of the information. If the scope of the evaluation is too small, then the results may not be as meaningful as they should.
- Selecting participants: During the knowledge elicitation workshops (Processes 1–3), staff members from multiple organizational levels will contribute their knowledge about the organization. It is important for these people to understand their operational areas. They should be assigned to workshops because of their knowledge and skills, not solely based on who is available.

The preparation activities for the OCTAVE Method address the issues listed above. The goal of preparing is to make sure that the evaluation is scoped and scheduled properly, that the organization's senior managers support the evaluation, and that everyone participating in the process understands his or her role and receives any training that is required. The following are the activities required when preparing to conduct the OCTAVE Method:

- Obtain senior management sponsorship of OCTAVE: The planning activities for the OCTAVE Method start with senior management sponsorship. Usually, the champion would perform this activity. This could require briefings to senior management to help them understand the process.
- Select analysis team members: Representatives from both the business and information technology parts of the organization will be on the analysis team. The size of the analysis team is three to five people. Senior managers should be involved in the selection of team members. In addition, it is helpful if some of the members come from the operational areas that will be participating in the evaluation.
- Train analysis team: The analysis team needs to be trained in the OCTAVE Method. Each member of the analysis team needs to understand his or her role during each workshop.
- Select operational areas to participate in OCTAVE: A key part of the planning process is selecting the operational areas that will participate in the OCTAVE Method. This scopes the evaluation. The analysis team will lead this activity with senior management input.
- Select participants: Participants for the knowledge elicitation workshops (Processes 1–3) need to be selected. Also, people with special skills to augment the analysis team at certain points in the process need to be selected. The analysis team members will lead the selection of participants. They need to get input from the senior managers as well as the managers for each of the operational areas participating in the evaluation.

- Coordinate logistics: The analysis team members need to ensure that rooms and equipment are available for all workshops.
- Brief all participants: The analysis team should conduct a briefing for all participants prior to their participation in the process.

Once the preparation is completed, the organization is ready to start the evaluation.

Phase 1: Build Asset-Based Threat Profiles

The OCTAVE Method enables decision makers to develop relative priorities based on what is important to the organization. This involves examining both organizational practices and the installed technology base to identify risks to the organization's important information assets. A comprehensive information security risk evaluation, like the OCTAVE Method, involves the entire organization, including personnel from the information technology department and the business lines of the organization.[9]

The purpose of a risk evaluation is to help decision makers select cost-effective countermeasures by balancing the cost of addressing a risk with the benefit derived from avoiding a potential negative impact to the organization. The result of the evaluation is a mitigation plan for applying countermeasures designed to reduce the organization's risks.

In the OCTAVE Method, the analysis team conducts the evaluation. The analysis team is interdisciplinary in nature, including participants with various backgrounds and job roles. It is responsible for conducting workshops with the organization's staff, for analyzing the information that is elicited, and for ensuring that the evaluation process proceeds as scheduled. The analysis team is composed of personnel from the organization undergoing the evaluation.

During Phase 1, the analysis team facilitates workshop interviews with staff from multiple organizational levels. During these workshops, the participants identify important assets and discuss the impact on the organization if the assets are compromised. These knowledge elicitation workshops are held for the following organizational levels:

- Senior management
- Operational area management (middle management)
- Staff (including IT staff)

You should note that the organizational levels are not mixed during the workshops. In addition, the information technology staff normally participates in a separate workshop from the general staff members. The purpose of the knowledge elicitation workshops is to identify the following information from each organizational perspective:

- Important assets and their relative values
- Perceived threats to the assets
- Security requirements
- Current protection strategy practices
- Current organizational vulnerabilities

An asset is something of value to the organization.[10] Assets can include information (data), systems, software, hardware, and people. The OCTAVE Method requires workshop participants to examine the relative priority of assets, based on the impact to the organization if the asset is lost. Participants are asked to examine threats to the highest-priority assets that they have identified. A threat is an indication of a potential undesirable event.[11]

It refers to a situation in which a person could do something undesirable (a hacker initiating a denial-of-service attack against an organization's e-mail server) or a natural occurrence could cause an undesirable outcome (a fire damaging an organization's information technology hardware). The participants create threat scenarios based on known sources of threat and typical threat outcomes (from the threat profile). Participants next examine security requirements. Security requirements outline the qualities of information assets that are important to an organization. The OCTAVE Method requires that personnel consider the following security requirements for each important asset:

- Confidentiality: The need to keep proprietary, sensitive, or personal information private and inaccessible to anyone who is not authorized to see it
- Integrity: The authenticity, accuracy, and completeness of an asset
- Availability: When or how often an asset must be present or ready for use

Finally, the participants examine their current protection strategy practices in relation to the catalog of practices. Security practices are actions that help initiate, implement, and maintain security within an organization.[12] Practices focus on strategic and operational issues. A specific security practice is normally focused on a specific audience. The audiences for practices include managers, users (general staff), and information technology staff. While security practices indicate what an organization is doing to protect its assets, organizational vulnerabilities focus on what the organization is not doing well. Organizational vulnerabilities are weaknesses in organizational policy or practice that can result in the occurrences of unauthorized access or modification. During this part of the workshop, the participants fill out a survey based on the catalog of practices, and then the analysis team leads a discussion around the survey questions.

You should note that the results of each workshop present the perspective of the participants from only that organizational level. During the fourth process of Phase 1, the analysis team consolidates all information, selects the organization's critical assets, and creates a threat profile for each critical asset. The remainder of this section describes the processes of Phase 1.

Process 1: Identify Senior Management Knowledge

The participants in this process are the organization's senior managers. The analysis team facilitates a knowledge elicitation activity with the managers in these activities:

- Identify assets and relative priorities: The first activity is to identify information assets and determine which are most important to the organization.
- Identify areas of concern: Participants construct plausible scenarios outlining concerns about the threats to important information assets. These areas of concern are likely to lack sufficient detail with respect to the components of threat, and they will be further examined in Process 4.
- Identify security requirements for the most important assets: The senior managers create and document the security requirements for each important asset with respect to its confidentiality, integrity, and availability.
- Capture knowledge of protection strategy practices and organizational vulnerabilities: The managers complete a survey to benchmark their security practices in relation to known good security practices. The results of this benchmarking will identify the current protection strategy practices of the organization as well as the organizational vulnerabilities.

Process 2: Identify Operational Area Management Knowledge

The participants in this process are the organization's operational area managers (middle managers). The analysis team facilitates a knowledge elicitation activity with the managers in these activities:

- Identify assets and relative priorities: The first activity is to identify information assets and determine which are most important to the organization.
- Identify areas of concern: Participants construct plausible scenarios outlining concerns about the threats to important information assets. These areas of concern are likely to lack sufficient detail with respect to the components of threat, and they will be further examined in Process 4.
- Identify security requirements for the most important assets: The operational area managers create and document the security requirements for each important asset with respect to its confidentiality, integrity, and availability.
- Capture knowledge of protection strategy practices and organizational vulnerabilities: The managers complete a survey to benchmark their security practices in relation to known good security practices. The results of this benchmarking will identify the current protection strategy practices of the organization as well as the organizational vulnerabilities.

Process 3: Identify Staff Knowledge

The participants in this process are the organization's staff members. The analysis team facilitates a knowledge elicitation activity with them in these activities:

- Identify assets and relative priorities: The first activity is to identify information assets and determine which are most important to the organization.
- Identify areas of concern: Participants construct plausible scenarios outlining concerns about the threats to important information assets. These areas of concern are likely to lack sufficient detail with respect to the components of threat, and they will be further examined in Process 4.
- Identify security requirements for the most important assets: The staff members create and document the security requirements for each important asset with respect to its confidentiality, integrity, and availability.
- Capture knowledge of protection strategy practices and organizational vulnerabilities: The staff members complete a survey to benchmark their security practices in relation to known good security practices. The results of this benchmarking will identify the current protection strategy practices of the organization as well as the organizational vulnerabilities.

Process 4: Create Threat Profiles

The participants in this process are the analysis team members. During Process 4, the information elicited from the different organizational levels during the previous processes is grouped, critical assets are chosen, and a threat profile is created for each critical asset. The following are the activities of Process 4:

- Group assets, security requirements, and areas of concern by organizational level: The analysis team creates an integrated view of the important information assets, the areas of concern, and the security requirements of the assets.

- Select critical assets: The analysis team examines the grouped information and identifies the assets that are most critical to meeting the mission of the organization. These are known as the critical assets.
- Refine security requirements for critical assets: The analysis team describes the security requirements for each critical asset. They build upon and refine any relevant security requirements that were generated during the knowledge elicitation workshops.
- Identify threats to critical assets: The analysis team builds a threat profile for each critical asset. They use the basic threat profile as a benchmark to create the range of threat scenarios that affect each critical asset.

After completion of the organization view, or Phase 1 of the OCTAVE Method, the organization is ready to move to the technological view. Phase 2 of the evaluation examines the organization's information technology infrastructure.

Phase 2: Identify Infrastructure Vulnerabilities

A vulnerability evaluation is a systematic examination of an organization's technology base to determine the adequacy of the organization's security measures, identify security deficiencies, provide data from which to predict the effectiveness of proposed security measures, and confirm the adequacy of security measures after implementation. A vulnerability is a weakness in an information system, security practices and procedures, administrative controls, internal controls, implementation of technology, or physical layout that could be exploited to gain unauthorized access to information or to disrupt information processing. An information security risk evaluation incorporates vulnerability information by showing how threat actors could use identified vulnerabilities to gain access to the organization's assets. Technology vulnerabilities can be grouped into the following categories:[13]

- Design vulnerability: A vulnerability that is inherent in the design or specification of the system's hardware or software. Even a perfect implementation of the design may result in the existence of a design vulnerability.
- Implementation vulnerability: A vulnerability that occurs from a flawed software or hardware implementation of a satisfactory design.
- Configuration vulnerability: A vulnerability stemming from system configuration or administration errors.

Each information technology system or component will have many specific technology vulnerabilities against which it can be benchmarked. The OCTAVE Method requires that technology be measured against a catalog of vulnerabilities. One catalog of vulnerabilities commonly used is the Common Vulnerabilities and Exposures (CVE). CVE is a list or dictionary that provides common names for publicly known vulnerabilities.[14] It enables open and shared information without any distribution restrictions.

Technology vulnerability evaluations target weaknesses in the installed technology base of the organization, including network services, architecture, operating systems, and applications. The following basic activities are performed during a technology vulnerability evaluation:

- Identify key information technology systems and components.
- Examine systems and components for technology weaknesses.

The focus of a vulnerability evaluation of systems and components is to identify and evaluate the configuration and strength of devices on the organization network(s). The following list includes examples of tests performed during a technology vulnerability evaluation:

- Reviewing firewall configuration
- Checking the security of public Web servers
- Performing a comprehensive review of all operating systems
- Identifying services running and/or available on hosts and systems
- Listing all system user accounts
- Identifying known vulnerabilities in routers, switches, remote access servers, operating systems, and specific services and applications
- Identifying configuration errors
- Looking for existing signs of intrusion (Trojan horses, backdoor programs, integrity checks of critical system files, etc.)
- Checking file ownership and permissions
- Testing password usage and strength

Over time, many tools have been developed to test systems for weaknesses. Vulnerability evaluations often mimic known or suspected threats by using common methods and tools to test systems and components and ultimately gain unauthorized access.

There are many software tools available to help automate the evaluation process, including tools for file integrity checking, virus scanning, password protection, system scanning, network scanning, and network mapping. These tools can be used during Phase 2 of the OCTAVE Method to identify the technology vulnerabilities. The remainder of this section describes the processes of Phase 2.

Process 5: Identify Key Components

The participants in this process are the analysis team and selected members of the information technology (IT) staff. Prior to the workshop, the analysis team must ensure that documentation of the present state of the computing infrastructure is available. The network topology diagrams used by the organization's IT group to conduct its business are sufficient for this activity. The key is that the network topology information must be current. During Process 5, components to be evaluated for technology vulnerabilities are selected using these activities:

- Identify system of interest: The analysis team and IT staff determine which system is most closely related to each important asset.
- Identify key classes of components: The analysis team and IT staff examine network access paths to the system of interest in the context of threat scenarios to identify the key classes of components for critical assets. This will help them to determine which classes of components are important for each important asset.
- Identify infrastructure components to examine: The analysis team and IT staff select specific components from the key classes to include in the vulnerability evaluation, and they determine an approach for conducting the vulnerability evaluation.

Process 6: Evaluate Selected Components

The participants in this process are the analysis team and selected members of the IT staff. A technology vulnerability evaluation supported by software tools is conducted prior to the workshop. The analysis team and IT staff review the results of the evaluation during the workshop in these activities:

- Run vulnerability evaluation tools on selected infrastructure components. A technology vulnerability evaluation supported by software tools is performed. The evaluation can be conducted by the organization's information technology staff or by external experts, depending on the approach that was selected during Process 5. The security posture of the networked environment should be assessed from three perspectives: outside the organization, inside the organization, and from individual systems within the organization. This is completed prior to the workshop.
- Review technology vulnerabilities and summarize results. The analysis team and selected members of the IT staff review the technology vulnerabilities and create a summary of results. If external experts conducted the vulnerability evaluation, then they should also participate in the workshop.

After the organization completes the technology view, or Phase 2 of the evaluation, it is ready to develop a protection strategy and mitigation plans. During Phase 3 of the OCTAVE Method, the analysis team identifies the risks to its critical assets, develops a protection strategy for the organization, and develops mitigation plans for the risks to the critical assets.

Phase 3: Develop Security Strategy and Plans

Once the assets, threats, and vulnerabilities have been identified, an organization is positioned to analyze the information and to identify the information security risks. The analysis team leads the risk analysis effort. The goal is to determine how specific threats affect specific assets. A risk is essentially a threat plus the resulting impacts to the organization based on these outcomes:

- Disclosure of a critical asset (a violation of confidentiality)
- Modification of a critical asset (a violation of integrity)
- Loss or destruction of a critical asset (a violation of availability)
- Interruption of a critical asset (a violation of availability)

A risk is a measure of the expected loss in the absence of any mitigation actions or countermeasures. Measurement of loss, or impact, can be either qualitative or quantitative in nature. Qualitative information requires a nominal or ordinal scale. Quantitative information requires a cardinal or ratio scale.[15] Assessing information security risks can be more difficult than assessing other types of risk because data on threat probability and asset value are often limited. In addition, risk factors are constantly changing. Because of these limitations, many organizations use qualitative measures when analyzing risks.[16] The OCTAVE Method uses qualitative measures of impact in its risk analysis process.

The analysis of risks in the OCTAVE Method is based on scenario planning. The analysis team constructs a range of risk scenarios, or a risk profile, for each critical asset. The risk profile for a critical asset comprises the threat profile for the critical asset and a narrative description of the resulting impact(s) to the organization. Because data on threat probability are limited for the scenarios, the risks are assumed to be equally likely.[17] Thus, the analysis team establishes priorities based on the qualitative impact values assigned to the scenarios. After the risk analysis has been completed, the goal is to reduce risk through a combination of these actions:

- Implementing new security practices within the organization
- Taking the actions necessary to maintain the existing security practices
- Fixing identified vulnerabilities

Information security affects the entire organization. It is ultimately a business problem whose solution involves more than the deployment of information technology. An organization must take a strategic view to address its information security risks. An information security risk evaluation can help an organization evaluate organizational practice as well as the installed technology base and make decisions based on the potential impact to the organization.

The remainder of this section describes the processes of Phase 3.

Process 7: Conduct Risk Analysis

The participants in this process are the analysis team members. The goal of the process is to create a risk profile. The following are the activities of Process 7:

- Identify the impact of threats to critical assets: A risk profile is created for each important asset by describing the impact of each outcome in the risk profile (disclosure, modification, loss/destruction, and interruption).
- Create risk evaluation criteria: The analysis team establishes organization-specific evaluation criteria, a benchmark by which impacts are evaluated. Evaluation criteria are based on a qualitative scale (high, medium, low).
- Evaluate the impact of threats to critical assets: The analysis team assigns an impact value to each impact description using the evaluation criteria as a benchmark.

Process 8: Develop Protection Strategy

Process 8 consists of two workshops. The goal of Process 8 is to develop a protection strategy for the organization, mitigation plans for the risks to the critical assets, and an action list of near-term actions. The participants in the first workshop for Process 8 are the analysis team members and selected members of the organization (if the analysis team decides to supplement its skills and experience for protection strategy development). The following are the activities of the first workshop of Process 8:

- Consolidate protection strategy information: Data consolidation must be completed prior to the workshop. One or more analysis team members can consolidate the data; it is not required that the entire team work on the consolidation of data. The results of the activity to benchmark security practices from the first three processes of the OCTAVE Method are consolidated, providing the analysis team with information about the current protection strategy practices used by the organization as well as organizational vulnerabilities.
- Create protection strategy: The analysis team members review the risk and protection strategy information. They then propose a protection strategy for the organization intended to maintain the good practice that is present in the organization and to address the organizational vulnerabilities.
- Create mitigation plans: The analysis team proposes mitigation plans to reduce the risks to the critical assets.

- Create action list: As the analysis team members develop the protection strategy and mitigation plans, they should capture any near-term actions that are identified. In this activity, the analysis team formally documents the action items in an action list.

In the second workshop of Process 8, the analysis team presents the proposed protection strategy, mitigation plans, and action list to senior managers in the organization. The senior managers review and revise the strategy and plans as necessary and then decide how the organization will build on the results of the evaluation. The following are the activities of the second workshop of Process 8:

- Review risk information: The analysis team provides context to the senior managers by providing a summary of the risk profiles for each critical asset. They also provide a summary of the results of the organization's protection strategy surveys, current security practices, and organizational vulnerabilities.
- Review and refine protection strategy, mitigation plans, and action list: The analysis team presents the protection strategy, risk mitigation plans for the critical assets, and the action list. The senior managers review them and revise, change, and add to them as appropriate.
- Create next steps: The senior managers decide how they will build on the results of the evaluation and how they can support an ongoing security improvement initiative.

After the organization has developed the protection strategy and risk mitigation plans, it is ready to implement them. This completes the OCTAVE Method.

Chapter Summary

- Once vulnerabilities are identified and ranked, a strategy to control the risks must be chosen. Four control strategies are avoidance, transference, mitigation, and acceptance.
- Controls can be placed into one of four categories: control functions, architectural layer controls, strategy layer controls, and information security principles.
- Economic feasibility studies determine and compare costs and benefits from potential controls (often called a cost-benefit analysis). Other forms of feasibility analysis include analyses based on organizational, operational, technical, and political factors.
- An organization must be able to place a dollar value on each collection of information and the information assets it owns. This value is based on one of several options that must be determined by each organization.
- Single loss expectancy (SLE) is based on the value of the asset and the expected percentage of loss that would occur from a single successful attack. Annualized loss expectancy (ALE) represents the potential loss per year.
- Cost-benefit analysis (CBA) determines whether a control alternative is worth its associated cost. CBA calculations are based on costs before and after controls are implemented and the cost of the controls. Other feasibility analysis approaches can also be used.

- Organizations may choose alternatives to feasibility studies to justify applying information security controls, including: benchmarking with either metrics-based measures or process-based measures, due care and/or due diligence, best security practices up to and including the near-mythic gold standard, and/or baselining.

- Risk appetite defines the quantity and nature of risk that organizations are willing to accept, as they evaluate the trade-offs between perfect security and unlimited accessibility. Residual risk is the amount of risk unaccounted for after the application of controls.

- It is possible to repeat risk analysis using estimates based on a qualitative assessment. Delphi techniques can be used to obtain group consensus on risk assessment values.

- Once a control strategy has been implemented, the effectiveness of controls should be monitored and measured.

- The OCTAVE Method provides a methodology to risk management that represents an alternative to the approach presented in Chapter 7 and this chapter.

Review Questions

1. What is competitive advantage? How has it changed over the years since the IT industry began?
2. What is competitive disadvantage? Why has it emerged as a factor?
3. What are the four risk control strategies?
4. Describe risk avoidance, risk transference, risk mitigation, risk acceptance, and residual risk.
5. What four types of controls or applications can be used to avoid risk?
6. Describe how outsourcing can be used for risk transference.
7. What three planning approaches are discussed in this chapter as opportunities to mitigate risk?
8. How does a disaster recovery plan differ from a business continuity plan?
9. How does an incident response plan differ from a disaster recovery plan?
10. What conditions must be met to ensure that risk acceptance has been used properly?
11. What is risk appetite? Explain why risk appetite varies from organization to organization.
12. What is the difference between a detective control and a preventive control?
13. In which architectural layers are controls implemented?
14. What is a cost-benefit analysis?
15. What is the difference between intrinsic value and acquired value?
16. What is single loss expectancy? What is annual loss expectancy?
17. What is the difference between benchmarking and baselining? What is the difference between due diligence and due care?
18. What is the difference between organizational feasibility and operational feasibility?
19. What is the difference between qualitative measurement and quantitative measurement?
20. What is the OCTAVE Method? What does it provide to those who adopt it?

Exercises

1. Using the following table, calculate the SLE, ARO, and ALE for each threat category listed.

    XYZ Software Company, Major Threat Categories for New Applications Development (Asset value: $1,200,000 in projected revenues)

	Cost per Incident	Frequency of Occurrence
Programmer Mistakes	$5000	1 per week
Loss of Intellectual Property	$75,000	1 per year
Software Piracy	$500	1 per week
Theft of Information (Hacker)	$2500	1 per quarter
Theft of Information (Employee)	$5000	1 per 6 months
Web Defacement	$500	1 per month
Theft of Equipment	$5000	1 per year
Viruses, Worms, Trojan Horses	$1500	1 per week
Denial-of-Service Attack	$2500	1 per quarter
Earthquake	$250,000	1 per 20 years
Flood	$250,000	1 per 10 years
Fire	$500,000	1 per 10 years

2. How did the XYZ Software Company arrive at the values in the table in Exercise 1? For each entry, describe the process of determining the cost per incident and the frequency of occurrence.

3. How do the values in the table in Exercise 1 differ from the calculations presented in the text? How can we determine SLE if there is no percentage given? Which method is easier for determining the SLE: a percentage of value lost or cost per incident?

4. Assume a year has passed and XYZ has improved its security. Using the following table, calculate the SLE, ARO, and ALE for each threat category listed.

XYZ Software Company, Major Threat Categories for New Applications Development
(Asset value: $1,200,000 in projected revenues)

	Cost per Incident	Frequency of Occurrence	Cost of Controls	Type of Control
Programmer Mistakes	$5000	1 per month	$20,000	Training
Loss of Intellectual Property	$75,000	1 per 2 years	$15,000	Firewall/IDS
Software Piracy	$500	1 per month	$30,000	Firewall/IDS
Theft of Information (Hacker)	$2500	1 per 6 months	$15,000	Firewall/IDS
Theft of Information (Employee)	$5000	1 per year	$15,000	Physical Security
Web Defacement	$500	1 per quarter	$10,000	Firewall
Theft of Equipment	$5000	1 per 2 year	$15,000	Physical Security
Viruses, Worms, Trojan Horses	$1500	1 per month	$15,000	Antivirus
Denial-of-Service Attack	$2500	1 per 6 months	$10,000	Firewall
Earthquake	$250,000	1 per 20 years	$5000	Insurance/Backups
Flood	$50,000	1 per 10 years	$10,000	Insurance/Backups
Fire	$100,000	1 per 10 years	$10,000	Insurance/Backups

Why have some values changed in the following columns: Cost per Incident and Frequency of Occurrence? How could a control affect one but not the other?

5. Assume the costs of controls presented in the table for Exercise 4 were unique costs directly associated with protecting against that threat. In other words, don't worry about overlapping costs between threats. Calculate the CBA for each control. Are they worth the costs listed?

6. Using the Web, research the costs associated with the following items:

   ■ Managed antivirus software licenses for 500 workstations

   ■ A FW-1 firewall

   ■ A Tripwire Host–based IDS for 10 servers

   ■ A Java programming continuing education training program for 10 employees

   ■ Checkpoint Firewall solutions

Case Exercises

Mike and Iris were meeting to review the asset valuation worksheets that had been collected from all over the company. After a few minutes of review, Mike said, "Iris, the problem as I see it is that no two managers used the same criteria to assess the asset values or rank the priority of their asset lists."

Iris nodded and said, "I agree. Some of the worksheets have only one of the four asset valuations filled in. This is going to be very difficult to merge into a single, uniform list of information assets. We're going to have to visit each manager and figure out what basis was used and how the assets were ranked."

1. If you could have spoken to Mike Edwards before he distributed the asset valuation worksheets, what advice would you have given him to make the consolidation process easier?

2. How would you advise Mike and Iris to proceed with the worksheets they already have in hand?

Endnotes

1. Jack M. Greenberg. Corporate press release: first worldwide social responsibility report. *McDonald's Corporation Online.* Accessed April 15, 2002 [Cited June 19, 2002]. Available from the World Wide Web at http://www.mcdonalds.com/corporate/press/corporate/2002/04152002/index.html.

2. Thomas J. Peters and Robert H. Waterman. *In Search of Excellence: Lessons from America's Best-Run Companies.* New York: Harper and Row, 1982.

3. National Institute of Standards and Technology. *Risk Management Guide for Information Technology Systems.* SP 800-30. January 2002.

4. Peter Gourlay. Playing it safe. *U.S. Business Review Online,* December 2001 [Cited June 19, 2002]. Available from the World Wide Web at http://www.usbusiness-review.com/0112/02.html.

5. Frederick M. Avolio. Best practices in network security. *Network Computing,* March 20, 2000, 60–66.

6. Thomas Mann. Politics is often defined as the art of the possible. Speech in the Library of Congress, Washington, DC, May 29, 1945.

7. Gamma Secure Systems. First measure your risk. *Gamma Online,* January 2, 2002 [Cited June 19, 2002]. Available from the World Wide Web at *http://www.gammassl.co.uk/inforisk/.*

8. Christopher J. Alberts, Sandra G. Behrens, Richard D. Pethia, and William R. Wilson. *Operationally Critical Threat, Asset, and Vulnerability Evaluation (OCTAVE) Framework, Version 1.0* (CMU/SEI-99-TR-017, ADA 367718). Pittsburgh, PA: Software Engineering Institute, Carnegie Mellon University, June 1999.

9. U.S. General Accounting Office. *Executive Guide: Information Security Management* (GAO/AIMD-98-68). Washington, DC: GAO, May 1998.

10. Arthur E. Hutt, Seymour Bosworth, and Douglas B. Hoyt. *Computer Security Handbook,* 3rd ed. New York: John Wiley & Sons, 1995.

11. National Security Telecommunications and Information Systems Security Committee. *Index of National Security Telecommunications Information Systems Security Issuances* (NSTISSI No. 4014). Fort Mead, MD: NSTISSC Secretariat, January 1998.

12. British Standard Institution. *Information Security Management, Part 1: Code of Practice for Information Security Management of Systems* (BS7799: Part 1: 1995). London, UK: British Standard Institution, February 1995.

13. John D. Howard and Thomas A. Longstaff. *A Common Language for Computer Security Incidents* (SAND98-8667). Albuquerque, NM: Sandia National Laboratories, 1998.

14. M. S. Merkow and J. Breithaupt. *The Complete Guide to Internet Security.* New York: AMACOM, American Management Association, 2000, 95–109.

15. Robert N. Charette. *Software Engineering Risk Analysis and Management.* New York: Intertext Publications/Multiscience Press, 1989.

16. U.S. General Accounting Office. *Information Security Risk Assessment, Practices of Leading Organizations* (GAO/AIMD-00-33). Washington, DC: GAO, November 1999.

17. Kees Van der Heijden. *Scenarios: The Art of Strategic Conversation.* Chichester, UK: John Wiley & Sons, 1997.

Protection Mechanisms 9

People are the missing link to improving Information Security. Technology alone can't solve the challenges of Information Security.
THE HUMAN FIREWALL COUNCIL

ONE NIGHT TOWARD THE END OF his shift, a technician at RWW, Inc., received a call from his wife; one of his children was ill, and she wanted the technician to pick up some medicine on his way home from work. He decided to leave a few minutes early.

Like all watch-standing employees in the operations center, he had a procedures manual, which was organized sequentially. He used the checklists for everyday purposes, and had an index to look up anything else he needed. Only one unchecked box remained on the checklist when he snapped the binder closed and hurriedly secured his workstation.

Since he was the second shift operator and RWW did not have a third-shift in its data center, the technician carefully reviewed the shutdown checklist next to the door, making sure all the room's environmental, safety, and security systems were set correctly. He activated the burglar alarm, exited the room and the building, and was soon on his way to the drugstore.

At about the same time, a tenth-grader in San Diego was up late, sitting at her computer. Her parents assumed that she was listening to music while "chatting" with school friends online. In fact, she had become bored with chatting and had discovered some new friends on the Internet—friends who shared her interest in programming and Perl script writing. One of these new friends had sent the girl a link to a new warez (illegally copied software) site.

From this site the seventh-grader downloaded a kit called Blendo, which helped hackers create attack programs that combined a mass e-mailer with a worm, a macro virus, and a network scanner. She clicked her way through the configuration options, clicked a button labeled "custom scripts," and then pasted in a script that one of her new friends had e-mailed

361

to her. This script was built to exploit a brand-new vulnerability (announced only a few hours before). Although she didn't know it, the anonymous middle-schooler had created new malware that was soon to bring the Internet to a standstill. She exported the attack script, attached it to an e-mail, and sent it out to an anonymous remailer service to be forwarded to as many e-mail accounts as possible. She had naively set up a mailback option to an anonymous e-mail account so she could track the progress of her creation.

Thirty minutes later, she checked that anonymous e-mail account. She had more than 8000 new messages, and her mailbox was full.

Back at RWW, the e-mail gateway was hard at work sorting and forwarding all of the incoming e-mail. The account sales@rww.biz always received a lot of traffic, as did service@rww.biz. Tonight was no exception. Unfortunately for RWW, and for the second-shift operator who had failed to install the patch download that fixed the new vulnerability announced by the vendor, the seventh-grader's attack code tricked the RWW mail server into running the program. The RWW mail server, with its high-performance server and high-bandwidth Internet connection, began to do three things at once: It sent an infected e-mail to everyone with whom RWW had ever traded e-mail, it infected every RWW server that the e-mail server could reach, and it started deleting files, randomly, from every folder on each infected server.

Within seconds, the network intrusion detection system had determined that something was afoot. By then, it was too late to stop the infection, but the system sent a message to Iris's PDA anyway.

LEARNING OBJECTIVES

Upon completion of this material, you should be able to:

- Know and understand access control approaches, including authentication, authorization, and biometric access controls

- Define and identify the various types of firewalls and the common approaches to firewall implementation

- Discuss the current issues in dial-up access and protection

- Identify and describe the types of intrusion detection systems and the two strategies on which they are based

- Discuss cryptography and the encryption process, and compare and contrast symmetric and asymmetric encryption

Introduction

Information security is an emerging discipline that combines the efforts of people, policy, education, training, awareness, procedures, and technology to improve the confidentiality, integrity, and availability of an organization's information assets. Technical controls alone cannot ensure a secure IT environment, but they are usually an essential part of information security programs. Managing the development and use of technical controls requires some knowledge and familiarity with the technology that enables them. Technical controls, when properly managed, enhance the confidentiality, integrity, and availability of information in each of its three states (storage, transit, and processing). In this chapter, you will learn about firewalls, intrusion detection systems, encryption-based systems, and some other widely used security technologies. The chapter is designed to help you evaluate and manage the many classes of technical controls for use in information security programs. Note, however, that those seeking expertise in the configuration and maintenance of technical control systems will require additional education and training beyond the overview presented here.

Technical controls can enable policy enforcement where human behavior is difficult to regulate. Consider, for example, a password policy that specifies composition requirements (for example, mixed case) and periodic password changes, and that prohibits the reuse of passwords. While this policy is difficult to enforce on an employee-by-employee basis, it can usually be automatically enforced by implementing common operating system software controls.

Although technical controls can be an important part of an information security program, they must be combined with sound policy and education, training, and awareness efforts. Figure 9-1 illustrates how technical controls can be implemented at a number of points in the technical infrastructure. The technical controls that defend against threats from outside the organization are shown on the left side of the diagram. The controls that defend against threats from within the organization are shown on the right side of the diagram. Because individuals inside an organization often have direct access to the information, they can circumvent many of the most potent technical controls. Controls that can be applied to this human element are also shown on the right side of the diagram.

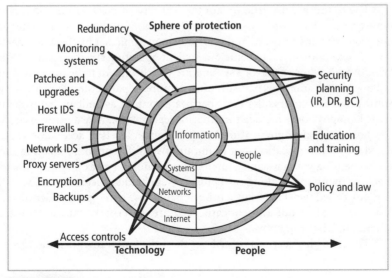

FIGURE 9-1 Sphere of Security

Among the most powerful and widely used technical security mechanisms are the following:

- Access controls
- Firewalls
- Dial-up protection
- Intrusion detection systems
- Scanning and analysis tools
- Cryptography

Access Controls

Access control encompasses two processes: confirming the identity of the entity accessing a logical or physical area (**authentication**), and determining which actions that entity can perform in that physical or logical area (**authorization**). A successful access control approach—whether intended to control physical access or logical access—always consists of both authentication and authorization.

Authentication

There are four types of authentication mechanisms:

- Something you *know* (for example, passwords and passphrases)
- Something you *have* (such as cryptographic tokens and smart cards)
- Something you *are* (including fingerprints, palm prints, hand topography, hand geometry, and retina and iris scans)
- Something you *produce* (such as voice and signature pattern recognition)

The technical infrastructure for the first type of mechanism—something you know, for example, a password—is already built into commonly used computer and network operating systems software, and is already in use unless it has been deliberately disabled. A notable exception arises in some older client operating systems such as Windows 95 and Windows 98, whose password systems are widely known to be insecure. Implementing other authentication mechanisms often requires separate supplemental physical devices. Some product vendors offer these hardware controls as built-in features; for example, some laptop vendors include thumbprint readers as standard features on certain models.

Some logical or physical areas require higher levels of access controls and, therefore, use **strong authentication**—at minimum two different authentication mechanisms (usually something you have and something you know). For example, access to a bank's ATM machine requires a banking card plus a personal identification number (PIN). Such systems are called two-factor authentication, because two separate identification mechanisms are used. Strong authentication requires that one of the mechanisms be something other than what you know.

The following sections describe each of the four authentication mechanisms in turn.

Something You Know

This type of authentication mechanism verifies the user's identity by means of a password, passphrase, or other unique authentication code, such as a personal identification number (PIN).

A **password** is a private word or combination of characters that only the user should know. One of the biggest debates in security focuses on the complexity of passwords. A password should be difficult to guess, which means it cannot be a word that is easily associated with the user, such as the name of a spouse, child, or pet. Nor should it be a series of numbers easily associated with the user, such as a phone number, Social Security number, or birth date. At the same time, the password must be something the user can easily remember, which means it should be short or have an association the user can remember but that is not accessible to others.

A **passphrase** is a plain-language phrase, typically longer than a password, from which a **virtual password** is derived. For example, while a typical password might be 23skedoo, a passphrase could be *May The Force Be With You Always*, from which the virtual password *MTFBWYA* is derived. Another way to create a virtual password is to use a set of construction rules applied to facts you know very well, such as the first three letters of your last name, a hyphen, the first two letters of your first name, an underscore, the first two letters of your mother's maiden name, a hyphen, and the first four letters of the city in which you were born. This may sound complicated, but once memorized the construction rules are easy to use. If you add another rule to substitute numeric digits for certain letters—1 for L, 0 for O, and 3 for E, and capitalize the first letter of each section, then you have a very powerful virtual password that you can easily reconstruct. Using the preceding rules would create a virtual password for Charlie Moody (born in Atlanta, mother's maiden name Meredith) of *M00-Cha_M3-At1a*, a very strong password.

Another method for creating strong passwords is to use a password memory support device like the PassWheel from Surelock Security Products. The PassWheel, as shown in Figure 9-2, allows the user to create a complex password by using the simple multi-alphabet dials. You simply use a reference word (e.g., MIKE), align the four wheels to spell that word, move the marker a predetermined number of letters to the left or right of the reference word, and then read 4–12 letters on the other side. Using the PassWheel, you can change common letters to numbers and mix capitalization. The result is a complex, powerful password that cannot be easily broken, even if someone found the PassWheel device (as long as you scramble it after use).

How important is it to have a long, not obvious password? As shown in Table 9-1, the longer the password, the lower the odds of it being guessed in a brute-force attack using random bit combinations (you will learn more about such attacks later in this chapter). A good rule of thumb is to require that passwords be at least eight characters long and contain at least one number and one special character.

Source: Surelock Security Products Pty Ltd

FIGURE 9-2 PassWheel Password Generator

Table 9-1 Password Power

Case-Insensitive Passwords

Number of characters	Odds of cracking: 1 in	Estimated time to crack
1	68	0.000009 second
2	4624	0.0006 second
3	314,432	0.04 second
4	21,381,376	2.7 seconds
5	1,453,933,568	3 minutes, 2 seconds
6	98,867,482,624	3 hours, 26 minutes
7	6,722,988,818,432	9 days, 17 hours, 26 minutes
8	457,163,239,653,376	1 year, 10 months, 1 day
9	31,087,100,296,429,600	124 years, 11 months, 5 days
10	2,113,922,820,157,210,000	8495 years, 4 months, 17 days

Table 9-1   Password Power   (continued)

Case-Sensitive Passwords

Number of characters	Odds of cracking: 1 in	Estimated time to crack
1	94	0.00001 second
2	8836	0.011 second
3	830,584	0.1 second
4	78,074,896	9.8 seconds
5	7,339,040,224	15 minutes, 17 seconds
6	689,869,781,056	23 hours. 57 minutes, 14 seconds
7	64,847,759,419,264	3 months, 3 days, 19 hours
8	6,095,689,385,410,820	24 years, 6 months
9	572,994,802,228,617,000	2302 years, 8 months, 9 days
10	53,861,511,409,490,000,000	216,457 years, 4 months

*Estimated Time to Crack is based on a Pentium 4 computer performing 8 million guesses per second. The estimates take into consideration all keyboard characters, some of which are not allowed by some systems.

Something You Have

This authentication mechanism makes use of something (a card, key, or token) that the user or the system has. While there are many implementations of this mechanism, one example is a **dumb card**, a category that includes ID and ATM cards with magnetic strips containing the digital (and often encrypted) PIN against which user input is compared. A more capable object is the **smart card**, which contains a computer chip that can verify and validate other information in addition to PINs.

Another device often used is the cryptographic token, a computer chip in a card that has a display. This device contains a built-in seed number that uses a formula or a clock to calculate a number that can be used to perform a remote login authentication. Tokens may be either synchronous or asynchronous. Once **synchronous tokens** are synchronized with a server, each device (server and token) uses the time to generate the authentication number that is entered during the user login. **Asynchronous tokens** use a challenge-response system, in which the server challenges the user with a number. That is, the user enters the challenge number into the token, which in turn calculates a response number. The user then enters the response number into the system to gain access. Only a person who has the correct token will be able to calculate the correct response number and thus log into the system. This system does not require synchronization and does not suffer from mistiming issues. Figure 9-3 shows two examples of access control tokens.

Source: RSA Security

FIGURE 9-3 Access Control Tokens

Something You Are

This authentication mechanism takes advantage of something inherent in the user that is evaluated using biometrics, which you will learn more about later in this chapter. Biometric authentication methods include the following:

- Fingerprints
- Palm scan
- Hand geometry
- Hand topology
- ID cards (face representation)
- Facial recognition
- Retina scan
- Iris scan

Most of the technologies that scan human characteristics convert these images to obtain some form of **minutiae**—that is, unique points of reference that are digitized and stored in an encrypted format. Each subsequent scan is also digitized and then compared with the encoded value to determine whether users are who they claim to be. One limitation of this technique is that some human characteristics can change over time, due to normal development, injury, or illness. Among the human characteristics currently employed for authentication purposes, only three are considered truly unique:

- Fingerprints
- Retina (blood vessel pattern)
- Iris (random pattern of features found in the iris, including freckles, pits, striations, vasculature, coronas, and crypts)

DNA or genetic authentication would be included in this category, if it ever becomes a cost-effective and socially accepted technology.

Something You Produce

This type of authentication makes use of something the user performs or produces. It includes technology related to signature recognition and voice recognition, for example. Signature recognition has become commonplace. Many retail stores already use signature recognition, or at least signature capture, for authentication during a purchase. Customers sign a special pad, using a stylus; the signatures are then digitized and either compared to a database for validation or simply saved for future reference. Signature capture is much more widely accepted than signature comparison, because signatures can vary due to a number of factors, including age, fatigue, and the speed with which they are written.

Voice recognition for authentication captures the analog waveforms of human speech, and compares these waveforms to a stored version. Voice recognition systems provide the user with a phrase that they must read—for example, "My voice is my password, please verify me. Thank you."

Another pattern-based approach is keystroke pattern recognition. This authentication method relies on the timing between key signals when a user types in a known sequence of keystrokes. When measured with sufficient precision, this pattern can provide a unique identification.

Figure 9-4 depicts some of these biometric and other human recognition characteristics.

FIGURE 9-4   **Recognition Characteristics**

THREAT MANAGEMENT

Password Attacks

Passwords must be protected against all of the following types of password attacks, each of which is defined more fully in Chapter 2.

Dictionary Attack

A dictionary attack is an attempt to identify your password by using common words, names of loved ones, names of pets, birth dates, addresses, and phone numbers. A dictionary attack begins with the dictionary, essentially a database of commonly used words to which the attacker can add custom words or conduct a forensic analysis, in which software scans text documents and adds all words to the dictionary. The odds of you using a piece of your password in a document are greater than you might think. Dictionary attack systems can substitute ones for L's, zeros for O's, and threes for E's, as well as use a long list of other popular substitution techniques. To protect against a dictionary attack, follow good password techniques as outlined earlier. Don't use easy-to-guess passwords, or even real words. Passphrases, if they are sufficiently long and complex enough, are impossible to guess in a dictionary attack.

Brute Force Attack

A brute force attack is an attempt to identify your password by systematically evaluating the bits that make up the password. Simply put, the computer starts at 1, then 01, then 10, then 11, and so on. Modern cracking programs are capable of making 8 million guesses per second. Unfortunately, most people use short passwords, typically six or fewer characters. As noted in Table 9-1, this practice results in a relatively easy-to-break password. By being password savvy, you can avoid having the password broken in this manner.

In addition, systems should disable accounts that are being attacked by password-guessing strategies. Some organizations are content to disable an account for a period of time after a certain number of unsuccessful attempts, thereby preventing further access to that account from a few minutes up to an hour or longer, after which time the account returns to a normal status. This tactic prevents brute force and dictionary attacks from trying many passwords. Other organizations prefer to permanently disable an account after a certain number of failed login attempts. This requires a system administrator or help desk technician to reset the account before it can be used again. Either approach will greatly reduce the odds of an unauthorized individual using random guessing or an automated dictionary attack to compromise someone else's account.

Man-in-the-Middle Attack

In this type of attack, a fake login screen is substituted for the real one; user names and passwords entered on this screen are then sent directly to the attacker. Often the fake screen provides a false "password incorrect" message (and who hasn't fat-fingered their password at least once or twice?), and then redirects the user to the real login screen. The best way to avoid this type of attack is to carefully scrutinize your login screens. Check the page's properties and make sure that the normal secure protocols (e.g., SSL) are in place. Use caution, and report suspected attacks.

A common attack strategy employs an e-mail that purports to be from an Internet service provider (ISP) or other service provider alerting you to a problem with your

(continued)

account billing. This message directs you to a convenient Web page where you can "resolve" the issue by typing in your credit card information. Unfortunately, the link has been spoofed, and it sends you to a Web server controlled by some other entity who will harvest your credit information for its own misuse.

Social Engineering Attack

In a social engineering attack, someone attempts to obtain your password, while masquerading as a support technician or other authorized individual who needs your login information, rely on social engineering. **Never** give system access information to someone; in almost every possible case, authentic support personnel have all the authorization they need to accomplish their assignments. In the state of Georgia, those convicted of assuming a false identity to perpetrate a crime face a $5000 fine and up to a year in jail.

Keyboard Attack

In a keyboard attack, the perpetrator installs keystroke capture software or hardware on the victim's computer. Widely available hackerware then sends all keystrokes to a remote location, or devices installed between the keyboard and computer record up to several hundred kilobytes of data. To prevent this type of attack, check regularly to make sure nothing "extra" is attached to your keyboard cable, and check for unknown, active software icons on your toolbar. A variation on this type of attack is remote system monitoring. Hacker versions of software like PCAnywhere or Timbuktu, which legitimately allow a user to view or control a remote system, can be used to spy on your other computer activity and to obtain login and other personal information. Like keystroke logging software, these programs typically display a software icon when active.

Conflicts over password complexity have yet to be resolved. Systems administrators want very complex passwords that are difficult to crack, while users want simple passwords that are easy to remember. Users who have difficult—or multiple—passwords are likely to write them down, often defeating the purpose of password security. We have all heard stories about passwords on Post-it notes stuck on the monitor, on slips of paper in desk drawers, and inside user manuals. Can passwords be somehow recorded without compromising security? The answer is yes. A number of software applications for computers and PDAs store system access information in an encrypted format. You log in to a "keychain" to view user name and password information. If others want to try to access this information, well, they have to guess the password first, don't they?

Authorization

The authorization process begins with an authenticated entity—a person, or a virtual identity like another computer program. In general, authorization can be handled in one of three ways:

- Authorization for each authenticated user, in which the system performs an authentication process to verify the specific entity and then grants access to resources for only that entity: This quickly becomes a complex and resource-intensive process in a computer system environment.

- Authorization for members of a group, in which the system matches authenticated entities to a list of group memberships, and then grants access to resources based on the group's access rights: This is the most common authorization method.

■ Authorization across multiple systems, in which a central authentication and authorization system verifies entity identity and grants a set of credentials to the verified entity: These credentials (sometimes called an **authorization ticket**) are honored by all systems within the authentication domain. Sometimes called single sign-on (SSO) or reduced sign-on, this approach is becoming more common, and is frequently enabled using a shared directory structure such as the Lightweight Directory Access (LDAP) protocol.

Evaluating Biometrics

Two of the four authentication mechanisms (something you are and something you produce) are considered to be biometric—literally, life measurement. Biometric technologies are generally evaluated according to three basic criteria:

■ The false reject rate: the percentage of authorized users who are denied access
■ The false accept rate: the percentage of unauthorized users who are allowed access
■ The crossover error rate: the point at which the number of false rejections equals the false acceptances

False Reject Rate

The **false reject rate** is the rate at which authentic users are denied or prevented access to authorized areas, as a result of a failure in the biometric device. This failure is also known as a Type I error or a false negative. Rejection of an authorized individual represents not a threat to security but an impedance to legitimate use. Consequently, it is often not seen as a serious problem until the rate increases to a level high enough to irritate users.

False Accept Rate

The **false accept rate** is the rate at which fraudulent users or non-users are allowed access to systems or areas, as a result of a failure in the biometric device. This failure, known as a Type II error or a false positive, represents a serious security breach. Often, multiple authentication measures must be used to back up a device whose failure would otherwise result in erroneous authorization.

Crossover Error Rate

The **crossover error rate (CER)**, also called the equal error rate, is the point at which the rate of false rejections equals the rate of false acceptances. It is the optimal outcome for biometrics-based systems. CERs are used to compare various biometrics and may vary by manufacturer. A biometric device that provides a CER of 1% is considered to be superior to one with a CER of 5%, for example.

Acceptability of Biometrics

A balance must be struck between the acceptability of a system to its users and the effectiveness of the same system. Many of the reliable, effective biometric systems are perceived as being somewhat intrusive by users. Organizations implementing biometrics must carefully balance a system's effectiveness against its perceived intrusiveness and acceptability to users. Note that the rated effectiveness of a system is roughly inverse to its acceptability, as shown in Table 9-2.

Table 9-2 Orders of Effectiveness and Acceptance	
Effectiveness of Biometric Authentication Systems Ranking from Most Secure to Least Secure	Acceptance of Biometric Authentication Systems Ranking from Most Accepted to Least Accepted
■ Retina pattern recognition	■ Keystroke pattern recognition
■ Fingerprint recognition	■ Signature recognition
■ Handprint recognition	■ Voice pattern recognition
■ Voice pattern recognition	■ Handprint recognition
■ Keystroke pattern recognition	■ Fingerprint recognition
■ Signature recognition	■ Retina pattern recognition

Source: Harold F. Tipton and Micki Krause. *Handbook of Information Security Management.* Boca Raton: CRC Press, 1998: 39–41.

Managing Access Controls

To appropriately manage access controls, an organization must have in place a formal **access control policy**, which determines how access rights are granted to entities and groups. This policy must include provisions for periodically reviewing all access rights, granting access rights to new employees, changing access rights when job roles change, and revoking access rights as appropriate. Without an access control policy, systems administrators may implement access controls in a way that is inconsistent with the organization's overall philosophy. Once a policy is in place, implementing access controls becomes a technical issue.

A good example of an access control policy comes from Charles Cresson Wood's book *Information Security Policy Made Easy:*

Access Control

Access Philosophy—Access to Public and Internal Use Only information is not restricted with access controls that discriminate by specific user. [...] Access to Confidential or Secret information must be granted only when a legitimate business need has been demonstrated and access has been approved in advance by the information Owner. Access to special hardware and software must be restricted based on business need.

Access Approval Process—A worker's manager must initiate the access control approval process, and the privileges granted remain in effect until the worker's job changes or the worker leaves Company X. If either of these two events occurs, the manager must notify the Information Security department immediately. All non-employees, contractors, consultants, temporaries, and outsourcing organizations must also go through a similar access control request and authorization process initiated by the project manager. The privileges of these non-employees must be immediately revoked by the Information Security department when the project is complete, or when the non-employees stop working with Company X. The relevant project manager must review the need for the continuing privileges of non-employees every three months.

Default Facilities—By default, all users must be granted basic information systems services such as electronic mail and word processing facilities. These basic facilities will vary by job title and be determined jointly by Information Security and the Information Systems department. All other system capabilities must be provided through job profiles or by special request directed to the Owner of the involved information. The existence of certain access privileges does not, in and of itself, mean that an individual is authorized to use these privileges. If users have any questions about access control privileges, they must direct these questions to the Information Security department.

Departures from Company X—When a user leaves Company X, all system privileges and access to Company X information must cease immediately [… and] all Company X information disclosed to users must be returned or destroyed. […]

Unique User IDs—Each user must be assigned their own unique user ID. This user ID follows an individual as they move through the organization. It must be permanently decommissioned when a user leaves Company X. Re-use of user IDs is not permitted. Every Company X user ID and related password is intended for the exclusive use of a specific individual. While user IDs can be shared in electronic mail messages and in other places, passwords must never be shared with anyone. […] User IDs are linked to specific people, and are not associated with computer terminals, departments, or job titles. […]

Privilege Deactivation—After a period of no activity defined in minutes by the Information Security department, online sessions with multi-user machines must be terminated automatically. […] Dormant user IDs on multi-user computers that have no any activity for a period defined in weeks by the Information Security department must have their privileges automatically revoked and the related files archived. Users who return from an extended vacation or a leave of absence must have their manager contact Information Security to reestablish their privileges.

User Authentication—All production information system user IDs must have a linked password or a stronger mechanism such as a dynamic password token, to ensure that only the authorized user is able to utilize the user ID. Users are responsible for all activity that takes place with their user ID and password or other authentication mechanism. A user must change their password immediately if they suspect that it has been discovered or used by another person. Users must notify Information Security if other access control mechanisms are broken or if they suspect that these mechanisms have been compromised.

Fixed Password Management

Choosing Passwords—Users must choose difficult-to-guess passwords. Fixed passwords must not be found in the dictionary and must not be a reflection of the user's personal life. All fixed passwords must be at least 10 characters, and this minimum length must be enforced automatically where systems support it. Users must choose fixed passwords that include both alphabetic and numeric characters.

Changing Passwords—User-chosen fixed passwords must not be reused or recycled. Where systems support it, fixed passwords must be required to change every 60 days and passwords must be changed the first time they are used. If a user suspects that somebody else may know his or her password, the password must be changed immediately.

The Information Systems department's Help Desk will not reset user passwords unless a user is identified.

Protecting Passwords—Users must not share a fixed password with anyone, including managers and co-workers. Users must employ authorized mechanisms to share information such as local server shared directories, electronic mail, intranet pages, or floppy disks. Users must not store fixed passwords in any computer files, such as logon scripts or computer programs, unless the passwords have been encrypted with authorized encryption software. Passwords must not be written down unless a transformation process has concealed them, or they are physically secured, such as placed in a locked file cabinet. All fixed passwords set by default by the hardware or software vendor must be changed before the involved system can be used for Company X business activities.[1]

Biometrics-based systems pose a particular set of management challenges, some of which you learned about earlier in this chapter. Foremost among these management challenges is probably cost; biometric technology is expensive, averaging more than $100 per user for a simple thumbprint reader. For a large organization, adoption of such a security mechanism means a substantial increase in the total cost of operating its systems. Another challenge is interoperability: Most biometric components come from independent vendors, whose efforts to standardize the technical capabilities are not complete. The social challenge—getting users to accept unfamiliar, relatively invasive authentication methods—requires training and education.

Firewalls

A physical firewall in a building is a concrete or masonry wall running from the basement through the roof to prevent fire from spreading. In the aircraft and automotive industries, a firewall is an insulated metal barrier that keeps the hot and dangerous moving parts of the motor separate from the inflammable interior where the passengers sit. In information security, a **firewall** is any device that prevents a specific type of information from moving between the outside world, known as the **untrusted network** (e.g., the Internet), and the inside world, known as the **trusted network**. The firewall may be a separate computer system, a service running on an existing router or server, or a separate network containing a number of supporting devices.

The Development of Firewalls

Firewalls have made significant advances since their earliest implementations. First-generation firewall devices were routers that could perform only simple packet filtering operations. Later generations have offered ever more complex capabilities, including the increased security and convenience of demilitarized zones (DMZs, described later in this chapter). Currently, there are some widely recognized generations of firewalls, which can be implemented in a wide variety of architectures.

The first generation of firewalls, **packet filtering firewalls**, are simple networking devices that filter packets by examining every incoming and outgoing packet header. They can selectively filter packets based on values in the packet header, accepting or rejecting packets as needed. These devices can be configured to filter based on IP address, type of packet, port request, and/or other elements present in the packet. The filtering examines packets for compliance with or violation of rules configured into the firewall's database. The rules most commonly implemented in packet filtering firewalls are based on a combination of IP source and destination address, direction (inbound or outbound), and/or source and destination port requests. Figure 9-5 shows how such a firewall typically works.

FIGURE 9-5 Packet Filtering Firewall

The ability to restrict a specific service is now considered standard in most modern routers, and is invisible to the user. Unfortunately, these systems are unable to detect whether packet headers have been modified, as occurs in IP spoofing attacks.

Early firewall models examined one aspect of the packet header: the destination address and the source address. For example, consider the rules listed in Table 9-3.

Table 9-3 Packet Filtering Example Rules

Source Address	Destination Address	Service Port	Action
10.10.x.x	172.16.126.x	Any	Deny
192.168.x.x	10.10.x.x	Any	Deny
172.16.121.1	10.10.10.22	FTP	Allow
10.10.x.x	x.x.x.x	HTTP	Allow
x.x.x.x	10.10.10.25	HTTP	Allow
x.x.x.x	10.10.10.x	Any	Deny

Notes: These rules apply to a network at 10.10.x.x.

This table uses special, nonroutable IP addresses in the rules for this example. In reality, a firewall that connects to a public network will use real address ranges.

With the rules shown in Table 9-3, any attempt to make a connection from any computers or network devices in the 10.10.x.x address range is blocked from all services offered at the network with the address 172.16.126.x. This first rule might be used to block objectionable content found at that particular address, for example. At the same time, the fourth rule allows all other 10.10 addresses to access any HTTP services at any other address. The second rule blocks any devices in the 192.168 network from any access to the 10.10 network, effectively blacklisting that external network from connecting to this network. The third rule allows a specific computer found at 172.16.121.1 to access a certain FTP server found at 10.10.10.22. The fourth rule allows all internal users to browse the entire Internet, unless blocked by an earlier rule, and the fifth rule allows any outside user to access the Web server at 10.10.10.25 unless otherwise blocked by an earlier rule. The final rule enforces an exclusionary policy that blocks all access not specifically allowed.

The second generation of firewalls, known as **application-level firewalls**, often consists of dedicated computers kept separate from the first filtering router (called an edge router); they are commonly used in conjunction with a second or internal filtering router. This second router is often called a **proxy server**, because it serves as a proxy for external service requests to internal services.

With this configuration, the proxy server, rather than the Web server, is exposed to the outside world from within a network segment called the **demilitarized zone** (**DMZ**). The DMZ is an intermediate area between a trusted network and an untrusted network (see Figure 9-8 later in this chapter). Using this model, additional filtering routers are placed between the proxy server and internal systems, thereby restricting access to internal systems to the proxy server alone. If these servers store the most recently accessed pages in their internal caches, they may also be called **cache servers**.

Suppose an external user wanted to view a Web page from an organization's Web server. Rather than expose the Web server to direct traffic from the users and potential attackers, the organization can install a proxy server, configured with the registered domain's URL. This proxy server receives Web page requests, accesses the Web server on behalf of external clients, and then returns the requested pages to users.

The primary disadvantage of application-level firewalls is that they are designed for a specific protocol. As a consequence, they cannot easily be reconfigured to work with protocols for which they were not originally designed.

The third generation of firewalls, **stateful inspection firewalls**, keeps track of each network connection established between internal and external systems using a **state table**. State tables track the state and context of each exchanged packet by recording which station sent which packet and when. Like first-generation firewalls, stateful inspection firewalls perform packet filtering, but they take matters a step further. Whereas simple packet filtering firewalls merely allow or deny certain packets based on their addresses, a stateful inspection firewall can restrict incoming packets by restricting access to packets that constitute responses to internal requests. If the stateful inspection firewall receives an incoming packet that it cannot match in its state table, then it defaults to its ACL to determine whether to allow the packet to pass.

The primary disadvantage of this type of firewall is the additional processing requirements of managing and verifying packets against the state table, which can expose the system to a DoS attack. In such an attack, the firewall is subjected to a large number of external packets, slowing it down as it attempts to compare all of the incoming packets first to the state table and then to the ACL. On the positive side, these firewalls can track connectionless packet traffic such as User Datagram Protocol (UDP) and remote procedure call (RPC) traffic.

Whereas static filtering firewalls, such as those in the first and third generations, allow entire sets of one type of packet to enter in response to authorized requests, a fourth-generation firewall, called a **dynamic packet filtering firewall**, allows only a particular packet with a specific source, destination, and port address to pass through the firewall. It does so by understanding how the protocol functions, and by opening and closing "doors" in the firewall based on the information contained in the packet header.[2] Dynamic packet filters are an intermediate form, between traditional static packet filters and application proxies.

Firewall Architectures

Each of the firewall generations can be implemented in a number of architectural configurations. These configurations are sometimes mutually exclusive but sometimes can be combined. The configuration that works best for a particular organization depends on the uses of its network, the organization's ability to develop and implement the architectures, and the available budget. Although literally hundreds of variations exist, four architectural implementations of firewalls are especially common: packet filtering routers, screened-host firewalls, dual-homed host firewalls, and screened-subnet firewalls.

Packet Filtering Routers

Most organizations with an Internet connection use some form of router between their internal networks and the external service provider. Many of these routers can be configured to block packets that the organization does not allow into the network. This is a simple but effective means of lowering the organization's risk of external attack. Such an architecture lacks auditing and strong authentication, and the complexity of the access control lists used to filter the packets can grow and degrade network performance. Figure 9-5 shows an example of this type of architecture.

Screened-Host Firewall Systems

Screened-host firewall systems combine the packet filtering router with a separate, dedicated firewall such as an application proxy server. This approach allows the router to screen packets to minimize the network traffic and load on the internal proxy. The application proxy examines an application layer protocol, such as HTTP, and performs the proxy services. This separate host, which is often referred to as a **bastion host**, represents a single, rich target for external attacks, and should be very thoroughly secured. Because it stands as a sole defender on the network perimeter, it is also commonly referred to as the **sacrificial host**.

Even though the bastion host/application proxy actually contains only cached copies of the internal Web documents, it can still present a promising target. Compromise of the bastion host can disclose the configuration of internal networks and possibly provide external sources with internal information. To its advantage, the proxy requires the external attack to compromise two separate systems before the attack can access internal data. As a consequence, the bastion host protects the data more fully than the router alone. Figure 9-6 shows a typical configuration of a screened-host architectural approach.

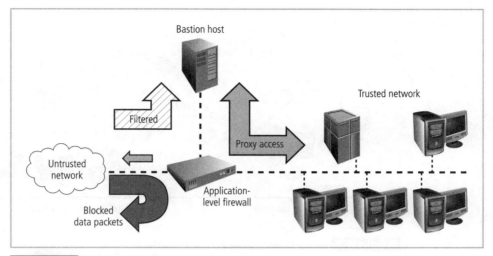

FIGURE 9-6   Screened-Host Firewall

Dual-Homed Host Firewalls

The next step up in firewall architectural complexity is the dual-homed host. In this configuration, the bastion host contains two network interfaces: one that is connected to the external network, and one that is connected to the internal network. All traffic *must* go through the firewall to move between the internal and external networks.

A technology known as **network–address translation (NAT)** is often implemented with this architecture. NAT is a method of converting real, valid, external IP addresses to special ranges of internal IP addresses. It creates a barrier to internal intrusion because these internal addresses cannot be routed over the public network. These special, nonroutable addresses consist of three different ranges:

- Organizations that need very large numbers of local addresses can use the 10.x.x.x range, which has more than 16.5 million usable addresses.
- Organizations that need a moderate number of addresses can use the 192.168.x.x range, which has more than 65,500 addresses.
- Organizations with smaller needs can use the 172.16.0.0 to 172.16.15.0 range, which has approximately 4000 usable addresses.

Taking advantage of NAT prevents external attacks from reaching internal machines with addresses in specified ranges. This type of translation works by dynamically assigning addresses to internal communications and tracking the conversations with sessions to determine which incoming message is a response to which outgoing traffic. Figure 9-7 shows a typical configuration of a dual-homed host firewall that uses NAT and proxy access to protect the internal network.

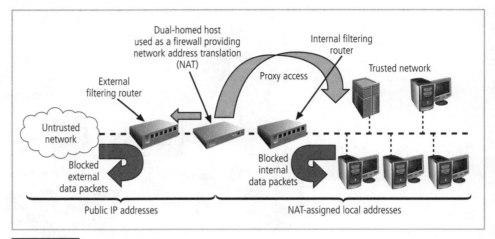

FIGURE 9-7   Dual-Homed Host Firewall

A dual-homed host is able to translate between the protocols of two different data link layers, such as Ethernet, Token Ring, Fiber Distributed Data Interface (FDDI), and asynchronous transfer method (ATM). This approach has two disadvantages, however:

- If the dual-homed host is compromised, it can take out the connection to the external network.
- As traffic volume increases, the dual-homed host can become overloaded.

Overall, however, this architecture provides strong protection with minimal expense compared to more complex solutions.

Screened-Subnet Firewalls (with DMZ)

The screened-subnet firewall consists of one or more internal bastion hosts located behind a packet filtering router, with each host protecting the trusted network. Many variants of the screened-subnet architecture exist. The first general model uses two filtering routers, with one or more dual-homed bastion hosts between them. In the second general model, as illustrated in Figure 9-8, the connections are routed as follows:

- Connections from the outside or untrusted network are routed through an external filtering router.
- Connections from the outside or untrusted network are routed into—and then out of—a routing firewall to the separate network segment known as the DMZ.
- Connections into the trusted internal network are allowed only from the DMZ bastion host servers.

As depicted in Figure 9-8, the screened subnet is an entire network segment that performs two functions: It protects the DMZ systems and information from outside threats, and it protects the internal networks by limiting how external connections can gain access to internal systems. Although extremely secure, the screened subnet can be expensive to implement and complex to configure and manage; the value of the information it protects must justify the cost.

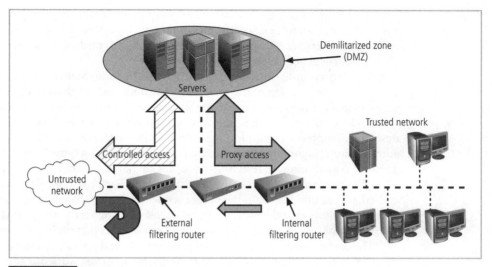

FIGURE 9-8   Screened-Subnet (DMZ)

The screened-subnet firewall architecture provides an intermediate area between the trusted network and the untrusted network—that is, a DMZ. This DMZ can be a dedicated port on the firewall device linking a single bastion host or it can be connected to a screened subnet or DMZ as shown in Figure 9-8. Until recently, servers providing services via the untrusted network were commonly placed in the DMZ. Examples include Web servers, File Transfer Protocol (FTP) servers, and certain database servers. More recent strategies utilizing proxy servers have provided much more secure solutions.

Selecting the Right Firewall

When evaluating a firewall for your networks, you should ask the following questions:[3]

1. What type of firewall technology offers the right balance between protection and cost for the needs of the organization?
2. What features are included in the base price? What features are available at extra cost? Are all cost factors known?
3. How easy is it to set up and configure the firewall? How accessible are the staff technicians who can competently configure the firewall?
4. Can the candidate firewall adapt to the growing network in the target organization?

Question 2 addresses the second most important issue, cost. The cost of a firewall may put a certain make, model, or type out of reach for a particular security solution. As with all security decisions, the budgetary constraints stipulated by management must be taken into account.

Managing Firewalls

Any firewall device—whether a packet filtering router, bastion host, or other firewall implementation—must have its own set of configuration rules that regulate its actions.

With packet filtering firewalls, these rules may be simple statements regulating source and destination addresses, specific protocol or port usage requests, or decisions to allow or deny certain types of requests. In all cases, a policy regarding the use of a firewall should be articulated before it is made operable.

In practice, configuring firewall rule sets can be something of a nightmare. Logic errors in the preparation of the rules can cause unintended behavior, perhaps allowing access instead of denying it, specifying the wrong port or service type, or causing the network to misroute traffic. These and any one of myriad other mistakes can turn a device designed to protect communications into a choke point. For example, a novice firewall administrator might improperly configure a virus screening e-mail gateway (think of it as a type of e-mail firewall), resulting in the blocking of all incoming e-mail, instead of screening only e-mail that contains malicious code. Each firewall rule must be carefully crafted, placed into the list in the proper sequence, debugged, and tested. The proper rule sequence ensures that the most resource-intensive actions are performed after the most restrictive ones, thereby reducing the number of packets that undergo intense scrutiny.

The ever-present balance between performance and restrictions imposed by security practices is very obvious in the use of firewalls. If users can't work due to a security restriction, then the security administration will most likely be told by management to remove the safeguard. Organizations are much more willing to live with a potential risk than certain failure.

Using a computer to protect a computer is fraught with problems that must be managed by careful preparation and continuous evaluation. Automated control systems, including firewalls, for the most part cannot learn from mistakes, and they cannot adapt to changing situations. They are limited by the constraints of their programming and rule sets in the following ways:

- Firewalls are not creative and cannot make sense of human actions outside the range of their programmed responses.

- Firewalls deal strictly with defined patterns of measured observation. These patterns are known to possible attackers and can be used to their benefit in an attack.

- Firewalls are computers themselves and are thus prone to programming errors, flaws in rule sets, and inherent vulnerabilities.

- Firewalls are designed to function within limits of hardware capacity and thus can only respond to patterns of events that happen in an expected and reasonably simultaneous sequence.

- Firewalls are designed, implemented, configured and operated by people and are subject to the expected series of mistakes from human error.[4]

There are also a number of management challenges to administering firewalls:

1. No training. Most managers think of a firewall as just another device, more or less similar to the computers already buzzing in the rack [...] if you get time to read manuals, you are lucky.

2. Firewalls are quite different. You have mastered your firewall and now every new configuration requirement is just a matter of a few clicks in the telnet window; however, the new e-commerce project just brought you a new firewall running on a different OS.

3. Responsible for security. Since you are the firewall guy, suddenly everyone assumes that anything to do with computer security is your responsibility.

4. Daily administration tasks. Being a firewall administrator for a medium or large organization should be a full-time job by itself; however, that's hardly the case.[5]

Some of the best practices for firewall use are described below:[6]

- All traffic from the trusted network is allowed out. This allows members of the organization to access the services they need. Filtering and logging outbound traffic is possible when indicated by specific organizational policy goals.

- The firewall device is never accessible directly from the public network. Almost all access to the firewall device is denied to internal users as well. Only authorized firewall administrators access the device via secure authentication mechanisms, with preference for a method based on cryptographically strong authentication using two-factor access control techniques.

- Simple Mail Transport Protocol (SMTP) data is allowed to pass through the firewall, but all of it should be routed to a well-configured SMTP gateway to securely filter and route messaging traffic.

- All Internet Control Message Protocol (ICMP) data should be denied. Known as the ping service, it is a common method for hacker reconnaissance and should be turned off to prevent snooping.

- Telnet (terminal emulation) access to all internal servers from the public networks should be blocked. At the very least, Telnet access to the organization's Domain Name Service (DNS) server should be blocked to prevent illegal zone transfers, and to prevent hackers from taking down the organization's entire network. If internal users need to reach an organization's network from outside the firewall, use a virtual private network (VPN) client or other secure authentication system to allow this kind of access.

- When Web services are offered outside the firewall, HTTP traffic should be prevented from reaching your internal networks by implementing some form of proxy access or DMZ architecture. That way, if any employees are running Web servers for internal use on their desktops, the services will be invisible to the outside Internet. If your Web server is located behind the firewall, you need to allow HTTP or HTTPS (SHTTP) data through for the Internet at large to view it. The best solution is to place the Web servers containing critical data inside the network and to use proxy services from a DMZ (screened network segment). It is also advisable to restrict incoming HTTP traffic to internal network addresses such that the traffic must be responding to requests originating at internal addresses. This restriction can be accomplished through NAT or firewalls that can support stateful inspection or are directed at the proxy server itself. All other incoming HTTP traffic should be blocked. If the Web servers contain only advertising, they should be placed in the DMZ and rebuilt when (not if) they are compromised.

Good firewall management is based on sound firewall policy. Here are a few policy notes from Charles Cresson Wood on the subject:

Policy Objective and Scope—Firewalls are an essential component of the Company X information systems security infrastructure. Firewalls are defined as security systems that control and restrict network connectivity and network services [...]

Playing the Role of Firewalls—In some instances, systems […] may be functioning as though they are firewalls when they are not formally known as firewalls. All Company X systems playing the role of firewalls, whether they are formally called firewalls, must be managed according to the rules defined in this policy […]

Required Documentation—Prior to the deployment of every Company X firewall, a diagram of permissible paths with a justification for each, and a description of permissible services accompanied by a justification for each, must be submitted to the Information Security manager. […]

Default to Denial—Every connectivity path and service that is not specifically permitted by this policy and supporting documents issued by the Information Security department must be blocked by Company X firewalls. […]

Regular Testing—Because firewalls provide such an important control measure for Company X networks, their strength and proper configuration must be tested on a regular basis. […]

Logs—All changes to firewall configuration parameters, enabled services, and permitted connectivity paths must be logged. […] These logs must be reviewed periodically to ensure that the firewalls are operating in a secure manner.

Intrusion Detection—All Company X firewalls must include intrusion detection systems approved by the Information Security department. […]

Extended User Authentication—Inbound traffic, with the exception of Internet electronic mail, regular news distributions, and push broadcasts previously approved by the Information Security department, that accesses Company X networks through a firewall must in all instances involve extended user authentication measures approved by the Information Security department. Examples of approved extended user authentication systems include dynamic passwords and digital certificates.

Virtual Private Networks—To prevent unauthorized disclosure of sensitive and valuable information, all inbound traffic, with the exception of Internet mail, approved news services, and push broadcasts, that accesses Company X networks must be encrypted with the products approved by the Information Security department […]

Firewall Access Mechanisms—All Company X firewalls must have unique passwords or other access control mechanisms. The same password or access control code must not be used on more than one firewall. […]

Firewall Access Privileges—Privileges to modify the functionality, connectivity, and services supported by firewalls must be restricted to a few technically trained individuals with a business need for these same privileges. […]

Demilitarized Zones—All Internet commerce servers including payment servers, database servers, and web servers must be protected by firewalls, and be located within a demilitarized zone (DMZ), a subnet that is protected from the Internet by one or more firewalls. An internal network, such as an intranet, is also protected from the DMZ subnet by one or more firewalls. […]

Posting Updates—Company X firewalls must be running the latest release of software to repel these attacks. […]

Monitoring Vulnerabilities—Company X staff members responsible for managing firewalls must subscribe the Computer Emergency Response Team advisories and other relevant sources providing current information about firewall vulnerabilities. Any vulnerability that appears to affect Company X networks and systems must promptly be brought to the attention of the Information Security department. [...]

Firewall Physical Security—All Company X firewalls must be located in locked rooms accessible only to those who perform authorized firewall management and maintenance tasks approved by the Information Technology department management [...].[7]

Dial-Up Protection

Before the Internet emerged as a public network, organizations created private networks and allowed individuals and other organizations to connect to them using dial-up or leased-line connections. In the current networking environment, firewalls are used to safeguard the connection between an organization and its Internet (public network) connection. The equivalent level of protection has always been and continues to be needed to protect connections among private networks. While internal network connections via private networks are now less popular due to the high cost of installation, maintenance, and protection, dial-up connections remain quite common.

It is a widely held view that unsecured dial-up access represents a substantial exposure to attack. An attacker who suspects that an organization has dial-up lines can use a device called a **war-dialer** to locate the connection points. A war-dialer is an automatic phone-dialing program that dials every number in a configured range (e.g., 555-1000 to 555-2000), and checks whether a person, answering machine, or modem picks up. If a modem answers, the war-dialer program makes a note of the number and then moves to the next target number. The attacker then returns at a later time and attempts to hack into the network through the identified modem connection using a variety of techniques.

Network connectivity using dial-up connections is usually much simpler and less sophisticated than Internet connections. For the most part, simple user name and password schemes are the only means of authentication. Some newer technologies have improved this process, including RADIUS systems, Challenge Handshake Authentication Protocol (CHAP) systems, and even systems that use strong encryption. The most prominent of these approaches are RADIUS and TACACS.

RADIUS and TACACS

RADIUS and TACACS are systems that authenticate the credentials of users who are trying to access an organization's network via a dial-up connection.

Typical dial-up systems place the responsibility for the authentication of users on the system directly connected to the modems. If the dial-up system includes multiple points of entry, such an authentication scheme is difficult to manage. The **Remote Authentication Dial-In User Service (RADIUS)** system centralizes the management of user authentication by placing the responsibility for authenticating each user in the central RADIUS server. When a remote access server (RAS) receives a request for a network connection from a dial-up client, it passes the request along with the user's credentials to the RADIUS server. RADIUS then validates the credentials and passes the resulting decision (accept or deny) back to the accepting RAS. Figure 9-9 shows the typical configuration of a Microsoft Remote Access Server (RAS) system making use of RADIUS authentication.

1. Remote worker dials RAS and submits username and password.
2. RAS passes user name and password to RADIUS server.
3. RADIUS server approves or rejects request and provides access authorization.
4. RAS provides access to authorized remote worker.

FIGURE 9-9 RADIUS Configuration

Similar in function to the RADIUS system is the **Terminal Access Controller Access Control System (TACACS)**. This remote access authorization system is based on a client/server configuration. It makes use of a centralized data service, such as the one provided by a RADIUS server, and validates the user's credentials at the TACACS server. Three versions of TACACS exist: TACACS, Extended TACACS, and TACACS+. The original version combines authentication and authorization services. The extended version authenticates and authorizes in two separate steps, and records the access attempt and the requestor's identity. The plus version uses dynamic passwords and incorporates two-factor authentication.[8]

Managing Dial-Up Connections

Many organizations that once operated large dial-up access pools are now reducing the number of telephone lines they support, in favor of Internet access secured by VPNs. Organizations that offer VPN technology face other issues, which are covered later in this chapter in the section on cryptography.

Organizations that continue to offer dial-up remote access must deal with a number of thorny issues:

- Determine how many dial-up connections the organization has. Many organizations don't even realize they have dial-up access, or they leave telephone connections in place long after they have stopped fully using them. This creates two potential problems: (1) The organization continues to pay for telecommunications circuits it is not using; and (2) these circuits may remain connected, permitting unmonitored access to your networks. For example, an employee may have installed a modem on an office computer to do a little telecommuting without management's knowledge. The organization should scan its internal phone networks periodically with special software to detect available connections. It should also integrate risk assessment and risk approval into the telephone service ordering process.

■ Control access to authorized modem numbers. Only those authorized to use dial-up access should be allowed to use incoming connections. Furthermore, although there is no security in obscurity, the numbers should not be widely distributed and the dial-up numbers should be considered confidential.

■ Use call-back whenever possible. Call-back requires an access requestor to be at a preconfigured location, which is essential for authorized telecommuting. Users call into the access computer, which disconnects and immediately calls the requestor back. If the caller is an authorized user at the preconfigured number, the caller can then connect. This solution is not so useful for traveling users, however.

■ Use token authentication if at all possible. Users can be required to enter more than user names and passwords, which is essential when allowing dial-up access from laptops and other remote computers. In this scheme, the device accepts an input number, often provided by the computer from which access is requested, and provides a response based on an internal algorithm. The result is much stronger security.

Intrusion Detection Systems

Information security **intrusion detection systems (IDSs)** work like burglar alarms. When the alarm detects a violation of its configuration (such as an opened or broken window), it activates the alarm. This alarm can be audible and visible (noise and lights), or it can be a silent alarm that sends a message to a monitoring company. With almost all IDSs, administrators can choose the configuration and alarm levels. Many IDSs can be configured to notify administrators via e-mail and numerical or text paging. The systems can also be configured to notify an external information security service organization, just as burglar alarms do. Like firewall systems, IDSs require complex configurations to provide the level of detection and response desired. These systems are either network based to protect network information assets, or host based to protect server or host information assets. IDSs use one of two detection methods: signature based or statistical anomaly based. Figure 9-10 depicts two typical approaches to intrusion detection where IDSs are used to monitor both network connection activity and current information states on host servers.

Host IDS: Examines the data in files stored on the host
and alerts systems administrators to any changes

External router

Untrusted
network

Header

Network IDS: Examines packets on the network
and alerts systems administrators to unusual patterns

FIGURE 9-10   Intrusion Detection Systems

Host-Based IDS

A **host-based IDS** works by configuring and classifying various categories of systems and
data files. In many cases, IDSs provide only a few general levels of alert notification. For
example, an administrator might configure an IDS to report changes to certain folders,
such as system folders (e.g., C:\Windows or C:\WINNT), security-related applications
(C:\TripWire), or critical data folders; at the same time, the IDS might be instructed to
ignore changes to other files (e.g., C:\Program Files\Office). Administrators might configure the system to instantly page or e-mail them for high-priority alerts but to simply
record other lower-priority activity. Most administrators are concerned only if unauthorized changes occur in sensitive areas. After all, applications frequently modify their internal files, such as dictionaries and configuration templates, and users constantly update
their data files. Unless the IDS is very precisely configured, these benign actions can generate a large volume of false alarms. Some organizations will use a variable degree of
reporting and recording detail. During times of routine operation, the system will provide alerting only for a few urgent reasons and recording only for exceptions. During
periods of increased threat, however, it may send alerts on suspicious activity and record
all activity for later analysis.

Host-based IDSs can monitor multiple computers simultaneously. They do so by
storing a client file on each monitored host and then making that host report back to the
master console, which is usually located on the system administrator's computer. This
master console monitors the information from the managed clients and notifies the
administrator when predetermined attack conditions occur.

Network-Based IDS

In contrast to host-based IDSs, which reside on a host (or hosts) and monitor only activities on the host, **network-based IDSs** monitor network traffic. When a predefined condition occurs, the network-based IDS notifies the appropriate administrator. Whereas host-based IDSs look for changes in file attributes (create, modify, delete), the network-based IDS looks for patterns of network traffic, such as large collections of related traffic that can indicate a denial-of-service attack or a series of related packets that could indicate a port scan in progress. Consequently, network IDSs require a much more complex configuration and maintenance program than do host-based IDSs. Network IDSs must match known and unknown attack strategies against their knowledge base to determine whether an attack has occurred. These systems yield many more false-positive readings than do host-based IDSs, because they are attempting to read the network activity pattern to determine what is normal and what is not.

Signature-Based IDS

IDSs that use signature-based methods work like antivirus software. In fact, antivirus software can be classified as a form of signature-based IDS. A **signature-based IDS** or **knowledge-based IDS** examines data traffic for something that matches the signatures, which comprise preconfigured, predetermined attack patterns. The problem with this approach is that the signatures must be continually updated, as new attack strategies emerge. Failure to stay current allows attacks using new strategies to succeed. Another weakness of this method is the time frame over which attacks occur. If attackers are slow and methodical, they may slip undetected through the IDS, as their actions may not match a signature that includes factors based on duration of the events. The only way to resolve this dilemma is to collect and analyze data over longer periods of time, which requires substantially larger data storage ability and additional processing capacity.

Statistical Anomaly-Based IDS

Another popular type of IDS is the **statistical anomaly-based IDS (stat IDS)** or **behavior-based IDS**. The stat IDS first collects data from normal traffic and establishes a baseline. It then periodically samples network activity, based on statistical methods, and compares the samples to the baseline. When the activity falls outside the baseline parameters (known as the **clipping level**), the IDS notifies the administrator. The baseline variables can include a host's memory or CPU usage, network packet types, and packet quantities.

The advantage of this approach is that the system is able to detect new types of attacks, because it looks for abnormal activity of any type. Unfortunately, these IDSs require much more overhead and processing capacity than do signature-based versions, because they must constantly attempt to pattern matched activity to the baseline. In addition, they may not detect minor changes to system variables and may generate many false-positive warnings. If the actions of the users or systems on the network vary widely, with unpredictable periods of low and high activity levels, this type of IDS may not be suitable, as dramatic swings from one level to another will almost certainly generate false alarms. As a result, this type of IDS is less commonly used than the signature-based approach.

Managing Intrusion Detection Systems

Just as with any alarm system, if there is no response to an alert, then an alarm does no good. An IDS does not remove or deny access to a system by default and, unless it is programmed to take an action, merely records the events that trigger it. IDSs must be configured using technical knowledge and adequate business and security knowledge to differentiate between routine circumstances and low, moderate, or severe threats to the security of the organization's information assets.

A properly configured IDS can translate a security alert into different types of notification—for example, log entries for low-level alerts, e-mails for moderate-level alerts, and text messages or paging for severe alerts. Some organizations may choose to configure systems to automatically take action in response to IDS alerts, although this technique should be carefully considered and undertaken only by organizations with experienced staff and well-constructed information security procedures. A poorly configured IDS may yield either information overload—causing the IDS administrator to shut off the pager—or failure to detect an actual attack. When a system is configured to take unsupervised action without obtaining human approval first, then the organization must be prepared to take accountability for these IDS actions.

Also, note that the human response to false alarm can lead to behavior that can be exploited by attackers. For example, consider the following tactic:

One possible car theft strategy exploits human intolerance for technological glitches that cause false alarms. In the early morning hours—say, 2:00 A.M.—a thief deliberately sets off the target car alarm, and then retreats to a safe distance. The owner comes out, resets the alarm, and goes back to bed. Twenty to thirty minutes later, the thief does it again, and then again. After the third or fourth time, the owner assumes that the alarm is faulty and turns it off, leaving the vehicle unprotected. The thief is then free to steal the car without having to deal with the now disabled alarm.

Most IDSs monitor systems by means of agents. An **agent** is a piece of software that resides on a system and reports back to a management server. If this piece of software is not properly configured and does not use a secure transmission channel to communicate with its manager, then an attacker could compromise and subsequently exploit the agent or the information from the agent.

A valuable tool in managing an IDS is the consolidated enterprise manager. This software allows the security professional to collect data from multiple host- and network-based IDSs and look for patterns across systems and subnetworks. An attacker might potentially probe one network segment or computer host, and then move on to another target before the first system's IDS caught on. The centralized manager not only collects responses from all IDSs, thereby providing one central monitoring station, but also can be used to identify these cross-system probes and intrusions.

Scanning and Analysis Tools

Although not always perceived as defensive tools, scanners, sniffers, and other analysis tools can enable security administrators to see what an attacker sees. Scanner and analysis tools can find vulnerabilities in systems, holes in security components, and other unsecured aspects of the network. Unfortunately, they cannot detect the unpredictable behavior of people.

Some of these devices are extremely complex; others are very simple. Some are expensive commercial products; others are available for free from their creators. Conscientious administrators will have several hacking Web sites bookmarked, and should frequently browse for discussion of new vulnerabilities, recent conquests, and favorite assault techniques. This activity can also enable them to discover the best tools for identifying weaknesses in security defenses. There is nothing wrong with security administrators using the tools used by hackers to examine their own defenses and search out areas of vulnerability. A word of caution is in order, however: Many of these tools have distinct signatures, and some ISPs scan for these signatures. If the ISP discovers someone using hacker tools, it may choose to deny access to that customer and discontinue service. It's best to establish a working relationship with the ISP and notify it before using such tools.

Scanning tools collect the information that an attacker needs to succeed. Collecting information about a potential target is known as footprinting. **Footprinting** is the organized research of the Internet addresses owned or controlled by a target organization. Attackers may use public Internet data sources to perform keyword searches to identify the network addresses of the organization. They may also use the organization's Web page to find information that can be used in social engineering attacks. For example, the Reveal Source option on most popular Web browsers allows users to see the source code behind the graphics on a Web page. A number of clues can provide additional insight into the configuration of an internal network: the locations and directories for Common Gateway Interface (CGI) script bins, and the names or possibly addresses of computers and servers.

A scanner can be used to augment the data collected by a common browser. A Web scanner, such as Sam Spade (www.samspade.org), can scan entire Web sites for valuable information, such as server names and e-mail addresses. It can also do a number of other common information collection activities, such as sending multiple ICMP information requests (pings), attempting to retrieve multiple and cross-zoned DNS queries, and performing common network analysis queries—all powerful diagnostic and/or hacking activities. Sam Spade is not usually considered to be hackerware (or hacker-oriented software), but rather is a useful utility for network administrator and potential attackers alike.

The next phase of the pre-attack data gathering process, **fingerprinting**, entails the systematic examination of all of the organization's Internet addresses (collected during the footprinting phase). By means of the tools described in the following section, fingerprinting yields a detailed network analysis that reveals useful information about the targets of the planned attack. Note that the tool discussions here are necessarily brief; readers who want to attain true expertise in the use and configuration of these tools will require more specific education and training.

Port Scanners

Port scanning utilities (or **port scanners**) can identify (or fingerprint) computers that are active on a network, as well as the active ports and services on those computers, the functions and roles fulfilled by the machines, and other useful information. These tools can scan for specific types of computers, protocols, or resources, or they can launch generic scans. It is helpful to understand the environment that exists on and in the network you are using, so that you can select the best tool for the job. The more specific the scanner is, the more detailed and useful the information it provides. However, you should keep a generic, broad-based scanner in your toolbox as well, to help locate and identify rogue nodes on the network of which administrators may not be aware.

A **port** is a network channel or connection point in a data communications system. Within the TCP/IP networking protocol, TCP and User Datagram Protocol (UDP) port numbers differentiate among the multiple communication channels used to connect to network services that are offered on the same network device.[9] Each service within the TCP/IP protocol suite has either a unique default port number or a user-selected port number. Table 9-4 shows some of the commonly used port numbers. In total, there are 65,536 port numbers in use. The well-known ports are those from 0 through 1023. The registered ports are those from 1024 through 49151, and the dynamic and private ports are those from 49152 through 65535.

Table 9-4 Commonly Used Port Numbers

Port Numbers	Description
20 and 21	File Transfer Protocol (FTP)
25	Simple Mail Transfer Protocol (SMTP)
53	Domain Name Services (DNS)
67 and 68	Dynamic Host Configuration Protocol (DHCP)
80	Hypertext Transfer Protocol (HTTP)
110	Post Office Protocol (POP3)
161	Simple Network Management Protocol (SNMP)
194	IRC Chat port (used for device sharing)
443	HTTP over SSL
8080	Proxy services

The first order of business in securing a system is to secure open ports. Why? Simply put, an **open port** can be used to send commands to a computer, gain access to a server, and exert control over a networking device. As a general rule, you should secure all ports, and remove from service any ports not required for essential functions. For instance, if an organization doesn't host Web services, there is no need for port 80 to be available in its network or on its servers.

Vulnerability Scanners

Vulnerability scanners, which are variants of port scanners, are capable of scanning networks for very detailed information. As a class, they identify exposed user names and groups, show open network shares, and expose configuration problems and other server vulnerabilities. An example of a vulnerability scanner is Nmap, a professional freeware utility available from www.insecure.org/nmap. Nmap identifies the systems available on a network, the services (ports) each system is offering, the operating system and operating system version they are running, the type of packet filters and firewalls in use, and dozens of other characteristics. LANguard Network Scanner is another example of a vulnerability scanner. Several commercial products are offered in this area as well, including products from ISS, Inc. and NetIQ, Inc.

Packet Sniffers

A **packet sniffer** is a network tool that collects and analyzes copies of packets from the network. It can provide a network administrator with valuable information to diagnose and resolve networking issues. In the wrong hands, it can be used to eavesdrop on network traffic. The commercially available and open-source sniffers include Sniffer (a commercial product) and Snort (open-source software). An excellent free network protocol analyzer is Ethereal (www.ethereal.com), which allows the administrator to examine both live network traffic and previously captured data. Ethereal offers a variety of features, including a language filter and TCP session reconstruction utility.

Typically, to use a packet sniffer most effectively, you must be connected directly to a local network from an internal location. Simply tapping into any public Internet connection will flood you with more data than you can process, and technically constitutes a violation of wiretapping laws. To use a packet sniffer legally, you must satisfy the following criteria: (1) be on a network that the organization owns, not leases; (2) be under the direct authorization of the network's owners; (3) have the knowledge and consent of the content creators (users); and (4) have a justifiable business reason for doing so. If all four conditions are met, the administrator can selectively collect and analyze packets to identify and diagnose problems on the network. Conditions 1 and 2 are self-explanatory, and condition 3 is usually a stipulation for using the company network. Incidentally, these conditions are the same requirements for employee monitoring in general.

Content Filters

Another type of tool that effectively protects the organization's systems from misuse and unintentional denial-of-service conditions is the **content filter**. Technically not a firewall, a content filter is a software program or a hardware/software appliance that allows administrators to restrict content that comes into a network. The most common application of a content filter is the restriction of access to Web sites with non–business-related material, such as pornography or entertainment. Another application is the restriction of spam e-mail from outside sources. Content filters can consist of small add-on software for the home or office, such as NetNanny or SurfControl, or major corporate applications, such as Novell's Border Manager.

Content filters ensure that employees are not using network resources inappropriately. Unfortunately, these systems require extensive configuration and constant updating of the list of unacceptable destinations or incoming restricted e-mail source addresses. Some newer content filtering applications come with a service consisting of downloadable files that update the restricted database automatically, similar to an antivirus program. These applications work by matching either a list of disapproved or approved Web sites, for example, and by matching key content words, such as "nude" and "sex." Content creators, of course, are working to bypass such restrictions by suppressing these trip words, creating additional problems for networking and security professionals.

Trap and Trace

Another set of technologies, known as trap and trace applications, is growing in popularity. Trap function describes software designed to entice individuals who are illegally perusing the internal areas of a network. These individuals either discover directly or find indicators of rich content areas on the network, which are actually set up exclusively to attract potential attackers. Better known as **honey pots**, these directories or servers distract the attacker while the software notifies the administrator of the intrusion.

The newest accompaniment to the trap is the trace. Similar in concept to the Caller ID service used with telephones, the *trace is* a process by which the organization attempts to determine the identity of someone discovered in unauthorized areas of the network or systems. If this individual is someone within the organization, administrators should follow the organization's policies in this area and report the intruder to the appropriate internal or external authorities. If the identified individual is outside the security perimeter, then policy will guide the process of escalation to law enforcement or civil authorities.

The most popular professional software suites for this type of functionality are ManTrap and ManHunt, from Recourse Technologies (www.recourse.com). ManTrap, a honey pot application, presents a virtual network running from a single server. The Man-Hunt IDS includes a TrackBack function, which traces a detected intruder as far as the administrator wishes, usually to an administrative boundary. This technology makes it possible to coordinate with an ISP that has similar technology and to hand off a trace to the upstream provider. By enabling the trace to traverse the administrative boundary at the ISP connection point, the ISP could be entitled to take action where the organization cannot.

Managing Scanning and Analysis Tools

It is vitally important that the security manager be able to see the organization's systems and networks from the viewpoint of potential attackers. Therefore the security manager should develop a program using in-house resources, contractors, or an outsourced service provider, to periodically scan his or her own systems and networks for vulnerabilities with the same tools that an typical hacker might use.

There are a number of drawbacks to using scanners and analysis tools, content filters, and trap and trace tools:

■ These tools are not human and thus cannot simulate the more creative behavior of a human attacker.

■ Most tools function by pattern recognition, so only previously known issues can be detected. New approaches, modifications to well-known attack patterns, and the randomness of human behavior can allow them to misdiagnose the situation, thereby allowing vulnerabilities to go undetected or threats to go unchallenged.

■ Most of these tools are computer-based software or hardware, and so are prone to errors, flaws, and vulnerabilities of their own.

■ All of these tools are designed, configured, and operated by humans and are subject to human errors.[10]

■ The old adage applies: You get what you pay for. Use of hackerware may actually infect a system with a virus, or open the system to outside attacks or other unintended consequences. Always view a hacker kit skeptically before using it in any way and especially before connecting it to the Internet. Never put anything valuable on the computer that houses the hacker tools. Consider segregating it from other network segments and disconnect it from the network when not in use.

■ Some governments, agencies, institutions, and universities have established policies or laws that protect the individual user's right to access content, especially if it is necessary for the conduct of his or her job. There are also situations where an entire class of content has been proscribed and mere possession of that content is a criminal act, specifically child pornography.

- Tool usage and configuration must comply with an explicitly articulated policy, and the policy must provide for valid exceptions. This mandate prevents administrators from becoming arbiters of morality as they create a filter rule set.

Cryptography

Although not a specific application or security tool, cryptography represents a sophisticated element of control that is often included in other information security controls. In fact, many security-related tools use embedded encryption technologies to protect sensitive information. The use of the proper cryptographic tools can ensure confidentiality by keeping private information concealed from those who do not need to see it. Other cryptographic methods can provide increased information integrity by providing a mechanism to guarantee that a message in transit has not been altered by using a process that creates a secure message digest, or hash. In e-commerce situations, some cryptographic tools can be used to assure that parties to the transaction are authentic, so that they cannot later deny having participated in a transaction, a feature often called nonrepudiation.

Encryption is the process of converting an original message into a form that cannot be understood by unauthorized individuals. That way, anyone without the tools and knowledge to convert an encrypted message back to its original format will be unable to interpret it. The science of encryption, known as **cryptology**, actually encompasses two disciplines: cryptography and cryptanalysis. **Cryptography**—from the Greek words *kryptos,* meaning "hidden," and *graphein,* meaning "to write"—describes the processes involved in encoding and decoding messages so that others cannot understand them. **Cryptanalysis**—from *analyein,* meaning "to break up"—is the process of deciphering the original message (or **plaintext**) from an encrypted message (or **ciphertext**), without knowing the algorithms and keys used to perform the encryption.

Cryptology is a very complex field based on advanced mathematical concepts. The following sections provide a brief overview of the foundations of encryption and a short discussion of some of the related issues and tools in the field of information security. Those students who would like more information about cryptography should seek out two books by Bruce Schneier: *Applied Cryptography: Protocols, Algorithms, and Source Code in C,* which provides a technical tutorial in the discipline, and *Secrets and Lies: Digital Security in a Networked World,* which discusses many of the theoretical and practical considerations in the use of cryptographic systems.

Encryption Definitions

You can better understand the tools and functions popular in encryption security solutions if you know some basic terminology:

- Algorithm: The mathematical formula or method used to convert an unencrypted message into an encrypted message
- Cipher: The transformation of the individual components (characters, bytes, or bits) of an unencrypted message into encrypted components

- Ciphertext or cryptogram: The unintelligible encrypted or encoded message resulting from an encryption
- Cryptosystem: The set of transformations necessary to convert an unencrypted message into an encrypted message
- Decipher: To decrypt or convert ciphertext to plaintext
- Encipher: To encrypt or convert plaintext to ciphertext
- Key: The information used in conjunction with the algorithm to create the ciphertext from the plaintext; it can be a series of bits used in a mathematical algorithm, or the knowledge of how to manipulate the plaintext
- Keyspace: The entire range of values that can possibly be used to construct an individual key
- Plaintext: The original unencrypted message that is encrypted and results from successful decryption
- Steganography: The process of hiding messages; for example, if messages are hidden within the digital encoding of a picture or graphic, it becomes almost impossible to detect that the hidden message even exists
- Work factor: The amount of effort (usually expressed in units of time) required to perform cryptanalysis on an encoded message

Encryption Operations

Encryption is accomplished by using algorithms to manipulate the plaintext into the ciphertext for transmission. Some widely used encryption operations are explained in the sections that follow.

Common Ciphers

In encryption the most commonly used algorithms include three functions: substitution, transposition, and XOR. In a **substitution cipher**, you substitute one value for another. For example, using the line labeled "input text," you can substitute the message character with the character three values to the right in the alphabet by looking at the aligned text in the line labeled "output text."

Input text:	ABCDEFGHIJKLMNOPQRSTUVWXYZ
Output text:	DEFGHIJKLMNOPQRSTUVWXYZABC

Thus a plaintext of BERLIN becomes EHUOLQ.

This is a simple enough method by itself, but it becomes very powerful if combined with other operations. Incidentally, this type of substitution is based on a **monoalphabetic substitution**, as it uses only one alphabet. More advanced substitution ciphers use two or more alphabets, and are referred to as **polyalphabetic substitutions**. To continue the previous example, consider the following block of text:

Input text:	ABCDEFGHIJKLMNOPQRSTUVWXYZ
Substitution cipher 1:	DEFGHIJKLMNOPQRSTUVWXYZABC
Substitution cipher 2:	GHIJKLMNOPQRSTUVWXYZABCDEF
Substitution cipher 3:	JKLMNOPQRSTUVWXYZABCDEFGHI
Substitution cipher 4:	MNOPQRSTUVWXYZABCDEFGHIJKL

In this example, the plaintext is matched character by character to the input text row. The next four lines are four sets of substitution ciphers. In this example, you can encode the word TEXT as WKGF, as you select letters from the second row for the first letter, letters from the third row for the second letter, and so on. This type of encryption would be substantially more difficult to decipher without the algorithm (rows of ciphers) and key (use of the second row for the first letter, the third row for the second letter, and so on). It is also easy to completely randomize the cipher rows to create more complex substitution operations.

Another simple example of the substitution cipher is the daily cryptogram in your local newspaper, or the well-known Little Orphan Annie decoder ring. Julius Caesar reportedly used a three-character shift to the right (using the Roman alphabet), in which A becomes D and so on, giving that particular substitution cipher his name—the Caesar cipher.

Like the substitution operation, transposition is simple to understand but can be complex to decipher if properly used. Unlike the substitution cipher, the **transposition cipher** (or **permutation cipher**) simply rearranges the values within a block to create the ciphertext. This can be done at the bit level or at the byte (character) level. Here is an example:

Plaintext: 001001010110101110010101010101001001
Key: $1 \to 3, 2 \to 6, 3 \to 8, 4 \to 1, 5 \to 4, 6 \to 7, 7 \to 5, 8 \to 2$

(Read as bit 1 moves to position 4, and so on, with bit position 1 being the rightmost bit.)

The following shows the plaintext broken into 8-bit blocks (for ease of discussion) and the corresponding ciphertext, based on the application of the preceding key to the plaintext:

Plaintext 8-bit blocks:	00100101	01101011	10010101	01010100
Ciphertext:	11000100	01110101	10001110	10011000

To make this easier to follow, consider the following example in character transposition:

Plaintext: MY DOG HAS FLEAS. (Spaces count as characters.)
Key: Same key as above but characters are transposed, rather than bits. (Note that spaces are transposed as well.)

Plaintext 8-character blocks:	MY DOG H	AS FLEAS
Ciphertext:	G YDHMO	E ASFSAL

Transposition ciphers and substitution ciphers can be used together in multiple combinations to create a very secure encryption process. To make the encryption stronger (more difficult to cryptanalyze), the keys and block sizes can be made much larger (64 bit or 128 bit), resulting in substantially more complex substitutions or transpositions.

In the **XOR cipher conversion**, the bit stream is subjected to a Boolean XOR function against some other data stream, typically a key stream. Two symbols commonly used to represent the XOR function are " ∧ " and " $\otimes$ ". XOR works as follows:

'0' XOR'ed with '0' results in a '0'. ($0 \otimes 0 = 0$)
'0' XOR'ed with '1' results in a '1'. ($0 \otimes 1 = 1$)
'1' XOR'ed with '0' results in a '1'. ($1 \otimes 0 = 1$)
'1' XOR'ed with '1' results in a '0'. ($1 \otimes 1 = 0$)

Simply put, if the two values are the same, you get "0"; if not, you get "1". Suppose you have a data stream in which the first byte is 01000001. If you have a key stream in which the first "byte" is '0101 1010', and you XOR them:

'0100 0001'   Plaintext

$\otimes$ '0101 1010'   Key stream

'0001 1011'   Ciphertext

This process is reversible. That is, if you XOR the ciphertext with the key stream, you get the plaintext.

Vernam Cipher

Also known as the one-time pad, the Vernam cipher was developed at AT&T and uses a set of characters that are used for encryption operations only one time and then discarded. The values from this one-time pad are added to the block of text, and the resulting sum is converted to text. When the two sets of values are added, if the resulting values exceed 26, 26 is subtracted from the total (a process called modulo 26). The corresponding results are then converted back to text. The following example demonstrates how the Vernam cipher works:

Plaintext:	MYDOGHASFLEAS
Corresponding values:	13 25 04 15 07 08 01 19 06 12 05 01 19
One-time pad:	F P Q R N S B I E H T Z L
Pad corresponding values:	6 16 17 18 14 19 2 9 5 8 20 26 12

Results

Plaintext:	13	25	4	15	7	8	1	19	6	12	5	1	19
One-time pad:	6	16	17	18	14	19	2	9	5	8	20	26	12
Sum:	19	41	21	33	21	27	3	28	11	20	25	27	31
Subtraction (modulo 26):		15		7		1		2				1	5
Ciphertext:	P	O	U	G	U	A	C	B	K	T	Y	A	E

Book or Running Key Cipher

Another method, used in the occasional spy movie, is the use of text in a book as the algorithm to decrypt a message. The key relies on two components: (1) knowing which book to use, and (2) a list of codes representing the page number, line number, and word number of the plaintext word. For example, using a copy of a particular popular novel, one might send the following message: 67,3,1;145,9,4;375,7,4;394,17,3. Dictionaries and thesauruses are the most popular sources as they provide every needed word, although almost any book will suffice. If the receiver knows which book is used for the preceding example, he or she goes to page 67, line 3, and selects the first word from that line; then goes to page 145, line 9, and uses the fourth word; and so forth. The resulting message `cancel operation target compromised` can then be deciphered. When using dictionaries, it is necessary to use only a page and word number. An even more sophisticated version of this cipher can use multiple books, with a new book in a particular sequence for each word or phrase.

Symmetric Encryption

Each of the methods of encryption and decryption described above requires the same algorithm and key are used to both encipher and decipher the message. This is known as **private key encryption**, or **symmetric encryption**. In this approach to encryption, the same key—a **secret key**—is used to encrypt and decrypt the message. Symmetric encryption methods are usually extremely efficient, requiring easily accomplished processing to encrypt or decrypt the message. The problem is that both the sender and the receiver must possess the encryption key. Of course, if either copy of the key becomes compromised, an intermediary can decrypt and read the messages. One challenge in symmetric key encryption is getting a copy of the key to the receiver, a process that must be conducted out-of-band (meaning through an alternate channel or band rather than the one carrying the ciphertext) to avoid interception. Figure 9-11 illustrates the concept of symmetric encryption.

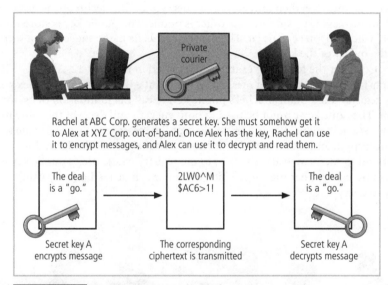

FIGURE 9-11   Symmetric Encryption

A number of popular symmetric encryption cryptosystems are available. One of the most familiar is Data Encryption Standard (DES). DES was developed in 1977 by IBM and is based on the Data Encryption Algorithm (DEA), which uses a 64-bit block size and a 56-bit key. With a 56-bit key, the algorithm has 2^{56} (more than 72 quadrillion) possible keys.

DES is a federally approved standard for nonclassified data (see Federal Information Processing Standards Publication 46-2). It was cracked in 1997 when the developers of a new algorithm, Rivest-Shamir-Aldeman (RSA, which you will learn about later in this chapter) offered a $10,000 reward for the first person or team to crack the algorithm. Fourteen thousand users collaborated over the Internet to finally break the encryption. **Triple DES (3DES)** was developed as an improvement to DES and uses as many as three keys in succession. It is substantially more secure than DES, not only because it uses as many as three keys instead of one, but also because it performs three different encryption operations.

The successor to 3DES is **Advanced Encryption Standard** (**AES**). It is based on the Rinjndael Block Cipher, which features a variable block length and a key length of either 128, 192, or 256 bits. In 1998, it took a special computer designed by the Electronic Freedom Frontier (www.eff.org) more than 56 hours to crack DES. It would take the same computer approximately 4,698,864 quintillion years (4,698,864,000,000,000,000,000) to crack AES.

Asymmetric Encryption

Another category of encryption techniques is **asymmetric encryption**, also known as **public key encryption**. Whereas symmetric encryption systems are based on a single key to both encrypt and decrypt a message, asymmetric encryption uses two different keys. Either key can be used to encrypt or decrypt the message. However, if Key A is used to encrypt the message, then only Key B can decrypt it; conversely, if Key B is used to encrypt a message, then only Key A can decrypt it. This technique is most valuable when one of the keys is private and the other is public. The public key is stored in a public location, where anyone can use it. The private key, as its name suggests, is a secret known only to the owner of the key pair.

Consider the following example, illustrated in Figure 9-12. Alex at XYZ Corporation wants to send an encrypted message to Rachel at ABC Corporation. Alex goes to a public key registry and obtains Rachel's public key. Recall the foundation of asymmetric encryption: The same key cannot be used to both encrypt and decrypt the same message. Thus, when Rachel's public key is used to encrypt the message, only her private key can be used to decrypt it, and that private key is held by Rachel alone. Similarly, if Rachel wishes to respond to Alex's message, she goes to the registry where Alex's public key is held and uses it to encrypt her message, which of course can be read only by using Alex's private key to decrypt it.

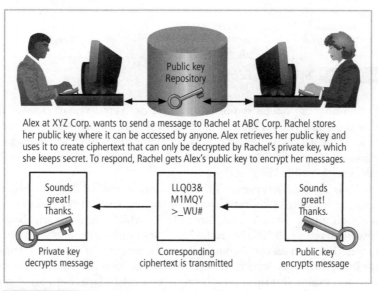

FIGURE 9-12   Public Key Encryption

The problem with asymmetric encryption is that it requires four keys to hold a single conversation between two parties. If four organizations want to frequently exchange messages, each must manage its private key and four public keys. It can be confusing to determine which public key is needed to encrypt a particular message. With more organizations in the loop, the problem grows. Also, asymmetric encryption is not as efficient in its use of CPU resources as symmetric encryptions when performing the extensive mathematical calculations. As a result, the hybrid system described in the section "Public Key Infrastructure" (later in this chapter) is more commonly used.

Digital Signatures

When the asymmetric process is reversed—the private key encrypts a (usually short) message, and the public key decrypts it—the fact that the message was sent by the organization that owns the private key cannot be refuted. This **nonrepudiation** is the foundation of digital signatures. **Digital signatures** are encrypted messages that are independently verified by a central facility (registry) as authentic. They are often used in Internet software updates (see Figure 9-13). The pop-up window shows that the downloaded files did, in fact, come from the purported agency and thus can be trusted. A **digital certificate** is an electronic document, similar to a digital signature, attached to a file certifying that the file is from the organization it claims to be from and has not been modified from the original format. A **certificate authority (CA)** is an agency that manages the issuance of certificates and serves as the electronic notary public to verify their origin and integrity.

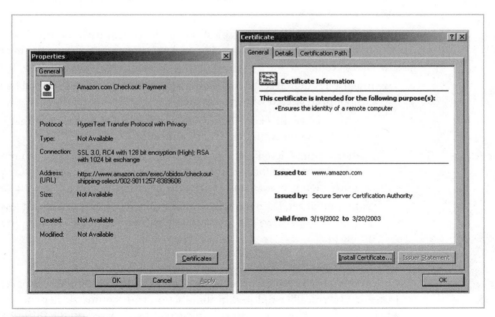

FIGURE 9-13 Digital Signature

RSA

One of the most popular public key cryptosystems is a proprietary model known as RSA. (RSA stands for Rivest-Shamir-Aldeman, the surnames of its developers.) It is the first public key encryption algorithm developed for commercial use. RSA is very popular and has been integrated into both Microsoft Internet Explorer and Netscape Navigator. A number of extensions to the RSA algorithm exist, including RSA Encryption Scheme— Optimal Asymmetric Encryption Padding (RSAES-OAEP) and RSA Signature Scheme with Appendix—Probabilistic Signature Scheme (RSASSA-PSS).

Public Key Infrastructure

A public key infrastructure (PKI) is the entire set of hardware, software, and cryptosystems necessary to implement public key encryption. PKI systems are based on public key cryptosystems and include digital certificates and certificate authorities. Common implementations of PKI include the following:

- Systems to issue digital certificates to users and servers
- Encryption enrollment
- Key-issuing systems
- Tools for managing the key issuance
- Verification and return of certificates
- Key revocation services
- Other services that specific vendors may choose to bundle into the product that are associated with PKI

The use of cryptographic tools is made more manageable when using PKI. PKI can increase the capabilities of an organization in protecting its information assets by providing the following services:[11]

- Authentication: Digital certificates in a PKI system permit individuals, organizations, and Web servers to authenticate the identity of each of the parties in an Internet transaction.

- Integrity: A digital certificate demonstrates that the content signed by the certificate has not been altered while in transit.

- Confidentiality: PKI keeps information confidential by ensuring that it is not intercepted during transmission over the Internet.

- Authorization: Digital certificates issued in a PKI environment can replace user IDs and passwords, enhance security, and reduce some of the overhead required for authorization processes and controlling access privileges for specific transactions.

- Nonrepudiation: Digital certificates can validate actions, making it less likely that customers or partners can later repudiate a digitally signed transaction, such as an online purchase.

Hybrid Systems

Pure asymmetric key encryption is not widely used except in the area of certificates. Instead, it is typically employed in conjunction with symmetric key encryption, creating a hybrid system. The hybrid process in current use is based on the **Diffie-Hellman key exchange method**, which provides a way to exchange private keys using public key encryption without exposure to any third parties. In this method, asymmetric encryption is used to exchange symmetric keys, so that two organizations can conduct quick, efficient, secure communications based on symmetric encryption. Diffie-Hellman provided the foundation for subsequent developments in public key encryption.

As illustrated in Figure 9-14, the process works like this: Because symmetric encryption is more efficient than asymmetric encryption for sending messages, and because asymmetric encryption doesn't require out-of-band key exchange, asymmetric encryption can be used to transmit symmetric keys in a hybrid approach. Suppose Alex at ABC Corporation wants to communicate with Rachel at XYZ Corporation. First, Alex creates a session key. A **session key** is a symmetric key for limited-use, temporary communications. Alex encrypts a message with the session key, and then gets Rachel's public key. He uses her public key to encrypt both the session key and the message that is already encrypted. Alex transmits the entire package to Rachel, who uses her private key to decrypt the package containing the session key and the encrypted message, and then uses the session key to decrypt the message. Rachel can then continue the electronic conversation using only the more efficient symmetric session key.

FIGURE 9-14 Hybrid Encryption

Using Cryptographic Controls

Cryptographic controls are often misunderstood by those new to the area of information security. While modem cryptosystems can certainly generate unbreakable ciphertext, that is possible only when the proper key management infrastructure has been constructed and when the cryptosystems are operated and managed correctly. As in many InfoSec endeavors, the technical control is valuable, as long it remains within programs that are founded on sound policy and managed with an awareness of the fundamental objectives of the organization. Unfortunately, many vendors of cryptographic controls have sold products to organizations that were not able to deploy them to improve their security programs. This may have been due to poor project planning, errors in executing the implementation plans, or failures to put sound policies in place before acquiring the controls. Whatever the causes, many organizations have failed to make full use of their investment in cryptographic controls.

For those organizations with the need and the capability to use cryptographic controls, they can be used to support several aspects of the business:

- Confidentiality and integrity of e-mail and its attachments
- Authentication, confidentiality, integrity, and nonrepudiation of e-commerce transactions
- Authentication and confidentiality of remote access through VPN connections
- A higher standard of authentication when used to supplement access control systems

E-mail Security

A number of encryption cryptosystems have been adapted to add security to e-mail, a notoriously insecure method of communication. Some of the more popular adaptations include Secure Multipurpose Internet Mail Extensions, Privacy Enhanced Mail, and Pretty Good Privacy.

Secure Multipurpose Internet Mail Extensions (S/MIME) builds on the Multipurpose Internet Mail Extensions (MIME) encoding format by adding encryption and authentication via digital signatures based on public key cryptosystems. **Privacy Enhanced Mail (PEM)** has been proposed by the Internet Engineering Task Force (IETF) as a standard that will function with public key cryptosystems. PEM uses 3DES symmetric key encryption and RSA for key exchanges and digital signatures. **Pretty Good Privacy (PGP)** was developed by Phil Zimmerman and uses the IDEA Cipher, a 128-bit symmetric key block encryption algorithm with 64-bit blocks for message encoding. Like PEM, it uses RSA for symmetric key exchange and to support digital signatures. PGP relies on a "web of trust" model to allow its users to share key information easily, albeit with some loss in the degree of control and trust in the key information. With PGP, if user A has established a trusting relationship with user B, and user B has a trusting relationship with user C, then user A is presumed to have a trusting relationship with user C and can exchange encrypted information with that user.

Securing the Web

Just as PGP, PEM, and S/MIME help to secure e-mail operations, a number of cryptosystems help to secure Web activity, especially transactions between customers' browsers and the Web servers at electronic commerce sites. Among the protocols used for this purpose are Secure Electronic Transactions, Secure Sockets Layer, Secure Hypertext Transfer Protocol, Secure Shell, and IP Security.

Secure Electronic Transactions (SET) was developed by MasterCard and VISA in 1997 to provide protection from electronic payment fraud. It works by encrypting the credit card transfers with DES for encryption and RSA for key exchange, much as other algorithms do. SET provides the security for both Internet-based credit card transactions and the encryption of card swipe systems in retail stores.

Secure Sockets Layer (SSL) was developed by Netscape in 1994 to provide security for online electronic commerce transactions. It uses a number of algorithms, but mainly relies on RSA for key transfer and on IDEA, DES, or 3DES for encrypted symmetric key-based data transfer. Figure 9-13 shows the certificate and SSL information that are displayed when you check out of an e-commerce site. If the Web connection does not automatically display the certificate, you can right-click in the window and select Properties to view the connection encryption and certificate properties.

Secure Hypertext Transfer Protocol (SHTTP) is an encrypted solution to the unsecured version of HTTP. It provides an alternative to the aforementioned protocols and can provide secure e-commerce transactions as well as encrypted Web pages for secure data transfer over the Web, using a number of different algorithms.

Secure Shell (SSH) is a popular extension to the TCP/IP protocol suite, sponsored by the IETF. It provides security for remote access connections over public networks by using tunneling. It provides authentication services between a client and a server and is used to secure replacement tools for terminal emulation, remote management, and file transfer applications.

IP Security (IPSec) is the primary and now dominant cryptographic authentication and encryption product of the IETF's IP Protocol Security Working Group. It is used to support a variety of applications, just as SSH does. A framework for security development within the TCP/IP family of protocol standards, IPSec provides application support for all uses within TCP/IP, including VPNs. This protocol combines several different cryptosystems:

- Diffie-Hellman key exchange for deriving key material between peers on a public network
- Public key cryptography for signing the Diffie-Hellman exchanges to guarantee the identity of the two parties
- Bulk encryption algorithms, such as DES, for encrypting the data
- Digital certificates signed by a certificate authority to act as digital ID cards[12]

IPSec has two components: (1) the IP Security protocol itself, which specifies the information to be added to an IP packet and indicates how to encrypt packet data; and (2) the Internet Key Exchange (IKE), which uses asymmetric key exchange and negotiates the security associations.

IPSec works in two modes of operation: transport and tunnel. In **transport mode**, only the IP data is encrypted—not the IP headers themselves. This allows intermediate nodes to read the source and destination addresses. In **tunnel mode**, the entire IP packet is encrypted and inserted as the payload in another IP packet. This requires other systems at the beginning and end of the tunnel to act as proxies to send and receive the encrypted packets. These systems then transmit the decrypted packets to their true destinations.

IPSec and other cryptographic extensions to TCP/IP are often used to support a **virtual private network (VPN)**. A VPN is a private, secure network operated over a public and insecure network. It keeps the contents of the network messages hidden from observers who may have access to public traffic. Using the VPN tunneling approach described earlier, an individual or organization can set up a network connection on the Internet and send encrypted data back and forth, using the IP-packet-within-an-IP-packet method to deliver the data safely and securely. VPN support is built into most Microsoft Server software, including Windows 2000, and client support for VPN services is included in Windows XP. While true private network services can cost hundreds of thousands of dollars to lease, configure, and maintain, a VPN can be established for much less.

Securing Authentication

A final use of cryptosystems is to provide enhanced and secure authentication. One approach to this issue is provided by **Kerberos**, named after the three-headed dog of Greek mythology (spelled *Cerberus* in Latin) that guarded the gates to the underworld.

Kerberos uses symmetric key encryption to validate an individual user's access to various network resources. It keeps a database containing the private keys of clients and servers that are in the authentication domain that it supervises. Network services running on the servers in the shared authentication domain register with Kerberos, as do clients that wish to use those services.[13] The Kerberos system knows these private keys and can authenticate one network node (client or server) to another. For example, it can authenticate a client to a print service. To understand Kerberos, think of a typical multi-screen cinema. You acquire your ticket at the box office, and the ticket-taker then lets you in to the proper screen based on the contents of your ticket. Kerberos also generates temporary session keys—that is, private keys given to the two parties in a conversation. The session key is used to encrypt all communications between these two parties. Typically a user logs into the network, is authenticated to the Kerberos system, and is then authenticated by the Kerberos system to other resources on the network.

Kerberos consists of three interacting services, all of which rely on a database library:

- Authentication Server (AS), which is a Kerberos server that authenticates clients and servers.
- Key Distribution Center (KDC), which generates and issues session keys.
- Kerberos Ticket Granting Service (TGS), which provides tickets to clients who request services. An authorization ticket is an identification card for a particular client that verifies to the server that the client is requesting services and that the client is a valid member of the Kerberos system and, therefore, authorized to receive services. The ticket consists of the client's name and network address, a ticket validation starting and ending time, and the session key, all encrypted in the private key of the server from which the client is requesting services.

Kerberos works by means of the following principles:

1. The KDC knows the secret keys of all clients and servers on the network.
2. The KDC initially exchanges information with the client and server by using the secret keys.
3. Kerberos authenticates a client to a requested service on a server through TGS and by issuing temporary session keys for communications between the client and the KDC, the server and the KDC, and the client and the server.
4. Communications takes place between the client and server using the temporary session keys.[14]

Kerberos may be obtained free of charge from MIT at http://web.mit.edu/is/help/kerberos. If you decide to get it, however, be aware of some concerns in its operation. If the Kerberos servers are subjected to denial-of-service attacks, no client can request (or receive) any services. If the Kerberos servers, service providers, or clients' machines become compromised, their private key information may also be compromised.

Managing Cryptographic Controls

Cryptographic controls require close management attention. Some of the more important managerial issues are described here:

- Don't lose your keys. Any key-based system is contingent upon the physical security of the keys used by the system. If the keys are compromised, so is all communication.

If the keys are lost, any data encrypted with those keys may be lost as well. Unlike your car keys, which the dealer can replace, cryptographic keys are not known to the software vendors and are usually not recoverable. The purpose of the encryption algorithm is to prevent unauthorized entities from viewing the data. Unless your organization has made an investment in a key management solution that enables key recovery, if you lose your key, you may lose your data or the service being protected. Loss of unrecoverable keys will deny access to everyone. Given the current state of cryptographic technology, breaking the code is very likely impossible.

- Know who you are communicating with. One of the most popular encryption-based attacks is the man-in-the-middle attack. In this case, the attacker pretends to be the second party in a conversation, and relays the traffic to the actual second party. The attacker collects, decrypts, reads, possibly modifies, reencrypts, and transmits the information. This type of operation is possible only if the attacker is involved in the initial key exchange. Always verify the public keys in a public key exchange.

- It may be illegal to use a specific encryption technique when communicating to some nations. Federal export regulation still restricts the countries with which you can share strong encryption. Check the U.S. Department of Commerce's export FAQs for more information (www.bis.doc.gov/Encryption/Oct2KQandAs.html).

- Every cryptosystem has weaknesses. Make sure you can live with the weaknesses of any system you choose. Research your selection by searching for additional information before trusting any cryptosystem.

- Give access only to those users, systems, and servers with a business need, a principle known as least privilege. Don't load cryptosystems on systems that can be easily compromised.

- When placing trust into a certificate authority, ask the following question: *Quis custodiet ipsos custodes?* That is, who watches the watchers? CAs don't assume any liability for the accuracy of their information, which is strange given that their purpose is to validate the identity of a third party. However, if you read the fine print on the CA agreement, you'll most likely find statements to that effect.

- There is no security in obscurity. Just because a system is secret doesn't mean it is safe. It is better to put your trust in a tried-and-true tested solution.

Security protocols and the cryptosystems they use are subject to the same rules as firewalls and IDS. They are all installed and configured by humans, and thus they are only as good as their installers. VPNs are particularly vulnerable to direct attacks; compromise of the remote client can directly result in compromise of the trusted system. Home computing users frequently use the Windows "remember passwords" function, which could present a real problem if these systems are compromised. Don't let telecommuters use this option.

As with all other information security program components, make sure that your organization's use of cryptography is based on well-constructed policy and supported with sound management procedures. The tools themselves may work exactly as advertised, but if they are not used correctly and managed diligently, your organization's secrets may soon be public knowledge.

VIEWPOINT

Leveraging Protection Mechanisms to Provide Defense in Depth

By Todd E. Tucker, CISSP, CISA, CPA

Defense in depth is a protection strategy with a long history. It is characterized by layers of protection that, while not impenetrable, provide the advantage of increasing the time and resources necessary to penetrate through every layer of defense. Perhaps the best-known physical example of defense in depth comes from the archetypal fortress, built with high walls, manned by armed guards, and placed behind a protective moat.

In information security, protection mechanisms are essential for providing defense in depth. Each mechanism, when considered alone, may provide little protection against today's sophisticated attacks. However, information security architects build systems and networks by implementing layers of protection. For example, architects leverage a secured physical perimeter to protect media and hardware, implement firewalls to secure the internal networks from untrusted ones, install antivirus applications to detect and eradicate malicious code, implement intrusion detection and prevention systems to identify and inhibit attacks, and harden critical platforms to reduce vulnerabilities. These protection mechanisms become the walls, guards, and moats of today's electronic fortresses and effectively provide defense in depth.

Defense in depth provides several advantages to organizations. The obvious benefit is the added security that results from requiring an attacker to spend more time and resources to break in. Another benefit is the flexibility it provides in responding to specific threats. For example, consider a worm that exploits databases via a specific TCP port. The options for responding to the threat include shutting down the port the worm uses, hardening the database directly, or perhaps setting intrusion detection rules to spot and terminate an attack. Flexibility is important in production environments, where one action may adversely impact mission critical systems, requiring other actions to be considered.

Defense in depth provides a major disadvantage, too—complexity. Defense in depth increases the number of protection mechanisms implemented. It requires architects and administrators to consider the overall design of the network. Moreover, they must consider all the protection mechanisms to ensure they adequately protect against threats and do not conflict with one another.

As you learn about protection mechanisms, think not just about their technical aspects and the security they provide. Think about their ability to work with other mechanisms to provide defense in depth. How can they work together to increase the overall security of the system? Also, consider the management implications of each mechanism. Remember that these mechanisms are often implemented on a large scale and each one requires maintenance, administration, and monitoring. One of the greatest challenges in information security today is in managing the protection mechanisms on an enterprise-scale and effectively leveraging them to provide defense in depth.

Mr. Tucker is an information security expert focused on the areas of vulnerability management, intrusion management, and security metrics. He is currently a senior product manager at NetIQ Corporation.

Chapter Summary

- Authentication is the validation of a user's identity. Authentication devices can depend on one or more of four factors: what you know, what you have, what you are, and what you produce.

- Authorization is the process of determining which actions an authenticated entity can perform in a particular physical or logical area.

- To obtain strong authentication, a system must use two or more authentication methods.

- Biometric technologies are evaluated on three criteria: the false reject rate, the false accept rate, and the crossover error rate.

- A firewall in an information security program is any device that prevents a specific type of information from moving between the outside world (the untrusted network) and the inside world (the trusted network).

- Types of firewalls include packet filtering firewalls, application-level firewalls, stateful inspection firewalls, and dynamic packet filtering firewalls. There are four common architectural implementations of firewalls: packet filtering routers, screened-host firewalls, dual-homed firewalls, and screened-subnet firewalls.

- A host-based IDS resides on a particular computer or server and monitors activity on that system. A network-based IDS monitors network traffic; when a predefined condition occurs, it responds and notifies the appropriate administrator.

- A signature-based IDS, also known as a knowledge-based IDS, examines data traffic for activity that matches signatures, which are preconfigured, predetermined attack patterns. A statistical anomaly-based IDS (also known as a behavior-based IDS) collects data from normal traffic and establishes a baseline. When the activity is outside the baseline parameters (called the clipping level), the IDS notifies the administrator.

- The science of encryption, known as cryptology, encompasses cryptography (from the Greek words *kryptos*, meaning "hidden," and *graphein*, meaning "to write") and cryptanalysis. Cryptanalysis is the process of obtaining the original message from an encrypted code, without the use of the original algorithms and keys.

- In encryption, the most commonly used algorithms employ either substitution or transposition. A substitution cipher substitutes one value for another. A transposition cipher (or permutation cipher) rearranges the values within a block to create the ciphertext.

- Symmetric encryption uses the same key, also known as a secret key, to both encrypt and decrypt a message. Asymmetric encryption (public key encryption) uses two different keys for these purposes.

- A public key infrastructure (PKI) encompasses the entire set of hardware, software, and cryptosystems necessary to implement public key encryption.

- A digital certificate is an electronic document, attached to a file, certifying that the file is from the organization it claims to be from and has not been modified.

- A number of cryptosystems have been developed to make e-mail more secure. Examples include Pretty Good Privacy (PGP), Secure Multipurpose Internet Mail Extensions (S/MIME), and Privacy Enhanced Mail (PEM).

- A number of cryptosystems work to secure Web browsers, including Secure Electronic Transactions (SET), Secure Sockets Layer (SSL), Secure Hypertext Transfer Protocol (SHTTP), Secure Shell (SSH), and IP Security (IPSec).

Review Questions

1. What is the difference between authentication and authorization? Can a system permit authorization without authentication? Why or why not?
2. What is the most widely accepted biometric authorization technology? Why do you think this is the case?
3. What is the most effective biometric authorization technology? Why do you think this is the case?
4. What is the typical relationship between the untrusted network, the firewall, and the trusted network?
5. How is an application layer firewall different from a packet filtering firewall? Why is an application layer firewall sometimes called a proxy server?
6. What special function does a cache server perform? Why does this function have value for larger organizations?
7. How does screened-host firewall architecture differ from screened-subnet firewall architecture? Which offers more security for the information assets that remain on the trusted network?
8. What is a DMZ? Is this really a good name for the function that this type of subnet performs?
9. What is RADIUS? What advantage does it have over TACACS?
10. How does a network-based IDS differ from a host-based IDS?
11. What is network footprinting? What is network fingerprinting? How are they related?
12. Why do many organizations ban port scanning activities on their internal networks? Why would ISPs ban outbound port scanning by their customers?
13. Why is TCP port 80 always of critical importance when securing an organization's network?
14. What kind of data and information can be found using a packet sniffer?
15. What are the main components of cryptology?
16. Explain the relationship between plaintext and ciphertext.
17. Define steganography. Why would it be of interest to the information security professional?
18. One tenet of cryptography is that increasing the work factor to break a code increases the security of that code. Why is that true?
19. Explain the key differences between symmetric and asymmetric encryption. Which can the computer process faster? Which lowers the costs associated with key management?
20. What is a VPN? Why are VPNs widely used?

Exercises

1. Create a spreadsheet that takes eight values input into eight different cells and then applies a transposition cipher to them. Next, create a row that takes the results and applies a substitution cipher to them (substitute 0 for 5, 1 for 6, 2 for 7, 3 for 8, 4 for 9, and vice versa).
2. Using the Web, search for information about a technology called personal firewalls. Examine the various alternatives and compare their functionality, cost, features, and type of protection.
3. Go to the Web site of Verisign, one of the market leaders in digital certificates. Determine whether Verisign serves as a registration authority, certificate authority, or both. Download its free guide to PKI and summarize Verisign's services.

4. Using the Web, go to http://csrc.nist.gov and locate FIPS 197. What encryption standard does this address use? Examine the contents of this publication and describe the algorithm discussed. How strong is it? How does it encrypt plaintext?

5. Using the Web, locate vendors of biometric products. Find one vendor with a product designed to examine each characteristic mentioned in Figure 9-4. What is the CER associated with each product? Which would be more acceptable to users? Which would be preferred by security administrators?

Case Exercises

Iris's PDA beeped. Frowning, she glanced at the screen, expecting to see another junk e-mail. "We've really got to do something about the spam!" she muttered to herself. She scanned the header of the message. "Uh-oh!" She looked at her watch, grabbed her cell phone, and while looking at her incident response pocket card, dialed the home number of the on-call systems administrator. When he answered, she asked "Seen the alert yet? What's up?"

"Wish I knew—some sort of virus," he replied. "A user must have opened an infected attachment."

Iris made a mental note to remind the awareness program manager to restart the refresher training program for virus control. Her users should know better, but some new employees had not been trained yet.

"Why didn't the firewall catch it?" Iris asked.

"It must be a new one," he replied. "It slipped by the pattern filters."

"What are we doing now?" Iris was growing more nervous by the minute.

"I'm ready to cut our Internet connection remotely, then drive down to the office and start our planned recovery operations—shut down infected systems, clean up any infected servers, recover data from tape backups, and notify our peers that they may receive this virus from us in our e-mail. I just need your go-ahead." The admin sounded uneasy. This was not a trivial operation, and he was facing a long night of intense work.

"Do it. I'll activate the incident response plan and start working the notification call list to get some extra hands in to help." Iris knew this situation would be the main topic at the weekly CIO's meeting. She just hoped her colleagues would be able to restore the systems to safe operation quickly. She looked at her watch: 12:35 A.M.

1. What can be done to minimize the risk of the situation recurring? Can these types of situations be completely avoided?

2. If you were in Iris's position, how would you approach your interaction with the second-shift operator?

3. How should RWW go about notifying its peers? What other procedures should Iris have the technician perform?

4. When would be the appropriate time to begin the forensic data collection process to analyze the root cause of this incident? Why?

Endnotes

1. Charles Cresson Wood. *Information Security Policies Made Easy,* 9th ed. NetIQ Corporation, 2003:466–467.
2. Fred Avolio and Chris Blask. Application gateways and stateful inspection: a brief note comparing and contrasting. *Avolio Consulting Online,* January 22, 1998. [Cited 1 July 2002]. Available from the World Wide Web at http://www.avolio.com/apgw+spf.html.
3. Elron Software, Inc. Choosing the best firewall for your growing network. *Elron Online,* April 22, 2002. [Cited 1 July 2002]. Available from the World Wide Web at http://www.elronsoftware.com/connection/story67a.html.
4. Kevin Day. *Inside the Security Mind: Making the Tough Decisions.* Upper Saddle River, NJ: Prentice-Hall, 2003: 220.
5. Adrian Grigorof. Challenges in managing firewalls. [Accessed June 28, 2003]. http://www.eventid.net/show.asp?DocId=18.
6. Laura Taylor. Guidelines for configuring your firewall rule-set. *Tech Update Online,* April 12, 2001. [Cited July 1, 2002]. Available from the World Wide Web at http://techupdate.zdnet.com/techupdate/stories/main/0,14179,2707159,00.html.
7. Charles Cresson Wood. *Information Security Policies Made Easy,* 9th ed. NetIQ Corporation, 2003:551–554.
8. Shon Harris. *CISSP Certification: All in One Exam Guide.* Berkeley: Osborne McGraw-Hill, 2001:163.
9. FOLDOC. User Datagram Protocol. *FOLDOC Online,* June 19, 2002. [Cited July 1, 2002]. Available from the World Wide Web at http://wombat.doc.ic.ac.uk/foldoc/foldoc.cgi?query=port&action=Search.
10. Kevin Day. *Inside the Security Mind: Making the Tough Decisions.* Upper Saddle River, NJ: Prentice-Hall, 2003:225.
11. Verisign. Understanding PKI. *Verisign Online.* [Cited July 1, 2002]. Available from the World Wide Web at http://verisign.netscape.com/security/pki/understanding.html.
12. Cisco Systems, Inc. White Paper: IPSec. *Cisco Online,* November 21, 2000. [Cited July 1, 2002]. Available from the World Wide Web at http://www.cisco.com/warp/public/cc/so/neso/sqso/eqso/ipsec_wp.htm.
13. Jennifer G. Steiner, Clifford Neuman, and Jeffrey I. Schiller. An authentication service for open network systems (paper presented for Project Athena, March 30, 1988). Available from the World Wide Web at ftp://athena-dist.mit.edu/pub/kerberos/doc/usenix.txt.
14. Ronald L. Krutz and Russell Dean Vines. *The CISSP Prep Guide: Mastering the Ten Domains of Computer Security.* New York: John Wiley and Sons, 2001:40.

Personnel and Security

10

> I'll take fifty percent efficiency to get one hundred percent loyalty.
>
> **SAMUEL GOLDWYN (1882–1974), U.S. FILM PRODUCER**

MIKE EDWARDS STUCK HIS HEAD INTO Iris's office and said, "Iris, are you free for the next hour or so?"

Iris glanced at her calendar and said, "Sure. What's up?"

Mike was standing in the hall with Erik Paulson, the manager of RWW's help desk. Both men looked grave. Mike said. "Can you bring the human resources policy manual with you?"

Without asking any further questions, Iris pulled the manual from her bookshelf and joined the pair. As they walked down the hall, Mike filled her in on the brewing situation.

In the meeting room that adjoined the CEO's office, three people were already seated. Mike and Paul took seats at the table, and Iris took a chair along the wall. Robin Gateere, RWW's CEO, cleared her throat and said, "Okay. Let's get started."

Jerry Martin from Legal was facilitating the meeting. The other person in the room was Gloria Simpson, Senior Vice President of Human Resources. Mike had asked Iris to join this upper-level management meeting because of her familiarity with human resources policy regarding information security.

Jerry began, "Recent events have caused us to revisit our hiring policies. Last week, one of our employees was arrested, and our company name was plastered all over the newspapers and on television. It turns out that the employee was on parole for sexual assault. He was hired into our IT department to work at the help desk. The police have since discovered that he is running a Web-based pornography site. His parole was revoked, and he's now in the

413

state prison. The questions are, How did he come to be an employee of this company in the first place, and What do we do now?"

Robin said, "As to the second question, we terminated his employment for cause since he did not report to work because he is in jail. As to the first question, ..." She looked pointedly at Erik and said, "What do you know?"

Erik looked uneasy. He said, "This is the first time I became aware that Sam had trouble with the law. As a matter of fact, I was the hiring manger who recruited him, and all of this is news to me. Of course, we followed the usual human resources procedures when we hired him, although I have always wondered why hiring managers don't get to see the whole personnel file for new hires."

Gloria spoke up. "I agree that practice seems odd in light of this case. According to his file, Sam did write about his conviction and parole status on his application. In fact, we did an identity check and received a criminal background report that confirmed the conviction and his parole status. He didn't lie on his application, but it's beyond me how Erik was ever cleared to make him a job offer."

Erik lifted the folder he was holding. "Here's the whole manager's file on Sam. The standard clearance to extend an offer is right here." He slid it down the table to Gloria, who looked at the approval signature on the form.

Iris realized several things: Some of the byzantine practices in human resources were about to change, somebody in human resources was in lot of trouble, and it was time for her to revisit all of the company's personnel information security policies.

LEARNING OBJECTIVES

Upon completion of this material, you should be able to:

- Identify the skills and requirements for information security positions
- Recognize the various information security professional certifications, and identify which skills are encompassed by each
- Understand and implement information security constraints on the general hiring processes
- Understand the role of information security in employee terminations
- Describe the security practices used to control employee behavior and prevent misuse of information

Introduction

Maintaining a secure environment requires that the InfoSec department be carefully structured and staffed with appropriately credentialed personnel. It also requires that the proper procedures be integrated into all human resources activities, including hiring, training, promotion, and termination practices.

The first part of this chapter discusses information security personnel hiring issues and practices, including information about the most sought-after professional certification credentials. Some aspects of managing InfoSec personnel—such as the placement of the information security department within the organization—were covered in Chapter 5. This chapter provides more details about the proper staffing (or adjusting the staffing plan) of the information security function. It also describes how to adjust IT job descriptions and documented practices to fulfill information security requirements throughout the organization.

The second part of the chapter presents strategies for integrating information security policies into an organization's general hiring practices. This effort requires collaboration between the general management community of interest and information security professionals.

Staffing the Security Function

Selecting an effective mix of information security personnel for a given organization requires that you consider a number of criteria. Some of these criteria are within the control of the organization; others are not, such as the supply and demand of varied skills and experience levels. In general, when the demand for any commodity—including personnel with critical information security technical or managerial skills—rises quickly, the initial supply often fails to meet it. As demand becomes known, professionals entering the job market or refocusing their job skills seek to gain the required skills, experience, and credentials. Until this new supply can meet the demand, however, competition for the scarce resource will continue to drive costs up. Once the supply is level with or higher than demand, organizations can become more selective, and no longer need to pay a premium for those skills.

This process swings back and forth like a clock pendulum, because the real economy, unlike an econometric model, is seldom in a state of equilibrium. For example, there was excess demand for experienced ERP professionals in the 1990s, and for experienced COBOL programmers at the turn of the twenty-first century, because of concerns about Y2K issues. At the time of this writing, the poor economic climate has precluded hiring to meet the great need for skilled information security professionals. Many economic forecasters expect this deferred demand to become active as the economy once again begins to expand.

Qualifications and Requirements

Because of the relatively recent emergence of information security as a distinct discipline, many organizations are not certain of the qualifications that competent information security personnel should have. In many cases, the information security staff lacks established roles and responsibilities. To move the information security discipline forward, organizations should take the following steps:

- The general management community of interest should learn more about the requirements and qualifications for both information security positions and relevant IT positions.
- Upper management should learn more about information security budgetary and personnel needs.

- The IT and general management communities of interest must grant the information security function—in particular, the chief information security officer—an appropriate level of influence and prestige.

In most cases, organizations look for a technically qualified information security generalist, with a solid understanding of how organizations operate. In many other fields, the more specialized professionals become, the more marketable they are. In information security, over-specialization can actually be a drawback.

When hiring information security professionals at all levels, organizations frequently look for individuals who have the following abilities:

- Understand how organizations are structured and operated
- Recognize that information security is a management task that cannot be handled with technology alone
- Work well with people in general, including users, and communicate effectively using both strong written and verbal communication skills
- Acknowledge the role of policy in guiding security efforts
- Understand the essential role of information security education and training, which helps make users part of the solution, rather than part of the problem
- Perceive the threats facing an organization, understand how these threats can become transformed into attacks, and safeguard the organization from information security attacks
- Understand how technical controls (e.g., firewalls, IDSs, and antivirus software) can be applied to solve specific information security problems
- Demonstrate familiarity with the mainstream information technologies, including Disk Operating System (DOS), Windows NT/2000, Linux, and UNIX
- Understand IT and InfoSec terminology and concepts

Entering the Information Security Profession

Many information security professionals enter the field after having prior careers in law enforcement or the military, or careers in other IT areas, such as networking, programming, database administration, or systems administration. Recently, college graduates who have tailored their degree programs to specialize in information security have begun to enter the field in appreciable numbers. Figure 10-1 illustrates these possible career paths.

Many information technologists believe that information security professionals must have an established track record in some other IT specialty. However, IT professionals who move into information security tend to focus on technical problems and solutions, to the exclusion of general information security issues. Organizations can foster greater professionalism in the information security discipline by clearly defining their expectations and establishing explicit position descriptions.

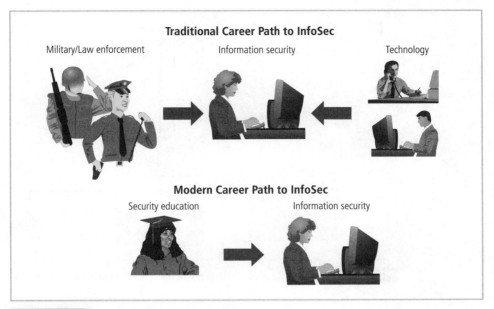

FIGURE 10-1 Information Security Career Paths

Information Security Positions

Standardizing job descriptions can increase the degree of professionalism in the field of information security, as well as improve the consistency of roles and responsibilities among organizations. Organizations can find complete information security job descriptions in Charles Cresson Wood's book *Information Security Roles and Responsibilities Made Easy*. Excerpts from this book are provided later in this chapter.[1]

A study of information security positions by Schwartz, Erwin, Weafer, and Briney found that positions can be classified into one of three areas: those that *define,* those that *build,* and those that *administer*.

> Definers provide the policies, guidelines and standards ... They're the people who do the consulting and the risk assessment, who develop the product and technical architectures. These are senior people with a lot of broad knowledge, but often not a lot of depth. Then you have the builders. They're the real techies, who create and install security solutions. ... Finally, you have the people who operate and [administer] the security tools, the security monitoring function, and the people who continuously improve the processes. This is where all the day-to-day, hard work is done. What I find is we often try to use the same people for all of these roles. We use builders all the time ... If you break your infosec professionals into these three groups, you can recruit them more efficiently, with the policy people being the more senior people, the builders being more technical, and the operating people being those you can train to do a specific task.[2]

One could find a number of position titles that fit these three roles. The following sections discuss some specific job titles that follow this model. Figure 10-2 shows typical information security job positions and the departmental hierarchy.

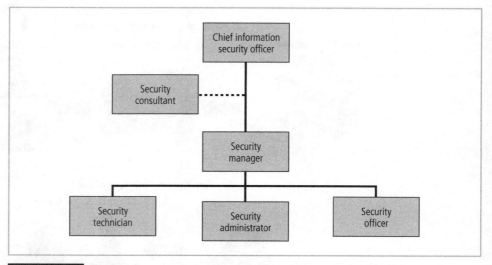

FIGURE 10-2 Possible Information Security Positions and Reporting Relationships

Chief information Security Officer (CISO)

The CISO is typically considered the top information security officer in the organization. As indicated in earlier chapters, the CISO is usually not an executive-level position and frequently reports to the CIO. Although these individuals are business managers first and technologists second, they must be conversant in all areas of information security, including technology, planning, and policy. The CISO is expected to draft or approve a range of information security policies. He or she works with the CIO on strategic planning, develops tactical plans, and works with security managers on operational planning. The CISO also develops information security budgets based on available funding and makes decisions or recommendations about purchasing, project and technology implementation, and the recruiting, hiring, and firing of security staff. This individual is the spokesperson for the security team and is responsible for the overall information security program.

Qualifications and Position Requirements. The most common qualification for the CISO is the Certified Information Systems Security Professional (CISSP), which is described later in this chapter. A graduate degree in criminal justice, business, technology, or another related field is usually required as well. A candidate for this position should have experience as a security manager, as well as in planning, policy, and budgets. As mentioned earlier, some organizations prefer to hire individuals with law enforcement experience.

Charles Cresson Wood's *Information Security Roles and Responsibilities Made Easy* defines and describes the CISO position, which he calls the Information Security Department Manager, as follows:

> **Information Security Department Manager**
> **Job Title:** Information Security Department Manager [also known as Information Security Manager, Chief Information Security Officer (CISO), or in high-tech firms, simply Chief Security Officer (CSO)]
> **Reports to:** Chief Information Officer (CIO)
> **Dotted Line:** Board of Directors Audit Committee

Summary: The Information Security Department Manager directs, coordinates, plans, and organizes information security activities throughout Company X. He or she acts as the focal point for all communications related to information security, both with internal staff and third parties. The Manager works with a wide variety of people from different internal organizational units, bringing them together to manifest controls that reflect workable compromises as well as proactive responses to current and future information security risks.

Responsibilities and Duties: The Information Security Department Manager is responsible for envisioning and taking steps to implement the controls needed to protect both Company X information as well as information that has been entrusted to Company X by third parties. The position involves overall Company X responsibility for information security regardless of the form that the information takes (paper, blueprint, floppy disk, audio tape, embedded in products or processes, etc.), the information handling technology employed (mainframes, microcomputers, fax machines, telephones, local area networks, file cabinets, etc.), or the people involved (contractors, consultants, employees, vendors, outsourcing firms, etc.).

Threats to information and information systems addressed by the Information Security Department Manager and his or her staff include, but are not limited to: information unavailability, information corruption, unauthorized information destruction, unauthorized information modification, unauthorized information usage, and unauthorized information disclosure. These threats to information and information systems include consideration of physical security matters only if a certain level of physical security is necessary to achieve a certain level of information security (for example, as is necessary to prevent theft of portable computers).

- Acts as the central point of contact within Company X when it comes to all communications dealing with information security problems, issues, and concerns
- Establishes and maintains strong working relationships with the Company X groups involved with information security matters (Legal, Internal Audit, Physical Security, Information Security Management Committee, etc.)
- Establishes, manages, and maintains organizational structures and communications channels with those responsible for information security; these responsible parties include individuals within Company X departments (such as Local Information Security Coordinators) as well as Company X business partners (outsourcing firms, consulting firms, etc.)
- Assists with the clarification of individual information security responsibility and accountability so that necessary information security activities are performed as needed, according to pre-established polices and standards
- Coordinates the information security efforts of all internal groups that have one or more information security-related responsibilities, to ensure that organization-wide information security efforts are consistent across the organization, and that duplication of effort is avoided [this is a shared responsibility with the Physical Security Department Manager]
- Coordinates all multi-application or multi-system information security improvement projects at Company X [a good example would be converting all operating system access control systems to a standard minimum password length]

- Represents Company X and its information security related interests at industry standards committee meetings, technical conferences, and the like [smaller or less visible organizations will generally dispense with this duty]

- Investigates the ways that information security related technologies, requirements statements, internal processes, and organizational structures can be used to achieve the goals found in the Company X strategic plan [this effort should include consideration of the long-range information systems plan, which in turn should be an intermediate link between the business strategic plan and the information security plan]

- Creates a strategic information security plan with a vision for the future of information security at Company X (utilizing evolving information security technology, this vision meets a variety of objectives such as management's fiduciary and legal responsibilities, customer expectations for secure modern business practices, and the competitive requirements of the marketplace)

- Understands the fundamental business activities performed by Company X, and based on this understanding, suggests appropriate information security solutions that uniquely protect these activities

- Develops action plans, schedules, budgets, status reports, and other top management communications intended to improve the status of information security at Company X

- Obtains top management approval and ongoing support for all major information security initiatives at Company X (or supervises others in their efforts with these proceedings)

- Brings pressing information security vulnerabilities to top management's attention so that immediate remedial action can be taken

- Performs and/or oversees the performance of periodic Company X risk assessments that identify current and future security vulnerabilities, determines what level of risk is acceptable to management, and identifies the best ways to reduce information security risks to this acceptable level [in a general sense, the Information Security Department Manager performs information security risk management or else establishes a management structure that has others (such as line managers) perform this function]

- Examines information security from a cross-organizational viewpoint including Company X's participation in extranets, electronic data interchange (EDI) trading networks, ad hoc Internet commerce relationships, and other new business structures, and makes related recommendations to protect Company X information and information systems [the prior paragraph discussing risk assessments deals with internal information systems, while this paragraph is advisable whenever new multi-organizational networks are contemplated or deployed]

- Directs the development of or originates self-assessment questionnaires and other tools that assist user department managers and other members of the management team in their efforts to determine the degree of compliance with information security requirements within their respective organizational units

- Periodically initiates quality measurement studies to determine whether the information security function at Company X operates in a manner consistent with standard industry practices (these include customer satisfaction surveys, benchmarking studies, peer comparison efforts, and internal tests)

- Coordinates and directs the development, management approval, implementation, and promulgation of objectives, goals, policies, standards, guidelines, and other requirements needed to support information security throughout Company X as well as within Company X business networks (such as extranets)

- Provides managerial guidance on the development of local, system-specific, and application-specific information security policies, guidelines, standards, and procedures

- Assists with the establishment and refinement of procedures for the identification of Company X information assets as well as the classification of these information assets with respect to criticality, sensitivity, and value [...]

- Coordinates internal staff in their efforts to determine Company X information security obligations according to external requirements (contractual, regulatory, legal, ethical, etc.)

- Closely monitors changes in society's information security related ethics, values, morals, and attitudes with an eye toward changes that Company X should make in response to these developments

- Designs and manages business processes for the detection, investigation, correction, disciplinary action, and/or prosecution related to information security breaches, violations, and incidents [these efforts would include an intrusion detection system, also known as an IDS]

- Manages internal Company X activities pertaining to the investigation, correction, prosecution, and disciplinary action needed for the resolution of information security breaches, violations, and incidents (whether actual or alleged)

- Prepares post-mortem analyses of information security breaches, violations, and incidents to illuminate what happened and how this type of problem can be prevented in the future

- Directs the preparation of information systems contingency plans and manages worker groups (such as Computer Emergency Response Teams or CERTs) that respond to information security relevant events (hacker intrusions, virus infections, denial-of-service attacks, etc.)

- Works with public relations and top management to develop suitable public responses to information security incidents, violations, and problems

- Acts as an external representative for Company X in the event of a hacker break-in or some other information security relevant event [this may involve news media interviews, discussions with concerned customers, etc.]

- Acts as an expert witness in information security related legal proceedings involving Company X

- Initiates and manages special projects related to information security that may be needed to appropriately respond to ad hoc or unexpected information security events

- Provides technical support consulting services on matters related to information security such as the criteria to use when selecting information security products

- Performs management and personnel administration functions associated with Company X's Information Security Department (coaches employees, hires and fires employees, disciplines employees, reviews employee performance, recommends salary increases and promotions, counsels employees, establishes employee task lists and schedules, trains staff, etc.)

- Acts as the primary liaison and decision maker regarding the work of information security consultants, contractors, temporaries, and outsourcing firms
- Provides technical information security consulting assistance for Company X staff disciplinary measures, civil suits, and criminal prosecutions
- Stays informed about the latest developments in the information security field, including new products and services, through online news services, technical magazines, professional association memberships, industry conferences, special training seminars, and other methods[3]

In addition to taking on these roles and responsibilities, the CISO must demonstrate competency in a number of areas, as shown in Table 10-1.

Table 10-1 Job Competencies for the CISO

1. Job-Specific Competency: Provides organization information security oversight.

- Maintains current and appropriate body of knowledge necessary to perform the information security management function.
- Effectively applies information security management knowledge to enhance the security of the open network and associated systems and services.
- Maintains working knowledge of external legislative and regulatory initiatives. Interprets and translates requirements for implementation.
- Develops appropriate information security policies, standards, guidelines, and procedures.
- Works effectively with other organization information security personnel and the committee process.
- Provides meaningful input, prepares effective presentations, and communicates information security objectives.
- Participates in short- and long-term planning.
- Monitors information security program compliance and effectiveness.
- Works with committees and management professionals to accomplish information security goals.
- Coordinates and prioritizes activities of the Office of Information Security in support of the mission.
- Acts as a resource for matters of information security. Provides pertinent and useful information.
- Oversees and conducts information security reviews and liaison visits to organization [system practices]. Makes recommendations and reports to Regional Practice Administration.
- Coordinates and performs reviews of contracts, projects, and proposals. Assists information technology proponents with standards compliance.
- Conducts investigations of information security violations and computer crimes. Works effectively with management and external law enforcement to resolve these instances.
- Reviews instances of noncompliance and works effectively and tactfully to correct deficiencies.

2. Job-Specific Competency: Manages Office of Information Security personnel.

- Determines positions and personnel necessary to accomplish information security goals. Requests positions, screens personnel, and takes the lead in the interviewing and hiring process.
- Develops meaningful job descriptions. Communicates expectations and actively coaches personnel for success.
- Prioritizes and assigns tasks. Reviews work performed. Challenges staff to better themselves and advance the level of service provided.
- Provides meaningful feedback to staff on an ongoing basis and formally appraises performance annually.
- Assists information technology proponents with standards compliance.
- Conducts investigations of information security violations and computer crimes. Works effectively with management and external law enforcement to resolve these instances.
- Reviews instances of noncompliance and works effectively and tactfully to correct deficiencies.

Source: AAMC-GASP. *Job Descriptions.* Accessed July 17, 2003. www.aamc.org/members/gir/gasp/jobdescriptions.pdf.

Security Manager

Security managers are accountable for the day-to-day operation of the information security program. They accomplish objectives identified by the CISO and resolve issues identified by the technicians. Security managers are often assigned specific managerial duties by the CISO, including policy development, risk assessment, contingency planning, and operational and tactical planning for the security function. They often liaise with managers from other departments and divisions in joint planning and development sections, such as security functions in human resources hiring and termination procedures, plant operations in environmental controls, and physical security design.

Management of technology requires an understanding of the technology administered, but not necessarily proficiency in its configuration, operation, or fault resolution. Management of a technology or area is very different from administration of it. For example, systems administrators are expected to be very technically proficient in the technology used by the systems under their control, and are responsible for ensuring that systems are used in compliance with the organization's policies. They may have some management functions, but they are not held accountable as managers. Within the information security community, security managers are those true managers given responsibility for specific tasks, assigned resources to control and apply to those tasks, and held responsible and accountable for the accomplishment of those tasks.

Qualifications and Position Requirements.   It is not uncommon for a security manager to have a CISSP. These individuals must have experience in traditional business activities, including budgeting, project management, personnel management, and hiring and firing, and they must be able to draft middle- and lower-level policies as well as standards and guidelines. Experience with business continuity planning is usually considered a plus. Several types of information security managers exist, and the people who fill these roles tend to be much more specialized than CISOs. For instance, a Risk Manager performs a different role than a manager hired to administer the SETA program. A careful reading of the job description is required to determine exactly what a particular employer is looking for.

Wood's job description for the Information Security Department Manager (provided earlier in this chapter) assumes that a single management-level professional performs all information security management functions for the organization. In such a case, the security manager and the CISO would be the same person. However, larger organizations that require 24-7 management oversight generally have several positions that collaborate to fulfill the functions that Wood describes. For example, an information security manager-of-managers—the CISO—may supervise managers who are accountable for specialized areas. These managers directly supervise the analysts, technicians, and support staff, and often have additional managerial responsibilities.

Security Technician

Security technicians are technically qualified individuals who configure firewalls and IDSs, implement security software, diagnose and troubleshoot problems, and coordinate with systems and network administrators to ensure that security technology is properly implemented. The role of security technician is the typical information security entry-level position, albeit a technical one. One dilemma for those seeking employment in the field is that it does require a certain level of technical skill, which can be difficult to obtain without experience. As a result, security technicians tend to be information technology technicians who have adopted a different career path.

Like network technicians, security technicians tend to be specialized, focusing on one major security technology group (firewalls, IDS, servers, routers, and software), and then further specializing in one particular software or hardware package within the group (e.g., Checkpoint firewalls, Nokia firewalls, or Tripwire IDS). These areas are sufficiently complex to warrant this level of specialization. Security technicians who want to move up in the corporate hierarchy must expand their technical knowledge horizontally, and obtain an understanding of the general organizational side of information security as well as all technical areas.

Qualifications and Position Requirements. The technical qualifications and position requirements for a security technician vary. Organizations typically prefer expert, certified, proficient technicians. Job requirements usually include some level of experience with a particular hardware and software package. Sometimes familiarity with a particular technology is enough to secure an applicant an interview; however, experience using the technology is usually required.

Information Security Engineer
Job Title: Information Security Engineer
Reports to: Information Security Department Manager
Summary: An Information Security Engineer provides technical assistance with the design, installation, operation, service, and maintenance of a variety of multi-user information security systems such as virtual private networks (VPNs). A hands-on technical specialist, an Engineer handles the complex and detailed technical work necessary to establish security systems such as firewalls and encryption-based digital signatures. An Engineer configures and sets up information security systems such as firewalls, or else trains Access Control System Administrators, Systems Administrators, Network Administrators, and/or Database Administrators to do these tasks themselves.
Responsibilities and Duties:

- Provides hands-on technical consulting services to teams of technical specialists working on integrating either centralized or networked systems that will offer enhanced levels of information security [examples include an active data dictionary, a data warehouse, or a data mart]

- Provides technical assistance with the initial set-up and secure deployment of systems that support information security, including virus detection systems, firewall content filtering systems, and software license management systems

- Offers technical information security consulting services to distributed personnel who are responsible for one or more information security systems; these people include Network Administrators, Systems Administrators, and Database Administrators

- Evaluates information system bug reports, security exploit reports, and other information security notices issued by information system vendors, government agencies, universities, professional associations, and other organizations, and as needed, makes recommendations to internal management to take precautionary steps [an example of these notices is the periodic reports issued by the CERT at Carnegie Mellon University]

- Runs or works with others who periodically run vulnerability identification software packages and related tools to immediately highlight errors in systems configuration, the need for the application of fixes and patches, and other security related changes [to leave this task solely to Systems Administrators introduces a conflict of interest because the results of such software will often indicate that Systems Administrators need to perform additional work]

- With management authorization, collects, securely stores, and utilizes software that is able to decrypt encrypted files, automatically guess user passwords, copy software that has been copy-protected, or otherwise circumvent information security measures

- Maintains and, as necessary, documents a collection of software that is able to trace the source of and otherwise investigate attacks on Company X systems

- Conducts selected tests of information security measures in accordance with specific instructions provided by the Information Security Department Manager [this effort usually includes penetration attacks]

- Interprets information security policies, standards, and other requirements as they relate to a specific internal information system, and assists with the implementation of these and other information security requirements

- Redesigns and reengineers internal information handling processes so that information is appropriately protected from a wide variety of problems, including unauthorized disclosure, unauthorized use, inappropriate modification, premature deletion, and unavailability

- Regularly attends conferences, professional association meetings, and technical symposia to remain aware of the latest information security technological developments

Other Position Titles

Organizations often find that many (if not all) non-information security job descriptions must define information security roles and responsibilities. The following list of positions with information security elements is drawn from *Information Security Roles and Responsibilities Made Easy* and shows the breadth of job titles that may be affected. The job description elements have been grouped according to the community of interest.

Information Security Community:

- InfoSec Department Manager
- Access Control System Administrator
- Internal InfoSec Consultant
- InfoSec Engineer
- InfoSec Documentation Specialist
- InfoSys Contingency Planner
- Local InfoSec Coordinator

IT Community:

- Chief Information Officer
- InfoSys Analyst/Business Analyst
- Systems Programmer
- Business Applications Programmer
- Computer Operations Manager
- Computer Operator
- InfoSys Quality Assurance Analyst
- Help Desk Associate
- Archives Manager/Records Manager
- Telecommunications Manager
- Systems Administrator/Network Administrator
- Web Site Administrator/Commerce Site Administrator
- Database Administrator
- Data Administration Manager

General Business Community:

- Physical Security Department Manager
- Physical Asset Protection Specialist
- Building and Facilities Guard
- Office Maintenance Worker
- Internal Audit Department Manager
- EDP Auditor
- Internal Intellectual Property Attorney
- Human Resources Department Manager
- Human Resources Consultant
- Receptionist
- Outsourcing Contract Administrator
- In-House Trainer
- Insurance and Risk Management Department Manager
- Insurance and Risk Management Analyst
- Business Contingency Planner
- Public Relations Manager
- Chief Financial Officer
- Purchasing Agent
- Chief Executive Officer[5]

Information Security Professional Credentials

As you learned in Chapter 2, many organizations rely to some extent on recognizable professional certifications to ascertain the level of proficiency possessed by any given candidate. Many of the certification programs are relatively new, and consequently their precise value is not fully understood by most hiring organizations. The certifying bodies work diligently to educate their constituent communities on the value and qualifications of their certificate recipients. Employers struggle to match certifications to position requirements, while potential information security workers try to determine which certification programs will help them in the job market. This section identifies widely recognized information security certification programs and describes their test contents and methodologies.

Certified Information Systems Security Professional (CISSP) and Systems Security Certified Practitioner (SSCP)

Considered the most prestigious certification for security managers and CISOs, the CISSP is one of two certifications offered by the International Information Systems Security Certification Consortium [(ISC)²; www.isc2.org]. (The SSCP is the other.) The CISSP certification recognizes mastery of an internationally recognized common body of knowledge (CBK) in information security. To sit for the CISSP exam, the candidate must have at least three years of direct, full-time security professional work experience in one or more of ten domains (see below).

The CISSP exam consists of 250 multiple-choice questions and must be completed within six hours. It covers ten domains of information security knowledge:

- Access control systems and methodology
- Applications and systems development
- Business continuity planning
- Cryptography
- Law, investigation, and ethics
- Operations security
- Physical security
- Security architecture and models
- Security management practices
- Telecommunications, network, and Internet security

The CISSP certification requires both successful completion of the exam and, to ensure that the applicant meets the experience requirement, endorsement by a qualified third party (typically another CISSP, the candidate's employer, or another licensed, certified, or commissioned professional). The breadth and depth covered in each of the ten domains makes it one of the most challenging to obtain of the various information security certifications available. Holders of the CISSP must earn a specific number of continuing education credits every three years to retain the certification.

Because it is difficult to master all ten domains covered on the CISSP exam, many security professionals seek other less rigorous certifications, such as (ISC)²'s SSCP certification. Like the CISSP, the SSCP certification is more applicable to the security manager than the technician, as the bulk of its questions focus on the operational nature of information security. The SSCP focuses "on practices, roles and responsibilities as defined by experts from major IS industries."[6] Nevertheless, the information security technician seeking advancement can benefit from this certification.

The SSCP exam consists of 125 multiple-choice questions and must be completed within three hours. It covers seven domains:

- Access controls
- Administration
- Audit and monitoring
- Risk, response, and recovery
- Cryptography
- Data communications
- Malicious code/malware

Many consider the SSCP to be the little brother of the CISSP. It is a valid certification and is easier to obtain than the CISSP. The seven domains are not a subset of the CISSP domains, but rather contain slightly more technical content. Just as with the CISSP, a SSCP holder must earn continuing education credits to retain the certification, or else retake the exam.

(ISC)[2] has recently unveiled its latest certification program, the (ISC)[2] Associate. This program is geared toward individuals who wish to take the CISSP or SSCP exams before obtaining the requisite experience for certification. "The Associate of (ISC)[2] program is a mechanism for information security professionals, who are still in the process of acquiring the necessary experience to become CISSPs or SSCPs, to become associated with (ISC)[2] and obtain career-related support during this early period in his or her information security career."[7]

Global Information Assurance Certification (GIAC)

In 1999, the System Administration, Networking and Security Organization (SANS; www.sans.org) developed a series of technical security certifications known as the Global Information Assurance Certification (www.giac.org). At the time, no other technical security certifications existed. Those working in the technical security field could only obtain networking or computing certifications like the Microsoft Certified Systems Engineer (MCSE) or Certified Novell Engineer (CNE).

GIAC certifications not only test for knowledge, but also require candidates to demonstrate application of that knowledge. While a growing number of entry-level certifications are available, GIAC currently offers the only advanced technical certifications. The GIAC family of certifications can be pursued independently or combined to earn a comprehensive certification called GIAC Security Engineer (GSE). The GIAC Information Security Officer (GISO) is an overview certification that combines basic technical knowledge with an understanding of threats, risks, and best practices, similar to the SSCP. Unlike other certifications, the GIAC certifications require the applicant to complete a written practical assignment that tests the applicant's ability to apply skills and knowledge. These assignments are submitted to the SANS Information Security Reading Room for review by security practitioners, potential certificate applicants, and others with an interest in information security. Only when the practical assignment is complete is the candidate allowed to take the online exam.

To obtain any GIAC certification you must meet the following requirements:

- Complete a practical/research paper and one or two exams (depending on your certification track).
- Your practical must receive a passing grade before you will be authorized to take the exams.
- Complete the online exams for that particular subject via the GIAC Web site. Most exams are 75 questions (multiple choice) and must be completed within two hours. A few of the exams are 90 questions and must be completed within three hours.
- If you submit an acceptable practical and pass your exams, you will be GIAC certified.[8]

The individual GIAC certifications are as follows:

- GIAC Security Essentials Certification (GSEC)
- GIAC Certified Firewall Analyst (GCFW)
- GIAC Certified Intrusion Analyst (GCIA)
- GIAC Certified Incident Handler (GCIH)
- GIAC Certified Windows Security Administrator (GCWN)
- GIAC Certified UNIX Security Administrator (GCUX)
- GIAC Information Security Officer—Basic (GISO–Basic)
- GIAC Systems and Network Auditor (GSNA)
- GIAC Certified Forensic Analyst (GCFA)
- GIAC Security Leadership Certificate (GSLC)

The GIAC Certified Engineer is considered the pinnacle of GIAC certifications. Candidates must earn all of the track certifications (GIAC Certified Firewall Analyst, GIAC Certified Intrusion Analyst, GIAC Certified Incident Handler, GIAC Certified Windows Security Administrator, and GIAC Certified UNIX Security Administrator), and receive honors recognition in at least one, before they are permitted to sit for this final certification.

Security Certified Program (SCP)

One of the newest certifications in the information security discipline is the Security Certified Program (www.securitycertified.net). The SCP offers two tracks: the Security Certified Network Professional (SCNP) and the Security Certified Network Architect (SCNA). Both are designed for the security technician and emphasize technical knowledge; the latter also includes authentication principles. The tests focus on network security, rather than on general networking concepts, making them distinct from the MSCE and the CNE. The SCNP track targets firewalls and intrusion detection, and requires two exams:[9]

- Network Security Fundamentals (NSF)
- Network Defense and Countermeasures (NDC)

The SCNA program includes authentication areas, including biometrics and PKI. It requires two certification exams:

- PKI and Biometrics Concepts and Planning (PBC)
- PKI and Biometrics Implementation (PBI)

While not as detailed as the GIAC certifications, these programs provide a useful way for a professional to demonstrate the knowledge needed to work in new areas of security, while developing a vendor-neutral core of practitioner knowledge evaluation.

TruSecure ICSA Certified Security Associate (TICSA)

TruSecure ICSA Certified Security Associate certifications are among the first vendor-sponsored certifications. TruSecure Corporation is a well-known security organization and is promoting a vendor-neutral approach that focuses on providing "certifications that are skills- and knowledge-based, technology specific, and pragmatic."[10] As in some other certification programs, a candidate must demonstrate appropriate experience and a training foundation before being allowed to sit for the examinations. The promoters of the certifications describe their programs as "complementary to CISSP, in as much as it is designed for the IT practitioner responsible for ensuring security principles are applied in the context of their daily job scope; and it represents a stepping stone toward higher-level security management." In fact, the managing director of (ISC)[2] has endorsed TICSA, which is much more technical than the SSCP and is targeted to network and systems administrators. According to TruSecure, to attain the TICSA, a candidate must meet the following requirements:

- Demonstrate experience or training as follows:
  - Have two years of experience in network security administration, LAN security management, database security, creation of security products or protocols, persistent writing, teaching, or creation of other original work in the area of computer or data security or privacy, including knowledge or practice in one or more of TruSecure's six categories of risk.

  or

  - Demonstrate attendance of at least 48 hours of approved computer security or privacy conference or seminars and/or successful completion of at least 48 hours of computer security training or courses acceptable to the TruSecure certification oversight board and published on the TruSecure ICSA security practitioner training page.
- Successfully complete the TICSA written multiple-choice examination, which requires understanding of the TruSecure security methodologies, which differentiates it from other security certification programs.
- Affirm at the time of examination the TruSecure ICSA Security Practitioner Code of Ethics.[11]

The examination is based largely on the TruSecure methodology (so it isn't purely vendor neutral) and the TruSecure Six Categories of Risk, which are as follows:

- Electronic
  - External and internal
  - Hacking and sniffing
  - Spoofing
- Malicious Code
  - Viruses, worms
  - Java, ActiveX
  - Trojans
- Physical
  - Theft, terminal hijack

- Human
  - Social engineering
- Privacy
- Down time
  - DoS attacks
  - Bugs
  - Power
  - Civil unrest
  - Natural disasters

The exam consists of approximately 70 multiple-choice questions, which must be completed within 90 minutes.

TruSecure is currently developing an expert certification, the TICSE. It will be a follow-up to the TICSA and will require knowledge levels approaching those of the security manager. The TICSE candidate must demonstrate proficiency in the following areas:

- Firewall implementation, including proxy-based and multiple- and single-firewall installations, and packet filtering
- Security policy formulation and implementation
- Risk analysis
- Attack method identification and solutions
- Bastion hosts and system hardening techniques
- Proxy server filtering properties
- VPN deployment
- Operating system security
- Applied cryptography (PGP, S/MIME, VPNs)
- Key management issues and solutions
- Incident response planning
- Biometrics
- Network and computer forensics

TICSE candidates also complete both written and practical exams. The exam formats and durations have not yet been published.

Security+

From CompTIA (www.comptia.com)—the organization that offered the first vendor-neutral professional IT certifications, the A+ series—comes another certification program, the Security+ certification. "The CompTIA Security+ certification tests for security knowledge mastery of an individual with two years on-the-job networking experience, with emphasis on security. The exam covers industrywide topics including communication security, infrastructure security, cryptography, access control, authentication, external attack, and operational and organization security. CompTIA Security+ curricula are being taught at colleges, universities, and commercial training centers around the globe. CompTIA Security+ is being used as an elective or prerequisite to advanced vendor-specific and vendor-neutral security certifications."[12] The exam covers five domains, as shown in Table 10-2.

Table 10-2	Domains Covered in the CompTIA Security+ Exam	
Domain	**Percentage of Exam**
1.0 General Security Concepts	30%
2.0 Communication Security	20%
3.0 Infrastructure Security	20%
4.0 Basics of Cryptography	15%
5.0 Operational/Organizational Security	15%

Source: CompTIA. *CompTIA Security+ Certification*. Accessed July 17, 2003. www.comptia.com/certification/security/default.asp.

Certified Information Systems Auditor (CISA) and Certified Information Security Manager (CISM)

The Certified Information Systems Auditor certification, while not specifically a security certification, does include many information security components. The Information Systems Audit and Control Association and Foundation (ISACA), which is the sponsoring organization for the CISA, touts the certification as being appropriate for auditing, networking, and security professionals. The CISA requirements are as follows:

- Successful completion of the CISA examination
- Experience as an information systems auditor, with a minimum of five years' professional experience in information systems auditing, control, or security
- Agreement to the Code of Professional Ethics
- Payment of maintenance fees, a minimum of 20 contact hours of continuing education annually, and a minimum of 120 contact hours during a fixed three-year period
- Adherence to the Information Systems Auditing Standards

The exam covers the following areas of information systems auditing:

- The IS audit process (10%)
- Management, planning, and organization of IS (11%)
- Technical infrastructure and operational practices (13%)
- Protection of information assets (25%)
- Disaster recovery and business continuity (10%)
- Business application system development, acquisition, implementation, and maintenance (16%)
- Business process evaluation and risk management (15%)

The CISA exam is offered only once a year, so planning in advance is a must.

The Certified Information Security Manager certification program is also offered by ISACA. The CISM credential is geared toward experienced information security managers and others who may have information security management responsibilities. The CISM can assure executive management that a candidate has the required background knowledge needed for effective security management and consulting. This exam is also offered annually. The CISM examination covers the following practice areas:

- Information security governance
- Risk management

- Information security program management
- Information security management
- Response management

In order to be certified, the applicant must:
- Pass the examination
- Adhere to a code of ethics promulgated by ISACA
- Pursue continuing education as specified
- Complete five years of information security work experience with at least three years in information security management in three or more of the defined areas of practice

Certified Information Forensics Investigator (CIFI)

The Information Security Forensics Association (IFSA; www.infoforensics.org) is developing an examination for a Certified Information Systems Forensics Investigator. This program will evaluate expertise in the tasks and responsibilities of a security administrator or security manager, including incident response, working with law enforcement, and auditing. Although the certification exam has not been finalized yet, the body of knowledge has been tentatively defined to include the following aspects of information security:

- Countermeasures
- Auditing
- Incident response teams
- Law enforcement and investigation
- Traceback
- Tools and techniques

Certification Costs

Certifications cost money, and the preferred certifications can be expensive. Individual certification exams can cost as much as $500, and certifications that require multiple exams can cost many hundreds or thousands of dollars. In addition, the cost for formal training to prepare for the certification exams can be significant. While you should not wholly rely upon certification preparation courses as groundwork for a real-world position, they can help you round out your knowledge and fill in gaps. Some certification exams, such as the CISSP, are very broad; others, such as the components of the GIAC, are very technical. Given the nature of the knowledge needed to pass the examinations, most experienced professionals find it difficult to do well on them without at least some review. Many prospective certificate holders engage in individual or group study sessions, and purchase one of the many excellent exam review books on the subject.

Certifications are designed to recognize experts in their respective fields, and the cost of certification deters those who might otherwise take the exam just to see if they can pass. Most examinations require between two and three years of work experience, and they are often structured to reward candidates who have significant hands-on experience. Some certification programs require that candidates document certain minimum experience requirements before they are permitted to sit for the exams. Before attempting a certification exam, do your homework. Look into the exam's stated body of knowledge as well as its purpose and requirements to ensure that the time and energy spent pursuing the certification are well spent. Figure 10-3 shows several approaches to preparing for security certification.

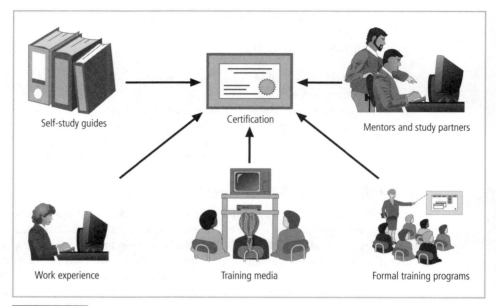

Self-study guides   Certification   Mentors and study partners

Work experience   Training media   Formal training programs

FIGURE 10-3 Preparing for Security Certification

Charles Cresson Wood has this to say about professional certification for information security practitioners:

> With résumé fraud on the rise, one of the sure-fire methods for employers to be sure that the people they hire are indeed familiar with the essentials of the field is to insist that they have certain certifications. The certifications can then be checked with the issuing organizations to make sure that they have indeed been conferred on the applicant for employment. This chapter lists the major certifications relevant to the information security field. There are others, but these are the ones that the practitioner will encounter most frequently, and these are the ones that have the greatest credibility.
>
> The [...] professional certifications are relevant primarily to centralized information security positions. They are not generally relevant to staff working in decentralized information security positions, unless these individuals intend to become information security specialists. You may also look for these certifications on the résumés of consultants and contractors working in the information security field.
>
> You may wish to list these designations in help wanted advertisements, look for them on résumés, and ask about them during interviews. Automatic résumé scanning software can also be set up to search for these strings of characters.[13]

VIEWPOINT

Finding Your Path

By Herb Mattord, CDP, CISSP

I started my IT career in 1977 using COBOL on a mainframe. I had a good academic record, a good attitude, many aspirations, and lots of hope for the future. But I did not see a path leading to a career as a university professor and author.

I learned early in my career that certification is an important part of the IT profession. My first certification was the Certificate in Data Processing, earned in 1979. While that certification was never the single most critical factor in my career, it helped me understand the power of external validation. That's why in the 1990s I pursued the Microsoft Certified Systems Engineer (MCSE) credential. I took most of the required exams, yet always managed to stay one exam short of certification, and then my career took a different turn.

Inexorable corporate forces drew me to information security in the late 1990s. To gain skills and to demonstrate my professionalism, I decided to pursue another certification, the Certified Information Systems Security Professional (CISSP). A quick look at my byline shows that I was successful in that pursuit.

I take my credentials seriously, finding ways to contribute to the success of my own career and to the future of the profession. When I began the CISSP certification program, I hoped for a positive performance review and another career credential. In fact, I gained a lot more than that: I started on a trail that led me out of corporate information security and into academia. Now, I am privileged to teach and stress the value of quality certifications to my students.

How did the CISSP come to redirect my career path? I suppose the only answer comes from Joseph Campbell. He said:

> If you follow your bliss, you put yourself on a kind of track that has been there all the while, waiting for you, and the life that you ought to be living is the one you are living. Wherever you are—if you are following your bliss, you are enjoying that refreshment, that life within you, all the time.[14]

The CISSP gave me the opportunity and the courage to follow my own sense of what gives me fulfillment. This pursuit of satisfaction is truly what Campbell had in mind when he said to follow your bliss.

As you progress in your own career, look for opportunities, and be aware that they may be very well camouflaged. What looks like a precipice might just be the springboard for your dreams.

Employment Policies and Practices

The general management community of interest should integrate solid information security concepts across all of the organization's employment policies and practices. The following sections examine important concepts associated with recruiting, hiring, firing, and managing human resources. Including information security responsibilities into every employee's job description and subsequent performance reviews can make an entire organization take information security more seriously.

Hiring

From an information security perspective, the hiring of employees is laden with potential security pitfalls. The CISO, in cooperation with the CIO and relevant information security managers, should establish a dialogue with human resources personnel so that information security considerations become part of the hiring process. Figure 10-4 highlights some of the hiring concerns.

Background checks

Certifications

Policies

Covenants and agreements

Contracts

FIGURE 10-4 Hiring Issues

Job Descriptions

Integrating information security into the hiring process begins with reviewing and updating job descriptions to include information security responsibilities. Organizations that provide complete job descriptions when advertising open positions should omit the elements of the job description that describe access privileges.

Interviews

Some interviews are conducted by members of the human resources staff; others include members of the department that the employee will eventually join. When a position within the information security department opens up, the security manager can take the opportunity to educate human resources personnel on the various certifications, the specific experience each credential requires, and the qualifications of a good candidate. In general, information security should advise human resources to limit the information provided to the candidates on the access rights of the position. When an interview includes a site visit, the tour should avoid secure and restricted sites, because the visitor could observe enough information about the operations or information security functions to represent a potential threat to the organization.

New Hire Orientation

New employees should receive, as part of their orientation, an extensive information security briefing. This orientation should cover policies, security procedures, access levels, and training on the secure use of information systems. By the time employees are ready to report to their positions, they should be thoroughly briefed on the security component of their particular jobs, as well as the rights and responsibilities of all personnel in the organization.

On-the-Job Security Training

Organizations should conduct the periodic security awareness and training activities described in Chapter 5 to keep security at the forefront of employees' minds and minimize employee mistakes. Formal external and informal internal seminars also increase the level of security awareness for all employees, but especially for InfoSec employees.

Security Checks

A background check should be conducted before the organization extends an offer to any candidate, regardless of job level. A background check can uncover past criminal behavior or other information that suggests a potential for future misconduct or a vulnerability that might render a candidate susceptible to coercion or blackmail. A number of regulations govern which areas organizations are permitted investigate and how the information gathered can influence the hiring decision. The security and human resources managers should discuss these matters with legal counsel to determine which local and state regulations apply.

Background checks differ in their levels of detail and depth. In the military, background checks are used to help determine the individual's security clearance. In the business world, the thoroughness of a background check can vary with the level of trust required for the position being filled. Candidates for information security positions should expect to undergo a reasonably detailed and thorough background check. Those applying for jobs in law enforcement or high-security positions may be required to submit to polygraph tests. Some of the common types of background checks are as follows:

- Identity checks: personal identity validation
- Education and credential checks: institutions attended, degrees and certifications earned, and certification status
- Previous employment verification: where candidates worked, why they left, what they did, and for how long
- Reference checks: validity of references and integrity of reference sources
- Worker's compensation history: claims from worker's compensation
- Motor vehicle records: driving records, suspensions, and other items noted in the applicant's public record
- Drug history: drug screening and drug usage, past and present
- Medical history: current and previous medical conditions, usually associated with physical capability to perform the work in the specified position
- Credit history: credit problems, financial problems, and bankruptcy

- Civil court history: involvement as the plaintiff or defendant in civil suits
- Criminal court history: criminal background, arrests, convictions, and time served

Organizations must comply with federal regulations regarding the use of personal information in employment practices. Among those is the Fair Credit Reporting Act (FCRA), which governs the activities of consumer credit reporting agencies as well as the uses of the information procured from these agencies.[15] Credit reports contain information on a job candidate's credit history, employment history, and other personal data.

Among other things, FCRA prohibits employers from obtaining a credit report unless the candidate gives written permission for such a report to be released. This regulation also allows the candidate to request information on the nature and type of reporting used in making the employment decision, and to know the content of these reports and how they were used in making the hiring decision. FCRA restricts the time period that these reports can address. Unless the candidate earns more than $75,000 per year, they can contain only seven years of adverse information.

Contracts and Employment

Once a candidate has accepted a job offer, the employment contract becomes an important security instrument. Many of the policies discussed in Chapter 6 require an employee to agree in writing to monitoring and nondisclosure agreements. It is important to have these contracts and agreement in place at the time of the hire, because existing employees cannot necessarily be compelled to sign, nor can they be denied access to the systems that enable them to perform their duties. Job candidates, on the other hand, can be offered "employment contingent upon agreement," whereby they are not offered a position unless they agree to the binding organizational policies. While such a policy may seem harsh, it is a necessary component of the security process. Once candidates sign the security agreements, the remainder of the employment contracts may be executed.

Security as Part of Performance Evaluation

To heighten information security awareness and change workplace behavior, organizations should incorporate information security components into employee performance evaluations. Employees pay close attention to job performance evaluations, and including information security tasks in them will motivate employees to take more care when performing these tasks.

Termination Issues

An organization can downsize, be bought out, be taken over, shut down, go out of business, or simply lay off, fire, or relocate its workforce. In any event, when an employee leaves an organization, a number of security-related concerns arise. Chief among these is the continuity of protection for all information to which the employee had access. When an employee leaves an organization, the following tasks must be performed:

- The former employee's access to the organization's systems must be disabled.
- The former employee must return all removable media.
- The former employee's hard drives must be secured.
- File cabinet locks must be changed.
- Office door locks must be changed.

- The former employee's keycard access must be revoked.
- The former employee's personal effects must be removed from the premises.
- The former employee should be escorted from the premises, once keys, keycards, and other business property have been turned over.

In addition to performing these tasks, many organizations conduct an **exit interview** to remind the employee of any contractual obligations, such as nondisclosure agreements, and to obtain feedback on the employee's tenure in the organization. At this time, the employee should be reminded that failure to comply with contractual obligations could lead to civil or criminal action.

Of course, most employees are allowed to clean out their own offices and collect their personal belongings, and are simply asked to return their keys. From a security standpoint, however, regardless of the level of trust in the employee or the level of cordiality in the office environment, the voluntary or involuntary termination of employee inevitably brings a risk of exposure of organizational information. Two methods for handling employee outprocessing, depending on the employee's reasons for leaving, are as follows:

- Hostile departure (usually involuntary), including termination, downsizing, lay-off, or quitting: Security cuts off all logical and keycard access, before the employee is terminated. As soon as the employee reports for work, he or she is escorted into the supervisor's office to receive the bad news. The individual is then escorted from the workplace and informed that his or her personal property will be forwarded, or is escorted to his or her office, cubicle, or personal area to collect personal effects under supervision. No organizational property is allowed to leave the premises, including diskettes, pens, papers, or books. Terminated employees can submit, in writing, a list of the property they wish to retain, stating their reasons for doing so. Once personal property has been gathered, the employee is asked to surrender all keys, keycards, and other organizational identification and access devices, PDAs, pagers, cell phones, and all remaining company property, and is then escorted from the building.
- Friendly departure (voluntary) for retirement, promotion, or relocation: The employee may have tendered notice well in advance of the actual departure date, which can make it much more difficult for security to maintain positive control over the employee's access and information usage. Employee accounts are usually allowed to continue, with a new expiration date. The employee can come and go at will and usually collects any belongings and leaves without escort. The employee is asked to drop off all organizational property before departing.

In either circumstance, the offices and information used by departing employees must be inventoried, their files stored or destroyed, and all property returned to organizational stores. It is possible in either situation that departing employees have collected organizational information and taken home files, reports, data from databases, and anything else that could be valuable in their future employment. This outcome may be impossible to prevent. Only by scrutinizing system logs during the transition period and after the employee has departed, and sorting out authorized actions from system misuse or information theft, can the organization determine whether a breach of policy or a loss of information has occurred. If information has been illegally copied or stolen, it should be treated as an incident and the appropriate policy followed. Figure 10-5 illustrates some termination concerns and procedures.

Information disclosure agreements   Audit system use and storage

Changing of system access

Equipment inventory   Exit interview

Changing of locks

FIGURE 10-5   Termination Issues

Personnel Security Practices

There are various ways of monitoring and controlling employees to minimize their opportunities to misuse information. **Separation of duties** is used to make it difficult for an individual to violate information security and breach the confidentiality, integrity, or availability of information. This control is particularly important in financial matters. For example, banks typically require two employees to issue a cashier's check. The first is authorized to prepare the check, acquire the numbered financial document, and ready the check for signature. The second, usually a supervisor, is authorized to sign the check. If one person has the authority to do both task, then that person can prepare checks made out to co-conspirators, sign them, and steal large sums from the bank.

Separation of duties can also be applied to critical information and information systems. For example, one programmer might update the software in the systems, and a supervisor or coworker might then apply the tested update to the production system following the procedures of the change management process. Alternatively, one employee might be authorized to initiate backups to the system, while another mounts and dismounts the physical media. This checks-and-balances method requires two or more people to conspire to commit a theft or other misadventure, which is known as **collusion**. The odds that two people will be able to successfully collaborate to misuse the system are much lower than the odds of one person doing so. A practice similar to separation of duties, known as **two-man control**, requires that two individuals review and approve each other's work before the task is considered complete. Figure 10-6 illustrates separation of duties and two-man control.

Another control used to prevent personnel from misusing information assets is job rotation. **Job rotation** requires that every employee be able to perform the work of at least one other employee. If that approach is not feasible, an alternative is **task rotation**, in which all critical tasks can be performed by multiple individuals. Both job rotation and task rotation ensure that no one employee is performing actions that cannot be knowledgeably reviewed by another employee. In general, this overlap of knowledge is just good business sense. Among the many threats to an organization's information, a major concern is the inability to perform the tasks of an employee who is unable or unwilling to perform them. If everyone knows at least part of another person's job (a human RAID system), the organization can survive the loss of any single employee.

Two-man control

Team members review each other's work

Separation of duties

Work is divided up; each team member performs a portion of the task sequence

FIGURE 10-6 Personnel Security Controls

For similar reasons, each employee should be required to take a **mandatory vacation**, of at least one week per year. This policy gives the organization a chance to perform a detailed review of everyone's work. Employees who are stealing from an organization or otherwise misusing information or systems are reluctant to take vacations, for fear that their actions will be detected if they are not present to conceal them.

Finally, another important way to minimize opportunities for employee misuse information is to limit access to information. That is, employees should be able to access only the information they need, and only for the period required to perform their tasks. This idea is referred to as the principle of **least privilege**. Similar to the need-to-know concept, least privilege ensures that no unnecessary access to data occurs. If all employees can access all the organization's data all the time, it is almost certain that abuses—possibly leading to losses in confidentiality, integrity, and availability—will occur.

Security of Personnel and Personal Data

Organizations are required by law to protect sensitive or personal employee information, including personally identifying facts such as employee addresses, phone numbers, Social Security numbers, medical conditions, and even names and addresses of family members. This responsibility also extends to customers, patients, and anyone with whom the organization has business relationships. While personnel data is, in principle, no different than other data that information security is expected to protect, certainly more regulations cover its protection. As a result, information security procedures should ensure that this data receives at least the same level of protection as the other important data in the organization. You will learn more about privacy and information security in Chapter 11.

Security Considerations for Nonemployees

Many individuals who are not employees often have access to sensitive organizational information. Relationships with individuals in this category should be carefully managed to prevent threats to information assets from materializing. Some of the categories of nonemployees, and the security considerations specific to them, are discussed in the sections that follow.

Temporary Workers

Temporary workers—often called temps—are brought in by organizations to temporarily fill positions or to supplement the existing workforce. In many cases, they are actually employees of a temp agency, a company that is paid to supply specially qualified individuals to an organization. Temps frequently provide secretarial or administrative support but can be used to fill almost any position in an organization, including executives. These workers are often exposed to a wide range of information as they perform their assigned duties. Because they are not employed by the organization for which they're working, however, they may not be subject to the contractual obligations or general policies that govern other employees. If these individuals violate a policy or cause a problem, the strongest action that the host organization can take is to terminate the relationship with the individual and request that he or she be censured. The employing agency is under no contractual obligation to do so, but may seek to appease a powerful or lucrative client. Unless specified in its contract with the organization, the temp agency may not be liable for losses caused by its workers.

From a security standpoint, access to information for these individuals should be limited to what is necessary to perform their duties. The organization can attempt to have temporary employees sign nondisclosure agreements and fair use policies, but the temp agency may refuse to go along, forcing the host organization to either dismiss the temp workers or allow them to work without such agreements. This can create an awkward—and potentially dangerous—situation. It may be impossible to limit a temp's access to information that is beyond the scope of his or her assigned tasks. The only way to combat this threat is to ensure that employees who are supervising temporary workers restrict their access to information, and to make sure that all workers—whether employees or temps—follow good security practices, especially clean desk policies and securing classified data. Temps can provide great benefits to the organizations, but they should not be employed at the cost of sacrificing information security.

Contract Employees

Contract employees—often called contractors—are typically hired to perform specific services for the organization. In many cases, they are hired via a third-party organization rather than as individuals. Typical contract employees include groundskeepers, maintenance services staff, electricians, mechanics, and other repair people, but can include professionals such as attorneys, technical consultants, and IT specialists.

While professional contractors may require access to virtually all areas of the organization to do their jobs, service contractors usually need access only to specific facilities, and they should not be allowed to wander freely in and out of buildings. In a secure facility, all service contractors are escorted from room to room, and into and out of the facility. When these employees report for maintenance or repair services, someone must verify that services are actually scheduled or requested. As mentioned earlier in this book, attackers have been known to dress up as telephone repairmen, maintenance technicians, or janitors to gain physical access to a building; therefore, direct oversight is a necessity. Any service agreements or contracts should contain the following regulations: The facility requires 24 to 48 hours' notice of a maintenance visit; the facility requires all on-site personnel to undergo background checks; and the facility requires advance notice for cancellation or rescheduling of a maintenance visit.

Consultants

Organizations sometimes hire self-employed or agent contractors—typically called consultants—for specific tasks or projects. Consultants have their own security requirements and contractual obligations. They should be handled like contract employees, with special requirements, such as information or facility access requirements, being integrated into the contract before they are given free access to the facility. In particular, security and technology consultants must be prescreened, escorted, and subjected to nondisclosure agreements to protect the organization from intentional or accidental breaches of confidentiality. Consultants tend to brag about the complexity of a particular job or an outstanding service provided to another client. If the organization does not want a consultant to make the relationship public or to disclose any detail, however small, about its particular system configuration, the organization must write these restrictions into the contract. Although these professionals typically request permission to include the business relationship on their résumés or promotional materials, the hiring organization is not obligated to grant this permission and can explicitly deny it.

Just because you pay security consultants, it doesn't mean that protecting your information is their number one priority. Always remember to apply the principle of least privilege when working with consultants.

Business Partners

Businesses sometimes engage in strategic alliances with other organizations, so as to exchange information, integrate systems, or enjoy some other mutual advantage. In these situations, a prior business agreement must specify the levels of exposure that both organizations are willing to tolerate. Sometimes one division of an organization enters a strategic partnership with another organization that directly competes with one of its own divisions. If the strategic partnership evolves into an integration of the systems of both companies, competing groups may be provided with information that neither parent organization expected. For this reason, there must be a meticulous, deliberate process of determining what information is to be exchanged, in which format, and to whom. Nondisclosure agreements are an important part of any such collaborative effort. The level of security of both systems must be examined before any physical integration takes place, as system connection means that vulnerability on one system becomes vulnerability for all linked systems.

THREAT MANAGEMENT

Social Engineering

The most nontechnical attack involves people. For this reason, this book dedicates a great deal of space to reinforcing the concept that security is a people problem, not a technological one. Every day thousands of systems are attacked successfully by individuals who take advantage of the natural gullibility of people. This gullibility is usually the result of a simple lack of computing knowledge and experience.

(continued)

Social engineering (SE) uses persuasive techniques to gain the confidence of an individual in an effort to obtain information. Contrary to popular myth, most social engineering attacks don't come in as a phone call from "Joe in technology services" asking for your user name and password to fix your computer problem. Most attacks are subtle, collecting small bits of seemingly harmless information until a base of insider knowledge is built and then deployed to gain access to systems or information. According to the infamous Kevin Mitnick, who used social engineering as the primary means of gaining access to an organization's systems: "'(As) the media characterizes social engineering, hackers will call up and ask for a password,' Mitnick said. 'I have never asked anyone for their password.'"[16] The former super-hacker turned security consultant served five years for his crimes. How do you succeed at SE attacks? "You try to make an emotional connection with the person on the other side to create a sense of trust," he said. "That is the whole idea: to create a sense of trust and then exploit it."[17]

Some forms of SE attacks are so prevalent that there are formal warnings about them:

> The CERT/CC has received reports of social engineering attacks on users of Internet Relay Chat (IRC) and Instant Messaging (IM) services. Intruders trick unsuspecting users into downloading and executing malicious software, which allows the intruders to use the systems as attack platforms for launching distributed denial-of-service (DDoS) attacks. The reports to the CERT/CC indicate that tens of thousands of systems have recently been compromised in this manner. Other reports indicate that Trojan horse and backdoor programs are being propagated via similar techniques. Here is an example of one such message:
>
> *You are infected with a virus that lets hackers get into your machine and read your files, etc. I suggest you to download [malicious URL] and clean your infected machine. Otherwise, you will be banned from [IRC network].*[18]

Many people will recognize these types of e-mails, IMs, and pop-ups for what they are. However, individuals with little computer experience may fail to discriminate between legitimate virus warnings and SE attacks.

A similar attack has been conducted recently to propagate the Slammer virus, among others. An e-mail arrives, apparently from Microsoft (see Figure 10-7), insisting that the user immediately download a critical patch or upgrade to avoid leaving his or her system open to attack. Because Microsoft does not e-mail individuals directly, experienced computer users simply delete the message. To the untrained eye, the message appears legitimate, however, and consequently it may be activated.

Social Engineering Attack Detection

It can be quite difficult to detect a social engineering attack. Indeed, attackers are becoming increasingly sophisticated. Sometimes they ask for seemingly innocuous information, such as the name or telephone number of a coworker. Many employees may have given

(continued)

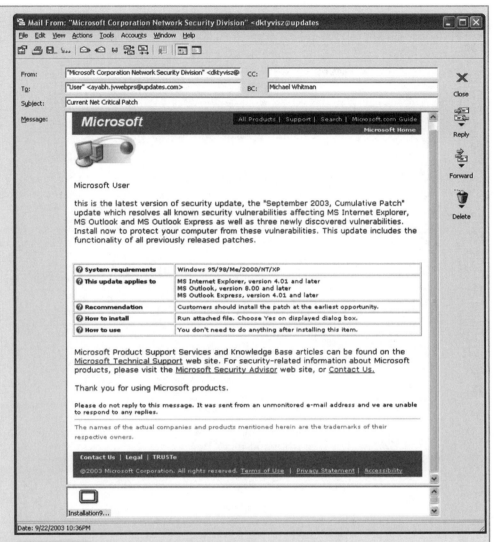

FIGURE 10-7   Social Engineering Attack

this information out routinely, without a second thought, allowing an attacker to begin building a story to get more information from the next person. To detect an SE attack, employees should be trained to detect anomalies in a conversation, e-mail, or pop-up window. These anomalies include "refusal to give contact information, rushing, name-dropping, intimidation, small mistakes (misspellings, misnomers, odd questions), and requesting forbidden information. Look for things that don't quite add up." [19]

(continued)

SE Attack Prevention

The number one method of preventing SE attacks is preparation. All employees must be trained and aware of the potential for these types of attacks. Security education, training, and awareness programs that focus on SE attacks can provide the organization with invaluable preparation and prevention techniques. Some additional prevention methods, along with the attacks they intend to thwart, are presented in Table 10-3.

Table 10-3 Social Engineering Tactics and Strategies

Area of risk	Hacker tactic	Combat strategy
Phone (help desk)	Impersonation and persuasion	Train employees and help desk personnel to never give out passwords or other confidential information by phone
Building entrance	Unauthorized physical access	Use tight badge security, provide employee training, and have security officers present
Office	Shoulder surfing	Don't type in passwords with anyone else present (if you must, do it quickly!)
Phone (help desk)	Impersonation on help desk calls	Assign all employees a PIN specific to help desk support
Office	Wandering through halls looking for open offices	Require all guests to be escorted
Mailroom	Insertion of forged memos	Lock and monitor the mailroom
Machine room/ phone closet	Attempting to gain access, remove equipment, and/or attach a protocol analyzer to grab confidential data	Keep phone closets, server rooms, and other facilities locked at all times and keep an updated inventory of equipment
Phone and PBX	Stealing phone toll access	Control overseas and long-distance calls, trace calls, and refuse transfers
Dumpsters	Dumpster diving	Keep all trash in secured, monitored areas, shred important data, and erase magnetic media
Intranet-internet	Creation and insertion of mock software on intranet or internet to steal passwords	Maintain continual awareness of system and network changes, and provide training on password use
Office	Stealing sensitive documents	Mark documents as confidential and require them to be locked
General–psychological	Impersonation and persuasion	Keep employees on their toes through continued awareness and training programs

Source: S. Granger. *Social Engineering Fundamentals, Part II: Combat Strategies Security Focus.* January 9, 2002. Accessed September 24, 2003. www.securityfocus.com/infocus/1533.

(continued)

SE Attack Defense

The first thing an employee must do to defend against an SE attack is to tell someone. That is, the organization should have an established procedure for reporting suspected SE attacks. If the organization uses some form of Caller ID, the number of the suspected SE attacker should be documented and reported. The organization's incident response team should log these attacks and treat them no differently than any other form of attack.

A paper by David Gragg overviews a multilayered defense against SE. In this paper he defines the following layers of defense:[20]

Foundational Level: Security Policy Addressing Social Engineering
Parameter Level: Security Awareness Training for All Users
Fortress Level: Resistance Training for Key Personnel
Persistence Level: Ongoing Reminders
Gotcha Level: Social Engineering Land Mines (SELM)
- The Justified Know-It-All
- Centralized Security Log
- Call Backs by Policy
- Key Questions
- "Please Hold" by Policy

Offensive Level: Incident Response

It is not difficult to protect against SE attacks, but first employees must know what they are and how they are conducted. Through these educational efforts, SE attacks can become your least dangerous threat, rather than the most dangerous one.

Chapter Summary

- The hiring of information security personnel is affected by a number of factors, among them the law of supply and demand.

- In most cases, organizations look for a technically qualified information security generalist, with a solid understanding of how the organization conducts its business, to serve as the chief information security officer.

- Many information security professionals enter the field through one of two career paths: (1) as former members of law enforcement or the military, or (2) as IT professionals. A relatively new trend is the emergence of university-trained information security specialists.

- During the hiring process, applying standard job descriptions can increase the degree of professionalism in the information security field and improve the consistency of roles and responsibilities among organizations.

- Many organizations use recognizable certifications to identify the level of proficiency associated with the various security positions.

- Management should integrate information security concepts and practices into the organization's employment activities.

- Organizations need the special services of nonemployees—temps, contractors, and consultants—and these relationships must be carefully managed to prevent information security breaches.

- Separation of duties, two-man control, job and task rotation, mandatory vacations, and least privilege are among the practices and methods recommended to minimize employees' opportunities to misuse information.

- Government-mandated requirements for the privacy and security of personnel and personal data must be met by the organization's information security program.

Review Questions

1. When an organization undertakes an information security-driven review of job descriptions, which job descriptions must be reviewed? Which IT jobs not directly associated with information security should be reviewed?

2. List and describe the criteria for selecting information security personnel.

3. What are some of the factors that influence an organization's hiring decisions?

4. What attributes do organizations seek in a candidate when hiring information security professionals? Prioritize this list of attributes and justify your ranking.

5. What are the critical issues that management must consider when dismissing an employee? Do these issues change based on whether the departure is friendly or hostile?

6. How do the security considerations for temporary or contract workers differ from those for regular employees?

7. Which two career paths are often used as entrees into the information security discipline? Are there other paths? If so, describe them.

8. Why is it important to have a body of standard job descriptions for hiring information security professionals?

9. What functions does the CISO perform, and what are the key qualifications and requirements for the position?

10. What functions does the security manager perform, and what are the key qualifications and requirements for the position?

11. What functions does the security technician perform, and what are the key qualifications and requirements for the position?

12. What functions does the internal security consultant perform, and what are the key qualifications and requirements for the position?

13. What is the rationale for acquiring professional credentials?

14. List and describe the certification credentials available to information security professionals.

15. In your opinion, who should pay for the expenses of certification? Under what circumstances would your answer be different? Why?

16. List and describe the standard personnel practices that are part of the information security function. What happens to these practices when they are integrated with information security concepts?

17. Why shouldn't you show a job candidate secure areas during interviews?

18. List and describe the types of nonemployee workers often used by organizations. What special security considerations apply to such workers, and why are they significant?

19. What is separation of duties? How can this method be used to improve an organization's information security practices?

20. What is least privilege? Why is implementing least privilege important?

Exercises

1. Using the Web, find at least five job postings for security administrators. What qualifications do the listings have in common?

2. Go to the (ISC)^2 Web site (www.isc2.org). Research the body of knowledge requirements for the CISSP and the SSCP. Which required areas are *not* covered in this text?

3. Using the Web, search for three different employee hiring and termination policies. Review each and look carefully for inconsistencies. Does each have a section addressing security of information requirements? What clauses should a termination policy contain to prevent disclosure of the organization's information? Create your own variant of either a hiring or a termination policy.

4. Using your local telephone directory, locate a service that offers background checks. Select one at random and call to determine the costs of conducting such checks. How much should an organization spend on conducting these checks, if it interviews dozens of potential employees?

5. Using the descriptions given in the chapter, write a job description for Iris's new position, described in the following Case Exercise. What qualifications and responsibilities should be associated with this position?

Case Exercises

Iris reviewed the scant stack of applications for the newly created security manager position and frowned. There should have been many more than just three applicants for the position.

After the human resources incident earlier in the month, she had been extremely careful in crafting the job description, and was elated when Mike Edwards approved the hire. The new security manager was to assist in the drafting of security policies and plans, a need that had been highlighted by the recent problem.

Iris called Cheryl in human resources. "I'm worried about the number of applicants we've had," she said. "I really thought there would be more than three given the way the economy's slowed down."

Cheryl replied, "Oh, there were dozens, but I prescreened them for you."

"What do you mean?" Iris asked. "Prescreened how?"

Cheryl elaborated. "Well, we pass on only the most qualified applicants. According to our criteria, applicants for information security positions must have a CISA certification or some level of GIAD."

"You mean GIAC?" Iris asked, her uneasiness building.

"No, the file says GIAD," Cheryl replied confidently.

"Well, for this position we need a CISSP or CISM, not a GIAD or CISA. Those certifications don't match the job description I wrote, and I don't remember specifying any required certifications."

"You don't have to," Cheryl said. "We've determined that the best people for the jobs are the ones who have the most certifications. We don't really look at anyone who isn't certified. Is there a problem?"

1. If you were Iris, how would reply to Cheryl's question?

2. What, if anything, is wrong with the human resources focus depicted here? Examine the relationship between certifications and experience. Do certifications alone identify the job candidates with the most appropriate expertise and work experience?

Endnotes

1. Charles Cresson Wood. *Information Security Roles and Responsibilities Made Easy.* Houston: PentaSafe, 2002: 55–94.

2. Eddie Schwartz, Dan Erwin, Vincent Weafer, and Andy Briney. Roundtable: Infosec staffing help wanted! *Information Security Magazine Online,* April 2001. [Cited July 22, 2002]. Available from the World Wide Web at www.infosecuritymag.com/articles/april01/features_roundtable.shtml.

3. Charles Cresson Wood. *Information Security Roles and Responsibilities Made Easy.* Houston: PentaSafe, 2002: 57–59.

4. Charles Cresson Wood. *Information Security Roles and Responsibilities Made Easy.* Houston: PentaSafe, 2002: 63.

5. Charles Cresson Wood. *Information Security Roles and Responsibilities Made Easy.* Houston: PentaSafe, 2002: Table of contents.

6. International Information Systems Security Certification Consortium. About SSCP certification. *ISC² Online* [Cited July 22, 2002]. Available from the World Wide Web at www.isc2.org/cgi/content.cgi?category=20.

7. ISC². *The Associate ISC² Program.* Accessed June 15, 2003. https:// www.isc2.org/cgi/content.cgi?category=84#cat07.

8. Global Information Assurance Certification. GIAC: steps to certification general instructions. *SANS Institute Online* [Cited July 22, 2002]. Available from the World Wide Web at www.giac.org/steps.php#instructions.

9. Security Certified Programs. Certifications. *Ascendant Learning, LLC Online* [Cited July 22, 2002]. Available from the World Wide Web at www.securitycertified.net/certifications.htm.

10. Trusecure. TICSA certification. *Trusecure Online* [Cited July 22, 2002]. Available from the World Wide Web at www.truesecure.com/solutions/certifications/ticsa/.

11. Ibid.

12. CompTIA. *CompTIA Security+ Certification.* Accessed July 17, 2003. www.comptia.com/certification/security/default.asp.

13. Charles Cresson Wood. *Information Security Roles and Responsibilities Made Easy.* Houston: PentaSafe, 2002: 169.

14. Joseph Campbell and Bill Moyer. *The Power of Myth.* New York. Doubleday. 1988.

15. Background Check International. BCI. *BCI Online* [Cited July 22, 2002]. Available from the World Wide Web at www.bcint.com/legal.html.

16. R. Lemos. Mitnick teaches "social engineering." *Ziff-Davis News Net,* July 17, 2000. Accessed September 24, 2003. www.zdnet.com/filters/printerfriendly/0,6061,2604480-2,00.html

17. Ibid.

18. CERT. *Social Engineering Attacks via IRC and Instant Messaging,* CERT Incident Note IN-2002-03, March 19, 2002. Accessed September 26, 2003. www.cert.org/incident_notes/IN-2002-03.html.

19. S. Granger. *Social Engineering Fundamentals, Part II: Combat Strategies Security Focus,* January 9, 2002. Accessed September 24, 2003. www.securityfocus.com/infocus/1533.

20. D. Gragg. A multi-level defense against social engineering. *SANS Institute,* December 2002. Accessed September 26, 2003. www.sans.org/rr/paper.php?id=920.

Law and Ethics

> In law a man is guilty when he violates the rights of others. In ethics he is guilty if he only thinks of doing so.
>
> **IMMANUEL KANT (1724–1804)**

IRIS WAS JUST OVER HALFWAY THROUGH her morning e-mail ritual when she came to a message that caught her attention. Just a few weeks ago RWW had set up a new Web server that allowed anyone, anywhere, to send anonymous e-mail to the company's most senior executive. The message had in fact been sent by the CEO's executive assistant. It read as follows:

```
To: Iris Majwabu
From: RWW Anonymous Ethics Mailbox
Date: 2006-11-18 07:45 AM
Subject: FW: Anonymous Ethics Report — 2006-11-17 02:46 AM
Iris, you better look at this. I pulled the text out and
encrypted it. I am briefing a special executive meeting with
Robin, Jerry and Mike at 10:00. You should be there too.
Meeting invitation follows...
— Cassandra
```

Iris opened her safe and mounted her secure document drive, then exported the file to it. She opened the decryption program, fumbling with her badge carrier to read the randomized key from her security token. The text of the anonymous e-mail appeared on her screen:

```
To: RWW Anonymous Ethics Mailbox
From: A Friend
Date: 2006-11-17 02:46 AM
Subject: Anonymous Ethics Report — 2006-11-17 02:46 AM
```

```
You might want to look at the nile.com auction site at
www.nile.com/auctions/ref=19085769340
Iris opened her browser window and typed in the URL. She saw:
Item #19085769340
RWW, Inc. Customer and key accounts list
Starting bid: US $10,000.00
Time left: 2 days 22 hours 50 mins 3-day listing
History: 0 bids
Location: Cityville WI
```

Iris reached for her incident response plan binder. She knew it was going to be a busy morning and a busy afternoon, too.

LEARNING OBJECTIVES

Upon completion of this material, you should be able to:

- Differentiate between law and ethics
- Identify major national and international laws that relate to the practice of information security
- Understand the role of culture as it applies to ethics in information security
- Access current information on laws, regulations, and relevant professional organizations

Introduction

This chapter covers information security law and ethics. Although the two topics are intertwined, the first part of this chapter focuses on relevant legislation and regulations concerning the management of information in an organization. The second part of the chapter discusses ethics and information security and offers a summary guide to professional organizations with established ethical codes. You can use this chapter both as a reference guide to the legal aspects of information security and as an aide in planning your professional career.

As a future information security professional, it is vital that you understand the scope of an organization's legal and ethical responsibilities. The information security professional should play an important role in an organization's approach to controlling liability for privacy and security risks. In the modern litigious societies of the world, sometimes laws are enforced in civil courts, and plaintiffs are awarded large payments for damages or to punish defendants. To minimize these liabilities the information security practitioner must understand the current legal environment and keep apprised of new laws, regulations, and ethical issues as they emerge. By educating employees and management about their legal and ethical obligations and the proper use of information technology and information security, security professionals can keep an organization focused on its primary objectives.

Law and Ethics in Information Security

Within modern society, individuals elect to trade some aspects of personal freedom for social order. As Jean Jacques Rousseau explains in *The Social Contract Or Principles Of Political Right*[1] (1762), the rules the members of a society create to balance the individual's right to self-determination with the needs of the whole are called laws. **Laws** are rules adopted and enforced by governments to codify expected behavior in modern society. Laws are largely drawn from the **ethics** of a culture, which define socially acceptable behaviors that conform to the widely held principles of the members of that society. The key difference between law and ethics is that law carries the sanction of a governing authority and ethics do not. Ethics are based on **cultural mores**: relatively fixed moral attitudes or customs of a societal group. Some ethics are often described as universal across cultures. For example, murder, theft, and assault are commonly accepted as actions that deviate from ethical and legal codes in the civilized world.

The Legal Environment

The information security professional and managers involved in information security must possess a rudimentary grasp of the legal framework within which their organizations operate. This legal environment can influence the organization to a greater or lesser extent depending on the nature of the organization and the scale on which it operates. The following pages outline, in general terms, the current legal environment.

Types of Law

There are a number of ways to categorize laws. **Civil law** embodies a wide variety of laws pertaining to relationships between and among individuals and organizations. **Criminal law** addresses violations harmful to society and is actively enforced and prosecuted by the state. **Tort law** is a subset of civil law which allows individuals to seek recourse against others in the event of personal, physical, or financial injury. Tort law is pursued in civil court, and is not prosecuted by the state.

Legislation that affects the individual in the workplace can be categorized as private law or public law. **Private law** regulates the relationships among individuals and among individuals and organizations, and encompasses family law, commercial law, and labor law. **Public law** regulates the structure and administration of government agencies and their relationships with citizens, employees, and other governments. Public law includes criminal, administrative, and constitutional law.

Relevant U.S. Laws

Historically, the United States has led the development and implementation of information security legislation to prevent misuse and exploitation of information and information technology. The development of information security legislation promotes the general welfare and creates a stable environment for a solid economy. In its capacity as a global leader, the United States has demonstrated a clear understanding of the problems facing the information security field and has identified necessary penalties for the individuals and organizations that fail to follow the requirements set forth in the U.S. civil statutes. Table 11-1 summarizes the U.S. federal laws relevant to information security.

Table 11-1 Key U.S. Laws of Interest to Information Security Professionals

Area	Act	Date	Web resource location	Description
Criminal intent	National Information Infrastructure Protection Act of 1996	1996	http://policyworks.gov/ policydocs/14.pdf	Categorizes crimes based on defendant's authority to access a protected computer system *and* criminal intent
Terrorism	USA Patriot Act of 2001 (H.R. 3162)	2001	thomas.loc.gov/ cgi-bin/bdquery/z?d107: H.R.3162:	Defines stiffer penalties for prosecution of terrorist crimes
Threats to computers	Computer Fraud and Abuse Act (also known as Fraud and Related Activity in Connection with Computers) (18 U.S.C. 1030)	1986 (amended 1994, 1996, and 2001)	www.usdoj.gov/ criminal/cybercrime/ 1030_new.html	Defines and formalizes laws to counter threats from computer-related acts and offenses
Telecommunications	Communications Act of 1934 Updated By The Telecommunications Deregulation And Competition Act of 1996	1934 (amended 1996 and 2001)	www.fcc.gov/Reports/ 1934new.pdf	Regulates interstate and foreign telecommunications
Federal agency information security	Computer Security Act of 1987	1987	www.cio.gov/ Documents/computer_ security_act_Jan_ 1998.html	Requires all federal computer systems that contain classified information to have surety plans in place, and requires periodic security training for all individuals who operate, design, or manage such systems
Privacy	Federal Privacy Act of 1974	1974	www.usdoj.gov/ foia/privstat.htm	Governs federal agency use of personal information

Table 11-1 Key U.S. Laws of Interest to Information Security Professionals (continued)

Area	Act	Date	Web resource location	Description
Cryptography	The Electronic Communications Privacy Act of 1986	1986	www.itpolicy.gsa.gov/itpolicy/5.pdf	Regulates interception and disclosure of electronic information; also referred to as the Federal Wiretapping Act
Banking	Gramm-Leach-Bliley Act of 1999 (GLB) or The Financial Services Modernization Act	1999	www.senate.gov/~banking/conf/	Focuses on facilitating affiliation among banks, insurance, and securities firms. It has significant impact on the privacy of personal information used by these industries
Trade secrets	The Economic Espionage Act (EEA) of 1996	1996	www.ncix.gov/pubs/online/eea_96.htm	Designed to prevent abuse of information gained while employed elsewhere
Accountability	The Sarbanes-Oxley Act of 2002 or Public Company Accounting Reform and Investor Protection Act	2002	http://news.findlaw.com/hdocs/docs/gwbush/sarbanesoxley072302.pdf	Intended as enforced accountability for executives at publicly traded companies, this law is having ripple effects throughout the accounting, IT, and related units of many organizations

General Computer Crime Laws

There are several key laws relevant to the field of information security. The Computer Fraud and Abuse Act of 1986 (CFA Act) is the cornerstone of many computer-related federal laws and enforcement efforts. It was amended in October 1996 by the National Information Infrastructure Protection Act of 1996, which modified several sections of the previous act, and increased the penalties for selected crimes. The punishment for offenses prosecuted under this statute varies from fines to imprisonment up to 20 years, or both. The penalty depends on the value of the information obtained and whether the offense is judged to have been committed for one of the following reasons:

1. For purposes of commercial advantage
2. For private financial gain
3. In furtherance of a criminal act

COMPUTER FRAUD AND ABUSE ACT OF 1986

(Section 1030, Chapter 47, Title 18 USC)

Fraud And Related Activity In Connection With Computers. Whoever having knowingly accessed a computer without authorization or exceeding authorized access, and by means of such conduct having obtained information that has been determined by the United States Government ... to require protection against unauthorized disclosure for reasons of national defense or foreign relations, or any restricted data ... with reason to believe that such information so obtained could be used to the injury of the United States, or to the advantage of any foreign nation, willfully communicates, delivers, transmits, or causes to be communicated, delivered, or transmitted, or attempts to communicate, deliver, transmit or cause to be communicated, delivered, or transmitted the same to any person not entitled to receive it, or willfully retains the same and fails to deliver it to the officer or employee of the United States entitled to receive it; intentionally accesses a computer without authorization or exceeds authorized access, and thereby obtains information contained in a financial record of a financial institution, or of a card issuer ... , or contained in a file of a consumer reporting agency on a consumer ...; information from any department or agency of the United States; or information from any protected computer if the conduct involved an interstate or foreign communication; intentionally, without authorization to access any nonpublic computer of a department or agency of the United States, accesses such a computer of that department or agency that is exclusively for the use of the Government of the United States or, in the case of a computer not exclusively for such use, is used by or for the Government of the United States and such conduct affects that use by or for the Government of the United States; knowingly and with intent to defraud, accesses a protected computer without authorization, or exceeds authorized access, and by means of such conduct furthers the intended fraud and obtains anything of value, unless the object of the fraud and the thing obtained consists only of the use of the computer and the value of such use is not more than $5,000 in any 1-year period; knowingly causes the transmission of a program, information, code, or command, and as a result of such conduct, intentionally causes damage without authorization, to a protected computer; intentionally accesses a protected computer without authorization, and as a result of such conduct, recklessly causes damage; or intentionally accesses a protected computer without authorization, and as a result of such conduct, causes damage; knowingly and with intent to defraud traffics ... in any password or similar information through which a computer may be accessed without authorization, if such trafficking affects interstate or foreign commerce; or such computer is used by or for the Government of the United States; with intent to extort from any person, firm, association, educational institution, financial institution, government entity, or other legal entity, any money or other thing of value, transmits in interstate or foreign commerce any communication containing any threat to cause damage to a protected computer.

The CFA Act was further modified by the USA Patriot Act of 2001—the abbreviated name for "Uniting and Strengthening America Act by Providing Appropriate Tools Required to Intercept and Obstruct Terrorism Act of 2001," which provides law enforcement agencies with broader latitude to combat terrorism-related activities. Some of the laws modified by the Patriot Act date from the earliest laws created to deal with electronic technology.

USA PATRIOT ACT OF 2001

(H.R. 3162)

Authority to Intercept Voice Communications in Computer Hacking Investigations. Under previous law, investigators could not obtain a wiretap order to intercept wire voice communications for violations of the Computer Fraud and Abuse Act. The Patriot Act identifies specific crimes under which investigators may obtain a wiretap order for wire communications by adding felony violations of the Computer Fraud and Abuse Act to the list of offenses. This authority will sunset December 31, 2005.

Obtaining Voice-mail and Other Stored Voice Communications. Previously, the Electronic Communications Privacy Act (ECPA) governed law enforcement access to stored electronic communications like e-mail, but not stored wire voice communications (voice mail). Instead, the wiretap act regulated these actions primarily because the definition of "wire communication" included stored voice communications; therefore, investigators were required to obtain a wiretap order from a judge to confiscate and review voice mail or answering machine messages. What was not envisioned when the original ECPA was developed was the creation of hybrid systems that stored voice communications as digital messages (digital voice mail). The Patriot act alters the way that the wiretap statute and ECPA apply to stored voice communications. The amendments delete "electronic storage" of wire communications from the definition of "wire communication" and insert language to ensure that stored wire communications are covered under the same rules as stored electronic communications, allowing investigators to search these messages using standard search warrants, rather than wiretap orders. Sunset: December 31, 2005.

Emergency Disclosures by Communications Providers. Previous law relating to voluntary disclosures by communication service providers (like ISPs) contained no special provision allowing providers to disclose customer records or communications in emergencies. If an ISP voluntarily provided account information or subscriber information to law enforcement officials, it risked being subject to civil suit, even if the information pointed to a potential crime or terrorist attack.

This Patriot Act permits, but does not require, ISPs to disclose customer information if it suspects an immediate risk of death or serious physical injury to any person. ISPs are also allowed to disclose such information to protect their property and rights.

Intercepting the Communications of Computer Trespassers. The wiretapping act permits owners of computers and computer systems to monitor their systems to protect rights and property. However, it does not provide clear guidance as to what extent these owners can ask for assistance in this monitoring from the law enforcement community. The Patriot Act allows computer system owners to monitor trespassers on their systems and obtain support from law enforcement officials in conducting this monitoring. This provision also stipulates that *if* the owners or operators of the system authorize law enforcement to monitor a suspected trespassers traffic, *and* the individual intercepting the traffic is engaged in a lawful investigation, *and* the investigator has reason to suspect that the intercepted traffic is vital to the investigation, *and* only those communications conducted by the trespasser will be intercepted, *then* it is legal to intercept the wire or electronic communications of a computer trespasser—even if acting "under color of law" or as an agent of the law. A computer trespasser is defined as "any person who accesses a protected computer without authorization." The definition explicitly excludes individuals "known by the owner or operator of the protected computer to have an existing

(continued)

contractual relationship with the owner or operator for access to all or part of the computer." Sunset: December 31, 2005.

Nationwide Search Warrants for E-mail. Current law requires the government to use a search warrant to compel a provider to disclose unopened e-mail less than six months old. Changes resulting from the Patriot Act allow investigators to obtain warrants for computer records outside their native jurisdiction. Sunset December 31, 2005.

Deterrence and Prevention of Cyberterrorism. This section makes a number of changes to the Computer Fraud and Abuse act, increasing penalties for hackers from 10 to 20 years and clarifying the definition of intent to make explicit that a hacker need only intend damage. It created new offenses for special types of computer crime, such as those targeting national security or the criminal justice system. It also allows aggregation of computer criminal offenses in order to meet some of the minimum requirements for stiffer penalties.

Development and Support of Cybersecurity Forensic Capabilities. This section requires the Attorney General to establish and fund a number of regional computer forensic laboratories as well as provide support for existing labs.

The Communications Act of 1934 was revised by the Telecommunications Deregulation and Competition Act of 1996, which attempts to modernize the archaic terminology of the older act. These much-needed updates were included as part of the Communications Decency Act (CDA), a subset of the TC Act. The CDA was immediately ensnared in a thorny legal challenge on First Amendment grounds over the attempt to define indecency, which through major efforts sponsored by the Internet Blue Ribbon Campaign and by the Electronic Freedom Frontier (www.eff.org), quickly reached the Supreme Court. The subsequent Supreme Court ruling left weak and ineffective controls in place of the more aggressive and ambitious ones originally intended, still leaving unclear the ability to enforce offenses such as harassment through fax or e-mail.

COMMUNICATIONS DECENCY ACT

Whoever in interstate or foreign communications by means of a telecommunications device knowingly makes, creates, or solicits, and initiates the transmission of, any comment, request, suggestion, proposal, image, or other communication which is obscene, lewd, lascivious, filthy, or indecent, with intent to annoy, abuse, threaten, or harass another person; by means of a telecommunications device knowingly makes, creates, or solicits, and initiates the transmission of any comment, request, suggestion, proposal, image, or other communication which is obscene or indecent, knowing that the recipient of the communication is under 18 years of age regardless of whether the maker of such communication placed the call or initiated the communication; makes a telephone call or utilizes a telecommunications device, whether or not conversation or communication ensues, without disclosing his identity and with intent to annoy, abuse, threaten, or harass any person at the called number or who receives the communications; makes or

(continued)

causes the telephone of another repeatedly or continuously to ring, with intent to harass any person at the called number; or makes repeated telephone calls or repeatedly initiates communication with a telecommunications device, during which conversation or communication ensues, solely to harass any person at the called number or who receives the communication; or knowingly permits any telecommunications facility under his control to be used for any activity prohibited; intent that it be used for such activity, shall be fined or imprisoned not more than two years, or both.

Whoever knowingly within the United States, by means of telephone, makes (directly or by recording device) any obscene communication for commercial purposes to any person, regardless of whether the maker of such communication placed the call; or permits any telephone facility under such person's control to be used for an activity prohibited; shall be fined, or imprisoned not more than two years, or both.

Whoever knowingly within the United States, by means of telephone, makes (directly or by recording device) any indecent communication for commercial purposes which is available to any person under 18 years of age or to any other person without that person's consent, regardless of whether the maker of such communication placed the call; or permits any telephone facility under such person's control to be used for an activity prohibited; shall be fined not more than $50,000 or imprisoned not more than six months, or both.

Whoever in interstate or foreign communications knowingly uses an interactive computer service to send to a specific person or persons under 18 years of age, or uses any interactive computer service to display in a manner available to a person under 18 years of age, any comment, request, suggestion, proposal, image, or other communication that, in context, depicts or describes, in terms patently offensive as measured by contemporary community standards, sexual or excretory activities or organs, regardless of whether the user of such service placed the call or initiated the communication; or knowingly permits any telecommunications facility under such person's control to be used for an activity prohibited, with the intent that it be used for such activity, shall be fined, or imprisoned not more than two years, or both.

Another key law that is of critical importance to information security professionals is The Computer Security Act of 1987. This legislation was one of the first attempts to protect federal computer systems by establishing minimum acceptable security practices. The Computer Security Act of 1987 charged the National Bureau of Standards, in cooperation with the National Security Agency, with the following tasks:

- Developing standards, guidelines, and associated methods and techniques for computer systems
- Developing uniform standards and guidelines for most federal computer systems
- Developing technical, management, physical, and administrative standards and guidelines for the cost-effective security and privacy of sensitive information in federal computer systems
- Developing guidelines for use by operators of federal computer systems that contain sensitive information in training their employees in security awareness and accepted security practice
- Developing validation procedures for, and evaluate the effectiveness of, standards and guidelines through research and liaison with other government and private agencies[2]

The Computer Security Act also established a Computer System Security and Privacy Advisory Board within the Department of Commerce. This board identifies emerging managerial, technical, administrative, and physical safety issues relative to computer systems security and privacy, and it advises the Bureau of Standards and the Secretary of Commerce on security and privacy issues pertaining to federal computer systems. The board reports to the Secretary of Commerce, the Director of the Office of Management and Budget, the Director of the National Security Agency, and the appropriate committees of the Congress.

The Computer Security Act of 1987 also amended the Federal Property and Administrative Services Act of 1949. The amendments required the National Bureau of Standards to distribute standards and guidelines pertaining to federal computer systems, making such standards compulsory and binding to the extent to which the secretary determines necessary to improve the efficiency of operation or security and privacy of federal computer systems. It also permitted the head of any federal agency to employ more stringent standards than those distributed.

Another provision of the Computer Security Act requires mandatory periodic training in computer security awareness and accepted computer security practice for all employees who are involved with the management, use, or operation of each federal computer system. This training for federal employees is intended to enhance their awareness of the threats to, and vulnerability of, computer systems and to encourage the use of improved computer security practices. It also provides guidance to federal agencies about who is responsible for computer systems security and privacy, requires the identification of systems that contain sensitive information, and outlines the requirements for formal security plans.

Privacy Laws

Privacy has become one of the hottest issues in information security at the beginning of the 21st century. Many organizations collect, trade, and sell personal information as a commodity, and many individuals are becoming aware of these practices and looking to the governments to protect their privacy. In the past it was not possible to create databases that contained personal information collected from multiple sources. Today, the aggregation of data from multiple sources permits unethical organizations to build databases with alarming quantities of personal information.

The number of statutes addressing individual privacy rights has grown; however, **privacy** in this context is not absolute freedom from observation, but rather it is defined as the "state of being free from unsanctioned intrusion."[3] To better understand this rapidly evolving issue, some of the more relevant privacy laws are presented in the pages that follow.

Some of the regulations represented in the U.S. code (the compilation of current U.S. laws) specify the responsibilities of common carriers (organizations that process or move data for hire) for the protection of the confidentiality of customer information, including that of other carriers. The Privacy of Customer Information Section of the section of regulations covering common carriers[4] specifies that any proprietary information shall be used explicitly for providing services, and not for any marketing purposes. It also stipulates that carriers cannot disclose this information except when necessary to provide its services, or by customer request, and then the disclosure is restricted to that customer's information only. This law does permit the use of aggregate information (which is created by combining nonprivate data elements) as long as the same information is provided to all common carriers, and the carrier in question conducts business with fair competition. The use of aggregate information raises privacy concerns because an organization could assemble data from a variety of sources in ways that would allow correlation of seemingly harmless information into something more intrusive. For example, the mapping of a government census database with telephone directory information, cross-indexed to bankruptcy court records, could be used to facilitate marketing efforts to people experiencing financial difficulties.

While this common carrier regulation controls public carriers use of private data, The Federal Privacy Act of 1974 regulates the government's use of private information. The Federal Privacy Act was created to ensure that government agencies protect the privacy of individuals' and businesses' information, and holds those agencies responsible if any portion of this information is released without permission. The act states that: "No agency shall disclose any record which is contained in a system of records by any means of communication to any person, or to another agency, except pursuant to a written request by, or with the prior written consent of, the individual to whom the record pertains…"[5] The following agencies are exempted from some of the regulations so that they can perform their duties:

- Bureau of the Census
- National Archives and Records Administration
- U.S. Congress
- Comptroller General
- Certain court orders
- Credit agencies

Also, individuals can access information controlled by others if they can demonstrate that it is necessary to protect their health or safety.

The Electronic Communications Privacy Act of 1986 is a collection of statutes that regulates the interception of wire, electronic, and oral communications. These statutes are frequently referred to as the federal wiretapping acts. They address the following areas:[6]

- Interception and disclosure of wire, oral, or electronic communications
- Manufacture, distribution, possession, and advertising of wire, oral, or electronic communication intercepting devices
- Confiscation of wire, oral, or electronic communication intercepting devices
- Evidentiary use of intercepted wire or oral communications
- Authorization for interception of wire, oral, or electronic communications
- Authorization for disclosure and use of intercepted wire, oral, or electronic communications
- Procedure for interception of wire, oral, or electronic communications
- Reports concerning intercepted wire, oral, or electronic communications
- Injunction against illegal interception

These statutes work in cooperation with the Fourth Amendment of the U.S. Constitution, which prohibits search and seizure without a warrant.

The Health Insurance Portability & Accountability Act Of 1996 (HIPPA), also known as the Kennedy-Kassebaum Act, is an attempt to protect the confidentiality and security of health care data by establishing and enforcing standards and by standardizing electronic data interchange. HIPPA affects all health care organizations, including small medical practices, health clinics, life insurers, and universities, as well as some organizations which have self-insured employee health programs. It provides for stiff penalties for organizations that fail to comply with the law, with up to $250,000 and or 10 years imprisonment for knowingly misusing client information. Organizations were required to comply with the act as of April 14, 2003.[7]

HIPPA affects the field of information security in a number of ways. It requires organizations that retain health care information to use information security mechanisms to protect this information, as well as policies and procedures to maintain them. It also requires a comprehensive assessment of the organization's information security systems, policies, and procedures. HIPPA provides guidelines for the use of electronic signatures based on security standards ensuring message integrity, user authentication, and nonrepudiation. There is no specification of particular security technologies for each of the security requirements; only that security must be implemented to ensure the privacy of the health care information.

The privacy standards of HIPPA severely restrict the dissemination and distribution of private health information without documented consent. The standards provide patients the right to know who has access to their information and who has accessed it. The privacy standards also restrict the use of health information to the minimum required for the health care services required.

HIPPA has five fundamental privacy principles:

1. Consumer control of medical information
2. Boundaries on the use of medical information
3. Accountability for the privacy of private information
4. Balance of public responsibility for the use of medical information for the greater good measured against impact to the individual
5. Security of health information

The Financial Services Modernization Act or Gramm-Leach-Bliley Act of 1999 contains a number of provisions that affect banks, securities firms, and insurance companies. This act requires all financial institutions to disclose their privacy policies, describing how they share nonpublic personal information, and describing how customers can request that their information not be shared with third parties. The act also ensures that the privacy policies in effect in an organization are fully disclosed when a customer initiates a business relationship, and distributed at least annually for the duration of the professional association.

Export and Espionage Laws

The need to protect national security, trade secrets, and a variety of other state and private assets has led to several laws affecting what information and information management and security resources may be exported from the United States (see, for example, Figure 11-1). These laws attempt to stem the theft of information by establishing strong penalties for related crimes.

In an attempt to protect intellectual property and competitive advantage, Congress passed the Economic Espionage Act (EEA) in 1996. This law attempts to protect trade secrets "from the foreign government that uses its classic espionage apparatus to spy on a company, to the two American companies that are attempting to uncover each other's bid proposals, or to the disgruntled former employee who walks out of his former company with a computer diskette full of engineering schematics."[8]

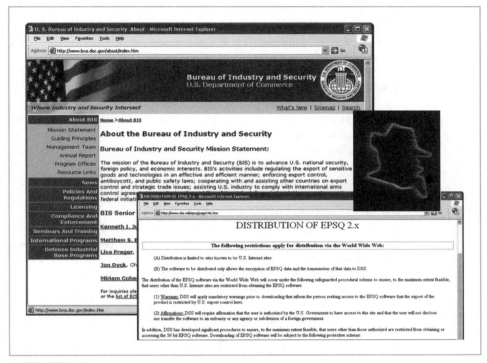

Export Restrictions

The Security and Freedom through Encryption Act of 1997 provides guidance on the use of encryption, and institutes measures of public protection from government intervention. Specifically, the Act:

- Reinforces an individual's right to use or sell encryption algorithms, without concern for the impact of other regulations requiring some form of key registration. Key registration is when a cryptographic key (or its text equivalent) is stored with another party to be used to break the encryption of the data under some circumstances. This is often called key escrow.

- Prohibits the federal government from requiring the use of encryption for contracts, grants, and other official documents, and correspondence

- States that the use of encryption is not probable cause to suspect criminal activity

- Relaxes export restrictions by amending the Export Administration Act of 1979

- Provides additional penalties for the use of encryption in the commission of a criminal act

U.S. Copyright Law

U.S. copyright law extends protection to intellectual property, which includes words published in electronic formats. The doctrine of fair use allows material to be quoted for the purpose of news reporting, teaching, scholarship, and a number of other related activities, so long as the purpose is educational and not for profit, and the usage is not excessive. Proper acknowledgement must be provided to the author and/or copyright holder of such works, including a description of the location of source materials by using a recognized form of citation.

Freedom of Information Act of 1966 (FOIA)

All federal agencies are required under the Freedom of Information Act (FOIA) to disclose records requested in writing by any person. However, agencies may withhold information pursuant to nine exemptions and three exclusions contained in the statute. The FOIA applies only to federal agencies and does not create a right of access to records held by Congress, the courts, or by state or local government agencies. Each state has its own public access laws that should be consulted for access to state and local records.

Sarbanes-Oxley Act of 2002

In the wake of the Enron and WorldCom financial scandals and the damage done to financial markets from criminal violations of the federal securities laws, the U.S. Congress enacted a law designed to enforce accountability for the financial record keeping and reporting at publicly traded corporations. While this law on its face would not seem to affect information security or even general IT functions, in fact its effects are being felt in many organizations.

The law requires that the CEO and chief financial officer (CFO) assume direct and personal accountability for the completeness and accuracy of a publicly traded organization's financial reporting and record-keeping systems. As these executives attempt to ensure that the systems used to record and report are sound—often relying upon the expertise of CIOs and CISOs to do so—the related areas of availability and confidentiality are also emphasized.

International Laws and Legal Bodies

It is important for IT professionals and information security practitioners to realize that when their organizations do business on the Internet, they do business globally. Many domestic laws and customs do not apply to international trade, which is governed by international treaties and trade agreements. It may seem obvious, but it is often overlooked, that there are a variety of laws and ethical practices in place in other parts of the world.

A number of different security bodies and laws are described in the following sections. Because of the political complexities of the relationships among nations and cultural differences, there are currently few international laws relating to privacy and information security. Therefore these international security bodies and regulations are sometimes limited in scope and enforceability.

European Council Cyber-Crime Convention

Recently the Council of Europe drafted the European Council Cyber-Crime Convention, which empowers an international task force to oversee a range of Internet security functions, and to standardize technology laws across international borders. It also attempts to improve the effectiveness of international investigations into breaches of technology law. This convention is well received by advocates of intellectual property rights, since it provides for copyright infringement prosecution.

As with any complex international legislation, the Cyber-Crime Convention lacks any realistic provisions for enforcement. The overall goal of the convention is to simplify the acquisition of information for law enforcement agents in certain types of international crimes, as well as the extradition process. The convention has more than its share of skeptics who see it as an overreaching attempt by the European community to exert undue influence in an attempt to control a complex problem. Adversaries of the convention say that it could create more problems than it resolves. As the product of a number of governments, the convention tends to favor the interests of national agencies over the rights of businesses, organizations, and individuals.

Digital Millennium Copyright Act (DMCA)

The Digital Millennium Copyright Act (DMCA) is a U.S.-based international effort to reduce the impact of copyright, trademark, and privacy infringement especially via the removal of technological copyright protection measures. The European Union also put forward Directive 95/46/EC of the European Parliament and of the Council of 24 October 1995 that increases individual rights to process and freely move personal data. The United Kingdom has already implemented a version of this directive called the Database Right.

United Nations Charter

To some degree, the United Nations Charter provides information security during information warfare. **Information warfare (IW)** is the use of information technology to conduct offensive operations as part of an organized and lawful military operation by a sovereign state. IW is a relatively new method of warfare, although the military has been conducting electronic warfare and counterwarfare operations for decades, jamming, intercepting, and spoofing enemy communications.

State and Local Regulations

Each state or locality may have a number of laws and regulations that affect the use of computer technology. It is the responsibility of information security professionals to understand state laws and regulations and ensure that their organization's security policies and procedures comply with the laws and regulations.

For example, the State of Georgia recently passed the Georgia Computer Systems Protection Act, which has various computer security provisions, and establishes specific penalties for use of information technology to attack or exploit information systems in organizations. These laws do not affect individuals outside the state unless they do business or have offices in the state. The key provisions of this law are as follows:

GEORGIA COMPUTER SYSTEMS PROTECTION ACT

(Section 90 et seq., Chapter 9, Title 16, Official Code of Georgia Annotated)

Computer Theft. Any person who uses a computer or computer network with knowledge that such use is without authority and with the intention of: Taking or appropriating any property of another, whether or not with the intention of depriving the owner of possession; Obtaining property by any deceitful means or artful practice; or Converting property to such

(continued)

person's use in violation of an agreement or other known legal obligation to make a specified application or disposition of such property shall be guilty of the crime of computer theft.

Computer Trespass. Any person who uses a computer or computer network with knowledge that such use is without authority and with the intention of; deleting or in any way removing, either temporarily or permanently, any computer program or data from a computer or computer network; obstructing, interrupting, or in any way interfering with the use of a computer program or data; or altering, damaging, or in any way causing the malfunction of a computer, computer network, or computer program, regardless of how long the alteration, damage, or malfunction persists shall be guilty of the crime of computer trespass.

Computer Invasion of Privacy. Any person who uses a computer or computer network with the intention of examining any employment, medical, salary, credit, or any other financial or personal data relating to any other person with knowledge that such examination is without authority shall be guilty of the crime of computer invasion of privacy.

Computer Forgery. Any person who creates, alters, or deletes any data contained in any computer or computer network, who, if such person had created, altered, or deleted a tangible document or instrument would have committed forgery under Article 1 of this chapter, shall be guilty of the crime of computer forgery. The absence of a tangible writing directly created or altered by the offender shall not be a defense to the crime of computer forgery if a creation, alteration, or deletion of data was involved in lieu of a tangible document or instrument.

Computer Password Disclosure. Any person who discloses a number, code, password, or other means of access to a computer or computer network knowing that such disclosure is without authority and which results in damages (including the fair market value of any services used and victim expenditure) to the owner of the computer or computer network in excess of $500.00 shall be guilty of the crime of computer password disclosure.

Penalties. Any person convicted of the crime of computer theft, computer trespass, computer invasion of privacy, or computer forgery shall be fined not more than $50,000.00 or imprisoned not more than 15 years, or both. Any person convicted of computer password disclosure shall be fined not more than $5,000.00 or incarcerated for a period not to exceed one year, or both.

Computer Trademark Infringement. It shall be unlawful for any person, any organization, or any representative of any organization knowingly to transmit any data through a computer network or over the transmission facilities or through the network facilities of a local telephone network for the purpose of setting up, maintaining, operating, or exchanging data with an electronic mailbox, home page, or any other electronic information storage bank or point of access to electronic information if such data uses any individual name, trade name, registered trademark, logo, legal or official seal, or copyrighted symbol to falsely identify the person, organization, or representative transmitting such data or which would falsely state or imply that such person, organization, or representative has permission or is legally authorized to use such trade name, registered trademark, logo, legal or official seal, or copyrighted symbol for such purpose when such permission or authorization has not been obtained; provided, however, that no telecommunications company or Internet access provider shall violate this Code section solely as a result of carrying or transmitting such data for its customers.[9]

The Georgia legislature also passed the Georgia Identity Theft Law in 1998 (Section 120 et seq., Chapter 9, Title 16, Official Code of Georgia Annotated). This law requires that:

A business may not discard a record containing personal information unless it:

1. Shreds the customer's record before discarding the record;
2. Erases the personal information contained in the customer's record before discarding the record;
3. Modifies the customer's record to make the personal information unreadable before discarding the record; or
4. Takes actions that it reasonably believes will ensure that no unauthorized person will have access to the personal information contained in the customer's record for the period between the record's disposal and the record's destruction.[10]

Personal information is defined as:

A. Personally identifiable data about a customer's medical condition, if the data are not generally considered to be public knowledge;
B. Personally identifiable data which contain a customer's account or identification number, account balance, balance owing, credit balance, or credit limit, if the data relate to a customer's account or transaction with a business;
C. Personally identifiable data provided by a customer to a business upon opening an account or applying for a loan or credit; or
D. Personally identifiable data about a customer's federal, state, or local income tax return.[11]

Failure to properly dispose of customer information can result in a fine of $500 per instance up to a total of $10,000.

"Consumer victim" means any individual whose personal identifying information has been obtained, compromised, used or recorded in any manner without the permission of that individual.

"Identifying information" shall include, but not be limited to:

- Current or former names
- Social Security numbers
- Driver's license numbers
- Checking account numbers
- Savings account numbers
- Credit and other financial transaction card numbers
- Debit card numbers
- Personal identification numbers
- Electronic identification numbers
- Digital or electronic signatures
- Medical identification numbers
- Birth dates
- Mother's maiden name
- Selected personal identification numbers
- Tax identification numbers
- State identification card numbers
- Any numbers or information which can be used to access a person's or entity's resources

Policy versus Law

As an information security professional, you must be aware of the legal environment in which your organization operates, and of how information security is maintained by means of policy. Most organizations develop and formalize descriptions of acceptable and unacceptable employee behavior, which are called policies (covered in detail in Chapter 4). Properly defined and enforced policies function in an organization the same way as laws, complete with penalties, judicial practices, and sanctions. Because policies function like laws, they must be crafted with the same care as laws to ensure that the policies are complete, appropriate, and fairly applied to everyone in the workplace. The key difference between policy and law is that ignorance is an acceptable defense, and therefore policies must be:

- Distributed to all individuals who are expected to comply with them
- Readily available for employee reference
- Easily understood, with multilingual translations and translations for visually impaired or low-literacy employees
- Acknowledged by the employee, usually by means of a signed consent form

Only when all of these conditions are met does the organization have the reasonable expectation that policy violations can be appropriately penalized without fear of legal retribution.

VIEWPOINT

Law, Ethics, and Information Security: Setting a Higher Standard

By Lee Imrey, CISSP, CISA

What if a speeding driver loses control of a car, and he and his passengers die in an accident? Or the captain of an ocean liner fails to read the weather report, and hits an iceberg? Or a pharmaceutical manufacturer mislabels the dosage on a shipment of medication?

Each of these is an example of a critical lapse in judgment, yet the impact of each is markedly different. Each successive example either affects, or has the potential to affect, a substantially greater number of people.

What if an insurance provider fails to adequately protect the sensitive data of half a million people?

If the address, telephone numbers, and names of family members are compromised, how does the impact of that lapse in judgment compare to that of the previous examples?

As we place increasing reliance on computers to manage sensitive information, it is incumbent upon us that we place appropriately effective controls on the systems. In most business environments, the information system controls are managed by information

(continued)

security professionals. In those environments that lack an information security specialist, the role is generally assumed by network and system administrators. In either case, the information system controls can frequently be bypassed by those who installed them.

How do we mitigate the risk that these *trusted parties* will abuse our trust? We do this by applying legal and ethical requirements to those we trust to secure our information.

We hope that our information security professionals will not abuse the power with which we entrust them, in much the same way that we trust that law enforcement professionals will not abuse their power. Yet we know from experience that not all professionals live up to their professed ethical standards.

Setting ethical expectations is not enough. Society needs another layer of assurance. This is provided by the adaptation of current legal code to the unique environment of information systems, and by the creation of new laws where existing law is not applicable.

Legal systems of various nations and states are all struggling to keep up with our rapidly changing environment. However, the ubiquitous and global nature of our information systems render many of the individual laws unenforceable, in any practical sense. Even acts of corporate espionage, incidents of computer hacking, and the writing of computer viruses and worms are judged by varying standards, depending on the circumstances and the forum.

Given the complex and fluid environment in which information security decisions are made, and the critical nature of these decisions, it is imperative that we be able to rely on the advice of our information security advisor. For this reason, we must hold these professionals to higher legal and ethical standards. There's too much at stake not to.

Lee Imrey, CISSP, CISA, is a Program Development Manager and Lead Instructor for (ISC)². He is a member of the ASIS IT Security Council, and he is currently Chair of the Information Systems Security Association's Professional Ethics Committee.

Ethical Concepts in Information Security

Some consider ethics to be the organized study of how humans ought to act. Others consider ethics to be a consideration of rules we should live by. The student of information security is not expected to study the topic of ethics in a vacuum, but within a larger ethical framework. However, those employed in the area of information security may be expected to be more articulate about the topic than others in the organization, and often must withstand a higher degree of scrutiny. The Ten Commandments of Computer Ethics (see the following Offline) are a useful guide to the ethical standards of the industry .

OFFLINE

The Ten Commandments of Computer Ethics

—from The Computer Ethics Institute[12]

1. Thou shalt not use a computer to harm other people.
2. Thou shalt not interfere with other people's computer work.
3. Thou shalt not snoop around in other people's computer files.
4. Thou shalt not use a computer to steal.
5. Thou shalt not use a computer to bear false witness.
6. Thou shalt not copy or use proprietary software for which you have not paid.
7. Thou shalt not use other people's computer resources without authorization or proper compensation.
8. Thou shalt not appropriate other people's intellectual output.
9. Thou shalt think about the social consequences of the program you are writing or the system you are designing.
10. Thou shalt always use a computer in ways that ensure consideration and respect for your fellow humans.

Differences in Ethical Concepts

Studies reveal that individuals of different nationalities have different perspectives on the ethics of computer use. Difficulties arise when one nationality's ethical behavior does not correspond to that of another national group. For example, Westerners view some of the ways in which Asians use computer technology as software copyright piracy.[13] This conflict arises from Asian traditions of collective ownership, which clashes with the Western notions of intellectual property.

A recent study has examined computer-use ethics among nine countries: Singapore, Hong Kong, United States, England, Australia, Sweden, Wales, Great Britain, and the Netherlands. This study selected a number of computer-use vignettes (see Offline: The Use Of Scenarios In Computer Ethics Studies later in this chapter) and presented them to students in universities in these nine countries. This study did not categorize or classify the responses as ethical or unethical, but indicated a degree of "ethical sensitivity" about the performance of the individuals in the short case studies. The results were grouped into three categories of ethical computer use: software license infringement, illicit use, and misuse of resources. The following sections are taken from the study, "Cross-National Differences In Computer-Use Ethics: A Nine Country Study," published in *The Journal of International Business Studies*. [14]

Software License Infringement

Overall, most of the countries studied had similar attitudes toward software piracy. Statistically speaking, only the United States and the Netherlands had attitudes that differed substantially from the other countries examined. The United States was significantly less tolerant of piracy, while the Netherlands was significantly more permissive. Although a number of studies have reported that the Pacific Rim countries of Singapore and Hong Kong are software piracy hotbeds, the study found their tolerance for copyright infringement to be moderate, as were the attitudes of England, Wales, Australia, and Sweden. This could mean that the individuals surveyed understood what software license infringement was, but either felt their use was not piracy, or that their society permitted it anyway. Peer pressure, the lack of legal disincentives, the lack of punitive measures, or any one of a number of other reasons could also explain why these reported piracy centers were not oblivious to intellectual property laws.

Although the Netherlands displayed a more permissive attitude towards piracy, which reflects their general culture, they only ranked third in piracy rates of the countries represented in this study.

Illicit Use

All of the individuals studied condemned viruses, hacking, and other forms of system abuse as unacceptable behavior. There were however, differences in groups as to just how tolerant individuals were. Singapore and Hong Kong proved to be significantly more tolerant than the United States, Wales, Great Britain, and Australia. Sweden and the Netherlands were also significantly more tolerant than Wales and Australia and significantly less tolerant than Hong Kong. The low overall degree of tolerance for illicit system use may be a function of the easy association between the common crimes of breaking and entering, trespassing, theft, and destruction of property to their computer-related counterparts.

Misuse of Corporate Resources

The scenarios used to examine the levels of tolerance in this category each represented different kinds of personal use of corporate assets, with no indication of established policy toward personal use of company resources. In general, individuals displayed a rather lenient view of personal use of company equipment. Only Singapore and Hong Kong view personal use of company equipment as unethical. There were several substantial national differences in this category, with the Netherlands reporting the most lenient view. Regardless of cultural background, many individuals feel that if an organization does not specifically forbid the use of its computing resources for personal use, then such use is acceptable. In fact, only the two Asian samples, Singapore and Hong Kong, reported generally intolerant attitudes toward personal use of organizational computing resources. The reasons behind this are unknown. Perhaps the formal Asian work ethic provides stricter guidance on duty to the company versus personal rights and privileges.

Overall, the researchers found that there is a general agreement among nationalities as to what is acceptable or unacceptable computer use. There is however, a range of degrees of tolerance of unethical behavior.

> "Thus, the results of this study underscore inter-cultural similarities as much as they describe inter-cultural differences. The study also found little to support, from an ethical perspective, the popular media's portrayal of Asians as 'digital bandits'. In fact, the Hong Kong and Singapore respondents were not consistently the most permissive nationalities among those studied. As noted earlier, the higher piracy rates in Singapore and Hong Kong may be less a function of ethical difference and more a function of the lack of legal and financial disincentive to engage in software copyright infringement. The only country that consistently ranked as 'most tolerant' was the Netherlands. However, this level of tolerance does not seem to have completely manifested itself in action; although the Netherlands has a higher piracy rate than the United States, Australia, Wales, England, and Sweden, it still ranks behind Singapore and Hong Kong."[15]

OFFLINE

The Use Of Scenarios In Computer Ethics Studies

The following vignettes can be used in an open and frank discussion of computer ethics. Review each scenario carefully and respond to each question using the following statement, choosing the description you feel most appropriate. Then, justify your response. *I feel the actions of this individual were (very ethical / ethical / neither ethical nor unethical / unethical / very unethical).*

Ethical Decision Evaluation

1. A scientist developed a theory that required proof through the construction of a computer model. He hired a computer programmer to build the model, and the theory was shown to be correct. The scientist won several awards for the development of the theory, but he never acknowledged the contribution of the computer programmer. *The scientist's failure to acknowledge the computer programmer was:*

2. The owner of a small business needed a computer-based accounting system. He identified the various inputs and outputs he felt were required to satisfy his needs, showed his design to a computer programmer, and asked the programmer if she could implement such a system. The programmer knew she could implement the system, because she had developed much more sophisticated systems in the past. In fact, she felt this design was rather crude and would soon need several major revisions. But she didn't say anything about the design flaws, because the business owner didn't ask her and she thought she might be the one hired to implement the needed revisions later. *The programmer's decision not to point out the design flaws was:*

3. A student suspected and found a loophole in the university computer's security system that allowed him access to other students' records. He told the system administrator about the loophole, but continued to access other records until the problem was corrected two weeks later.
The student's action in searching for the loophole was:
The student's action in continuing to access others' record for two weeks was:
The system administrator's failure to correct the problem sooner was:

4. A computer user called a mail-order computer program store to order a particular accounting system. When he received his order, he found that the store had accidentally sent him a very expensive word-processing program as well as the accounting package that he had ordered. The invoice listed only the accounting package. The user decided to keep the word-processing program. *The user's decision to keep the word-processing program was:*

5. A programmer at a bank realized that he had accidentally overdrawn his checking account. He made a small adjustment in the bank's accounting system so that his account would not have an additional service charge assessed. As soon as he deposited funds that made his balance positive again, he corrected the bank's accounting system. *The programmer's modification of the accounting system was:*

6. A computer programmer enjoyed building small computer systems (programs) to give to his friends. He would frequently go to his office on Saturday when no one was working and use his employer's computer to develop systems. He did not hide the

(continued)

fact that he was going into the building; he had to sign a register at a security desk each time he entered.

The programmer's use of the company computer was:

If the programmer sold the programs his actions would have been:

7. A student enrolled in a computer class was also employed at a local business part-time. Frequently her homework in the class involved using popular word-processing and spreadsheet packages. Occasionally she worked on her homework on the office computer at her part-time job, on her coffee or meal breaks.

The student's use of the company computer was:

If the student had worked on her homework during "company time" (not during a break), the student's use of the company computer would have been:

8. A student at a university learned to use an expensive spreadsheet program in her accounting class. The student would go to the university microcomputer lab and use the software to complete her assignment. Signs were posted in the lab indicating that copying software was forbidden. One day, she decided to copy the software anyway to complete her work assignments at home.

If the student destroyed her copy of the software at the end of the term, her action in copying the software was:

If the student forgot to destroy her copy of the software at the end of the term, her action in copying the software was:

If the student never intended to destroy her copy of the software at the end of the term, her action in copying the software was:

9. A student at a university found out that one of the local computer bulletin boards contained a "pirate" section (a section containing a collection of illegally copied software programs). He subscribed to the board, and proceeded to download several games and professional programs, which he then distributed to several of his friends.

The student's actions in downloading the games were:

The student's actions in downloading the programs were:

The student's actions in sharing the programs and games with his friends were:

Ethics and Education

Differences in computer use ethics are not exclusively cultural. Differences are found among individuals within the same country, within the same social class, and within the same company. Key studies reveal that the overriding factor in leveling the ethical perceptions within a small population is education. Employees must be trained and kept up to date on information security topics, including the expected behaviors of an ethical employee. This is especially important in areas of information security, as many employees may not have the formal technical training to understand that their behavior is unethical or even illegal. Proper ethical and legal training is vital to creating an informed, well-prepared, and low-risk system user.

Deterring Unethical and Illegal Behavior

It is the responsibility of information security personnel to do everything in their power to deter unethical and illegal acts, using policy, education and training, and technology as controls or safeguards to protect the information and systems. Many security professionals understand technological means of protection, but many underestimate the value of policy.

There are three general categories of unethical behavior that organizations and society should seek to eliminate:

- Ignorance: As you learned earlier, ignorance of the law is no excuse, but ignorance of policies and procedures is. The first method of deterrence is education. Organizations must design, publish, disseminate organizational policies and relevant laws, and employees must explicitly agree to abide by them. Reminders, training and awareness programs support retention, and one hopes, compliance.

- Accident: Individuals with authorization and privileges to manage information within the organization have the greatest opportunity to cause harm or damage by accident. The careful placement of controls can help prevent accidental modification to systems and data.

- Intent: Criminal or unethical intent refers to the state of mind of the individual committing the infraction. A legal defense can be built upon whether or not the accused acted out of ignorance, by accident, or with the intent to cause harm or damage. Deterring those with criminal intent is best done by means of litigation, prosecution, and technical controls. As you learned in Chapter 2, intent is only one of several factors to consider when determining whether a computer-related crime has occurred.

Deterrence is the best method for preventing an illegal or unethical activity. Laws, policies, and technical controls are all examples of deterrents. However, it is generally agreed that laws and policies and their associated penalties only deter if three conditions are present.

- Fear of penalty: To be deterred, people must fear the penalty. Threats of informal reprimand or verbal warnings may not have the same impact as the threat of imprisonment or forfeiture of pay.

- Probability of being caught: There must be a strong possibility that perpetrators of illegal or unethical acts will be caught.

- Probability of penalty being administered: The organization must be willing and able to impose the penalty.

THREAT MANAGEMENT

Wireless Network Attacks: War Driving

Introduction

With the popularity of movies like *War Games* emerged a generation of individuals seeking to identify and exploit organizational network connections by scanning access points—in this case, phone numbers—looking for an available and unprotected connection. This practice is known as war dialing. While most hackers have moved on to exploits that use Internet connections, war dialing is still a viable threat. A new variant of war dialing has recently emerged, which seeks to exploit the growing home and business use of wireless networks, which are often not configured properly, allowing anyone

(continued)

with a compatible network card to seek and gain access to the network. This new generation of war drivers has escalated hacking to a sport. While driving through business and residential districts, they "count coup" by tracking exactly how many networks they can connect to in a short amount of time. While seemingly harmless, war drivers reveal a very real threat to information security, since many networks are established quickly with little concern for the protection of information.

This phenomenon depends upon people not realizing that their radio packet network—a wireless network is basically broadcast radio—can penetrate walls, ceilings, and floors, and thus has different security requirements than older, more secure, cable-based versions. While a cable based local area network is relatively secure until you hook it to another network, like the Internet, wireless networks can be more easily penetrated.

In order to engage in war driving—which is also known as LAN-jacking—all a perpetrator needs is transportation, a notebook/laptop computer with a wireless network card, and an antenna. Ingenious war drivers frequently convert cans and other similar objects into directional antennae, although commercially produced versions are available for under $75. The driver then traverses an area, residential or commercial or both, looking for wireless networks that can be detected and accessed. To make this easier, war drivers can use a program known as Network Stumbler, which scans for wireless networks and logs the network IDs, addresses, quality of signal information, and length of connection. Once in, they can simply record their success and move on; or, they may be able to access another network (for example, the Internet), or stop and conduct data espionage or some other kind of attack. It is reported that some war drivers use global positioning systems to plot the location of successful network accesses to determine the range of a wireless network.

To find out more about this phenomenon, a security manager "conducted an unobtrusive test that demonstrated war driving is more than just theoretical. While driving at 65 mph between Leesburg, VA, and Dulles International Airport near Washington, D.C., he detected dozens of unsecured wireless LANs."[16]

Detection

Detecting a war driver can be as simple as determining what connections are active on the wireless access point (WAP) or as complex as determining if you have a hacker in the network. While detecting a war driver depends on the skills of the system or security administrator, for the most part, war drivers strike quickly, grabbing what they can (if anything) and moving on before detection. Host-based intrusion detection systems can determine if files are changed, added or deleted, but may not report simple viewing or copying.

Prevention

If a company or individual implements a wireless network there are a number of measures they can use to protect their data, including the Wired Equivalent Privacy (WEP) encryption standard, Virtual Private Networks (VPNs), and firewalls. It is also possible to restrict access via the wireless network card's MAC address. This is especially useful in small or personal networks where all possible users are known. Reliance on any one control is marginally better than no control at all. WEP itself only encrypts the data being transmitted.

(continued)

A research group from the University of California at Berkeley recently published a report citing "major security flaws" in WEP that left WLANs using the protocol vulnerable to attacks (called *wireless equivalent privacy attacks*). In the course of the group's examination of the technology, they were able to intercept and modify transmissions and gain access to restricted networks. The Wireless Ethernet Compatibility Alliance (WECA) claims that WEP—which is included in many networking products—was never intended to be the sole security mechanism for a WLAN, and that, in conjunction with traditional security practices, it is very effective.[17]

With the low cost of wireless networks, war driving and other intrusions are becoming more frequent. Wireless networks provide a low cost alternative to wired networks, because of the difficult and often expensive problem of running cable in existing structures. The downside is that the footprint of the radio packets is difficult to manage. Users want sufficient power to ensure quality connections within the building, but not enough to allow those outside the building to receive them.

Certifications and Professional Organizations

A number of professional organizations have established codes of conduct and/or codes of ethics that members are expected to follow. Codes of ethics can have a positive effect on an individual's judgment regarding computer use[18]. Unfortunately, many employers do not encourage their employees to join these professional organizations. However, the loss of accreditation or certification due to a violation of a code of conduct can be a deterrent, as it can dramatically reduce the individual's marketability and earning power.

In general, research has shown that some certifications have little impact on the long-term earning potential of practitioners, while other certifications, notably those in information security, have a lingering effect on the economic prospects of certificate holders.[19] The long-term value of an information security certification adds leverage to the certification granting authority to exert influence over its members, including influence in matters of ethical responsibility.

It remains the individual responsibility of security professionals to act ethically and according to the policies and procedures of their employers, their professional organizations, and the laws of society. It is likewise the organization's responsibility to develop, disseminate, and enforce its policies. The following sections describe several of the relevant professional associations.

Association of Computing Machinery (ACM)

The ACM (www.acm.org) is a respected professional society, originally established in 1947, as "the world's first educational and scientific computing society." It is one of the few organizations that strongly promotes education, and provides discounted membership for students. The ACM's code of ethics requires members to perform their duties in a manner befitting an ethical computing professional. The code contains specific references to protecting the confidentiality of information, causing no harm (with specific references to viruses), protecting the privacy of others, and respecting the intellectual property and copyrights of others.

The ACM also publishes a wide variety of professional computing publications, including the highly regarded *Communications of the ACM*.

International Information Systems Security Certification Consortium, Inc. (ISC)²

The (ISC)² (www.isc2.org) is not a professional organization in the strictest sense, and has no member or membership services, but is a nonprofit organization that focuses on the development and implementation of information security certifications and credentials. The (ISC)² manages a body of knowledge on information security and administers and evaluates examinations for information security certifications. Currently the (ISC)² offers two professional certifications in the information security arena: the Certification for Information Systems Security Professionals (CISSP), and the Systems Security Certified Professional, or SSCP.

The code of ethics put forth by (ISC)² is primarily designed for information security professionals who have earned one of their certifications. This code includes four mandatory canons:

- Protect society, the commonwealth, and the infrastructure
- Act honorably, honestly, justly, responsibly, and legally
- Provide diligent and competent service to principals
- Advance and protect the profession.[20]

Through this code, (ISC)² seeks to provide sound guidance that will enable reliance on the ethicality and trustworthiness of the information security professional as the guardian of the information and systems.

System Administration, Networking, and Security Institute (SANS)

The System Administration, Networking, and Security Institute, or SANS (www.sans.org), is a professional organization with a large membership dedicated to the protection of information and systems. Founded in 1989, SANS is a professional research and education cooperative organization with currently over 156,000 security professionals, auditors, system administrators, and network administrators. SANS offers a set of certifications called the Global Information Assurance Certification, or GIAC, as described in Chapter 10.

These certifications can be pursued independently or combined to earn the comprehensive certification called the GIAC Security Engineer (GSE). The newest GIAC certification, the Information Security Officer (GISO), is an overview certification that combines basic technical knowledge with understanding of threats, risks, and best practices. Unlike other certifications, the GIAC certifications require the applicant to complete a written practical assignment. This assignment requires applicants to demonstrate their abilities and skills by putting them into practice. These assignments are submitted to the SANS Information Security Reading Room for review by security practitioners, potential certificate applicants, and others with an interest in information security.

Information Systems Audit and Control Association (ISACA)

The Information Systems Audit and Control Association, or ISACA (www.isaca.org), is a professional association with a focus on auditing, control, and security. The membership comprises both technical and managerial professionals. ISACA focuses on providing IT control practices and standards. They offer the Certified Information Systems Auditor (CISA) certification, which does not focus exclusively on information security but does contain many information security components.

The ISACA also has a code of ethics for its professionals. It requires many of the same high standards for ethical performance as the other organizations and certifications.

Computer Security Institute (CSI)

The Computer Security Institute (www.gocsi.com) provides information and certification to support the computer, networking, and information security professional. Established in 1974, the CSI sponsors a number of conferences. This organization is renowned for its technical expertise and scope. CSI also publishes a newsletter and threat advisory, and is well known for its annual computer crime survey of threats developed in cooperation with the FBI. While CSI does not promote a particular certification as do the (ISC)² and SANS, it does provide a range of technical training classes in the areas of Internet security, intrusion management, network security, forensics, as well as technical networking.[21]

Information Systems Security Association

The **Information Systems Security Association (ISSA)** (www.issa.org) is a nonprofit society of information security professionals. As a professional association, its primary mission is to bring together qualified practitioners of information security for information exchange and educational development. ISSA provides conferences, meetings, publications, and information resources to promote information security awareness and education.[22] ISSA also promotes a code of ethics, similar to those of (ISC)², ISACA, and the ACM, "promoting management practices that will ensure the confidentiality, integrity, and availability of organizational information resources."[23]

Other Security Organizations

There are a number of professional and private societies and organizations that play a key role in the development and dissemination of information security practices and technologies. A few of the more prominent ones are discussed here.

The **Internet Society** or ISOC (www.isoc.org) is a nonprofit, nongovernmental, international professional organization. It promotes the development and implementation of education, standards, policy, and education and training to promote the Internet. At the time of this publication, global membership was free. While the general membership does not actively promote education, standards, and policy, there are a number of ISOC organizations that do actively review and promote these issues, and one of these is the **Internet Engineering Task Force (IETF)**. The IETF consists of individuals from the computing, networking, and telecommunications industries, and is responsible for developing the Internet's technical foundations. Standards developed by the IETF are then reviewed by the Internet Engineering Steering Group (IESG), with appeal to the Internet Architecture Board, and promulgated by the Internet Society as international standards.

Standards are reviewed and published through Requests for Comments (RFCs) and may be viewed at www.rfc-editor.org, as well as through numerous mirror sites. These RFCs are rich sources of information on the development and standardization of commonly used protocols for both the Internet and related technologies.

The **Computer Security Division (CSD)** of the National Institute for Standards and Technology (NIST) runs the Computer Security Resource Center (CSRC)—an essential resource for any current or aspiring information security professional. This Web site (csrc.nist.gov) houses one of the most comprehensive sets of publicly available information on the entire suite of information security topics.

The CSD is involved in five major research areas related to information security:

1. Cryptographic standards and applications
2. Security testing
3. Security research and emerging technologies
4. Security management and guidance
5. Outreach, awareness, and education

The **CERT Coordination Center,** or CERT/CC (www.cert.org), is a center of Internet security expertise which is part of the Software Engineering Institute, a federally funded research and development center operated by Carnegie Mellon University. The CERT/CC studies security issues and provides publications and alerts to help educate the public to the threats facing information security. The center also provides training and expertise in the handling of computer incidents. CERT/CC acts both as a research center and outside consultant in the areas of incident response, security practices, and programs development.

Computer Professionals for Social Responsibility (CPSR) is a public organization for technologists and anyone with a general concern about the impact of computer technology on society. CPSR promotes ethical and responsible development and use of computing, and seeks to inform public and private policy and lawmakers on this subject. It acts as an ethical watchdog for the development of ethical computing.

Table 11-2 provides summary information about the organizations described in this section.

Table 11-2   Professional Organizations of Interest to Information Security Professionals

Focus	Professional Organization	Web Resource Location	Description
Certifications in the field of information security	International Information Systems Security Certification Consortium, Inc., (ISC)²	www.isc2.org	**The Certified Information Systems Security Professional** (CISSP) is a broad certification requiring mastery of 10 domains of information security **Systems Security Certified Professional** (SSCP) is a certification for operational planning for information security with a focus in operational rather than managerial, on seven domains of information security
Ethics of security professionals	Association of Computing Machinery	www.acm.org	Code of 24 imperatives of personal and ethical responsibilities of security professionals

Table 11-2   Professional Organizations of Interest to Information Security Professionals (continued)

Focus	Professional Organization	Web Resource Location	Description
Information security certification for advanced technical subject areas	SANS Institute	www.giac.org	The **Global Information Assurance Certification** (GIAC) consists of twelve individual technical certifications that can be tied into six tracks, or culminate in the GIAC Security Engineer certification
Tasks and knowledge required of the information systems audit professional	Information Systems Audit and Control Association	www.isaca.org	The **Certified Information Systems Auditor** (CISA) and the **Certified Information Security Manager** (CISM)
Individual training courses and tracks (not certification)	Computer Security Institute	www.gocsi.com	Policy development, risk analysis, security awareness, and other vital aspects of information protection; practical insights into the technical problems of network security
Professional security information sharing	Information Systems Security Association	www.issa.org	Professional association of information systems security professionals; provides education forums, publications, and peer networking for members
Internet leadership and development	Internet Society	www.isoc.org	Professional association of individuals and organizations with an interest in promoting the growth of and leadership for the Internet
Promotion of national awareness of information security	Computer Security Division of the National Institute of Standards and Technology	csrc.nist.gov	Raising awareness of information technology security, especially in new and emerging technologies

Key U.S. Federal Agencies

There are a number of key U.S. federal agencies charged with the protection of U.S. information resources, and the investigation of threats to, or attacks on, these resources. These include the Federal Bureau of Investigation's National Infrastructure Protection Center, the National Security Administration, and the U.S. Secret Service.

The Federal Bureau of Investigation's **National Infrastructure Protection Center (NIPC)** (www.nipc.gov) was established in 1998 and serves as the U.S. government's focal point for threat assessment and the warning, investigation, and response to threats or attacks against critical U.S. infrastructures.[24] A key part of the NIPC's efforts to educate, train, inform, and involve the business and public sector in information security is the National InfraGard Program. Established in January of 2001, the **National InfraGard Program** began as a cooperative effort between the FBI's Cleveland field office and local technology professionals. The FBI sought assistance in establishing a more effective method of protecting critical national information resources. The resulting cooperative formed the first InfraGard chapter as a formal effort to combat both cyber and physical threats. Since then, every FBI field office has established an InfraGard chapter and collaborates with public and private organizations and the academic community to share information about attacks, vulnerabilities, and threats. The National InfraGard Program serves its members using the following tools:

- Intrusion alert network using encrypted e-mail
- Secure Web site for communication about suspicious activity or intrusions
- Local chapter activities
- Help desk for questions

InfraGard's dominant contribution is the free exchange of information to and from the private sector in the subject areas of threats and attacks on information resources.[25] Another key federal agency is the **National Security Agency (NSA)**. The NSA is:

the Nation's cryptologic organization. It coordinates, directs, and performs highly specialized activities to protect U.S. information systems and produce foreign intelligence information…. It is also one of the most important centers of foreign language analysis and research within the Government.[26]

The NSA is responsible for signal intelligence and information system security. The NSA's Information Assurance Directorate (IAD) provides information security "solutions including the technologies, specifications and criteria, products, product configurations, tools, standards, operational doctrine and support activities needed to implement the protect, detect and report, and respond elements of cyber defense."[27] The IAD also develops and promotes an Information Assurance Framework Forum, developed in cooperation with commercial organizations, and academic researchers. This framework provides strategic guidance as well as technical specifications for security solutions. IAD's Common Criteria is a set of standards designed to promote understanding of information security.

Prominent among the NSA's information security efforts and activities are its information security outreach programs. The NSA recognizes universities that offer information security education opportunities, and that have integrated information security philosophies and efforts into their internal operations. These recognized "Centers of Excellence in Information Assurance Education," can display this recognition on their Web sites and in other materials, and are named on the NSA's Web site. Additionally, the NSA has an information security curriculum certification program. The Information Assurance Courseware Evaluation process reviews an institution's information security course offerings, and gives three-year accreditation to those that meet their standards. Graduates of these programs receive certificates recognizing this accreditation.

The **U.S. Secret Service** is a department within the Department of the Treasury. In addition to its well-known mission to protect key members of the U.S. government, the Secret Service is also charged with the detection and arrest of any person committing a U.S. federal offense relating to computer fraud, as well as false identification crimes.[28] This is an extension of its original duty to protect U.S. currency. After all, the communications networks of the U.S. carry more funds, in the form of electronic data, than all of the armored cars in the world combined. Protect the networks, protect the data, and you protect money, stocks, and other financial transactions.

The Patriot Act (Public Law 107-56) increased the Secret Service's role in investigating fraud and related activity in connection with computers. In addition the Act authorized the director of the Secret Service to establish nationwide electronic crimes taskforces to assist law enforcement, the private sector, and academia in detecting and suppressing computer-based crime; the act increases the statutory penalties for the manufacturing, possession, dealing and passing of counterfeit U.S. or foreign obligations; and the act allows enforcement action to be taken to protect our financial payment systems while combating transnational financial crimes directed by terrorists or other criminals.

The Department of Homeland Security is established with the passage of Public Law 107-296 which in part, transfers the United States Secret Service from the Department of the Treasury, to the new department effective March 1, 2003.

Organizational Liability and the Need for Counsel

What if an organization does not support or even encourage strong ethical conduct on the part of its employees? What if an organization does not behave ethically? Even if there is no criminal conduct that can be prosecuted under criminal code, there can be liability. **Liability** is the legal obligation of an entity and can be applied to conduct even when no law or contract has been breached. Liability for a wrongful act includes the obligation to make payment or **restitution**—compensation for the wrong. If an employee, acting with or without the authorization, performs an illegal or unethical act, causing some degree of harm, the organization can be held financially liable for that action. An organization increases its liability if it refuses to take measures—**due care**—to make sure that every employee knows what is acceptable and what is not, and the consequences of illegal or unethical actions. **Due diligence** requires that an organization make a valid and ongoing effort to protect others. Because of the Internet, it is possible that a person wronged by an organization's members could be anywhere, in any state, or any country, around the world. Under the U.S. legal system, any court can impose its authority over an individual or organization if it can establish **jurisdiction**—a court's right to hear a case if the act was committed in its territory or involving its citizenry. This is sometimes referred to as **long-arm jurisdiction**, as the long arm of the law reaches across the country or around the world to pull an accused individual into its court systems. Trying a case in the injured party's home area usually favors the injured party or parties, as it creates a home court advantage.[29]

Chapter Summary

- Laws are formally adopted rules for acceptable behavior in modern society. Ethics are socially acceptable behaviors. The key difference between laws and ethics is that laws bring to bear the sanction of a governing authority and ethics do not.

- Organizations formalize desired behaviors in documents called policies. Policies must be read and explicitly agreed to by employees before they are binding.

- Civil law represents a wide variety of laws that regulate relationships between and among individuals and organizations. Criminal law addresses violations that harm society and that are prosecuted by the state. Tort law is a subset of civil law that deals with lawsuits by individuals rather than criminal prosecution by the state.

- The desire to protect national security, trade secrets, and a variety of other state and private assets has led to several laws affecting what information and information management and security resources may be exported from the U.S.

- U.S. copyright law extends intellectual property rights to the published word, including electronic publication.

- Studies of ethical sensitivity to computer use have determined that individuals of different nationalities have various perspectives on the ethics of computer use.

- Deterrence can prevent an illegal or unethical activity from occurring. Successful deterrence requires the institution of severe penalties, the probability of apprehension, and an expectation that penalties will be enforced.

- As part of an effort to sponsor positive ethics, a number of professional organizations have established codes of conduct or codes of ethics that their members are expected to follow.

- There are a number of key U.S. federal agencies tasked with the protection of American information resources, and the investigation of threats to, or attacks on, these resources.

Review Questions

1. What is the difference between criminal law and civil law?
2. What is tort law and what does it permit an individual to do?
3. What are the primary examples of public law?
4. Which law amended the Computer Fraud and Abuse act of 1986, and what did it change?
5. Which organization led the efforts to overturn the Computer Decency Act? What happened to the law they opposed?
6. What is privacy, in the context of information security?
7. What is another name for the Kennedy-Kassebaum Act (1996), and why is it important to organizations that are not in the health care industry?
8. If you work for a financial service organization (such as a bank or credit union) which law from 1999 affects your use of customer data? What other affects does it have?
9. Which 1997 law provides guidance on the use of encryption?
10. What is intellectual property? Is it offered the same protection in every country of the world? What laws currently protect it in the U.S. and Europe?
11. What is a policy? How does it differ from a law?

12. What are the three general categories of unethical and illegal behavior?

13. What is the best method for preventing an illegal or unethical activity?

14. Of the professional organizations listed in this chapter, which has been established for the longest time? When was it founded?

15. Of the professional organizations listed in this chapter, which is focused on auditing and control?

16. Of the professional organizations listed in this chapter, which sponsors a certification called the Global Information Assurance Certification (GIAC)?

17. Which U.S. federal agency sponsors the InfraGard program?

18. What is due care? Why would an organization want to make sure it exercises due care in its usual course of operations?

19. What can be done to deter someone from committing a crime?

20. How does due diligence differ from due care? Why are both important?

Exercises

1. What does CISSP stand for? Using the Internet, find out what continuing education is required in order for the holder of a CISSP to remain current and in good standing.

2. For what kind of information security jobs does the NSA recruit? Use the Internet to visit their Web page and find a listing.

3. Using the resources available in your library, find out what laws your state has passed to prosecute computer crime.

4. Using the Web, go to the site www.eff.org. What are the current top concerns of this organization?

5. Using the ethical scenarios presented in the chapter, answer each question, and bring your answers to class to compare your answers with those of your peers.

Case Exercises

Iris was a little unsure of what to do next. She had just left the meeting with the other executives of RWW, Inc. At that meeting they confirmed the need for action on the matter of the critical information offered for sale on a public auction site. That was the last point of agreement. This was a risk they had simply not planned for and they were completely unprepared.

Just before the meeting broke up, they had made assignments to various people in the meeting. Robin, the CEO, was going to contact the members of the Board of Directors to brief them, so that if the story became public they would not be surprised. Jerry, the corporate counsel, was going to start an intensive effort to discover what peer companies had done in situations like this. Mike, the CIO, was assigned to contact the auction site to get the auction shut down and lay the groundwork for working with whatever authorities were brought in for the criminal aspects of the case.

Iris was assigned to investigate which law enforcement agency should be involved in the investigation. She reached for her business card box and began thumbing through the contacts she had.

1. With which agency do you think she should start? On what factors do you base that recommendation?

2. What criminal acts do you think are involved in this? What do you think the relationship of the perpetrator to RWW, Inc. might be?

Endnotes

1. J. B. Noone. *Rousseau's Social contract : a conceptual analysis.* University of Georgia Press,1981.
2. www.house.gov/science_democrats/archive/compsec1.htm.
3. *The American Heritage Dictionary of the English Language: Fourth Edition.* 2000.
4. www4.law.cornell.edu/uscode/47/222.html.
5. www.usdoj.gov/foia/privstat.htm.
6. www4.law.cornell.edu/uscode/18/pIch119.html.
7. www.hipaadvisory.com/regs/HIPAAprimer1.htm.
8. www.cybercrime.gov/usamay2001_6.htm.
9. www.gsu.edu/doc/crime-act.html.
10. OCGA. Official Code of Georgia Annotated §10-15-1. Definitions.
11. OCGA. Official Code of Georgia Annotated §10-15-2. Business must properly dispose of identifying information.
12. www.cpsr.org/program/ethics/cei.html.
13. Mike Magee. Software piracy in Asia exposed. *The Inquirer*, Jan. 29, 2002. Available from the World Wide Web at www.theinquirer.net/piracy1.htm.
14. M. E. Whitman, A. M. Townsend, and A. R. Hendrickson. Cross-National Differences In Computer-Use Ethics: A Nine Country Study. *The Journal of International Business Studies*, 30(4), 1999, 673–687.
15. Ibid.
16. Miller, S. "War Driving", Information Security Magazine, November 2001, http://infosecuritymag.techtarget.com/articles/november01/technology_wardriving.shtml.
17. Ibid.
18. S. J. Harrington. The Effects of Codes of Ethics and Personal Denial of Responsibility on Computer Abuse Judgment and Intentions. *MIS Quarterly*, September 1996, 257–278.
19. Foote Partners, LLC. Press release, August 18, 2003, New Canaan, CT.
20. www.isc2.org/cgi-bin/content.cgi?category=12.
21. www.gocsi.com/infosec/wkshop.html.
22. www.issa.org/.
23. www.issa.org/codeofethics.html.
24. www.nipc.gov/about/about.htm.
25. www.fbi.gov/pressrel/pressrel01/infragard.htm.
26. www.nsa.gov/about_nsa/index.html.
27. www.nsa.gov/isso/brochure/index.htm.
28. www.secretservice.gov/mission.html.
29. R. J. Aalberts, A. M. Townsend, and M. E. Whitman. The Threat of Long-arm Jurisdiction to Electronic Commerce. *Communications of the ACM*, 41(12), December 1998, 15–20.

Information Security Project Management

> I find that the harder I work, the more luck I seem to have.
>
> **THOMAS JEFFERSON (1743–1826)**

"COME IN," SAID IRIS TO Maria Rodriguez, one of the technicians in the Information Security department. "Have a seat, please." As Iris closed her office door, Maria settled at the small table by the window.

Iris began. "Maria, we've been working together since I joined RWW. I've been very happy with your work as the team leader for the network vulnerability assessment team. You and the others have done a good job finding holes and fixing them across the company. I know how much collaboration and teamwork goes into that process. Now I'm ready to offer you another opportunity in a different part of the security group. Are you ready for some new challenges?"

"Yes!" said Maria.

"Good." Iris continued. "I think it would be good for you to start training Marion on the vulnerability team to be the team leader while we get you started as project manager for the deployment of our upgraded intrusion detection system."

Maria said, "I don't have any experience with project management, but I'm willing to learn."

Iris nodded. "Maria, you have a great track record as a developer and a system administrator here at RWW. You've got the right attitude for this job, and I'm here to make sure you get the right skills. I would like you to take the next week to work out the transition of your team lead role, and then you'll spend a week at a project management class that I asked the RWW Training Department to arrange for you. I've already ordered you a license for Microsoft Project, which is the software that you'll need for the class."

Maria thought about it for just a second, and then said, "I'm ready."

LEARNING OBJECTIVES:

Upon completion of this material, you should be able to:

- Understand basic project management
- Apply project management principles to an information security program
- Evaluate available project management tools

Introduction

The need for project management skills within the practice of information security may not at first be self-evident. It has been emphasized throughout this book that information security is a process, not a project. However, each element of an information security program must be managed as a project, even if it is an ongoing one. Organizations routinely require technically skilled IT or information security experts to lead projects, or they assign experienced project and general managers to lead information security projects. Some organizations use both approaches at the same time, sometimes assigning project management tasks to technical managers and sometimes assigning those tasks to a general manager, so that all elements of the information security program are completed with quality deliverables, on a timely basis, and within budget.

The job posting shown in Figure 12-1 shows the typical job requirements for an information security analyst.

While there is no guarantee that project management and organizational skills will be part of every information security analyst position description, there is much evidence that employers are seeking individuals that couple their information security focus and skills with strong project management skills. Consider the following from a consulting services company that offers security policy services:

Project management
[Company] certified consultants can orchestrate the complete implementation of your information security policy solution—coordinating the equipment and personnel needed to meet your target dates and avoid budget overruns. Their experience in managing security projects of all sizes can either augment or lead your implementation project team."[1]

Many consulting firms now offer information security services in conjunction with, or in the context of, project management.

But how can information security be both a process and a project? In fact, it is a continuous series, or chain, of projects. As illustrated in Figure 12-2, each link in this chain is a specific project. As the chain progresses, the security systems development life cycle (SecSDLC) guides the management of each individual project.

Information Security Analyst

The Information Security Analyst will be responsible for managing and performing end-to-end technical security reviews, solutions, and implementations for all applications and interfaces within Google. Works with the members of the security team to provide product development input, and assure the security of the company's infrastructure. This is a highly technical hands-on role. Review existing service offerings and suggest improvements. Perform security architectural reviews of existing/planned IT and production infrastructure. Act as a resource to internal departments (Engineering, Operations, Product Development, HR, QA) for security related topics.

Responsibilities:

- Conduct information security risk assessments and risk management services throughout the company, providing security risk evaluation, mitigation and solutions to projects and initiatives.
- Stay abreast of industry best practices in risk management techniques and integrate new methods and tools as appropriate.
- Coordinate efforts between the Information Security and development and production teams.
- Work with the members of the security team to develop and implement strategies to balance security recommendations with business needs.
- Provide guidance and consultation for security related questions from users, developers, and managers.
- Provide technical support for corporate security initiatives such as intrusion detection, virus and malicious code protection, operating systems (Windows XP and Linux) security support, networking, and firewall administration.

Requirements:

- Bachelor's degree, preferably in a technical discipline; or equivalent.
- Expert knowledge and experience of Information Security best practices and business controls.
- Experienced in facilitating Information Security risk assessments for major processes, systems and projects.
- Excellent verbal and written communication skills, including facilitation and team leadership skills.
- Strong project management and organization skills.
- Teamwork/interpersonal ability to gain agreement effectively.
- Results oriented, high energy, self-motivated.
- Knowledge of computer applications design, software and network architectures, protocols, and standards.
- Technical knowledge and demonstrated technical expertise in at least two of the following areas: operating systems, networking, database, client server and web technologies.
- Minimum of 4 years experience in Information Security or IT auditing related fields.

Source: Association of American Medical Colleges. Reprinted with permission.

FIGURE 12-1 Position Posting for an Information Security Analyst

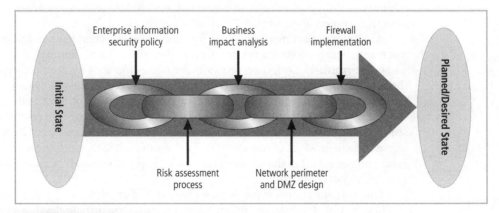

FIGURE 12-2 The Information Security Program Chain

To be sure, some aspects of information security are not project based; rather, they are managed processes. These managed processes include the monitoring of the external and internal environments during incident response, ongoing risk assessments of routine operations, and continuous vulnerability assessment and vulnerability repair. These activities are called **operations** and are ongoing.

Projects, on the other hand, are discrete sequences of activities with starting points and defined completion points. In other words, a "project is a temporary endeavor undertaken to create a unique product or service."[2] Although each individual information security project has an end point, larger organizations never completely finish the information security improvement process; they periodically review progress and realign planning to meet business and IT objectives. This realignment can lead to new goals and projects, as well as the modification, cancellation, or reprioritization of existing projects.

Project Management

The *Guide to the Project Management Body of Knowledge* by W. R. Duncan (hereafter called the *PMBoK*) defines **project management** as:

> the application of knowledge, skills, tools, and techniques to project activities to meet project requirements. Project management is accomplished through the use of processes such as: initiating, planning, executing, controlling, and closing.[3]

In other words, project management—which makes use of many of the approaches discussed in the management sections of Chapter 1—is focused on achieving the objectives of the project.

Unlike ongoing operations, project management involves the temporary assemblage of a group that completes the project, and whose members are then released, and perhaps assigned to other projects. Projects are sometimes seen as development opportunities that enable employees and managers to extend their skills in readiness for promotion to larger opportunities. This can lead to one of the common pitfalls in organizations that have operations groups and project teams: the *prima donna* effect, where certain groups are perceived as elite or more skilled than others. This effect is often seen when workers in operations support roles or software maintenance are seen as less dynamic or capable than their project-focused peers.

Although project management is focused on projects that have end points, this does not mean these projects are necessarily one-time occurrences. Some projects are iterative, and occur regularly. Budgeting processes are one example of iterative projects. Each year the budget committee meets, designs a proposed budget for the following year, and then presents it to the appropriate manager. The committee may not meet again for six to nine months until the next budget cycle. Another common practice is the creation of a sequence of projects, with periodic submission of grouped deliverables. Each project phase has a defined set of objectives and deliverables, and the authorization to progress to future phases is tied to the success of the preceding phase as well as availability of funding or other critical resources.

Some organizational cultures have a long record of relying on project management and have put in place training programs and reward structures to develop a cadre of highly skilled project managers and a corresponding group of trained technical personnel. Other organizations implement each project from scratch, and define the process as they go. Organizations that make project management skills a priority accrue many benefits, including:

- Implementation of a methodology—such as the SecSDLC—ensures that no steps are missed.

- Creation of a detailed blueprint of project activities serves as a common reference tool, and make all project team members more productive by shortening the learning curve when getting projects underway.
- Identification of specific responsibilities for all involved personnel lessens ambiguity and reduces confusion when individuals are assigned to new or different projects.
- Clear definition of project constraints, including time frame, budget, and minimum-quality requirements increases the likelihood that the project stays within them.
- Establishing measures of performance and creation of project milestones simplifies project monitoring.
- Early identification of deviations in quality, time, or budget enables early correction.

Successful project management relies on careful and realistic project planning coupled with aggressive proactive control. The project success may be defined differently in each organization, but in general a project is deemed a success when:

- It is completed on time or early as compared to the baseline project plan.
- It comes in at or below the expenditures planned for in the baseline budget.
- It meets all specifications as outlined in the approved project definition, and the deliverables are accepted by the end user and/or assigning entity.

Applying Project Management to Security

In order to apply project management to information security, you must first identify an established project management methodology. Just as information security systems analysts use the SecSDLC, information security project managers often follow methodologies based on the Project Management Body of Knowledge (PMBoK), a methodology promoted by the Project Management Institute. While other project management approaches exist, the PMBoK is considered the industry best practice. In the following sections, the PMBoK is examined in the context of information security project management.

PMBoK Knowledge Areas

The PMBoK identifies the project management knowledge areas shown in Table 12-1. Each of these areas is discussed in the following sections.

Table 12-1 Project Management Knowledge Areas

Knowledge Area	Focus	Processes
Integration	Elements are coordinated	• Project plan development • Project plan execution • Overall change control
Scope	Including all necessary work	• Initiation • Scope planning • Scope definition • Scope verification • Scope change control

Table 12-1   Project Management Knowledge Areas (continued)

Knowledge Area	Focus	Processes
Time	On-time completion	• Activity definition • Activity sequencing • Activity duration estimating • Schedule development • Schedule control
Cost	Completion within budget	• Resource planning • Cost estimating • Cost budgeting • Cost control
Quality	Satisfying target needs	• Quality planning • Quality assurance • Quality control
Human Resource	Effectively using workers	• Organizational planning • Staff acquisition • Team development
Communications	Efficiently processing information	• Communications planning • Information distribution • Performance reporting • Administrative closure
Risk	Minimizing impact of adverse occurrences	• Risk identification • Risk quantification • Risk response development • Risk response control
Procurement	Acquiring needed resources	• Procurement planning • Solicitation planning • Solicitation • Source selection • Contract administration • Contract closeout

Project Integration Management

Project integration management includes the processes required to ensure that effective coordination occurs within and between the project's many components, including personnel. Most projects include a wide variety of elements: people, time, information, financial resources, internal coordination units (other departments), outside coordination units (regulatory agencies, standards organizations), computing resources, and physical resources (meeting rooms), to name a few.

The major elements of the project management effort that require integration include:

- The development of the initial project plan
- Monitoring of progress as the project plan is executed
- Control of the revisions to the project plan
- Control of the changes made to resource allocations as measured performance causes adjustments to the project plan

Project plan development is the process of integrating all of the project elements into a cohesive plan with the goal of completing the project within the allotted work time using no more than the allotted project resources. As shown in Figure 12-3, these three elements—work time, resources, and project deliverables—are core components used in the creation of the project plan. Changing any one element usually affects the accuracy and reliability of the estimates of other two, and likely means that the project plan must be revised. For instance, changing the quality or quantity of project deliverables requires changes in work time or resource allocations in order for the project plan to remain realistic.

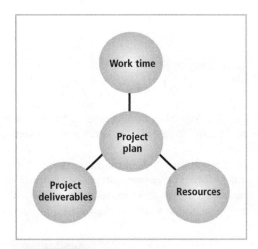

FIGURE 12-3   Project Plan Inputs

When integrating the disparate elements of a complex information security project, complications are likely to arise. Among these complications are:

Conflicts among communities of interest.   When business units do not perceive the need or purpose of an information security project, they may not fully support the project. When IT staff are not completely aligned with the objectives of the information security project, or do not fully understand its impact or criticality, they may be less than fully supportive and may make less than a complete effort towards ensuring its success. It is incumbent on the information security community to educate and inform the other communities so that information security projects are afforded the same degree of support as other IT and non-IT projects.

Far-reaching impact.   Many information security projects span the enterprise and may affect every user of an organization's IT systems. Some parts of the organization may not have the same degree of motivation to participate and, in fact, may be opposed to the goals of the project. The project manager may have to build consensus across the far reaches of the organization and must allow for any necessary education, training, and systems integration efforts when estimating work time and resource demands.

New technology.   Often, information security projects introduce new technologies. Depending on an organization's appetite for risk, a project may deploy technology-based controls that are new to the industry as well as new to the organization. Sometimes the disparate constituencies that are needed to make a project successful are not open to new or different technologies and the project manager becomes engaged in debates about technology selections, or is required to build consensus around technology choices. Project team members, as well as other workers in the organization, may require special training when new technologies are introduced. This increases the risk of human resource turnover, because personnel trained in a new, high-demand skill are more likely to leave the organization for opportunities elsewhere. Proactive steps, such as retention bonuses or gain-sharing arrangements, may help mitigate this risk, but the project plan should include contingency plans for personnel turnover.

VIEWPOINT

Okay, Go Ahead and Do It

By Henry Bonin

Congratulations! You made it this far learning about the various components of information security management. Now it's time to sew all the pieces together to make information security actually happen.

You and your team have gone through all the steps of planning (Units 2 and 3) and analyzing (Units 4 and 5) your concept for some element of an information security system, and you have presented a proposal to the decision maker. You convinced the boss that this is the right thing to do, and he or she has just given you the go-ahead. Is your response "Yikes!" or "Cool!"?

The last step is to demonstrate (prove) that this portion of the information security system can be installed and configured to do the things you claimed it would. That's what this final chapter is about. This last step will have as profound an affect on your information security project and total information security program as will the technology you have selected, the process you have designed, and the personnel you have chosen. Failure here will have no less an impact than a failure of the technology itself.

Projects can have high failure rates, and failure is usually traceable to a failure to follow an accepted methodology or a lack of experience in project management. Information security projects introduce a third reason for possible failure: the incorrect assumption that information security projects are just another IT project. They are not, as you are learning in this chapter.

I just left one of the many conferences I attend every year, put on by one of the major IT vendors. At this conference, the theme was low-cost computing. Rosy pictures of some future state or end points were shown—the future of your organization, if you implement the ideas presented at the conference. Most of the presentations avoid illustrating the less picturesque process of getting from here to there. That process is project management. By practicing and mastering the project management methods described in this chapter, the journey between here and there will be a smoother one.

Henry Bonin is a former member of the MIS Department faculty at San Jose State University in San Jose, California and is now a consultant for IT services management at Andromeda Sciences.

Project Scope Management

Project scope management includes the processes required to ensure that the project plan includes those activities—and only those activities—necessary to complete it. One issue that undermines many projects once they are underway is a phenomenon known as scope creep. **Scope creep** occurs when the quantity or quality of project deliverables is expanded from the original project plan. Stopping scope creep can pose a challenge to many project managers, who seek to meet the objectives expressed to them by project sponsors. Experienced project managers, exposed to project scope creep in the past, are prepared to ask for a corresponding expansion of project work time or project resources or both.

The major processes of this stage include:

- Initiation
- Scope planning
- Scope definition
- Scope verification
- Scope change control

Project Time Management

Project time management includes the processes required to ensure that the project is finished by the identified completion date while meeting its objectives. The failure to meet project deadlines is one of the most frequently cited failures in project management. Many completion deadlines are tied to such external requirements as market demands, business alliances, or government regulations. Missing a deadline can sometimes make project completion moot.

Many missed deadlines are rooted in poor planning. While poor performance by project managers and project resources can cause missed deadlines, it is more often the case that project planners impose unrealistic and often impossible deadlines. The hope that the gap between realistic and unrealistic planning can be closed by hard work may be realized from time to time, but far too often projects that begin with unrealistic timetables only get worse. An experienced project manager becomes adept at estimating the time and resources required to complete projects. Such a project manager, with a track record of success, is in a position to stick to accurate and realistic estimates in the face of management resistance.

The fact is that a given result (the deliverable of the project) costs a certain amount of time and resources (money, people, equipment, and so on) to accomplish. Management wishes notwithstanding, trimming time or resources from these amounts requires reducing the quantity or quality of the deliverables. Some believe that most of the projects that fail do so in the planning phase, when management underestimates the necessary time and resources, or overestimates the quantity and quality of project deliverables given the available resources.

This management area includes the following processes:

- Activity definition
- Activity sequencing
- Activity duration estimating
- Schedule development
- Schedule control

Project Cost Management

Project cost management includes the processes required to ensure that a project is completed within the resource constraints placed upon it. Some projects are planned using only a financial budget from which all resources—personnel, equipment, supplies, and so forth—must be procured (see the section entitled Project Procurement Management later in this chapter). Other projects have a variety of resources cobbled together, with no real financial support, just whatever the managers can scrounge.

The earlier description of the components of planning—deliverables, work time, and resources—emphasizes the interrelated nature of these three components. Beyond this level of interdependence, note that project work time directly influences the consumption of resources. Some resources have associated costs based on reserved time, regardless of whether or not they are actually used. If a project manager arranges for 20 computer workstations, but only has five developers at work, cost of the unused workstations is wasted. Planning for resource usage is among the more complex processes in project management, and many project management tools (covered later in this chapter) focus on the development of efficient resource planning.

This management area includes the following processes:

- Resource planning
- Cost estimating
- Cost budgeting
- Cost control

Project Quality Management

Project quality management includes the processes required to ensure that the project adequately meets the project specifications. The common use of the word "quality" may seem vague—what is a quality product to one individual may not be to another. In fact, the definition of quality is quite clear: if the project deliverables meet the requirements specified in the project plan, the project has met its quality objective; if they do not, it has not met its quality objectives. Unfortunately, far too often, poorly planned projects do not provide clear descriptions of what the project is to deliver, whether it is a product, a service, or a revised process. As the quotation from Yogi Berra that opened Chapter 2 said, "You got to be careful if you don't know where you're going, because you might not get there."

A good plan defines project deliverables in unambiguous terms against which actual results are easily compared. This enables the project team to determine at each step along the way whether all components are being developed to the original specifications. As noted above in the section on scope management, changes made along the way can threaten the overall success of the project. Any change to the definition of project deliverables must be codified, and then the other two areas of project planning—work time and resources—must be reconciled to the changes.

This focus of management includes the following processes:

- Quality planning
- Quality assurance
- Quality control

Project Human Resource Management

Project human resource management includes the processes necessary to ensure the personnel assigned to a project are effectively employed. Staffing a project requires careful estimates of the number of worker hours required. Too few people working on a project almost guarantees it will not be completed on time. Too many people working on a project may be an inefficient use of resources, and may cause the project to fail to stay within its resource limits.

In general, human resource management faces some complications, including:

- Not all workers operate at the same level of efficiency; in fact, wide variance in the productivity of individuals is the norm. This can pose complexities for the project manager as they must accommodate the work style of each project resource while encouraging every worker to be as efficient as possible.

- Not all workers begin the project assignment with the same degree of skill. An astute project manager attempts to evaluate the skill level of some or all of the assigned resources to better match them to the needs of the project plan.

- Skill mixtures among actual project workers seldom match the needs of the project plan. This means that in some circumstances workers may be asked to perform tasks for which they are not necessarily well suited, and therefore tasks take longer and/or cost more than planned.

- Some tasks may require skills that are not available from sources on hand. This might require the project manager to go outside normal channels for a key skill, almost always resulting in delays and higher costs.

In information security projects, human resource management has additional complexities, including:

- Extended clearances may be required. Since some information security projects involve working in sensitive areas of the organization, project managers may have restrictions placed on which resource can be used (for example, only those with the requisite clearances). While this is not yet a common restriction in most commercial organizations, organizations in the financial sector (banking and brokerage) as well as many government agencies face this issue.

- Often, information security projects deploy technology controls that are new to the organization, and so there is not a pool of resources skilled in that area from which to draw. This can occur in any project that faces a skill shortage, but is more likely in an information security project than in a routine development project.

The major processes that take place in this management area include:

- Organizational planning
- Staff acquisition
- Team development

Project Communications Management

Project communications management includes the processes necessary to convey the details of activities associated with the project to all involved parties. This includes the creation, distribution, classification, storage, and ultimately destruction of documents, messages, and other associated project information.

Overcoming resistance to change may be more of a challenge in information security projects than in traditional development projects. In some cases, users and IT partners may be uncertain about the reasons for the project and wary of its effect on their work lives. In extreme cases, a project may face hostility from the future users of the system. The only way to change this situation is to initiate education, training, and awareness programs. The project manager, usually working in conjunction with the SETA program within the Information Security department, should communicate the need for the project as early as possible, and should answer any questions about the effect on users of the deployment of the project deliverables.

The major processes associated with this area of project management include:

- Communications planning
- Information distribution
- Performance reporting
- Administrative closure

Project Risk Management

Project risk management includes the processes necessary to assess, mitigate, manage, and reduce the impact of adverse occurrences on the project. Project risk management is very similar to normal security risk management, except the scope and scale are usually much smaller, because the area to be protected is the individual project and not the entire organization. In many cases, simply identifying and rating the threats facing the project and assessing the probability of the occurrence of these threats is sufficient. The usual purpose of this component of project management is to identify large risks and to plan the mitigation of adverse events should the risks manifest themselves.

Information security projects do face risks that may be different from other types of projects, as noted in the preceding sections. Those projects that face higher than normal risks should include appropriate planning, and perhaps preemptive action to mitigate these risks.

The major processes involved in this area are:

- Risk identification
- Risk quantification
- Risk response development
- Risk response control

Project Procurement Management

Project procurement management includes the processes necessary to acquire needed resources to complete the project. Depending on the common practices of the organization, project managers may simply requisition human resources, hardware, software, or supplies from the organization's stocks. Or, they may have to specify the required resources, request and evaluate bids, and then negotiate contracts for them.

Information security projects may have more complex procurement needs than other types of projects, because they may be more likely than other projects to need different software or hardware products and/or differently skilled human resources than other common types of IT projects.

The major processes involved in this area of project management are:

- Procurement planning
- Solicitation planning
- Solicitation
- Source selection

- Contract administration
- Contract closeout

Additional Project Planning Considerations

The sections below discuss important considerations for project planners as they decide what to include in the project plan, how to break tasks into subtasks and action steps, and how to accomplish the objectives of the project.

Financial Considerations

Regardless of the information security needs within the organization, the effort that can be expended depends on the funds available. A cost-benefit analysis (CBA), usually prepared earlier in the project planning effort, must be verified prior to the finalization of the project plan. The CBA identifies the impact that a specific technology or approach can have on the organization's information assets, and what it may cost.

Each organization has its own approach to the creation and management of budgets and expenses. In many cases, the information security budget is a subsection of the overall IT budget. In some organizations, information security is a separate budget category that may have parity with the IT budget. Regardless of where information security is located in the budget, monetary constraints determine what can be accomplished. Both public and private organizations have budgetary constraints, albeit of a different nature.

Publicly funded organizations (notably government agencies) are the most predictable in their budget processes. Based on the results of legislative budget meetings, they usually know in advance the amount of the next fiscal year's budget. If during a fiscal year additional funding is needed for operations such as information security, the funds must come from a different spending category. In addition, some public organizations rely on temporary or renewable grants. The expenses must be determined when the grants are written. If new expenses arise, funds must be requested in new grant applications. Grant expenditures are usually audited and cannot be misspent. Also, many public institutions have a budget requirement that's rarely present in the private sector: all budgeted funds must be spent in one fiscal year. If not, the budget is reduced by that amount the next fiscal year. The result can be an "end-of-fiscal-year spend-a-thon." This is often the best time to acquire that remaining piece of information security technology.

Nonprofit organizations face many of the same regulatory and financial complications of publicly funded organizations, but in addition also face a perennial shortage of reliable funding and the need to find contributors for most activities that do not directly address the core mission of the organization. Information security activities are rarely construed as contributing to the core mission.

Profit-driven (for-profit) organizations have different budgetary constraints that are governed by the marketplace, not a legislative body. If a for-profit organization does not generate adequate revenue, there is often no funding available for discretionary information security expenditures.

When a for-profit organization needs to fund a project to improve security, the funding comes from the company's capital and expense budgets. Each for-profit organization determines its capital budget and the rules for managing capital spending and expenses differently, but in any case, the budget significantly guides the implementation of information security. For example, a less desirable technology or solution may be chosen over the preferred one simply because it is more affordable.

To justify a budget for a security project in either a public or for-profit organization, it may be useful to benchmark expenses of similar organizations. Most for-profit organizations publish the components of their expense reports. Publicly funded organizations are generally required to show how funds were spent. The savvy security project manager can find a number of similarly sized organizations with larger expenditures for security and use these as justification for planned expenditures. While such tactics may not improve this year's budget, they could improve the budget in future years. Attacks can also help to justify the information security budget. If, during the year, attacks have successfully compromised secured information systems, management may be more willing to support the information security budget.

Priority Considerations

In general, the most important information security controls in the project plan should be scheduled first. As with budgetary constraints, however, there are also constraints when assigning priorities. As discussed in Chapters 7 and 8, risk management is the procedure used to identify controls applied to the information assets that are threatened. A control that costs a little more and is a little lower on the prioritization list but addresses many more vulnerabilities and threats may be implemented before a less expensive, higher-priority component that only addresses one particular vulnerability (such as encryption).

Time and Scheduling Considerations

Time is another constraint that has a broad impact on the development of the project plan. Time can affect a project plan at dozens of points in its development, including the following: time to order and receive a security control; time to install and configure the control; time to train the users; and time to realize the return on investment of the control. If a control must be in place before a new electronic commerce product can be implemented, the selection of a technology may be influenced by differences in acquisition and implementation time lines.

Staffing Considerations

The lack of qualified, trained, and available personnel also constrains the project plan. Experienced staff is often needed to implement available technologies and to develop and implement policies and training programs. If no staff members are trained to configure a firewall that is being purchased, someone must be trained, or someone must be hired who is experienced with that particular technology.

Scope Considerations

The project plan should not attempt to implement the entire security system at one time. In addition to the difficulty of handling so many complex tasks at one time, there are interrelated conflicts between the installation of information security controls and the daily operations of the organization. In addition, new information security controls may conflict with existing controls. For example, installing a new packet filtering router and a new application proxy firewall at the same time can cause a conflict between the controls, and as a result, the organization's users could be blocked from accessing the Web. Which technology caused the conflict? Was it the router, firewall, or an interaction between the two? As this example shows, it is best to limit the scope of implementation to manageable tasks. This does not mean that the project can allow change to only one component at a time; it does mean that it is prudent to cut back on the number of tasks that are planned to occur at the same time in a single department.

Procurement Considerations

There are a number of constraints on the selection process of equipment and services in most organizations, specifically in the selection of certain service vendors or products from manufacturers and suppliers. For example, in a recent situation, a lab administrator was considering an automated risk analysis software package. The leading candidate promised to deliver a solution that met all requirements at a cost within the budget limits. Unfortunately, the vendor was not among those authorized by the organization's procurement unit and the vendor could not be qualified in the time remaining before the budget authorization expired.

Organizational Feasibility Considerations

Another consideration is the ability of the organization to adapt to change. New policies require time to develop and new technologies require time to be installed, configured, and tested. In addition, employees need training on both the new policies and new technology components. Employees need to understand how the new information security program affects their working lives. Changes to security components should be transparent to systems users, unless the new technology requires changes to procedures, such as requiring additional authentication or verification. The organization must develop and conduct training sessions that minimize the impact of the changes before the new technologies come online. Waiting until the processes are in place can create tension and resistance, and possibly undermine security operations altogether. Unless properly trained, users may develop ways to work around difficult or unfamiliar security procedures, bypassing controls and creating additional vulnerabilities. Conversely, users should not be prepared so far in advance that they forget the new training techniques and requirements. The optimal time is usually one to three weeks before the new policies and technologies come online.

Training and Indoctrination Considerations

The size of the organization and the normal conduct of business may preclude a single large training program covering new security procedures or technologies. Therefore, the organization should conduct a pilot approach to implementation, such as roll-out training for one department at a time, or conduct the training in phases. In the case of policies, it may be sufficient to brief all supervisors on new policy and assign them the task of updating users in regularly scheduled meetings. All employees should receive compliance documents, and be required to read, understand, and agree to the new policies.

Technology Governance and Change Control Considerations

Other factors that determine the success of an organization's IT and information security programs are technology governance and change control processes. Technology governance is a complex process that organizations use to manage the affects and costs of technology implementation, innovation, and obsolescence. This process determines how frequently technical systems are updated, and how technical updates are approved and funded. Technology governance also facilitates communication about technical advances and issues across the organization.

Medium-sized or large organizations deal with the impact of technical change on operations by means of a change control process. By managing the process of change the organization can:

- Improve communication about change across the organization.
- Enhance coordination among groups within the organization as change is scheduled and completed.
- Reduce unintended consequences by having a process to resolve potential conflicts and disruptions that uncoordinated change can introduce.
- Improve quality of service as potential failures are eliminated and groups work together.
- Assure management that all groups are complying with the organization's policies regarding technology governance, procurement, accounting, and information security.

Effective change control is an essential part of the IT operation in all but the smallest organizations. The information security group can also use the change control process to ensure that essential process steps, which assure confidentiality, integrity, and availability, are followed as systems are upgraded across the organization.

Controlling the Project

Once a project plan has been defined and all of the preparatory actions are complete, the project gets underway. The following sections discuss project supervision and execution.

Supervising Implementation

Some organizations may choose to designate a champion from the general management community of interest to supervise the information security project. In this case, groups of tasks are delegated to individuals or teams from the IT and information security communities of interest. An alternative is to designate a senior IT manager or the CIO of the organization to lead the implementation. In this case, the detailed work is delegated to cross-functional teams. The optimal approach is usually to designate a suitable person from the information security community of interest, because the focus is on the information security needs of the organization. Each organization must find the leadership that best suits its specific needs and the personalities and politics of the organizational culture.

Executing the Plan

Once a project is underway, it is managed using a process known as a **negative feedback loop** or cybernetic loop, which ensures that progress is measured periodically. The measured results are compared to expected results. When significant deviation occurs, corrective action is taken to bring the task that is deviating from plan back into compliance with the projection, or else the estimate is revised in light of new information. Figure 12-4 illustrates this process.

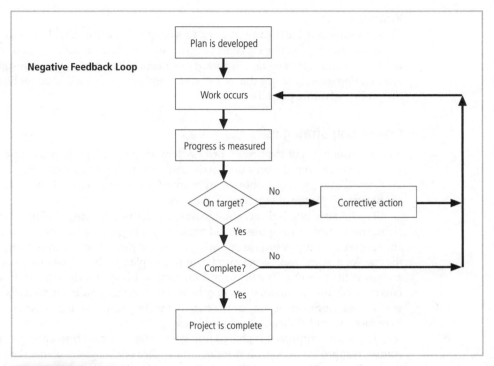

Negative Feedback Loop

Plan is developed

Work occurs

Progress is measured

On target? — No → Corrective action

Yes

Complete? — No

Yes

Project is complete

FIGURE 12-4 Negative Feedback Loop

Corrective action is required in two basic situations: the estimate is flawed, or performance has lagged. When an estimate is flawed, as when an incorrect estimate of effort-hours is made, the plan should be corrected and downstream tasks updated to reflect the change. When performance has lagged, perhaps because of a high turnover of skilled employees, correction is accomplished by adding resources, lengthening the schedule, or by reducing the quality or quantity of the deliverable. These corrective actions are usually expressed in terms of trade-offs.

Often a project manager can adjust one of the three following planning parameters for the task being corrected:

- Effort and money allocated
- Elapsed time or scheduling impact
- Quality or quantity of the deliverable

When a task is lagging behind expectations, it is failing in one or more of these parameters. When too much effort and money is being spent, you can either slow down and take longer, or lower the deliverable quality or quantity. If the task is taking too long to complete, you can add more resources in staff time or money, or else lower the quality or quantity of the deliverable. If quality is too low, you can add more staff time or money, or take longer to complete the task. Of course, these simplistic solutions do not serve in all cases, but this simple trade-off model can help a project manager to analyze available options.

Wrap-Up

Project wrap-up is usually a procedural task assigned to a mid-level IT or information security manager. These managers collect documentation, finalize status reports, and deliver a final report and a presentation at a wrap-up meeting. The goal of the wrap-up is to resolve any pending issues, critique the overall effort, and draw conclusions about how to improve the process in future projects.

Conversion Strategies

As the components of the new security system are planned, provisions must be made for the changeover from the previous method of performing a task to the new method. There are four basic approaches—borrowed from information systems changeover strategies—to changing from the old method to the new.

The first method is **direct changeover**; also known as going cold turkey, a direct changeover involves stopping the old method and beginning the new. Some cases of direct changeover are simple, such as requiring a new password with stronger authentication at the start of a work week; some may be more complex, such as disabling an old firewall and activating the new one. The primary drawback to this approach is that if the new system fails or needs modification, users may be without services while the system's bugs are worked out. Complete testing of the new system in advance of the direct changeover helps to reduce the probability of these problems.

The second approach is phased implementation. **Phased implementation** is the most common approach and involves rolling out a piece of the system across the entire organization. This could mean that the security group implements only a small portion of the new security profile, giving users a chance to get used to it, and resolving small issues as they arise. This is usually the best approach to security rollouts.

The next strategy is pilot implementation. **Pilot implementation** involves implementing all security improvements in a single office, department, or division, and resolving issues within that group before expanding to the rest of the organization. Pilot implementation works well when an isolated group can serve as a guinea pig without dramatically affecting the performance of the organization as a whole. Implementing security improvements in a research and development group, for example, may not affect the real-time operations of the organization and could assist security in resolving issues that emerge.

The final strategy is parallel operation. **Parallel operation** involves running the new methods alongside the old methods. In information systems, this means running two systems concurrently. Although parallel operation may be too complex for general use when deploying information systems, in security it may be justifiable. For instance, it can involve running two firewalls concurrently, and allowing the old systems to back up the new systems if they fail or are compromised. Drawbacks to parallel operation usually include the need to manage both systems and having to maintain two sets of procedures.

To Outsource or Not

Not every organization needs to develop project management capability within its Information Security department. Just as some organizations outsource part of or all of their IT operations, so too can organizations outsource part of or all of their information security programs, especially developmental projects. The expense and time it takes to develop effective information security project management skills may be beyond the reach—as well as the needs—of some organizations, and it is in their best interest to hire competent professional services.

When an organization has outsourced most or all of its IT services, information security should be part of the contract arrangement with the service provider. When an organization retains its own IT department, it may choose to outsource some of the more specialized information security projects. It is not at all unusual for small and medium-sized organizations to hire outside consultants for penetration testing and information security program audits in addition to information security deployment projects. It is also common for organizations of all sizes to outsource monitoring the quality of service of the network and monitoring the network for intrusions.

Because of the complex nature of outsourcing—whether for IT, information security, or other infrastructure and corporate services—organizations should hire the best available specialists, and then obtain capable legal counsel to negotiate and verify the legal and technical intricacies of the contract.

Dealing With Change

The prospect of change, shifting the familiar to the unfamiliar, can cause employees to be unconsciously or consciously resistant. Whether the changes are perceived as good, such as information security implementations, or bad, such as a downsizing or massive restructuring, employees prefer the old way of doing things. Even when employees embrace changes, the stress of making changes and adjusting to the new procedures can increase the probability of mistakes or create vulnerabilities in systems. By understanding and applying some of the basic tenets of change management, you can lower the resistance to change, and even build resilience for change, thus making ongoing change more palatable to the entire organization.

The basic foundations of change management require that those making the changes understand that there is a fundamental culture that reflects the organizational mood and philosophy. Changes that disrupt this model must be managed to minimize their effects. One of the oldest models of change management is the Lewin change model, which consists of:[4]

- Unfreezing
- Moving
- Refreezing

Unfreezing is the thawing of hard and fast habits and established procedures. Moving is the transition between the old way and the new. Refreezing is the integration of the new methods into the organizational culture, by creating an atmosphere in which the changes are accepted as the preferred way of accomplishing tasks.

Unfreezing

The process of unfreezing can be broken down into three subprocesses, each of which must be effective for employees to feel ready and motivated to change:

1. Disconfirmation: You must instill the belief among employees that unless they change to the new standards, they will fail to achieve their goals (survival anxiety), or to perform their duties to their own satisfaction (survival guilt). This is a necessary part of getting the employees to break with their old habits.

2. Induction of survival guilt or survival anxiety: To reinforce these feelings, employees must feel that the reasons behind their survival guilt are valid. The validity of these feelings can be thwarted by learning anxiety—the fear that you must change because you are imperfect or flawed (learning anxiety). Learning anxiety can promote fear and lead to a loss of self-esteem or effectiveness. The change process can accommodate this risk by creating some degree of psychological safety as planning for change occurs.

3. Creation of psychological safety or overcoming learning anxiety: "The key to effective change management, then, becomes the ability to balance the amount of threat produced by disconfirming data with enough psychological safety to allow the change target to accept the information, feel the survival anxiety, and become motivated to change."[5]

Moving

Like unfreezing, the process of moving is composed of three subprocesses that are necessary for change to be realized.

1. Cognitive redefinition: Moving is the process of enabling the employees to realize that there is no loss of honor in accepting the new learning. Cognitive redefinition is when a group of individuals redefine what acceptable and desirable behavior is. Cognitive redefinition results in cognitive restructuring, also known as frame breaking or reframing. Restructuring occurs when new information enables employees to accept the new way of doing things.

2. Imitation and positive or defensive identification with a role model: The easiest way to get the employees to accept new procedures is to use role models. An organization can designate as a role model an employee who is respected by others, who adopts the new methods, and demonstrates that the new methods do not threaten status or well-being. If no positive role models exist, then you have to create the environment for scanning.

3. Scanning (also called insight, or trial-and-error learning): Scanning is the process whereby employees learn by scanning their environment, talking to coworkers, and generally learning new methods on their own. The problem with scanning is that it is easy for employees to assimilate poor or negative reinforcement. Change agents—trained employees or consultants—can support scanning, if they meet with employees in training sessions and demonstrate the positive results of the change process. Once the new learning has occurred, employees go through a period of trial and error. During this time, if the new learning is not reinforced, it results in a new scanning process.

Refreezing

For change to become permanent, it must be refrozen through personal and relational refreezing. Personal refreezing occurs when each individual employee comes to an understanding that the new way of doing things is the best way. Relational refreezing occurs when a group comes to a similar decision. Both can be accomplished by means of group training in the new procedures and methods. Each individual applies the new training in the work environment, reinforcing the group learning, and solidifying the personal refreezing.

Considerations for Organizational Change

Steps can be taken to make an organization more amenable to change. These steps reduce resistance to change at the beginning of the planning process and help the organization to be more flexible as changes occur during project implementation.

Reducing Resistance to Change from the Start

The more ingrained the previous methods and behaviors, the more difficult the change. It's best to start in the early phases of a project to establish the interaction between the affected members of the organization and the project planners. The interaction between these groups is improved through a three-step process: communication, education, and involvement.

Communication is the first and most crucial step. You should notify employees that a new security process is being considered, and solicit their feedback. You should also update employees on the progress of the project and provide information on the expected completion dates. This ongoing series of updates prevents the process from being a surprise, and helps employees to accept the change when it finally arrives.

The updates should also educate employees on exactly how the proposed changes will affect them, both individually and across the organization. While detailed information may not be available in earlier stages, as the project progresses, more details become available. Education also involves teaching employees to use the new systems once they are in place. This means a high-quality training program delivered at the appropriate times.

Finally, involvement means getting key representatives from user groups to serve as members of the development team. In systems development this is referred to as joint application development, or JAD. Users who are part of the development team report to their coworkers on the progress of the project, and report to the project team on the concerns of their coworkers. This representative approach serves the team well in early planning stages, when potential problems accepting the project are addressed.

Developing a Culture that Supports Change

An ideal organization fosters resilience to change. This resilience means the organization accepts that change is a necessary part of the culture, and that embracing change is more productive than fighting it. To develop such a culture, the organization must successfully accomplish many projects that require change. A resilient culture can be either cultivated or undermined by management's approach. Strong management support for change, with a clear executive-level champion, enables others in the organization to recognize the necessity and strategic importance of change. Weak management support, with delegated responsibility and no champion, sentences projects to certain failure, as employees perceive and mirror this weak support.

THREAT MANAGEMENT

SQL Injection

By John Lampe

Definition

SQL injection is an Application layer (or layer 7) attack. As of this writing, it is one of the more popular attack methods employed by professional penetration testers as well as hackers. SQL injection attacks exploit a flaw in the way that a programmer fails to properly validate input data, and are a common root cause of many of the popular Application layer attacks.

Within SQL statements, certain characters have a special meaning. For instance, the semicolon tells the SQL engine to stop processing the statement, and the keyword OR changes the logic of the SQL statement. When an application fails to strip out one of these special characters or strings, the logic of the SQL statement can be compromised. This can, in turn, lead to unauthorized system or data access. SQL injection attacks commonly use a "front-end" (or ingress) machine as their attack vector. Typically, many Web sites are connected to a back-end SQL server. The attacker typically tests the Web server for CGI scripts or forms that return error codes regarding SQL. Another technique (called blind SQL injection) does not rely on error codes, but instead looks for changes of return code based on an SQL query. Once an attacker finds a script or form which does not validate the user input, it is usually a short time before the attacker gains full access to the SQL server.

Detection/Testing for Vulnerability

Many intrusion detection systems (IDS) can detect SQL injection attempts. SQL and application logs can also serve as an alert mechanism. To test for this vulnerability, there are many automated tools. You can also test for the vulnerability manually; however, this can be very time consuming. Some tools which check for SQL injection include Nessus (www.nessus.org), WebInspect (www.spidynamics.com), and SPIKE (www.immunitysec.com).

To manually check for SQL injection flaws (not recommended), you must first identify the ingress point of the SQL statement (i.e., the Web form, CGI, etc.) and map out each of the input parameters.

For example, www.thisNEwidget.com/orderform.asp is a Web form which accepts four input variables (text boxes named box, box2, box3, and box4). A typical order might, in the browser address bar, look like:

```
http://www.thisNEwidget.com/orderform.asp?box=Joe%20
Smith&box2=Atlanta%20GA&box3=widget%20order&box4=654333
```

(Note that %20 is just how the browser represents a space.)

In this imaginary order, a user named Joe Smith from Atlanta, Georgia, is placing a widget order for item number 654333. From the browser window, you can tinker with the values of the four variables. By changing the URL to

```
http://www.thisNEwidget.com/orderform.asp?box=Joe%20
Smith&box2=Atlanta%20GA&box3=widget%20order&box4=;
```

(note that the final character is a semicolon)

(continued)

you may receive a SQL or database error. If you get one of these errors, then the site is probably vulnerable to SQL injection. Once a SQL injection flaw is found, it is typically manually exploited. Common exploit methods include calling a stored procedure (such as xp_cmdshell, a Microsoft SQL default stored procedure), creating a SQL query which dumps all table data to an HTML table, and copying a file (like cmd.exe) into the Web root directory.

Protection

The best way to protect your application from SQL injection attacks is to validate all user input. Programmers must be taught the tenets of secure programming. If a variable should only be alphanumeric, then the application must strip out all nonalphanumeric values from the variable. Many large sites utilize a single server-side include (SSI) to filter all special characters. There is a caveat to this sort of blanket approach, however. Some forms may require a certain special character. If you are utilizing a single SSI to validate all Web server forms, then there is a loss of granularity in your validation. It is recommended that each application individually validate each separate variable.

Many Web servers also support custom input filters, which can be utilized to parse data. Application layer firewalls may also catch these sorts of attacks. In addition, there are also application firewalls, which run as a dedicated service on each Web server.

Applications should be audited on a regular basis. Monthly penetration testing can help to catch these flaws before a hacker does.

For more information, see the SecurIteam SQL Injection paper at www.securiteam.com/securityreviews/5DP0N1P76E.html.
Other useful links in this area are:
NESSUS: www.nessus.org/
SPIKE: www.immunitysec.com
WebINSPECT: www.spidynamics.com

John Lampe is a consultant to the KSU Center for Information Security Education and Awareness Extension Service.

Project Management Tools

There are many tools that support the management of the diverse resources in complex projects. Some of these tools are modeling approaches, such as PERT or CPM, and others involve the use of software. Most project managers combine software tools that implement one or more of the dominant modeling approaches. A few of the more common models are discussed here. If you are planning to become a project manager, seek out the proper level of training to acquire the needed skills and background to be successful. The most successful project managers gain sufficient skill and experience to earn a certificate in project management.

The Project Management Institute (PMI) is project management's leading global professional association, and sponsors two certificate programs, which it describes as follows:

- The Project Management Professional (PMP): PMP certification is the profession's most globally recognized and respected certification credential. The PMP designation following your name tells current and potential employers that you have a solid foundation of project management knowledge that can be readily applied in the workplace. To be eligible for the PMP certification, you must first meet specific education and experience requirements and agree to adhere to a code of professional conduct. The final step in becoming a PMP is passing a multiple-choice examination designed to objectively assess and measure your project management knowledge.

- Certified Associate in Project Management (CAPM): A logical stepping stone to the PMP, and a boon to your overall professional development, is the CAPM. The CAPM is intended for those practitioners who provide project management services but are relatively new to the profession. ...Like the PMP, CAPM candidates must first meet specific education and experience requirements and then pass an examination.[7]

Most project managers engaged in the execution of project plans that are nontrivial in scope use tools to facilitate scheduling and execution of the project. A project manager usually determines that certain tasks cannot be performed until prerequisite tasks are complete. It is almost always advantageous to determine in what order tasks must be performed. It is equally important to determine what tasks must not be delayed in order to avoid holding up the entire project.

Using complex project management tools often results in a complication called projectitis, which is a common pitfall of IT and information security projects. **Projectitis** occurs when the project manager spends more time documenting project tasks, collecting performance measurements, recording project task information, and updating project completion forecasts than accomplishing meaningful project work. The development of an overly elegant, microscopically detailed plan before gaining consensus for the work and related coordinated activities that it requires may be a precursor to projectitis. However, the proper use of project tools can help project managers organize and coordinate project activities, and can enhance communication among the project team.

The following sections discuss some of the more commonly used project management tools.

Work Breakdown Structure

A project plan can be created using a very simple planning tool, such as the **work breakdown structure (WBS)** shown in Table 12-2. The WBS can be prepared with a simple desktop PC spreadsheet program, as well as with more complex project management software tools.

In the WBS approach, the project plan is first broken down into a few major tasks. Each of these major tasks is placed on the WBS task list. The minimum attributes that should be determined for each task are:

- The work to be accomplished (activities and deliverables)
- Estimated amount of effort required for completion in hours or workdays
- The common or specialty skills needed to perform the task
- Task interdependencies

As the project plan develops, additional attributes can be added, including:

- Estimated capital expenses for the task
- Estimated noncapital expenses for the task

- Task assignment according to specific skills
- Start and end dates, once tasks have been sequenced and dates projected

Each major task on the WBS is then further divided into either smaller tasks or specific action steps. For simplicity, the sample WBS later in this chapter divides each task only into action steps. In an actual project plan, tasks are often more complex than in the example, and may require the subdivision of major tasks before action steps can be determined and assigned. Although there are few hard-and-fast rules as to the appropriate level of detail, generally a task or subtask becomes an action step when it can be completed by one individual or skill set, and when it includes a single deliverable, as defined later.

Work To Be Accomplished

The first step in the WBS is to identify the work to be accomplished in the task or task area. This encompasses both activities and deliverables. A deliverable is a completed document or program module that is either the beginning point for a later task or an element of the finished project deliverables. Ideally, the project planner provides a label for the task followed by a thorough description. The description should be complete enough to avoid ambiguity during the later tracking process, but not so detailed as to make the WBS unwieldy. For instance, if the task is to write firewall specifications for the preparation of a request for proposal (RFP), the planner would note that the deliverable is a specification document suitable for distribution to vendors.

Amount of Effort

Planners need to estimate the effort required to complete each task, subtask, or action step. Estimating effort hours for technical work is a complex process. Even when an organization has formal governance, technical review processes, and change control procedures, it is always good practice to ask the individuals who are most familiar with the work or with similar types of work to make the estimates. Then, all individuals assigned to action steps should review the estimated effort hours, understand the tasks, and agree with the estimates.

Skill Sets/Human Resources

The project planner should describe the skill set or individual (often called a human resource) needed to accomplish the task. Naming individuals should be avoided in the early planning efforts. Instead of assigning individuals, the plan should focus on roles or known skill sets. For example, if any of the engineers in the networks group can write the specifications for a router, the assigned resource would be "network engineer" on the WBS. As planning progresses to a more detailed level, however, the specific tasks and action steps should be assigned to specific individuals. For example, when only the manager of the networks group can evaluate the responses to the RFP and make an award for a contract, the planner identifies the network manager by name as the resource.

Task Dependencies

Planners should note wherever possible when a task or action step is dependent upon other tasks or actions steps. The tasks or action steps that come before a particular task are called predecessors. Tasks or action steps that come after a particular task are called successors. Note that there is more than one type of dependency; most courses on project management cover this subject in detail.

Estimated Capital Expenses

Planners need to estimate the expected capital expenses for the completion of each task, subtask, or action item. While each organization budgets and expends capital according to its own established procedures, most differentiate between expenses for durable assets and expenses for other purposes. Be sure to determine the practices in place at the organization where the plan is to be used. For example, a firewall device costing $5000 may be a capital expense for a given organization, but the same organization might not consider a $5000 software package to be a capital expense.

Estimated Noncapital Expenses

Planners need to estimate the expected noncapital expenses for the completion of each task, subtask, or action item. Some organizations require that this cost include a recovery charge for staff time, while others exclude employee time and only plan contract or consulting time as a noncapital expense. Organizations follow their own established procedures in classifying different kinds of expenses as being capital or noncapital. As mentioned earlier, it is important to determine the practices in place at the organization where the plan is to be used. For example, an information security management program costing $600,000 may be considered a noncapital expense, but a network router that costs $600 may be considered a capital expense.

Start and End Dates

In the early stages of planning, the project planner should focus on determining completion dates only for major milestones within the project. A milestone is a specific task completion point in the project plan that has a noticeable effect on the progress of the project plan as a whole. For example, the date for sending the final RFP to vendors is considered a milestone, because it signals that all RFP preparation work is complete. Early in the planning process, assigning too many dates to too many tasks can be a symptom of projectitis. By assigning only key or milestone start and end dates early in the process, planners can avoid this pitfall. Later in the planning process, additional start and end dates can be added as needed.

An example project plan is provided below to help you better understand the process of creating one. The project is to design and implement a firewall for a single small office. The hardware is a standard organizational product and will be installed at a location that already has a network connection. The first step is to list the major tasks:

1. Contact the field office and confirm network assumptions.
2. Purchase standard firewall hardware.
3. Configure firewall.
4. Package and ship firewall to the field office.
5. Work with local technical resource to install and test.
6. Coordinate vulnerability assessment by penetration test team.
7. Get remote office sign-off and update all network drawings and documentation.

Table 12-2   Early Draft Work Breakdown Structure

Task	Effort (hours)	Skill	Dependencies
1. Contact field office and confirm network assumptions	2	Network architect	
2. Purchase standard firewall hardware	4	Network architect and purchasing group	1
3. Configure firewall	8	Network architect	2
4. Package and ship to field office	2	Intern	3
5. Work with local technical resource to install and test	6	Network architect	4
6. Complete network vulnerability assessment	12	Network architect and penetration test team	5
7. Get remote office sign-off and update all network drawings and documentation	8	Network architect	6

After the project manager has compiled the draft WBS and consulted with specific participants of the project team, additional detail is added and more dates are assigned to tasks. Another, more detailed version emerges, as shown in Table 12-3. The project plan has been further developed and illustrates the breakdown of tasks 2 and 6 into action steps.

Table 12-3   Later Draft Work Breakdown Structure

Task	Effort (hours)	Skill	Dependencies	Capital expenses	Noncapital expenses	Start and end dates
1. Contact field office and confirm network assumptions; notify penetration test team of intent for test	2	Network architect		0	200	S:9/22 E:9/22
2. Purchase standard firewall hardware						
2.1 Order firewall through purchasing group	1	Network architect	1	4500	100	S:9/23 E:9/23
2.2 Order firewall from group manufacturer	2	Purchasing group	2.1		100	S:9/24 E:9/24

Table 12-3	Later Draft Work Breakdown Structure (continued)					
Task	Effort (hours)	Skill	Dependencies	Capital expenses	Noncapital expenses	Start and end dates
2.3 Firewall delivered	1	Purchasing group	2.2		50	E:10/3
3. Configure firewall	8	Network architect	2.3		800	S:10/3 E:10/5
4. Package and ship to field office	2	Intern	3		85	S:10/6 E:10/15
5. Work with local technical resource to install and test	6	Network architect	4		600	S:10/22 E:10/31
6. Penetration test						
6.1 Request penetration test	1	Network architect	5		100	S:11/1 E:11/1
6.2 Perform penetration test	9	Penetration test team	6.1		900	S: 11/2 E:11/12
6.3 Verify results of penetration test	2	Network architect	6.2		200	S: 11/13 E:11/15
7 Get remote office sign-off and update all network drawings and documentation	8	Network architect	6.3		800	S: 11/16 E:11/30

Once the project manager has completed the WBS by breaking tasks into subtasks, estimating effort, and forecasting the necessary resources, the work phase—during which the project deliverables are prepared—may begin. A more complex project may require the use of more complex models to complete the task-sequencing effort.

Task-Sequencing Approaches

Sequencing tasks and subtasks in a large and complex project can be truly daunting. Once a project reaches even a relatively modest size, say a few dozen tasks, there can be almost innumerable possibilities for task assignment and scheduling. Fortunately, a number of approaches are available to assist the project manager in this sequencing effort.

Network Scheduling

One method for sequencing tasks and subtasks in a project plan is known as network scheduling. The word "network" in this context does not refer in any way to computer networks; rather, it refers to the web of possible pathways to project completion from the beginning task to the ending task. For example, activity A must occur before activity B, which in turn must occur before activity C; a network diagram illustrating this network dependency is shown in Figure 12-5.

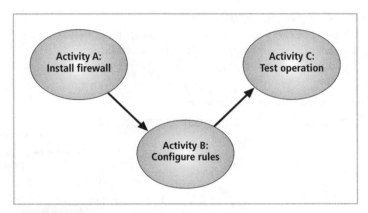

FIGURE 12-5 Simple Network Dependency

While this illustration is very simple, this method of depiction gains value as the number of tasks and subtasks increase and information is added about the effort and type of resources necessary to complete each activity. If multiple activities can be completed concurrently, the diagram can show that. If a single activity has two or more prerequisites, or is the common prerequisite for two or more activities, this can also be depicted, as shown in Figure 12-6.

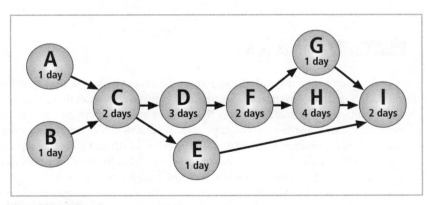

FIGURE 12-6 Complex Network Dependency

The most popular of networking dependency diagramming techniques is the **Program Evaluation and Review Technique (PERT)**. PERT was originally developed in the late 1950s to meet the needs of the rapidly expanding engineering projects associated with government acquisitions, such as weapons systems. About the same time, a similar project, called the **Critical Path Method**, was being developed in the industry. The PERT diagram, as illustrated in Figure 12-7, shows a number of events followed by key activities and their duration. It is possible to take a very complex operation and diagram it in PERT if you can answer three key questions about each activity[8]:

1. How long will this activity take?
2. What activity occurs immediately before this activity can take place?
3. What activity occurs immediately after this activity?

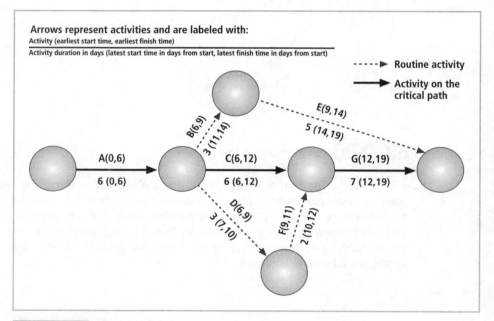

Arrows represent activities and are labeled with:
Activity (earliest start time, earliest finish time)
Activity duration in days (latest start time in days from start, latest finish time in days from start)

- - - → Routine activity
——→ Activity on the critical path

B(6,9)
3 (11,14)

E(9,14)
5 (14,19)

A(0,6)
6 (0,6)

C(6,12)
6 (6,12)

G(12,19)
7 (12,19)

D(6,9)
3 (7,10)

F(9,11)
2 (10,12)

FIGURE 12-7 PERT Example

By determining the path through the various activities, you can determine the critical path. The **critical path** is the sequence of events or activities that requires the longest duration to complete, and identifies the series of events or activities that cannot be delayed without delaying the entire project. As each possible path through the project is analyzed, the difference in time between the critical path and any other path is called **slack time**, an indication of how much time is available for starting a noncritical task without delaying the project as a whole. Should a delay be introduced, whether due to poor estimation of time, unexpected events, or the need to reassign resources to other paths such as the critical path, the tasks with slack time are the logical candidates for delay. In Figure 12-7, the critical path is the sequence of events A → C → G as shown by the heavier arrows. It is possible to have more than one critical path in a project, if two or more paths have the same total time requirement. In the example shown in Figure 12-7, the noncritical path A → D → F → G has one day of slack time. This path can incur a delay of up to one day without adversely affecting the overall completion of the project.

There are several advantages to the PERT method, such as it:

- Makes planning large projects easier by facilitating the identification of pre- and post activities.
- Allows planning to determine the probability of meeting requirements (i.e., timely delivery through calculation of critical paths).
- Anticipates the impact of changes on the system. Should a delay in one area occur, how does it affect the overall project schedule?
- Presents information in a straightforward format that both technical and nontechnical managers can understand and refer to in planning discussions.
- Requires no formal training. After a brief explanation most people understand it thoroughly.

Disadvantages of the PERT method include:

- Diagrams can become awkward and cumbersome, especially in very large projects.
- Diagrams can become expensive to develop and maintain, due to the complexities of some project development processes.
- Can be difficult to place an accurate "time to complete" on some tasks, especially in the initial construction of a project; inaccurate estimates invalidate any close critical path calculations.

The Critical Path Method is similar in design to the PERT method.

Gantt Chart

Another popular project management tool is the bar or Gantt chart, named for Henry Gantt, who developed this method in the early 1900s. Like network diagrams, Gantt charts are easy to read and understand, and thus easy to present to management. These simple bar charts are even easier to design and implement than the PERT diagrams, and yield much of the same information.

The Gantt chart lists activities on the vertical axis of a bar chart, and provides a simple time line on the horizontal axis. A bar represents each activity, with its starting and ending points coinciding with the appropriate points on the time line. The length of the bar thus represents the duration of that particular phase. Activities that overlap can be performed concurrently. Those that do not must be performed sequentially. A vertical reference line can be used to evaluate the current date. Some implementations of the Gantt chart use a fill method to show percentage completion of particular activities. As shown in Figure 12-8, the Gantt chart can provide a wealth of information in a simple format. Activity A has been completed; Activity B is ahead of schedule; Activity C is behind schedule. Milestones can be added to individual activities, and are usually represented by a numbered triangle just above the bar. These milestones might include the completion of a key report, or a component that requires outside interventions. Whatever the case, this method of tracking has proven so simple to use, yet so effective, that it is frequently the preferred method of tracking project progress.

FIGURE 12-8 Project Gantt Chart

Automated Project Tools

Microsoft Project is a commonly used project management tool. While it is not the only automated project management tool (there are quite few), and is not universally perceived as the best (that is matter of heated opinion among project managers), it is generally acknowledged to be the most widely used. If you're considering using an automated project management tool, keep the following in mind:

- A software program cannot take the place of a skilled and experienced project manager who understands how to define tasks, allocate scarce resources, and manage the resources that are assigned. While an automated tool can be powerful in the hands of someone who knows how to use it, it can temporarily disguise the shortcomings of an unprepared project manager.

- A software tool can get in the way of the work. A project manager who spends more than a small amount of time using a tool to record progress and forecast options is on the way to projectitis. Sufferers of this condition spend many hours tweaking project details and calculating trade-offs without making any measurable progress toward completing the project. When project workers are required to use unfamiliar procedures to report progress in minute detail, they may not be as productive as possible. When status meetings turn into multi-hour slideshows detailing each aspect of progress, experienced project managers will want to know why everyone isn't at work in their assigned tasks.

- Choose a tool that you can use effectively. Any project manager is better served using a tool they know than an overly complex tool they cannot use to good effect. Multi-million dollar projects have been brought in on time and under budget using nothing more than a simple spreadsheet and lots of hard work. On the other hand, a project manager using state-of-the-art tools can trim weeks from a schedule and save thousands of dollars while meeting every deliverable requirement.

Chapter Summary

- Employers looking for security personnel often seek individuals that couple their information security mindset and skills with strong project management skills.

- Operations are activities that are ongoing events without discernable end. Projects are discrete sequences of activities with known starting points and defined completion points.

- Each link in a chain of projects accomplishes a specific goal toward the completion of the overall objective of information security program improvement.

- Project management is the application of knowledge, skills, tools, and techniques to project activities to meet project requirements. Project management is accomplished through the use of processes that include initiation, planning, execution, controlling, and closing.

- There are nine areas that make up the component process of project management: integration, scope, time, cost, quality, human resource, communications, risk, and procurement.

- The amount of effort that can be expended on information security programs depends on the funds available. All organizations have budgetary constraints, albeit of a different nature.

- Once a project is underway, it is managed using a negative feedback loop, which ensures that progress is measured periodically. Corrective action is taken if either the estimate was flawed or performance has lagged.

- Provisions must be made for the changeover from the previous method of performing a task to the new method. Four methods exist: direct changeover, phased implementation, pilot implementation, and parallel operation.

- Organizations can choose to outsource part or all of their information security programs, and are more likely to outsource developmental projects.

- Through change management, the resistance to change can be lowered, and resilience for change can be built.

- One of the oldest models of change is the Lewin change model, which consists of unfreezing, moving, and refreezing.

- The creation of a project plan can be accomplished using a very simple planning tool, such as the work breakdown structure (WBS).

- A set of methods which can be used to sequence the tasks and subtasks in a project plan is known as network scheduling. Popular techniques include the Program Evaluation and Review Technique (PERT), the Critical Path Method, and the Gantt chart.

- Automated project management tools can assist experienced project managers in the complexities of managing a large project, but may get in the way when used by novice project managers or when used on simple projects.

Review Questions

1. Why are project management skills important to the information security professional?
2. How can security be both a project and a process?
3. What is an operation, and how does it differ from a project?
4. What are the benefits to an organization that emphasizes project management skills?
5. What are the nine areas that make up the component process of project management?

6.   What complications can information security projects face in complex projects?

7.   What are the respective drawbacks of having too many or too few people working on a project?

8.   What differences between publicly funded and for-profit institutions affect how projects are budgeted?

9.   Why is change management important in organizations?

10. What benefits can organizations gain by actively managing change?

11. What is a negative feedback loop and how is it used to keep a project in control?

12. What are the three planning parameters that can be adjusted when a project is not being executed according to plan?

13. What are the risks and benefits of outsourcing an information security program?

14. What are the three stages of the Lewin change model?

15. What is resilience to change?

16. Name three tools that can be used to help manage projects.

17. What is a work breakdown structure and why is it important?

18. What is projectitis and how can it be prevented?

19. List the various approaches to task sequencing.

20. How does the PERT/CPM method help to manage a project?

Exercises

1.   Using a Web search engine, search for the terms "information security" *and* "project management." What information can you find that incorporates both search terms?

2.   Using only pencil and paper, draft a Gantt chart outlining the process of registering for classes. Identify key resources needed and constraints on the process.

3.   Draft a work breakdown structure for the task of implementing and using a PC-based virus detection program (one that is not centrally managed).

4.   Your instructor has been provided with an Instructor Resources Kit that includes several MS Project files. If you have access to MS Project and can access the file MoIS_12_01.mpp, you can perform this exercise.

     Open the project file. Make a note of the project completion date as shown in the Gantt chart (you can easily see this date by selecting Project | Project Information from the menu bar). Now, change the predecessors in task G from 3, 7 to 3, 6. Check the completion date again. What happened? Why?

5.   Your instructor has been provided with an Instructor Resources Kit that includes several MS Project files. If you have access to MS Project and can access the file MoIS_12_02.mpp, you can perform this exercise.

     Open the project file. When is the project scheduled to begin? When will it be completed? Which phase will take the longest to complete?

Case Exercises

Charlie looked up from his coffee as Iris sat down across from him. "How's it going?" he asked.

"I don't know how much longer I'll be able to squeeze time in for these coffee meetings," she replied, looking exhausted.

"Why's that?" Charlie asked.

"It seems I spend all my time in meetings, and when I'm not in a meeting I'm explaining some aspect of the job to one of my security managers."

"Really?" Charlie asked, concealing a smile.

"Really!" Iris replied. "Just today I spent half an hour with Maria going over the basics of project management, much of which I had to dredge up from my old college textbook. I mean, I know how to manage a project, but I don't remember all of the technical components."

"A project management text? What in the world are you doing that requires a project management text?" Charlie asked.

"I've assigned Maria to head the deployment of our new IDS. I felt it was a perfect opportunity for her to show me what she can do, and complete some of her background education at the same time."

"So you're the master now, grasshopper?" Charlie laughed.

Iris looked confused, and then began to laugh. "Yes, sensei...and my Kung Fu is strong."

For the next hour Iris explained how she integrated project management techniques into the development and implementation of key security components. Before long Charlie pulled out a yellow pad and began scribbling notes. Iris was proud that she had mastered the lessons offered by her former boss and was now able to teach him something in return.

1. What other components of information security could Iris have used project management techniques to control?

2. How could Charlie have made it as far as he has in the IT and information security industry without any formal project management education?

Endnotes

1. Solsoft. Project Management WWW document, accessed 9/7/2003. www.solsoft.com/solsoft.cfm?pageid=52.
2. W. R. Duncan. A Guide to the Project Management Body of Knowledge. Project Management Institute, 3.
3. W. R. Duncan. A Guide to the Project Management Body of Knowledge. Project Management Institute, 6.
4. Edgar H. Schein. Kurt Lewin's Change Theory in the Field and in the Classroom: Notes Toward a Model of Managed Learning, Working paper, MIT Sloan School of Management. [Cited 20 July 2002]. Available from the World Wide Web, www/sol-ne.org/res/wp/10006.html#one.
5. Edgar H. Schein. Kurt Lewin's Change Theory in the Field and in the Classroom: Notes Toward a Model of Managed Learning, Working paper, MIT Sloan School of Management. [Cited 20 July 2002]. Available from the World Wide Web, www/sol-ne.org/res/wp/10006.html#one.
6. www.pmi.org/info/PDC_CertificationsOverview.asp?nav=0401 cited on 9/27/03.
7. H. Kerzner. *Project Management: A Systems Approach to Planning, Scheduling, and Controlling*, 6th ed. New York: Van Nostrand Reinhold Publishing, 1999: 646.

Glossary

3DES Synonymous with Triple DES. An enhancement to the Data Encryption Standard (DES). An algorithm that uses up to three keys to perform three different encryption operations.

A

access The ability to use, manipulate, modify, or affect an object.

access control A security measure such as a badge reader that admits or prohibits users from entering sensitive areas.

access control list (ACL) A list of people or other entities permitted to access a computer resource.

accountability Characteristic of information that exists when every activity involving the information can be attributed to a named person or automated process.

accreditation The state of having been reviewed by an authority and being recognized as having approved processes, programs, or skills. Individual persons are often accredited via certification testing and the fulfillment of experience requirements. The term can also be used to describe the requirement to demonstrate that processes or programs comply with government sanctioned rules before an IT system is authorized to process, store, or transmit information.

acquired value The value an asset has gained over time within an organization.

Advanced Encryption Standard (AES) A Federal Information Processing Standard (FIPS) specified cryptographic algorithm for use within the U.S. government to protect unclassified information.

after-action review A detailed examination of the events that occur from the first detection of a security breach to the final recovery.

agent A piece of software that resides on a system and reports back to a management server.

alert message A scripted description of a security breach that points the recipient to a specific section of a response plan for immediate action.

alert roster A document containing contact information for the individuals to be notified in the event of a security breach.

analysis phase The portion of the SDLC that assesses the organization's readiness, its current systems status, and its capability to implement and then support the proposed systems.

annualized loss expectancy (ALE) The element of a formula for calculating the overall loss an organization could incur from the specified threat over the course of an entire year. ALE=SLE X ARO (annualized loss expectancy equals single loss expectancy times annualized rate of occurrence).

annualized rate of occurrence (ARO) The element of a formula for calculating the overall loss an organization could incur from a potential risk that represents the anticipated rate of occurrence of a loss from the specified threat. ALE=SLE X ARO (annualized loss expectancy equals single loss expectancy times annualized rate of occurrence).

application-level firewall A device, typically a computer, that provides a defense between a network inside the firewall and a network outside the firewall (the Internet) that could pose a threat to the inside network. All traffic to and from the network must pass through the firewall, so that unauthorized traffic can be blocked.

asset valuation The process of assigning financial value or worth to each information asset.

asymmetric encryption Synonymous with public key encryption. A method of communicating on a network using two different but related keys, one to encrypt and the other to decrypt messages.

asynchronous token A device that uses a challenge-response method, in which a server challenges a user during login with a numerical sequence. The user places the sequence into a token, which generates a response that is entered to gain access.

attack An act that is an intentional or unintentional attempt to compromise the information and/or the systems that support it.

attack profile A detailed description of the activities that occur during an attack.

attack scenario end case The summary that describes an attack, the most likely outcome from that attack, and the associated costs from that outcome.

authentication Proof that a user is indeed the person or entity requesting authorized access to a system or facility.

authorization Permission by the proper authority to access, update, or delete the contents of an information asset.

authorization ticket In a client/server environment, a token issued to a particular client that verifies to a server that the client is requesting services on behalf of an authorized user and that the client is a valid member of a system and therefore authorized to receive services.

availability A quality or state of information characterized by being accessible and correctly formatted for use without interference or obstruction.

avoidance The risk control strategy that attempts to prevent the exploitation of the vulnerability.

B

baseline A value or profile of a performance metric against which changes in the performance metric can be usefully compared.

bastion host A dedicated server that receives screened network traffic, which is usually prepared with extra attention to detail and hardened for use in an unsecured or limited security zone. Sometimes referred to as a sacrificial host.

behavior-based intrusion detection system (IDS) Synonymous with statistical anomaly-based IDS. A device that collects data from normal traffic to establish a baseline. The IDS compares periodic data samples with the baseline to highlight irregularities.

behavioral feasibility Synonymous with operational feasibility. The examination of user acceptance of proposed security measures.

benchmarking The process of seeking out and studying the organizational practices that produce desired results.

benefit The value that an organization recognizes by using controls to prevent losses associated with a specific vulnerability.

best business practices Synonymous with best practices and recommended practices. Procedures that provide a superior level of security for an organization's information.

best security practices Security efforts that seek to provide a superior level of performance in the protection of information.

blueprint The basis for the design, selection, and implementation of security controls.

bottom-up approach A method of establishing security policies that begins as a grassroots effort in which systems administrators attempt to improve the security of their systems.

British Standard BS 7799 A code of practice adopted as an international standard framework for information security by the International Organization for Standardization (ISO) and the International Electrotechnical Commission (IEC) as ISO/IEC 17799 in 2000.

bull's-eye model An implementation model in which information security issues are addressed from the general to the specific, always starting with policy.

business continuity plan (BCP) A plan for the continuation of business activities if a catastrophic event occurs, such as the unrecoverable loss of an entire database, building, or operations center.

business impact analysis (BIA) The first phase in the development of the continuity planning process. It extends the risk assessment process to determine the priority for risks in the area of information security.

C

cache server The server used by proxy servers to temporarily store frequently accessed pages.

capabilities table A list that specifies data items or physical devices (for example printers) that users are authorized to access.

CERT Coordination Center A center of Internet security expertise located at the Software Engineering Institute, a federally funded research and development center operated by Carnegie Mellon University.

certificate authority (CA) An agency that manages the issuance of digital certificates and serves as the electronic notary public to verify their worth and integrity.

certification   The process of reviewing processes, programs, or skills for compliance with a standard or expected level of performance. Individuals achieve certification by means of testing and the fulfillment of experience requirements. Organizations can obtain certification by demonstrating that processes or programs comply with government or other sanctioned rules.

Certified Information Security Manager (CISM)   A credential sponsored by The Information Systems Audit and Control Association and Foundation (ISACA) that requires mastery in specified information security management skills and attainment of the required number of years of experience.

Certified Information Systems Auditor (CISA)   A credential sponsored by The Information Systems Audit and Control Association and Foundation (ISACA) for individuals that can demonstrate the specified information system auditing skills and who possess the required number of years of experience.

champion   An executive who manages a security project.

Chief Information Officer (CIO)   The senior technology officer responsible for aligning the strategic efforts of the organization into action plans for the information systems or data processing division of the organization.

Chief Information Security Officer (CISO)   The senior security officer responsible for the assessment, management, and implementation of securing the information in the organization.

C.I.A. triangle   The industry standard for computer security since the development of the mainframe. It is based on three characteristics that describe the utility of information: confidentiality, integrity, and availability.

ciphertext   A message that is formed when plaintext data is encrypted by a cryptosystem.

civil law   A wide variety of laws that are recorded in volumes of legal code available for review by any citizen.

clipping level   As detected by an intrusion detection system, a level of network activity that is higher than an established baseline and therefore suspect.

cold site   An alternate site that can be used by an organization if a disaster occurs at the home site. Contains rudimentary services and facilities.

collusion   The act of conspiring to circumvent laws, policies, or information security controls.

communications security   The protection of an organization's communications media, technology, and content, and its ability to use these tools to achieve the organization's objectives.

community of interest   A group of individuals united by shared interests or values within an organization.

competitive advantage   The leverage gained by an organization that supplies superior products or services. Establishing a competitive business model, method, or technique allows an organization to provide a product or service that is superior to others in the marketplace.

competitive disadvantage   The leverage lost by an organization that supplies products or services perceived to be inferior to other organizations.

Computer Security Division (CSD) of the National Institute of Standards and Technology   An organization that raises the awareness of issues on information security, especially on new and emerging technologies.

confidentiality   The quality or state of information that prevents disclosure or exposure to unauthorized individuals or systems.

consultant   A self-employed individual who is hired for a specific, one-time purpose. Sometimes used as a senior position title for very experienced employees within large organizations.

content filter   A software device that allows administrators to work within a network to restrict accessibility to information.

contingency planning (CP)   The program developed to prepare for, react to, and recover from events that threaten the security of the information assets of an organization.

control   Synonymous with safeguard and countermeasure. A security mechanism, policy, or procedure that can counter system attack, reduce risks, limit losses, and resolve vulnerabilities.

cost avoidance   The money saved by using a control to avoid the financial impact of an incident.

cost benefit analysis (CBA)   Synonymous with economic feasibility study. The comparison of the cost of protecting an asset with the worth of the asset or the costs of the compromise of an asset.

criminal law   Laws that address violations harmful to society and that are actively enforced through prosecution by the state.

crisis management   The actions taken during and after a disaster.

critical path   The sequence of project events/activities that requires the longest duration to complete; it identifies the series of events/activities that cannot be delayed without delaying the entire project.

Critical Path Method   A networking dependency project diagramming technique similar to PERT.

crossover error rate (CER)   Evaluation criteria for biometric technologies, the crossover rate is the point at which the number of false rejections (denial-of-access to authorized users) equals the number of the false acceptances (granting of access to unauthorized users).

cryptanalysis   The methodologies used to obtain information from encoded messages when the cryptographic algorithm and/or keys are unknown.

cryptography   From the Greek work *kryptos*, meaning hidden, and *graphein*, meaning to write. The enciphering and deciphering of coded messages.

cryptology   The science of encryption; a field of study that encompasses cryptography and cryptanalysis.

cultural mores   Fixed moral attitudes or customs of a particular group.

cyberactivism   The use of computer-related technologies to advance a political agenda.

cybernetic control   The process of monitoring progress toward completion, and making necessary adjustments to achieve desired objectives.

cyberterrorist   The act of hacking to conduct terrorist activities via network or Internet pathways.

D

data custodians   Individuals responsible for the storage, maintenance, and protection of information.

data owners   Individuals who determine the level of classification associated with data.

data user   Synonymous with end user. An individual who uses computer applications for his daily work.

database shadowing   A process that duplicates data in real-time using databases at a remote site or to multiple servers.

decisional role   Management role that involves selecting from among alternative approaches, and resolving conflicts, dilemmas, or challenges.

Delphi technique   Named for the oracle at Delphi, a process in which a group rates or ranks asset values or threats to assets.

demilitarized zone (DMZ)   An intermediate area between a trusted network and an untrusted network.

denial-of-service (DoS)   An attack in which the abuser sends a large number of connection or information requests to overwhelm and cripple a target.

detective control   A measure that warns organizations of violations of security principles, organizational policies, or of attempts to exploit vulnerabilities.

deterrence   Discouraging illegal or unethical activity by punishing violators of laws, policies, and technical controls.

Diffie-Hellman key exchange method   A method for exchanging private keys using public key encryption.

digital certificate   An electronic document attached to a file that certifies the file is from the organization it claims to be from and has not been modified from the original format.

digital signature   An encrypted message that is independently verified as authentic by a central facility (registry).

direct changeover   A modification to work practices that involves stopping the old method and beginning the new.

disaster recovery plan (DRP)   A program to limit losses during a disaster and resume business afterwards.

due care   The actions that demonstrate that an organization makes sure that every employee knows what is acceptable or not acceptable behavior, and knows the consequences of illegal or unethical actions.

due diligence   The actions that demonstrate that an organization has made a valid effort to protect others.

dumb cards   ID cards or ATM cards with magnetic stripes containing the digital (and often encrypted) user personal identification number (PIN) against which a user input is compared; performs no computation as contrasted with smart cards, which can perform some computations using an onboard processor.

dumpster diving   The retrieval of information from refuse that could prove embarrassing to the company or could compromise the security of information.

Dynamic Host Control Protocol (DHCP)   A standard within TCP/IP that reassigns IP numbers to devices as needed, making the use of IP numbers as part of the asset identification process very difficult.

dynamic packet filtering firewall   A firewall that allows only a particular packet with a particular source, destination, and port address to enter through the firewall.

E

economic feasibility study   Synonymous with cost benefit analysis. The comparison of the cost of protecting an asset with the worth of the asset or the costs if the asset is compromised.

electronic vaulting   The transfer of large batches of data to an off-site facility.

encryption   The process of converting an original message into a form that is unreadable by unauthorized individuals.

end user   Synonymous with data user. An individual who uses computer applications for his daily work.

enterprise information security policy (EISP)   A policy document that establishes the strategic direction, scope, and tone for all of an organization's security efforts.

ethical hacker   Synonymous with tiger team, white-hat hacker, and red team. Consultants or outsourced contractors who are hired to perform controlled attacks to compromise or disrupt systems by using documented vulnerabilities.

ethics   Behaviors that are socially acceptable.

event-driven   The impetus to begin a SDLC-based project that is in response to some event in the business community, inside the organization, or within the ranks of employees, customers, or other stakeholders.

exit interview   A discussion at the end of employment that reminds an employee of contractual obligations, such as nondisclosure agreements, and obtains feedback on the employee's tenure in the organization.

exploit   A technique used to compromise a system.

F

false accept rate   The percentage or value associated with the rate at which fraudulent users or nonusers are allowed access to systems or areas as a result of a failure in the biometric device.

false reject rate   The percentage or value associated with the rate at which authentic users are denied or prevented access to authorized areas as a result of a failure in the biometric device.

field change order (FCO)   An authorization issued by an organization for the repair, modification, or update of a piece of equipment.

file hashing   Method for ensuring information validity. Involves a file being read by a special algorithm that uses the value of the bits in the file to compute a single large number called a hash value.

fingerprinting   A data-gathering process that discovers the assets that can be accessed from a network, usually performed in advance of a planned attack. It is the systematic examination of the entire set of Internet addresses of the organization.

firewall   Synonymous with application firewall and application-level firewall. A computer that provides a defense between a network inside the firewall and a network outside the firewall (the Internet) that could pose a threat to the inside network. All traffic to and from the network must pass through the firewall, so that unauthorized data can be blocked.

footprinting   The identification of the Internet addresses that are owned or controlled by an organization.

framework   The outline from which a detailed security blueprint evolves.

G

general business community   A group of nontechnical business managers and professionals within an organization.

Global Information Assurance Certification (GIAC)   A professional qualification consisting of twelve individual technical certifications that can be tied into six tracks, or culminate in the GIAC Security Engineer certification.

goal   The end result of a planning process.

guidelines   Instructions to employees that explain how to comply with organizational policy.

H

hacktivist   Synonymous with cyberactivist. An individual who uses technology as a tool for civil disobedience.

hash value   Synonymous with message digest. A single large number created when a file is read by a special algorithm that uses the value of the bits in the file to compute the number. The hash value ensures information validity.

hierarchical roster   A list of names of people who are called in the case of an emergency. Each person in turn calls the next person.

honeypot   A computer server configured to misdirect hackers by resembling a production system that contains substantial information.

host-based intrusion detection system (IDS)   Device that is installed on a computer system to monitor the status of files stored on that system and protect them from security breaches.

hot site   Synonymous with business recovery site. A remote location with systems identical or similar to a home site for use after a disaster.

I

identification   The ability of an information system to recognize individual users.

implementation phase   The portion of the SDLC during which the organization develops, acquires, and integrates necessary software.

incident   An attack on an organization's information assets.

incident candidate   An event that may or may not be an attack on an organization's information systems.

incident classification   The process of determining whether an incident candidate is an actual security breach.

incident response   Activities taken to plan for, detect, and correct the impact of an incident on information assets.

incident response planning (IRP)   A process to establish procedures an organization's staff would follow if it were attacked.

information security (InfoSec)   The protection of information and the systems and hardware that use, store, and transmit that information.

information security policy   A set of rules designed to protect the information assets of an organization.

Information Systems Audit and Control Association (ISACA)   A professional association focused on auditing, control, and security.

Information Systems Audit and Control Association's Certified Information Systems Auditor (CISA)   A certificate that focuses on auditing information security, business process analysis, and information security planning.

Information Systems Security Association (ISSA)   A nonprofit society of information security professionals.

information technology community   A group of technology professionals that supports the business objectives of the organization by supplying and supporting information technology.

information warfare   An offensive organized and lawful operation conducted by a sovereign state that involves the use of information technology.

informational role   A management role that seeks to collect, process, and evaluate information that can affect decisions and outcomes

integrity   The quality or state of being whole, complete, and uncorrupted.

International Information Systems Security Certification Consortium (ISC)² , Systems Security Certified Professional (SSCP)   An international consortium dedicated to improving the quality of security professionals.

International Standard Organization (ISO) model   An approach that provides a five-layer structure to the administration and management of networks and systems.

Internet Engineering Task Force (IETF)   A group of professionals in the fields of computing, networking, and telecommunications who develop the Internet's technical foundations.

Internet Society (ISOC)   A nonprofit, nongovernmental, international professional organization that promotes the development and implementation of education, standards, policy, and education and training to promote the Internet.

Internet vulnerability assessment   The process of finding and documenting the vulnerabilities that may be present in the public-facing network of an organization.

interpersonal role   A management role that includes interacting with superiors, subordinates, outside stakeholders, and others that influence or are influenced.

intrinsic value   The essential worth of an asset.

intrusion detection systems (IDSs)   Devices that inspect data communication flows to identify patterns that may indicate that hacking is underway.

IP Security (IPSec)   The primary and now dominant cryptographic authentication and encryption product of the IETF's IP Protocol Security Working Group.

investigation phase   The portion of the SDLC that identifies the problem that the system being developed is to solve.

issue-specific security policy   A program that addresses specific areas of technology and contains a statement on the organization's position on each specific issue.

J

job rotation   Synonymous with task rotation. A security check that requires that every employee is trained to perform the work of another employee.

jurisdiction   A court's right to hear a case because a wrong was committed in its territory or involving its citizenry.

K

Kerberos   A cryptosystem that uses symmetric key encryption to validate an individual user to various network resources.

knowledge-based intrusion detection system (IDS) Synonymous with signature-based IDS. A device that examines data traffic for signature matches with predefined, preconfigured attack patterns.

L

lattice-based access control   A matrix of authorizations that control access to data.

laws   Rules adopted by society for determining expected behavior; drawn from ethics.

leadership   A management role that addresses the direction and motivation of human resources.

least privilege   A security measure by which employees are provided access to the minimum amount of information for the least duration of time necessary for them to perform their duties.

liability   The legal obligation of an entity that includes responsibility for a wrongful act and the legal obligation to make restitution.

logical design phase   Portion of the SDLC in which the information obtained during the analysis phase is used to create a proposed system-based solution for the business problem.

long arm jurisdiction   A law that reaches across the country or around the world to pull an accused individual into its court systems.

M

maintenance phase   Portion of the SDLC during which tasks necessary to support and modify the system for the remainder of its useful life cycle are executed.

management   The process of achieving objectives using a given set of resources.

manager   A member of an organization who coordinates the work of employees order to accomplish organizational goals.

management controls   Synonymous with managerial controls. Organizational processes that are designed and implemented to reduce risk to the organization by using the role of the manager to enforce policy compliance.

managerial controls   Synonymous with management controls. Organizational processes that are designed and implemented to reduce risk to the organization by using the role of the manager to enforce policy compliance.

mandatory vacation   A policy requiring that all employees take at least one week of vacation per year.

methodology   A formal approach to solving a problem based on a structured sequence of procedures.

minutiae   In biometrics, unique points of reference that are digitized and stored in an encrypted format for comparison with scanned human characteristics.

mission statement   A written declaration of an organization's purpose and its intended areas of operations.

mitigation   A control approach that attempts to reduce the impact caused by the exploitation of vulnerability through planning and preparation.

monoalphabetic substitution   In encryption, the substitution of one value for another using a single alphabet.

mutual agreement   A contract between two or more organizations that specifies how each assists the other in the event of a disaster.

N

National InfraGard Program   A cooperative effort of the FBI and local technology professionals to protect critical national information.

National Infrastructure Protection Center (NIPC) An organization that serves as the U.S. government's center for threat assessment, warning, investigation, and response to threats or attacks against critical U.S. infrastructures.

National Security Agency (NSA)   The organization responsible for signal intelligence and information system security.

need-to-know   A principle within a data classification scheme that limits individuals' access to information to that which is required to perform their jobs.

negative feedback loop Synonymous with cybernetic loop. A process to manage a project that insures that progress is measured periodically and that measured results are compared to expected results.

network address translation (NAT) A method of mapping real, valid, external IP addresses to special ranges of internal IP addresses, creating a barrier to internal intrusion.

network-based intrusion detection systems (IDSs) Devices that are installed on networks to monitor patterns of network traffic to detect unusual and therefore threatening activity.

network review board Synonymous with technical architecture team. A group that directs the orderly introduction of change in information technology across the organization.

network security The protection of an organization's data networking devices, connections, and contents, and the ability to use the network to accomplish the organization's data communication functions.

nonrepudiation A message characteristic wherein the fact that a message was sent by a particular entity cannot be refuted.

O

objective An intermediate point at which you can measure progress toward the goal

open port A network channel or device used to send commands to a computer, gain access to a server, and exert control over a networking device.

operational controls Measures that deal with the operational functionality of security in an organization.

operational feasibility Synonymous with behavioral feasibility. The examination of user acceptance of proposed security measures.

operations Managed, ongoing processes.

operations security The safeguarding of the organization's ability to fulfill operational activities without interruption or compromise.

organization The management principle dedicated to the structuring of resources to support the accomplishment of objectives.

organizational feasibility A comparison of how proposed information security alternatives contribute to the efficiency, effectiveness, and overall operation of an organization.

P

packet filtering firewall Networking devices that filter data packets based on their headers as they travel in and out of an organization's network.

packet sniffer A network tool that collects copies of packets from the network and analyzes them.

parallel operations A method of modifying work practices that involves using the new methods alongside the old methods.

passphrase A series of characters, typically longer than a password, from which a virtual password is derived.

password A private word or combination of characters that only the user knows.

penetration testing A simulation performed by security personnel to compromise or disrupt their own systems by exploiting documented vulnerabilities.

permutation cipher Synonymous with transposition cipher. The rearranging of values within a block to create coded information.

personal security The protection of the people within an organization.

phased implementation An approach to implementing new security systems that involves rolling out a piece of a new system across the entire organization.

physical design phase Portion of the SDLC during which the team selects specific technologies that support the alternatives identified and evaluated in the logical design phase.

physical security An aspect of information security that addresses the design, implementation, and maintenance of countermeasures that protect the physical resources of an organization.

pilot implementation The changing of work practices that involves implementing all security improvements in a single office, department, or division, and resolving issues within that group before expanding to the rest of the organization.

plaintext Synonymous with cleartext. The unencrypted message that will be encrypted into ciphertext for transmission over an unsecured channel.

plan-driven The impetus for a project that is the result of a carefully developed planning strategy.

planning The process that develops, creates, and implements strategies for the accomplishment of objectives.

policy The set of organizational guidelines that describe acceptable and unacceptable behaviors of employees in the workplace.

political feasibility An examination of the acceptability of limits placed on an organization and its employees' actions or behaviors.

polyalphabetic substitutions In encryption, the substitution of one value for another, using two or more alphabets.

port A network channel or connection point in a data communications system.

port scanners The tools used to identify (or fingerprint) computers that are active on a network.

practices Methods or processes used by an organization to accomplish its objectives.

Pretty Good Privacy (PGP) A hybrid cryptosystem that combines some of the best available cryptographic algorithms. PGP is the open source *de facto* standard for encryption and authentication of e-mail and file storage applications.

preventive control The implementation of an organizational policy or a security principle, such as authentication or confidentiality, to protect a vulnerability.

privacy The state of being free from unauthorized observation, or in the legislative sense, the ability to exercise control over how others use personal information collected from individuals.

Privacy Enhanced Mail (PEM) A standard proposed by the Internet Engineering Task Force (IETF) that will function with public key cryptosystems. PEM uses 3DES symmetric key encryption and RSA for key exchanges and digital signatures.

private key encryption Synonymous with symmetric encryption. A method of communicating on a network using a single key to both encrypt and decrypt a message.

private law Laws that regulate the relationship between the individual and the organization, and that encompass family law, commercial law, and labor law.

procedures Methods or processes, usually detailed, put in place by an organization in order to accomplish its objectives.

program A collection of steps, often many of them being projects, performed within the organization to improve security.

project management The application of knowledge, skills, tools, and techniques to meet planned objectives.

projectitis The phenomenon of becoming so engrossed in project administration that meaningful project work is neglected.

proxy server Synonymous with proxy firewall. A server that is configured to look like a Web server, and which performs actions on behalf of that server to protect it from hacking.

public key encryption Synonymous with asymmetric encryption. A method of communicating on a network using two different keys, one to encrypt and the other to decrypt a message.

public law Laws that regulate the structure and administration of government agencies and their relationships with citizens, employees, and other governments.

Q

qualitative assessment The evaluation of an organization's assets using their relative values to the organization.

quantitative assessment The evaluation of an organization's assets using actual values or estimates.

R

rapid onset disasters Episodes—often natural disasters—that occur suddenly, with little warning, taking the lives of people, and destroying the means of production.

readiness and review The domain of the security maintenance model concerned with keeping the information security program functioning as designed and keeping it continuously improving over time.

recommended practices Synonymous with best practices and best business practices. Procedures that provide a superior level of security for an organization's information.

red team Synonymous with ethical hacker, tiger team, and white-hat hacker. Consultants or outsourced contractors who are hired to perform controlled attacks to compromise or disrupt systems by using documented vulnerabilities.

Remote Authentication Dial-in User Service (RADIUS) A system that authenticates the credentials of users who are trying to access an organization's network through a dial-up connection.

remote journaling The transfer of live transactions to an off-site facility.

residual risk The risk that remains to an information asset after an existing control has been applied.

resource An individual or skill set whose function is detailed in a project plan.

restitution The compensation for a misdeed.

risk The probability that something can happen.

risk analysis Synonymous with risk assessment. The analysis of a danger to assign a risk rating or score to an information asset.

risk appetite The quantity and nature of risk that organizations are willing to accept.

risk assessment Synonymous with risk analysis. The analysis of a danger to assign a risk rating or score to an information asset.

risk management The process of identifying vulnerabilities in an organization's information system and taking steps to assure its confidentiality, integrity, and availability.

role-based control A type of access control in which individuals are allowed to use data based on their positions in an organization.

S

sacrificial host Synonymous with bastion host. A dedicated firewall that enables a router to prescreen data packets to minimize the network traffic and load on a proxy server.

safeguard Synonymous with control and countermeasure. A security mechanism, policy, or procedure that can counter system attacks, reduce risks, and resolve vulnerabilities.

scope creep A project phenomenon that occurs when the quantity or quality of project deliverables is expanded from the original project plan.

secret key In symmetric encryption, the single key shared by both parties. In asymmetric encryption, the private key retained by the owner for use in decrypting messages encrypted with owner's public key.

Secure Electronic Transactions (SET) A standard developed by MasterCard and VISA in 1997 to provide protection from electronic payment fraud. It works by encrypting the credit card transfers with DES for encryption and RSA for key exchange.

Secure Hypertext Transfer Protocol (SHTTP) A protocol designed to enable secure communications across the Internet. SHTTP is the application of SSL over HTTP, which allows the encryption of all information passing between two computers through a protected and secure virtual connection.

Secure Multipurpose Internet Mail Extensions (S/MIME) A specification developed to increase the security of e-mail that adds encryption and user authentication.

Secure Shell (SSH) A popular extension to the TCP/IP protocol suite, sponsored by the IETF. It provides authentication services between a client and a server and is used to secure replacement tools for terminal emulation, remote management, and file transfer applications.

Secure Sockets Layer (SSL) A protocol for transmitting private information securely over the Internet.

security To be protected from the threat of loss; protection from that which would do harm, intentionally or otherwise.

security education, training, and awareness (SETA) program An education program designed to reduce the number of security breaches that occur through a lack of employee security awareness.

Security Management Index (SMI) A survey developed by the Human Firewall Council that gathers information on how organizations manage security.

security manager A member of an organization accountable for the day-to-day operation of the information security program, accomplishing the objectives identified by the CISO, and resolving issues identified by technicians.

security model A collection of security rules that represents the implementation of a security policy.

security systems development life cycle (SecSDLC) A methodology for the design and implementation of security for information systems.

security technicians The technically qualified individuals who configure firewalls and IDSs, implement security software, diagnose and troubleshoot problems, and coordinate with systems and network administrators to ensure that security technology is properly implemented.

separation of duties A control used to reduce the chance of an individual violating information security and breaching the confidentiality, integrity, or availability of the information.

sequential roster A list of people who are called by a single person in the case of an emergency.

service bureau A service agency that provides a service for a fee.

session key A limited-use symmetric key for encrypting electronic communication.

signature-based intrusion detection system (IDS)
Synonymous with knowledge-based IDS. A device that examines data traffic for signature matches with predefined, preconfigured attack patterns.

single loss expectancy (SLE) The calculation of the cost incurred in a single instance when a specific asset within an organization is attacked.

slack time The difference in time between the critical path and any other path. It identifies how much time is available for starting a non-critical task without delaying the project as a whole.

slow onset disasters Episodes that occur over time and slowly deteriorate the capacity of an organization to withstand their effects.

smart card A device that contains memory and a processor that can verify and validate a number of pieces of information about an individual beyond recording facts.

standard A detailed statement of what employees of an organization must do to comply with a policy.

state table A process used by a server that tracks the state and context of each connection to authenticate the exchange of packets by recording which host sent which packet, when, and to which remote host

stateful inspection firewall Devices that track network connections that are established between internal and external systems.

statistical anomaly-based intrusion detection system (IDS) Synonymous with behavior-based IDS. A device that collects data from normal traffic to establish a baseline. The IDS compares periodic data samples with the baseline to highlight irregularities.

strategic planning Synonymous with strategy. The process of moving an organization towards its vision by accomplishing its mission.

strategy Synonymous with strategic planning. The process of moving an organization towards its vision by accomplishing its mission.

strong authentication The use of two or more authentication mechanism types to authenticate a single transaction or session; for example, the use of something you have and something you know as occurs when making an ATM banking transaction

substitution cipher In encryption, the substitution of one value for another.

symmetric encryption Synonymous with private key encryption. Symmetric encryption is a method of communicating on a network using a single key to both encrypt and decrypt a message.

synchronous tokens Authentication devices that are synchronized with a server so that each device (server and token) uses the time or a time-based database to generate a number that is entered during the user login phase.

systems development life cycle (SDLC) A methodology for the design and implementation of an information system.

Systems Security Certified Professional (SSCP) A certification for operational planning for information security with an operational focus on seven domains of information security.

systems-specific policy (SysSP) A policy document that addresses the particular use of certain systems. This could include firewall configuration policies, systems access policies, and other technical configuration areas.

T

task rotation Synonymous with job rotation. A security check that requires that every employee is trained to perform the work of another employee.

task-based control A type of data access control in which individuals are allowed to use data, based on their job responsibilities.

technical controls Control measures that use or implement a technical solution to reduce risk of loss in an organization, as well as issues related to examining and selecting the technologies appropriate to protecting information.

technical feasibility An examination of whether an organization has or can acquire the technology and expertise necessary to implement and support specific control alternatives.

Terminal Access Controller Access Control System (TACACS) A remote access system that validates a user's credentials.

threat An object, person, or other entity that represents a risk of loss to an asset.

threat agent A specific instance or component that represents a danger to an organization's assets. Threats can be accidental or purposeful, for example, lightning strikes or hackers.

threat identification The examination of a danger to assess its potential to impact an organization.

tiger team Synonymous with ethical hacker, white-hat hacker, and red team. Consultants or outsourced contractors who are hired to perform controlled attacks to compromise or disrupt systems by using documented vulnerabilities.

timeshare A site that is leased by an organization in conjunction with a business partner for use if a disaster occurs at the home site.

top-down approach A methodology of establishing security policies that is initiated by upper management.

tort law The body of law that allow individuals to seek recourse against others in the event of personal, physical, or financial injury.

transference The control approach used by an organization to shift the risks from one asset to another.

transport mode One of the two modes of operation of the IP Security Protocol. In transport mode, only the IP data is encrypted, not the IP headers.

transposition cipher Synonymous with permutation cipher. The rearranging of values within a block to create coded information.

triple DES Synonymous with 3DES. An enhancement to the Data Encryption Standard (DES). An algorithm that uses up to three keys to perform three different encryption operations.

trusted network A network segment that has had some degree of protection established (such as an intranet that is inside an organization's firewall) and is therefore perceived as being less susceptible to attack or loss.

tunnel mode One of the two modes of operation of the IP Security Protocol. In tunnel mode, the entire IP packet is encrypted and placed as payload into another IP packet.

two-man control A security check that requires that two individuals review and approve each other's work in order to complete a task.

U

U.S. military classification scheme A categorization method used by the U.S. Department of Defense to assign key documents to groups based on sensitivity levels.

U.S. Secret Service A unit within the Department of the Treasury that provides protective services for key members of the U.S. government and has enforcement responsibility for certain criminal acts, including crimes involving U.S. currency (counterfeiting) and some aspects of computer and technology crimes.

untrusted network A network segment perceived as uncontrolled, such as the Internet.

user involvement The inclusion of users in the organizational process of developing security systems.

V

values statement A formal set of organizational principles, standards, and qualities.

virtual password A password calculated or extracted from a passphrase that meets system storage requirements.

virtual private networks (VPNs) A network within a network that typically allows a user to use the Internet as a private network.

vision statement A written declaration of the organization's long-term goals.

vulnerability A weakness or fault in a system or protection mechanism that exposes information to attack or damage.

vulnerability assessment The process of identifying and documenting specific and provable flaws in the organization's information asset environment.

vulnerability scanner A device that scans servers to identify exposed usernames, shows open network shares, and exposes configuration problems and other vulnerabilities.

W

war dialer An automatic phone-dialing program that dials every number on a list or in a configured range (e.g., 555-1000 to 555-2000), and checks to see if a person, answering machine, or modem picks up.

warm site An alternate site that can be used by an organization if a disaster occurs at the home site. Frequently includes computing equipment and peripherals with servers but not client workstations.

white-hat hacker Synonymous with ethical hacker, tiger team, and red team. Consultants or outsourced contractors who are hired to perform controlled attacks to compromise or disrupt systems by using documented vulnerabilities.

work breakdown structure (WBS) A planning approach that breaks a project plan into specific action steps.

X

XOR cipher conversion A programming algorithm that uses the Boolean XOR function to combine binary digits from two data streams, one with a clear text and the other with an encryption key, to produce an encrypted data stream.

Index